MW00851068

SALES FORCE MANAGEMENT

By

Gregory A. Rich

CHICAGO
BUSINESS PRESS

CHICAGO
BUSINESS PRESS

For product information or assistance, visit: www.chicagobusinesspress.com

ISBN 978-0-9971171-3-4

SALES FORCE MANAGEMENT

BRIEF CONTENTS

Chapter 1 Introduction to Sales Force Management *1*
Chapter 2 Strategy *29*
Chapter 3 The Personal Selling Process *57*
Chapter 4 Sales Force Organization *83*
Chapter 5 Profiling and Recruiting Salespeople *119*
Chapter 6 Selecting and Hiring Salespeople *149*
Chapter 7 Sales Training *183*
Chapter 8 Motivating a Sales Force *211*
Chapter 9 Sales Force Compensation *241*
Chapter 10 Sales Force Quotas and Expenses *271*
Chapter 11 Leadership of a Sales Force *307*
Chapter 12 Forecasting and Budgets *335*
Chapter 13 Sales Territories *371*
Chapter 14 Sales Volume Analysis *401*
Chapter 15 Cost And Profitability Analysis *421*
Chapter 16 Evaluating a Salesperson's Performance *445*
Chapter 17 Ethics and Laws *473*
      Company Index *493*
      Subject Index *495*

CONTENTS

Chapter 1 Introduction To Sales Force Management   *1*

Scope and Focus of This Book   *2*
Personal Selling and The Marketing Mix   *3*

The Nature of Personal Selling   *3*
Relationship Marketing and The Role of Personal Selling   *4*
The Nature of Sales Jobs   *4*
How Sales Jobs Differ From Other Jobs   *7*
New Dimensions of Personal Selling: The Professional Salesperson   *8*

The Nature of Sales Management   *9*
Role and Skills of a Sales Manager   *10*
Administration—A Distinct Skill   *11*
Levels of Sales and Sales Management Positions   *12*
How Sales Managers' Job Differ From Other Management Jobs   *14*
In Our Economy   *14*
In An Individual Organization   *15*
To You, The Student   *15*

Challenges Facing Sales Force Management   *16*
Summary   *19*
Key Terms   *20*
Questions and Problems   *20*
Experiential Exercises   *21*
Endnotes   *28*

Chapter 2 Strategy   *29*

The Marketing System   *30*
External Environment   *30*

The Marketing Concept and Marketing Management   *32*
Internal Variables   *32*
Evolution of Marketing Management   *33*
Evolution of Selling In The United Stages[9]   *35*
Relationship Marketing   *37*
Integrating Marketing and Sales Functions   *40*
Integrating Production and Sales   *40*
Objectives   *41*
Strategies   *41*

Strategic Planning   *41*
Tactics   *42*
Strategic Planning for The Total Company   *43*
Strategic Marketing Planning   *44*

Sales Force Strategy   *45*
Social Selling   *45*
Strategic Trends   *45*
Hybrid Sales Channels   *46*
Multiple Relationship Strategies   *46*
Marketing Management's Social Responsibility   *47*
Summary   *47*
Key Terms   *48*
Questions and Problems   *49*
Experiential Exercises   *50*
Endnotes   *55*

Chapter 3   The Personal Selling Process   *57*
Prospecting   *58*
Identifying Leads   *59*
Qualifying Leads   *60*
Pre-Approach: Planning The Sale   *62*
Customer Research   *62*
Planning The Sales Presentation   *62*
The Approach   *63*
Need Assessment   *63*
The Presentation   *65*
Product Demonstrations   *66*
Prepared Sales Presentations   *67*
Developing Effective Presentations   *67*
Meeting Objections   *68*
Price Or Value Objections   *69*
Product/Service Objections   *69*
Procrastinating Objections   *70*
Hidden Objections   *70*
Gaining Commitment (Aka The Close)   *71*
Follow-Up   *72*
Summary   *73*
Key Terms   *74*
Questions and Problems   *74*
Experiential Exercises   *75*
Endnotes   *81*

Chapter 4   Sales Force Organization   *83*
Nature of Sales Organizations   *84*
Sales Force Organization and Strategic Planning   *84*
Characteristics of a Good Organization   *85*
Role of An Informal Organization   *86*
Basic Types of Organizations   *87*
Specialization Within a Sales Department   *89*
Geographic Specialization   *90*
Product Specialization   *90*
Market Specialization   *92*
Combination of Organizational Bases   *94*

Introduction To The Running Case Study   *95*
Sales Force Specialization   *95*
Key Account Management   *97*
Additional Strategic Organizational Alternatives   *97*
Buying Centers and Team Selling   *99*
Independent Sales Organizations   *101*
E-Commerce and Inside Sales   *104*
Organizing for International Sales   *106*
Home-Country Intermediaries   *107*
Foreign-Country Intermediaries   *107*
Summary   *108*
Company Sales Force Operating Abroad   *108*
Key Terms   *109*
Questions and Problems   *110*
Experiential Exercises   *111*
Endnotes   *117*

Chapter 5   Profiling and Recruiting Salespeople   *119*
Sales Force Selection and Strategic Planning   *120*
Adding Minority Reps To The Sales Force   *121*
Importance of a Good Selection Program   *121*
The Law and Sales Force Selection   *122*
Scope of Sales Force Staffing Process   *124*
The Planning Phase   *124*
The Recruiting Phase   *124*
The Selection Phase   *125*
The Hiring and Assimilation Phases   *125*
Determining The Number of People Needed   *125*
Developing a Profile of The Type of People Needed   *126*
Job Analysis   *127*
Job Description   *127*
Qualifications Needed To Fill The Job   *128*
Methods of Determining Qualifications   *129*
Need for Many Recruits   *131*
Recruiting and Its Importance   *131*
Finding and Maintaining Good Recruiting Sources   *132*
Referrals   *133*
Sources for Recruiting Sales Representatives   *133*
Current Employees   *134*
Other Companies: Competitors, Customers…   *134*
Job Advertisements   *135*
Company Website   *137*
Educational Institutions   *137*
Diversity   *138*
Employment Agencies   *138*
Part-Time Workers   *138*
Minority Groups   *139*
Recruiting Evaluation   *140*
Women   *140*

Summary   141
Key Terms   141
Questions and Problems   142
Experiential Exercises   143
   Case Exhibit 5-A   *Sample Job Description of a Salesperson   144*
Endnotes   148

Chapter 6   Selecting and Hiring Salespeople   *149*
  Selection Tools   *150*
    Resumes/Application Forms   *152*
    Personal Interviews   *152*
    Employment Testing   *158*
    References and Other Outside Sources   *162*
    Assessment Centers   *163*
  The Job Offer Decision   *164*
  The Hiring Phase   *164*
    Ranking The Recruits   *164*
    Communicating With Applicants   *164*
    Extending The Offer   *165*
    Extending a Job Offer   *165*
  Socialization and Assimilation   *166*
    Preentry Socialization   *166*
    Assimilation of New Hires   *167*
  Meeting Social and Psychological Needs   *169*
  Summary   169
  Key Terms   170
  Questions and Problems   171
  Experiential Exercises   172
  Endnotes   182

Chapter 7   Sales Training   *183*
  The Value of Sales Training   *184*
  Sales Training and Strategic Planning   *185*
  Training Assessment   *185*
    What Are The Training Program Objectives?   *186*
    Who Should Be Trained?   *187*
    What Are The Training Needs of The Individual Rep?   *188*
    Training for An Experienced Sales Rep   *189*
    How Much Training Is Needed?   *190*
    Who Should Do The Training?   *191*
  Program Design   *191*
    When Should The Training Take Place?   *193*
    Where Should Training Take Place?   *194*
    What Should The Content of The Training Be?   *196*
    What Teaching Methods Should Be Used?   *199*
  Reinforcement   *202*
  Training Evaluation   *203*
  Summary   203
  Key Terms   204

Questions and Problems   204
Experiential Exercises   205
Endnotes   210

Chapter 8 Motivating a Sales Force   *211*
  Motivation—What Is It? *212*
    Dimensions of Sales Motivation   *212*
    Motivation and Strategic Planning   *213*
    Unique Nature of The Sales Job   *213*
    Individuality of Salespeople   *213*
  Importance and Difficulty of Motivation   *213*
  Behavioral Concepts of Motivation   *214*
    Diversity In Company Goals   *214*
    Changes In Market Environment   *214*
    Expectancy Theory   *215*
    Maslow's Hierarchy of Needs Theory   *216*
    Dual-Factor Theory   *217*
    Role Theory   *218*
    Attribution Theory   *219*
  Salesperson Characteristics   *220*
  Career Stages and The Plateaued Salesperson   *220*
  Financial Rewards   *222*
    Compensation   *223*
    Other Financial Rewards   *223*
    Sales Contests   *223*
    The Sales Contest   *225*
  Nonfinancial Rewards   *226*
    Job Enrichment and Support   *226*
    Recognition and Honor Awards   *227*
    Promotions   *227*
  Sales Meetings   *228*
    Encouragement and Praise   *228*
    Customer Feedback   *228*
    Corporate Culture   *228*
    Purposes of Sales Meetings   *228*
    Planning for Sales Meetings   *229*
  Motivation and Performance   *229*
  Summary   230
  Key Terms   231
  Questions and Problems   231
  Experiential Exercises   233
  Endnotes   240

Chapter 9 Sales Force Compensation   *241*
  Sales Force Compensation and Strategic Planning   *242*
  Objectives of a Compensation Plan   *242*
    The Company's Perspective   *242*
    The Salesperson's Perspective   *245*
  Designing a Sales Compensation Plan   *246*

Review Job Descriptions   *247*
Identify Specific Objectives   *247*

Establishing The Level of Compensation   *247*
Reps Selling Too Many Low-Profit Products   *248*

Developing The Method of Compensation   *249*
Basic Types of Compensation Plans   *250*
Straight Salary Plans   *251*
Straight Commission Plans   *252*
Combination Plans   *255*

Indirect Monetary Compensation   *258*
Linking The Method To The Objective   *258*
Introducing The Plan To The Sales Force   *259*

Pretest and Install The Plan   *259*
Summary   *260*
Key Terms   *261*
Questions and Problems   *262*
Experiential Exercises   *263*
Endnotes   *270*

Chapter 10   Sales Force Quotas and Expenses   *271*

Sales Quotas   *272*
Relation To Sales Potential   *272*
Sales Quotas and Strategic Management   *272*
Indicate Strong Or Weak Spots In The Selling Structure   *273*
Furnish Goals and Incentives for The Sales Force   *273*
Control Salespeople's Activities   *273*
Evaluate Productivity of Salespeople   *273*

Purposes of Sales Quotas   *273*

Types of Quotas   *274*
Improve Effectiveness of Compensation Plans   *274*
Control Selling Expenses   *274*
Evaluate Sales Contest Results   *274*
Sales Volume Quotas   *276*
Gross Margin (Or Profit) Quotas   *276*
Expense Quotas   *277*
Activity Quotas and Customer Satisfaction   *277*
Combination Quotas   *277*

Calculating Quota Attainment   *278*

Basis for Setting a Sales Volume Quota   *278*
Quotas Based On Sales Potential   *278*
Adjustments To Potential-Based Quotas   *279*
Quotas Based On Factors Other Than Potential   *279*
Typical Administrative Weaknesses   *281*

Administration of Sales Quotas   *281*

Sales Force Expenses   *282*
Gaining Sales Force Acceptance of a Quota Plan   *282*

Sales Force Expenses and Strategic Planning   *283*

Internal Revenue Service Regulations   *283*

Legitimate Travel and Business Expenses   *283*

Reduction In Travel Expense   285
No Net Gain Or Loss for The Reps   285
Characteristics of a Sound Expense Plan   285
Equitable Treatment of The Reps   286
No Curtailment of Beneficial Activities   286
Minimal Detail and Administrative Expense   286
Clarity   286
Company Control of Expenses and Elimination of Padding   286
Salespeople Pay Own Expenses   287
Unlimited-Payment Plans   287
Methods of Controlling Expenses   287
Limited-Payment Plans   288
Combination Plans   289
Control of Sales Force Transportation   289
Ownership Or Leasing of Automobiles   290
Reimbursement Plans for Employee-Owned Cars   291
Other Methods of Expense Control   294
Training and Enforcement   294
Credit Cards   294
The Expense Bank Account   295
Change In Nature of Entertainment   295
Telemarketing/Email   295
Careful Travel Planning   295
Summary   296
Key Terms   297
Questions and Problems   297
Experiential Exercises   299
Endnotes   305

Chapter 11   Leadership of a Sales Force   307
Leadership Characteristics and Skills   308
Personal Characteristics   308
Managerial Skills   308
Transactional Leadership   309
Leadership Style⁵   309
Transformational Leadership   310
Situational Leadership   312
Leadership and Strategic Planning   312
Personal Contact   313
Tools and Techniques of Leadership   313
Sales Reports   314
Information Communication   315
Published Materials   316
Meetings   316
Indirect Supervisory Aids   316
Outcomes of Effective Leadership   318
Well-Trained Salespeople   318
Trust Among Salespeople   318
Citizenship Behaviors   319

Better Performance   *319*
Sales Force Morale   *319*
Problems Encountered In Leadership   *320*
Poor Performance   *320*
A Sales Rep Objects To Harassment   *321*
Substance Abuse   *321*
Expense Accounts   *323*
Unethical Behavior   *323*
Sexual Harassment[17]   *323*
Summary   325
Key Terms   326
Questions and Problems   326
Experiential Exercises   327
Endnotes   333

Chapter 12   Forecasting and Budgets   *335*
Market Potential and Sales Potential   *337*
Sales Forecast   *337*
The Basic Ideas Used In Forecasting   *337*
Estimating The Potential for a Market and Sales   *338*
Customer Analysis   *338*
Market-Factor Derivation   *339*
Surveys of Buyer Intentions   *340*
Test Markets   *340*
Territory Potentials   *341*
Difficulty of Sales Forecasting   *343*
Sales Forecasting Periods   *343*
Sales Forecasting   *343*
Factors Influencing The Sales Forecast   *344*
Sales Forecasting Methods   *345*
Executive Opinion   *346*
Sales Force Composite   *346*
Moving Average Technique   *347*
Exponential Smoothing Models   *348*
Regression Analysis   *349*
"Must-Do" Forecasts   *350*
Capacity-Based Forecasts   *351*
Some Guiding Princples for Forecasting   *351*
Fit The Method To The Product/Market   *352*
Use More Than One Method   *352*
Minimize The Number of Market Factors   *353*
Recognize The Limitations of Forecasting   *353*
Use The Minimum/Maximum Technique   *353*
Understand Math and Statistics   *353*
Review The Forecasting Process   *353*
Account Managers Underestimate Sales Forecasts   *354*
Planning   *355*
Coordination   *355*

Developing Budgets   *355*
Purposes of Budgeting   *355*
Determining The Sales Budget   *356*
  Evaluation   *356*
  Percentage-Of-Sales Method   *356*
  Objective-And-Task Method   *356*
  The Sales Budget   *357*
  The Selling-Expense Budget   *357*
Budgets for Sales Department Activities   *357*
The Budget Process for The Firm   *358*
  The Administrative Budget   *358*
Budget Periods   *360*
Managing With Budgets   *360*
Summary   *360*
Key Terms   *361*
Questions and Problems   *362*
Experiential Exercises   *363*
Endnotes   *369*

Chapter 13   Sales Territories   *371*
Nature of Territories   *372*
  Benefits of Territories   *372*
  Potential Problems With Territories   *373*
  When Territories Are Unnecessary   *373*
Designing Territories   *374*
  Determine Basic Control Unit for Territorial Boundaries   *374*
  Determine Location and Potential of Customers   *376*
  Determine Basic Territories   *377*
  Buildup Method   *377*
Using Technology In Territory Design[5]   *380*
Assigning Salespeople To Territories   *383*
Revising Sales Territories   *383*
  Indications of Need for Adjustment   *384*
  Claim Jumping By Account Manager Formerly In a Territory   *386*
  Why Are So Many Sales Territories Unbalanced?[10]   *386*
Territorial Coverage—Managing a Salesperson's Time   *387*
  Routing The Sales Force   *388*
Summary   *390*
Key Terms   *391*
Questions and Problems   *391*
Experiential Exercises   *393*
Endnotes   *399*

Chapter 14   Sales Volume Analysis   *401*
  Relation of Performance Evaluation To Sales Control   *402*
  A Marketing Audit: a Total Evaluation Program   *403*
  A Sales Management Audit   *404*
  The Evaluation Process   *404*
  Components of Performance Evaluation   *405*

The Nature of Misdirected Marketing Effort: The 80/20
Principle   *405*
Reasons for Misdirected Effort   *406*
The Need for Detailed Data   *407*
Basis for Analyzing Sales Volume   *407*
Total Sales Volume   *408*
Sales By Territories   *409*
Sales By Products   *410*
Sales By Customer Classifications   *411*
The Insufficiency of Sales Volume Analysis   *412*
Summary   414
Key Terms   415
Questions and Problems   415
Experiential Exercises   416
Endnotes   419

Chapter 15 Cost and Profitability Analysis   *421*
Nature and Scope of Marketing Cost Analysis   *422*
Marketing Cost Analysis and The Accounting System   *422*
Marketing Cost Analysis Compared With Production Cost
Accounting   *422*
Analysis of Ledger Expenses   *423*
Analysis of Activity Expenses   *423*
Types of Marekting Cost Analysis   *423*
Analysis of Activity Costs By Market Segments   *426*
Allocating Costs   *429*
Problems In Marketing Cost Analysis   *429*
The Contribution-Margin Versus Full-Cost Controversy   *431*
Territorial Decisions   *433*
Use of Findings From Profitability Analysis   *433*
Products   *434*
Customer/Size of Order   *434*
Return On Investment: An Evaluation Tool   *436*
Summary   438
Key Terms   439
Questions and Problems   439
Experiential Exercises   441
Endnotes   443

Chapter 16 Evaluating a Salesperson's Performance   *445*
Nature and Importance of Performance Evaluation   *446*
Concept of Evaluation and Development   *446*
Concept of Evaluation and Direction   *446*
Importance of Performance Evaluation   *446*
Difficulties Involved In Evaluating Performance   *447*
Importance of a Good Job Description   *447*
Program for Evaluating Performance   *448*
Step 1. Establish Some Basic Policies   *448*
Step 2. Select Bases for Evaluation   *449*

Step 3. Set Performance Standards   *454*
Step 4. Compare Performance With Standards   *454*
Step 5. Discuss The Evaluation With The Salesperson   *458*
An Account Manager Objects To His Evaluation   *459*
Using Evaluation Data: An Example   *460*
Joe's Sales Performance   *461*
Gus's Sales Performance   *463*
Paula's Sales Performance   *463*
Summary   *464*
The Sales Manager's Decisions   *464*
Key Terms   *465*
Questions and Problems   *465*
Experiential Exercises   *466*
Endnotes   *471*

Chapter 17   Ethics and Laws   *473*
Business Ethics and Sales Management   *474*
The Legal-Ethical Confusion   *474*
The Pressure To Compromise Personal Ethics   *475*
The Problem of Determining Ethical Standards   *476*
Relations With The Sales Force   *477*
Relations With The Company   *477*
Relations With Customers   *478*
Establishing An Ethical Climate   *480*
Take a Long-Run Point of View   *480*
Put Guidelines In Writing   *480*
Reinforce The Ethical Climate   *481*
Public Regulation and Sales Managers   *482*
Provide Ethical Training   *482*
Price Discrimination   *482*
Unfair Competition   *483*
Green River Ordinances   *484*
Cooling-Off Laws   *484*
Account Manager Accused of Passing Confidential
Information   *485*
Current Problems   *485*
Summary   *486*
Key Terms   *486*
Questions and Problems   *487*
Experiential Exercises   *488*
Endnotes   *492*

Company Index   *493*

Subject Index   *495*

PREFACE

For firms with an outside sales force, the activities involved in personal selling typically include more people and cost more money than any other phase of the firm's marketing program. Moreover, the success experienced by sales managers and their team of salespeople usually is a major factor in determining the success enjoyed by the firm. Consequently, the topic of this book – *Sales Force Management* – is a very important part of a firm's overall strategy.

The book presents a blend of leading-edge research and real-world strategy in a highly readable, student-friendly writing style. The focus is on the challenges faced by *today's* sales managers – and so, the book covers the latest on technology, globalization, social selling, hybrid sales channels, and host of other contemporary issues.

The book is divided into five main parts:

1. **Introduction to sales force management (Chapters 1, 2, 3).** The first three chapters set the scene for the rest of the book. After establishing the nature, scope, and importance of personal selling and sales force management, the book demonstrates how sales force planning relates to the firm's overall strategic plan. The final chapter in this section presents an overview of the personal selling process – which is necessary background information for sales managers.

2. **Organization, staffing, and training a sales force (Chapters 4, 5, 6, 7).** After explaining how to organize a sales force, this section makes the case that *selecting the right people* is the most important activity in the entire management process. In fact, this is a basic managerial philosophy that permeates the entire book.

3. **Directing sales force operations (Chapters 8, 9, 10, 11).** In this section, we present motivation, compensation and leadership theories and practices. This includes discussion on how salespeople respond to both financial and nonfinancial rewards.

4. **Sales planning (Chapters 12, 13).** This part picks up on the strategy concepts introduced in chapter 2, and presents a comprehensive explanation on sales forecasting and territory design – which are two critical parts of the planning process of a sales organization.

5. **Evaluating sales performance (Chapters 14, 15, 16, 17).** Finally, the textbook closes with a set of chapters on evaluation. After describing how to analyze the sales volume and marketing cost and profitability of the entire sales force, the book discusses how to conduct performance reviews of each member of the sales team. The final chapter covers evaluation of ethical and legal responsibilities.

A particular strength of this book are the cases, which are designed to generate lively in-classroom discussions. Each chapter closes with two to three short cases that delve into the latest issues associated with the chapter topics. In addition, there is a running case about Shiderlots Elevator, a fictional company portrayed as one of the world's leading manufacturers of – and service providers to – elevators, escalators and moving walkways. Shiderlots sales manager, Adam Dark, and his sales team are introduced in Chapter 4, and the cases continue throughout the book. Several of the cases have data, and thus lend themselves to the type of quantitative analysis that sales managers must do.

To accompany *Sales Force Management,* an extensive set of teaching supplements have been prepared by the textbook author. This includes:

- Case notes.
- Answers to end-of-chapter questions.
- PowerPoint slides for each chapter.
- An extensive, revised test bank of objective true-false and multiple choice questions.
- Classroom quizzes on Kahoot!, which is a free game-based learning platform that allows students to respond to questions with their own device (i.e., smartphone, laptop, etc.)

Finally, I would like to recognize and acknowledge the many people who have been instrumental in the creation of *Sales Force Management.* William Stanton and Rosann Spiro have had major influences on the book. In addition, Jason Heaster from Fastenal, Matt Maurer from Reynolds Consumer Products, Jerry Foy from Liberty Mutual Insurance, and Adam Drake from Otis Elevator are extended my sincere thanks. These four sales professionals provided extensive, up-to-date information on the latest sales force management practices in a series of in-depth interviews. Finally, I would like to recognize, with grateful appreciation, the creative efforts of Paul Ducham and his team from Chicago Business Press. This textbook would not have been possible without the contributions of these generous and talented individuals.

Gregory A. Rich

1

Introduction to Sales Force Management

Getting things done through people has never been more challenging than it is today. This is especially true for sales managers, whose job is to generate more sales through salespeople. What makes this so difficult is that sales managers must continually adapt to a number of dramatic changes to their field. Customers are more knowledgeable, more analytical and have higher expectations about salespeople, who customers expect will truly add value to their business.[1] Of course, changes in technology add to the challenge, as customers are increasingly accessing information through social media and other online sources. This results in them being more than halfway through the purchase process before a salesperson even gets to talk to them.[2] Finally, globalization and the ensuing fierce competition continues to be more and more a part of the everyday life of the sales function.[3] The sales manager is expected to keep up with these trends, and then provide the leadership necessary to guide the sales organization to success. Never has the field of sales management been more important to study!

The answers are not always intuitive. Microchip Technology is a large semiconductor company headquartered near Phoenix. This company realized that the selling function was becoming more and more sophisticated. The easy, routine functions, which salespeople used to focus on, had become automated. They needed their account managers to shift toward interpreting information to clients, instead of just dispensing it. They needed to solve complicated problems for clients, and sell insights and solutions, rather than just the tangible product. In the end, what made the shift possible was a dramatic move away from commission-based compensation, to a salary with a small, team-based bonus. The fact that this tactic (of moving away from incentive-based pay) was successful was quite surprising to most traditional, business-to-business sales professionals.[4]

According to customers, the number one reason salespeople are not successful is that *they talk too much, and don't listen enough*.[5] Listening builds trust, and is how salespeople can understand the needs of their customers. Figure 1-1 shows the results from another survey about what customers do not like about salespeople. Again, this points to how sophisticated today's selling is, and how salespeople often do meet customer expectations. The sales manager can play a critical role in this. This role includes hiring the right people (i.e., people who *listen*), implementing the proper training program, and then motivating and leading the salespeople to do the job.

The world is changing, and the field of selling and sales management is changing right along with it. Sales executives have no choice but to keep up with and adapt to these changes. Only then can they be successful in "getting things done through people!" We introduce the dynamic field of sales force management by explaining the scope and focus of this book.

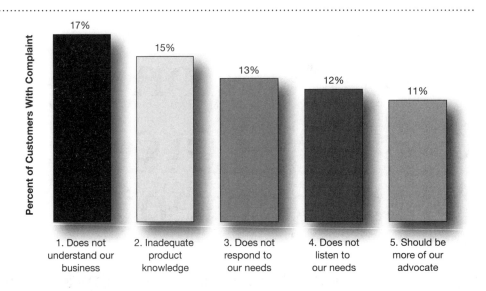

FIGURE 1-1

Top Five Customer Complaints about Salespeople
Source: The HR Chally Group, Ten Year Research Report, *2002.*

SCOPE AND FOCUS OF THIS BOOK

This is a book about **sales management**—also called sales force management. We define sales management as the management of the personal selling component of an organization's marketing program. The central focus of the book is the design of sales management strategies and tactics that will help an organization achieve its marketing goals.

Specifically, this book deals almost entirely with the management of what is known as an **outside sales force**, that is, a sales force that calls in-person on prospective customers. Outside selling stands in contrast with situations in which customers come to the salespeople—called across-the-counter selling. An outside sales force makes in-person sales calls, usually at the customer's home or place of business. Managing an outside sales force presents a unique set of problems, since most of the salespeople are geographically outside the organization's offices.

There are many different types of outside sales forces, each requiring a different strategy to be successful. Outside sales forces can be either in business-to-business sales (e.g., Firestone selling tires to Ford) or in business-to-consumer sales (e.g., State Farm selling auto insurance directly to consumers). Further, the salesperson in business-to-business sales calls on three distinct types of business customers: manufacturers (e.g., Ford), intermediaries (e.g., Dick's Sporting Goods), and institutions (e.g., Harvard University). All salespeople sell products that are goods, services, or most commonly—some combination of the two, and that are being purchased for the purpose of consumption, incorporation, or resale. Figure 1-2 lists some examples of these different types of outside sales forces.

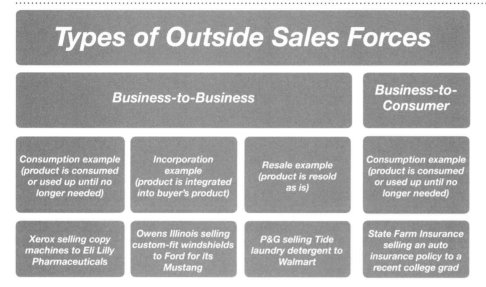

FIGURE 1-2

Examples of Consumption, Incorporation, or Resale

Further, many firms also contact customers by methods that are not face to face. For example, **inside sales (or telemarketing)** is used to contact customers by telephone; and **e-commerce** refers to an online system of commercial transactions, which involves contacting customers via the internet. These systems are used as either the primary method or a supplemental method of interacting with customers.

THE NATURE OF PERSONAL SELLING

We just said that sales management is the management of the personal selling effort in an organization. So let's begin by looking at some aspects of personal selling to see what it is that sales managers manage.

Personal Selling and the Marketing Mix

The term **marketing mix** describes the combination of the four ingredients that constitute the core of a company's marketing system. When these four ingredients—product, price, distribution, and promotion—are effectively blended, they form a marketing program that provides want-satisfying goods and services to the company's market.

Promotional activities form a separate sub-mix that we call the **promotional mix**, or the **communication mix**, in the company's marketing program. The major elements in the promotional mix are the company's advertising, sales promotion, and personal selling efforts. Publicity and public relations are also part of the promotional activities, but typically they are less widely used than the first three elements. In the American economy, personal selling is the most important of the big three elements in terms of people employed, dollars spent, and sales generated.

Relationship Marketing and the Role of Personal Selling

In the face of intense competition, companies today are trying to improve their performance in every dimension of their operations. As a result, companies expect more from their suppliers. Salespeople who represent these suppliers are expected to make a contribution to their customers' success. To do this, salespeople must understand their customers' needs and be able to discover customers' problems and/or help solve those problems.

At the same time, companies are finding it harder to develop or sustain product-based competitive advantages. Most product-based advantages are soon copied by competitors. For example, Apple Computer began selling the first modern tablet computer in 2010, but at the Computer Electronics Show in 2011, Motorola, Samsung, Blackberry and many others released their own tablets to compete with the iPad. Thus, companies must focus on strengthening the value-added components of their offerings. **Value-added components** are those that augment the product itself, such as information and service.

To understand customer needs and to provide customers with value-added solutions to their problems, salespeople must develop close long-term relationships with their customers. These relationships are built on *cooperation*, *trust*, *commitment*, and *information*. The process by which a firm builds long-term relationships with customers for the purpose of creating mutual competitive advantages is called **relationship marketing**, or **relationship selling**. Salespeople who are engaged in relationship selling concentrate their efforts on developing trust in a few carefully selected accounts over an extended period, rather than calling on a large number of accounts. Relationship selling is distinct from the traditional **transaction selling**, whereby salespeople focus on the immediate one-time sale of the product. Although chapter 2 discusses relationship marketing in greater detail, these are the main differences:

Transaction Selling	Relationship Selling
Get new accounts	Retain existing accounts
Get the order	Become the preferred supplier
Cut the price to get the sale	Price for profit
Manage all accounts to maximize short-term sales	Manage each account for long-term profit
	Concentrate on high-profit-potential accounts
Sell to anyone	

The Nature of Sales Jobs

In Figure 1-2 we identified different types of salespeople based on the different types of products they sell. However, most sales jobs, even within the same product category, are quite different from one another and generally are different from non-sales jobs. Further, most sales jobs today are quite different from those of the past. Before we discuss each of these differences, we interject a note on pertinent terminology. The most common job title for a salesperson is account manager, and another very common title is sales representative (or sales rep). We tend to use these terms interchangeably. Note that some sales professionals make a distinction between these two job titles (account manager and sales representative)—and argue that the former focuses on retaining existing accounts, whereas the latter focuses on generating new accounts. However, we find that in common practice both of these job titles tend to be involved with both tasks (i.e., the tasks of retaining existing and generating new business).

Wide Variety of Sales Responsibilities

No two selling jobs are alike. The types of jobs and the requirements needed to fill them cover a wide spectrum. The job of a Pepsi-Cola salesperson who calls in routine fashion on a group of retail stores is in another world from that of the IBM client manager who heads up a team of product specialists dedicated to serving the information needs of a specific industry. Similarly, an Avon Products representative who sells door-to-door has a job only remotely related to that of a Cessna Aircraft Company rep who sells airplanes to large firms.

The wide variety of sales jobs differs greatly with respect to the amount of problem-solving and selling required, from very complex to simple. Some salespeople are creative order-getters, others are unimaginative order-takers, and some never ask for or receive orders at all—they merely provide support. A recent survey of over 1,000 salespeople from a wide variety of industries identified the following six categories of contemporary sales jobs:[6]

1. **Consultative seller.** This type of sales rep uses relationship selling techniques to demonstrate how his or her company's products will contribute to the customer's well-being or profit. They are creative, problem solvers who serve as consultants to their customers. For example, strategic account managers at 3M are consultative sellers. Recently, the 3M account reps helped redesign one of IBM's manufacturing processes with 3M materials that were less sensitive to static than the ones that had been in use. This cooperative problem-solving led to a much stronger relationship between the two companies and to a tenfold increase in 3M's sales to IBM.[7]

2. **Key account seller.** There are many similarities between key account sellers and consultative sellers. The key difference is that key account sellers focus on a smaller number of big, important customers (i.e., key accounts). For example, Owens Corning, a manufacturer of insulation and other building materials, has teams of key account sellers focused on Home Depot, Lowes, and other big-box retailers. The goal of these sellers is to maintain and penetrate the existing accounts, as opposed to generating new customers.

3. **New business seller.** More than any other category, this salesperson focuses on prospecting for customers and generating new accounts. Typically, the goal is to earn the trust of prospects, get the initial order, and turn them into long-term customers. In some cases, the customer is turned over to a **sales support** person (see next category) after the account is established, and the new business seller moves onto what he or she does best: finding new customers. Other times, the new business seller keeps and maintains the accounts and gradually becomes more of a consultative seller. New business sellers typically face rejection on a daily basis, so they need to be highly motivated self-starters.

4. **Sales support.** These salespeople support the actual selling done by the reps in the other categories. Support personnel perform sales promotional activities and work with customers in training and educational capacities. Sometimes these reps may be part of the sales team brought in to assess customer needs and provide information before the sale or after the sales to help solve customer problems, but they are not responsible for *selling* the product.

   Some support people who are product specialists—**sales engineers**—work with customers to assist with technical problems. These reps may either help adapt a customer's system to the seller's products or help the seller design new products to fill the customer's particular needs. Shell Oil Company's sales engineers help out when the company's sales representatives need specialized expertise to solve a customer problem. Essentially, all support reps assist in getting or keeping the customer by providing assistance and information about the products and their applications to customer needs.

5. **Missionary seller.** The term missionary salespeople is commonly used to describe a type of sales support salesperson. By definition, missionary salespeople do not solicit orders. They work for a manufacturer, calling on customers in order to provide product information and generally promote goodwill about the product. These salespeople sometimes introduce new lines of products to customers or assist in conducting special promotional activities. Pharmaceutical sales reps are missionary salespeople, since doctors do not order drugs directly from them. Rather, doctors write prescriptions when they are with their patients, who then buy the drug from a pharmacy.

6. **Delivery seller.** These are maintenance salespeople that facilitate sales to consumers or to business accounts that have already been established. Delivery sellers take orders, but they do not engage in as much creative problem solving as the consultative or key account sellers. Examples include Coca-Cola reps or Hostess brand food reps, who deliver product and stock shelves at retail food and drugstore chains. This work is fairly routine. Both selling and problem solving are left to key account salespeople higher in the organization, while the primary responsibility of the local reps is to ensure that their products are getting as much shelf space and promotional attention as possible.

Note that the previously described six categories of sales jobs are not completely distinct. That is, the responsibilities of many salespeople do not neatly fall into a single category. The specific activities of each salesperson depend on both the type of product being sold and the specific needs of customers. Of course, this presents a leadership challenge for sales executives, because it is their job to define the roles and responsibilities for the salespeople in their firm.

Wide Variety of Companies, Products, and Customers
Salespeople have different responsibilities because they work for different types of companies, selling different types of products to different types of customers. For example, salespeople for Quaker Oats, Ford Motor Company, Eli Lilly, and Coca-Cola sell consumer products to wholesalers, institutions, or retailers.

Mary Kay sells to the final consumer as well as to some retailers. Companies such as South-Western Educational Publishing sell only to the final consumer. The reps for any of these companies may be consultative sellers, new business sellers, and/or sales support employees.

Salespeople from Du Pont, Alcoa, Inland Steel, Textron, Georgia-Pacific, IBM, Xerox, Merck, and Airborne Express generally sell industrial and business products to manufacturers, wholesalers, and institutions. These reps are usually consultative salespeople and sales support personnel. It should be noted that most large companies employ more than one type of salesperson because they sell to more than one type of customer.

How Sales Jobs Differ from Other Jobs

Why is it useful to study management of a sales force separately from the management of other classes of business personnel? Why are there no courses in the management of accountants or finance personnel? The answer is that a sales job is different from other jobs and is vital to a company's financial well-being. Figure 1-3 provides an overview of the activities for which a salesperson may be responsible. Not all reps perform all of these activities. Which activities they perform depends on the types of products they sell and the types of customers to whom they sell. Let's take a closer look at some of the key differentiating features of a sales job:

- *The sales force is largely responsible for implementing a firm's marketing strategies in the field.* Moreover, the sales reps generate the revenues that are managed by the financial people and used by the product people.
- *Salespeople are among the few employees authorized to spend company funds.* They are responsible for spending company money for entertainment, rooms, food, transportation, and so on. Their effectiveness in discharging this responsibility significantly influences marketing costs and profits.
- *Salespeople represent their company to customers and to society in general.* Opinions of the firm and its products are formed on the basis of impressions made by these people in their work and outside activities. The public ordinarily does not judge a company by its factory or office workers.
- *Salespeople represent the customer to their companies.* As noted earlier in the chapter, salespeople are primarily responsible for transmitting information on customer needs and problems back to the various departments in their own firms.
- *Sales reps operate with little or no direct supervision and require a high degree of motivation.* For success in selling, a sales rep must work hard physically and mentally, be creative and persistent, and show considerable initiative.
- *Salespeople frequently face rejection.* Sales reps do not get the sale every time. They must be able to handle the negative feelings that come with "losing the sale."
- *Salespeople need more tact and social intelligence than other employees on the same level in the organization.* Many sales jobs require the rep to socialize with customers, who frequently are upper-level people in their companies. Considerable social intelligence also may be needed in dealing with difficult buyers.

Generate sales:	Provide service to customers:	Territory management:	Professional development:	Company service:
Pre-call planning	Provide consulting	Gather and analyze information on customers, competitors' general market developments	-Participate in sales meetings	-Train new salespeople
Prospecting	Oversee installations and repairs		-Join professional associations	-Perform civic duties
Make sales presentations	Check inventory levels		-Attend training programs	
Overcome objections	Stock shelves	Disseminate information to appropriate personnel within salesperson's company		
Close / ask for order	Provide merchandising assisting			
Arrange for delivery	Oversee product and equipment testing			
Entertain		Develop sales strategies and plans, forecasts, and budgets		
Arrange for financing	Train wholesalers' and retailer's salespeople			
Collect payments				
Participate in trade shows				

FIGURE 1-3
Selected Activities of salespeople

- *Sales jobs frequently require considerable travel and time away from home and family.* This places additional physical and mental burdens on salespeople who already face much pressure and many demands.
- *Salespeople have large role sets.* The salesperson's role requires that individuals in this position interact with large numbers of people. At each customer firm, the salesperson usually works with many people, such as buyers, engineers, and production and finance personnel. In their own firms, they also must work with people from a variety of departments such as marketing research, product design, product management, finance, and production—as well as with other sales personnel.
- *Salespeople face role ambiguity, role conflict, and role stress.* As consultative sellers, salespeople often must provide innovative solutions to problems and, in doing so, must satisfy many different people. As a result, salespeople often experience **role conflict**, whereby they feel caught in the middle between the conflicting demands of the people they must satisfy. Also, reps are not supervised very closely, so they frequently find themselves in situations where they are uncertain about what to do; thus, they experience **role ambiguity**. Because of role conflict and ambiguity, along with the expectation that salespeople will contribute increasing revenues to their companies, many sales positions have greater **role stress** than other jobs.

New Dimensions of Personal Selling: The Professional Salesperson

Personal selling today is quite different from what it was years ago. The cigar-smoking, backslapping, joke-telling salesman (and virtually all outside sales reps were men in those days) is generally gone from the scene. Moreover, his talents and methods would likely not be effective in today's business environment.

Instead, a new type of sales representative has emerged—a professional salesperson who is also a marketing consultant. This new breed works to relay consumer wants back to the firm so that appropriate products may be developed. Its representatives engage in a *total* consultative, non-manipulative selling; they are expected to solve customers' problems, not just take orders. For example, Medtronic, a leader in the design and manufacture of high-tech surgical devices, sells to surgeons. These doctors often want the sales rep to be in the operating room during surgery to advise them in the best use of the product.[8] The vice president of sales and marketing for Lucent Technologies states that Lucent's overall goal is "to have all of our customers say that we are vital to their business success."[9] Of course, this is difficult given the rising expectations of customers.

The new-style reps also serve as *territorial profit managers.* They have the autonomy they need to make decisions that affect their own territory's profitability. Many decisions that in the past would have been made by the sales manager are today made by the salesperson. Salespeople are *empowered* to act in the best interests of their firms. A recent survey of salespeople's competencies found those salespeople who excel at aligning the strategic objectives of both customers and suppliers, and who understand the *business issues* underlying their customers' needs, are the most successful.[10] To a large extent, technology has empowered salespeople to increase the quality of contact and service they provide to their customers by allowing them to tap into huge data banks.

What factors are important to customers when selecting a sales force? More than anything else, customers want their salespeople to provide service that solves problems and responds to their needs. Other important factors are shown in the following list. Clearly, this provides further evidence that customers' expectations are very high and getting higher!

The ten most important factors for professional sales forces
The professional sales force...
Provides service that solves problems and responds to customer needs
Has excellent product knowledge
Serves as an advocate for the customers within the selling firm.
Keeps customers up-to-date
Sells a high-quality product
Offers superior technical support
Has accessible personnel that are available locally
Sells a wide variety of products that offer a total solution
Understands the customers' business
Sells the product for a competitive price

SOURCE: The HR Chally Group, *Ten Year Research Report,* 2002.

THE NATURE OF SALES MANAGEMENT

During the early stages in the evolution of marketing management, sales management was narrow in scope. The major activities were recruiting and selecting a sales force, and then training, supervising, and motivating these people. Today, personal selling and sales management have much broader dimensions. Many sales executives are responsible for strategic planning, forecasting,

CONSIDER THIS...

The Value of Silence in Selling

As discussed in the chapter, listening is one of the most important skills sales. However, salespeople can only listen if they are *silent*—and patiently wait for their client to fully explain the issue. This is not always easy. People tend to be uncomfortable with silence. Salespeople, in particular, often are inclined to keep talking just to fill the noise gap. However, successful salespeople understand that silence is a powerful tool in selling. They learn to nod their head, and listen quietly and intently to what the prospect is saying.

By learning to be silent, salespeople can demonstrate empathy to prospects, gain knowledge about their full range of needs, and then deliver value by satisfying those needs they have identified.

SOURCE: Rachel Clapp Miller, "The Value of Silence in Your Discovery Process," *Growth Play Sales Effectiveness Blog*, July 8, 2016. Available at: http://blog.growthplay.com/the-value-of-silence-in-your-discovery-process. Accessed July 11, 2016.

budgeting, territory design, and sales and cost analyses, as well as the more traditional activities. Sales managers must see that all of these tasks are integrated. Figure 1-4 illustrates how each of the sales management activities is linked with the others, and generally maps them onto the chapter topics of this book. If one of these activities is performed poorly, it will have a ripple effect on the others. For example, if the wrong people are hired, efforts to train and motivate them will almost always result in failure.

Furthermore, it is the sales manager's responsibility to see that all of the activities—such as production, advertising, and distribution—that support the sales of products and services are coordinated with the efforts of the sales department.

Role and Skills of a Sales Manager

As the role of the salesperson has changed, so has that of the sales manager. With high-quality empowered sales forces, sales managers are more likely to provide support and resources than to direct and control salespeople. They focus on internal coordination of the sales efforts so that their salespeople can spend more time with their customers. Increasingly, they will be asked to manage multiple sales channels—for example, field sales, inside sales and e-commerce might all have to be coordinated.

The demanding, controlling, volume-oriented sales manager is a dying breed. Today, the most successful sales managers are seen as *team leaders* rather than *bosses*. They still direct and advise people, but they do so through collaboration and empowerment rather than control and domination. To be successful, sales managers, like salespeople, will need to adapt their strategies, styles, and attitudes. Some of the critical changes are:

- Developing a detailed understanding of customers' business.
- Treating salespeople as equals and working with them to achieve profitability and customer satisfaction.
- Applying flexible motivational tools to a hybrid sales force of tele-sellers, direct marketers, and field salespeople.
- Keeping up to date on the latest technologies affecting buyer-seller relationships.

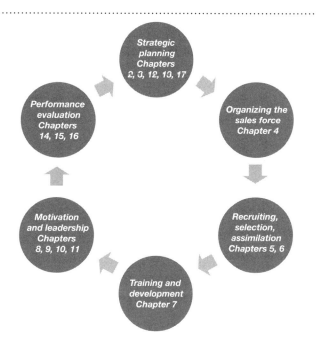

FIGURE 1-4
Sales management
responsibilities

- Working closely with other internal departments as a member of the corporate team seeking to achieve customer satisfaction.
- Continually seeking ways to exceed customer expectations and bring added value to the buyer-seller relationship.
- Creating a flexible learning and adapting environment.[11]

In terms of abilities, "people skills" are more important than analytical and evaluative skills. The ability to develop team-oriented relationships is particularly important. Today's sales manager must be sensitive to individual needs and skills, caring more about communicating and coaching than monitoring and controlling.

Administration—A Distinct Skill

A sales manager is first and foremost a manager—an administrator—and management is a distinct skill. Only during the past few decades has management, or administration (we use these terms synonymously), been recognized as a separate body of knowledge. One of the ironies of sales force management is that sales managers were usually promoted into the executive ranks because of their talent as salespeople. But from then on, their success or failure depended on their administrative skills—skills that may or may not have been developed during their time as sales reps.

Sales Ability Is Not Enough

Although many people with outstanding technical abilities make good administrators, there is considerable evidence that sales talent does not necessarily correlate with managerial skill. The same concept holds true in many fields. In the sports world, for example, many successful managers and coaches were only average players, and some excellent players do not turn out to be excellent managers. In the sales field, it is widely recognized that the best salesperson may not even be a passable sales manager.[12] The very factors that create an outstanding salesperson often cause failure as an administrator. For example, many successful salespeople have strong, aggressive personalities. This can be a liability when working closely with others in an organization. Also, the detailed reporting that most sales personalities detest are essential duties of a sales manager. However, we should not jump to the conclusion that top sales producers never make good sales managers. A firm's top salespeople certainly should be considered when a management opportunity develops. In identifying a potential sales manager, particularly from among the ranks of salespeople, some important qualities to look for are

- A willingness to share information.
- Structure and discipline in work habits.
- An ability to work well in teams or groups.
- Skill at selling internally.
- An ego that is not overinflated.[13]

While sales skills alone do not make a good administrator, some proficiency in the field is needed. It is difficult to imagine a successful sales manager who has little or no knowledge of selling. Also, the sales force must be confident that the sales manager can lead the group; successful sales experience can inspire such confidence.

Management Can Be Learned

One top executive who was a leader in the Young Presidents Organization confessed to a group of business students that she was a terrible manager in her first job. She set out to overcome this deficiency by volunteering for charitable work. In this way, she learned how to organize people and get them to cooperate.

Another young president reported that he learned a great deal about administration by studying executives and how they behaved in managing their enterprises. Observing the tactical behavior of both successful and unsuccessful managers helped him form ideas about managing people. The continuing growth of management development programs indicates that there is a body of management knowledge that can be taught and learned.

Levels of Sales and Sales Management Positions

In the administrative structure of many firms with outside sales forces, several levels are involved in sales force management, as shown in Figure 1-5. These titles and levels vary greatly across firms and industries—and the compensation levels also vary, including within firms. That is, top account managers might be making five times more than their low performing colleagues—and it is also not unusual for these top performers to be making significantly more than their boss, the sales manager! Following are some comments about lower-, middle-, and top level sales professionals from Figure 1-5.

Lower-Level Sales Professionals

The entry-level sales management position, especially in traditional firms with a large sales force, is typically that of a *sales supervisor, sales manager,* or *branch manager.* This person provides day-to-day supervision, advice, and training for

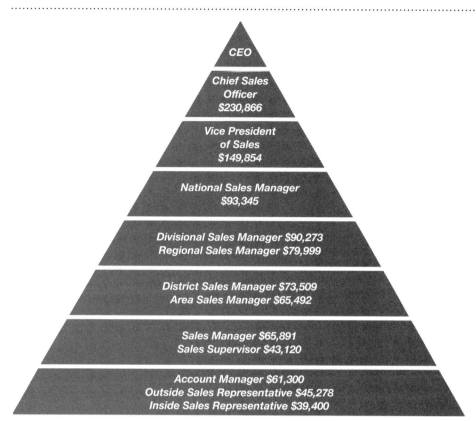

FIGURE 1-5
Levels of Sales Positions with Estimates of Annual Compensation
Source: PayScale.com, GlassDoor.com

a small number of salespeople in a limited geographical area. In firms that have adopted a team selling approach, the first managerial position is typically a *client team leader,* who coordinates the efforts of a multifunctional team. Usually these leaders are people with client sales or service experience.

Middle-Level Sales Professionals
The next step up the executive ladder is a mid-level manager, typically with the job title of *area sales manager* or *district sales manager.* This person manages the activities of sales supervisors or team leaders and also participates in some sales planning and evaluation activities in the district. The next step in many firms is the *regional* or *divisional sales manager.* This middle-level sales manager is generally responsible for several sales districts. This position also may be eliminated in a firm that is using team selling.

Top-Level Sales Professionals
The highest levels in sales management are *national sales manager, vice president of sales,* and *chief sales officer (CSO).* The national sales manager is generally in charge of the large, key accounts—so for a consumer goods manufacturer, these accounts might be Walmart, Home Depot, and/or Kroger. The VP of sales and the CSO are responsible for designing an organizations long-run sales strategies and other companywide strategic sales planning activities. These executives act as the sales department's liaison to the top executive in finance, production, and other major functional areas of the firm.

Flatter Organizations

It is important to note that many organizations are becoming flatter; that is, they have eliminated some of the levels of management. Typically, these are the organizations using cross-functional teams to serve their clients. As noted above, team leaders replace lower-level management positions, and often the middle levels are eliminated as well. Thus, the team leader may report directly to the chief sales officer and/or the chief marketing officer (CMO).

Staff Sales Management Positions

In addition to the sales management positions discussed above, most medium-sized and large companies employ staff executives to head activities that provide assistance to the sales executives and the sales force. Sales training, sales planning, and sales and marketing cost analyses are examples of these staff activities. A key point is that these executives have only an advisory relationship with the line sales executive and the sales force. Staff executives do not have line authority in the sales executive hierarchy. However, within a staff activity area—sales training, for example—the staff executives do have line authority over the people in that area.

How Sales Managers' Job Differ from Other Management Jobs

Probably the most significant differentiating feature of an outside personal selling job is that the salespeople work away from the company's main facilities. Thus, sales managers cannot directly supervise each rep's work in person on a daily basis. The geographical deployment of an outside sales force makes sales managers' jobs different in several respects from other management jobs.

In sales training, for example, a sales manager can provide on-the-job training usually to only one person at a time, so other training tools and methods must be used. Communication with outside salespeople is often more difficult because it is not face-to-face communication. Similarly, motivating a sales force is a problem when a sales manager cannot regularly spend one-on-one time with the salespeople.

Another problem is evaluating a sales rep's performance when the sales manager cannot personally see the rep's work. It is also difficult to monitor the ethical behavior of workers who are geographically separated from the company. Finally, sales managers frequently face morale problems among outside salespeople. Being physically separated from co-workers, the sales reps don't have the same group morale support network as do inside employees.

IMPORTANCE OF PERSONAL SELLING AND SALES MANAGEMENT

From any viewpoint in our total economy, in an individual organization, or even to you as a student, personal selling—and consequently its management—is tremendously important.

In Our Economy

Selling has certainly been very important to our economy. First, just look at the number of sales jobs. According to the U.S. Bureau of Labor Statistics, there are about 14 million sales jobs in the United States—and experts project a 6 percent employment growth for sales representatives by 2024.[14]

Second, the United States economy has been a strong *buyers' market* for many years. That is, the available supply of goods and services has generally far surpassed demand. There has been relatively little difficulty in producing most products. The real problem has been in *selling* them. Particularly during recessions, businesspeople soon realize that it is a slowdown in selling that forces cutbacks in production. This is why companies spend more on professional selling than they do on advertising; in fact. As Red Motley, a noted sales trainer and writer, once said, "Nothing happens until somebody sells something."

In an Individual Organization

When a firm stresses marketing management, executive attention is devoted to sales and market *planning*. Such emphasis may be well placed, but ordinarily the sales force in the field must carry out the sales plan. No plan is of much value unless it is implemented properly. If salespeople cannot sell successfully because they are improperly selected, trained, or compensated, then the efforts devoted to sales planning are of little value. About the only exceptions are firms that do not rely on their own sales force but instead primarily use advertising or agent intermediaries, such as brokers or manufacturers' agents, to move the products. Since the sales force is critical to the success of a concern's marketing venture, sound management of these representatives is important.

The cost of managing and operating a sales force is usually the largest single operating expense for most firms. Public attention and criticism often focus on the amounts a firm spends for television or magazine advertising. Yet a firm's total advertising expenditures may be only 3 or 4 percent of net sales. The total expenses related to salespeople may be 15 or 20 percent of net sales.

To You, the Student

Okay, so selling and sales management are important in our economy and in an individual organization. But why should you study sales management? What's in it for you?

The primary benefit of studying sales management is related to your career aspirations. There are more positions available in sales than in any other professional occupation. As a result, there are also a lot of sales management jobs in today's world. A firm with a medium-sized or large sales force has many sales executive positions (sales supervisors, sales team leaders, district sales managers, regional sales managers) but only a few executives in finance, production, personnel, advertising, or marketing research. And the pay is usually much higher in sales management jobs than in other areas of management.

Within two or three years after graduation, you may be serving as a sales supervisor or a district sales manager. Even as a salesperson, you may engage in managerial activities, such as visiting your alma mater to do employee recruiting. You may be asked to do some sales forecasting for your territory or to offer suggestions regarding a proposed compensation or quota plan. All of these activities will require knowledge of sales management.

CHALLENGES FACING SALES FORCE MANAGEMENT

As explained earlier in this chapter, sales organizations must learn how to adapt to a continuously changing environment that revolves around customers with higher and higher expectations. This presents several specific challenges that sales managers and salespeople must overcome to be successful. Specifically, sales professionals must develop greater expertise in the following areas. Each of these areas is discussed in varying depth later in the book.

1. **Selling by, and to, executives.** Because customers are so demanding, selling firms must increasingly rely on their top executives to be involved in the sales process. Customers—especially important customers—expect to interact and negotiate with the highest levels of the organization.[15] For example, every senior officer and every vice president at Xerox is assigned to specific major accounts, such as Kinko's and ADP.[16] In fact, each of these major accounts has a team of Xerox employees assigned to it, and the top-level executive works closely with the team. This structure is sometimes called *strategic or key account management.* In addition, salespeople are increasingly finding themselves selling to high level executives (also called C-level executives because their titles begin with that letter, such as *chief executive officer*). This is a different kind of sale. On one hand, it is more difficult because these people do not have much time and are hard to see; however, if a salesperson can make this appointment, this executive often has the power to make the buying decision right away—so it can be a shorter sales process.[17]

2. **Customer relationship management (CRM) and Sales Force Automation (SFA).** CRM and SFA both refer to the comprehensive software programs that help companies manage customer information. These programs have become mainstream technology for sales organizations. As shown in Figure 1-6, the CRM industry is growing rapidly. The leading companies include Salesforce.com and NetSuite, but there are many others. Some sales organizations develop their own

FIGURE 1-6
Growth of CRM Industry in Total Revenues
Source: Gartner annual market share releases, as reported by Chuck Schaeffer, "CRM Market Share Report," CRM Search. Available at http://www.crmsearch.com/crm-market-share.php. Accessed July 11, 2016.

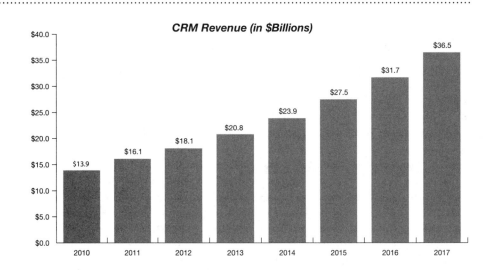

CRM Revenue (in $Billions)

Year	Revenue
2010	$13.9
2011	$16.1
2012	$18.1
2013	$20.8
2014	$23.9
2015	$27.5
2016	$31.7
2017	$36.5

system—Fastenal Company, for example, internally developed a program it calls its Sales Management System. In fact, Fastenal's sales force is being equipped with tablet computers for the purpose of making it easier for salespeople to remotely enter data into the system. But for some firms, the transition to this technology has not always gone well, as sales managers tend to struggle with how to use it to drive the performance of their teams.[18] The challenge is that salespeople often do not see the benefit as much as their manager does—and in fact, many salespeople have not yet adapted to using these programs. This stems from several reasons. First, salespeople sometimes feel that the CRM or SFA program takes away their freedom in that it allows management to spy on them. Another concern is that salespeople feel their system is not user friendly in that it takes too much time to enter the information the system asks for.[19] These concerns can be avoided through proper training and effective leadership by the sales executives.

3. **Sales force diversity.** Over the past few decades, more and more women and minorities have successfully pursued careers in personal selling and are advancing into sales management positions. In fact, over half of sales workers in the United States are now women.[20] This is surprising since sales was once dominated by men. Sexual discrimination still exists in the U.S. workplace, as evidenced by the over 20,000 sex-based lawsuits filed each year. Yet great strides have been made.

   A controversial issue in this area involves the criteria used for hiring women into sales. Select industries, such as pharmaceutical sales, have been criticized for emphasizing physical attractiveness over professional qualifications. "There's a saying that you'll never meet an ugly drug rep," says one industry expert who charges that seduction is a deliberate industry strategy.[21] Pharmaceutical companies deny that sex appeal has anything to do with whom they hire. This is very possibly true. Regardless, all sales organizations must be careful that they do not perpetuate the negative stereotypes that have long been associated with the selling profession.

   Minority groups present another opportunity and a different set of challenges for sales management because minorities have been more difficult to recruit in large numbers for outside sales jobs. The United States has long been a nation of ethnic diversity. About one-third of American workers are minorities, and the percent is growing every year. To remain competitive, sales managers need to capitalize on the strengths of *everyone* in our diverse population.

   The bottom line for sales managers of women and minority groups is this: These groups are here to stay in selling, and they must be managed effectively. As a matter of self-interest, sales managers cannot afford to waste the brainpower (and selling power) of over half our population. Moreover, executives simply will not be able to adequately fill the available sales jobs in the foreseeable future unless they recruit qualified women and minorities.

   Additionally, today's salespeople are much more educated than in the past. Over 65 percent of salespeople have college degrees, and the number holding postgraduate degrees has increased as well to 6.5

percent.[22] The more-educated salesperson will desire challenges and rewards that differ from those his or her less-educated counterpart desired in the past. Finally, as our population grows older, sales managers will be faced with managing a greater proportion of seniors in their sales forces. In many cases, these senior salespeople will place less emphasis on financial rewards than will their younger counterparts, but they will still need to be motivated to maintain and improve their performance.

4. **Complex channels of distribution.** Many sales managers will be asked to manage increasingly complex channels of distribution. They will oversee a hybrid sales force, which might include both outside field sales reps, and inside salespeople. Their work—organizing and coordinating the efforts of these diverse salespeople—will become more strategic. The successful sales managers of the future will be adaptive enough to handle both complexity and rapid change. Sony Electronics, for example, sells its products through three distinct channels: (1) company-owned retail stores with the Sony name; (2) traditional retailers such as Best Buy, Circuit City, and Wal-Mart; and (3) online through its company-owned Web site. Sony's president of consumer sales is faced with the challenge of creating synergy among these channels such that the sum is greater than its three parts.

5. **Globalization.** Today the U.S. market has reached the saturation point for many consumer and industrial products. At the same time, many global markets are emerging and growing rapidly. Growth for many companies in the coming decades will come from their development of these international markets. Some companies, such as Coca-Cola, Colgate-Palmolive, and Avon, are already earning the greatest proportion of their revenues outside the United States. Differences in cultures and ways of doing business in foreign countries pose real challenges for American sales management.

   Additionally, in the United States, American sellers face increasing competition from many foreign firms. This competition is bound to increase as economies expand in Asian and eastern European countries, and as a result of the general trend of the elimination of trade barriers between countries. Sales executives must manage their sales forces to meet foreign competition in this country and to improve their company's personal selling efforts in other countries.

6. **Ethical behavior and social responsibility.** "Salespeople are dancing in the spot where there's the greatest likelihood for unethical behavior," says a lawyer for PricewaterhouseCoopers' governance risk management and compliance practice. Indeed, salespeople have been involved in a number of recent financial accounting scandals. In one aspect of the most famous case, Enron salespeople were accused of using wildly optimistic estimates for the forward price of commodities and other factors. This created the appearance that deals were profitable when they were actually losing money.[23] In a case that is similar, a salesperson for Kraft Foods agreed to what he thought was a simply, harmless request from one of his biggest customers, a grocery wholesaler. This customer wanted the Kraft salesperson to sign a letter to confirm that certain payments were to

cover a "shortfall" in past accounts. In reality, these payments were for something else. This allowed the customer to appear to be more profitable than it was, which misleads investors.[24] Salespeople must realize that these activities are not only dishonest and unethical, but illegal. The U.S. Securities and Exchange Commission is becoming more and more aggressive in pursuing these cases, and this includes taking legal action against specific salespeople! Sales executives have the challenge of first staying up to date on these laws, and then informing their salespeople through proper training.

For centuries, the institution of business, and especially its personal-selling component, has been accused periodically of unethical behavior. Yet it is commonly accepted that outside selling today is on an ethical plane far above that of a few decades ago and in a different world from that of a century or two in the past. Today, sales managers have no choice but to strive to maintain their ethical standards in personal selling and sales management, for the alternative can put them out of business or even into prison.

SUMMARY

This is a book about managing a sales force—that is, managing the personal-selling component of an organization's marketing program. Specifically, this book deals with the management of an outside sales force where the salespeople go to the customer. Outside selling contrasts with across-the-counter selling, where the customers come to the salespeople. By any measure—people employed, dollars spent, or sales generated—personal selling is by far the most important element in a company's promotional mix.

In the face of intense competition, many companies today practice relationship marketing or relationship selling, which is very different from the traditional transaction-oriented selling that focused on the one-time sales of the product. In contrast, relationship selling focuses on developing trust in a few selected accounts over an extended period.

There are a wide variety of sales jobs in which salespeople work for a wide variety of companies, selling many different products, and serving a wide variety of customers. The sales job is also different in a number of ways from other jobs. Further, a new type of sales representative is emerging, one who acts as a marketing consultant for the customer and for his or her own firm.

The role of the sales manager is also expanding. Today, the most successful sales managers are seen as team leaders rather than bosses. Sales managers are administrators, and administration (management) is a distinct skill. Sales talent alone does not make a good manager, but management can be learned. There are several levels of sales management positions, and sales managers' jobs also differ from other management positions.

The importance of personal selling and sales management may be viewed from the perspective of our total economy; individual organizations; or you, the student. To manage a sales force effectively in the coming decades, sales executives must develop greater expertise in the following areas: (1) selling by executives, (2) customer relationship management (CRM) and sales force automation (SFA), (3) sales force diversity, (4) complex channels of distribution, (5) globalization, and (6) ethical behavior and social responsibility.

KEY TERMS

Communications mix
Complex distribution
   channels
Consultative seller
Customer relationship
   management (CRM)
E-commerce
Inside sales (or
   telemarketing)
Key account seller

Marketing mix
Missionary salespeople
New business seller
Outside sales force
Promotional mix
Relationship marketing
Relationship selling
Role ambiguity
Role conflict
Role stress

Sales engineers
Sales force automation
   (SFA)
Sales force diversity
Sales management
Sales support
Selling by executives
Transaction selling
Value-added
   components

QUESTIONS AND PROBLEMS

1. Explain how and why customers' expectations are changing.
2. What is an outside sales force? Is this type of sales force used only by producers and wholesalers? Is it used only in business-to-business selling?
3. How can a salesperson add value to his or her customers' business?
4. How does relationship oriented selling differ from transaction-oriented selling?
5. Study the six categories of sales jobs (i.e., consultative seller, etc.) and answer these questions:
   a. In which types of jobs is the sales rep most free of close supervision?
   b. Which types of jobs are likely to be the highest paid?
   c. For which groups is a high degree of motivation most necessary?
6. We said that today's professional sales representative is a marketing consultant and a manager of a market—his or her territory. Explain how a sales rep can be a marketing consultant and manager.
7. What can sales managers do to increase the professionalism of their salespeople?
8. How does a sales job differ from other jobs?
9. How will the trend toward flatter organizations affect the job of the middle-level sales manager?
10. Why do many successful salespeople fail to become successful sales managers?

11. Assume that you are a sales manager. What characteristics would you look for, or what criteria would you use, when promoting a salesperson to the position of district sales manager?

12. It has been said, "Nothing happens until somebody sells something." How would you explain this to a student who is majoring in accounting, finance, or engineering?

13. Should someone who is not majoring in marketing take a course in personal selling? In sales management?

14. Review your activities of the past week and identify those in which you did some personal selling.

15. Assume that your company, which sells paper products, has 60 percent of the business at your largest account. What factors would make it relatively easy for you to get a larger share of that customer's business, and what factors would make it harder?

EXPERIENTIAL EXERCISES

1. Interview sales managers from three different companies concerning their responsibilities and what they do. Compare and contrast their positions. Then explain which one you would prefer and why.

2. Interview a salesperson from each of three different companies about the nature of their selling responsibilities and their relationships with their customers. Then describe each of these sales positions and explain whether the selling is more similar to transactional selling or to relationship selling and why.

3. Visit the following two websites, which focus on selling and sales management issues: www.smei.org and www.salesandmarketing.com. What services do they offer, and how might these services be of use to sales managers?

KV HOMES
Making the transition from salesperson to sales manager

KV Homes is a $300 million family-owned company that builds and sells residential homes throughout the state of Illinois. The company takes pride in its quality, custom-built homes, which generally sell for between $400,000 and $700,000. KV Homes currently is developing eight neighborhood communities throughout Illinois. In each of these developing neighborhoods, a sales force works from a model home.

In the model home of each neighborhood, there are typically three salespeople. These salespeople have one of two job titles: assistant sales consultant or sales consultant. The typical model home contains one assistant sales consultant and two sales consultants—but this varies from community to community. The assistant sales consultants are in a training phase that lasts approximately 20 weeks. They work closely with one of the sales consultants, who serves as a mentor, and then are eventually promoted. In total, there are currently 21 salespeople across the eight communities that are being developed. These salespeople are directly managed by the sales manager, Damien Badenhop.

The company has a simple line-type organization that is relatively small. Sales manager Damien Badenhop reports directly to the vice president of marketing, Jen Lehatny. Lehatny—along with the vice presidents of manufacturing, finance, and operations—reports to the company president, Kyle Vee.

Damien Badenhop was recently promoted into the manager's job. KV Homes has a policy of promoting from within and Damien was selected from among the salespeople based on the strong recommendation of Jen Lehatny. She felt that even though he was not the top salesperson, he was the best choice to move into management. He clearly had the best administrative skills of the group, he was an excellent mentor of the younger salespeople, and he was respected throughout the organization. In her mind, Damien had seemed to be the logical choice; but now she was wondering if she had made a mistake.

The sales manager for KV Homes has a large amount of the responsibility for planning the sales effort and total responsibility for organizing and managing the sales force. In the area of planning, he (or she) assists in the preparation of the sales forecast. This involves estimating expected sales within each community, based on past history, forecasts of economic conditions, and competitive developments. On the basis of the final forecasts, he also prepares the expense budgets and the sales quotas for the individual reps. He then breaks these budgets down into monthly and quarterly dollar figures, which he uses in evaluating the reps and determining their incentive pay.

The sales manager has total responsibility for recruiting and selecting new salespeople, which is a continual process for KV Homes. Most new recruits are recent college graduates. So, the sales manager maintains relationships with several Illinois universities and then conducts on-campus interviews in the fall. The sales manager then spends two to three weeks training the new salespeople before assigning them to mentoring sales consultants in their specific neighborhoods. This training involves acquainting new reps with company objectives and operating policies, providing them with background knowledge about the construction industry, and teaching them the sales process through the use of role plays.

Supervision, motivation, and evaluation also are essential components of this position. The manager provides all reps with refresher training, teaching them to allocate their time properly and to keep current with regard to trends in the construction industry. He is responsible for weekly sales meetings and continuing training programs. Further, on a quarterly basis, he must spend time in each community model home in order to formally evaluate performance of all salespeople. In conjunction with the evaluation, he designs and administers the recognition and compensation programs. Of course, the sales manager also acts as a troubleshooter when any of the sales consultants needs assistance with a client.

In the past, the sales managers at KV Homes had always continued to sell homes, at least on a part-time basis. However, Jen felt that because the size of the sales force had doubled in the last few years and because the responsibilities of the sales manager had expanded, it was time that the sales manager devote 100 percent of his time to managing the sales effort. Therefore, when she offered the manager's position to Damien Badenhop, she asked him to give up all of his selling responsibilities. His compensation package would consist of salary, plus a commission on all the consultants' sales, plus a bonus for making the sales and expense targets. This package would more than compensate for the loss of income from his sales commissions.

Damien was really excited about the opportunity to become KV Homes sales manager. But he was somewhat surprised that he had been chosen because he did not have seniority among the consultants. However, when Jen told him about giving up selling entirely to focus on the administrative duties of the sales manager, he countered that he didn't want to do that and that it was not in KV Homes' best interests. Jen recalled his comment: "I don't understand why you're changing the policy. Bob Burton (the last sales manager) continued to sell part-time—and I thought it worked out well. In fact, I think that I'll stay more in touch with the market if I can continue to sell. This will make me a better manager because I'll be more knowledgeable about what my salespeople are facing."

Damien also explained that after a slow start, the homes in his community are really starting to move. "I've developed the trust of the several people that I know are going to buy from me in the coming months. It doesn't seem fair to hand these people over to someone else."

Damien was persistent in arguing his case to Jen, who finally relented. He was promoted to sales manager, and continued to sell three mornings a week. At first this arrangement worked pretty well. However, in the last several months, Damien began having problems with both the managing and the selling aspects of his job. His paperwork was way behind, his sales figures had slipped a little, and some of the reps had complained to Jen about the lack of support from Damien.

Jen did not have a good solution. If she forced Damien to give up selling entirely, she thought there was a good chance he might quit KV Homes. The additional compensation Damien received from his own sales was a significant boost to his sales manager's compensation. If he quit, she really did not have anybody else she felt she could put in his position. She would have both a manager and a sales consultant to replace. If she asked him to give up the manager's job and go back into full-time selling, he might quite in that situation as well.

Question:

1. Should Jen ask Damien to give up his accounts? How do you think Jen should handle this problem?

G.W. PERGAULT, INC.
Salespeople feeling threatened by the company website

Mr. Ken Sutton, sales manager for G.W. Pergault, directly oversees 15 salespeople that serve clients in and around Milwaukee, Wisconsin. He is currently in a tough spot. The new president of the company, Ms. Celia Fiorni, has a vision for e-commerce that Sutton's salespeople strongly oppose. Sutton feels caught in the middle—between his boss and his subordinates.

Ms. Fiorni had become president of G.W. Pergault just six months ago. Her previous job was CEO/president of a very successful—but relatively small—technology firm that sold computer hardware to consumers. Ms. Fiorni is an enthusiastic, charismatic leader who has brought a fresh outside perspective to G.W. Pergault.

Given her background in the computer industry, Ms. Fiorni not surprisingly is a fervent believer in new technology. Her first task was to spend over $20 million updating G.W. Pergault's website. With this accomplished, her next goal is to move a much larger percentage of the reps' sales to the company website. Further, she feels that the company's salespeople should take the lead role in encouraging and training their customers to order products through the website.

G.W. Pergault is an established, $4.2 billion supplier of maintenance, repair, and operations (MRO) products. The company sells pipe fittings, light bulbs, ladders, and literally hundreds of thousands of other MRO products to business customers throughout North America. Established in 1952, G.W. Pergault traditionally has sold these products through its extensive mail-order catalog, which has grown to over 4,000. In 1997, the catalog was put online. Online sales have increased each year since but are still dwarfed by catalog sales.

The business customers that buy these products vary greatly in size. Most are relatively small accounts that purchase supplies directly through either the paper catalog or website without ever seeing or talking to a G.W. Pergault salesperson. Even though these smaller businesses represent about 80 percent of the customers, the aggregate sales generated from them is still only about 20 percent of G.W. Pergault's total sales.

Alternatively, the remaining 20 percent of the customers tend to be much larger accounts. The sales generated from these bigger customers represent about 80 percent of G.W. Pergault's total sales. These are the customers that are regularly called upon and serviced by G.W. Pergault's sales force. These sales reps personally process the vast majority of orders from their customers.

President Fiorni, however, believes that it is highly inefficient for these customers to order all their products through salespeople. First, it is needlessly time-consuming and keeps salespeople from more important, creative-selling activities. Second, it is costly. She feels that G.W. Pergault could save hundreds of thousands of dollars by insisting that existing customer reorder their supplies through the website. The savings, she says, will stem primarily from eliminating steps in the order process.

Currently, the ordering process starts as the G.W. Pergault sales rep personally meets with a purchasing agent from the customer firm. The sales rep writes up the order by hand as the purchasing agent makes his requests. After the meeting, the rep submits the order to G.W. Pergault—usually by fax. A member of G.W. Pergault's data-entry clerical staff receives the form and enters the information into the system for delivery. The order is packaged and shipped, usually within three business days from when it was made.

The new company website, of course, provides an interface that allows customers to complete their own order, which then is directly entered into the system as soon as the customer clicks on the submit button. This allows for the order to be processed more quickly, saving at least one day in delivery time. In addition, it significantly reduces the chance of order-entry error by either the salesperson or the data-entry clerk.

As Ms. Fiorni says, "It's a no-brainer. By ordering through the website, customers will not only get their supplies sooner, they can be much more assured that they will get exactly what they asked for."

Ken Sutton could see the logic in his new president's thinking. A recent customer satisfaction survey revealed that mistakes were made in about one out of every 20 orders that come in through salespeople. He feels that this error rate is much too high. Further, he believes that his sales reps are not even close to reaching the full potential for his market in and around Milwaukee. "The reps spend too much time taking orders, and not enough time explaining to customers how our *other products* can meet their needs," he says.

At the same time, his reps have expressed strong opposition to the plan. In fact, his top rep for the past two years had just called him yesterday. In a somewhat angry tone, the rep told him what he thought of the new president. "Fiorni doesn't understand that selling is about building personal relationships, and you can't have a relationship with website. Customers buy from G.W. Pergault not just because they like our products, but also because they like me. I'm sorry, but I refuse to tell my best customers, 'I'm too busy to take your order. Go surf the Internet!'"

Other reps have told Sutton that customers who have tried the new website did not like it. Some of the complaints were that it was too glitzy with too many distracting graphics. "We don't care about the bells and whistles; we just want to buy supplies in a convenient and quick way," said one purchasing agent. "It's so much easier to just meet with our rep and tell her what we want. Frankly, the website is too complicated and confusing!"

Sutton thinks that customers might be less confused if their salespeople would do a better job of showing them how to use the website. After all, G.W. Pergault offers over 500,000 different products, which can be overwhelming to sort through. Sutton believes that some of his reps may have trouble finding specific products on the website. He also acknowledges that G.W. Pergault has not made much of an effort to train its own sales force on the ins and outs of ordering online through the company website.

There are two other key issues that help explain why the sales force is so strongly opposed to the president's new vision. Ken Sutton believes these are the most critical reasons for the objections. First, over half of the typical salesperson's compensation is earned through commission. When customers buy through the website, reps don't earn any commission! Why would a sales rep convince a customer to do something that reduces the rep's pay?

And, finally, many of the reps feel that the website is a threat to their future with the company—even though Ms. Fiorni is on record saying that she does not want to eliminate the sales force. In a recent company address, she said, "G.W. Pergault needs more—not less—people selling. We simply need a shift of focus toward selling new products to our best customers. We also need sales to focus on opening new accounts." Nevertheless, some reps feel that this initiative is the first step to a pink slip.

Next week, Ms. Fiorni is scheduled to come to Milwaukee and talk to Sutton and his reps. She understands that her plan has not been well received by sales. G.W. Pergault reps from all around the country feel the same way that Sutton's reps do. In fact, she will be visiting various sales groups from around the country to try to get a better idea of why there is such resistance.

Sutton believes his new boss is a reasonable person, and is looking forward to her visit. Through telephone conversations, he gets the sense that she will listen to his advice on the matter—but he is not sure exactly where he stands! Al he knows is that Fiorni's e-commerce goal will not be achieved without salesperson buy-in, and that the salespeople are not buying the plan in its current form.

Questions:

1. What advice should sales manager Ken Sutton give to his company president, Celia Fiorni, in order to improve her plan and make it successful?

2. What should Ken Sutton do to make his salespeople more accepting of the new initiative?

THE CORNELL COMPANY
Selection of a Sales Manager

Mrs. Paula Ruiz, vice president of marketing for the Cornell Company of Chicago, knew she had to make a decision on who to select to manager the company's 56-percent sales force. Seven months previously, the former sales manager resigned to accept the sales manager position for Cornell's major competitor. Since that time, Mrs. Ruiz had assumed direct control of the sales force, but she clearly saw that, in doing so, she was not only neglecting her other responsibilities but also doing a poor job of managing the sales force.

Mrs. Ruiz's search for a new sales manager had narrowed down to two people, Gordon Price and Janice Wilson, both of whom seemed eminently qualified for the job.

The Cornell Company was one of the nation's leading manufacturers of special-purpose metal fasteners and metal fastening systems used by metal fabricating manufacturers. The sales reps worked closely with both the engineers and purchasing agents of customers' organizations in developing product designs and specifications for solving their problems. While there was some calling on new accounts, the bulk of the sales rep's time was spent working with long-standing established accounts.

The sales manager was charged with the full responsibility for maintaining an effective field sales force, which include hiring firing, training, supervising, compensating, controlling, and evaluate the salespeople. The manager was accountable for the entire department's paperwork, which included budget preparation, expense account auditing, and sales force planning. At times, the manager had to work closely with salespeople in handling special accounts or particularly important or difficult contracts. There were no field supervisors to help the salespeople; however, close communications were maintained with them by the home office through the extensive use of modern electronic technology.

Each rep had a company smartphone and choice between a tablet computer or laptop, which allowed immediate contact with the home office and its databases. Customer information and IT support were immediately available to all sales reps through the company's CRM system and staff. The sales manager had an assistant in the home office who handled all communications between the reps and the manager. A large portion of the manager's time was spent in meetings with other members of management to coordinate sales force activities with all other functions of the business. The manager had to work particularly closely with Mrs. Ruiz.

Mrs. Ruiz had taken the files on the two prospective managers home for the weekend to contemplate her decision. She had decided to announce her selection Monday morning.

As she reviewed Gordon Price's file, she fully realized that if Gordon were not made sales manager, some repercussions might be felt. Gordy was not only the firm's best sales rep, but was well regarded throughout the organization. He had sold for the company for 20 plus years and prior to that had worked in production for 5 years after graduation from high school. Now 45 years old, he had outsold all other reps for the last 10 years and always exceeded quotas by more than 20 percent, even in difficult times. Since the sales force was paid on a commission basis, Gordy had become moderately wealthy. His average earnings over the past decade exceeded $150,000; last year he earned $185,000. Gordon was married to an understanding women of considerable charm. Their three children were high school and college age and, to Mrs. Ruiz's knowledge, were outstanding youngsters. The Prices were extremely adept at entertaining and socializing with people. Hardly a month passed that they did not have some sort of social event at their home.

Although Gordon had not attended college, Mrs. Ruiz knew that he was intelligent and had acquired considerable business know-how. He had accumulated an impressive library of business books and had participated in many meaningful self-improvement programs.

When he learned of the previous sales manager's resignation, Gordon had come directly to Mrs. Ruiz and requested the position. He outlined his achievements for the company and then gave a brief account of the goals that he would work toward as manager. Mrs. Ruiz recalled acknowledging at the time that Gordon was certainly a prime candidate for the job and that he could be assured that he would be given every consideration. However, she told Gordon that the decision was not entirely hers to make. The president had suggested that a thorough search be made in order to ensure that the best person available was placed in the position, since he felt keenly that the company had prospered largely because of its excellent sales force and he wanted to do nothing to jeopardize that success formula.

Privately, Mrs. Ruiz had some reservations about making Gordy sales manager, but she was hesitant to bring her thoughts into the open for fear of engendering animosities that would later haunt her. First, she was fearful that if she promoted Gordy, she would be losing a good sales rep and getting a poor sales manager. She had seen it happen in other companies, and sales management literature was full of warnings that top salespeople may not make good sales managers. The two jobs required different skills. Second, Mrs. Ruiz was worried that Gordon would be unhappy with the sales manager's salary of $140,000, despite his insistence that he would be happy with it. Third, she was afraid that Gordy's preference for customer contact would result in his not staying in the office enough to do the required paperwork. Finally, she was concerned by Gordy's relationships with the other salespeople. He was extremely well liked by most of the men, who felt that he "would give you the shirt off his back" if you needed it. However, a several of the 14 women on the sales force had communicated to her that they felt that Gordy was a bit too macho for their liking. However, none of the women had indicated that Gordon had been anything but very proper and pleasant in his behavior toward them.

Gordon had forced Mrs. Ruiz to make a selection soon, appearing in her office Friday morning to issue a rather strong ultimatum: he had been offered a sales manager position with a significant competitor and had to give an answer in two weeks. He made it clear that he did not want to leave, but he would do so to become a sales manager if that opportunity was not to be his with the Cornell Company. Mrs. Ruiz inwardly rebelled at this holdup play but realized that it was a fair tactic. The last sales manager had given no warning of his impending departure. She thought that at least it was nice to be forewarned for a change.

Mrs. Ruiz proceeded to review her other leading candidate, Janice Wilson, with whom she had been acquainted for more than four years. They were members of several clubs together and, while not close friends, had known each other from their college days. Janice was the sales manager for an electronic instrumentation company and had developed an enviable reputation in the industry for building an outstanding sales force. She was just 32 years old—several years younger than Gordon. And she was the mother of two preschool children. She came across as friendly and likable, yet all evidence indicated that she ran a tight ship. She demanded high performance from her sales team, and seemed to get it.

Mrs. Ruiz casually mentioned her job opening to Mrs. Wilson one day at one of their club meetings—she thought Janice might know some good person that she could recommend for the job. Mrs. Wilson had hesitated for a moment, then replied, "Let's talk."

She then confided that her firm was about to be acquired by a larger firm and she was not at all enthralled about what she knew of its management. "They are not my kind of people," she went on to say. "From what I know of you and your operation, I think I would like very much to be considered for the job." The two went on to have a long conversation. The more she heard, Mrs. Ruiz became more and more impressed with her friend.

Mrs. Ruiz began to seriously contemplate the situation; she felt that this was going to be a tough decision.

Questions:

1. What are the pros and cons of each candidate?
2. Whom would you make sales manager? Explain your answer.

ENDNOTES

[1] Ken Dooley, "4 things you need to know about today's customers," *Customer Experience Insight,"* September 5, 2014. Available at http://www.customerexperienceinsight.com/4-things-you-need-to-know-about-todays-customers/. Accessed July 11, 2016.

[2] Emma Brudner, "6 Surprising Statistics on Social Selling That all Salespeople Should Know," *HubSpot Sales Blog,* March 2, 2016. Available at http://blog.hubspot.com/sales/surprising-statistics-on-social-selling-that-all-salespeople-should-know. Accessed July 11, 2016.

[3] Hansen J, Tanuja S, Weilbaker D, Guesalaga R. "Cultural Intelligence In Cross-Cultural Selling: Propositions And Directions For Future Research," *Journal of Personal Selling & Sales Management* [serial online]. Summer2011 2011; 31(3):243-254. Available from: Business Source Complete, Ipswich, MA. Accessed July 11, 2016.

[4] Frank V. Cespedes, "Putting Sales at the Center of Strategy," *Harvard Business Review*, October 2014. Available at: https://hbr.org/2014/10/putting-sales-at-the-center-of-strategy. Accessed July 11, 2016.

[5] Jim Giuliano, "The biggest complaint about salespeople," *BusinessBrief.com*, June 15, 2009. Available at: http://www.businessbrief.com/the-no-1-complaint-customers-have-about-salespeople/. Accessed July 11, 2016.

[6] William C. Moncrief, Greg W. Marshall, and Felicia G. Lassk, "A Contemporary Taxonomy of Sales Positions," *Journal of Personal Selling & Sales Management* 26, no. 1 (Winter 2006), pp. 55-65.

[7] Erika Rasmusson, "3M's Big Strategy for Big Accounts," *Sales & Marketing Management*, September 2000, p. 92.

[8] James Champy, "Heading in New Directions," *Sales & Marketing Management*, January 1997, pp. 32-33.

[9] Andy Cohen, "The Traits of Great Sales Forces," *Sales & Marketing Management*, October 2000, pp. 70-71.

[10] Bernard L. Rosenbaum, "Seven Emerging Sales Competencies," *Business Horizons*, January/February 2001, pp. 33-36.

[11] Chad Kaydo, "The New Skills of Top Managers," *Sales & Marketing Management*, May 2000, p. 16.

[12] Erin Stout, "Movin' On Up," *Sales & Marketing Management*, March 2001, p. 63.

[13] Ibid.

[14] Frank Cespedes, "Why Reports of the Death of the Salesman Are Greatly Exaggerated," *Reuters*, November 6, 2014. Available at: http://blogs.reuters.com/great-debate/2014/11/06/why-reports-of-the-death-of-the-salesman-are-greatly-exaggerated/. Access on July 11, 2016.

[15] David Goldsmith, "Leadership Selling," *Sales & Service Excellence Essentials* [serial online]. December 2010; 10(12):15. Available from: Business Source Complete, Ipswich, MA. Accessed July 11, 2016.

[16] Julie Barker, "In Depth: Leading Men," *Sales & Marketing Management*, December 2005.

[17] Stuart Leung, "Selling to Executives: Bringing Your Sales 'A' Game to the C-Level," *Salesforce.com Blog*, February 24, 2014. Available from: https://www.salesforce.com/blog/2014/02/selling-to-c-level-executives.html. Accessed July 11, 2016.

[18] Martin Zeman, "The 2 Biggest CRM Mistakes and What to Do About Them," *Sales & Marketing Management,* April 1, 2016. Available from: https://salesandmarketing.com/content/2-biggest-crm-mistakes-and-what-do-about-them. Accessed July 11, 2016.

[19] Andy Levi, "Here's Why Salespeople Hate CRM," Spiro Technologies' Sales Blog. Accessed 3/8/2016 from https://spirohq.com/heres-why-salespeople-hate-crm/

[20] U.S. Equal Employment Opportunity Commission, "Occupational Employment in Private Industry by Race/Ethnic Group/Sex, and by Industry, United States, 2006." https://www.eeoc.gov/eeoc/statistics/employment/jobpat-eeo1/2006/national.html. Accessed July 11, 2016.

[21] Stephanie Saul, "Gimme an Rx! Cheerleaders Pep Up Drug Sales," *New York Times*, November 28, 2005, p. 1.

[22] Christian P. Heide, *Dartnell's 30th Sales Force Compensation Survey* (Chicago: Dartnell Corporation, 1999), p. 173.

[23] Wendy Zellner et al., "Jeff Skilling: Enron's Missing Man," *BusinessWeek*, February 11, 2002, p. 38.

[24] Michael T. Burr, "Salespeople Get Caught in SEC's Governance Net," *Corporate Legal Times*, July 2005, p. 16.

2

Strategy

SAP is the world leader in enterprise resource planning (ERP) systems—the software that allows businesses to run efficiently by integrating accounting, marketing, production and other functions. This German company has locations in 130 countries, and its products are used by the vast majority of Fortune 1000 companies.

The global financial crisis that began in 2008, as well as the shift toward cloud-based solutions, has changed the way businesses buy ERP systems. When calling on customers, SAP salespeople must now deal with more stakeholders, including many high-level executives with no information technology (IT) background. To reach this new target market, the company turned to social selling tools, such as LinkedIn's Sales Navigator.

According to SAP sales executive Mark Ghaderi, this new sales tactic enabled SAP "...to transform our sales process by finding and engaging the right decision makers with relevant content and key insights in a programmatic way." In other words, social selling not only helped SAP connect to the right people, but also provided a way for its reps to enhance their credibility through the posting of helpful, product-related information.

As this scenario demonstrates, sales needs to be at the center of the firm's corporate strategy and marketing plans. Too often, people think of sales as an activity that is separate from marketing. In fact, marketing and sales often operate as if they are engaged in some sort of win-lose contest in which neither side cooperates with the other. The reality is that the marketing objectives can be achieved only when sales becomes an integral part of the marketing strategy— the part that carries out strategy. By working together as a team, marketing and sales personnel become key contributors to the success of the overall strategic plan for the business.

The purpose of this chapter is to place sales force management within the context of the total marketing program. To make wise strategic decisions about the sales force, the sales manager must understand how the field-selling effort fits into the strategic marketing plan and how that fits into strategic planning for the total company.

FIGURE 2-1

A company's complete marketing system: a framework of internal resources operating within a set of external forces

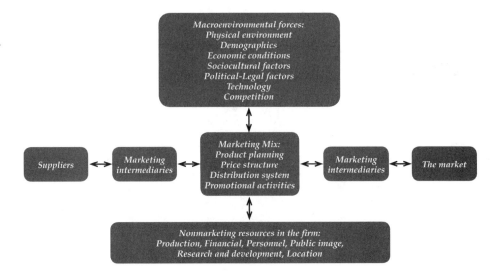

THE MARKETING SYSTEM

A **marketing system** is the network of buyers, sellers and other actors (such as intermediaries and suppliers) that come together for the creation, promotion, distribution and exchange of a company's products. This system operates within a framework of forces—its environment. Two sets of these forces are external to the company, and another two sets are internal. Their relationship is seen in Figure 2-1.

External Environment

The first set of external forces are macro-environmental and impinge considerably on any company's marketing system, yet they generally are not controllable by management. These forces are defined below, along with examples of how a company's marketing activities might be impacted by changes in these forces.

1. **Physical environment** consists of the aspects of the natural world, including general climate and weather conditions, and also natural resources such as water, oil, and other minerals. This can have a major impact on a company's marketing system. When it rains in New York City, street vendors selling umbrellas suddenly appear out of nowhere! When Hurricane Sandy ravaged parts of New Jersey in 2012, it had an impact on 300,000 businesses—and several of these were forced to go out of business. At the same time, the event resulted in increased business for plumbers, carpenters, tree surgeons, trash haulers, carpet cleaners, scrap dealers and several other businesses that helped with the cleanup.[1]

2. **Demography** is the measurement of basic characteristics of the human population such as age, sex, race, income, and stage in family life-cycle. Customer demographics can have a major impact on a firm's marketing system, which, of course, includes the sales force. For example, since the

aging baby boomer generation are beginning to retire, sales opportunities have grown for those organizations that build and operate retirement communities. This includes a number of niche retirement communities that are created for retirees who share a common identity, such as religion, artistic inclination, sexual orientation, or membership in a particular labor union.[2]

3. **Economic conditions** simply refer to the overall health of the economy. This has a huge impact on a variety of industries, including home sales. For example, the financial crisis of 2008 led to a recession, during which banks became much less willing to approve mortgages and new home sales plummeted. The economy is much stronger today. The National Association of Realtors showed existing-home sales rising at healthy levels, and banks are selling mortgages at a rate not seen for several years.[3]

4. **Sociocultural factors** are the fundamental values and beliefs of society. Americans, for example, have placed a high priority on fitness and health in recent years. This trend benefits those who sell memberships to fitness centers. Life Time Fitness Inc. has found success with a relatively new health club concept: a chain of family-oriented centers that offer lush décor, child care, restaurants, meeting rooms, and other amenities.[4]

5. **Political-legal factors**—laws, ordinances, regulations—can impact sales organizations in many ways. For example, the Occupational Safety and Health Act (i.e., OSHA) has a significant impact on the sales force of Fastenal Company. Fastenal salespeople are sometimes required to go through safety training before they are allowed into certain customers' facilities. Also, OSHA creates opportunities for Fastenal to sell a variety of safety products that help customers fulfill OSHA requirements. A more comprehensive discussion on laws that impact salespeople can be found in Chapter 17.

6. **Technology** includes inventions, innovations, and advances in scientific knowledge. Such advances have had a tremendous effect on day-to-day jobs of salespeople. For example, most travel agents have disappeared due to the efficiency of travel websites, such as Expedia.com and Priceline.com. In fact, many observers originally thought that the internet would replace face-to-face selling entirely. Instead, people who work in direct sales have learned to use technology to better serve their customers and enhance their productivity; and data from the U.S. Bureau of Labor Statistics shows that the percent of workers in sales occupations has actually slightly increased since 1999.[5]

7. **Competition** involves the marketing activities of rival firms. In most cases, this force has the greatest impact on the sales organization. In a survey of over 500 CEOs, "changes in type and/or level of competition" were identified as the top marketplace challenge (number two was "impact of the internet").[6]

In addition to these seven macro-environmental forces, the second set of external forces a company faces are a *direct* part of the firm's marketing system. These are the company's market, its suppliers, and its marketing intermediaries (primarily middlemen). While generally classed as uncontrollable, these three elements are susceptible to a greater degree of company influence than are the macroenvironmental forces. Note the two-way flows between the company and these three external elements in Figure 2-1. The company receives products and promotional messages from its suppliers. In return, the company sends out payments and marketing information. The same types of exchanges occur between the company and its market. Any of these exchanges can go through one or more intermediaries.

Internal Variables

To reach its marketing goal, management has at its disposal two sets of internal, controllable forces: (1) the company's resources in non-marketing areas and (2) the components of its marketing mix. Figure 2-1 shows these internal forces in relation to the forces in the external environment. The result is the company's total marketing system set within its environment.

Recall from Chapter 1 that the term **marketing mix** describes the combination of four ingredients that constitute the core of a company's marketing system. When effectively blended, these four—product, price, distribution, and promotion—form a marketing program designed to provide want-satisfying goods and services to the company's market. Also recall that promotional activities form a separate sub-mix in the company's marketing program that we call the *promotional mix* or the *communications mix.* The **promotional mix** is defined as the specific set of advertising, sales promotion, public relations and personal selling activities used by the selling firm.

THE MARKETING CONCEPT AND MARKETING MANAGEMENT

As business people have come to recognize marketing's vital importance to a firm's success, a way of business thinking—a philosophy—has evolved. Called the **marketing concept,** this philosophy holds that the overriding goal of an organization is to *identify the needs and wants of a target market, and then satisfy those needs and wants better than the competition does.* As shown in Figure 2-2, there are three keys to being successful with this philosophy. First, all employees and business functions of the firm must be focused on the customer. Second, there must be good communication throughout the firm such that the various marketing activities work together. And third, the firm must efficiently manage

FIGURE 2-2
Marketing Concept Success
Factors

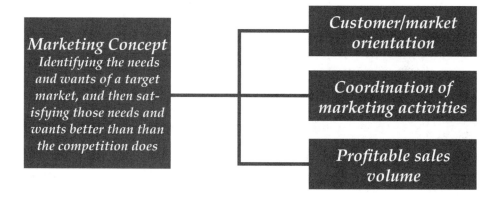

margins and minimize cost so that a profit is generated over the long run. Stated another way, these are the three elements of an effective marketing concept:

1. Company planning and operations should be *customer-oriented* or *market-oriented.*
2. Marketing activities in a firm should be *organizationally coordinated.*
3. The goal of the organization should be to generate *profitable sales volume over the long run.*

FIGURE 2-3
The evolution of marketing management

Evolution of Marketing Management

Marketing management is the process of planning, implementing, and coordinating all marketing activities and integrating them into the overall operations of the firm. In most successful firms, this process is the responsibility of the chief marketing executive and is guided by the marketing concept. In other words, the needs and wants of customers should be at the center of marketing management, but this is not always the case.

Marketing management evolves through four stages: production orientation, sales orientation, marketing orientation, and relationship orientation (see Figure 2-3). As explained below, the marketing concept is embraced by firms in the third and fourth stages, but not by those in the first two stages. The stages have direct implications for how salespeople deal with customers.

Production-Orientation Stage

During the first stage, a company is typically production oriented. The executives in production and engineering shape the company's objectives and planning. The focus is on taking advantage of economies of scale and mass-producing a limited variety of products for as little cost as possible. The function of the sales department is simply to sell the production output at the price set by production and financial executives.

With this stage, marketing is not recognized. In fact, the top "marketing" executive is the sales manager, who leads a sales department that is essentially within manufacturing. Salespeople are mere order takers, as the product tends to sell itself. This stage is more likely to exist when demand greatly exceeds supply. For example, Ford Motor Company embraced this orientation one century ago when selling its very popular Model T automobile. Henry Ford famously quipped that customers could buy the Model T in any color, "as long as it's black." No automobile maker could be successful today with this same attitude!

Sometimes production-orientation is confused with product-orientation. They are similar in certain ways, but we argue that they are distinct (see box entitled "Henry Ford…").

Sales-Orientation Stage

When supply catches up to demand, the first reaction of many companies is to engage in the aggressive, "hard sell" approach. In this stage, companies focus

CONSIDER THIS...

Henry Ford, Steve Jobs and Ralph Waldo Emerson

Marketing scholars sometimes refer to a product-orientation stage that is similar to—but subtly distinct from—production-orientation. Here are the differences:

Production-orientation focuses on mass producing products at low cost. Demand tends to greatly exceed supply, and so the products sell themselves. Salespeople are mere order takers, and marketing executives have very little say or power. This approach does not reflect the marketing concept. The best example of this was Ford during Model-T heyday, when Henry Ford famously quipped that customers could buy the Model T in any color, "as long as it's black."

Product-orientation focuses on continually improving the product through creative and innovative means. Salespeople are tech-savvy, highly knowledgeable, and fervent ambassadors of the products they represent. Marketing executives lead these companies with their out-of-box thinking that arguably goes beyond customer needs. The best example of this was Apple during its string of innovative products, such as the iPod and iPhone. In fact, Apple's Steve Jobs is sometimes said to be the greatest marketer of all time.

Product-orientation is consistent with this quote attributed to Ralph Waldo Emerson: "Build a better mousetrap, and the world will beat a path to your door."

Question: Do you agree with Emerson's quote? What are the pros and cons of embracing a product-orientation?

SOURCE: Tim Nudd, "The Greatest Marketer of the Age," *Adweek Blog*, Retrieved June 16, 2016 from: http://www.adweek.com/news/advertising-branding/greatest-marketer-age-135597

on selling their product to any and all prospects, regardless of their needs. Salespeople do not take "no" for an answer, and might even engage in trickery to get the sale. Of course, this style of high-pressure selling continues to give salespeople a bad reputation, even though most modern, professional salespeople are not at all like this. This orientation is much more likely to be found in transactional (one-time) selling than in relationship selling.

Marketing-Orientation Stage

The marketing concept first emerges in the marketing-orientation stage. In this third stage, companies use a coordinated marketing management strategy directed toward the twin goals of customer satisfaction and profitable sales volume. Attention focuses on identifying and meeting customer needs, rather than on high-pressure selling. The top executive is a marketing manager or the vice president of marketing. In this stage, several activities—traditionally the province of other executives—become the responsibility of the marketing manager. For instance, inventory control, warehousing, and aspects of product planning are often turned over to the marketing manager.

Ideally, a marketing-oriented firm goes beyond its own boundaries and coordinates its marketing activities with a select group of customers and suppliers. After all, customer needs and wants can be more easily understood and responded to if the selling firm has developed a close working relationship with its customers.

Relationship-Orientation Stage

The relationship-orientation stage is characterized by relationship building and is a natural extension of the marketing-orientation stage. Relationship-oriented firms continue to embrace the marketing concept. At the same time, the buyer and seller make a commitment to do business with each other *over a long time.* Thus, a given sale is not viewed as a solitary transaction. Because of this ongoing relationship, salespeople better understand their customers' business and can become more like consultants. Their goal is to improve each customer's overall profitability rather than just to sell products. Over time, salespeople earn the customer's trust, which adds significant value to the relationship from the customer's perspective.[7] As noted in Chapter 1, this process of close cooperation and collaboration between selling and buying firms is called **relationship marketing**.

Interestingly, the evolution of marketing management has not necessarily progressed in a uniform, chronological manner. There are still firms today in the early production-orientation and sales-orientation stages. This tends to vary by industry. For example, a few years ago there were many firms in the finance sector that specialized in making home loans to consumers with poor credit history. This involved salespeople using high-pressure tactics and failing to disclose all fees to the borrowers.[8] These were unethical practices by modern companies with an outdated, sales-oriented approach to business. Many say these practices led to a severe recession.

Evolution of Selling in the United Stages[9]

Selling has evolved along with marketing management. Over the past two centuries, American businesses have put forth extraordinary effort toward organizing, training, and further developing their sales forces. Increasingly, "salesmanship" has been approached as a science, as opposed to an art. That is, U.S. firms systematically have adapted and refined their business strategies to make their sales forces as effective and efficient as possible. To appreciate the sophistication of the modern sales organization, it is useful to examine how sales jobs have evolved over time.

Independent **peddlers** were the dominant form of salespeople in the first century of the United States. These peddlers were similar to those that had existed in Europe for centuries. They worked for themselves, traveling across the country selling pots, pans, clocks, medicines, and many other small goods, which they carried in large trunks or wagons. Peddlers sold directly to consumers, who were mostly farmers (since the vast majority of the American work force lived and worked on farms). The profession was not well respected by the general public, who generally distrusted these strangers who came knocking on their doors. At the same time, the U.S. economy was not very advanced, and there were not many other options for consumers, such as retail stores. To become a peddler, little investment was required, but, of course, the job did require lots of travel. It appealed mostly to young, unmarried men. Bartering was a way of life in this time period. And since most of the peddlers' customers were farmers, who grew and made most of what they consumed, peddlers would often trade their goods in exchange for blankets, pillows, scarves or some other item that had been made by the farmer's family. The new goods would then be added to the peddler's wagon to potentially sell to the next customer.

As the U.S. economy developed in the later 1800s, more and more manufacturers came into existence. To gain a larger market, many of these companies opted to sell through their own sales force consisting of salespeople known as **canvassers.** Canvassers were paid straight commission (no salary). Like the peddlers, they tended to sell small goods, door-to-door. However, canvassers sold a product line from a single manufacturer, unlike peddlers who typically sold a wide variety of products. Further, canvassers would sell goods "by subscription," meaning that the customer would commit to the sale, make a down payment, and then the good would be delivered at a later date. This was possible for the first time due to the increasing sophistication of the product distribution system, which relied on trains and canal boats. In addition, this was an era in which selling was first considered a science. These companies studied the psychology of persuasion and provided canvassers with elaborate sales kits. Canvassers, therefore, used intricate sales tactics, which tended to be high-pressure. Common products sold this way were lightning rods, brushes, seeds, bulbs, roots, shrubs, fruit trees and anything that might improve life or lighten the workload for farmers.

At the same time, large book publishers hired salespeople called **book agents**. These agents were similar to canvassers in most respects, except that females were hired more often to be book agents (essentially all peddlers and canvassers were men). One of the most successful campaigns carried out by book agents was the selling of the memoirs of President Ulysses S. Grant—a national best-seller.

Toward the end of the 19th century, most manufacturers distributed their goods through large wholesale companies. These wholesale companies hired traveling salesmen, typically called **drummers**, to sell *the goods of the many manufacturers they represented* to owners of general stores. Drummers usually were paid a mixture of salary and commission. The typical drummer was a white, Protestant man (they were almost all men), who was very entertaining with a seemingly endless number of jokes and stories. Ironically, drummers approached selling in a much less *scientific* manner than did canvassers, who emerged before them. This was an era in which demand exceeded supply, and so the products essentially sold themselves. Yes, the drummer had a close relationship with customers, but the relationship was personal (not business-focused). Drummers were not consultative salespeople like we see today.

In the 1920s, drummers began to be replaced by what could be viewed as the modern sales force. With technological advancements, especially in the areas of transportation, the reliability and efficiency of distribution greatly increased. This allowed manufacturers to sell directly to retailers *with their own sales force.* Two of the leading examples of this time were the sales organizations of Singer Sewing Machine and National Cash Register. Although this was the era in which a production-orientation was predominate, the salespeople of these companies were sophisticated, well-respected professionals that were successful to the extent they understood customer needs.

Figure 2-4 shows the evolution of selling in a cartoon that was first published in 1927. The purpose of this cartoon was to contrast "The Salesman of Today" (i.e., the salesman of 1927) with two "outdated" sales types: the drummer and the solicitor (the solicitor is like the canvasser described above). Of course, there have been many changes and advances since that cartoon was drawn 90 years ago—yet the cartoon's portrayal of the right way to approach sales is just as true today. Unfortunately, the old styles of selling are also still around today, and this sometimes disgraces the sales profession. It is important to understand, however, that salespeople have a long history of helping customers and solving problems. In fact, the growth and development of selling and **sales** management has helped the United States become the largest and most technologically powerful economy in the world.

RELATIONSHIP MARKETING

Relationship marketing is a process of collaboration between the buying and selling firms that results in economic benefits for *both* firms. Instead of being adversarial, the relationship between firms is built on cooperation, trust, commitment, and information. Typically, the firms align their operating functions, such as order processing, accounting and budgeting, information systems, merchandising processes, and the like.

FIGURE 2-4
Selling styles, 1927
SOURCE: 52 letters to Salesmen, Chicago: Stevens-Davis Co., © 1926-1927

The sales manager and salespeople play a key role in these activities, and, thus, relationship marketing is often called **relationship selling**. In particular, sales must facilitate the following four key issues: promoting open communication, empowering employees, involving customers in the planning process, and working in teams.[10] Each of these is discussed below.

Open Communication

Because relationship marketing is often complex, the selling and buying firms must exchange extensive amounts of information. Open communication is the lifeblood of relationship marketing. It fosters trust and provides the information and knowledge necessary to carry out the cooperative and collaborative activities. Nobody in the selling firm knows more about the customer than the salesperson, who is therefore a key coordinator of the information flow. That is, a salesperson's responsibilities include collecting information from the customer and then dispensing that information to the appropriate person or department in their own organization. Of course, the salesperson also represents the firm and thus keeps the customer informed of events within that firm.

Employee Empowerment

In relationship marketing, salespeople do more than simply sell their product to customers—they help solve customer problems. They can only do this if they have the skills, responsibility, and authority to make decisions and take action. Thus, companies must encourage and reward their salespeople for taking initiative and using creativity to solve customer problems. Further, managers must foster an environment in which salespeople do not fear losing their jobs if they make a mistake.

Customers and the Planning Process

Close, effective collaboration exists between firms when they agree on what tactics should be performed to carry out strategies that will lead to the accomplishment of goals. In other words, the selling firm should allow the customer to be involved in the seller's planning process. This ensures the customer's support in the implementation of the plan. In most cases, it is not feasible to involve all customers, but selling firms should at least solicit input from the larger firms among its customer base. Again, the salesperson is the key facilitator of this process; he or she is responsible for keeping the customer apprised of the latest planning decisions and for collecting feedback about those decisions.

Teamwork

"It's never an individual who closes a sale. It's an effort by your entire team," says a Senior VP of Sales for IBT Media.[11] Certainly, a firm engaged in relationship marketing must encourage teamwork—both among its own employees and among those of its partner firm. As indicated above, the relationship is often complex, with various operating processes of the two firms being closely aligned. Consequently, to effectively provide meaningful service and value to the buyer, the seller must use **team selling**, involving a team of people with diverse, complementary skills. In addition to one or more salespeople, the selling team is composed of design engineers, financial experts, customer service representatives, quality control engineers—anyone and everyone who can contribute to solving customer problems and thus keeping the relationship on good terms.

Salespeople play a key role in coordinating the many different actions of the diverse team, which interacts with an equally diverse group of individuals from the customer firm. This group or team of people from the customer firm is known as the **buying center**. The buying center is made up of functional specialists from purchasing, manufacturing, engineering, and/or product development who view the purchase from a strategic perspective. Team selling has many benefits in the business-to-business realm; and is arguably the most widespread and significant trend to influence sales in recent years. Here are six benefits of having a close knit sales team that works together:

1. Fosters Creativity and Learning—Similar to brainstorming, combining the unique perspectives of a variety of people stimulates the imagination.
2. Blends Complementary Strengths—The whole is greater than the sum of the parts, because each member of a team tends to take on tasks that they are especially good at.
3. Builds Trust—When people rely on each other and accomplish tasks together, strong relationships form.
4. Teaches Conflict Resolution Skills—When conflict occurs within a team, members tend to solve the problems themselves instead of relying on management.
5. Promotes a Wider Sense of Ownership—Working toward a common goal as a cohesive unit makes team members feel more connected to the firm.
6. Encourages Healthy-Risk Taking—The members of a team tend to take more risks because they have the support of their teammates to fall back on if failure were to happen.

SOURCE: Dave Mattson, "6 Benefits of Teamwork in the Workplace," Sandler Training blog, February 19, 2015, Retrieved on June 16, 2016 from the following website:
HTTPS://WWW.SANDLER.COM/BLOG/6-BENEFITS-OF-TEAMWORK-IN-THE-WORKPLACE

Interestingly, these relationship marketing concepts, such as employee empowerment and working in teams, emerged in the 1990s as part of the **total quality management (TQM)** movement. TQM is the process by which a company strives to improve customer satisfaction through the continuous improvement of all its operations. The entire supply chain focuses on improving product quality through eliminating manufacturing defects, and collaboration with both customers and suppliers. Thus, firms that embrace the TQM philosophy are necessarily engaged in relationship marketing. Again, salespeople play a critical role in these relationships as they oversee the transfer of relevant, accurate, and timely information between firms.

If a company is successful in implementing a relationship marketing program, it can expect to have higher-quality products, higher customer satisfaction, more loyal customers, and greater profitability.[12] As more and more companies focus on customer relations and satisfaction as a measure of the effectiveness of their marketing programs, sales managers and salespeople will be expected to assume greater responsibility for directing and coordinating the marketing efforts of the firm.

Integrating Marketing and Sales Functions

One common problem in marketing management is the lack of integration between a firm's marketing department and its sales function.[13] The marketing department typically develops a firm's overall marketing strategy, which includes decisions about how to promote, distribute, and price the product line. The salespeople ultimately determine success or failure of the strategy, because they have the responsibility of implementing it in the field. Thus, integration between the activities of the marketing and sales functions is critical to the success of the firm.

The marketing strategy can be effective only when it is clearly understood and embraced by the sales force. This is more likely to happen when salespeople are involved in the strategy development process. After all, salespeople are an invaluable source of information in this regard, given their unique position of working closely with customers. Further, the marketing department must assist the salespeople in carrying out the marketing strategy by providing them with the right marketing tools, such as advertising, support services, and sales promotions. But if salespeople don't like a particular tool, they probably won't use it—or at least they won't use it as effectively as they could.

One company that understands the importance of integrating marketing and sales is Ecolab Inc., which has a long history of manufacturing and selling detergents and other cleaning products to hotels and restaurants. Ecolab trains its salespeople to listen to customers, and then it listens to its salespeople in the development of marketing strategy. For example, one salesperson relayed to the company that many customers were having significant problems with insect control. Ecolab responded by creating its pest-elimination service, which is now one of the world's largest killers of cockroaches![14] Like many other companies embracing the marketing concept, Ecolab expects salespeople to do more than simply sell things—they solve customer problems.

Integrating Production and Sales

Coordinating the activities of the sales force and the production function is also critical to the overall success of the firm. Materials requirements and production schedules are developed according to sales forecasts. Therefore, firms avoid operational problems by integrating the plans of the production and sales functions. When the amount sold exceeds production output, customers become dissatisfied because the products they ordered do not arrive on time. Of course, the opposite situation is also a serious problem, because high levels of unsold inventory become extremely costly to the firm.

In spite of the intuitive connection between production and sales, many companies do a poor job of coordinating the activities of these two business functions. The problem stems from the fact that salespeople for a given company are often dispersed across many different territories throughout the world. This makes it difficult for the company to keep up to date on the needs of each sales territory. A-dec, Inc., a dental equipment manufacturer, is one of the many companies using web-based technology to improve the coordination of its planning processes. Previously, A-dec would develop a sales forecast during its annual meeting—which was the one time all year when the sales managers from the company's 75 territories would come together. Typically, the forecast was extremely inaccurate, causing excess inventory for some products and long production lead times for others. The solution to these problems was a secure website. The site's advanced web-based software application enabled sales managers from around the world to constantly update their sales forecasts—they can now communicate about the product mix they need, and when they need it. This technology-facilitated integration has led to many benefits for A-dec and its customers. Lead times are shorter, excess inventory has been eliminated, and customers get the right product at the right time.[15]

STRATEGIC PLANNING

When shaping sales force management strategy, sales executives are guided and limited by both the firm's overall **strategic planning**, which is the process of identifying the firm's general direction, and making decisions on allocating resources to successfully reach its goals. For example, in the early 1990s, IBM made some significant changes in its overall strategic approach to the personal computer market. For several years, IBM concentrated on selling networks to big businesses and more or less ignored the individual, the educational, and the small-business market segments that Apple Computer solicited. However, Apple's success in its markets forced IBM to reconsider its own company strategies. IBM altered its marketing strategies accordingly, and IBM sales management planning also soon reflected the new company strategies.

Three concepts—objectives, strategies, and tactics—are the heart of planning at any level in the organizational hierarchy. All sales managers should have a thorough understanding of these concepts—what they are and how to use them.

Objectives

Objectives are goals around which a strategic plan is formulated. Without goals, it is impossible to create a meaningful plan. Objectives must be more than platitudes. Such clichés as "We should be of service to our customers and treat our employees fairly" are only hazy guideposts for making business decisions. To be useful, objectives must be specific and measurable.

Once the firm's objectives are agreed on, all decisions should align with them. Decisions incompatible with the objectives only hinder the company's realization of its goals. This alignment seems simple and obvious, but it is not easy to achieve. For instance, goals of a 15 percent return on investment and a 10 percent rate annual growth rate can clash. Heublein, Inc., encountered this difficulty when it acquired Hamm's beer. One of Heublein's objectives was a 15 percent rate of return on its investment. It also had ambitious growth objectives. Hamm's large sales volume fit the company's growth objective. However, profits in the beer business are far less than 15 percent—Hamm's realized about a 5 percent return on investment. To satisfy its growth objective, Heublein would have had to sacrifice its profit objective. A few years after acquiring the brand, Heublein sold Hamm's at a loss.

Strategies

The terms *objectives*, *strategies*, and *tactics* gain more meaning when viewed in relation to each other, as in Figure 2-5. Companies set objectives first and then

FIGURE 2-5
Relationship of objectives,
strategies, and tactics

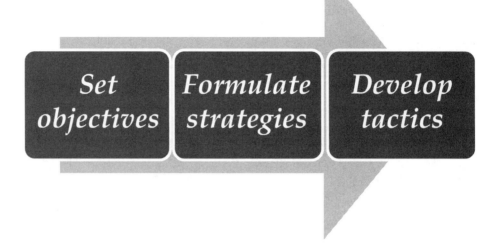

develop **strategies**, or plans of action, to achieve the objectives. For instance, the sales manager may have the goal of achieving a certain dollar volume of sales in a coming period. She proceeds to formulate strategies to accomplish this goal. These strategies may include entering new markets or covering the existing markets more intensely.

Strategies should be followed with some degree of perseverance. Some strategies require time to be effective. Impatient managers eager for results may not allow certain programs time to bear fruit. These managers often take new products off the market before the products have had a fair chance to develop a following. One sales manager fired a rep that had been sent to open up a new territory because dealers were not buying the product as fast as the manager had expected. The fault was not that the sales rep was inefficient, but rather that the manager had unrealistic expectations.

Tactics

After all the talking, the firm implements its chosen strategies. Some work must be done. **Tactics** are the activities that people must perform in order to carry out the strategy.

There are no perfect tactics, and in most situations there is no one best tactic that should always be used. Rather, managers must evaluate the situation and choose those tactics they feel are consistent with the strategy and have the highest probability of success at a given time.

Generally, when a company changes its strategies, it also must change its tactics. However, many administrators use the same tactics repeatedly, regardless of the circumstances, because those tactics worked for them in the past. But success can be lulling. There comes a time when the tactic will not work, and that is usually the most critical time.

A classic example of using an inappropriate tactic occurs when a company changes its sales strategy from transactional selling to consultative selling yet does not make any changes in its compensation plan (as we will learn in

Chapter 9, straight-commission plans do not work well with consultative selling). The following discussion of strategic planning further illustrates the relationship among objectives, strategies, and tactics at different levels within the corporation.

STRATEGIC PLANNING AT THE COMPANY, MARKETING, AND SALES FORCE LEVELS

Several of the administrative concepts we just discussed are involved in the strategic planning process for the total company, its marketing program, and its sales force operations. The strategic planning on all levels in a firm should be well integrated and highly coordinated.

Marketing must create a strategic plan that is consistent with the strategic plan of the total company. In turn, planning by the sales department is determined by the strategic marketing plan. In this sense, the planning starts at the top and works its way down, guiding the entire organization.[16] At the same time, planning is a bottom-up process—those creating the strategic plan for the total company must listen carefully to the input of employees at all levels of the organization. Of course, this includes salespeople, who work closely with customers and thus have valuable insight into what direction the firm should take.

Strategic Planning for the Total Company

Strategic planning for the total company involves determining the organization's mission, the broad objectives (goals) that will enable the company to fulfill its mission, and the strategies and tactics needed to achieve the objectives. Thus, strategic planning starts with identifying the organization's fundamental **mission**. Management should ask two questions: "What businesses are we in?" and "What business should we be in?" The answers may or may not be the same. A television manufacturer may say it is in the "indoor entertainment" business. But after further analysis of its market opportunities, it may decide that it should be in the "entertainment and education" business.

Once it determines the company's mission, management can set objectives consistent with that mission. For example, the company may aim either to earn a 20 percent return on investment next year or to increase its market share from the present 8 percent to 20 percent in three years.

The next step is to select the strategy to be used to reach the objectives. As examples, consider the following relationships:

Objectives	Possible Strategies
1. Earn 20 percent return on investment next year.	a) Reduce production and marketing costs b) Increase the rate of capital turnover
2. Increase market share from present 8 percent to 20 percent in three years.	a) Intensify marketing efforts in domestic markets. b) Expand into foreign markets. c) Buy out a competitors

The tactics selected to implement the strategy depend, of course, on the strategy chosen. Thus, if the chosen strategy is to reduce marketing costs, management can use such tactics as cutting advertising expenses by 10 percent or closing two

CONSIDER THIS...

An International Perspective

The international marketplace is booming, and thus strategic planning for most U.S. companies involves a global dimension. While the objectives or ultimate goals might be the same in all countries served, the best salespeople develop tactics unique to each specific culture.

For example, American salespeople generally find that the sales cycle is longer in almost every country outside the United States. That is, it takes more time for the salesperson to close a deal after making initial customer contact. This means that in order to be productive, American salespeople selling abroad must work simultaneously with more accounts than they would back home.

The reasons for the longer sales cycle tend to vary across cultures. The following observations are based on comments from salespeople with oversees experience:

In Germany, longer sales cycles stem from Germans' tendency to be thorough. Germans expect multiple references and do extensive background research on all competitive products before committing to the sale.

In Spain and Italy, customers expect weeks and weeks of schmoozing and entertaining before committing to the sale. In fact, U.S. salespeople are often asked to attend social gatherings with the customer's spouse, children, and maybe even siblings, parents, aunts, and uncles!

In England, the British do not commit before extensive negotiation about the price and thorough double-checking of facts and figures.

In Turkey, the sales cycle takes longer due to an unstable economy. American businesspeople have learned to ask for payment up front, and to insist on dealing with U.S. currency rather than the seriously devalued Turkish lira.

Note that these are general tendencies observed by a few salespeople. Clearly, not all customers in a given country or culture are identical!

SOURCE: Lisa Bertagnoli, "Selling Oversees Complex Endeavor," *Marketing News* 35, no. 16 (July 30, 2001), p.4

branch offices. To implement the strategy of intensifying the domestic marketing effort, management might add 20 more sales reps or change the compensation plan to provide greater motivation for the sales force.

Strategic Marketing Planning

Once the total company planning process is completed, essentially the same procedure can be repeated for the marketing program. The objectives, strategies, and tactics at the marketing level are closely related to those at the corporate level. A corporate strategy often translates into a marketing strategy. To illustrate:

Company Objective	Company Strategy	Marketing Strategy
1. Earn 20 percent return on investment.	Cut marketing costs by 15 percent this year.	Reduce direct selling efforts by using wholesalers to reach small accounts
2. Increase market share from 8 percent to 20 percent.	Intensify marketing efforts in domestic markets.	Enter new markets.

Sales Force Strategy

Once the strategic planning process for the entire marketing program has been completed, the role of the sales force has largely been established. That is, the objectives, strategies, and tactics adopted by sales managers generally are limited and guided by the strategic marketing plan. To illustrate:

Company Objective	Company Strategy (Marketing Goal)	Marketing Strategy (Sales Force Goal)
Increase market share from 8 percent to 20 percent in two years.	Intensify market efforts in domestic markets to increase sales volume by $3 million next year.	a) Enter new geographic markets and sell to new types of customers, or b) Cover existing geographic markets more aggressively.

Now, whether the company elects to pursue marketing strategy (sales force goal) a or b will make a big difference in the choice of sales force strategies and tactics. Tactical decisions in the areas of organizational design, selection, training, compensation, supervision, and evaluation must all be aligned with the sales strategy. These principles may be illustrated as follows:

Marketing Strategy	Sales Force Strategy	Sales Force Tactics
a) Enter new markets	Build long-term customer relations.	1. Stress missionary selling in sales training and supervision. 2. Stress salary element in compensation plan.
b) Sell aggressively in existing markets.	Increase sales force motivation.	1. Conduct more sales contests 2. Stress commission feature in pay plan. 3. Increase field supervision.

In many companies, this strategic sales force planning is cascaded down the organizational hierarchy. That is, sales force goals and strategies are established for regional sales divisions, and even for individual sales reps and key accounts.

STRATEGIC TRENDS

Several strategic trends emerging in the past decade continue to have a major impact on the sales strategies of today. These include social selling, hybrid sales channels, and multiple relationship strategies. We elaborate on each trend below.

Social Selling

Social media was first utilized by customers who became empowered by learning about the relative pros and cons of products and companies. Not surprisingly, salespeople have followed suit. Recent research in sales management has shown that both business-to-business and business-to-consumer salespeople are using relationship-oriented social media tools to a substantial extent.[17] This practice, known as **social selling**, involves the use of relationship-oriented social media tools to identify the right prospects, and turn them into close, long-term customers. This chapter's opening scenario, which focused on SAP's use of LinkedIn's Sales Navigator, is one example of this. Facebook, Twitter, YouTube and Salesforce.com's chatter can similarly be used by salespeople to achieve sales goals.

Through social selling, sales organizations can enhance their professional brand image, which ultimately leads to more sales. In part, this is done when account managers post relevant content and/or publish articles that catch the eye and inform prospects. Experts say that relative to traditional sales approaches, social selling is better at helping salespeople connect with the right prospects, engage them in a meaningful exchange of information, and build trust.[18]

Hybrid Sales Channels

To maintain existing customer bases, cut costs, and expand market coverage, many firms use **hybrid sales channels**. That is, a company might sell its products through three distinct channels: a direct sales force, a network of distributors, and its own e-commerce website. This allows that company to reach different segments of customers in different ways for the sake of efficiency. Often, the guiding principle in designing these hybrid systems is to use less-expensive selling methods for tasks that do not require face-to-face contact. The trade-off that must be considered is between the need for personalized customer service and the cost of providing that service.

Originally, IBM's selling tasks were handled by the company's direct sales force only. But as IBM faced increasing competition, it expanded its sales efforts to include independent dealers, catalogs, direct mail, and telemarketing. Apple Computer, in contrast, started with a dealer network and later added a direct sales force. Cosmetics seller Mary Kay Inc. has added telemarketing (or inside sales) to its more traditional personal selling methods. These various approaches all serve to allow these companies to reach different segments of buyers.

The addition of new channels requires changes in the structure and policies of the sales organization. These changes may be accompanied by a certain amount of resistance from the existing salespeople. Sales managers must manage this conflict as well as the coordination within and across channels. Specific guidelines must be established that clearly delineate who is responsible for which customers and tasks in the hybrid system. Utilizing multiple channels undoubtedly makes the sales manager's job more complex. But in spite of the potential problems, the use of multiple channels is likely to increase throughout the next decade.

Multiple Relationship Strategies

A firm might use a single sales channel of its own direct sales force, yet segment customers according to what kind of relationship the company has (or wants to develop) with the sales force. For example, a selling firm might reach some customers through transactional selling and other customers through consultative selling. This is called a **multiple relationship strategies** approach.

That is, on one end of the continuum, transactional selling (discussed in Chapter 1) is targeted at customers who are not interested in, or who are unable to afford, the value-added services offered by the selling firm. With this approach, the salesperson does not follow up with the customer after the sale and is not concerned about cultivating a long-term relationship.

Alternatively, **consultative selling** is used for those customers interested in the value-added services. Consultative selling involves salespeople who have in-depth knowledge of their customers' company and business. In fact, a team of individuals from the selling firm might be involved since it is often difficult for a single salesperson to provide all the necessary knowledge. Consultative salespeople or sales teams create value for their customers by identifying problems and finding mutually beneficial solutions.

Interestingly, the different relationships do not always correspond to the size of the customer. For example, Microsoft has a wide range of relationships with its many customers, including *transactional relationships with some of its largest national accounts*. Certain firms simply have corporate cultures that resist forming close partnerships and sharing proprietary information with vendors.[19]

Marketing Management's Social Responsibility

Global warming, toxic waste, pollution, and other concerns have led to another important development in the evolution of marketing management: Marketing executives in this era must act in a socially responsible manner if they wish to succeed, or even survive. External pressures—consumer discontent, concern for environmental problems, and political-legal forces—influence marketing programs in countless firms.

In response to great pressure from environmentalists, Arco developed and now markets an unleaded regular gasoline with low emissions. The auto industry made many technical and design changes in its products in response to governmental and public pressure for safer vehicles. Grocery chains responded quickly to complaints about harmful chemicals sprayed on produce. Ralph's, a California supermarket chain, promotes its produce as being free of such chemicals. It would be difficult to find any firm that has not somehow had to alter its marketing behavior in response to external pressure.

Viewed more broadly, there is a growing concern for the management of human resources. We sense a change in emphasis from materialism to humanitarianism in our society. One mark of an affluent society is a shift in consumption from products to services and a shift in cultural emphasis from things to people. As we progress, marketing management must be concerned not only with establishing a better material standard of *living*, but also with creating and delivering a better quality of *life*.

SUMMARY

Modern sales managers understand that they are but one link in the total marketing strategy for the firm. Moreover, they understand the place of the firm's marketing strategy within the company's total strategic plan.

In addition, both managers and salespeople should understand the external environmental forces that affect their operations. Specifically, they must monitor and respond to any changes in the physical environment, demographics, economic conditions, sociocultural factors, political-legal factors, technology, and competition associated with their market. They also must understand their markets, their suppliers, and the marketing intermediaries (wholesalers and retailers).

To respond to their environment, marketing executives can manipulate the variables of the marketing mix, which include product, price structure, distribution system, and promotional activities. Personal selling is a major element of promotion.

With the advent of the marketing concept and its acceptance by most businesses, the job of the sales manager has been changed and sales operations have become but one portion of the firm's total marketing program. Marketing has evolved through several stages. It is now in the relationship-orientation stage, in which buyers and sellers make long-term commitments to do business with each other. For effective relationship marketing, all functions of the selling firm must work together as a team to help solve customer problems.

Setting specific, clear-cut objectives is an essential step in the management of a company. Once the company's objectives are set, management can develop appropriate strategies. Tactics are the organizational behaviors that execute the strategy.

Strategic planning across all levels in a firm should be coordinated. Strategic decisions at the top of the organization dictate what goes into the strategic marketing plan, which in turn guides the activities of the sales force. At the same time, top-level executives cannot plan effectively without listening to lower-level employees such as salespeople.

Several strategic trends have emerged in the past decade and are shaping the strategy of sales organizations. These include social selling, hybrid sales channels, and multiple relationship strategies. Finally, today's managers must act in a socially responsible manner if they wish to succeed.

KEY TERMS

Book agents	Marketing mix	Relationship selling
Buying center	Marketing system	Social selling
Canvassers	Mission	Sociocultural factors
Competition	Multiple relationship	Strategic planning
Consultative selling	strategy	Strategies
Demography	Objectives	Tactics
Drummers	Peddlers	Team selling
Economic conditions	Physical environment	Total quality manage-
External environment	Political-legal factors	ment (TQM)
Marketing concept	Promotional mix	Transactional selling
Marketing management	Relationship marketing	

QUESTIONS AND PROBLEMS

1. How can top management keep the sales manager abreast of changes in the environment that affect the company? How can the sales manager pass on such information to the sales force?

2. We said company planning should be customer oriented. Exactly what does that mean? In what way or by what stretch of the imagination might the planning of the firm's employee benefit package by affected by customer considerations?

3. Why should a company be concerned about the profitability of its customers?

4. What are some ways in which sales managers can empower their salespeople?

5. How do marketing people depend on salespeople? How do salespeople depend on marketing people?

6. Why should a sales manager prepare an annual operating plan?

7. If you, as a sales manager, were required to prepare an annual operating plan, what would you include in the plan?

8. As a sales rep, you are required to develop an annual sales plan for your territory. Would you include in your plan? *Hint:* Think in terms of objectives, strategies, and tactics.

9. What role does the quality of the information you possess have in your tactical behavior?

10. In what way is the existence of a sales force the reflection of a strategy?

11. One management writer observed that it is folly to expect behavior A when rewarding behavior B. How might his insight be applied to the problem of aligning sales force behavior with corporate goals?

12. What are some of the ways sales managers can limit the amount of conflict between various distributors if their company is using a multiple-channel strategy?

13. How should a company decide whether to use transaction selling or consultative selling with each of its customers?

14. How does a manager reward the team members in a team-selling situation?

15. In what industries are salespeople's jobs most likely to change due to the increasing predominance of the Internet in our society? Elaborate on how the sales job will change.

EXPERIENTIAL EXERCISES

1. Interview a marketing or product manager. Ask him or her to identify the primary sales objective for one of the company's products. Ask a sales manager and a sales representative at that company the same question for the same product. Compare and contrast the three viewpoints.

2. Interview a salesperson on how social media has impacted her or his job responsibilities. Which specific social media website or websites are liked, and which ones are not liked? Why is that?

3. Choose two companies and visit their websites. After examining each company's mission statement and other basic information, compare and contrast the marketing and sales strategies of the two companies. Which company is more customer-focused? Do the companies' sales organizations appear to use transactional selling or consultative selling?

4. Using a search engine (e.g., Google), enter "team-building exercises" or another similar search phrase. From the list of hits that is returned, find a few specific exercises that you feel would be most likely to help a sales team bond and work together, and describe these briefly. Then try to find price information. If you were a sales manager, would you pay to have your salespeople go through any such programs? Why or why not?

CARDINAL CONNECTORS, INC.
E-Commerce and a Hybrid Sales Channel Strategy

Ms. Sarah Miko, a sales manager for Cardinal Connectors Inc., is suddenly frightened about losing her job! She just stepped out of a meeting with her company's president, Mr. Bill Evans. In the meeting, Mr. Evans outlined a revolutionary e-commerce strategy that would dramatically alter Cardinal's distribution channel in the name of enhanced efficiency and overall productivity. That is, Mr. Evans has begun to believe that Cardinal's customers might be better-served through a company website that actually replaces its current sales force, as well as its network of intermediary wholesalers.

With 100 employees and $10 million in annual sales, Cardinal Connectors Inc. is a relatively small manufacturer of custom-design circuit-board connectors. Cardinal has a loyal base of customers, which consist of firms in the telecom, networking, and auto industries. Currently, these customers are serviced through a hybrid sales channel strategy. The bigger customers, which represent about 60 percent of total revenue, are deal with directly through Cardinal's 15-person full-time sales force. The remaining 40 percent of revenue is generated from smaller customers, which buy the product indirectly through one of five intermediary electronics wholesaler firms.

Ms. Sarah Miko has been a loyal and successful sales executive for Cardinal Connectors for over 20 years. She began as a sales representative with Cardinal right out of college, and eventually came to be one of Cardinal's most consistent sales performers. Seven years ago, Ms. Miko was promoted to sales manager and has received consistently high evaluations from Mr. Evans, the company president.

Ms. Miko prides herself on her ability to train and coach young sales reps into being professional, consultative salespeople. Above all, Ms. Miko preaches about the importance of relationship selling, and says that Cardinal sales reps are not doing their job unless they are adding value to the interfirm relationship between buyer and seller. For a Cardinal sales rep, most of the creative selling effort involves showing existing customers how they can solve their problems through the purchase of more Cardinal products. Thus, the emphasis is on increasing customer share—as opposed to market share.

Cardinal's sales force, however, does not service all customers. As stated above, a significant portion of revenue is generated from smaller customers who buy Cardinal products through intermediaries. But again, Ms. Miko believes that these intermediaries provide end-user customers with a host of valuable services that Cardinal could never offer itself through any website. These services include access to inventory, parts delivery, engineering support, and chip programming.

Mr. Evans is not so sure that either the direct sales force or the intermediaries are truly adding value. Evans believes that Cardinal circuit-board connectors are unmatched in quality and performance, and, thus, current customers will remain loyal to Cardinal as the sales function is moved to the Internet. Evans says this will be especially true since the e-commerce strategy will result in cost savings that can be passed on to the customer. The savings will stem from two sources. First, Cardinal can eliminate the high costs of paying for salesperson compensation and benefits; and, second, it will no longer have to offer margins to intermediaries. In addition, Mr. Evans thinks that customers will prefer dealing with a well-designed, interactive website, which (unlike salespeople and intermediaries) can be reached from anywhere at any time! And because a website is a great way to organize information, customers can find out all they want about Cardinal products simply by surfing and clicking. Further, Cardinal Connectors' competitors have started to move toward selling product through their company website. However, Mr. Evans is convinced that it is just a matter of time before that happens, and he wants to be the first in the industry to capitalize on the many new e-commerce tools and capabilities that are now available.

Although respectful of Mr. Evans's bold, future-oriented thinking, Sarah Miko still believes in the merits of many aspects of the current system. She feels that Mr. Evans's e-commerce initiatives are too extreme and should be down-scaled and better integrated with the existing hybrid sales channel strategy. At the same time, she knows it will take a convincing argument to persuade the very strong minded Mr. Evans to consider anything else!

Mr. Evans has called another meeting in a few days to discuss the specifics of his strategy. Of course, Ms. Miko is greatly troubled by the thought of eliminating Cardinal's direct sales force. She is proud of the effort and accomplishments of her salespeople—many of whom she has personally trained. But in addition, Ms. Miko truly believes that Mr. Evans's e-commerce strategy is not in the best interests of Cardinal Connectors Inc. Consequently, she wants to come to that meeting prepared to make a case for the benefits of their current strategy.

Questions:

1. What are the pros and cons of Mr. Evans's e-commerce strategy?

2. What is the best argument that Ms. Miko can make to keep her sales force intact?

3. In your opinion, should Cardinal Connectors Inc. eliminate its sales force? Explain.

MATSUSHITA ELECTRIC CORPORATION OF AMERICA
Sales Force Strategy

John Cunningham was the national sales manager of the Lighting Products Department, Special Products Division, of Matsushita Electric Corporation, a huge industrial complex in Japan with total sales worldwide of 6,660 billion yen ($60 Billion). He was immediately concerned with the operational sales strategy for a new line of compact, energy-efficient, fluorescent light bulbs (lamps) for both the consumer and industrial markets. The company had many years of experience selling lamps in the Orient, where it was a major factor in the market. For strategic reasons, Matsushita marketed its wide line of consumer and industrial products in the United States under the trade name Panasonic.

John Cunningham, after graduation as a marketing major from the University of South Florida in 1988, began his career selling light bulbs (lamps) for Westinghouse and subsequently North American Philips when it purchased the lamp division from Westinghouse. His outstanding sales record attracted the attention of Mitsubishi, which was trying to build distribution for a new line of energy-efficient light bulbs it had developed. However, that venture was terminated when the new bulbs were found to infringe on patents held by Phillips. Mitsubishi transferred John to selling its gigantic Diamond Vision television screens now seen in most of the sports stadiums in the country. His outstanding performance attracted the attention of the managers of Matsushita' light bulb operations, who were looking for someone to manage sales and distribution in the United States. After much conversation, several interviews, and a thorough investigation, John was hired. While his previous experience working for a Japanese company, combined with his knowledge of the Japanese business culture, were important factors in his selection, his outstanding sales record and establishment of a distribution network with Mitsubishi's compact fluorescent lamp operation was instrumental in the hiring decision.

Matsushita's basic marketing strategy was to introduce compact, energy-efficient, fluorescent lamps. A 15-watt fluorescent lamp would provide the same lumens (light) as a 75-watt incandescent lamp, thus yielding significant savings in power consumption. Such savings were important in the Far East markets where electricity costs were much higher than in the United States. Further, the life of the lamp was about 10 times that of an incandescent lamp. Research in the United States indicated that most people considered longevity the product's prime benefit. Social, political, and economic forces strongly supported such energy-saving innovations.

Despite John's outstanding performance, Panasonic's share of the U.S. consumer lamp market was small. It was a new player in a very competitive market dominated by such powerful names as General Electric and Phillips. Even such name as Westinghouse had been driven out of the business. At a meeting at the company's headquarters in Osaka, Japan, he was asked a direct question by one of the firm's top executives: "What would it take for us to significantly increase our share of the market for our fluorescent bulbs?"

John knew that he was expected to make the company a major player in the market; Matsushita management did not like being a minor factor in any of its markets. John had studied the situation intensely and was waiting with his answer. "We need to develop an electronic chip to replace the ballast. Present ballasts hum, flicker when started, are bulky, and are not rheostatable. They are either off or on. If a small electronic chip could be designed to replace the traditional ballast, we'd have technological feature that would significantly increase our market share."

John's superiors took note of his request and, within a short time, the company R&D people gave him exactly what he had requested—a small electronic chip to replace the ballast in fluorescent bulbs. It could be available for distribution in about 10 months. A planning meeting was held in Osaka at which John was asked to provide sales forecasts and budgets for marketing the new line of lamps. John was responsible only for the marketing of lamps under the Panasonic brand name. Matsushita also sold huge quantities of goods directly to other manufacturers and to large distributive organizations that sold them under their own brand names. For example, while Matsushita sold compact disc machines under its brand name Panasonic, it also made essentially the same product, with minor cosmetic alterations, for many other companies to market under their brand names. Matsushita company policy was to encourage OEM sales since it was felt that, by so doing, the company would be able to sell a much larger portion of the total market.

One basic corporate goal was to keep the factories in Japan busy, at full employment. Matsushita was not caught up with the penchant of many American corporations for controlling significant shares of a market through their own brands. It would sell to any firm that could provide significant volume for the factories.

John was informed at the meeting that the new technology would be offered to all other manufacturers. General Electric would have the same technology to sell as Panasonic. John was somewhat dismayed but knew that he could do nothing about the policy. However, he negotiated two concessions. First, he was able to have his sales quotas reduced in view of the increased competition. Second, he was able to get a one-year lead time over the competition. Panasonic would have the innovation exclusively for one year before Matsushita would sell it to anyone else. John had some sales force planning to do.

The new bulbs would be sold through the channels that traditionally sold light bulbs: hardware stores, discount stores, supermarkets, drugstores, light fixture outlets, electrical wholesalers, industrial distributors, and so on. Many of these retail markets were dominated by such huge and powerful mass merchandising firms as Kmart, Wal-Mart, Home Depot, and the drug and grocery chains. All of these firms were national accounts. The task before John was to get adequate distribution of the new bulb in such distributive systems quickly while Panasonic had exclusive control of the product. It would require building a large sales system quickly.

John was inclined to build the sales system using manufacturers' rep organizations that had existing relationships with the target distributive organizations. Using such rep organizations was within Panasonic policy. Its small-appliance division sold Panasonic's wide line of appliances through independent sales reps who called on essentially the same accounts targeted by the lamp division.

However, one of John's peers in the Panasonic organization initiated a casual conversation at a company social event during which he suggested that perhaps now would be a good time for the company to consider hiring its own salespeople to sell directly to the particularly large national accounts such as Wal-Mart, Sears, Kmart, Home Depot, and others of such size. Such a sales force also could sell to the distributors that sold to smaller retail groups and could cover OEM buyers. He argued, "It's time for us to get some experience in managing a sales organization and we could well afford it on the 5 percent of sales we would have to pay the reps. And we'd have more control over them than we would the reps!" John nodded but said nothing.

Questions:

1. Should Panasonic initiate some efforts to build its own sales force to sell to selected target markets and distributor networks?

2. If not, what course of action would you recommend to John?

ENDNOTES

[1] Doyle Rice and Alian E. Dastagir, "One year after Sandy, 9 Devastating Facts," *USA Today*, October 29, 2013.

[2] Richard Eisenberg, "A Guide To The New Retirement Communities," *Forbes.com*, April 4, 2014. Retrieved from the following URL on June 17, 2016: http://www.forbes.com/sites/nextavenue/2014/04/04/a-guide-to-the-new-retirement-communities/

[3] Aaron Back, "Why Banks Are Back in Love With Mortgages, " *The Wall Street Journal*, April 27, 2016, p. C12.

[4] Dick Youngblood, "Entrepreneur Gets Healthy Return on His Investment," *Star Tribune* (Minneapolis, MN), November 5, 2000, p. 1D.

[5] Jason Jordan, "Salespeople vs. the Internet: Who Is Winning?" *Quotable* (a sales blog created by Salesforce.com). Retrieved from the following URL on June 17, 2016: https://www.salesforce.com/quotable/articles/salespeople-versus-the-internet/ ; Gregory A. Rich, "The Internet: Boom or Bust to Sales Organizations?" *Journal of Marketing Management* 18 (April 2002).

[6] Esther Rudis, Melissa A. Berman, and Chuck Mitchell, "The CEO Challenge: Top Marketplace and Management Issues 2001: A CEO Survey by Accenture and The Conference Board" (New York: Conference Board, 2001).

[7] Sandy D. Jap, "The Strategic Role of the Salesforce in Developing Customer Satisfaction across the Relationship Lifecycle," *Journal of Personal Selling & Sales Management* 21, no. 2 (Spring 2001), pp. 95-108.

[8] Jonathan Peterson, "Lenders Target State Laws," *Los Angeles Times*, December 28, 2005.

[9] This section based largely on Walter A. Friedman, *Birth of a Salesman: The Transformation of Selling in America* (Cambridge, MA: Harvard University Press, 2004).

[10] Atul Parvatiyar and Jagdish N. Sheth, "The Domain and Conceptual Foundations of Relationship Marketing," in *Handbook of Relationship Marketing*, ed. Jagdish N. Sheth and Atul Parvatiyar (Thousand Oaks, CA: Sage, 2000), pp. 3-38.

[11] Thomas Hammer, "Secrets of Top Sellers," *Folio: The Magazine for Magazine Management*, Jan/Feb 2016, Vol 45 (1), pp. 26-27.

[12] Joel R. Evans and Richard L. Laskins, "The Relationship Marketing Process: A conceptualization and Application," *Industrial Marketing Management* 23 (1994), pp. 439-52.

[13] Belinda Dewsnap and David Jobber, "The Sales-Marketing Interface in Consumer Packaged-Goods Companies: A Conceptual Framework," *Journal of Personal Selling & Sales Management*, Spring 2000, pp. 109-19.

[14] Weld Royal, "Manufacturers Introduce Services to Boost Revenues and Give Salespeople Expanded Roles," *Industry Week*, March 5, 2001, p. 41.

[15] "American's Largest Dental Equipment Manufacturer Creates 'Wow' Application with Comshare Business Intelligence Software," *Business Wire*, April 11, 2001.

[16] William Strahle, Rosann L. Spiro, and Frank Acito, "Marketing and Sales: Strategic Alignment and Functional Implementation," *Journal of Personal Selling & Sales Management*, Winter 1996, pp. 1-20.

[17] Jess N. Moore, Mary Anne Raymond, Christopher D. Hopkins, "Social Selling: A Comparison of Social Media Usage Across Process Stage, Markets, and Sales Job Functions," *Journal of Marketing Theory & Practice*, Winter 2015, Vol 23(1), pp. 1-20.

[18] Alex Pirouz, "How to Master Content Marketing on LinkedIn," *HubSpot*, July 20, 2015. Retrieved from the following URL on June 17, 2016: http://blog.hubspot.com/marketing/linkedin-content-marketing

[19] Neil Rackham and John R. DeVincentis, *Rethinking the Sales Force: Redefining Selling to Create and Capture Customer Value* (New York: McGraw-Hill, 1999), pp. 157-58.

chapter

3

The Personal Selling Process

As an account executive for Williams Scotsman, Inc., Ashley Lochtefeld says that she strives for three things in servicing her customers: growth, knowledge, and building relationships. In other words, she finds new customers, solves their problems through her expertise in the construction industry, and then keeps those customers by conscientiously following up with them after the sale. These tasks correspond to the steps of the personal selling process, which is what this chapter is about. This process describes what salespeople do every day in their jobs.

All other chapters in this textbook are about how a sales manager *manages* his or her salespeople. In fact, we have already established how different the sales job is from sales management. Often, top salespeople who are promoted into administrative roles are lousy sales managers; and conversely, excellent sales managers were not necessarily the top producers when they were in sales. However, to be effective, a sales manager must at least be familiar with what a salesperson does; and essentially all sales managers were once salespeople.

The goal of the sales process is to generate sales; yet the process is based on the concept that the best way to generate sales is to find customers who truly benefit from the product offering. Sales is about finding people you can help with your product or service; and so the steps of the sales process

explain the most effective way to make others successful.

Ironically, when a salesperson is bad at sales, people are quick to say "That salesperson is highly annoying; I hate sales." Yet when someone excels at the sales process, the customer sees that person as a trustworthy, valuable resource or consultant—not as a salesperson. That is, the word "sales" has a negative connotation for many people, if not the majority of the public. This is unfair. As the saying goes, "one bad apple should not spoil the whole barrel."

The sales process—when done the right way—solves problems and helps customers. This process is *absolutely not* about manipulating people into buying something they do want or need. Rather, it is the process that salespeople use to find and serve customers who will benefit from the product offering. This does involve salespeople convincing others to adopt their point of view about certain things—but that is something that must be done by everyone on a regular basis. In that sense, the sales process can be applied to not only all jobs, but to almost all aspects of life! (See "Sales and Dating" box).

The actual selling process can be likened to a chain, each link of which must be closed successfully or the seller will fail to get the order. However, each step overlaps others, and their sequence may be altered to meet the situation at hand.

The eight steps of the sales process are:

1. Prospecting
2. Pre-approach—planning the sale
3. Approach
4. Need assessment
5. Presentation
6. Meeting objections
7. Gaining commitment
8. Follow-up

PROSPECTING

Prospecting is the method or system used by the sales force to find new customers. This is a critical activity for all sales organizations—especially for those newer firms that are trying to become established. Twenty years ago, salespeople from Fastenal Company spent a large percentage of their time making sales calls to firms that had never heard of them. Often, the Fastenal reps would show up to these prospective accounts unannounced—which is called **cold calling**. Because this prospecting was successful, Fastenal has grown to become the largest distributor of fasteners in North America. This has allowed Fastenal to shift its focus away from prospecting and more toward servicing existing accounts. But still, prospecting is an activity that Fastenal reps still do on a regular basis. No sales organization can afford to forget about acquiring new customers.

CONSIDER THIS...

Sales and Dating

The sales process is often compared to dating, but not just any kind of dating. When done the right way, the sales process is especially similar to the process of matching up with your one, true love!

That is, great salespeople do the following:

- Engage in meaningful conversations early on to determine if the prospect is the right fit for a *long term* relationship.
- Listen in a genuine, active manner in a way that shows they have empathy for prospects.

- Persistently follow-up through texts, emails, phone calls and visits to make prospects feel like they are important—without being too aggressive so that it feels like stalking!
- Build relationships through direct and honest conversations that create an environment of mutual respect and trust.

In other words, being successful in sales is similar to asking for someone's hand in marriage—except without the romance!

SOURCE: Nick Hedges, "Sales and Dating," *Inc.com*, October 8, 2014. Retrieved from the following website on June 14, 2016: http://www.inc.com/nick-hedges/sales-and-dating-why-good-salespeople-operate-like-eharmony-vs-other-dating-site.html

There are two steps in successful prospecting. The first step is **identifying leads**—generating names of potential customers. The second step is **qualifying leads** according to who is most likely to buy.

Identifying Leads

Names and addresses of good prospects can be obtained in a number of ways:

- *Referrals.* Sales professionals generally agree that the best way to acquire new customers is through referrals, which means that a third-party (who knows and trusts the sales organization) is providing the name of a potential customer. Most commonly, referrals come from existing customers; but they can also come from sources inside the sales organization.
  - *Customer referrals.* Salespeople responsible for generating their own leads indicate that their number one source of referrals is their existing customers. A salesperson should ask for referrals whenever there is synergy between him- or herself and the customer. The best, most loyal customers are the ones most likely to be willing to refer their colleagues and peers. A great time to ask these customers for a referral is *after* the salesperson has resolved a sticky situation. And to keep them coming, sales organizations often thank the customers who provided the referrals through rewards, such as gift cards or electronics.[1]
  - *Internal referrals from sources such as the sales manager, the marketing department, or telemarketing (inside sales).* Customer inquiries may be generated from company advertising, direct mail, company websites, trade shows, and tele-prospecting efforts. For example, Liberty Mutual Insurance provides price quotes on a variety of types of insurance to those visiting the company website. After receiving the quote, the website visitor can then request to be contacted by a Liberty Mutual agent, who is sure to follow-up on this inquiry from what would be called a hot prospect (as discussed later in the chapter with regard to the sales pipeline).
- *Outside agencies and publications.* Some companies turn to outside agencies and/or publications for the generation and qualification of leads. For example, prospects can be found in published membership lists of various trade associations, local chambers of commerce, or other organizations. In recent years, a large number of website companies have begun to provide leads, as can be seen by searching Google for the phrase "sales leads." This search query returns millions of websites, many of them businesses that sell lists of prospects for pennies per name. One such agency is Sales Genie (www.salesgenie.com), which claims to offer 235 million consumer leads and 24 million business leads, such as the one shown in Figure 3-1—this could be a hot prospect for a sales rep selling pizza ovens! The popular social media site LinkedIn is also used extensively to identify leads (see box entitled "LinkedIn, Social Selling and Prospecting").
- *Networking by the salesperson.* Salespeople often use their friends and acquaintances to make new contacts. Many salespeople join professional and civic organizations in part to meet new people who may be potential

CONSIDER THIS...

LinkedIn, Social Selling, and Prospecting

Using social media to find and interact with customers is called social selling, and LinkedIn is the most popular website for this. LinkedIn has an optional, fee-based prospecting tool called Sales Navigator, which generates leads in an impressive manner. Sales Navigator not only keeps salespeople up to date on what their current prospects are doing, it analyzes current contacts and suggests potential organizations that fit a similar profile. This includes potential customers that the salesperson may have never heard of!

SOURCE: Ian Altman, "LinkedIn Paid vs. Free—A Review of Sales Navigator," *Forbes* http://www.forbes.com/sites/ianaltman/2015/09/01/linkedin-paid-vs-free-a-review-of-sales-navigator/ Accessed January 7, 2016.

customers or who may be able to provide leads. One example of this is Business Network International (BNI), which is reportedly the world's largest referral organization with 185,000 members across 60 different countries.[2]

- *Cold calling.* In years past, salespeople would routinely make *unannounced* calls—either in-person or by phone—on businesses that they thought might need the products they were selling. This approach, which is called cold calling, is no longer popular as it is very time-consuming and not very cost-effective due to the high rejection rate. By definition, cold calling does not involve the *qualifying lead process* discussed in the next section. However, a variation that some call warm-calling or smart-calling involves doing extensive research on the prospect before the call, such that the sales rep can effectively make a connection with the client, and perhaps build some rapport. The plethora of information found on the internet (e.g., through social media) makes this possible. Some sales experts claim that this can significantly improve the success rate relative to traditional cold calling.[3]

After the sales organization has identified the lead, the next step is to go through the process of qualifying leads.

Qualifying Leads

Whatever the source of the lead, it is important that the lead by qualified. Philosophically, professional salespeople do not want to bother people who have no

FIGURE 3-1

Sample record of a lead from Sales Genie

Source: Sales Genie Website, www.salesgenie.com, accessed Jan 6, 2016.

Company Name	Joe's Pizza
Street Address	123 Rob Martin Way
City	Omaha
State	NE
Zip Code	68022
Telephone	(402) 826-5290
LEAD STATUS	HOT LEAD!

need for their products. Moreover, it is very expensive for salespeople to make calls that have little chance of success because the customer does not need, does not want, or cannot afford the products. In order to qualify a prospect, the salesperson or the person providing the referral should determine whether the prospect is a good one. To determine this, the prospect must satisfy three conditions:

1. The customer has a need for the products being sold.
2. The customer can afford to buy the products.
3. The customer is receptive to being called on by the salesperson.

Traditionally, sales reps were expected to find their own prospects. That was part of the selling process, part of the job—a most important part of it. Today, however, many companies realize that the marketing department is in the best position to develop effective prospecting systems for the sales force.

Sales reps generally appreciate being relieved of the burden of developing a prospecting system, and the company benefits when its reps can spend more time actually making sales presentations to qualified prospects. However, studies have shown that salespeople often fail to follow up in contacting prospects—even when that prospect has expressed interest in buying the product.[4] Typically, this is due to the salespeople lacking skills in organization and time management, and, thus, presents a challenge to the sales manager.

One way to improve on prospect follow-up is to introduce the concept of the **sales pipeline** (Figure 3-2). The sales pipeline is simply a full listing of the names and contact information for all prospects, categorized by how likely they are to purchase the product. As the figure suggests, the sales process turns leads into qualified prospects, hot prospects, and eventually customers. Sales pipeline diagrams—with considerably more detail—are generated automatically by a number of customer relationship management (CRM) programs, such as Salesforce.com. Tracking prospects in this way keeps the salespeople focused on developing new clients, which is important for a firm's survival. After all, even the best companies lose customers from time to time. Further, sales managers understand that turning a lead into a new customer takes time, and thus trying to fill up the pipeline at the last minute is nearly impossible. Successful sales organizations keep the sales pipeline full because they understand that a well-managed and continuous process of prospecting is critical to sales success.

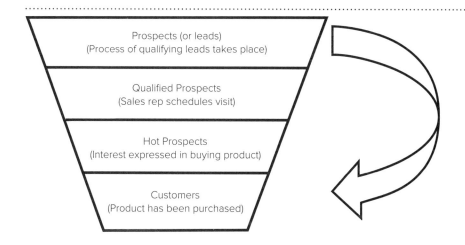

FIGURE 3-2
Sales pipeline

Of course, in order to personally meet with the prospect, the salesperson has to call and make an appointment. Interestingly, research shows that salespeople only pursue about 30% of the leads that are provided to them.[5] The 70% of potential customers that are being ignored is referred to as the sales lead black hole. This is often a point of contention between the sales force and the marketing department. Salespeople argue that many of the leads are not worth pursuing, but the marketing department, which is typically overseeing the lead generation, typically argues that the salespeople need to work harder to contact the prospect.

PRE-APPROACH: PLANNING THE SALE

The pre-approach step includes all the information-gathering activities salespeople perform to learn relevant facts about the prospects, their needs, and their overall situation. Then, on the basis of this information, salespeople plan their sales presentations, selecting the most appropriate objective for each call.

Customer Research

The sales rep should learn everything possible about the prospective customer's business—its size; its present purchasing practices; the location of its plants; the names of its executives; and, most important, the names of people who make the buying decision as well as those who influence the purchase. It is also helpful to learn something about the buyers' backgrounds, such as their education, social affiliations, or personalities. If the prospective buyer has been having problems, the seller, if possible, should become familiar with those problems.

When researching a current customer or one that has been called on previously by a salesperson from your company, start by reading the company files. They should provide a wealth of background information on the past sales call reports, and other relevant information. Many companies store information about their customers in a CRM or other database to which their salespeople have easy access using laptop or tablet computers.

For new customers, you can easily obtain a great deal of information by using the internet or online information services such as LexisNexis, Dialog, and Dow Jones News/Retrieval. Other sources include trade magazines, industrial directories, magazine and newspaper articles, chambers of commerce, and government publications, as well as the annual reports of companies. Sometimes the company's current suppliers, customers, and certain employees can provide information.

The goal of customer research is for salespeople to know as much as they can about the company, the decision makers, and their needs before making that first call. As Kenneth Ranucci, a senior account executive at Contempo Design, says, "In-depth research into prospects makes salespeople stand out."[6]

Planning the Sales Presentation

The most important part of planning the sales presentation is defining the objective or goal for the particular call. The goal is not necessarily to close or complete the sale on each call. In fact, salespeople report that, on average, it takes four calls to close a sale.[7] However, on each call, the salesperson does want to obtain from the buyer some type of commitment for action that moves the sale forward. For example, the salesperson may try to obtain a list of the customer's vendor selection criteria or get the buyer to set up a meeting with some of the other people who will be involved in the decision. The objective may be any agreement on an action that moves the sale forward.

Salespeople also may plan how they are going to approach the buyer and what kind of questions they want to ask. It is important that salespeople recognize differences across selling situations and adapt their presentations accordingly. On the basis of their pre-call customer research, they will make a tentative judgment as to which of their products best meet their customers' needs and then formulate a tentative plan for presenting the features and benefits of those products. Of course, the information gained by salespeople during the actual call often may cause them to alter their initial objectives or plans. This is called **adaptive selling**.[8]

THE APPROACH

Once the sales rep has the name of a prospect and adequate pre-approach information, the next step is the actual **approach**. Making an appointment to see the buyer increases the chances that the salesperson will have the buyer's attention during their meeting.

A good approach makes a favorable impression and establishes some degree of rapport between the salesperson and the buyer. In order to make a favorable impression with customers in the United States, the salesperson should have a firm handshake, be professionally attired, and make good eye contact. Usually each call starts with an introduction (unless the salesperson has called on this customer before) and a limited amount of small talk. Sometimes salespeople will draw attention to their products by handing the buyer a sample or by highlighting some benefit in which the buyer will likely be interested.

The approach usually takes up only the first minute or so of a call, but it can make or break the entire presentation. If the approach fails, the salesperson often does not get a chance to give a presentation. At the end of the approach, the salesperson must gain the buyer's agreement to move into the need assessment stage of the call.

NEED ASSESSMENT

Companies and consumers purchase goods and services to satisfy needs or to solve problems. In a business situation, the company's purchases are always related to the need to improve performance—to become more efficient and effective at fulfilling customer needs. **Need assessment** is the stage in which the salesperson must discover, clarify, and understand the buyer's needs. The best way to uncover and understand needs is by asking questions—and then of course genuinely listening to the answers (see box entitled, "How to Listen").

The need assessment step of the sales process has been strongly influenced by a book entitled *SPIN Selling* by sales researcher Neil Rackham. This book, which was written about 30 years ago, was recently identified as the top sales book of all time by *Inc.* magazine.[9] SPIN is an acronym that stands for Situation,

CONSIDER THIS...

How to Listen

Salespeople have the reputation of being good talkers. What separates the most productive salespeople from the pack, however, is a different communication skill: the ability to listen. The editors of *Selling Power* magazine identify the following behaviors of a good listener.

A good listener:

- Looks at you when you're speaking
- Asks questions to clarify what you're asking

- Shows concern by asking questions
- Repeats some of what you've said
- Doesn't rush you
- Is poised and controlled
- Responds with a nod, frown, or smile
- Pays close attention to what you're saying
- Doesn't interrupt
- Lets you stick to the subject until you've finished your thought

SOURCE: "Selling Tip: Can You Hear?" *Selling Power,* January 2016, p. 21

Problem, Implication and Need Payoff, which are the four categories of questions that successful salespeople ask:[10]

- **Situation questions.** These are basic data-gathering questions that ask for factual information about the buyer's current situation. Salespeople ask situation questions to get ideas about how the customers might be able to use their products. If salespeople do a good job of researching the customer during their pre-call planning, then they are able to use fewer situation questions. Examples are:
  - How often do you change the cutting oil in your drill presses?
  - Who is involved in the purchase decision for this product?
  - How much inventory of this product do you carry?

- **Problem questions.** These are questions used to uncover potential problems, difficulties, or dissatisfaction the customer is experiencing that the salesperson's products and services can solve. Salespeople use these questions to uncover customer needs around which they can build their presentation. Examples are:
  - Which part of your production process is the most difficult in terms of controlling quality?
  - Have you experienced any delays in getting those materials from your current suppliers?
  - Have you experienced any problems in servicing your presses?

- **Implication questions.** These questions are the next logical step because they ask about the impact or *implications* of the problems. The answers to these questions not only help the salesperson thoroughly understand the problems, but also can enlighten the buyer who might not fully realize the seriousness of these issues, and the potential negative consequences of *not* solving the problem. Examples of these questions are:
  - What impact do the quality consistency problems have on your production costs?

○ What effects do the delays in receiving the materials have on your operations?

○ How do these maintenance problems affect your operations?

- **Need-payoff questions.** Finally, need-payoff questions help the buyer see how valuable a solution to any problems would be. These are similar to implication questions because they reference a problem—but the point of these questions is to evoke *positive emotions* as the buyer describes how things would be different once the problem has gone away. That is, need-payoff questions are encouraging because they help buyers visualize a better world. Examples are:

○ If the rejection rate on your quality inspection was reduced to less than 1 percent, how much would that save you?

○ If we could minimize your downtime through a better maintenance program, how much more revenue could you generate?

○ Would it be useful to have an environmentally-friendly machine that cut your utility costs by 50%?

Salespeople ask these questions in the logical order just presented. The situation questions should be asked first, followed by the problem questions, the implication questions, and then the need-payoff questions. Each type naturally leads to the following type, and each one helps build the buyer's interest in hearing about the solutions the salesperson has to offer. It should be noted that studies by Neil Rackham of 35,000 sales calls demonstrate that the most successful salespeople are those who use fewer situational question and more implication and need-payoff questions.

Finally, a **trial close** is a type of question that asks for the prospect's opinion—such, as "How does that sound so far?" Trial closes are helpful *throughout* the sales process (not just during need assessment); and, in fact, may be even more appropriate during the presentation, which is the next step of the sales process.

THE PRESENTATION

After assessing the needs and desires of the customer, the salesperson moves into the main body of the sales process, the presentation. Effective presentation skills are critical to the success of all businesspeople—especially salespeople.[11] The **presentation** is primarily a discussion of those features of the product that provide a benefit to the customer. So, an effective presentation can only be done by a salesperson who understands the needs of the customer, which is why the need assessment step is so important. While most presentations are oral, they often include written proposals and supporting material as well as visual aids. The goal of the presentation is to convince the customer that the product being sold will satisfy the customer's needs better than that of a competitor.

Features describe the characteristics of the product, and **benefits** describe how the various features will help the buyer. A common mistake made by salespeople is that they focus only on the features, and assume that prospects understand how that feature helps them. Effective presentations clearly explain how the feature will benefit the prospect—and so, the salesperson should focus or elaborate on those features that will have the most impact on helping the customer's business be successful. That is, the benefits should be those that address specific needs mentioned by the customer. Following are some examples of the features and resulting benefits of four different products:

Product	Feature	Benefits
Copy machine	Ten service reps	Results in faster service that saves the customer time
Shoes	Inventory control system	Results in less inventory and thus more cost savings
Motor oil	Rust inhibitor	Results in fewer oil changes and longer engine life, which saves both time and money for the customer
Forklift truck	One-month trial	Results in the customer being sure that the product meets the needs of the customer, which can save both time and money

When making presentations, salespeople should also be aware of how the customer views them. Before they have earned the customers trust, salespeople should be careful to not be overly one-sided in their presentations. Research shows that customers who are suspicious of the ulterior motives of the salesperson respond better to presentations that are balanced, and thus explain both the pros *and cons* of a product offering.[12]

Product Demonstrations

A good sales presentation is built around a forceful product demonstration. If done well, demonstrations—demos for short—are a great way to engage the prospect, and this can lead to a more in-depth and easy-to-understand explanation for how the product can solve the customer's most pressing problems. Steve Jobs, the charismatic founder of Apple Computer, became famous for his dazzling product demonstrations, which he delivered alongside exciting, interesting images as opposed to bullet-points of text.

Technology has impacted the nature of presentations in many ways. There are a wide variety of computer-based tools that sales professionals are using to create striking and effective presentations, and many of these are available online for little or no cost.[13] Of course, the most common presentation software for over twenty years has been Microsoft PowerPoint, but the program has changed dramatically since its inception. That is, Microsoft has introduced a number of new design tools to make its presentations dynamic and engaging. Keynote, Prezi, Slideshark and Zoomit are just a few of many available slideware programs—but salespeople need to understand that fancy slides do not replace or compensate for a boring message (see box on "Presentation Fatique").

Social media is also used for product presentations. For example, The Vollrath Company is a manufacturer of food prep equipment and professional cookware. Vollrath has an extensive Youtube channel that shows off its product lines. The channel is a tool for the sales team to use with customers, and it creates a positive brand image among anyone who visits the website.[14]

Another trend that has impacted the nature of sales presentations is the shift from a goods-based to a service-based economy. Services are especially challenging to present or demonstrate because they are intangible (i.e., they cannot be touched or seen). Further, salespeople increasingly must make presentations over the telephone—especially to customers who do not have the time for an in-person meeting. Interestingly, recent research shows that telesales

CONSIDER THIS...

How to Overcome Presentation Fatigue

In today's high-tech world, most prospects have seen thousands of elaborate slide presentations using PowerPoint, Prezi, etc. This has led to presentation fatigue, especially among younger prospects who have graduated from college within the past ten years—as the vast majority of university courses rely on this type of technology to deliver content.

Experts say that the way to overcome presentation fatigue—and truly engage the audience—is through an interesting storyline that delivers a powerful, relevant message. That is, a sales presentation will succeed or fail on the strength of the message and how well the salesperson tells it. This has very little to do with the particular brand of presentation software that is used.

SOURCE: "Presentation Fatigue: 5 Ways the Struggle is Real for Your Prospect and Fatal For Your Sale," from the blog entitled *Performance Sales Training* (December 18, 2015). Retrieved January 8, 2016 from: http://performancesalesandtraining.com/presentation-fatigue-5-ways-the-struggle-is-real-for-your-prospect-and-fatal-for-your-sale/

presentations are perhaps more effective than face-to-face presentations when selling a service (as opposed to a good).[15] The results are perhaps preliminary given the sparse research on this topic. However, sales organizations that sell services should take notice of this, especially given the savings in travel and entertainment expense associated with telesales.

There are those who caution that when done too early in the sales cycle, demos can actually sabotage the sale. This is especially true when the salesperson is dealing with a lower-level employee who might be the product user, but not the ultimate decision-maker that understands the big picture. These lower-level employees might dismiss the product due to an irrelevant feature that they do not like. The product demonstration should be done with the person who is aware of the key business problem and committed to finding a solution.[16]

Prepared Sales Presentations

The advisability of using a prepared sales presentation, better known as a canned sales talk, is debatable. Without doubt, a prepared presentation done poorly and without feeling is a dismal experience. However, many firms do use canned talks successfully. The prepared presentation has several advantages:

- It gives new salespeople confidence.
- It can use tested sales techniques that have proven effective.
- It gives some assurance that the complete story will be told.
- It greatly simplifies sales training.

The use of a prepared presentation does *not* mean that sales reps must use someone else's words. Above all, the salesperson's own feelings and personality should be evident in the presentation.

Developing Effective Presentations

The task of developing a presentation is not an easy one. Some simple advice may be helpful here:

- **Keep the presentation simple.** The temptation to tell everything is overwhelming. Don't do it. The prospect can absorb only a limited amount of information at any one time. Don't overload their system.
- **Talk the prospect's language.** Don't build the presentation around industry jargon or product model numbers. If customers don't understand what the rep is talking about, they seldom say so. That would be an admission of ignorance. They usually pretend to understand and then say, "I'll have to think it over for a while."
- **Stress the application of the good or service to the prospect's situation.** Tailor the presentation to the application or person at hand. Even within the same firm, different individuals place different priorities on what is important about the product. You must adapt your presentation to the situation and person.
- **Above all, seek credibility at every turn.** The entire presentation is nothing if it is not believed. Each statement must be credible. Prove points one by one. A critical point is not complete until the prospect believes it. The real key to successful selling lies in this credibility.

MEETING OBJECTIONS

Objections are encountered in practically every presentation. They should be welcomed because they indicate that the prospect has some interest in the proposition, and they give the salesperson key information on the prospect's needs and concerns. Further, hearing no objections is often a bad sign, as a prospect who is not interested in buying is not engaged enough to think about potential problems.

Consequently, the salesperson should carefully and actively listen to the buyer. It is important to allow the buyer to fully complete what they are saying. Salespeople should not assume that they know what the buyer is going to say; and they should never interrupt—nothing annoys a buyer more! And throughout the objection, the salesperson should be sure to *respect* what the buyer is saying. Do not argue and do not get defensive.

After allowing the buyer to fully express the concern, the salesperson should proceed with deliberate caution (see box, "Overcoming Objections: The Silent Treatment"). Specifically, the rep should clarify, respond and confirm as described in the following:

1. *Clarify* the objection. It is critical that the salesperson is clear about the concern. So, the first step is to repeat and/or clarify the objection. This could involve asking for more information, using questions such as "Let me see if I understand you correctly, [repeating the objection as you understand it]. Is that correct?" The buyer may confirm that you are correct in your understanding or provide additional information. Sometimes this step can uncover a misunderstanding that the buyer has about your product and/or service.

2. *Respond* to the objection. It is important that you respond to the buyer's concern. The specific response to the objection depends on the type of objection it is. Ideally, the salesperson has planned for this objection during the pre-approach, and so is ready to answer it. But of course, that is often not the case.

CONSIDER THIS...

Overcoming Objections: The Silent Treatment

A good first step to handling a customer objection is often to do nothing! That is, remaining silent for a moment makes sense for the following reasons:

- Gives the salesperson time to think
- Demonstrates that the objection is being taken seriously
- May lead to the customer answering their own objection for the salesperson

Certainly, a moment of silence is much better than getting defensive and immediately arguing about the objection—which is what many rookie salespeople do as their natural first reaction.

Of course, after the silence, the salesperson should be sure to clarify, respond and confirm that the issue is no longer an issue.

SOURCE: Rachel Clapp Miller, "The Value of Silence in Your Discovery Process," *Growth Play Sales Effectiveness Blog,* July 8, 2016. Available at: http://blog.growthplay.com/the-value-of-silence-in-your-discovery-process. Accessed July 11, 2016.

3. *Confirm* that the objection is no longer an issue. This could be done by asking, "Have I addressed your concern?" or "Does this make more sense now?" Hopefully, the answer is "Yes!"

As these techniques suggest, the salesperson's response to the objection should not threaten the rapport that hopefully has been developed with the customer. Like all people, customers desire to be seen as competent, credible individuals; and want to be treated fairly. Salespeople must keep this in mind and carefully manage the rapport when overcoming customer objections.[17] The most common types of objections and specific strategies for handling them are discussed next.

Price or Value Objections

Buyers who say "I don't need it" or "It costs too much" are indicating that they don't think the *value* of solving the problem or meeting the need is *worth* the cost. In this case, the salesperson must convince the buyer of the importance of the problem and of the value of the solution. It may be necessary to go back to the need assessment part of the call to ask some additional problem, implication, and need-payoff questions to increase the buyer's perception of the seriousness of the problem and the importance of a solution. If the buyer acknowledges the importance of the problem but still feels that the company can't afford the product/service or that it is not a price-competitive solution, then the salesperson can offer some price value comparisons of alternative solutions.

Product/Service Objections

Sometimes the buyer acknowledges the importance of a problem but doubts whether the good or service can solve his problem or improve his operations. The buyer may disagree with the salesperson's assessment or, in some cases, even doubt the genuineness of the salesperson. In this case, the salesperson needs to convince the buyer that the product will do what she says. She must demonstrate or provide proof that the product has the capability to fulfill the need. Some of the proof-providing tactics are to offer the buyer one or more of the following: case histories, testimonials, independent tests, a demonstration, trial use and/or expert opinion.

Some objections relate to needs that your product cannot satisfy. In this case, it is best to first acknowledge that your product or service cannot meet the particular need. Then try to increase the perceived value of your product by reemphasizing those important needs your product *can* meet.

Procrastinating Objections

Procrastinating objections can be difficult to overcome. Some such objections are:

- Let me think about it a while.
- I have to talk it over with my boss.
- I have to wait until the next budget cycle.
- I have some other reps to talk to before I make a decision.

Procrastinating prospects use such excuses to avoid acting on a proposition immediately or to avoid admitting that they don't have the authority to make the decision.

In retail selling, a sale that cannot be closed on one call usually has little chance of completion. In many business sales, however, the prospect cannot be pushed into a sale without creating considerable ill will. In fact, businesses are taking more and more time before committing. Customers today are very thorough. They use the internet to research all options and are careful not to make a mistake. A survey of purchasers found that only 13 percent tend to buy within three months, while 44 percent require 6 to 12 months to decide. A full 20 percent of purchasers say they require a year or longer before a typical sale is complete.[18] The length of the **sales cycle** is the amount of time between these two points: (1) when the salesperson first identifies the name of a prospect and (2) when that prospect agrees to buy the product. Because the sales cycle is increasingly long, sales reps must remain a patient and trusted adviser to the customer.

The amount of aggressiveness must be modified to fit the prospect and the situation. Some people will not be pushed or rushed. In these situations, the best strategy is to ask for a commitment for some future action that will move the sales cycle forward. For example, the salesperson might ask for a meeting with the buyer and his boss or with whoever else seems to have substantial influence over the decision.

Hidden Objections

Prospects may state their objections to a proposition openly and give the salesperson a chance to answer them. This is an ideal circumstance, because everything is out in the open and the salesperson does not need to read the prospect's mind. Unfortunately, prospects often hide their real reasons for not buying. Further, stated objections may be phony. A prospect may say she does not like the looks of a product, when she really thinks the price is too high. The rep must determine the real barrier to the sale to be able to overcome it.

Some salespeople have developed special methods for getting the prospect to disclose what is blocking the sale. One saleswoman uses what she calls her "appeal for honesty" tactic. She says to the reluctant prospect, "You expect me to be honest with you, as you should. But haven't I the same right—to expect you to be honest with me? Now, honestly, what is bothering you about the proposition?" However, the best technique for discovering hidden objections is to ask questions that keep the prospect talking.

As we noted in the planning section, it is often necessary for salespeople to change their original objectives and strategies for the sales call. Salespeople must recognize the need and be willing to adapt their presentations when the buyer's objections signal that they may have initially chosen the wrong strategies. Another important principle to remember in handling most objections is to avoid arguments at any cost. The sales rep should ask questions that help clarify the prospect's thinking. This provides insights into the precise obstacles that are hindering the sale. Even if prospects are dead wrong, sales reps should never offend them. A sales rep can win an argument only to lose the sale.

GAINING COMMITMENT (AKA THE CLOSE)

If all objections are handled, the next logical step is to **close** the sale. A successful close involves the salesperson asking the customer to buy the product, and the customer saying "Yes!" However, as discussed previously, the sales cycle is increasingly long—and can take more than one year for some products. For example, imagine how long the sales cycle is for commercial furniture companies reaching out to Apple Inc. to sell products for its new Silicon Valley headquarters, which includes a massive, round building that will take several years to construct. This new building will surely require Apple to buy millions of dollars worth of office desks, chairs, etc. Certainly, this kind of a sale will not be finalized in the sales rep's first and only sales call.

Consequently, we prefer the term **gaining commitment** over "the close" for this step, because for many early sales calls with a new client, it is not realistic to *close* the sale. Rather, the salesperson's goal is often to move the sale forward by promising to return with more information at a future meeting. That is, the salesperson may return with more product samples, or promise to come back with an engineer that can answer technical questions. The rep may also ask for the customer's commitment to bring additional information to their next meeting. The keys to obtaining commitment are, first, to *plan realistic objectives for each sales call* and, second, to *ask for a commitment.* If the salesperson doesn't ask, then he or she won't move the sale forward.

Of course, in a relatively simple sale, it is important for the salesperson to get a commitment from the buyer to purchase the product *on the first call* (usually the only call) or she will have lost the sale. To ask for an action that in effect finalizes the sale, the salesperson may simply say, "Can I place an order for you today?" Or alternatively, there are other ways to ask for the sale. These closing techniques include (1) the assumptive close, (2) special offer close, and (3) summary close; and are discussed in the box titled "Common Sales Closes." These techniques tend to be more suited for simple products sold through transaction (as opposed to relationship) selling.

As the field has shifted toward relationship selling, the importance of closing techniques has diminished. Today, success in a sales job is much more about understanding the customer's business (through proper need assessment); and

CONSIDER THIS...

Common Sales Closes

The Assumptive Close. Assuming the prospect is going to buy (even though she/he never explicitly agreed to), the salesperson starts to take the order by asking questions such as: "Now, what size do you want?" or "When can we deliver this – today or tomorrow morning?" or "Will three dozen be enough, or should I send four?" If the prospect answers such questions, the close is underway.

Special-Offer Close. Adding a special deal (one that most others cannot get) if the customer signs the contract. For example: "I can see that you are very influential in this market, so I will give you a special 10% discount because I believe you will be so happy with this product that you will spread the word to others."

Standing-Room-Only Close. Suggesting scarcity—or that the product will be sold out soon, so the customer better act quickly. "These new touchscreen laptops are selling like hotcakes. I can't guarantee that they'll be available if you don't act today."

Summary Close. Providing a summary of the benefits that the buyer has already acknowledged and then to suggest an action for finalizing the sale. For example, the salesperson could say, "You have agreed that our products will be easier for the consumer to use and that our advertising support will convince the retailers to stock the product, correct? Then I suggest that you place your first order today so that you have it on the retailer's shelves when our advertising campaign kicks off."

To what extent are each of these common sales closes unethical?

then being sure to keep the customer satisfied after the sale through proper follow-up, which is the final step of the sales process.

FOLLOW-UP

Salespeople must learn that the sale is not over when they get the order. Good sales reps follow up in various ways. They make certain that they have answered all the buyer's questions and that the buyer understands the details of the contract. If the merchandise is delivered at a later date, the reps are present at the time of delivery or call soon afterward to ensure that everything is in order.

The follow-up step of the sales process has become critical to the success of contemporary sales organizations. This is especially true given recent sales management trends toward the concepts of relationship marketing and consultative selling. That is, instead of focusing on one-time, transactional sales, today's salespeople work to build and maintain long-term, mutually beneficial partnerships with their customers. Of course, customers would never form partnerships with organizations whose salespeople forget about them after the sale!

Indeed, the concepts of relationship marketing have made sales organizations rethink the steps of the sales process.[19] Organizations realize that it is much more expensive to acquire new customers than it is to retain existing customers. So, although generating new accounts is still important, salespeople must be careful not to sacrifice effective follow-up for prospecting. Further, effective

CONSIDER THIS...

Follow-Up on the Golf Course

There is a long history of salespeople building closer relationships with their clients (i.e., following up) through the game of golf. Many people debate whether this is becoming more or less popular; Case 3-1 Omnico, Inc., at the end of this chapter, is about this very issue.

On one hand, the game of golf is declining in popularity in the United States. The number of golfers and sales of golf equipment are both down, and there are more golf courses closing than opening.

On the other hand, there are those sales professionals who still swear by this tactic. For example, internet entrepreneur George Souri, owner of UltraPawn, claims to have closed hundreds of deals through golfing, though not necessarily while playing golf.

follow-up essentially consists of asking questions of customers in an ongoing attempt to monitor their needs. Thus, when dealing with loyal customers, salespeople must continually revisit the need assessment step of the sales process.

Interestingly, when the buyer and seller form a very close integrative partnership, it sometimes makes sense for someone other than the salesperson to maintain the relationship and perform the follow-up selling tasks. In these cases, an operational-level employee in the selling organization would replace the salesperson.[20] For example, Bose Corporation, a Massachusetts-based manufacturer of high-end stereo equipment, has formed close partnerships with select suppliers. Ultimately, the supplier salesperson who developed the account is replaced by a fellow employee who works full-time at an office within the Bose facility—even though the employee still draws a paycheck from the selling firm. Being part of the customer's social system makes the supplier employee especially effective as he or she places purchase orders and helps design products for the customer firm.

Whether managed by the salesperson or an operational-level employee, good follow-up is the key to building a loyal clientele. Satisfied customers voluntarily provide more business. People truly appreciate being served by good salespeople. Once they locate a person who pleases them, they are not likely to forget that individual in the future.

SUMMARY

As part of their jobs, salespeople perform a wide variety of activities. The majority of their time is spent in selling activities, which revolve around the eight steps of the personal selling process.

The first step is prospecting, which involves identifying and qualifying leads. There are a number of possible methods of generating leads. The most frequent source of leads is existing customers. In order to qualify a prospect—to decide if the prospect is a good one—it must be determined whether the prospect has a need for the product, can afford to buy the product, and is receptive to being called on by the salesperson.

The second step is pre-approach planning. This includes all of the information-gathering activities salespeople perform to learn about their prospective customers. Then, on the basis of this research, salespeople plan their presentations. As a part of their plan, they must decide on the objective for the call as well as on how they are going to approach the buyer and what kind of questions they will ask.

The third step is the approach, during which salespeople meet the buyer, introduce themselves, engage in momentary small talk, and, most important, gain the buyer's agreement to move forward into the need assessment part of the process.

During the fourth step, identified as "need assessment," the salesperson must discover, clarify, and understand the buyer's needs. The salesperson uses a variety of questions to encourage buyers to reveal their needs.

The presentation of the product and its features and benefits is the next step. The general goal for salespeople is to convince their customers that their company's product and supporting services will satisfy the customers' needs better than those of a competitor. Effective presentations often rely on software, graphics and other visual support readily available from a laptop or tablet computer.

The sixth step is handling the buyer's objections. Buyers often question the price or value of the product, or they may not believe that the product will improve their operations. The salesperson must be able to overcome these objections as well as others. Sometimes salespersons will find it necessary to adapt their presentations in order to move the presentation forward.

At the seventh step, the salesperson must ask the buyer to commit to some action that will move the buyer closer to the sale. Often it takes multiple calls before the buyer is ready to commit to the sale.

The final step of the personal selling process is follow-up, which takes place after the purchase. Given that selling today is consistent with relationship marketing concepts, follow-up is arguably the most important step. To effectively build relationships, the salesperson must ensure customer satisfaction by following through with value-added service after the sale.

KEY TERMS

Adaptive selling	Implication questions	Prospecting
Approach	Need assessment	Qualifying leads
Benefits	Need-payoff questions	Sales Cycle
Features	Personal selling process	Sales pipeline
Gaining commitment	Presentation	Situation questions
Identifying leads	Problem questions	Trial close

QUESTIONS AND PROBLEMS

1. Which step of the personal selling process has been most impacted by internet technology?
2. Should marketing or sales be responsible for generating leads?

3. How does the salesperson determine whether the lead is a good prospect?

4. Should the salesperson try to close on every call? Why or why not?

5. Identify what type of question each of the following is:

    a. If your inventory could be reduced by 20 percent, how much would that save you?

    b. Can you tell me how you recruit your new salespeople?

    c. How does the turnover in your sales force affect your operations?

    d. Have you experienced any problems in servicing your office equipment?

6. Identify a feature and a benefit for each of the following products: a camera, a backpack, fat-free ice cream, lawn care service.

7. What are the advantages and disadvantages of using prepared, or canned, sales presentations? Give examples of when using a canned presentation might be better than using a less structured presentation.

8. If the salesperson doesn't believe that the customer has been honest in giving her opinions about the product, what should he do?

9. If the customer says to the salesperson, "You seem like a nice guy and I would like to buy from you personally, but I don't think your company is worth a nickel!" What should the salesperson say?

10. It has often been said that salespeople are born, not made. Do you agree or disagree? Explain why.

EXPERIENTIAL EXERCISES

1. Spend a day with a salesperson from two different companies.

    a. Report in itinerary form how you spent each day.

    b. Describe each job, comparing and contrasting both.

    c. Tell which position you would prefer and why.

2. Identify prospects for a new brand of special occasion and novelty greeting cards.

3. Pick a product normally sold by a salesperson. Talk to a customer who has just purchased or has been considering purchasing the product and find out the important characteristics of the salesperson from the customer's point of view.

4. Search the Internet to identify a short list of prospects for each of the following types of sales organizations.

    a. Professional beauty/barber instruments—scissors, shears, manicure implements, and so on.

    b. Pharmaceutical sales.

    c. Safety equipment sales—work gloves, safety glasses, hard hats, and so on.

    d. A travel agency specializing in business travel

e. Law enforcement supplies—handcuffs, leg irons, mace, and so on.

f. Payroll services.

5. A few organizations now offer sales certification. Visit the two sites listed below and describe their sales certification processes. What does someone have to do to earn a sales certification? Who is eligible? What are the benefits of a certification?

a. Sales and Marketing Executives International (www.smei.org).

b. National Association of Sales Professionals (www.nasp.com).

OMNICO, INC.
Follow-Up on the Golf Course

"Follow-up, follow-up, follow-up! That's the key to success in sales. And there's no better place for follow-up to occur than on the golf course!" These are the words of Mr. Buddy Towers, sales manager of Omnico, Inc.

Truly a legendary figure at Omnico, Buddy started working there as a salesman 35 years ago immediately after graduating from the University of Michigan. He has never worked for any other company. His record at Omnico is outstanding. He's been the top-producing salesperson for 20 of the last 35 years—an especially impressive record, given that the Omnico sales force has over twenty salespeople.

This history of success stemmed from the fierce loyalty that Buddy inspired among his customers. Buddy sums up the reasons for this loyalty in one word: golf. "I simply could not have succeeded in sales without golf. Out on the golf course is where my customers and I learn to know and trust each other. That's what kept them coming back to me."

Buddy, however, is no longer out in the field. After his long, distinguished selling career, he assumed the administrative position of sales manager at Omnico about one month ago. He had grown tired of all the traveling. He is 55 years old and had just become a grandfather for the first time. He hated to be away from home so much.

When Buddy applied for sales manager, Omnico's CEO/president felt that he couldn't say no. "Buddy Towers *is* Omnico sales. He's done and made so much for this company over the years. In my opinion, he's earned the right to get what he wants around here."

Upon assuming the job, Buddy noticed a market research report that compared industry averages for customer retention. He discovered that Omnico was well below the average for their industry. In other words, relative to competitors, Omnico is not as likely to maintain long-term relationships with its clients. Buddy's conclusion is that Omnico salespeople fail to appreciate the importance of relationship selling. His number one goal is to change this. At his first sales meeting as manager, he went over financial data that demonstrated how much more expensive it is to acquire new customers than it is to keep current ones. He told them, "If we keep losing customers at this rate, we'll be out of business in three years!"

He then encouraged his sales force to go out and cultivate closer, more personal relationships with their key customers. And, of course, he advised them to do this on the golf course. He even offered to pay for golf lessons for those who need them.

Some of the salespeople were not so thrilled with Buddy's idea. Laura Kilburn, a successful rep who had worked for Omnico for five years, strongly objected. She spoke up in the meeting and said, "Buddy, you're old school. Today's customers don't come back to us because they're our golfing buddy; in fact, many of mine don't even golf. Customers re-buy from Omnico only when our products and service improve their bottom line. Follow-up is important, sure—but it involves a lot more than playing stupid games with the customer."

Questions:

1. Whose side are you on, Buddy's or Laura's? Why?

2. Notice that Omnico, Inc. is not identified with any particular industry. For which industries are buddy-buddy relationships (like those cultivated on a golf course) especially important? And for which industries are these relationships not important? Explain your answer.

WILLY'S WINDOWS, INC.
Evaluating Sales Leads

Willy's Windows manufactures commercial windows for major construction sites. The company has annual sales of $100 million. Scott is the new head of marketing for Willy's Windows. One of his initiatives has been his lead generation program, which provides 70 names of prospects to the sales force every week. The program is expensive, but he believes it results in the names of potential customers that are highly qualified. Scott is proud of the program.

These prospects are construction companies that have recently been approved to construct major commercial buildings in the Dallas-Fort Worth area. These firms are the key target market for Willy's Windows.

Missy is the top sales executive for the company. Missy tells Scott that every Friday afternoon, she goes through the list of sales leads that has been provided to her from the marketing department. And then, passes them out to the firm's 20 sales reps, who make an average of $120,000 in straight salary compensation.

Scott has recently discovered that through the CRM program, he can actually keep track of exactly how many of his program's leads are being contacted. What he learned has angered him! Scott discovered that only about 30% of the leads are called. That means that on typically 50 of the 70 leads he provides to sales every week are completely ignored.

Further, Scott has calculated that the leads on average cost the company about $100 apiece, and that about 2% of his leads become customers. He also knows that each signed contract is for an average of one million dollars in sales revenue, which contributes about 20% of that to the Willy's Windows bottom line. So, he is convinced that Missy and her sales department are wasting lots of money by ignoring all those leads.

Success is a numbers game to Scott, and he believes his lead generation program could grow Willy's Windows sales by as much as 50% if they would only fully commit to it.

Missy believes that her salespeople are working as hard as they possibly can; and they have no additional time to pursue the extra leads. Scott doubts this.

Further, Missy believes that the leads provided vary greatly in quality. Some are good, but many are bad. So she eliminates lots of the names because she feels that it would be a waste of time for her salespeople to call them. She tells Scott: "You have no experience in sales. Trust me. I throw out leads for valid reasons. Most of these leads are no good."

"How can you tell so quickly who's a good lead and who's not—who's going to buy and who's not?" Scott demands. "You have no proof!"

They go round and round on this issue. Scott thinks each and every inquiry should be followed up with at least a salesperson's phone call, if not a personal visit. Missy strongly disagrees.

In the midst of this argument between Scott and Missy, Willy walks into the room. Willy, the President of the company, asks "What is this fuss all about?"

Missy and Scott present their sides to Willy, who now must try to mediate this dispute and to recommend a course of action for the future.

Questions:

1. What evidence in the case suggests that Scott is right?

2. What evidence suggests that Missy is right?

3. What is your best estimate as to how much money is being lost because of the neglected leads? Be sure to state your assumptions and show your work.

4. What course of action should Willy recommend to settle this?

FLETCHER ELECTRIC, INC.
Partnering Relationship

Molly Stevens, account manager for Fletcher, was pondering her next move with Tymco, her largest account. Fletcher manufactures a line of pumps, electric motors, and controls that are sold to companies that use Fletcher's parts in manufacturing all kinds of equipment. Tymco, a maker of street sweepers and other specialized industrial products, had purchased Fletcher controls for the last five years, but also purchased controls from several small distributors for specific applications when Fletcher's products could not meet the specifications. Stevens originally sold the controls by proving to the engineering department that Fletcher's quality could meet their specifications and demonstrating the controls' accuracy and long life. Then she convinced the purchasing agent that the pricing would be more stable with one major vendor than with multiple distributors. Since then, Stevens has heard no complaints about Fletcher's products. Tymco even allowed a trade magazine to write an article about Tymco's experience with Fletcher controls.

Early last year, Stevens persuaded the purchasing agent for Tymco to switch to Fletcher electric motors for several applications. Although engineering was not involved in this decision, Stevens had to prove to the purchasing agent that the products were as good as the ones they were currently purchasing. Stevens estimated that Fletcher had about 30 percent of the Tymco motor business, 30 percent went to Visa SA from Mexico, and the remainder of the business belonged to Smart & Company, which actually distributed several lines of electric motors imported from the Pacific Rim.

Last month, Stevens received a call from the director of engineering asking for a meeting to discuss some issues with Fletcher motors. She was delighted, because one of the Fletcher engineers had suggested combining Fletcher motors and controls and shipping the units as one assembly.

Stevens believed such a meeting would be a perfect opportunity to present the new idea. She created and presented a proposal to the engineering department that, if accepted, would mean doubling Fletcher's share of the electric motor business. The proposal would require some redesign by Tymco, but the savings over two years would be more than the redesign costs. After that, Tymco could increase profits on those products by about 3 percent. But several engineers pointed out that Fletcher was unwilling to manufacture controls for all of Tymco's needs, and they were reluctant to make such a change with a company that was not willing to work more closely with them. In addition, one engineer seemed very unhappy that the purchasing department had switched to Fletcher motors. She thought the reject rate of 2 percent was too high; all of Tymco's other vendors were achieving less than 1 percent rejects. At the conclusion of the meeting, the director of engineering said to Stevens, "Molly, we've enjoyed a long and good relationship with Fletcher, and your idea is a good one. Right now, though, I don't think Fletcher is the company we should do that with. But we'll consider it and let you know."

Questions:

1. In what stage of partnering is the relationship between Fletcher and Tymco?

2. Is there anything Stevens could have done to set the stage for better acceptance of her proposal?

3. What should she do right now? If her visionary objective is to develop a strategic partnership with Tymco, is it still realistic? What should she do to achieve that visionary objective?

CENTENNIAL MARKETING, INC.
Closing Tactics

Marsha Dixon, president of Centennial Marketing, Inc., of Atlanta, had just finished talking with JD Spitler, the assistant athletic director of Borden State University. Spitler had asked Dixon for a personal appointment at 9:00 am the following Monday to discuss his university's relationship with Centennial Marketing.

"We Make Your Business Look Good" is the motto of Centennial Marketing, which has over 25 years' experience as a manufacturer of custom-printed specialty products. These products include customized pens, bags, coffee mugs, hats, t-shirts, key chains, and so forth. Centennial's printing equipment is sophisticated, with the capability of foil hot stamp, flexographic, screen, and digital four-color printing processes.

Borden State University is one of Centennial's largest customers. In particular, the BSU athletic department buys a wide variety of customized products to promote its various athletic teams. Recently, BSU purchased a large order of mini-footballs from Centennial. These min-footballs were imprinted with the Borden State logo and were being passed out by the cheerleaders to fans at all the home football games.

As president of Centennial, Marsha Dixon rarely became involved in sales calls, and so was confused as to why Spitler would call her. The BSU account was assigned to Jon Jacobs, who had only been with Centennial for a few months. Before Jacobs, the account had been handled for over 10 years by Marty Milligan, but was transferred to Jacobs upon Milligan's retirement.

In the just-finished phone call, Dixon could tell Spitler was angry. "I just don't trust that new sales guy you assigned to us," Spitler told Dixon. "Marty was great—I wish he hadn't retired. I felt like we were true partners. But Jon Jacobs is always using his high-pressure sales tactics to sell us what we don't need. The printing on these mini-footballs was not at all what we expected. Plus, he told us, 'if we order right-away, we'd get a great deal,' but I found out that you guys sold the same footballs to our rival university for 10 percent less!"

This reaction was all very surprising to Dixon, who thus far had been impressed with the new salesperson. In fact, Jacobs's sales performance in his first quarter with the company was especially strong. Dixon explained to Spitler that it was not really appropriate for the company president to get involved in negotiations between a salesperson and his client. But Spitler absolutely demanded that the two of them have face-to-face meeting. "I'll be there at 9 o'clock tomorrow morning!" Dixon agreed to the meeting only to end the conversation—and, after all, BSU was one of Centennial's biggest customers.

Dixon wondered what could have gone wrong. She recalled that Jon Jacobs's previous job was in real estate sales, which was an industry that did not focus as much on maintaining close relationships with customers. Dixon also wished that she would have spent more time training Jacobs—especially in the areas of need assessment, appropriate closing techniques, and follow-up.

Dixon leaned back in her chair and looked out at the Atlanta skyline. She wondered how she should handle the matter.

Questions:

1. Was it right for Dixon to agree to meet with Spitler? Should she invite Jacobs to the meeting?

2. How should Dixon handle the meeting with Spitler?

3. How do the steps of the sales process differ when a salesperson's priority is to maintain long-term relationships with customers?

[1] *The No Fuss Recipe for Hot Referral Leads*, eBook downloaded from www.influitive.com on January 6, 2016.

[2] BNI (Organization) entry in Wikipedia. https://en.wikipedia.org/wiki/BNI_(organization) accessed on January 6, 2016.

[3] Art Sobczak, *Smart Calling: Eliminate the Fear, Failure, and Rejection from Cold Calling, 2nd Edition* (Hoboken, New Jersey: John Wiley & Sons, 2013).

[4] Bob Donath, James W. Obermayer, Carolyn K. Dixon, and Richard A. Crocker, "When Your Prospect Calls," *Marketing Management* 3, no. 2 (1994), pp. 27-28.

[5] Gaurav Sabnis, Sharmila C. Chatterjee, Rajdeep Grewal, and Gary L. Lilien, "The Sales Lead Black Hole: On Sales Reps' Follow-Up of Marketing Leads," *Journal of Marketing*, January 2013, Vol 77 (1), pp. 52-67.

[6] Quoted in Ginger Trumfio, "Opening Doors," *Sales & Marketing Management*, May 1994, p. 81.

[7] Christian P. Heide, *Dartnell's 30th Sales Force Compensation Survey* (Chicago: Dartnell Corporation, 1999), p. 162.

[8] Rosann L. Spiro and Barton A. Weitz, "Adaptive Selling: Conceptualization, Measurement, and Nomological Validity," *Journal of Marketing Research*, February 1990, pp. 61-69.

[9] Geoffrey James, "Top 10 'How to Sell' Books of All Time," *Inc.* (February 27, 2013). http://www.inc.com/geoffrey-james/top-10-sales-books-of-all-time.html

[10] This discussion is based to a large extent on concepts developed by Neil Rackham, which in turn were based on a research study by the Huthwaite Corporation of 35,000 sales calls. These ideas were originally reported in Rackham's book *Spin Selling* (New York: McGraw-Hill 1988).

[11] Lillian Chaney and Catherine Green, "Effective Presentations," *American Salesman*, December 2014, Vol. 59 (12), pp. 8-13.

[12] Thomas E. DeCarlo and Michael J. Barone, "The Interactive Effects of Sales Presentation, Suspicion, and Positive Mood on Salesperson Evaluations and Purchase Intentions," *Journal of Personal Selling and Sales Management*, Winter 2013, Vol. 33 Issue 1, pp. 53-66.

[13] Fergal Glynn, "20 Tools for Creating and Delivering Amazing Presentations," *HubSpot Blogs*, October 16, 2014. Accessed on January 7, 2016 from the website: http://blog.hubspot.com/marketing/presentation-tools

[14] The Vollrath Company Youtube channel, https://www.youtube.com/user/TheVollrathCompany Accessed January 7, 2016

[15] David M. Szymanski, "Modality and Offering Effects in Sales Presentations for a Good versus a Service," *Journal of the Academy of Marketing Science* 29, no. 2 (Spring 2001), pp. 179-89.

[16] Darrin Fleming, "When Demos Sabatage the Sale," *Sales & Service Excellence Essentials*, December 2014, Vol 13 (12), p. 7.

[17] Kim Sydow Campbell and Lenita Davis, "The Sociolinguistic Basis of Managing Rapport When Overcoming Buying Objections," *Journal of Business Communication*, January 2006, pp. 43-66.

[18] John R. Graham, "Successful Selling: Learn the Customer's Buying Cycle," *The American Salesman*, March 2000, pp. 3-9.

[19] Nikolaos Tzokas, Michael Saren, and Panayiotis Kyziridis, "Aligning Sales Management and Relationship Marketing in the Services Sector," *Service Industries Journal*, January 2001, pp. 195-2010.

[20] David T. Wilson, "Deep Relationships: The Case of the Vanishing Salesperson," *Journal of Personal Selling and Sales Management*, Winter 2000, pp. 53-61.

4

Sales Force Organization

Owens Corning manufactures a wide variety of construction materials, including fiberglass insulation and roofing products. These products are sold to thousands of customers across the world—but not all customers are equal. For example, The Home Depot is the largest home improvement retailer in the United States; and so, it is one of Owens Corning's most important customers for many of its consumer-oriented products.

Consequently, when organizing its sales force, Owens Corning makes sure that The Home Depot is serviced by a *team* of knowledgeable, service-oriented people that focus exclusively on this key account. In fact, Jonathon Frezzo is the manufacturers' Director of Sales for The Home Depot, and he manages a team of nine salespeople all servicing the retail giant. In fact, even though Owens Corning is an Ohio-based company, the members of this sales team all live in the Atlanta-area because, of course, that is where The Home Depot is headquartered. This creates a close, win-win relationship between the two companies, as the key account managers work to grow business with Home Depot in several product categories.[1]

Owen Corning's decision to call The Home Depot a key account that is serviced by a team of people living in Atlanta is a sales force organization decision. To do this well, the firm should first establish its objectives and then plan the appropriate strategies and tactics to reach those goals. The fundamentals of the organization are essentially the same whether we are talking about organizing a sales force, a production department, a sorority, or any other group involved in a common effort.

NATURE OF SALES ORGANIZATIONS

An **organization** is simply an arrangement—a working structure—of activities involving a group of people. The goal is to arrange these activities so that the people involved can act better *together* than they can *individually.*

Organizational changes occur in companies' sales and marketing efforts as firms find that their existing structures are inappropriate to implement the marketing concept. As we noted in Chapter 2, one idea underlying the marketing concept is that all marketing activities should be organizationally integrated and coordinated.

In recent years, many firms have restructured their sales organizations to make them more responsive to the changing needs and, in some cases, demands of their customers. Companies are doing this by organizing around their customers.

"Our primary goal is to keep listening to our customers extremely well, so we are constantly evaluating our business and making adjustments," says a top executive from Microsoft, when explaining a recent realignment of its sales force.[2] This quote also indicates that organizing the sales force is an ongoing responsibility—it is not something firms do just once and then forget about it.

A trend in sales force restructuring is to move toward a flatter organization, in which coordination across activities is more important than top-down control. For example, in the realignment referred to above, Microsoft organized its sales force into product-focused teams, and then assigned each team to a single industry. This creates teams that are experts on how a particular product line can meet the needs of the target market.

In addition, Microsoft's realignment is consistent with the general trend toward flatter organizations, in which coordination across activities is more important than top-down control. In these organizations, salespeople are often part of cross-functional teams designed to serve specific customers. These changes are occurring because companies are changing the way they do business with their suppliers. These organizational trends are discussed in detail later in the chapter.

SALES FORCE ORGANIZATION AND STRATEGIC PLANNING

A close relationship exists between a company's sales force organizational structure and its strategic marketing and sales force planning. The organizational structure has a direct and significant bearing on the implementation of strategic planning. The key here is to design an organizational structure that will help those who work within it to successfully implement the strategic marketing and sales force planning.

An organizational structure—whether it is for a sales force or any other group involved in a joint effort to meet a goal—is a control-and-coordination mechanism. In addition to organizational structure, management has several other mechanisms it can use to direct the efforts of its sales force: its compensation plan, training program, supervisory techniques, and so on. But the organizational structure looms large because it typically is set up before these other mechanisms are established. Consequently, any mistakes in organization can result in reduced efficiencies in selection, compensation, training, and other tools of managerial control and guidance.

Therefore, as a control mechanism, the organizational structure guides the company—or in some cases, the sales force—in carrying out the strategic planning to pursue marketing and sales force goals. Often a sales force fails to reach its goals because the organizational structure hinders the effective implementation of the strategic sales force planning.

To illustrate, assume that a company's sales goal is to increase its market share to 20 percent next year and that its *sales strategy* is to increase its sales to large key accounts by 30 percent over last year. However, the company's sales force is structured so that each rep's efforts are spread thinly over accounts of all sizes. No sales executives are assigned to sell to key accounts. Under these organizational conditions, it is doubtful that this company will successfully implement its plan.

CHARACTERISTICS OF A GOOD ORGANIZATION

Several management generalizations that characterize a good organization are summarized in the list below. These principles of organization design apply to organizations in any field—not just sales management—and they are useful in the designing of a new organization or the revising of an existing one.

- **The organizational structure should reflect a marketing orientation.** When designing a sales organization, management should focus first on the market and the customer. Executives should consider the selling and marketing tasks necessary to capitalize on the market demand and to serve the firm's customers. From this base, an organizational structure can be built.
- **The organization should be built around activities, not around people.** This is sometimes difficult as strong personalities demand—and high-performers can handle—more responsibility than others. However, these people inevitably leave the organization, and the resulting organizational structure is often seriously problematic.
- **Responsibility and authority should be related properly.** When you give someone a job to do, also give the person the authority and the tools to do it. Sales managers must learn how to hire the right people and appropriately delegate.
- **Span of executive control should be reasonable.** The span of executive control is simply the average number of subordinates who report to each manager. The average span of control for U.S. sales forces is 10-12 salespeople per manager, but this varies widely depending on the industry (see box entitled "Span of Control.")
- **Organization should be stable but flexible.** An organization should be like a tree—firmly rooted but flexible enough so that a strong wind won't break it. *Stability* in an organization means having trained executive replacements available when needed. *Flexibility* refers more to short-run situations such as seasonal fluctuations in the number of workers needed. An organization might subcontract some work during peak seasons or hire a temporary sales force to deliver samples of new products.

- **Activities should be balanced and coordinated.** Balancing activities does not mean making all organizational units equal. Instead, balance means not letting one unit unduly become more important than another. Coordination is needed between sales and other functional areas, including the production operation, the finance/accounting team, and the marketing department.

All of these principles should be reflected throughout the firm's company handbook, which should include all job descriptions and relationships among the functional areas. This is known as the formal structure of the organization. However, in the real world, most firms need an additional element to make the formal structure work well. The key element is an **informal organization.**

CONSIDER THIS...

Span of Control

In sales, the span of control is defined as the average number of salespeople for each manager. Although the average span of control is 10-12 salespeople per manager, there is wide variation around this average.

Firms with complex products and large customers may have a span of control closer to 5 or 6 key account managers per sales executive. On the other end of the spectrum, consumer products companies sometimes have up to 50 salespeople called merchandisers (who stock shelves, set up displays, manage inventory for the retailer) for every manager.

How does a firm determine the right span of control for its sales force? The answer is to analyze what the sales managers are doing, what they should be doing, and how much time the various tasks might take. This analysis relates to these three broad management tasks:

- People management—includes hiring, supervising, coaching and conducting performance reviews. Span

of control can be larger when the sales cycle is short and relatively simple, when the firm has strong sales support units (e.g., information systems, training), and when the salespeople are knowledgeable, experienced and empowered to make their own decisions.

- Customer management—includes account planning, customer visits, and accompanying salespeople on their calls. Span of control depends on the size and needs of the customers, and the nature of manager selling responsibilities.

- Business management—includes time spent on budgeting, sales (and other) meetings, and other administrative requirements. Span of control must be reduced when sales managers control local budgets and resources, and/or when the organization is de-centralized such that each manager must adapt sales strategies to local needs.

SOURCE: Andris Zoltners, PK Sinha and Sally Lorimer, "Does Your Company Have Enough Sales Managers?" *Harvard Business Review*, April 1, 2014. Retrieved June 10, 2016 from https://hbr.org/2014/04/does-your-company-have-enough-sales-managers.

Role of an Informal Organization

A healthy organization is a self-adjusting one. Through its own devices, it finds ways to get a job done with minimum effort. A formal organization's well-being is maintained by the system known as the informal organization structure. This structure represents how things actually get done in a company, not how they are supposed to be done according to a formal organization chart.

The following example shows how an informal organization works. A sales manager's assistant opens a letter from a customer complaining about an overcharge on an order. If the lines of the formal organization chart were followed, the assistant would refer the letter to the sales manager. This manager would relay the message up through executive echelons until it reached the administrator in charge of the chief executives in sales and accounting. This top administrator would forward the complaint down through channels to the appropriate person in the billing division. The answer would follow the reverse path up and down through channels until the sales manager's assistant received it and could notify the customer. Such procedures are rather ridiculous, and most organizations would not follow them. Instead, the informal structure would be used. The sales manager's assistant would simply telephone or walk over to see a clerk in the billing department to find out what happened to the customer's order.

Frequently, salespeople do things that are above and beyond their formal job requirements, such as helping another rep prepare a quote or showing a new rep how to search the company's online product catalog. These behaviors, which are known as **citizenship behaviors**, are also part of the informal organization.[3]

BASIC TYPES OF ORGANIZATIONS

Most sales organizations can be classified mainly into one of four basic categories:

- A line organization
- A line-and-staff organization
- A functional organization
- A horizontal organization

A **line organization** shown in Figure 4-1 is the simplest form. Authority flows from the chief executive to the first subordinate, then to the second subordinate, and so on. This structure *per se* is hardly ever used (as usually there are at least a couple employees who are at the same level), but very small firms are organized in a way that is very close to a pure line organization. The key advantage of a line organization is that there is never any dispute about who is the boss of whom. It is also a low-cost structure that lends itself to quick decision-making. However, it is not feasible for organizations that have more than a few employees.

A **line-and-staff organization** shown in Figure 4-2 is probably the most widely used structure in sales organizations today. The structure is likely to be used when the sales force is large, and is a good structure for national companies that have a number of different products and customers. The key advantage over the line organization is that this allows for division of labor and specialization. That is, for each staff, the employees are focused on one set of activities, and are led by the staff executive (e.g., the sales manager) who has authority over the subordinates (e.g., the salespeople).

FIGURE 4-1
Line organization

In a line-and-staff organization, staff executives' formal line authority is limited to their direct subordinates, and so they merely have advisory authority over the subordinates of the other staffs. In other words, the market research manager can only *recommend and encourage* salespeople to administer a survey to customers—but ultimately, the sales manager can overrule that recommendation.

A **functional organization** differs from this in only one fundamental way: the advisory authority of the staff executives over the other staff subordinates changes to formal authority (again, see Figure 4-2). In other words, the functional organization allows the market research manager to formally order the salespeople to administer a survey to salespeople. This can be practical and useful. However, the problem with this is that the subordinates get orders from more than one manager, and sometimes these might be conflicting orders. In other words, the major drawback of the functional organization is that there can be too many bosses.

A drawback to both the line-and-staff and functional organizations is that they can generate multiple levels of middle managers, which leads to inefficiency as they become tangled in a web of relationships generating too many demands that often conflict. This is why there has been a strong trend in the past several years for organizations to cut out midlevel managers, and move toward a flatter structure.

A flatter structure in the purest form is the **horizontal organization,** which is the final basic type of organization discussed. This is a difficult organizational structure to show on a graphic. Figure 4-3 at least demonstrates

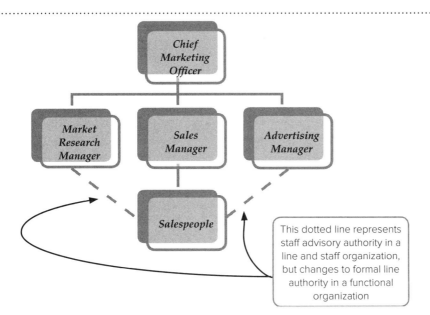

FIGURE 4-2
Line-and-staff organization
vs. Functional sales
organization

how a horizontal organization eliminates management levels and departmental boundaries, and thus consists of many people *at the same level*.

In this structure, a small group of senior executives at the top oversee the essential support functions, such as human resources and accounting. Everyone else is a member of multiple self-managed, cross-functional teams that each perform a different core process, including sales. This leads to the customers having direct access to a team of specialists, including someone from operations, research and development, etc. This selling team often works with a team of people from the customer firm. The horizontal organization reduces supervision and eliminates activities that are not necessary for the process.

The horizontal structure has been adopted by some of the biggest companies in the United States—such as AT&T, Du Pont, General Electric, and Motorola—to gain greater efficiencies and customer responsiveness.[4] Kraft Corporation recently restructured into a hybrid organization in which functional staff personnel provide advice to the horizontal customer teams.[5] Usually most medium- and large-sized firms will expand one of the basic structures in some specialized way so that the sales force can be more effective. We discuss specialization in sales organizations in the next section.

SPECIALIZATION WITHIN A SALES DEPARTMENT

In the organizational examples discussed earlier, the sales force has not been divided on any basis. As a sales force grows, the job of the executive managing the sales force becomes more difficult. The number and complexity of a company's products and/or markets also may call for some organizational division if the sales effort is to be effective.

The most common way to divide sales responsibilities is to split the sales force on some basis of sales specialization. There is a definite trend toward the

FIGURE 4-3

The horizontal organization

Source: © Jacob Morgan
(thefutureorganization.com)

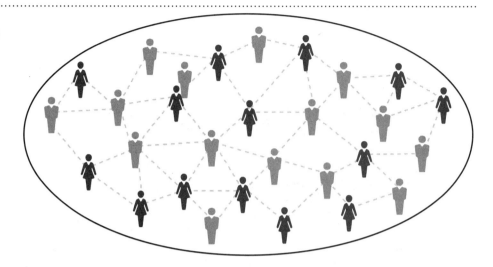

use of specialized sales forces in the United States. The key strategic question here is, *what should be the basis of the specialization*—geography, type of product, market-based divisions, or other criteria? To make this decision, management should carefully analyze many factors, including sales force abilities, market and customer considerations, nature of the product, and demands of the selling job.

Geographic Specialization

Probably the most widely used system for dividing responsibility and line authority over sales operation is the **geographic organization**—the sales force is grouped on the basis of physical territories. This sales specialization structure may assign each salesperson to a separate geographical area (or *territory*), in which to sell. As shown in Figure 4-4, companies with large sales forces often have multiple levels of geographic boundaries. For example, there might be multiple territories in each district, and multiple districts in each region. The territorial salespeople are supervised by district managers, who are supervised by regional sales managers—and at the top of this hierarchy is the general or *national sales manager*.

A firm can benefit in many ways from territorial specialization in its sales department. For example, this structure usually ensures better coverage of the entire market as well as better control over the sales force and sales operations. A firm can meet local competition and adjust to local conditions by having an executive responsible for a limited segment of the market. Local management also can act more rapidly in servicing customers and handling their problems.

A drawback in a geographical sales organization is that there is usually no specialization of marketing activities. Each district manager, for example, may have to work in advertising, sales promotion, and marketing research, in addition to managing a sales force.

Product Specialization

The type of product sold is another frequently used basis for dividing the responsibilities and activities within a sales department. The two most widely

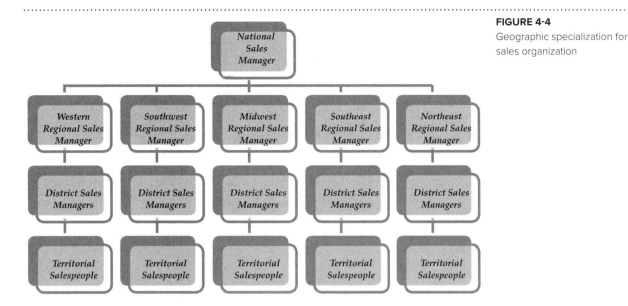

FIGURE 4-4
Geographic specialization for sales organization

used structures featuring **product specialization organization** are product operating and product staff organizations.

Product Operating Specialization

Companies that organize their sales force to focus on specific products or groups of products, while centralizing functions like advertising and customer service are using **product operating specialization**. In the company represented in Figure 4-5, products have been separated into two groups: A and B. Salespeople in each group sell only the products included in that group. This is similar to how 3M Corporation uses separate sales forces to sell its different product lines: One group of salespeople sells industrial adhesives and another sells safety equipment.

The product sales managers are strictly line-operating executives; they have no staff assistants. The staff executives in advertising, for example, are located in the home office and coordinate the advertising for all products.

Product operating specialization is likely to be used when a company is selling

- A variety of complex, technical products, as in the electronics field.
- Many thousands of products—a hardware wholesaler, for example.
- Very dissimilar, unrelated products—a rubber company may use three sales forces to sell (a) truck and auto tires, (b) rubber footwear, and (c) industrial rubber products such as belts, bushing, and insulating materials.

The major advantage of this form of organization is that the sales force can give specialized attention to each product line. Also, each line gets more executive attention because one person is responsible for a particular product group. Probably the biggest drawback is that sometimes more than one salesperson from a company calls on the same customer. Such duplication of coverage not only is expensive but also can evoke ill will from customers, who might be

FIGURE 4-5
Product Operating
Specialization for sales
organization

FIGURE 4-5
Product Operating
Specialization for sales
organization

frustrated over having to see two different salespeople from the same company. Product operating specialization also has the same weakness as the geographic type in that the product sales managers have no staff assistants in advertising, sales promotion, or other specialized marketing activities.

Product Staff Specialization

Figure 4-6 illustrates a **product staff specialization,** which is commonly used when management wants to use staff assistants who specialize by product. This structure utilizes staff executives called **product managers** (or, in some companies, brand or category managers). Each product manager bears responsibility for planning and developing a marketing program for one product line. These people have no line authority over the sales force or the sales force managers—they can only advise and make recommendations to them. The sales force is not specialized by product; in fact, it is typically organized via a geographic specialization where each salesperson sells all the products of the company.

A company can use this structure when it wants some of the advantages of specialization by product line at the planning level but does not need the specialization at the selling level. Thus, in one stroke the product staff organization corrects two of the weaknesses in a product operating structure: (1) the problems of duplicate calls on a customer and (2) the lack of specialization in planning the functional activities. Of course, a product staff organization loses any advantage of having salespeople specialize in a limited line or products. Product staff specialization is frequently used by consumer product companies such as Procter & Gamble or Quaker Oats.

Market Specialization

Many companies divide the line authority in their sales departments on the basis of type of customer, classed by industry, by channel of distribution or by customer size. This is called a **market specialization**. For example, a division

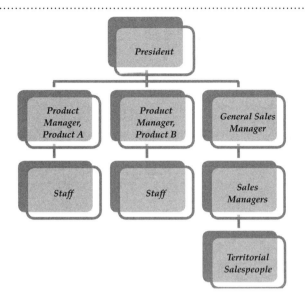

FIGURE 4-6
Product Staff Specialization
for sales organization

of Kimberly-Clark that sells Huggies diapers, Kleenex tissues, and a variety of feminine products uses separate sales forces to reach each distinct customer type; for example, one group of salespeople is focused on grocery stores, and another one sells to military bases.

A market specialization structure is shown in Figure 4-7. The sales manager in charge of each industry group is a line-operating executive with authority over one group of salespeople. These executives have no staff assistants under them. Each sales rep sells the full line of products used by the customer group.

Similarly, two types of Fastenal Company salespeople are outside sales representatives and account specialists. Outside sales representatives focus on smaller customers, and may service over 150 accounts. Account specialists, on the other hand, sell to just a few, large accounts within the territory. The higher level sales executives at Fastenal (e.g., the district managers) are also much more involved with these larger accounts. Note that this is a variation of strategic account management, which is discussed later in the chapter.

The use of market specialization in sales organizational structures has increased in recent years, while product specialization, at least in some industries, has declined. This trend is expected to continue. Certainly market specialization is consistent with the customer orientation philosophy that underlies the marketing concept. Among the companies that already have made the market specialization move in their sales organizations are such well-known names as Xerox, IBM, NCR, Hewlett-Packard, General Foods, and General Electric.

Xerox embarked on an ambitious three- to five-year program that eventually had its 4,000 to 5,000 sales reps selling the company's full line of office-automation products. In effect, the company switched from a product-oriented sales organization, consisting of several product sales forces, to a market-oriented structure. The company spent between $10 and $20 million a year in its training program to implement this organizational change.

FIGURE 4-7
Market Specialization for
sales organization

IBM reconfigured its sales force by industry; that is, reps are now assigned by industry, not necessarily by geography. The reps are industry experts who sell primarily to customers within specific industries. This focus on customers is widely credited for the company's double-digit sales growth. As one IBM client executive noted, "Customers were demanding that we focus our organization more closely on their industries, so IBM changed its organization to meet their demands. Now we have intimate knowledge of their businesses."[6] Although it overcomes some of the disadvantages of product specialization and conflict of interest between channels, market specialization does have some limitations. It causes overlap in territorial coverage and therefore is costly. Also, unless separating the sales force by markets results in some product specialization, the customer-based organization may include the disadvantages of full-line selling.

Combination of Organizational Bases

In the examples of organizational bases given earlier, we assumed that a company divides its sales force on only one basis, such as territory, product, or market. Actually, many firms use some combination drawn from the structures already discussed. For example, a firm may combine geographical specialization with product staff specialization (through the use of product managers). Or a sales force may combine market specialization with geographical specialization.

As we look at sales management today, it is evident that the trend toward specialized sales forces will continue. The basis of specialization—geography, product, market, or a combination—may vary from company to company, but some specialization is needed to remain competitive. In the following section, we discuss additional organizational alternatives that can benefit a company's selling effort.

Introduction to the Running Case Study

Shiderlots Elevators is one of the world's largest manufacturers of vertical transportation systems, which primarily consist of elevators and escalators. With $10 billion in revenue and over 50,000 employees, Shiderlots sells and services systems that can be found in almost every country of the world. During the recession of a few years ago, business was slow. But right now, the company is on track for a record year.

Adam Dark is a general sales manager for Shiderlots. Dark works out of the branch in Columbus, Ohio, where he supervises seven account managers that operate in his district. Each account manager is paid a base salary of $50,000, plus a commission of 3 percent on all sales in his or her territory. In addition, account managers receive an annual bonus depending on the extent to which they met their sales goals. Last year, about half of the sales force received this bonus, which averaged $12,000 (for those who got it). Overall, the median compensation level was $90,000 last year, with two salespeople making over $150,000. Shiderlots also paid all reasonable travel and entertainment expenses that were incurred by the reps.

The seven Shiderlots account managers that report to Adam Dark primarily sell maintenance service contracts—along with upgrades—to building managers of structures that are already equipped with elevators and/or escalators. They spend about half of their time following-up/checking on existing customers. The other half of the time, they work on gaining new accounts.

Shiderlots services the products of all manufacturers of elevators and escalators—so Shiderlots service personnel are capable of repairing and upgrading the products of any elevator manufacturer. Government regulations require that all buildings with elevators to have a valid permit. This is good as it essentially requires that each building have a service contract with Shiderlots or one of its competitors; however, competition in this industry is very fierce.

Shiderlots account managers must possess excellent product knowledge. Consequently, all account managers receive extensive and ongoing training so they can serve as well-informed *consultants* to the building managers. In fact, Shiderlots salespeople are all on call 24 hours a day—because when an elevator or escalator breaks down, it needs to be fixed as soon as possible.

Dark believes that selecting and retaining quality account managers is the most important part of his job. Of course, the best salespeople are highly sought after, and Dark is always concerned that his top performers will be hired—or "stolen away"—by another organization in the industry.

As a company, Shiderlots also sells new systems (i.e., new escalators and elevators) to major construction companies that erect commercial buildings, including skyscrapers. However, this is a very different kind of sale that is handled by key account managers from company headquarters in New York City. In other words, Dark's account managers focus almost all of their time on the maintenance contracts.

Throughout the textbook, we will use Shiderlots for case studies of the various operating problems facing Adam Dark's sales force. The problem of each case relates to the chapter topic. Consequently, the first case in the series is a problem in sales force organization.

Sales Force Specialization

Adam Dark, the general sales manager of Shiderlots Elevator, has seen his Columbus, Ohio, district grow at a tremendous rate since he started working there

RUNNING CASE
Shiderlots
Elevators, Inc.

ten years ago. This growth has created many exciting opportunities for him and his salespeople. Growing so fast, however, also presents many challenges.

When Dark started, for example, his account managers were responsible for selling both the service maintenance contracts and new product installations. Since selling the new product installations were so complicated and time consuming, that portion of the business was taken over by key account managers from company headquarters. And so, Dark's seven account managers now focus exclusively on selling the maintenance contracts. In other words, Shiderlots moved to a product operating specialization.

The current specialization structure of Dark's sales force is done by geography. That is, each of the account managers sells to and services all customers within his or her well-defined territory in the Columbus area. Claim jumping, which is the act of a salesperson selling in someone else's territory, is strictly forbidden—which means that the account managers are only allowed to call on customers in their own territory.

The seven territories have been carefully designed—and are continually revised—so that all of the account managers have the same sales potential and workload. Specifically, each account manager has a total of about 100 customers or potential customers in his or her territory. This means that the Columbus market has a total of about 700 firms that need service contracts for elevators and/or escalators. With a 50% market share, Shiderlots has about 350 current customers.

This is a large number of customers for each account manager! In fact, Dark has recently heard some complaints from his team that they were stretched too thin. And to make matters worse, he just learned that his most experienced account manager is retiring in one month! Dark knows a recent college grad named Phil Johnson, who had interned with Shiderlots. Dark believes Johnson has great potential, and knows he would take the job. However, Dark is not so sure Johnson is ready to handle the larger accounts in his market.

Given this impending new hire, Dark wondered if it might be a good time to restructure the sales force to enhance efficiency. He generated several customer detail reports from the company CRM system to look into the matter in some depth. The reports showed that about 80 percent of his district's sales originated from the 70 largest customers. The remaining 280 customers were much smaller, generating just 20 percent of sales. This brought Dark back to his college days learning about the 80/20 principle in business school (how 80 percent of sales tends to come from about 20 percent of the customers). He was struck by how closely that applied to his current situation.

The reports also showed how the larger customers required a great deal of time and attention from the account managers. However, he was also struck by how much time and effort his people were spending with in-person visits to the small accounts. He seriously questioned whether these visits were worth it.

Dark began to think about sales force specialization approaches other than geography. Inside sales (or telemarketing) even crossed his mind. The company president was scheduled to visit him next week, at which point he thought it might be a good time to propose something new.

Question: How might the sales force be restructured to remedy the current problems? Present at least two possible options, and explain the pros and cons of each.

CONSIDER THIS...

The Virtual Office

With the advent of technology, many companies such as IBM, AT&T, and Lucent Technologies have eliminated district sales offices. Instead the reps work out of virtual offices. These offices are called virtual because, although they are not "real" locations, reps can use them to do all of the things they once did in the district office or even in a home office. Virtual offices, which sometimes consist of nothing more than a cell phone and/or laptop, and can be set up almost anywhere at almost any time, not only reduce costs but also allow salespeople to respond to customer needs efficiently and effectively. However, sales managers today do not see their reps in person as much as they did in the past. Therefore, managers must be proficient at using the same tools to supervise and provide assistance to their reps.

ADDITIONAL STRATEGIC ORGANIZATIONAL ALTERNATIVES

In our discussion of organizational structures, we looked at an outside sales force that makes calls *in person* on accounts (customers). We implied that the reps are alone when they make these face-to-face sales calls, and we did not consider the impact of the size of the account on these organizational structures.

However, there are additional selling strategies with significant organizational implications that do include such factors as (1) account size, (2) team selling, (3) outside selling without in-person sales calls, and (4) the use of independent agents (see Figure 4-8.) These organizational alternatives, which have attracted increasing managerial attention in recent years, are likely to gain even greater acceptance going forward.

Key Account Management

As shown in the chapter introduction, some companies use a **key account management (KAM)** organizational structure to serve their major accounts—that is, their large volume customers. Large customers can range from firms with only local or regional markets to multinational corporations. **Strategic account management (SAM)** or **global account management (GAM)** are also commonly used as terms to describe this same structure of managing large customers (and some firms use the terms *national*, or *major account management*). However they are described, large customers are extremely important to a seller because they usually account for a *disproportionately large share* of a seller's sales volume and profit. In addition to their large buying size, major customers also are differentiated by the *complexity of their buying process.*

Several factors contribute to the complexity of the buying-selling process of key accounts. On the buyer's side, people in different geographical locations may be involved in the buying process. Even at one site, several executives, including top management, may influence the buying decision. Price concessions, special services, and customer-made products may be demanded by large buyers. Salespeople in different geographical areas may be calling on the same customer, and many customers do not want the confusion of dealing with

FIGURE 4-8
Organizational options

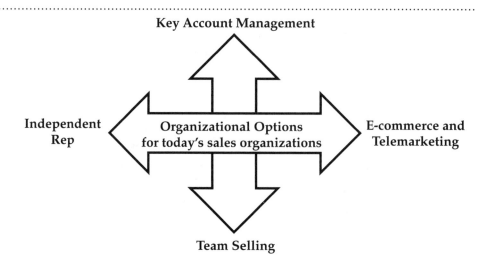

a different salesperson and a different contract for each site. Similar conditions on the seller's side add to the complexity and potential confusion. The large dollar volume involved usually attracts executives from other functional areas, and maybe even the company president.

Obviously there is a dramatic need for close organizational coordination both within the seller's company and between the buyer and seller. Many sales executives believe that the key accounts are too important to be handled only by the average territorial sales rep. Consequently, they are modifying their sales organizations to provide better treatment for these accounts. Three commonly used organizational approaches are

- **Creating a separate sales force.** In recent years, many firms have established separate sales forces to sell to key accounts. A variation is to have the strategic-account salespeople call on customers' home offices while using the regular sales force to service the customers' branch and field offices. Hewlett-Packard splits its sales force into three groups: the red team, the blue team, and the green team. The red team goes after only strategically important accounts in targeted industries; the green team calls on the wholesalers and distributors that are used to sell to the smaller accounts; and the blue team includes telesales and some other, less important accounts that don't fit in the other categories.[8] In contrast, Xerox key account managers work hand-in-hand with the local reps to develop strategies for approaching the customer on both the national and local levels.[9] 3M Corporation also has key account managers who work with local reps around the globe on corporate strategic accounts.[10]

- **Using executives.** Some companies use their top sales and marketing executives or their field sales executives for major-account selling. This approach is an alternative for firms that cannot afford a separate sales force. A company that has only a few large customers also may find this approach useful. Sending top executives to call on key accounts ensures that the salesperson has the authority to make decisions about prices and the allocation of manufacturing facilities. On the other hand, executive time spent on servicing key accounts is time taken away from planning and other management activities.

- **Creating a separate division.** A company may establish a separate division to deal with its key accounts. This option has been used by some apparel manufacturers that produce and sell private-label clothing for the large general-merchandise chains such as Sears and JCPenney. This organizational structure has the advantage of integrating the manufacturing and marketing (including the sales) activities related to the major accounts. On the other hand, this structure is expensive because it duplicates other units in the selling firm.

BUYING CENTERS AND TEAM SELLING

In Chapter 1 we stated that growing expertise among buyers would continue to challenge strategic sales management in the foreseeable future. Many business and government organizations have already developed and implemented the concept of a buying center in their buying process. The **buying center** may be defined as all the individuals involved in the purchasing decision process. Thus, a buying center usually includes people who play any of the following roles:

- *Users* of the product.
- *Influencers* who set the product specifications.
- *Deciders* who make the actual purchasing decision.
- *Gatekeepers* who control the flow of purchasing information.
- *Buyers* (purchasing agents) who process the purchase orders.

In contrast to consumer purchasing, organizational buying is generally based more on economic reasons than on emotional ones. Among the many factors buyers consider when choosing suppliers are the quality-price ratio, delivery reliability, reputation of the suppliers, information and market services provided by the suppliers, and previous experience with the supplier. It also should be noted that purchasing managers will continue to have increased status and authority within the firm as materials management grows in importance. This increased status and authority are reflected by such titles as vice president of materials management or vice president of supply chain management.

Team Selling

As noted in Chapter 2, a growing number of firms are using selling teams to call on the various individuals in the buying center. A **selling team** is a group of people representing the sales department and other functional areas in the firm, such as finance, production, and research and development (R&D).

Organizational Options for Team Selling

The organizational arrangements for team selling are quite flexible. Usually the functional specialists and management levels on the selling team match those from the buying center in any given purchase-sales transaction. Therefore, the functional and executive composition of a selling team varies from company to company, and from one selling situation to another within a given firm. Companies such as IBM and Compaq, which sell customized combinations of computer hardware and software, use teams of salespeople and technical experts who work closely with the customer's buying team. At IBM, for example, client executives manage teams, which include product reps, systems engineers, and consultants.[11] On the Monsanto customer team, IBM included research experts in molecular technology to help Monsanto with genetic engineering problems. As a result, IBM won a contract with Monsanto worth $1 billion.[12] At 3M Corporation, cross-functional teams have been formulated from each of the company's regions; these teams include people from logistics, management information systems, and sales.[13]

In recent years, there has been a trend toward including representatives from the customers' organization on the team. In order to serve its important customers, General Electric (GE) creates large teams that are both cross-functional and cross-company. It formed a 140-person cross-company team to help one customer, Southern California Edison, reduce the downtime on its steam turbine generators, which were purchased from GE. The team consisted of 60 people from GE and 80 from Southern California Edison. Medical equipment manufacturer Baxter International has gone even further by jointly setting targets and sharing the savings or the extra costs.[14] In these cases the two companies have entered into a partnership, as described in Chapter 2.

Some companies establish a separate location where sales teams meet with customer buying teams. At these **selling centers,** the selling team presents an integrated program that matches the account's needs. The agenda for the program is usually developed in consultation with the buying team. Xerox has six of these centers, which it calls executive briefing centers, and management believes that they stimulate openness, which improves communication and thus the relationship with the buying team.[15]

Strategic Considerations

A number of factors must be considered if a company chooses to adopt a team-selling approach. The size and the functional diversity of the team must be established. Management must determine how it will reward the individuals on the team as well as the team itself. To a large extent, these decisions should be based on the strategic objectives for the team. For example, if one of the primary responsibilities of the team will be to provide a great amount of after-sale support, and if that support will be provided by people other than the salesperson, it is often effective to include the support staff as part of the sales team. This enables the support personnel to develop a better understanding of the customer's support needs relatively quickly. Furthermore, with their expertise, support people can help close the sale.

However, there are some general guidelines that may affect strategic decisions. On the one hand, it has been found that individuals tend to exert less effort as team size increases, so there is some rationale for limiting the size of the team. On the other hand, there is evidence that greater skill diversity is related to increased effort and interaction on the part of the team members. Therefore, it is a good idea to form teams with individuals who are from several different functional areas or departments within the firm.

Team selling is not the best alternative in every situation. It is expensive and consequently is used only when there is potential for high sales volume and profit. For example, companies may use teams to call on their major accounts

CONSIDER THIS...

An Ethical Dilemma

A strong regional manufacturer decided several years ago to expand into a new geographic area. Although the company served all of its current customers with its own sales force, it chose to use a manufacturers' rep to expand into the new territory. The company was not certain how long it would take to build up the business in the new area, and using a rep organization would enable the company to limit its expenses during this developmental period.

During the next several years, the rep did an outstanding job of opening up new accounts for the manufacturer. The rep was well liked by her customers, and the company was very satisfied with the amount of effort that had been devoted by the rep to the company's products. In fact, management readily acknowledged that the rep's knowledge of the customers in her market had clearly been the primary factor that enabled the company to penetrate this market with such rapid success.

Sales in this territory were now at a level large enough to support the company's own captive rep, and so, the company was not planning on renewing its contract with the independent agent. Rather, it would replace her with one of its own salespeople.

Question: Is this company acting ethically if it replaced the independent rep with one of its own salespeople?

but not on their low-volume accounts. Even then, team selling is likely to be used only in complex situations involving a large capital expenditure, a long-term contract, customized products and services, or a new account.

The overriding consideration in the decision to use sales teams should be whether the approach is consistent with the needs of the buyer. If important customers or potential customers are using buying teams for the complex purchasing decisions, then the sales organization should consider using multifunctional sales teams to call on these customers.

Independent Sales Organizations

Most producers use some type of wholesaling or retailing intermediaries to get their products to the final customer. According to the most recent U.S. Census of Retail Trade, less than 5 percent of the dollar volume of products bought by household consumers is purchased directly from producers.[16] In business goods, the dollar volume of direct sales—producer to business user—is very high. But most business-goods producers also use some type of wholesaling intermediary. Most producers, then, rely in part on using someone else's sales force to move the product to market. At the same time, these intermediaries must be sold on representing a certain producer and selling the producer's products. In effect, an intermediary's organization becomes both a customer and a sales force for this producer.

The two major categories of these independent sales forces are independent agents (such as manufacturers' representatives) and wholesale distributors.

Independent Agents

Many producers, either with or without their own sales forces, rely heavily on the sales forces of **independent agents** to reach the market. These agents are wholesaling intermediaries that do not take ownership title to the products they sell, and they usually do not carry inventory stocks. Independent agents are paid a commission on the sales they make. Consequently, the commission is a variable expense to a producer—that is, a producer doesn't pay if no sale is made.

The most widely used type of agent is a **manufacturers' representative,** also called a **manufacturers' agent** or simply a **rep**. A single producer usually uses several manufacturers' agents, each having a specified geographical territory. Each agent has its own sales force and generally represents several manufacturers of related, but not directly competing, products. Manufacturers' reps are most often used in the following situations:

- When a manufacturer does not have a sales force. (The rep then does all the selling.)
- When a producer wants to introduce a new product but for some reason does not want its existing sales force to handle it.
- When a company wants to enter a new market that is not yet sufficiently developed for the seller to use its own sales force.
- When it is not cost-effective for a company to use its own reps to call on certain accounts because the sales potential does not justify the cost.

From a producer's point of view, there are advantages in using the sales forces of manufacturers' agents. These reps know their market and have already established relations with prospective accounts. An individual producer, on the other hand, especially one new in the market, probably will not have the same access to customers.[17] Another benefit of using reps is that it is less expensive in sparsely populated markets, with smaller accounts, or with a limited line of products. For example, Lucent Technologies uses independent reps to sell its smaller customers. These reps generate 10 percent of the company's revenues.[18]

Wholesale Distributors

Wholesale Distributors are another type of independent sales organization that producers may use to reach their final customers. Wholesalers—also called *jobbers, distributors,* or *industrial distributors,* depending on the industry—are intermediaries who take ownership title to the products they sell. They also carry a physical inventory of these products. Wholesalers may represent only one producer, but most often they represent many producers of related and competing products. A large percentage of producers, especially producers of business (industrial) products, use wholesale distributors.

Wholesalers can be very useful in selling situations where (1) individual sales are small, (2) the buying process is not highly specialized, or (3) rapid delivery and local service facilities are important.

Independent versus Company Reps

Whether to use independent or company reps depends on the specific market the firm is trying to serve. As a basis for making the decision, a company must establish clear objectives for each of the markets it is targeting. Then it must develop strategies to achieve those objectives. The strategies will dictate whether the company should use its own captive salespeople, independent reps, or some combination of both.

Often the decision revolves around three considerations:

1. Which type of rep is most effective in achieving your objectives for the market?
2. Which method is the most economical
3. Which gives you the necessary amount of control in order to achieve your objectives?

The answer to which method is most effective in achieving your objectives depends directly on what those objectives are. For example, if the primary objective is to quickly achieve wide distribution for a new product, manufacturers' reps may be the best alternative for a company without an established company sales force. If the long-term objective is to develop partnerships with a certain group of customers, then it is probably best to serve those customers directly even though this may be an expensive alternative.

As illustrated in Figure 4-9, the answer to which is the most economical method is a function of (1) the potential volume in the particular market and (2) the cost of sales that is directly related to the number of company salespeople that would be required to serve that market. It also can be seen that the direct sales force has a variable cost-to-sales ratio, and the independents have a fixed cost-to-sales ratio. When sales are low, the direct cost-to-sales ratio will be high, but it decreases as volume rises, whereas the ratio for the independents stays the same regardless of the volume. Because of this, the use of direct salespeople becomes more economical at higher volumes. Generally, the volume in a market must be fairly substantial before a company can cover the costs of serving the customers with direct salespeople.

The question of control should be decided on the basis of how much control is needed to achieve the desired objectives. When a firm uses independent reps, it loses control over the amount of time devoted to its product lines because these reps usually represent more than one company. It also loses control over the approach and attention given to its customers. If the firm's customers each require a specialized approach and a great deal of attention, using independent reps may not be the way to achieve sales objectives. However, control in itself is not an objective; sometimes the objectives may be achieved more efficiently and effectively using independent reps.

Choosing an Independent Agent.   It is important to pick the very best agent available. In particular, the agent should be one who best matches the market strategy and the culture of the parent organization. The goals of the two organizations should be compatible, and the selling philosophies of the two should be the same. The product lines that the agent carries should complement those of the manufacturer, and the manufacturers' products should be the primary line for the agent. In order to be compatible, a parent company should devote the same amount of resources (time and money) to the selection of its independent agents as it would to the selection of its own company reps.

Managing the Independent Sales Force.   It is difficult enough to run your own sales force, but you face further organizational challenges when you use independent sales reps—whether agents or distributors. The biggest and perhaps the most obvious challenge is the one mentioned above—that the producer has

FIGURE 4-9
Captive versus independent
sales force

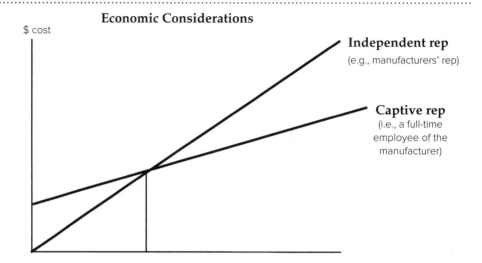

Economic Considerations

$ cost

Independent rep
(e.g., manufacturers' rep)

Captive rep
(i.e., a full-time
employee of the
manufacturer)

very little control over the independent sales force. This factor creates at least two managerial problems. First, a producer must compete with other firms for the selling time of the agent's or distributor's salespeople. This is a particularly tough challenge if the manufacturer and its products are not well known. Second, it is difficult to get manufacturers' reps to service an account and perform non-selling activities because they get no commission for such work.

There is no perfect solution to the second problem because the top independent agents will have their choice of companies to represent. They do not need your company to survive and will not put up with attempts to control their actions. Therefore, the best strategy is to provide your reps with the proper amount of support. This may involve training the salespeople of the agent or distributor. The manufacturer also can provide technical product information and can have a missionary sales force that does promotional work supporting the intermediary's efforts. Providing the appropriate level of support will alleviate the control problems. Furthermore, it is important to work with the reps as partners, making joint decisions on issues that affect the sales of products in the markets the reps serve.

E-Commerce and Inside Sales

In Chapter 1 we said that this book deals with the management of a sales force that goes to the customer. But an increasing number of firms—both large and small—have moved some selling efforts from outside to within the company. Instead of making face-to-face sales calls, salespeople are "going to the customer" by using telephones, email, screen-sharing software, video, and a variety of social media.

Telephone selling is not new. What is new today, however, is the innovative use of communication systems to aid selling efforts and other marketing activities. Generally, **inside sales** (or sometimes called telemarketing) refers to situations in which a customer is contacted by a sales rep via telephone, and **e-commerce** refers to situations in which communication with the customer is carried out through the internet (often via e-mail). Inside sales and e-commerce both generate hundreds of billions of dollars in sales revenues for business-to-business firms.[19] In fact, these revenues represent over one third of the total business-to-business market, and they are expected to continue to grow.[20]

Two main reasons for the growing use of e-commerce and inside sales as forms of sales specialization are (1) many buyers prefer them over personal sales calls in certain selling situations and (2) many marketers find that they increase selling efficiency. For a buyer, placing routine reorders or new orders for standardized products by computer or by telephone takes less time than fielding in-person sales calls. For a seller, keeping salespeople on the road means facing increasingly high costs, so any selling done via the internet or over the phone reduces such expenses. Also, using e-commerce or inside sales for routine selling allows the field sales force to devote more time to developmental selling; major-account selling; and other, more profitable selling activities.

In some cases, e-commerce or inside sales is the primary interface with the customer. For example, Dell Computer Company, with over $500 million in personal computer sales, launched its business through telephone sales and still does the majority of its business through this channel.[21] Owens Corning, the maker of Fiberglas, is another company that relies primarily on a variety of e-commerce platforms for serving its customers.[22] These companies used their reps exclusively to develop customer solutions for their most important accounts. On the other hand, many companies are trying to extend coverage by providing customers a choice of how they wish to do business: via email, online chat, video conferencing, phone, fax, or by meeting with a rep. Consolidated Freightways and Automatic Data Processing (ADP) have each extended this strategy even further by allowing customers to switch from making unassisted online transactions to speaking with a rep, either online or by telephone, merely by clicking the appropriate box on the company website.[23]

Some companies, such as Hewlett-Packard and IBM, use telephone reps or e-commerce to handle small or low-priority sales. This allows the direct sales reps to concentrate on bigger potential accounts.[24] In these inside sales programs, the rep is responsible for qualifying customers as to their sales potential, assessing their needs, recommending products and services, taking orders, and providing customer service.

As noted in Chapter 1, many companies us the internet and inside sales to assist the sales force. Estimates of the increases in sales in these situations range anywhere from 10 percent to 400 percent. Shachihata, which sells pre-inked rubber stamps through independent reps, created a consumer development department whose sole function is to follow up on leads and generate appointments for the reps. This led to an increase in appointments of four to five times the number generated the previous year.[25] Eastman Chemical customers can track orders, obtain account information, and receive technical assistance online 24 hours a day.[26] Other companies use inside sales to provide after-sale service to customers. General Electric (GE) is famous for its "Answer Center," whose 250 telephone operators answer 3 million inquiries a year concerning GE products that the customers have purchased or are considering purchasing.[27]

The selling activities performed by e-commerce or inside sales can be summarized as follows:

- Identification of prospective customers.
- Qualification of sales leads (including screening and referral).

CONSIDER THIS...

An International Perspective

Even when a company chooses to employ its own sales force, it still must decide whether to hire foreign reps or reps from its own country. Foreign nationals are familiar with the local customs and culture but unfamiliar with the product and the company's marketing practices. The company reps, on the other hand, know the product and the company but are unfamiliar with the local customs and culture.

The answer to this question can be found be examining the needs and desires of the customers. Research on similarity in sales has generally demonstrated that, all other things being equal, the customers would rather be served by someone who is similar to themselves. Therefore, it is probably better to hire a national from

your target market unless there are some overriding reasons not to. For example, some products are so complex that the salespeople may require extensive training and/or experience before they can sell these products. It may not be economically feasible to provide the amount of in-depth training that would be needed if the company hires inexperienced nationals, or it may not be possible to find enough qualified individuals in the target country.

If a company does hire foreign nationals, it should provide adequate product and company training. Likewise, if a company hires reps from its own country, it should provide extensive training in the cultural norms of the foreign market.

- Sales solicitation.
- Order processing.
- Product service support.
- Account management.
- Customer relations management.
- Competitive reporting.
- Expense reporting.

In most companies, inside sales or e-commerce is not the exclusive method used to generate and service sales. It has not replaced the direct selling effort, but rather it is used to supplement the direct efforts in some way. As we noted in Chapter 2, many companies are using hybrid selling channels to reach customers more efficiently; inside sales or e-commerce is often one of the channels.

ORGANIZING FOR INTERNATIONAL SALES

American sales organizations continue to go global at an increasing rate. In fact, the number of American businesses selling goods and services abroad has tripled since 1990. These firms are taking advantage of the tremendous and sustained economic growth of several developing countries—especially those in eastern Asia, such as China (*The Wall Street Journal*). Research shows that companies that engage in exporting are 9 percent less likely to fail in any given year than similar firms that do not.[28] Additionally, international trade is being actively promoted by a number of trade organizations and agreements that are lessening the trade barriers around the world. The most important of these is the **World Trade Organization (WTO)**, which currently has more than 140 member countries around the globe. Important agreements in the United States include both the **North American Free Trade Agreement (NAFTA)**, which was passed in 1994, and the **Central American Free Trade Agreement (CAFTA)**, signed in 2005. These agreements eliminate trade barriers between the United States and many of its fellow North American countries, and thus make it easier to sell in these places. This trend toward globalization presents challenges in terms of how to organize the sales force. A company has essentially three options with regard to distributing its products internationally: (1) turn over the export of its product to home-country intermediaries, (2) partner with foreign-country intermediaries, or (3) establish its own company sales force in the foreign country.

Home-Country Intermediaries

Depending on the products, there are a number of export intermediaries, located in the producing firm's country, who provide international marketing services from a domestic base. Firms such as export merchants, trading companies, export management companies, agents, and distributors all offer international sales and distribution services for those companies that do not wish to become immediately involved in the complexities of international sales or that want to sell abroad with a minimum financial and management commitment. Assistance in locating and selecting the proper intermediary is provided by a variety of sources, including the American Association of Exporters and Importers as well as the U.S. Department of Commerce.

Even in the case of minimum involvement, the company must make a number of critical sales management decisions. Sales managers must identify the appropriate agent or distributor and must reach an agreement with that intermediary regarding services and compensation. It also may be necessary to train personnel and to establish a system for monitoring sales results.

Foreign-Country Intermediaries

Many small and midsize firms that decide to establish a sales organization in a foreign country cannot afford to employ their own international sales forces. Therefore, many manufacturers set up a network of manufacturers' agents, distributors (wholesalers), and/or dealers (retailers) in foreign markets. In many cases, these independent organizations are already selling other products and services in the target country. In addition to personal selling, these intermediaries perform many services, including advertising products, providing market information, making repairs, collecting invoices, and settling disputes. In return, the American firms usually grant the intermediaries exclusive territorial sales rights and may grant one wholesaler the sole distributorship for an entire country.

In foreign markets without sufficient sales potential to justify establishing a company sales force, such as those in developing countries, distributors are used. Other markets are so large geographically that a company may use independent reps to cover the outlying areas and company salespeople to cover the population centers.

Cultural diversity also affects this decision. Some multilingual, culturally heterogeneous markets require several different reps to deal with customers from the varying cultural groups. This is often the case in the markets in Southeast Asia.

Foreign intermediaries are generally less aggressive and perform fewer marketing activities than their American counterparts, but some of the factors described above often make it difficult for the company to bypass them. If a company decides to use foreign-company intermediaries, it must first identify the prospective candidates. As with home-country intermediaries, the U.S. Department of Commerce is one of several sources that help companies locate the appropriate foreign-based intermediary for their products. Other sources include foreign consulates, foreign chambers of commerce, trade associations, and published directories, such as *The Standard Handbook of Industrial Distributors.*

Company Sales Force Operating Abroad

In a country where the volume and profit potential warrants it and government regulations allow it, an American firm may establish its own company sales force. These sales forces may sell directly to the final customers, or they may sell through local distributors and dealers. Using its own sales force enables a company to (1) promote products more aggressively and (2) control its sales effort more completely. For example, Boston Scientific Corporation, a manufacturer of medical devices, shifted from using local distributors to employing its own sales and marketing personnel in twenty international markets.[2] This ensures that customers receive the proper training and assistance; and thus, this approach is more common for complex products. In addition, the company's legal liability with regard to the use of its products also may compel them to use their own sales force.

Previously in this chapter, the concept of **global account management (GAM)** was discussed (along with key or strategic account management). GAM is a sales force structure that delivers service and products across the globe to the subsidiaries of multinational customers in a coordinated way. Consequently, GAM necessarily involves a company's sales force operating abroad. For example, Xerox uses a GAM structure that involves various sales teams, each being dedicated to a single, global customer. One such customer is BMW, the German automobile manufacturer. By dealing with BMW on a global basis, the Xerox sales team can provide a single set of prices to BMW for all of its many facilities across the world (of course, the prices may be adjusted for differing tariffs, transportation fees, etc.). In years past, these dealings were negotiated on a country-by-country basis, and thus were less efficient. The reason that many sales organizations have moved toward GAM is simple: Customers have demanded it!

SUMMARY

An organization is an arrangement of activities involving a group of people. The goal is to arrange the activities so that the people who are involved can work better *together* than they can *individually.* The sales force organizational structure has a significant influence on the implementation of a company's strategic planning.

The general characteristics of a good organization are (1) an organizational structure that reflects a market orientation; (2) an organization that is built around activities and not around the people performing these activities; (3) responsibilities that are clearly spelled out, and sufficient authority granted to meet the responsibilities; (4) a reasonable span of executive control; (5) stability combined with flexibility; and (6) balanced and coordinated activities both *within* the sales department and *between* sales and non-marketing departments.

Most sales organizations can be classified into one of three basic categories: a line organization, a line-and-staff organization, or a functional organization. A line organization is the simplest form of organization and is often appropriate for small firms. A line-and-staff organization enables a company to use staff assistants who are specialists in various areas of marketing. A functional organization carries specialization a step further by giving more line authority to the executive specialists. Also, a new horizontal structure being used by a number of firms is a much flatter organization with fewer levels of management.

In most medium- and large-sized companies, the sales forces are divided on some basis of sales specialization. The most frequently used bases are (1) geographical territories, (2) type of product sold, (3) classes of customer, or (4) some combination of these categories.

Giving each sales representative the responsibility for his or her own geographical territory is probably the most widely used form of sales force specialization. Specializing a sales force by type of product sold is often used when a company sells unrelated products, highly technical products, or several thousands of products. Product specialization also may involve the organizational concept of a product manager. Specialization by markets may be done on a channel-of-distribution basis or on an industry basis.

In the organization of an outside sales force, the use of the following four organizational strategies is increasing: key account management, team selling, independent sales forces, and e-commerce and inside sales. For key account management, firms may use a separate sales force or executives, or they may establish a separate division. Selling teams comprised of people from several departments are being used to match the needs of customer buying centers. Sometimes a firm cannot afford or does not want to have its own sales force; in that case, it will use some type of independent agent, such as manufacturers' reps or wholesale distributors. E-commerce and inside sales are sometimes used as the primary selling method, but often used only to assist the sales force.

Organizing for international sales also presents some difficult challenges for sales management. Companies must decide whether to use independent selling organizations in the home country or in the foreign country, or to employee their own salespeople. Even if the company decides to use its own salespeople, it must still determine whether it will hire reps from its own country or foreign nationals.

KEY TERMS

Buying center

Central American Free Trade Agreement (CAFTA)

Citizenship behaviors

E-commerce

Functional organization

Global account management (GAM)

Horizontal organization

Independent agent

Informal organization	Market specialization	Product staff
Inside sales (or	North American Free	specialization
telemarketing)	Trade Agreement	Selling centers
Key account manage-	(NAFTA)	Selling team
ment (KAM)	Organization	Strategic account man-
Line-and-staff	Product managers	agement (SAM)
organization	Product operating	Wholesale distributors
Line organization	specialization	World Trade Organiza-
Manufacturers'	Product specialization	tion (WTO)
representative	organization	

QUESTIONS AND PROBLEMS

1. What are the reasons for the lack of coordination that sometimes exists between advertising executives and field sales managers? What are some proposals for developing better coordination between these two groups?

2. Explain how each of the following factors may influence the organizational structure of a firm:

   a. Size of company.

   b. Nature of products.

   c. Nature and density of the market.

   d. Ability of executives.

   e. Financial condition of the company.

3. In your opinion, what are the best policies or procedures for solving the following problems, which are often found in a line-and-staff organization?

   a. A strong-willed staff executive tries to take on line authority instead of remaining an adviser

   b. A line executive consistently bypasses or ignores advice from staff departments.

4. What type of organizational specialization within the sales department do you recommend in each of the following companies?

   a. Manufacturer of high-quality women's sportswear with 100 salespeople selling to department stores and specialty stores throughout the nation.

   b. Plumbing wholesaler covering the southeastern quarter of the country with 50 salespeople.

   c. Manufacturer of chemicals used in fertilizers with 35 salespeople selling to 500 accounts located throughout the country.

   d. Manufacturer of office machines with 1,000 salespeople.

5. A regional hardware wholesaler in Detroit, Michigan, employed 20 salespeople, each of whom sold the full line of products. It became apparent that the list of products was simply too long for one

person to sell effectively. Which of the following two choices do you recommend?

   a.   Reorganizing the sales force by product lines or

   b.   Adding more representatives, reducing each person's territory, but still having each carry the full line.

6. A manufacturer of small aircraft designed for executive transportation in large companies has decided to implement the concept of a selling center. What people in this company should be on the selling teams? What problems is this firm likely to encounter when it uses team selling?

7. How does the quote: "Listen to the customer and act on what they tell you," relate to the concepts discussed in the first four chapters?

8. What courses of action would you propose for a company that wants to get its manufacturers' reps to devote more time to selling its products?

9. A manufacturer of small motors uses industrial distributors to reach its market. What can this producer do to encourage the distributors to spend more time selling the company's products?

10. A manufacturer of playground equipment now uses its own sales force to sell directly to customer groups such as city park departments, school districts, private day nurseries, and companies that maintain day care centers for employees' children. This producer would like to install a telemarketing system to reduce some of its field-selling costs. What are the problems that this seller is likely to encounter in this move toward inside sales? What recommendations do you have for solving these problems?

11. A U.S. manufacturer of industrial tools wants to market its products overseas. It is considering establishing sales organizations in several different countries. Discuss whether or not the manufacturer should use an independent selling organization or its own sales force—for each of the following countries:

   a.   Switzerland.

   b.   Malaysia.

   c.   Spain.

   d.   China

EXPERIENTIAL EXERCISES

1. Obtain an organizational chart for a firm that sells consumer products and a firm that sells industrial products. Compare and contrast the sales organization structure in terms of span of control, centralization, specialization, line-and-staff components, and so on.

2. Contact an executive from any small organization and ask about the formal organizational relationships. Without seeing the firm's organizational chart (if there is one), draw an organizational chart based on the information given to you by the executive. Does this organization

violate any of the principles of organizational design? Compare your organizational chart with the firm's official chart.

3. Contact a manufacturers' rep for any type of product. Find out what criteria reps use to select the manufacturers they are willing to represent. Also determine what types of assistance the various manufacturers they represent provide to the manufacturers' rep.

4. Visit the LinkedIn profiles of several salespeople/account managers and try to determine the specialization structure used by their companies--for example, is it by product, by type of customer, by geography, or some combination of these factors.

TELIN, INC.
Outsourcing Sales through Manufacturers' Reps

Telin is one of the world's largest manufacturers of semiconductors, also known as computer chips. Telin is an international company with over $30 billion in annual sales revenue, just under 100,000 employees, and a ranking of about 50 in the Fortune 500. Since its start in 1980, Telin has sold its semiconductors to the leading manufacturers of personal computers (PCs). Telin has sold these products through its own employee salespeople, who are highly educated and trained electrical engineers. These members of the Telin sales force pride themselves on the close relationship they have built with their customers, the PC makers.

However, after years of phenomenal growth, the PC market has begun to level off. This has led Telin to develop new lines of more specialized products. These products still use the same technology found in Telin's computer chips, but they are much more versatile. In other words, they can be integrated into a wide range of products *other than* PCs. The new Telin chips can be used in cell phones, video game machines, toys, and a variety of Internet data processing products.

The following exchange is between two Telin sales executives: Jim Pierce and Pam Mudge. These executives disagree as to how to organize the sales force that will be selling these new products. Jim Pierce believes Telin should sell the new line of products through its own product-specialized sales force (i.e., he wants Telin to hire a separate group of 20 salespeople that would exclusively sell the new product line to the manufacturers of cell phones, etc.). Pam Mudge, on the other hand, believes the new line could be sold more effectively and efficiently through manufacturers' reps.

Jim Pierce: You want to *outsource* the sales function? You're crazy!

Pam Mudge: Well, I think we should use manufacturers' reps to sell our new products—I didn't really think of that as "outsourcing" sales.

Jim Pierce: But that's exactly what you're proposing. Manufacturers' reps are not our employees. They're independent agents working for themselves—not us. To me, it's no different than outsourcing our payroll process or janitorial service, except that salespeople are much more important to our success.

Pam Mudge: You can call it "outsourcing" or whatever you want, but I still think it's the best idea.

Jim Pierce: Well, I think it's a terrible idea. Our salespeople are our link to the customers. Customers form their impression of Telin through the salespeople. I would hate to leave that to some manufacturers' rep who does not even work for us.

Pam Mudge: What do you think we should do?

Jim Pierce: I think we should hire 20 salespeople to focus exclusively on the new product lines. Our own captive product-specialized sales force is what we need. They could focus on developing relationships with our new set of clients. Building and maintaining those relationships was the key to our success with the PC makers.

Pam Mudge: Yes, but it took a long time to develop those relationships with IBM, Dell, and all the other PC manufacturers. Our brand name means next to nothing in these new markets, and we need to move fast. There are manufacturers' reps that have already established relationships with the companies in this new market. We have very little time. Hiring and training a whole new sales force could take a couple of years.

Jim Pierce: We'd hire salespeople with backgrounds in electrical engineering—they should catch on pretty quickly…

Pam Mudge: Did you ever think about how much it would cost to hire and then train all those engineers? I mean, they'd probably each expect a compensation package worth well over $100,000 apiece! Training them would cost tens of thousands of dollars more. Manufacturers' reps are experienced salespeople that are already trained, and we'd pay them 100 percent commission, so they'd only cost us money if they were successful. It's much less risky.

Jim Pierce: Yes, but how could they be successful at selling our products when Telin is just one of maybe 20 companies they represent! What percent of their time do you think they'll devote to *our products*?

Pam Mudge: I don't know, but actually these other products they sell *complement* our products—they don't compete with them! So the manufacturers' reps can provide total solutions to our customers. Sure, our own salespeople would focus 100 percent on Telin products, but customers might rather see a salesperson who is selling them everything they need.

Jim Pierce: I thought manufacturers' reps were for small companies that couldn't afford their own sales force. Our total sales revenue last year was over $30 billion!

Pam Mudge: Jim, there are lots of big companies that use manufacturers' reps, including Motorola, IBM, and Texas Instruments, to name a few.

Jim Pierce: I guess I didn't know that. But still, it scares me to outsource our sales function.

Pam Mudge: We have to think about new ways of organizing our business. I'm convinced that manufacturers' reps are the best way to pursue this new market.

Questions:

1. Evaluate the strengths and weaknesses of Telin using:

   a. Its own, product-specialized sales force for its new line of products.

   b. Manufacturers' reps to sell its new line of products.

2. Which side are you on? Explain your answer.

MICROPLASTICS, INC.
Need for Reorganization

"Perhaps a bit of history regarding our sales organization will help you in your coming weeks as our new sales manager," said Don Lopez, president of Microplastics, Inc., to Katie Curry, the firm's new sales manager. "The company had been organized twenty years ago to manufacture precise, small plastic parts that were sold directly to other manufacturers, particularly high-technology industries."

Lopez continued, "It seems as if our sales force has been in a constant state of upheaval for the past five years. A year hasn't gone by but that we reorganized it some way or another. But nothing seems to work. Let me go back to when we started, and trace our troubles for you. Our growth had been great in the early days of our industry. We had little direct competition and we were making plenty of money, sold everything we could make. Then competition came into the market and we hit a recession. Sales dropped 40 percent and profits turned to losses. At first we thought that it was happening to everyone, but soon we discovered that our competitors were not being hit as hard as we were. Their salespeople seemed to be able to sell into accounts where our people couldn't.

"We became most unhappy with our sales organization, which at the time consisted of 28 people who reported to one sales manager. We fired the sales manager and brought in a man from one of our most successful competitors. It cost some money to get him, but we were willing to pay it. Well, right off the bat this bozo wants to hire three assistant sales managers to supervise the sales force, a sales training director to train them, a sales analyst for the home office, and a home-office sales engineer to back up the field sales force technically."

That's a lot of money," Katie Curry commented when Lopez paused. "How did he justify it to you?"

"I remember it well because it scared me to death," Lopez said. "He said that if we wanted to be a big-time company, we would have to do things the way the big boys do them. He insisted that the key to success was to back up the field people with tremendous support from the home office and supervise them closely in the field."

"Well, how did it work out?"

"Need you ask? Sales stayed about the same but our costs skyrocketed. We lost our shirts. I never saw such confusion. No one seemed to know what they were supposed to do. So we fired the sales manager and promoted one of the sales reps to the job. He immediately cleaned out all of the staff the other fellow had hired, so we were back to square one. But not quite."

"Oh, did the new manager make some changes?" Curry asked.

"He felt that our real problem was that the reps couldn't sell to all types of customers, so he divided them into two groups. The first bunch of 10 reps was to sell to the large manufacturers, where there was a lot of engineering work to be done with the customer's people. The second group was to cover the smaller assemblers, where engineering was not so important and where you dealt with the owner directly," Lopez explained.

"What happened?"

"Mass confusion! The reps didn't want to give up their customers, so they held on to them as long as they could. And it didn't seem to help sales. We didn't sell any more large accounts than we were previously selling. The guy got tired of managing and asked to go back into the field where he felt he knew what to do.

"You can bet that the next sales manager was selected with a lot more care," Lopez continued. "We interviewed more than 20 people until we found this fellow who had a terrific record over at National Plastics. We thought we had a barn burner in him. He came in, surveyed the situation, and wrote a report for me on what had to be done."

"You're shaking your head. What went wrong?" Curry inquired.

"He personally spent a day with each sales representative to diagnose what was wrong with the operation," said Lopez. "On the basis of his judgment, 19 of our reps were incompetent, with no hope of ever becoming the type of salesperson he thought was needed to do the job. He planned to fire them immediately. Then he would call in the remaining nine reps for an intensive training program to teach them how to sell the way he wanted them to. I remember vividly how he leaned over my desk with his fists clenched and sternly said, 'My sales force will sell the way I want them to sell or they won't be around.' Well, we had some words over that report. I just could not let him fire 19 people who had been with us from the beginning and who had helped us build the company. I wanted him to train all of them, but he said it couldn't be done. They just weren't his 'type of people.' That kind of talk really gets my goat. He was putting these people down like they were dirt, and I told him so. Well, one thing led to another, and there went the new sales manager."

"And you had no inkling of this aspect of his personality before hiring him?" Curry asked.

Lopez drew a deep breath and confessed, "I must say that we did. His previous boss described him as one tough, driving guy who was hard to live with but who really got results. I guess all we wanted to hear was that he got results. We didn't stop to think about how he got them."

"And so here we are," Curry summarized. "You want to know what I have discovered and what I intend to do about it."

"That's it!" said Lopez. "Have you anything to report yet?"

"It's a bit premature now to lay out a program for you," she replied, "but the seeds of it are in everything that has happened previously. I'll be ready next Friday for a report on my proposed program."

"Fair enough," said Lopez.

Curry had already made up her mind about what needed to be done, but she did not want to reveal it until she had figured out how to go about it. She had quickly related to everything that had been told her. The sales manager who had wanted to reorganize for some staff support was right. The span of control was ridiculous, and the reps were getting little support from the home office. The second manager had been right in seeing that the reps were not equally effective in selling to all types of customers. The third manager was certainly correct in his appraisal of the reps. The sales force had some people with mediocre talents. For the most part, they constituted a seedy crew that had looked good in the early days of the industry before competition became a factor in the market. But she realized that here would be little she could do about this problem immediately. It would have to be worked on over a lengthy period. For the time being, she had to develop a means for working with these people, and that seemed to call for some sort of reorganization.

Questions:

1. What changes should the new sales manager recommend?

[1] Although this scenario is based on information gathered from studying LinkedIn profiles in June, 2016, the name of the key manager is fictional.

[2] Microsoft Corporation, "Q&A: Microsoft Realigns U.S. Sales Structure for Better Customer Service and Deeper industry Focus," press release, April 13, 2005, from http://www.microsoft.com/presspass/features/2005/apr05/04-13SalesStructure.mspx (accessed March 20, 2006). http://news.microsoft.com/2005/04/13/qa-microsoft-realigns-u-s-sales-structure-for-better-customer-service-and-deeper-industry-focus/ (accessed June 1, 2015).

[3] Phillip M. Podsakoff and Scott B. MacKenzie, "Organizational Citizenship Behaviors and Sales Unit Effectiveness," *Journal of Marketing Research*, August 1994, pp. 351-63.

[4] John A. Byrne, "The Horizontal Corporation," *BusinessWeek*, December 20, 1993, pp. 76-81.

[5] George S. Day, "Aligning the Organization to the Market," Prakash Nedungadi Memorial Lecture, Indiana University School of Business, January 1997.

[6] Geoffrey Brewer, "Brain Power," *Sales & Marketing Management*, May 1997, pp. 39-41.

[7] Sanjit Sengupta, Robert E. Krapfel, and Michael A. Pusateri, "An Empirical Investigation of Key Account Salesperson Effectiveness," *Journal of Personal Selling & Sales Management*, Fall 2000, p. 253.

[8] Daniel S. Levine, "Justice Served," *Sales & Marketing Management*, May 1995, pp. 53-58.

[9] Kerry J. Rottenberger-Murtha, "The Lean and the Green," *Sales & Marketing Management*, February 1993, pp. 68-71.

[10] Erika Rasmusson, "3M's Big Strategy for Big Accounts," *Sales & Marketing Management*, September 2000, pp. 92-98.

[11] Geoffrey Brewer, "Love the Ones You're With," *Sales & Marketing Management*, February 1999, pp. 40-41.

[12] Neil Rackham, "The Other Revolution in Sales," *Sales & Marketing Management*, March 2000, p. 36.

[13] Rahul Jacob, "Why Some Customers Are More Equal Than Others," *Fortune*, September 19, 1994, pp. 215-20.

[14] Ibid.

[15] Joseph Conlin, "Teaming Up," *Sales & Marketing Management*, October 1993, pp. 98-104.

[16] U.S. Census of Retail Trade, 2000.

[17] Kimberly Weisul, "Do You Dare Outsource Sales?" *BusinessWeek Online*, June 18, 2001.

[18] Dan Hoover, "Independents Day," *Sales & Marketing Management*, April 2000, pp. 66-67.

[19] Melinda Ligos, "Clicks and Misses," *Sales & Marketing Management*, June 2000, p. 69.

[20] "Telemarketing Cited as Chief Form of Direct Marketing," *Marketing News*, January 1, 1996, p. 9.

[21] Erika Rasmusson, "Best at E-Business," *Sales & Marketing Management*, July 2000, p. 72.

[22] Don Peppers and Martha Rogers, "Build Stronger Relationships," *Sales & Marketing Management*, July 2000, p. 50.

[23] Danielle Hall, "Get Closer to More Customers," *Sales & Marketing Management*, May 2000, p. 2; and Christine Galea, "Planning a Web Relaunch," *Sales & Marketing Management*, May 2000, p. 118.

[24] Tim Clark, "Sales Force Weaves New Strategies," *Business Marketing, May 1993, pp. 26, 32.*

[25] John F. Yarbrough, "Salvaging a Lousy Year," *Sales & Marketing Management*, July 1996, p. 72.

[26] Gabrielle Birkner, "Eastman Draws Customers On-Line," *Sales & Marketing Management*, June 2000, pp. 41-42.

[27] Aimee L. Stern, "Telemarketing Polishes Its Image," *Sales & Marketing Management*, June 1991, pp. 107-10.

[28] SBA Web site, www.sba.gov/managing/marketing/intlsales.html.

[29] Slade Sohmer, "Emerging as a Global Sales Success," *Sales & Marketing Management*, May 2000, pp. 124-25.

5

Profiling and Recruiting Salespeople

Fastenal, the world's largest distributor of hardware fasteners (e.g., screws, bolts, rivets, etc.), understands that its success is strongly tied to its ability to hire the right people for its sales force. In particular, this multibillion-dollar organization looks for ambitious, hardworking individuals that are adept at building relationships with its business customers through superior service. Profiling and recruiting salespeople is an ongoing, continuous process at Fastenal, which actively looks to fill its entry-level sales positions from a number of sources, including universities.

Jason Heaster, a District Sales Manager from Fastenal, explains why his company generally prefers to recruit college students over experienced salespeople: "From what we've found over the years in recruiting and trying to develop a good sales force, we find that students are easier to train because they don't have preconceived notions about how to sell. Experienced salespeople, on the other hand, sometimes are slower to adapt to our culture." But like almost all sales organizations, Fastenal does not focus exclusively on a single recruiting source. "We also place job ads on employment websites, like monster.com—and often we get names of excellent candidates from referrals made by members of our existing sales force."[1]

Companies look to several recruiting sources because finding the right salespeople is both difficult and important. In fact, most sales professionals agree that this is one of the greatest challenges in sales management today. The process is long, complicated and can be quite expensive. The costs associated with recruiting, interviewing, hiring, orienting and training one new employee are estimated to be more than the employee's annual compensation—easily into the six figure range.[2] These costs are higher due to the lost productivity during the transition time; because even after new hires start their job, they typically do not reach the performance levels of existing salespeople for a year or two.

Of course, hiring the *wrong* person for the job confounds the problem, and is especially expensive!

As we have learned in earlier chapters, there are a wide variety of roles and responsibilities of a sales manager; but *staffing the sales force is arguably the most important activity.* That is, it is absolutely critical for sales executives to effectively recruit and hire the right people; and this process should be ongoing and continuous—as it is at Fastenal.

CONSIDER THIS...

Employer Brand

A strong employer brand helps sales organizations successfully recruit the best people for the job. Google, Microsoft and Apple all have strong employer brands, which means that both current and prospective employees believe those companies are great places to work.

LinkedIn created a talent brand index to categorize companies into strong and weak employer brands. An analysis showed these three ways that a strong employer brand positively impacts a firm's recruiting efforts:

- The amount of applicants per job more than doubles.
- The cost per hire decreases by 43%.
- New hires are 40% less likely to leave after the first 6 months.

SOURCE: Alyssa Sittig, "LinkedIn Data Proves the Impact of a Strong Talent Brand," *LinkedIn Talent Blog*, March 17, 2015. Accessed June 9, 2016 from https://business.linkedin.com/talent-solutions/blog/2015/03/the-roi-of-talent-brand

SALES FORCE SELECTION AND STRATEGIC PLANNING

In most organizations, the sales force is the one group that directly generates the revenues for the organization. Thus, the sales force is the group most directly involved in carrying out the company's strategic marketing plans. How well these plans are implemented depends to a great extent on the choice of salespeople. Certainly the selection process should be consistent with the company's strategic marketing planning and its sales force planning.

Let's look at some practical applications of the relationship between sales force selection and strategic marketing planning. Assume that a company's goal is to maintain its leading market position and its market share. One major marketing strategy may be to provide considerable service to existing accounts. The sales rep's job consists primarily of existing-account maintenance rather than new-account development. This affects selection because the two tasks—maintenance and development—usually call for different types of salespeople.

As another example, the company may adopt a strategy of promoting from within as part of its strategic planning for the development of future executives. Hiring older, experienced sales reps at high salaries probably would not be a sound way to implement such a strategy.

The selection process also should be strategically integrated with all aspects of sales force management. If a company has no sales training program, it should not recruit inexperienced students just graduating from college. If management prefers to hire people right from college, the firm had better institute a training program.

Adding Minority Reps to the Sales Force

There were seldom any vacancies on the Shiderlots sales force, and sales manager Adam Dark was proud of that fact. He had several applications from available recruits on an informal waiting list, and he tried to keep the facts on these applicants up to date. Occasionally unsolicited applications were received, and some were from unusual types of applicants. For example, Dark had once been urged to hire an ex-convict. Currently, Shiderlots sales force was composed of 5 men and 2 women, all of whom were white (Caucasian). On more than one occasion, Dark had been asked why the company had no minority account managers. These questions had come from a variety of people, including company executives, customers, and public officials. They made Dark feel uncomfortable as he did not have a good answer.

One afternoon when Dark was visiting Shiderlots headquarters, he was asked to come to the office of the company president, Rosann Speer. He found himself in a conference with Speer, several department heads, and two men who were introduced as representatives of the Affirmative Action Program in the U.S. Department of Health and Human Services (HHS).

The visitors explained that Shiderlots Elevator had been loyally served for many years by minority employees in a variety of blue-collar and white-collar positions. However, no minority people had ever held an account management job in Dark's branch office—and this included the many years before Dark had assumed his managerial position. The HHS representatives directly requested that Dark hire minorities or suffer censure through national publicity. Further, the visitors even provided well-prepared dossiers on several minority candidates with solid sales experience. As nearly as Dark could judge during a quick examination of these files, the people easily met the minimum standards he had maintained in his recruiting efforts.

The meeting continued after the visitors left. Dark expressed his concern that minority salespeople might find "rough sledding" on his sales force from certain customers. Dark also pointed out that there were no openings on the sales force now or in the near future. To accommodate a new rep, Dark said he would be forced either to discharge a salesperson now or create a new and unnecessary territory.

In closing the meeting, Speer said, "We'll have to look at this thing positively. Life could get mighty unpleasant for us if we don't!

Question: What action should Adam Dark take in this situation?

RUNNING CASE
Shiderlots
Elevator, Inc.

IMPORTANCE OF A GOOD SELECTION PROGRAM

Good **selection** is vital to the firm because, as noted earlier, it is the sales force that directly generates revenues for the firm. In this section, we further explore the reasons why a good sales selection program is essential.

- **Qualified salespeople are scarce.** For many reasons, good salespeople are hard to find. Selling does not have the high social prestige of some other careers and therefore may not attract the most top-notch candidates from colleges and universities. Indeed, a survey of students in a large introductory marketing class found that most students viewed selling in a negative way, associating it with door-to-door activities or with less-than-desirable personal traits, such as being pushy or obnoxious.[3] Furthermore, many young people are not aware of the opportunities provided by jobs in outside selling. They often equate selling with clerking in a retail store.

- **Good selection improves sales force performance.** The salesperson-recruiting process has a strong impact on profits. When a firm hires a salesperson whose performance is just acceptable rather than outstanding, it is forgoing additional sales revenues and profits that the outstanding rep would have generated. Also, a good selection program is likely to reduce sales force turnover and thus lead to improved sales performance.

- **Good selection promotes cost savings.** A good selection program brings about both direct and indirect cost benefits. Substantial *direct* cost savings are often generated when sales force turnover is reduced. A beginning salesperson may cost a company well over $100,000 before reaching productive status. This figure includes recruiting and selection costs, training and supervision costs, and salary and travel expenses. Well-chosen reps will provide a good return on the investment the company has made in them. The *indirect* cost benefits of good selection don't show up in accounting records, but they include the prevention of lost sales that can result from poor selection.

- **Good selection eases other managerial tasks.** Proper training, compensation, supervision, and motivation are vital to successful management of a sales force. However, if a company selects the right people for the sales job, training is easier, less supervision is required, and motivation is less difficult.

- **Sales managers are no better than their sales force.** No matter how good a manager he or she is, an executive with a poor sales force cannot surpass a competitor who has much better salespeople.

THE LAW AND SALES FORCE SELECTION

Increasingly, firms are held responsible for the legality of their recruiting and selection policies. Although certain aspects of the selection process may be performed by the human resources department, the sales manager most often makes the final hiring decisions. Sales managers must therefore understand the complex laws that govern sales force selection policies. Figure 5-1 summarizes the particular laws and other regulations directly related to sales force selection. Federal legislation and related regulatory guidelines emphasize two concepts in employment: nondiscrimination and affirmative action. **Nondiscrimination** requires employers to refrain from discriminating against anyone with regard to age, race, religion, sex, national origin, disability, or status as a veteran— and to eliminate all existing discriminatory conditions, whether intentional or inadvertent. **Affirmative action** requires employees to do more than ensure neutrality—they must *make additional efforts* to recruit, employ, and promote qualified members of groups formerly excluded. These efforts must be made even if that exclusion cannot be traced to discriminatory actions of the employer.

**Civil Rights Act of 1964—Prohibits discrimination based
on race, color, religion, nationality, or sex.**

**Federal Contract Compliance, Executive Orders—Ensures that federal
contractors and subcontractors with 50 or more employees will comply
with federal legislation and submit affirmative action plans.**

**Age Discrimination in Employment Act (1967)—
Prohibits discrimination based on age.**

**Fair Employment Opportunity Act (1972)—Established the Equal
Employment Opportunity Commission (EEOC) to ensure compliance
with the Civil Rights Act for firms with 25 workers or more.**

**Rehabilitation Act of 1973—Requires affirmative action to hire and
promote persons with disabilities if the firm employs 50 or more
workers and is seeking federal contracts in excess of $50,000.**

**Vietnam Era Veterans Readjustment Act (1974)—Requires
affirmative action to hire Vietnam veterans and disabled veterans
of any war by firms holding contracts in excess of $10,000.**

**Uniform Guidelines on Employment Selection Procedures (1978)—The
EEOC, the U.S. Civil Service, and the Department of Justice and Labor jointly
issued these guidelines to prevent discriminatory practices in hiring.**

**Americans with Disabilities Act (1990)—Prohibits discrimination
based on handicaps or disabilities (either physical or mental).**

FIGURE 5-1

Key Laws and Regulations Affecting a Sales Force

If a qualified applicant suspects that a job rejection is discriminatory, he or she may file a lawsuit against the employer. If the company has as employees a disproportionately low number of people from the group represented by the applicant, that may be enough to establish discrimination.

Discrimination charges also can be filed against a firm that uses recruitment sources with few people from the protected classes. For example, if a firm that employs predominantly white males hires salespeople only from within the firm, then this recruiting practice may be discriminatory even if there wasn't any intent to discriminate. The easiest way the firm can protect itself from these charges is to recruit from multiple sources, some of which clearly include the protected classes. Similarly, in advertising the position, the firm must be very careful not to use any language that could be construed as discriminatory.

The guidelines set by the Equal Employment Opportunity Commission (EEOC) and the Office of Federal Contract Compliance (OFCC) cover the full scope of sales force selection activities—setting hiring specifications and recruiting and processing applicants. They also set prescribed limits regarding the use of various tools in the selection procedure, such as application blanks, interviews, and tests. These will be highlighted in Chapter 6.

Probably the greatest problem these agencies pose for sales executives is that the burden of proof to show that a company is complying with the regulations generally rests with the company. That is, the firm must be able to demonstrate (if called on to do so) that its recruiting and selection processes are *not* discriminatory and that all of its selection requirements, sources, and tools are predictive of performance in a given sales job.

SCOPE OF SALES FORCE STAFFING PROCESS

There are five major activities involved in staffing a sales force:

1. *Plan* the recruiting and selection process.
2. *Recruit* an adequate number of applicants.
3. *Select* the most qualified applicants.
4. *Hire* those people who have been selected.
5. *Assimilate* the new hires into the company.

The flowchart in Figure 5-2 illustrates these major activities. You will notice that planning, recruiting and selecting are broken down into several related steps.

The Planning Phase

As can be seen in Figure 5-2, the first step of the planning phase is to establish responsibility for recruiting and selection. These responsibilities may be assigned to the top sales executive, the field sales manager, the human resources department, or some combination of these positions. Second, the company must determine the number and type of people needed. This involves analyzing the market and the job and preparing a written job description. Planners also must establish the qualifications necessary to fill the job.

The Recruiting Phase

The recruiting phase includes identifying sources of recruits that are consistent with the type of person desired, selecting the source to be used, and contacting

FIGURE 5-2
Sales force staffing process

Plan for recruiting and selection

| 1. Establish responsibility for recruiting, selection, and assimilation | 2. Determine the number of people wanted | 3. Conduct job analysis | 4. Prepare job description | 5. Determine hiring qualifications |

Recruit applicants

| 1. Identify sources of recruits | 2. Select the source to be used | 3. Contact the recruits |

Select applicants

| 1. Design a system for measuring applicants | 2. Measure applicants against hiring qualifications | 3. Make selection decisions |

Hire the people

Assimilate new people into sales force

the recruits. Selecting the source entails an evaluation of its potential effectiveness versus its cost.

The Selection Phase

The selection phase has three steps. First, it is necessary to design a system for measuring the recruits against the standards that were established in the planning phase. Second, the system must be put into effect with those who have become applicants. Making the actual selections is the third step. Selection is covered more thoroughly in chapter 6.

The Hiring and Assimilation Phases

After the company has made an offer to a recruit, the job is not done. Sometimes the recruits have other job offers and you must convince them that your company offers them the best opportunity. The staffing process is complete when the new salespeople are successfully assimilated into your organization. Hiring and assimilation also are covered more thoroughly in Chapter 6.

ESTABLISHING RESPONSIBILITY FOR RECRUITING, SELECTION, AND ASSIMILATION

Management must decide who will be responsible for making the recruiting and selection decisions and who will be responsible for assimilating the new hires into the organization. How these decisions are made often is related to the size of the firm and the nature of the selling task. In a small firm, for example, it is usually the top-level sales executive or even the president who makes these decisions. Since the sales force is small, these decisions do not place too much of a burden on any one executive.

In a large firm, however, the large number of territories and the normal turnover in those territories mean that the job of recruiting and selecting new salespeople will be a continuous one. It would be very difficult for any one executive to make all of these decisions; therefore, the decisions are usually shifted to lower-level sales managers. Additionally, in large firms, the human resources department usually assists managers with their recruiting and selection responsibilities. The human resources department may do all of the recruiting and initial screening of the recruits, but it is usually the sales manager who makes the final hiring decisions.

DETERMINING THE NUMBER OF PEOPLE NEEDED

A company should try to accurately determine how many sales reps it needs and then hire that number. It should not employ more than are needed with the intent of weeding out some as time goes by. Such an action would indicate that the firm has no faith in its selection system and is using performance on the job as an additional selection tool.

Sales personnel needs should be forecast well in advance of the time the people will actually be employed. This policy forces the various sales units to

FIGURE 5-3
Determining the number of
salespeople needed

Strategic Plans						
New territories	− Eliminated/ combined territories	+ Promotions	+ Retirements	+ Terminations/ resignations	=	Total new reps needed
Expansion	MN and RI territories combined. Reps eliminated:	Two promotions expected:	Two retirements expected:	One termination expected:		
4	− 1	+ 2	+ 2	+ 1	=	8

plan systematically. It also allows better programming of recruiting, interviewing, and other steps in the selection procedure.

Additionally, management should first review any changes in the company's strategic marketing plan to determine how the plan will affect the number of salespeople needed. Planned increases and decreases in marketing expenditures lead to changes in the level of forecasted sales. This in turn will probably affect the number of salespeople needed. For example, is the company planning to continue with its present channels-of-distribution structure? A firm now using manufacturers' reps in a certain region may be planning to replace these reps with a company sales force. Is the company planning to cut sales force costs by using the Internet and reducing the size of the outside sales force?

For the specific estimates of the number of new salespeople that must be hired, management should consider the following factors, which are depicted in Figure 5-3:

- Reps needed for changes in the deployment of salespeople: new territories, eliminated territories, realigned territories.
- Promotions out of the sales force.
- Expected retirements from the sales force.
- Expected turnover including terminations and resignations.

The manager adds the total number for each of these categories to estimate the number of new reps that will have to be hired (see the example in Figure 5-3). The question of how many reps are needed to cover a particular area is discussed in Chapter 13, on sales territories.

DEVELOPING A PROFILE OF THE TYPE OF PEOPLE NEEDED

A sales manager needs detailed specifications when selecting salespeople. Otherwise, he or she cannot know what to look for. Certainly, a company should be as careful in buying the services of men and women as it is in buying the products these people use or sell.

There are three tasks associated with developing a profile of the type of people wanted:

- **Job analysis**—the actual task of determining what constitutes a given job.
- **Job description**—the document that sets forth the finding of the job analysis.

- **Job qualifications—**(sometimes called hiring specifications)—the specific, personal qualifications and characteristics applicants should possess to be selected for the given job.

These tasks are detailed next.

Job Analysis

There are many different types of sales jobs and specific skills associated with each of those jobs that will make someone a success or failure. Therefore, before it develops the selection process, the company should conduct a thorough job analysis. The analysis should clearly identify the specific tasks that salespeople will perform. Additionally, it should provide information on which activities are critical for job success.

Any member of the sales organization or the human resources department may conduct the analysis—or the company can hire an outside specialist. An effective analysis of a sales job usually requires extensive observation and interviewing. The person conducting this analysis should spend time traveling with several salespeople as they make their calls.

The analyst also should interview many of the people who in some way interact with the reps in the sales job. The analyst should start interviewing with the reps themselves and then include sales force managers, customers, and other executives who are directly involved with the personal selling activities of the company. Also, salespeople can complete time and duty sheets on which they record their activities and the specific times they performed the activities for a specified period.

Job Description

Once the job is analyzed, the resultant description should be put in writing. The job analysis and subsequent written description must be done in great detail. It is not enough to say that the salesperson is supposed to sell the product, call on the customers, or build goodwill toward the company.

Scope of Job Description

Most well-prepared job descriptions have similar items of information. The following points are usually covered:

- *Title of job*—a complete description so there is no vagueness, especially in a company that distinguishes between several different types of sales jobs.
- *Organizational relationship*—to whom do the salespeople report?
- *Types of products and services sold.*
- *Types of customers called on*—purchasing agents, engineers, plant managers, and so on.
- *Duties and responsibilities related to the job*—planning activities, actual selling activities, customer servicing tasks, clerical duties, and self-management responsibilities.
- *Job demands*—the mental and physical demands of the job, such as the amount of travel, autonomy, and stress.
- *Hiring specifications*—the qualifications an applicant needs to be hired for the job. While job qualifications technically are not part of a job analysis,

there is merit in presenting the job duties and the job qualifications in one document.

Case Exhibit 5-A (at the end of the chapter) is a sample job description for a salesperson.

Uses of Job Description

Conducting the job analysis and writing the job description become the first two steps in the selection process. As such, they provide strategic guidance for the steps that follow. Recruiters cannot talk intelligently to prospective applicants if they do not know in detail what the job involves. A firm cannot develop application forms, employment tests, and other selection tools if it has not first analyzed the job. If hiring criteria and selection tools are developed through job analysis, misplacement and turnover can be reduced.

However, hiring is only part of it. A *job description is probably the most important single tool used in the operation of a sales force.* A job analysis should be the foundation of a sales training program. By studying the description, the executive in charge of sales training knows in detail what the salespeople's duties are and what they must learn. Job descriptions also are used in developing compensation plans. If management does not have a clear idea of what the sales force is supposed to do, it is difficult to design a sound compensation structure. Also, a salesperson's periodic performance ratings will be more meaningful if the company designs an evaluation form that includes many of the detailed aspects of the sales job. Finally, a good job description enables management to determine whether each salesperson has a reasonable workload.

Qualifications Needed to Fill the Job

The next step in a selection program—determining the qualifications needed to fill the job—is probably the most difficult part of the entire selection process. This is because there is no generally accepted profile for success across selling positions. Each company should establish its own individualized set of hiring requirements for each type of sales job in that firm. Tailored recruitment and selection criteria, recognizing that various sales roles have distinct requirements, has been identified as a critical component in successful selection programs.[4] IBM, for example, hires client representatives and sales specialists. The client representatives are responsible throughout the sales process for driving revenue and ensuring customer satisfaction. The sales specialists, on the other hand, are responsibile for identifying new sales opportunities, which requires a higher degree of technical expertise.[5] It should be noted that a sales rep who fails in *one* company or territory might not necessarily fail in *all* companies or territories. Many people have become successful with one firm after failing in an earlier environment. Even within a given firm, salespeople sometimes perform poorly in one territory (because of social, ethnic, or other environmental factors) but are successful after transferring to another region.[6]

Though every selling situation is different, most managers, customers, and salespeople agree that there are some generally desirable characteristics for salespeople. These characteristics are presented in Figure 5-4.

It is also generally acknowledged that the salesperson of the future must be able to work with electronic communications and technology.[7] Salespeople

Trait	Related ability
Emotional intelligence	To understand customers, to adapt
Analytical intelligence	To solve problems
Creative intelligence	To sell idea, to adapt
Integrity	To build trust
Social competence	To build relationships
Risk taker	To be innovative
Optimism	To handle rejection
Resilience	To complete the sale
Self-motivation	To work hard
Cooperativeness	To work on team

FIGURE 5-4
Ten traits and abilities of top salespeople

have access to CRM data banks with extensive product, customer, and competitive information. They also have multimedia options for making presentations to their customers. Salespeople need to be comfortable with the technology in order to utilize the information options in a comprehensive manner.

Team selling is now the predominant method of serving key accounts. This has an important impact on the type of salesperson that companies desire. The box titled "Recruiting for the Team" highlights some of the important characteristics of the team salesperson.

Even though there are some generally desirable traits, we emphasize again that it is important for each company to develop its own set of criteria for selecting salespeople. The following major categories of traits are those for which specifics should be developed:

- Cognitive abilities (planning and problem-solving ability).
- Physical characteristics (appearance, neatness).
- Experience (sales and other business experience).
- Education (number of years, degrees, majors).
- Personality traits (persuasiveness, adaptiveness).
- Skills (communication, interpersonal, technological, job-specific).
- Socioenvironmental factors (interests, activities, memberships in organizations).

When dealing with qualifications in any of the categories listed above, management must be careful to comply with laws regarding nondiscrimination in employment (see again Figure 5-1). Many qualifications that once were used to screen sales force applicants—such as age, marital status, and ethnic background—can no longer be used. Similarly, an arrest (or even a conviction) cannot be used to screen out an applicant. Exceptions exist if the company can show that a requirement related to an otherwise-protected group is a bona fide occupational qualification (BFOQ). Chapter 6 discusses BFOQs in more detail.

Methods of Determining Qualifications

There is no single satisfactory method for every company to use in determining the qualifications needed in its sales force. Several different procedures are currently being used. Some are adaptable for companies that have large sales

CONSIDER THIS...

Recruiting for the Team

In this reengineered business environment, many companies are choosing partners, not product. Customers are demanding more value-added services and more follow-up after the sale than one person can provide. This makes teamwork essential!

Character traits long associated with salespeople, such as independence, self-sufficiency, and a need to control, are considered a handicap in the new selling order. Companies now seek salespeople who are very *adaptable*, with a *willingness* to share and the *ability to put the group's goal above their own*—in other words, people who show selfless behavior.

forces and have been in business for some time, and thus have recorded histories of background and performance. Other methods may be used by firms that are large or small, old or new. Some of these methods are discussed in this section.

Study of Job Description

Many hiring specifications can be deduced from a carefully prepared job description. Job description statements about the degree of sales supervision, for instance, indicate that the salesperson should have the resourcefulness to work alone. Statements about the nature of the product, viewed in light of the company's training program, indicate something about the desired technical background or experience qualifications.

Analysis of Personal Histories

A large company in business for several years can determine its job qualifications by analyzing the personal histories of its present and past salespeople. The company must be big enough and old enough for a sample of histories to make the findings reasonably reliable. The procedure is to analyze various characteristics of good and poor sales reps to determine whether there are certain traits present in the good reps and absent in the poor ones. The traits of the good sales reps are then used to develop a **job profile** of the kind of person the firm is seeking.

For example, assume that ABC Company has 200 account managers—and that we wish to analyze their personal histories with respect to their age at the time of hiring. As shown in Figure 5-5, we could examine the impact of this variable by a comparison across high and low performing salespeople. From this table, we find that those account managers most likely to succeed were between 25 and 35 years of age when hired. Eighty-two percent of these were high performers. Those salespeople who were under 25 or over 55 when hired seem to perform the most poorly.

Many other variables could be examined in this same way, and a set of distinguishing characteristics will emerge. This information can be used to develop a profile for successful salespeople. For example, Accenture did this type of analysis of its current sales consultants. The company discovered that students with part-time jobs and extracurricular activities were more likely to succeed than those with higher grade-point averages.[8]

Age at Hiring	High Performers	Low Performers	Total	Percent of High Performers
Under 25	5	15	20	25%
25-35	45	10	55	82%
36-45	30	20	50	60%
46-55	15	30	45	33%
Over 55	5	25	30	17%
Total	100	100	200	

FIGURE 5-5
Personal-history analysis

RECRUITING AND ITS IMPORTANCE

After the number and type of salespeople wanted have been determined, the next major step in selecting a sales force is to recruit applicants for the position to be filled. **Recruiting** includes all activities involved in securing individuals who will apply for the job. The concept does not include the actual selection of people by means of interviews, tests, or other hiring tools. That step is the topic of Chapter 6. A sound selection program cannot exist without a well-planned and well-operated system for recruiting applicants. If recruiting is done haphazardly, a company runs the risk of overlooking good sources of prospective salespeople. Also, there is a risk of hiring unsuitable people simply because the firm must select immediately from the available applicants.

The importance of recruiting grows in relation to increases in the costs of selecting salespeople and maintaining them in the field. Certainly, the direct costs of recruiting—costs such as maintaining recruiting teams and placing recruiting advertisements—are increasing. But more important than the *direct* cost of recruiting is the effect that recruiting may have on the *total* costs of selection and training. It may be desirable to increase the cost of the recruiting activity if it results in finding better-quality applicants.

The costs of having an open sales territory are also great. *If a firm must do a significant amount of recruiting, it should be done continuously.* Even when no immediate need for new salespeople exists, the firm should develop a list of potential recruits. Then when an opening does occur, the time and costs of filling that territory will be relatively low. Sales managers should be proactive in their recruiting efforts. They should anticipate openings, look constantly for potential recruits, and keep a file on those who might be able to fill a future need. As Brian Ely, an Aflac sales executive, stated, "It's important to always have a list of top sales talent at the ready so that when positions open up, there are candidates who could potentially fill the job quickly."[9]

Need for Many Recruits

A philosophy to follow in recruiting is to get enough qualified applicants to maximize the chances of finding the right person for the job. The shortage of qualified sales representatives makes it imperative for a business to screen several people for each opening. The following is a useful rule of thumb to determine the number of recruits needed to select one salesperson:

CONSIDER THIS...

Attracting Millennial Talent

Millennials, who are generally defined as those born between 1980 and 2000, represent the largest generation in the workforce. Sales organizations work hard to hire the best and the brightest from this group of young adults, but it is not easy! Millennials are motivated by a complex set of values that are much different than those of the generations that came before them.

Experts say that to hire elite millennial talent who will stick around, today's sales organizations should follow these five tips:

1. Create flexibility to support work-life balance that might involve working from home, or at least does not insist on a strict 9 to 5 schedule.
2. Offer regular training programs that create a leadership development culture.
3. Move away from annual reviews toward more continuous feedback on attainment of short-terms goals.
4. Articulate a sense of purpose to the job that is beyond the bottom line.
5. Cultivate a people-driven culture where team goals are more important than individual accomplishments.

SOURCE: Claire Groden, "Five Things You Can Do to Attract Millennial Talent," *Fortune*, March 15, 2016, Vol. 173(4), pp. 182-183.

- A recruiting effort may reach 20 people who are interested in the job.
- A review of application blanks will eliminate 10.
- The initial interview will eliminate another 6 or 7.
- The 3 or 4 finalists are screened further by interviews, tests, and other selection tools.
- One personal is finally hired.

Finding an adequate number of recruits may not be as easy as it sounds. Today's recruits, who are generally from the millennial generation, want a lot more than just a high salary. As shown in the box entitled "Attracting Millennial Talent," candidates for sales positions place a higher value on things other than salary. If companies want to succeed in recruiting salespeople in tight labor markets, then they must offer the advantages that recruits want.[10]

Finding and Maintaining Good Recruiting Sources

Most firms actively recruit sales reps from many sources. To determine the best sources, a recruiter should first find out where the company's best salespeople came from in the past. This assumes that there has been no substantial change in the job description or job qualifications. The evaluation of current sources will be discussed at the end of this chapter.

If a company is recruiting for the first time, or if its current sources are inadequate, then the job description and hiring specifications provide a useful starting point. These documents reveal factors that affect the recruiter's choice of sources. For example, the educational qualifications for the job may indicate whether colleges are a good source for recruits. If industry knowledge is a requirement, the recruiter may consider employees from other departments within the company.

Once satisfactory sources are located, management should maintain a continuing relationship with them, even when the firm is not hiring. Firms that want college graduates should keep in touch with professors who have furnished assistance in the past. Customers who have supplied leads to good people should be reminded periodically of the company's gratitude and be encouraged to suggest more prospects.

SOURCES FOR RECRUITING SALES REPRESENTATIVES

Recruiting sources are the places where firms identify the names of potential candidates (or applicants) to fill open sales positions. As shown in Figure 5-6, some frequently used recruiting sources are:

- Referrals.
- Current employees (i.e., promoting from within).
- Other companies (including competitors, customers).
- Advertisements in:
    - Employment websites (e.g., careerbuilder.com, monster.com)
    - Newspapers.
    - Trade journals.
- The hiring company's *own website.*
- Educational institutions.
- Employment agencies.
- Part-time workers.

Referrals

A **referral** is a recommendation by one individual that another be hired for a position. For example, a current salesperson might have a friend who works in sales for another company, and refer that person to the hiring manager. Note that this shows how there can be overlap between a referral and one of the other recruiting sources (such as other companies). Most sales executives say that referrals is their preferred source of sales recruits.

The reason why managers prefer referrals as a source of potential salespeople is because of the advantages they offer. Most referrals come from someone who works for the company. They know the job requirements and the recruit. Chances are pretty good that the recommended candidate will have the necessary skills as well as fit within the company culture. The current salespeople, for example, are an excellent source of leads to new recruits. They clearly know the job and the company, and they often meet reps and employees from other companies. Both Microsoft and Dr Pepper/Seven Up Inc. rely to a great extent on employee referrals as a recruiting source. Dr Pepper/Seven Up makes 40 percent of its new hires from referrals.[11]

The big disadvantage of using referrals is that you may not get enough of them. Southwest Airlines has found a good way to combat this problem. Southwest offers many different incentives to encourage its employees to make referrals, such as flight coupons and drawing for computers. At Microsoft and Dr Pepper/Seven Up employees receive a monetary reward if a referred person is hired and meets initial performance goals. Additionally, managers at Microsoft

FIGURE 5-6
Sources of sales force
recruits
*Source: The HR Chally
Group*, Ten Year Research
Report, *2002.*

believe that its strong corporate culture stimulates employee referrals.[12] Again, it should be noted that referrals often come from another recruiting source.

Current Employees

Some companies recruit their sales force from workers in their production plants or offices. Management has been able to observe these people and evaluate their potential as sales reps. These workers are acquainted with the product and also have been indoctrinated in company policies and programs. Their values fit with the company culture. Many companies like to recruit within their own organizations because these candidates are the least costly to recruit and train. Hiring salespeople from within the company also can be a great morale booster, because most plant and office workers consider transfer to the sales department to be a promotion. General Motors (GM) believes strongly in recruiting from within the company. In fact, in its formal training program, GM conducts cross-functional training for many different positions. Upon completion, employees can attain positions in new departments, including sales.[13]

Other Companies: Competitors, Customers...

A *competitor's* sales force is a major recruiting source for salespeople. However, there are different views about recruiting competitors' salespeople. On the one hand, they know the product and the market very well. They are also experienced sellers and therefore require little training. On the other hand, it may be harder for these people to unlearn old practices and make the adjustment to a new environment. Also, for some managers, recruiting from a competitor's sales force may present an ethical dilemma as it is sometimes called pirating (which suggests that the person was "stolen").

A firm may seek leads to prospects from its *customers.* Purchasing agents are often good sources of names. They have some knowledge of the abilities of the sales reps who call on them. Customers' employees themselves may be a source of salespeople. Often, retail clerks make good salespeople for wholesalers and manufacturers. These clerks know the product. They also know something of the behavior of the retailers—the market to which the hiring firm sells.

Sales reps working for *noncompeting companies* are another source, particularly if they (1) are selling products related to those sold by the recruiting firm or (2) are selling to the same market. A salesperson working for a supplier of the recruiting firm, for example, is a potential source of recruits. Presumably, recruits from this source have some sales ability and need relatively little training.

Recruiting from other firms raises some questions. Hiring the good employees of a customer obviously has drawbacks. The task must be handled very diplomatically to avoid losing the customer.

A firm that hires from the outside should determine (1) why the applicants are interested in changing jobs and (2) why they want to work for the hiring company. Applicants may figure that the quickest way to success is to move from one company to another, which might mean that they won't stay long.

A recruiting source many companies may overlook is *former employees.* It is interesting to note that many firms have established Internet "alumni" networks to maintain connections with those who have left. As Agilent Technologies' director of global talent states, "We want to be able to welcome back folks who have left and expanded their skills."[14]

Job Advertisements

One of the most common sources for recruiting sales representatives is through placing job advertisements in various media. Advertisements ordinarily produce many applicants, but the average quality of the applicants may be questionable. The cost of placing these advertisements is low; however, that cost is often offset by the resources required to screen through and weed out those who are not qualified. The most common media for job advertisements are employment websites, newspapers, and/or trade journals—each of which are discussed below.

Employment Websites

Many companies place job ads in online employment websites, such as Monster.com and Careerbuilder.com, to fill sales positions. These are nonprofit recruitment and human resources databases that post job listings from a huge variety of companies. These websites have thousands and thousands of job postings for sales positions, which include job titles such as sales representative, account manager, account executive, and business development manager. Indeed.com is a website service that behaves as a search engine for jobs, as it aggregates job listings from thousands of other websites. Indeed.com is one of the most visited sites on the web, with hundreds of thousands of job listings and over one hundred million unique visitors each month.[15] Although not an employment website *per se*, LinkedIn is a business-oriented social networking site that is used by organizations to fill sales positions—in fact, many organizations used the "Apply with LinkedIn" feature which streamlines the application process.[16]

Newspapers

Although the popularity of newspapers is declining, many sales organizations still rely on this medium to advertise job listings. Generally speaking, this method is used for trying to fill the less attractive type of sales jobs, such as in-home selling or clerking in a retail store. Placing a job ad in a local, small-town newspaper may be the most effective way to fill a sales position *in that particular geographic location.* On the other hand, there are national newspapers in which job ads can be placed, and these are right for certain kinds of positions. For example, *The Wall Street Journal* promotes its career and job classified ads section as a way to recruit for high-level, professional jobs.

Trade journals

As a way to improve the quality of applicants, sales organizations often place job ads in carefully selected trade journals (rather than in newspapers). In every industry, there are trade journals or magazines specific to its interests. Among the hundreds of examples are *Advertising Age, American Banker, Construction Today*—even *Portable Restroom Operator*! When organizations want to fill sales positions with someone who knows the industry, it makes sense to advertise in these focused journals.

When selecting employment websites, newspapers and/or trade journals for job ads, organizations consider the tradeoff between the quantity of applicants and the quality of applicants. Generally speaking, organizations like to have lots of applicants for its sales positions because it is nice to have options. However, it is better to have a few high quality applicants rather than lots of low quality applicants! And of course, it costs a lot more to screen through a large number of applicants.

Consequently, with respect to the various options of placing a job ad, organizations must consider three things: (1) cost of the job ad, (2) the expected number of applicants, and (3) the expected percent of suitable applicants that accept a job offer. These numbers can be combined to calculate the cost per hire, which is an important input into the decision making process. For example, consider a firm that can place job ads on salesjobs.com for $198 per month, which generates an average of 5.5 applicants per month, and it finds that it can successfully make a job offer to 10 percent of the applicants. With this scenario, the cost per applicant is $36 per month (or $198/5.5 applicants); but since the firm can only hire one out of 10 applicants, the cost per hire is $360 (or $36/10%).

Finally, when placing a job ad, the firm must decide what information to include in the advertisement. Here are some points to consider:

- **Company name?** The company name is usually included in the advertisement—especially if the company is well-known. However, some companies with a poor public image often choose to hide their identities.
- **Product?** Usually yes, unless it is a product that is likely to turn away prospects who otherwise might be interested once they learned more about the company and the job opportunities. For example, products associated with the funeral industry might fit into this category.

- **Territory?** Yes, especially if it is not in the area where the ad is run.
- **Hiring qualifications?** Yes, include enough of them so the ad serves as a useful screening device. But keep in mind the legal guidelines (discussed earlier in this chapter) when stating any hiring requirements.
- **Compensation plan, expense plan, and benefits?** Yes, include some information in these areas, especially if it is a strong point. A company paying straight salary is more likely to mention this point than is one that pays straight commission.
- **How to contact the employer?** The ad must have a phone number or a mailing address. The address in a blind ad is usually a post office box.

Job ads for sales positions can be readily found online at Monster.com and many other employment websites. Take a look at several and decide which are good, which are poor, and why.

Company Website

An excellent source of recruits for most companies is their own website—or at least it should be. Research has found that such website recruitment is more effective than printed job ads in terms of enhancing applicants' knowledge of—and attraction toward—the firm.[17] Companies should have a "Join Our Team" section that effectively *sells* potential employees about the vision, mission, values and culture of the company. Microsoft does this through its website, which generates over 500 applications per week. In fact, companies increasingly refer *all applicants* to their websites to complete the application process—this ensures that everybody is treated equally and fairly. The most positive aspect of web-based recruiting is that the cost of obtaining resumes is very small. Also, the voluntary applicants usually know something about the firm and have shown some initiative by submitting their resumes. However, the company does bear a significant cost in that it must establish a process for sorting through the large numbers of applicants to find those who qualify for the position.

Educational Institutions

Companies frequently use colleges and universities as a source of recruits for sales positions. This is a very cost-effective method of recruiting because college campuses provide large numbers of individuals who are educated and looking for jobs. Also, there typically is only a small fee for companies to attend university job fairs. Companies also may look beyond traditional four-year colleges to recruit from community colleges, vocational-technical schools, or even high school.

Some companies have developed distinctive identities with students by speaking to classes and student organizations, participating in job fairs or on advisory boards to marketing departments, and providing scholarships and summer internship opportunities.

Another trend for filling sales jobs is for companies to become involved in university sales competitions. For example, the National Collegiate Sales Competition is held annually at Kennesaw State University.[18] Scores of companies pay sponsorship fees to gain access to the over 100 sales-oriented students from over 50 plus universities across the country. The students compete in role play scenarios (selling the product of the lead sponsor); the employees from the sponsoring companies serve as judges—and of course also aggressively recruit these top students. Many other universities have similar competitions.

CONSIDER THIS...

Musicians as Part-Time Salespeople

Martin Miller's Gin was having difficulty recruiting and retaining a full-time sales force to sell its premium gin to the company's target market of clubs, trendy bars and hip restaurants. It was very expensive, and turnover was quite high.

The problem was solved by shifting focus to a new source of recruits: part-time workers. Specifically, the company realized that hiring musicians to sell Martin Miller's Gin to these establishments on a part-time basis made a lot of sense. Musicians were generally free during the day, during which they could call on these customers, make some much needed money—and then sometimes build a relationship with the bar manager that boosted their music career!

"Lots of artists have bar-hopped, trying to get a gig," says one Martin Miller sales rep/musician. "It's like I'm bar-hopping with the purpose of selling gin, and that's how the relationship starts. From there, I can do my own PR, and land more singing gigs. It's a very symbiotic relationship."

SOURCE: Cathy Huyghe, "Why a Gin Company Hired Musicians as Part-Time Salespeople," *Harvard Business Review*, September 10, 2015. https://hbr.org/2015/09/why-a-gin-company-hired-musicians-as-part-time-salespeople

Employment Agencies

Agencies that place salespeople are a frequently used source of recruits. If the agency is carefully selected and good relations are established with it, the dividends can be satisfying. The agency can do some of the initial screening, because presumably it will abide by the job specifications given. This is a relatively expensive source. Fees usually range from 10 to 40 percent of the new employee's first year's compensation, and they increase as the compensation goes up. Agencies where the employer pays the fee probably attract a better quality of sales recruit. The employer's cost for the agency's fee may be offset by the savings in the advertising and initial screening activities done by the agency.

Part-Time Workers

The use of part-time salespeople in outside selling jobs is increasing. Part-time workers are easy to contact, are readily available, and usually can work flexible hours. In-home selling organizations (which market products such as jewelry, cosmetics, housewares, food and fashion) hire part-time salespeople that prefer to work from home, often because of family obligations. See the box entitled "Musicians as Part-Time Salespeople" for the story of how and why a gin company has effectively used this source of recruits.

DIVERSITY

For outside selling jobs, firms can ensure **diversity** in recruiting by using a variety of the sources that we discussed in the preceding section. In this section, however, we call special attention to minorities and women as recruiting sources for two reasons. First, these groups are underemployed in outside sales jobs. That is, the percentage of minorities and women in *outside* sales jobs is far below their percentage in the total population. Second, the changing economic, demographic, and legal conditions in this country are bringing major changes to the sales field. As shown in Figure 5-7, the composition of the workforce will change to include a more culturally diverse group of people. The sales force of the future will be drawn from this culturally diverse group of workers, including women, American-born minorities, and immigrants.

Minority Groups

Many executives report only limited success in attracting minority groups to outside sales jobs. In fact, the outside sales force typically has the lowest percentage of minority employees of any department in a company. Many companies cite two reasons for this low percentage: (1) not many African Americans apply and (2) they don't have adequate recruiting sources. However, some companies have been successful in recruiting minorities by tapping into nontraditional sources such as the National Black MBA Association and the National Society of Hispanic MBAs.[19] Also most business schools have resource centers with hundreds of resumes on file.

As noted earlier, there are legal reasons to practice diversity. The Equal Employment Opportunity Commission, which strives to ensure that minorities have the same opportunities as whites, investigates as many as 30,000 cases of racial discrimination each year. In many cases, companies are forced to pay stiff fines and implement diversity programs. But practicing diversity is also good business. As minorities make up more of the labor force, so too will they be a greater percentage of the purchasing population. For some companies, such as AT&T and Levi Strauss & Co., ensuring sales force diversity is seen not only as the right thing to do but also as a key to success.[20]

FIGURE 5-7
The Growth Of Population Diversity

		In the year 2014	In the year 2060 (predicted)
	Total U.S. Population	319 million	417 million
Age Raw number (% of total)	Young (under 18)	74 million (23%)	82 million (20%)
	Working age (18-64)	199 million (62%)	236 million (57%)
	Older Americans (65+)	46 million (14%)	98 million (24%)
Diversity Raw number (% of total)	Non-Hispanic White	198 million (62%)	182 million (44%)
	Black/African American	42 million (13%)	60 million (14%)
	Asian	17 million (5%)	39 million (9%)
	Two or more races	8 (3%)	26 (6%)
	Hispanic	55 million (17%)	119 million (29%)

Based on U.S. Census data, this table shows the predicted changes that will occur in the U.S. population in the coming decades. Salespeople will be drawn from an older and more culturally diverse group of candidates. [Note that the diversity numbers do not add up exactly to the total population because Hispanic origin is considered an ethnicity, not a race (i.e., Hispanics may be of any race).]

SOURCE: Sandra L. Colby and Jennifer M. Ortman, *Projections of the Size and Composition of the U.S. Population: 2014 to 2060.* Issued March 2015 by the U.S. Census Bureau.

Women

Reports on the perceptions and experiences of sales executives concerning women in outside selling jobs are interesting and enlightening. Overall, these experiences and perceptions have been quite favorable. Furthermore, this favorable reaction is not limited to consumer products companies or service industries. Women also are performing well as sales recruits in industrial sales jobs. Many companies that may have originally recruited women as the "politically correct" thing to do have found that women are a vast untapped resource with a significant positive effect on the bottom line.[21]

Yet women are still grossly underrepresented in many outside sales forces. Women account for about 50 percent of the total labor force, yet in few companies do they account for more than 25 percent of the outside sales force. If one looks at sales management ranks, the picture is even worse—on average, only 14 percent are women.[22] There are still factors that inhibit the entry and progress of women in outside sales forces.

Nevertheless, the influx of women into outside sales forces will continue to increase. To counter the shortage of qualified salespeople, management must strongly recruit from the population segment that comprises over half of the labor force.

RECRUITING EVALUATION

To better direct its focus in the management of its recruiting sources, a company should continually evaluate the effectiveness of its recruiting program. To conduct **recruiting evaluation,** management might use some form of matrix approach, such as the one in Figure 5-8. Data on the evaluative criteria can be gathered for a time frame, such as the past two years. This information should

FIGURE 5-8
Recruiting evaluation matrix

Recruiting Source	Evaluative Criteria—For The Past Two Years				
	Number Of Recruits	Number Hired	Percent Retained	Cost Per Hire	Percent Performing Above Average
Referrals					
Current employees					
Other companies but not competitors					
Competitors					
Employment websites					
Newspaper job ads					
Trade journal job ads					
Voluntary applicants from company website					
Educational institutions					
Employment agencies					
Part-time workers					

enable management to determine which sources produced the best recruits. A spin-off benefit of recruiting evaluation is that it can be used in the performance ratings of sales executives who are involved in recruiting. That is, some companies use "recruiting effectiveness" as one factor in evaluating a sales manager's judgment and promotability.

SUMMARY

Selecting the right people (staffing the organization) is one of the most important steps in the management process. Sales force selection should be coordinated with an organization's strategic marketing and sales force planning because the sales force often plays a major role in implementing the plans. Sales executives must understand the various civil rights laws and other government regulations that have a substantial impact on all phases of sales force selection.

Sales selection includes five phases. First, management determine how many and what kind of people are wanted. The second phase involves recruiting a number of applicants. The third phase involves processing these applicants and selecting the most qualified. Then those selected must be hired and assimilated into the organization.

Management can determine the *number* of salespeople to be hired by conducting an analysis based on the company's past experiences and future expectations. To determine the *type* of person wanted, management should first conduct a job analysis and then write a job description for each position to be filled.

Determining the qualifications needed to fill the job is the most difficult part of the sales selection process. As yet, we simply have not been able to isolate the traits that make for success in selling. However, we do know that it is important to develop *individualized* hiring specifications for a given job in a given firm. As a starting point, management should study the job descriptions. They also should analyze the personal histories of their present and past salespeople to identify those characteristics that distinguish the successful reps from the less successful ones.

Firms should understand the pros and cons of the following sources of recruits: referrals, current employees, other companies, advertisements, the company website, educational institutions, employment agencies and part-time workers. To ensure diversity in their sales forces, firms should use a variety of these sources.

KEY TERMS

Affirmative action	Job profile	Recruiting evaluation
Diversity	Job qualifications	Recruiting sources
Job analysis	Nondiscrimination	Referral
Job description	Recruiting	Selection

QUESTIONS AND PROBLEMS

1. What is the best way for a company to avoid being sued for a lack of affirmative action?

2. Why would a company be willing to rehire someone who had earlier left the firm?

3. For IBM, how should the recruiting criteria for client representative differ from sales specialist?

4. If a person wants to be a top-notch professional career sales rep and has no interest in being a manager, is a college education necessary? Discuss. If your answer is no, why do so many firms recruit salespeople from colleges, and why is a college education so often listed as a qualification for a sales job?

5. Assume that a company wants to hire a sales engineer—that is, fill a position where the major emphasis is on technical product knowledge. Should this firm recruit engineers and train them to sell, or recruit sales reps and teach them the necessary technical information and abilities?

6. If you were recruiting from a university for the salesperson job description found in Case Exhibit 5-A, what college majors would you target? Which majors would you avoid?

7. Is it ethical for a sales manager to directly approach a competitor's salesperson with an outright offer of a better job?

8. How would the sources and methods of recruiting salespeople *differ* among the following firms?

   a. A company selling precision surgical equipment to hospitals.

   b. A coffee roaster and canner in Denver selling to wholesalers and retailers in the Southwest and the Rocky Mountain regions.

   c. A national firm selling baskets and other home decorative items by the party-plan method.

   d. A furniture manufacturer selling a high-quality product nationally through selected retail outlets.

9. One manufacturer of dictating machines recruits only experienced salespeople and does no recruiting among graduating college students. A competitor recruits extensively among colleges in its search for salespeople. How do you account for the difference in sources used by firms selling essentially the same products?

10. The following companies are looking for product salespeople and decide to use advertising to recruit applicants. For each firm, you are asked to select the specific advertising media and to write a recruiting advertisement for one of those media. You may supply whatever additional facts you need.

    a. Manufacturers' agent handling lighting fixtures for both the industrial and consumer markets.

    b. Manufacturer of snowboards.

    c. Wholesaler of lumber and building materials.

11. What are the 2 or 3 best recruiting sources to generate the names of qualified candidates to fill the position described in Case Exhibit 5-A? Explain your answer.

EXPERIENTIAL EXERCISES

1. Interview appropriate employees of one or more local firms with an outside sales force; gather information about the firms' entry-level sales positions; and then prepare detailed job descriptions for those positions.

2. Prepare a list of qualifications needed to fill each job you analyzed and described in the preceding exercise.

3. Visit various employments websites (such as, Monster.com), and/or a specific company sites, to find several sales positions in which you think you might be interested. Name the companies and describe the jobs and the application procedures. Describe what appeals to you about the particular positions that you have selected.

Case Exhibit 5-A Sample Job Description of a Salesperson

Sales Representative Job Responsibilities:
Serves customers by selling products; meeting customer needs.

Sales Representative Job Duties:

- Services existing accounts, obtains orders, and establishes new accounts by planning and organizing daily work schedule to call on existing or potential sales outlets and other trade factors.
- Adjusts content of sales presentations by studying the type of sales outlet or trade factor.
- Focuses sales efforts by studying existing and potential volume of dealers.
- Submits orders by referring to price lists and product literature.
- Keeps management informed by submitting activity and results reports, such as daily call reports, weekly work plans, and monthly and annual territory analyses.
- Monitors competition by gathering current marketplace information on pricing, products, new products, delivery schedules, merchandising techniques, etc.
- Recommends changes in products, service, and policy by evaluating results and competitive developments.

- Resolves customer complaints by investigating problems; developing solutions; preparing reports; making recommendations to management.
- Maintains professional and technical knowledge by attending educational workshops; reviewing professional publications; establishing personal networks; participating in professional societies.
- Provides historical records by maintaining records on area and customer sales.
- Contributes to team effort by accomplishing related results as needed.

Sales Representative Skills and Qualifications:
Customer Service, Meeting Sales Goals, Closing Skills, Territory Management, Prospecting Skills, Negotiation, Self-Confidence, Product Knowledge, Presentation Skills, Client Relationships, Motivation for Sales.

SOURCE: Monster.com, accessed on June 9, 2016 from http://hiring.monster.com/hr/hr-best-practices/recruiting-hiring-advice/job-descriptions/sales-representative-job-description-sample.aspx

GALACTICA
Recruiting Sources

Brenda Crohn, the recruiting director for a text-book publisher called Galactica, was in the middle of a heated argument with John Stubbins, the vice president of marketing. The argument revolved around where to place the ads to recruit candidates for sales positions. "I know that the quality of the applicants generated off salescareers.com may not be as good as those from our job ads in *The Journal of Academic Publishing;* but we can reach a lot more candidates through the Internet job site compared to our trade journal—and I really want a large pool of applicants to choose from. Even if we hire fewer of them, I think it's good to select from a bigger group," argued John.

Crohn was frustrated that the only criterion John seemed to be considering was the number of applicants the Internet job site ad would generate. "John," Crohn interrupted, "you are right about the number of applicants the ads will generate. Our current trade journal ads generate an average of 1.2 applicants per ad, and we could expect over twice that number from salescareers.com—in fact, I've been told that a reliable estimate is 4.5 applicants per posting. But you've got to consider the costs as well as the number of qualified applicants. We like to hire experienced reps who understand the industry, and those who respond to the Internet ads are much less likely to have the experience we prefer."

"So what are the differences in costs?" Stubbins asked.

Crohn replied, "Well the current trade journal ads cost $132 per posting, and salescareers.com charges $288 per ad. But as you acknowledged a minute ago, the quality of the internet applicant would be lower, and therefore we would surely make fewer successful offers than we currently do. We currently hire 50 percent of the applicants, but we estimate that we would only be able to hire 10 percent of those who applied through the Internet site.

"So what is the bottom line on all of this?" asked Stubbins. "The Internet ad costs us more, but we get a bigger pool of candidates. Even if we reject a higher number of them, it may actually cost Galactica less per rep hired. There is nothing more critical to our business than hiring good people; and given our growth rate, we will need to keep hiring steadily for the indefinite future. I think we should give the Internet a try!"

Crohn was not convinced. She told Stubbins, "I do not have a bottom line at this point, but I will have a recommendation as soon as I crunch the numbers. I'll get back to you later today. Then we can make an informed decision about whether or not we should switch to salescareers.com.

Questions:

1. Analyze the numbers in this case, and calculate the cost per hire for both the trade journal ads and the internet job site ads. Label all calculated numbers, and clearly show your work!

2. What other considerations (besides the financial analysis in the first question) should be taken into account when deciding between the two options.

3. Make a recommendation for using one of the two options—fully explaining your reasoning.

NOTEBOOK SERVICES CORPORATION
Improving the Recruiting Process

Sandy Paul, national sales manager for Notebook Services Corporation (NSC), was frustrated. The company's recruiting efforts this past spring had not yielded the number of recruits NSC needed to fill its open territories. This was not a new problem; it was a repeat of similar problems the company had faced for the past couple years.

NSC was a growing company—which for the most part was good. The problem, however, was that NSC was expanding into new markets, which created the need for new salespeople to be hired. They currently had about 85 salespeople that worked throughout the Western states, but they had at least 5 open territories. And Sandy Paul felt that he was way behind in identifying good people to fill these positions.

Located in Bakersfield, California, NSC, manufactured and sold a variety of small, durable laptop and tablet computers. These were niche products sold mostly to businesses in the healthcare, law enforcement, and utilities industries. NSC has been in business for about 15 years, and management is extremely proud of the company's consistent growth throughout that time.

NSC considers itself a customer-oriented company. The sales organization is responsible for implementing NSC's strategy of being a full-service, high-quality supplier. Because reorders provide the majority of sales for NSC's primary products, it is imperative that the sales reps maintain regular and close contact with their customers. To facilitate this close contact, NSC has over 30 branch offices throughout eight western states: Washington, Oregon, California, Nevada, Arizona, Wyoming, Colorado and New Mexico.

The salespeople are authorized to sell the entire NSC product line, which are all fairly complex, high-tech products. Each rep is responsible for a specific geographic area. The reps must learn their customers' business and identify ways to help their customers improve their operations and profits.

The reps access and input their job data into Salesforce.com, which is the number one customer relationship management (CRM) software in the world. Most reps like this system, and use it without a problem—though some of the older reps are a bit confused as to how to operate the program.

The salespeople are paid a base salary plus commission at a level that is well-above the norm for outside sales. In fact, in the increasingly competitive landscape, Sandy Paul is pressured to do more with less—and is sometimes told by his superiors that the sales force is overpaid. The excellent compensation has created a loyal sales force, as the turnover rate is much lower than the industry average. The reps are generally well-trained, solid performers.

Sandy Paul has had the most success recruiting new salespeople through referrals from the existing sales force. In fact, if a current sales rep provides the name of someone who ends up getting hired, then that rep is paid $1,000! This incentive system has worked quite well—at least, the system generates good quality reps. The only problem is that it does not provide *enough names.*

Sandy Paul has decided that he is going to have to start getting names from additional sources of recruits. One possibility he is considering is to begin to hire from universities. However, he has concerns about this source, because college students typically have very limited real world experience. He also has heard a lot of negative comments from a friend about how today's college students are "...lazy, entitled, narcissists."

There are a variety of other sources of recruits for salespeople, each with its pros and cons. Sandy Paul is going to spend the afternoon researching the issue, and then go to the company president to secure the resources to hire from at least one or two of these new sources.

Questions:

1. Explain the pros and cons of hiring from educational institutions for this particular company and situation.

2. Identify at least two or three other potential sources of recruits for NSC, and explain their pros and cons.

3. Make a comprehensive recommendation for how NSC can start to hire more salespeople (…through these additional sources of recruits).

ENDNOTES

[1] Interview with Jason Heaster, District Manager at Fastenal (3/8/2016).

[2] Josh Bersin, "Employee Retention Now a Big Issue: Why the Tide has Turned," *LinkedIn*, Aug 16 2013. Accessed 3/8/2016 from https://www.linkedin.com/pulse/20130816200159-131079-employee-retention-now-a-big-issue-why-the-tide-has-turned

[3] "Business Student Attitudes toward Business Positions," Kelley School of Business survey, 2006.

[4] Elana Harris, "Hire Power," *Sales & Marketing Management,* October 2000, p. 88.

[5] The Chally Group, "The Customer-Selected World Class Sales Excellence Ten-Year Research Report," 2003, p. 53.

[6] "Pop Quiz," *Sales & Marketing Management,* September 2005, p. 19.

[7] George Avlonitis and Despina A. Karayanni, "The Impact of Internet Use on Business-to-Business Marketing," *Industrial Marketing Management* 29 (2000), pp. 441-59.

[8] Nina Munk and Suzanne Oliver, "Think Fast," *Forbes,* March 24, 1997, pp. 146-51.

[9] Betsy Cummings, "Star Search," *Sales & Marketing Management*, June 2005, pp. 24-25.

[10] Erin Strout, "How to Win Today's Recruiting War," *Sales & Marketing Management*, March 2000, p. 85.

[11] Katharine Kaplan, "Help (Still) Wanted," *Sales & Marketing Management*, February 2002, pp. 38–43.

[12] Ibid.; Karen Renk and Patricia Childers, "Reward with Awards," *Occupational Health & Safety,* September 2002, pp. 56-58.

[13] Erin Strout, "Finding Your Company's Top Talent," *Sales & Marketing Management,* May 2000, p. 113.

[14] Abby Nickenson, "Alma Matters," *Sales & Marketing Management*, February 2002, p. 52.

[15] Pamela Skillings, "The Top 50 Best Job Search Sites You Need to Know About," *Big Interview*, October 23, 2014. Retrieved January 30 from http://biginterview.com/blog/2014/10/best-job-search-sites.html

[16] Susan Adams, "Five New Tips For Using LinkedIn To Find A Job," *Forbes.com*, December 12, 2014, p.8

[17] Matthias Baum and Rudiger Kabst, "The Effectiveness of Recruitment Advertisements and Recruitment Websites: Indirect and Interactive Effects on Applicant Attraction," *Human Resource Management*, May-June 2014, Vol. 53 (3), pp. 353-378.

[18] National College Sales Competition, visit http://ncsc-ksu.org/ Accessed January 30, 2016.

[19] Cummmings, "Star Search."

[20] Ibid.

[21] Christen P. Heide, *Dartnell's 30th Sales Force Compensation Survey* (Chicago: Dartnell Corporation, 1999), pp. 168-71.

[22] Ibid.

Selecting and Hiring Salespeople

As the leading consumer goods company in the world, Procter & Gamble has no trouble generating a very large applicant pool when posting for an Account Manager position. In fact, one estimate is that over 300 people apply for every P&G opening.[1] So, how does P&G sort through and screen all those applicants in order to select and hire the best salesperson for the job? The answer is that it uses a series of rigorous, well-researched selection tools.[2]

Specifically, P&G first has all candidates submit their resume and fill out an application form for the specific sales job posted on the company website (see box entitled "Sales Jobs at P&G"). This provides P&G with contact information, education level, work experience, and a variety of other basic qualifications (e.g., geographic preferences, driver's license, etc.). Next, P&G has all applicants complete an online employment test to assess a variety of work-related attitudes and

reasoning skills that are proven to correspond to future success in sales.

This information is analyzed by P&G human resources professionals, who then select a certain number of candidates to interview. This initial interview may be over the phone or at company headquarters. The interview questions will be focused on the candidates' past behaviors at work and/or school. The next step—for those who make it—is the more detailed final interview often with a panel of two to three interviewers consisting of at least some sales executives.

Finally, the P&G sales team makes a job offer to the one person who comes out on top—but only after this time-consuming, complicated and expensive process that screens out the hundreds of applicants.

CONSIDER THIS...

Sales Jobs at P&G

According to the Procter & Gamble website, sales jobs are by far the most common type of job opening at the firm. To sort through the hundreds of applicants that apply for each job, P&G uses multiple selection tools, including resumes, application forms, employment tests, and interviews.

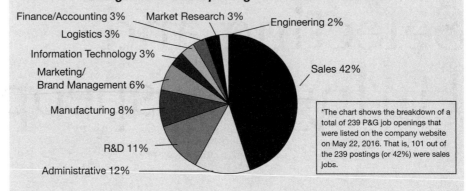

Categories of Job Openings at Procter & Gamble*

Finance/Accounting 3%
Market Research 3%
Engineering 2%
Logistics 3%
Information Technology 3%
Marketing/Brand Management 6%
Sales 42%
Manufacturing 8%
R&D 11%
Administrative 12%

*The chart shows the breakdown of a total of 239 P&G job openings that were listed on the company website on May 22, 2016. That is, 101 out of the 239 postings (or 42%) were sales jobs.

SOURCE: This graph created by the author from data found on the Procter & Gamble website http://us.pgcareers.com/

SELECTION TOOLS

The previous chapter presents tools and techniques to recruit a large applicant pool of viable candidates for open sales positions. We now present **selection tools** that are used to *screen* those applicants so that the sales organization can select and hire the best candidates for the job. The major selection tools are:

- Resumes/Application forms
- Personal interviews
- Employment testing
- Reference and credit reports
- Assessment centers

No single selection tool is adequate by itself. Like P&G does in the chapter introduction, companies should use a series of tools to carefully assess an applicant's qualifications, and attain a *complete profile* of the individual. For example, oral communication skills are better assessed by an interview than by an employment test yet the test is likely a better way to assess cognitive ability. In addition, the information derived from one tool often can complement or verify that derived from another.

The sequencing of these selection tools tends to vary across companies. At Fastenal Company, the first selection tool used is the resume and application form submitted by applicants through the company website. Fastenal human resources staff screens these documents and then conducts brief telephone interviews with those applicants who meet the established standards. The third step involves a longer, in-person interview with a higher-level sales manager. This process is consistent with idea that *the least costly selection tools should be used first.* In other words, the initial screening should be set up so that applicants who obviously do not possess the qualifications for the job are efficiently eliminated.

As discussed in chapter 5, there are a variety of laws that relate to recruitment and selection; so, sales managers must be sure that they are applying these selection tools in a way that does not unfairly discriminate against certain classes of people. As a result of these laws and their enforcement, there is certain information that employers should *not* request during the selection process. For example, questions about age, marital status, and religion should generally be avoided. Also, sales managers involved in this process should be sure to understand the concepts of **validation** and **bona fide occupational qualifications (BFOQs),** which are explained in the Hiring and the Law box.

CONSIDER THIS...

Hiring and the Law

As a result of laws and their enforcement by the Equal Employment Opportunity Commission (EEOC) and the Office of Federal Contract Compliance (OFCC), the selection tools should not screen out candidates based on factors not related to the job—especially if those factors lead to discrimination against legally protected classes of people, such as women, minorities, religious groups, and those with disabilities.

Hiring decisions should not be made on gut feeling. Rather, sales organizations should base their selection of employees on objective criteria, which are (1) independently measurable, (2) job related, and (3) predictive of performance. For most sales positions, previous years of sales experience meets these three criteria.

To meet affirmative action guidelines, companies should keep an "applicant flowchart" that lists the processed applicants by key demographic data, such as sex and ethnic group. If the company finds that it is rejecting a disproportionately high number of women or minority applicants, it should review each step in the hiring process to determine which tool is producing this result. Once identified, the particular tool must undergo a validation procedure if management wants to continue using it.

Validation is the process of statistically measuring the extent to which a given selection tool or hiring qualification is related to job performance. To reduce selection mistakes and possible legal hassles later,

companies should validate their selection tools as soon as possible—ideally, the tool should be validated *before* using it. This not only protects the hiring organization in legal disputes, but also increases its chances of hiring the best people for the job (by using the most appropriate selection criteria).

Note that some information that would be illegal to gather in most situations, can be gathered under *certain* situations. For example, human resource personnel may ask questions in sensitive areas *after* the person is hired, as in asking about age and marital status for insurance purposes. Further, interviewers may ask questions in sensitive areas during the interviews if they relate to **bona fide occupational qualifications (BFOQs).** Of course, age and sex are BFOQs when hiring an actor to play the lead role in *Annie the Musical*; and religion is a BFOQ when selecting clergy for a particular church.

Courts are careful to allow only very narrow exceptions to discriminating against protected groups, and so, there are not many examples of this in the hiring of sales professionals. It is legal, however, to hire only those who can lift so many pounds for certain food or beverage delivery seller positions where part of the sales job is to stock shelves, set up displays, etc. This strength qualification might disproportionately discriminate against women or those with disabilities, yet this is allowable given that it is a legitimate BFOQ.

Selection tools and procedures are only *aids* to sound executive judgment and not *substitutes* for it. They can eliminate obviously unqualified candidates and generally help recruiters spot extremely capable individuals. However, for the mass of recruits between these extremes, the tools currently used can only predict those who have the *potential* to be successful in the job. Executive judgment still plays a critical role in making the final choice.

Each of the five categories of selection tools is described in greater detail in the following sections.

Resumes/Application Forms

A resume and/or a completed application form fit into the same category of selection tools in that they both typically contain a record of the applicant's work experience, education, honors, special skills, relevant outside-of-work activities, and other accomplishments and experiences. Compared to an application form, a resume is more commonly used as a selection tool for business-to-business sales positions. Application forms *by themselves* tend to be used for lower level sales jobs, such as those in retail sales; however, many sales organizations have candidates apply by (1) submitting a resume and (2) completing an application form through the company website.

A resume is widely used in screening applicants; and in fact, is often the first selection tool used. Certainly, many applicants are *eliminated* because of a less than impressive resume, but few if any salespeople are ever *hired* based only on information found on a piece of paper. Those who do move past this step are typically further screened by the next selection tool: the interview.

In fact, the information found on a resume is often the basis for probing in an interview, as an interviewer often asks several follow-up questions about this information. Using an analysis of this information in relation to differences in performance for its current and past salespeople, a firm can determine whether certain characteristics should be weighted more heavily than others. For example, Total Quality Logistics analyzed the resumes of their existing sales force (i.e., the resumes that these salespeople had used to get hired); and found that those with typos on their resumes had significantly lower sales performance than those who had submitted error-free resumes! Consequently, TQL increased the importance of this in their selection process.

Personal Interviews

Virtually no salesperson is ever hired without a **personal interview,** and there are no satisfactory substitutes for this procedure. Much has been written about the relative advantages of the other selection tools, but nothing takes the place of getting to know applicants personally by talking to them.

A personal interview is used basically to determine a person's fitness for a job. Moreover, personal interviews disclose characteristics that are not always observable by other means. An interview is probably the best way to find out about the recruit's conversational ability, speaking voice, and social intelligence. By seeing the applicant in person, an executive can appraise physical characteristics such as general appearance and care given to clothes—and also, whether or not the applicant has visible tattoos! (See box titled "What Tattoos Tell Customers about Salespeople.") Research shows that image does have a

CONSIDER THIS...

What Tattoos Tell Customers about Salespeople

Many sales organizations have strict rules prohibiting visible tattoos on salespeople, but that is changing as tattoos have become more popular in recent years. A recent poll found that 1 out of every 5 adults (or 21 percent) has at least one tattoo; and that nearly 40 percent of younger adults (ages 18 to 29) have tattoos.

Research has shown that salespeople with tattoos are not automatically viewed negatively by customers. Not surprisingly, customers with tattoos trust and are more willing to work with tattooed salespeople than people who do not have tattoos. In other words, when selling to customer segments where tattoos are common, the presence of a tattoo should not affect the hiring decision.

SOURCE: Aaron D. Arndt and Myron Glassman, "What Tattoos Tell Customers about Salespeople: The Role of Gender Norms," *Marketing Management Journal,* Spring 2012 Vol. 22(1), pages 50-65.

direct impact on sales performance.[3] The interview also may reveal certain personality traits. The interviewer may note the applicant's poise under the strain of an interview, along with any tendency to dominate or lead a conversation.

Another purpose in interviewing is to get further information about or to interpret facts stated on the resume or applicant form. For example, an applicant may have referenced that he or she was a district manager in a previous job. The prospective employer may ask what their responsibilities were and how many employees they supervised.

Fundamentally, all the questions asked during an interview are aimed at learning four points about the applicant:

1. Is this person capable of excelling at this job?
2. How badly does this person want the job?
3. Will the job help this person realize his or her goals?
4. Will this person work to his or her fullest ability?

These points cover the applicant's past behavior, experiences, environment, and motivation. Another set of questions typically deals with an applicant's future goals. Within these broad categories of past behavior and future goals, each firm must select those inquiries that are pertinent for its sales positions.

Finally, the interview is not only a means by which a company determines an applicant's fitness for a job; it is also a tool for "selling" the position and the company to the recruit. The interviewer can help interest applicants by talking about the nature of the job, the compensation, the type of training and supervision provided, and the opportunities for the future.

Reliability of Personal Interviews as Predictors of Success

Interviews are the most widely used selection tool. Studies have found that interviews can be good predictors of success on the job—but only if they are done well.[4] For sales positions, the interview is probably even more valid as a predictor of success. This is due in part to the fact that the sales job requires skills similar to those on display in the interview. Also, it has been discovered that structured situation-based interviews are better predictors of subsequent success than other types of interviews.[5] (This type of interview is discussed later in this chapter).

Too often, however, interviews are not as effective as they could be. An inherent weakness is that the interviewing process is heavily dependent on the behavior of the interviewer. Unfortunately, many people do not know how to interview an applicant effectively, nor do they know how to interpret an applicant's responses. An interviewer's reactions, for example, can greatly affect an applicant's performance. It is so important, and yet so difficult, for an interviewer to remain completely neutral and consistent through a series of interviews with several applicants. Another problem is that an interviewer's first impression may be based on gut reaction instead of on an objective evaluation of the candidate's qualifications. This reaction is highly subjective and therefore may not be consistent with the impression that other interviewers have. Still another behavioral consideration is that most interviewers talk too much, listen too little, and ask the wrong questions. These factors tend to lower the value of the interviewing process as a selection tool. Consequently, most interviewers do not accomplish their intended goal of matching applicants with hiring specifications and thus predicting job performance. Yet, despite all of these potential shortcomings, a well-planned, properly conducted interview is a valid predictor of performance and should always be used in the selection process.

Improving the Validity of Interviews

There are ways to offset potential weaknesses and improve the validity of interviews as predictors of job performance. It is important for the recruiter to thoroughly review the applicant's resume or application before proceeding further in the selection process. Sometimes companies use a telephone interview or a brief in-person interview (such as a campus interview or a job fair interview) as part of the initial screening process. The screening step can weed out obviously unqualified or uninterested candidates. It also may highlight certain aspects of the candidate's background that are in need of further investigation.

It is also important to have more than one interview with each candidate. In general, a company should not depend on a single interview held in a single place with a single interviewer. This advice is based on the assumption that the more time a company spends with prospective recruits and the more people who talk with them, the greater the opportunity to get to know them well. Additionally, interviewers should use standardized rating forms that they fill out after each interview with an applicant. Those in charge of hiring can review the information on these forms, evaluate it, and use it for making comparisons among the applicants.

Another way to improve validity is to train interviewers on how to conduct interviews and how to use rating forms. Training sessions that involve practice interviews with a follow-up group discussion can increase the consistency of applicant ratings by the interviewers. Additional suggestions for improving the interviewing process are discussed below.

Interview Structure

Selection interviews can differ according to the extent to which the questions are detailed in advance and the conversation is guided by the interviewer. At one end of the scale is the totally structured or guided interview, and at the other end is the informal or nondirected type.

Guided Interviews

The procedure in a **guided interview** is highly standardized. All interviewers for a firm use the same guide sheet containing a series of questions. The interviewer asks these questions and makes notations concerning the candidate's responses. The guided interview seeks to overcome common problems encountered in using personal interviews as a selection technique. Many sales executives engaged in selection activities do not know what questions to ask. They may know the qualifications for the job, but they do not know what questions will tell them whether the applicant possesses these characteristics.

Also, because all of the applicants are asked the same questions and their responses are recorded, an interviewer working alone can readily compare and rate the candidates he or she has seen. Furthermore, several interviewers who have seen either the same or a different set of candidates have a good basis for comparing their evaluations. Some people criticize the guided interview as being inflexible. But this is not necessarily the case. Trained interviewers can use their judgment and make slight modifications without detracting from the full value of the guided form.

Nondirected Interviews

At the other end of the structured interview scale is the **nondirected interview.** Ordinarily, the interviewer asks a few questions to get the applicant talking on certain subjects, such as his or her business experiences, home life, or school activities. The interviewer does very little talking—just enough to keep the conversation rolling. The theory is that significant characteristics come to light if the applicant is encouraged to speak freely.

The major problem with the nondirected interview is that much time may be wasted unearthing little information. Some of what an applicant says may be irrelevant or impossible to evaluate. Also, the values of standardization are lost in the nondirected interview. Research has demonstrated that this type of interview is not a very accurate predictor of job performance.[6]

There are also legal concerns about nondirected interviews. Without a script or outline to follow, untrained interviewers are more likely to ask questions that cover sensitive topics that might discriminate against protected groups. For an overview of what sales managers can and cannot ask about during an interview, see the list of illegal interview questions in Figure 6-1.

Most firms today use an interview format somewhere between the guided and the nondirected interview, such as those described in the next section.

Interview Focus

Many companies now use interviews that focus on the applicant's behavior. One type poses questions concerning candidates' intended behaviors in defined situations (**situation-based**) or past behaviors (**behavior-based**) that relate to their sales aptitude. Another allows interviewers to observe candidates' performance on selling-related exercises (**performance-based**).

Situation- and Behavior-Based Interviews   Questions that focus on intended or past behaviors in sales situations are based on the premise that what a

FIGURE 6-1

Illegal Interview Questions

Illegal Question	Rationale
How Old Are You?	Any question that gets at the candidates' age is illegal to ask because the Age Discrimination in Employment Act protects people over 40. This includes questions about when they graduated from school, and/or how long have they worked...
Have You Ever Been Arrested?	Questions about whether they have been arrested are always illegal. However, if the sales job involves sensitive information (e.g., financial issues) for which trustworthiness is important, then candidates can be asked if they have ever been *convicted* of specific crimes.
How Is Your Health?	Any question about the candidates' general health is illegal. This includes questions about how much they weigh, how tall they are, how many sick days they used in a past job. It is also illegal to ask about disabilities; however, employers can ask about specific physical abilities related to specific tasks required for the job (e.g., Can you lift 50 pounds?).
Are You Married?	Any question referring to information about family plans (e.g., marriage, engagement, and child planning) is illegal. This is also viewed as an indirect way to ask someone about their sexual orientation, which is a protected class in most U.S. states.
What Is Your Religion?	Questions that ask about any aspect of religion are absolutely off limits during interviews. This includes general questions about any social or charitable organizations, because that could lead to candidates revealing participation in groups affiliated with religion (e.g., The Salvation Army). However, it is fine to ask about job-related organizations (e.g., The American Marketing Association).
What Is Your Nationality?	It is illegal to ask any question about where candidates were born—or even if they are a U.S. citizen. However, employers do have the right to determine whether candidates can legally work for them. Similarly, asking about what languages they speak is fine as long as (1) the question does not get into *where* they learned the language, and (2) language fluency is part of the job.
Do You Like To Drink Socially?	This question should be avoided as recovering alcoholics are protected under the American With Disabilities Act (ADA). In fact, questions about whether candidates smoke are also illegal—even if the company has a strict no-smoking policy.
Have You Ever Used Drugs In the Past?	This is a bad question first because it is so vague, as it refers to anything from illegal narcotics to prescription drugs. Note that employers can legally ask if candidates are *currently* using illegal drugs; however, asking about past drug use is off limits as the ADA protects those being treated for former addictions.

SOURCE: Patrick Allan, "The Most Common Illegal Job Interview Questions You Should Watch Out For," *Lifehacker*, May 26, 2015. Retrieved from the following URL on May 22, 2016: http://lifehacker.com/the-most-common-illegal-job-interview-questions-you-sho-1706238105

person says they will do in the future or what they have done in the past is indicative of what he or she will actually do in the future. Applicants who have performed successfully in the past are expected to be successful in the new job. As shown in Figure 6-2, Rubbermaid is a company that uses this type of interview. Looking for clues that indicate how the potential salesperson deals with other people, Rubbermaid's recruiters ask specific questions about how he or she has handled real situations in the past.[7]

Focusing on past behaviors is valid if the new job is similar to the old one. However, if the applicant has not had experiences similar to those in the new job, then exploring past behavior becomes less useful. In this case it may be better to ask about *intended behaviors*—how applicants think they would behave

Traditional	Behavior-Based	
Do you get along with people?	Tell me about an incident in your last job that caused conflict with a customer. How did you react to this?	
What is your biggest weakness?	Tell me about your greatest failure	
	Situation-Based	
What qualities do you think are important for success in this job?	A potential customer has just told you that your competition got the order. What do you do now?	

FIGURE 6-2

Types of interview questions

in job-related situations. This type of question is based on the premise that people's behavioral intentions are related to their subsequent behavior.

Performance-Based Interviews   Some companies ask candidates to perform *exercises simulating selling situations* (**performance-based interview**). For example, at Copyrite, Inc., candidates first review the annual report and videotapes on the company. Then they are asked to "sell the interviewer on the company from what they have learned." The Office Place, an office supply and equipment dealer, gives candidates a product ID number and asks them to be prepared to make a presentation on that product during their interviews.[8] Students doing role plays in university sales competitions are essentially doing a performance-based interview with the recruiters who serve as judges.

These exercises are valuable in showing how much time, effort, skill, and creativity the candidates bring to their presentations.

Stress Interviews   The **stress interview** is one in which the interviewer intentionally places the applicant under stress. For example, the applicant may be handed an object such as a pen or a notebook and asked to "sell" it to the interviewer. In recent years, a number of companies have been asking interviewees to solve brainteasers and riddles in order to gauge their ability to think quickly and creatively. The answer isn't as important as how one gets there—test yourself on the examples in the box titled "Brainteaser Interview Questions;" and remember, there is no "correct answer" to any of them. The purpose of asking these questions is to reveal how a candidate might work through a problem.

In some stress interviews, the interviewer may be intentionally rude, silent, or overly aggressive in questioning just to see how the candidate will react. The ultimate performance-based, stressful exercise in sales is one in which the candidate rides with a rep to observe several cold calls and then is asked to make a cold call on his or her own.

These techniques give the interviewer some idea of how the candidate will behave under the stress encountered in the sales job. However, these methods also can irritate applicants and lessen their interest in the job.

Timing and Method of the Interview

Because interviewing takes executives' valuable time, the interviewer should quickly find out whether the recruit is interested and qualified to move forward in the interview process. The interviewer should first give a brief job description and then ask a few questions concerning the minimum requirements. Many companies conduct an initial *telephone interview.* Figure 6-3 is an example

CONSIDER THIS...

Brainteaser Interview Questions

How many quarters—placed one on top of the other—would it take to reach the top of the Empire State Building?

How many times do a clock's hands overlap in a day?

How would you weigh a plane without scales?

Tell me 10 ways to use a pencil other than writing.

If you were an animal, which one would you want to be?

Why is there fuzz on a tennis ball?

If you could choose one superhero power, what would it be and why?

If you could get rid of any one of the US states, which one would you get rid of and why?

With your eyes closed, tell me step-by-step how to tie my shoes.

SOURCE: Thad Peterson, "Beat Interview Brainteasers," *Monster.com* website blog. Retrieved from the following URL on May 24, 2016: http://www.monster.com/career-advice/article/brainteaser-interviews

of a patterned interview form when a telephone interview is the initial screening device.

Some companies use a *face-to-face interview* as the initial screening device. For example, when recruiting teams visit college campuses, one or more team members may briefly interview a prospect to determine whether that person should be considered further. Initial screening interviews should last only 15 or 20 minutes. Figure 6-4 is an example of a form used to evaluate sales applicants during an interview.

With the increased availability of technology such as Skype, a number of companies have started using videoconferencing to interview candidates. The *videoconference interview* can then be recorded and replayed multiple times to all those who will take part in the hiring decision. It is expected that use of videoconferencing will continue to increase due to the savings in time and cost it allows.

Firms that do a thorough selection job ordinarily interview applicants several times before they are hired. After applicants pass through the initial screen, much remains for the company to learn about them before a final decision can be made. In turn, candidates must be told many things about the job. The more times a company spends with prospective recruits and the more people who talk with them, the greater the opportunity to get to know them well. Although telephone interviews and videoconferencing may be used in the earlier stages, final interviews will generally be conducted in person.

EMPLOYMENT TESTING

Employment testing, which is sometimes called psychological testing and includes everything from intelligence to personality tests, is another major tool often used in the sales selection process. Typically a company uses a battery of employment tests rather than a single test. Over the years, employment testing has undoubtedly been the most controversial of all the selection tools. Today the added burden of complying with legal guidelines has increased the complexity and controversy surrounding such testing. Even so, it is becoming increasingly popular as a selection tool.

Applicant	Interviewer	Date
1. Would you tell me about your current job? (Determine whether the applicant has related experience, training, interest, etc.)		
2. Why are you looking for a job at this time? (Determine whether reasons are acceptable).		
3. Why are you looking for this particular job with our company? (Determine whether the applicant's perceptions of the job are sufficiently accurate.)		
4. What background, qualifications, and abilities do you feel you have which would enable you to be successful on this job? (Determine whether the applicant can sell him/herself and whether these qualifications are beneficial.)		
5. What are your salary expectations? (Determine whether the applicant is realistic.)		
6. Where do you expect to be in five years from now? (Determine whether the applicant is realistic.)		
7. When would you be able to start? (Determine whether this fits into our needs.)		
Summary of Applicants Qualifications		
Apparent Strengths:		
Apparent Weaknesses:		
Interviewer's Recommendations		
A. Do you recommend this candidate for testing? Yes____ No____		
B. Areas requiring clarification in additional interviewers:		

FIGURE 6-3
Telephone Screen Evaluation

There are five different categories of employment tests used in selecting and hiring.

1. **Mental Intelligence Tests** are intended to measure a person's intelligence quotient (IQ) and general ability to learn. Some examples of these tests are (1) the Otis Self-Administering Test of Mental Ability and (2) the Wonderlic Personnel Test.
2. **Sales Aptitude Tests** are designed to measure a person's aptitude for selling. This category also includes tests that measure social aptitude (social intelligence). Some examples are (1) the Sales Aptitude Checklist, and (2) the General Sales Aptitude Test.
3. **Interest Tests** are designed to measure or compare a person's interests with the interests of successful people in specific occupations. Some examples are (1) the Strong-Campbell Interest Inventory and (2) the Kuder Occupational Interest Survey.

Candidate's Name:		Interviewer		Date	
Rating scale					
N = No opportunity to observe or assess	1 = Shows evidence of improvement needs in all Key Actions (i.e., ineffective in all)	2 = Shows evidence of improvement needs in most Key Actions (i.e., ineffective in most)	3 = Shows positive evidence of most Key Actions (i.e., effective in most); has small needs for improvement in one or two Key Actions.	4 = Shows positive evidence of most Key Actions (i.e., effective in most); has no significant needs for improvement.	5 = Shows positive evidence of all Key Actions (i.e., effective in all); has no need for improvement in any Key Action.

Job Dimension	Rating
Overall Technical Knowledge	_____
Sales Ability/Persuasiveness	_____
Personal Drive	_____
Customer Driven Approach	_____
Initiating Action	_____
Cross Functional Teamwork	_____
Motivational Fit	_____
Communication Skills	_____

Recommendation For The Position Of: _____
As Per Hiring Decision Guidelines (Check One)

_____ Hire = No more than one rating of less than 3; No ratings of 1

_____ Hold = No more than two ratings of less than 3; No ratings of 1

_____ Not Hire = More than two ratings of less than 3 and/or any rating of 1

Additional Comments:

FIGURE 6-4

Sales Interview Rating Form

4. **Personality Tests** are intended to measure various personality traits. These tests are the most risky and difficult to validate because of our inability to identify the traits needed for a particular sales job. Some examples of these tests are (1) the Bernreuter Personality Inventory, and (2) the Edwards Personal Preference Schedule.

5. **Drug Tests** are unique from the other categories, as they are a *physical* test of the applicants' blood, breath, urine, or hair; and are typically done in the final stages of selection—often *after* a job offer has been made. It is illegal to covertly test for drug use; in fact, employers face serious legal difficulties if the test is somehow performed without the knowledge or consent of the applicant.

The increased use of employment tests has occurred because studies have established the performance-related validity of these tests. In other words, certain personality characteristics (as discussed in the previous chapter) have been shown to be related to performance.[9] Finally, as the cost of making a poor selection decision continues to rise, employers are turning to testing as an additional means of improving their selection decisions.

Legal Aspects of Testing

Although federal legislation put restraints on the use of testing in the selection process, *testing is legal.* In fact, a testing and selection order issued by the Office of Federal Contract Compliance says that "properly validated and standardized employee selection procedures can significantly contribute to the implementation of nondiscriminatory personnel policies" and that "professionally developed tests … may significantly aid in the development and maintenance of an efficient work force." The key phrases in this quotation are *properly validated* and *professionally developed.* These requirements are discussed below.

A Framework for Testing

Ideally, tests should provide objective information about a candidate's skills and abilities. Companies can and should use this information to support what is discovered in the interview process or to uncover areas to explore during the interview. It is important to remember that no test can predict with 100 percent accuracy. Therefore, the results should *not* be used as the sole acceptance or knockout factor. Accordingly, the test results should not include a hiring recommendation. Rather, it is the responsibility of the hiring manager to decide whether the particular testing profile is correct for the job in question.[10]

Selecting and Developing Tests. In building a good testing program, a company should use tests that measure the criteria developed during the planning phase of the hiring process. The firm can develop in-house tests with the aid of company or outside psychologists. Alternatively, it can use tests professionally developed by outside consulting firms such as the Klein Behavioral Science Consultants or the Austin Technology Incubator (ATI) Company. Typically, tests developed outside have a broad usage base, which makes validation less complicated and less costly.

However, many testing specialists and managers agree that the variable requirements of different sales jobs call for customized tests. Many firms use customized sales aptitude tests to identify behaviors that are critical to a specific sales position.[11]

Companies should validate each test they use as part of the selection process. As discussed earlier in this chapter, this means that the company should be able to demonstrate a relationship between test results and the performance of its salespeople. If the company is using standard tests supplied by an outside consulting firm, the supplier should provide proof of the tests' validity. If the company has developed customized tests, it must validate them.

Problems in Testing[12]

Most testing procedures generate the concept of an average or normal type of employee. The implication is that this person is the best to hire for a given job. The danger is that a potentially successful sales representative may be screened out simply because he or she does not fit the stereotype. Testing may eliminate a truly creative person who does not fall in the average or normal range in testing. The creativity that does not measure well on a standardized test may be the very trait that would make that person an outstanding sales representative.

Another problem with testing is that tests are sometimes used as the sole deciding knockout factor. An applicant may look good based on the resume, interviews, and reference checks; but if the test scores are especially low, management may be reluctant to hire that person.

Tests are sometimes misused because executives fail to apply the concept of a *range* of scores. For many kinds of tests, psychologists agree that a range of scores is acceptable. All who fall within that range should be judged as *equally qualified for the job.* Unfortunately, most people tend to feel that a person scoring near the high end of the acceptable range is a better prospect than one scoring in the lower part of that range.

Another factor to watch for in testing is that applicants can fake the answers on some tests, especially on some personality or interest tests. Reasonably intelligent applicants for a sales job know they should indicate a preference for mixing with people, in contrast to staying home and reading a good book. Cultural bias is another situation that can creep into tests. A person may score poorly, not because of a lack of interest, aptitude, or native intelligence, but only because the test included questions that assumed a certain cultural background.

References And Other Outside Sources

When processing applicants for sales jobs, an administrator can get help from two general sources of information outside the company. In the first, the applicant furnishes the leads, name, phone number, e-mail address, or other contact information of a person who is familiar with his or her experience or aptitude; this is called a **reference**. In the other, the company solicits information on its own initiative; this source includes credit and insurance reports, school records, social media checks, and motor vehicle histories.

A company may check an applicant's references by letter, telephone, or personal visit. Each method has some limitations. A personal visit may take too much time, and it is not practical unless the reference is located near the prospective employer. Using a personal visit or the telephone is advantageous because nothing is in writing. However, some references, especially those at companies with strict policies in this area, will not supply information to a stranger over the telephone. A letter is probably used more frequently than the two other methods, but often it is of very little value. Firms hesitate to put anything derogatory in writing. This leads us to the big problem today with any kind of reference check. Companies are extremely leery about giving out meaningful information regarding former employees. Reference policies may, in effect, put a tight rein on the employee information they release. This situation has developed because companies fear being sued for defamation of character.

Despite the obstacles, management should not bypass references as a selection tool. If only one significant fact is uncovered, it makes the effort worthwhile. When talking with an applicant's former employer, a key question to ask is: Would you rehire this person? Additional questions that may provide some insights are: In which areas does the applicant need improvement? Why did the applicant leave? Did performance in the applicant's territory go up or down after he or she left? For the reasons noted above, companies generally give very positive references only to those people who deserve them and say little, except to verify information, about those whose performance was inadequate.

Most people list as references only those who are certain to give them a positive reference. In order to get a more balanced picture of the candidate, you can ask the reference for the names of several other people who would be familiar with the applicant's work. Also, if you are hiring salespeople with experience, the best reference source is the candidate's previous customers. They can provide an accurate picture of the salesperson's skills or personality. Questions that should be asked are: How would you rank this person compared to other salespeople who currently call on you? Was this person genuinely interested in serving your needs? Was the candidate efficient and dependable?

Background Checks

A special source of outside information is the **credit report**, or a report from some other investigating agency. These agencies specialize in pre-employment investigative interviews with former employers, co-workers, neighbors, and creditors. Reports from local credit bureaus, through their affiliation with their national association, can provide a wealth of information on a prospective salesperson. Often, former employers and other references give information to a credit bureau that they would not divulge to a prospective employer. Several companies—Equifax and Fidelifacts/Metropolitan New York, for example—specialize in providing pre-employment data to employers. Using information from several different databases, they provide summaries of the applicant's financial condition, criminal and driving records, and employment history.

Today, reference checks and other forms of background investigation are critical because, sad to say, too many job applicants lie about their backgrounds. Some applicants lie about their educational record, past salaries, and/or past job responsibilities. Career fraud—that's the fancy name for it—often goes undetected, simply because many companies don't take the time and effort needed to do a thorough background check.

Legal Considerations

Essentially any question that is illegal to ask a candidate is also illegal to ask a reference. All inquiries should be job related. One step companies can take to lessen the legal liability that occurs in checking references is to ask the candidate to sign a release form that gives the company permission to contact previous employers, educational institutions, and so on. Employers may run credit checks on applicants without informing them. But if candidates are rejected on the basis of a credit check, they must be informed of this.

Assessment Centers

An **assessment center** is another selection tool a company can use as part of its sales force hiring process. A company sets up an area in which it conducts a lengthy assessment experience. Candidates are given simulated exercises that they must perform as if they were in a real organization.[13] Such exercises may involve business games, case analyses, leaderless discussion groups, role-playing, or individual presentations. The assessment is conducted by trained executive observers and usually takes from one to three days. Assessment centers have been used primarily to evaluate people for promotion within a firm and to aid in an individual's professional development. However, they also have been used in selecting new salespeople. AT&T uses assessment centers to evaluate candidates for account management positions. The main factor limiting the use of this tool is probably its high cost.

THE JOB OFFER DECISION

When all the steps in the selection process have been completed, one thing remains to be done. A company must decide whether to make a job offer. This decision involves a review of everything known about each applicant. What detailed impressions have the applicants made? What are their qualifications, and what is their potential? What do they want, and what can the firm offer them? This last point is far broader than just the monetary aspects of the job. It involves all the hopes and ambitions of each applicant as matched against the opportunities and rewards offered by the job and the company.

Ranking the Recruits

The hiring company should develop two lists: The first is a list of the recruits in the order of the firm's preference for them; the second is a list of the recruits in the order of their preference for the firm. The second list can be developed by the firm's interviewers according to how interested the recruits seemed in joining the firm during the interviews.

Should the firm make offers to those who top its preference list regardless of their apparent interest? The decision depends on the depth of the list, the decrease in quality as people of lesser rank are considered, the amount of money involved, the time factors faced by both the recruits and the sales managers, and competing offers from other firms. The costly recruiting and selection process can be completely nullified if the person or people selected do not accept the firm's offer.

Communicating with Applicants

At this stage, it is important that the company not leave any applicant dangling. If the firm clearly has decided *not* to hire a certain applicant, an executive should gently, but clearly, tell the person. To those applicants who are still in contention for the job, an executive might say something like this at the close of an interview: "As you know, we have several people applying for this position. My hope is that we will move along in the process and be able to notify you one way or another in two weeks."

If the decision is to hire a certain person, the next step is to make a formal offer and persuade the person to accept it.

THE HIRING PHASE

A well-designed **hiring** process properly implemented tells the recruit that the firm is well managed and that it really wants the recruit as an employee. Sometimes firms inadvertently send a message of indifference to the recruit: "It's no big deal one way or the other to us if you take the job." Remember that everyone likes to feel important. People seek work environments in which they are made to feel that they somehow make a difference, that they are important to the company.

Extending the Offer

The most important part of the offer is, of course, the compensation that the salesperson will be paid. The type and amount of compensation are covered in detail in Chapter 9. The offer also should include the other benefits that will be part of the employment package. These might include any or all of the following: insurance, retirement contributions, vacation pay, educational benefits, profit sharing, and company car. In many cases, to alleviate some of the inconveniences of moving, the new employee's relocation expenses also are paid. Most large companies usually pay for moving expenses when they transfer employees.

A number of firms now also offer to help the potential employee's spouse or significant other find a job. While this may not need to be a part of the formal offer, it may be a very important consideration in the candidate's decision. As more families have come to include two people who are pursuing careers, it has become important that both people are able to find good employment opportunities in the same location. Helping the other person identify job opportunities will certainly create a very positive impression on the candidate—and could be the factor that causes the recruit to accept one firm's offer over another attractive offer.

Extending a Job Offer

RUNNING CASE
Shiderlots
Elevators, Inc.

"I need some time to think about your offer, Mr. Dark. I feel that changing jobs is a serious matter, and I don't want to act too suddenly. The job does appeal to me and definitely would be a step up for me. Can I give you an answer on March 15th?" asked Nicole Stuckey in her reply to Adam Dark's job offer over the telephone a dreary day in early February.

Dark had been under considerable pressure from his boss to hire a new Account Manager for the sales territory that had been vacated when one of the firm's older reps had retired. He had recruited and interviewed four experienced salespeople, all of whom were qualified for the job. However, Stuckey stood out as the most promising one. Further, Stuckey had experience in the elevator industry with one of Shiderlots competitors—which was why Adam told his colleagues that Nicole could really "hit the ground running."

After consulting with his boss, Dark had called Stuckey to make her the firm's standard job offer. He was somewhat surprised by her request for more time to think about it; he thought she wanted the job and was eager to get going.

Dark also was eager to get the position filled because many of the accounts in the territory had voiced some concern about the company's inattention to their needs during the past several weeks. Dark had been trying to cover the territory as best he could, but the time he could spend there was limited given all of his other managerial duties.

Dark stalled for a few moments, making some pleasant remarks about how happy he was that Stuckey liked Shiderlots—but he had to reply to her request for time *now.*

Question: Exactly what should Adam Dark say to Nicole Stuckey?

Who will make the offer? How will it be made? Will a contract be written up? Some firms want the sales manager for whom the recruit will be working to make the offer. Other firms leave such matters to professionals in the human resources department. Sometimes high-level executives, even the company president, may make the offer in the hope of impressing the recruit with the importance of the job.

Most job offers are initially made over the telephone. Before picking up the phone, the sales manager must make two important decisions: (1) how much time will be allowed for acceptance? And (2) what concession will be made if the recruit wants to negotiate some of the terms of the deal? Once on the telephone, the manager will have to make some quick decisions about these matters. Prior consideration greatly facilitates a smooth telephone offer. A formal letter follows only if the candidate accepts the telephone offer. This letter is very important and requires careful wording since it becomes a contract.

Aggressive managers often prefer to make job offers in person. This puts more pressure on the recruit to respond favorably and quickly. It is quite easy for the recruit to avoid giving direct answers over the telephone. Moreover, the telephone does not allow the manager to read the recruit's body language to make additional judgments about the negotiations.

SOCIALIZATION AND ASSIMILATION

Socialization is the process through which the new recruits take on the values and attitudes of the people who are already working for the firm. This process begins before recruits go to work for the company and continues until they are fully assimilated into the company's culture. Successful socialization of recruits and new salespeople helps them adjust to their new jobs. More important, it also leads to increased involvement and job satisfaction in the long run.

Preentry Socialization

Both before accepting the offer and during the pre-employment period, the recruits will start thinking about the experiences they are about to encounter, and they will begin to prepare themselves mentally. It is critical that the candidates by provided with realistic **job previews** that allow them to make informed employment decisions. Having accurate information about the job and the company helps the recruit form realistic expectations about the challenges to be faced and the level of effort and the kinds of skills required to meet these challenges. It also allows recruits to decide whether there is congruence between their values and those of the company. After a recruit accepts the offer, realism at the pre-employment stage will lead to greater satisfaction with the job and commitment to the company.[14]

Most firms start indoctrinating the recruit the minute initial contact is made. Booklets describe the operations of the company and its distinctive qualities. These publications are part of the recruiting process described in chapter 5. Further introductory work is done in the selection interviews, as discussed in this chapter. The sales executive describes the company's operations and answers the recruit's questions. The thoroughness of the interview will tell the recruit something about the organization even before the offer is made.

Many firms go a step further in presenting a realistic picture by asking recruits to view a video of the salesperson on the job. Northwestern Mutual Life, IBM, and Deloitte are among the firms providing the recruits with interactive programs filled with information on the job and the company. Deloitte information categories include information on the company's mission and shared values statement, an overview of the firm, details on training, employee benefits, and professional development opportunities.[15] Some firms ask recruits to spend a day making calls with a salesperson so that they will have a more realistic perspective of what the job entails.

For college students, a summer internship is one of the best ways to learn about a company before making a long-term commitment by accepting a job offer. Some of the most highly sought after internships for business students have been with tech firms such as Google, Facebook, and Twitter. The best internships not only pay well, but they also give interns an opportunity to interact with clients and do real work for the company.[16]

The more recruits understand about the company and its culture before making a decision, the more effective their self-selection will be. That is, those people who fit in the company's culture are more likely to accept the offer than those who don't. Also, the more information recruits get at this stage, the smoother their assimilation into the organization will be.

Assimilation of New Hires

The second stage in the socialization process—**assimilation**—begins when the recruits accept the position. The newly hired employees must learn how to perform the tasks associated with their jobs, and they must become familiar with the people in various work groups with whom they must interact. In many companies, a great deal of this information will be covered in an initial training program. However, assimilation cannot be accomplished exclusively through training. There must be a conscious effort made to provide recruits with information, experience, and the personal attention that will enable them to understand the informal as well as the formal norms and values of the corporate culture.

It is especially difficult to assimilate new sales reps when they are thrust into a sales territory with no home-office training. The new person has little opportunity to become integrated with the work group. For this reason, it is usually advisable to keep new salespeople around the home office long enough to get to know the employees in supporting departments very well.

The first few days are particularly trying, since the new person has not had time to develop communications with the other members of the organization and must look to the manager for answers. The manager should give as much time as possible to starting the trainee in the right direction. A good technique is to confer with the new employee at the beginning of each day, for a time, to answer questions and present new material. The trainee should be encouraged to ask questions about the job and the company.

New sales reps appreciate this attention. It makes them feel wanted and valued by the company—something most individuals earnestly seek. One of the quickest ways to affect people's attitudes adversely is to ignore them. New reps may interpret a lack of attention to mean that the sales manager does not care about them, even if the truth is that the executive is just preoccupied with operational problems. It comes as quite a blow to new workers to encounter such apparent lack of interest, since they were given so much attention while they were being interviewed. If the honeymoon ends abruptly, the new hires may believe their recruitment was just sales talk and they should have known better than to be taken in by it. The wise sales manager will try to prolong the honeymoon until the new people can take their places in the organization with confidence.

Relationships

A new rep needs to know from whom to take orders. The entire organizational plan should be explained so that the rep knows his or her relationship to others, who else reports to the rep's immediate boss, and to whom the boss reports in the department and the company. The support staff must be informed of their relationship to the new person. Those who report to the same boss must become acquainted with their new workmate, and other employees also should be informed about the position the new rep occupies.

Introductions are a two-way street—a new salesperson is eager to meet other employees and they want to meet him or her. The introductions should be so arranged that those involved have enough time to do more than just say hello. A short chat with each person is helpful. It allows people to form more than a quick impression of each other, and it helps them to remember names. Present employees should be given background information on the new salesperson so that they can converse on some common ground. The new rep should be briefed on the people to be met—who they are, what they do, and what their interests are.

Mentoring New Employees

A **mentor** is someone with knowledge, experience, rank, or power who provides personal counseling and career guidance for younger employees. Reports indicate that over 70 percent of Fortune 500 companies have formal mentoring programs.[17] The goals of these programs are to make the employees feel comfortable in their new jobs, to teach them the corporate culture, to give them someone to whom they can turn when they need support or advice, and, in some cases, to push them up the corporate ladder. Research has demonstrated that mentoring salespeople improves their performance in a number of ways, including greater sales volume.[18]

There are three types of mentoring programs. The first is one in which a senior manager is assigned to each of the new sales reps for a period of a year or sometimes a little longer. This manager advises, teaches, and helps the rep learn the corporate culture. Because this person is supposed to be a friend as well as an adviser, the mentor is never the employee's direct boss. Rather, the mentor should not have the authority to fire or promote the employee.

A second form of mentoring involves co-workers who are chosen to be the new reps' advisers/trainers. Senior salespeople are assigned to the new sales reps and are expected to teach them the ropes. In some cases, especially in small companies, the mentor is also the primary trainer, teaching product knowledge and basic selling skills. Again because of the importance of the personal relationship between the mentor and the employee, companies should take care to assign a mentor who does not or will not have any direct authority over the new rep.

The third type of mentoring is an informal process in which a senior executive selects a younger salesperson or manager and helps him or her climb the corporate ladder. A well-placed mentor inside the company can protect the reps' interests in the company's political arena as well as help them advance if their talents warrant it. The mentor knows the cast of characters and can provide valuable advice. Eli Lilly is a company that has this type of mentoring program. Lilly encourages its reps to find a mentor and its managers to become mentors.[19]

MEETING SOCIAL AND PSYCHOLOGICAL NEEDS

An individual's assimilation into the organization involves considerably more than just getting started on the job. He or she should be socially integrated into the new environment. Newly hired salespeople too often are thrust into a strange city, their children are upset, and their new home is not as comfortable as the old one—conditions that hardly foster efficiency at work. The sales manager is in a position to cushion the shock of social uprooting by providing some social activities and contacts.

The manager should take positive steps to see that recruits and their families get into activities in which they are interested. The golfer should be worked into a foursome, and the bridge player invited to join an established group.

SUMMARY

The third phase in the sales force selection process involves (1) developing a system of tools and procedures to measure the applicants against the predetermined hiring specifications and (2) actually using this system to select the salespeople. Processing applicants is a key activity in implementing a company's strategic planning. When using any selection tool, management must make certain that it is complying with all pertinent laws and regulatory guidelines.

The first selection tool typically applied to begin the screening process is the application form and/or resume. This selection tool is a good source for getting a candidate's basic work and personal history.

The personal interview, which is the most widely used of all selection tools, is designed to answer four questions regarding an applicant: (1) is the person capable of excelling at this job? (2) How badly does the person want the job? (3) Will the job help the person realize his or her goals? (4) Will the person work to his or her fullest ability?

Unfortunately, interviews are not always an accurate predictor of job performance, because too many people don't know how to interview. The predictive validity can be improved by using more than one interview, with more than one interviewer, in more than one place. Training the interviewers, providing a reasonable amount of structure to the interview, and using situations- and/or behavior-based interviews can also improve the process.

Interviews may vary according to (1) structure (guided versus nondirected interviews), (2) focus (behavior- or situation—versus performance-based interviews, or stress interviews), and (3) timing and method (early or late, telephone or face-to-face). Some companies are using videoconferencing to conduct interviews.

Employment testing is another major selection tool, and researchers consider it the best tool for predicting job performance. The most commonly used tests cover four areas—mental intelligence, aptitudes, interests, and personality. There are some problems in using tests as part of the hiring process. Also, testing is more likely to be successful when firms are hiring a large number of inexperienced people using inexperienced recruiters, when the cost of failure is high, and when executives are free to use their own judgment.

Reference checks are widely used in the sales selection process. A personal visit or a phone call to a reference usually is a better method than letter writing. A key question to ask is whether the reference would hire the applicant. Credit reports and other outside sources may supplement reference checks. Assessment centers, the final selection tool discussed briefly in this chapter, allow hiring companies to observe candidates performing simulated exercises.

Once acceptable recruits have been identified, the fourth phase of the staffing process begins: hiring. During preoffer planning, the acceptable recruits should be ranked. Then the company must decide what will be included in the offer and how it will be extended. The offer should include the compensation and the benefits. Some firms also offer to help the spouse or significant other find a job. Most offers specify a time by which the offer must be accepted.

Much of the sales recruit's long-run success with a company depends on the fifth and final phase of the staffing process: socialization and assimilation. There is much to learn about the company, its people, and how things are done in the organization. The initial socialization begins during the pre-employment period as the reps hear and read about the jobs they will soon begin. The second stage is the actual assimilation into the firm. During this period, the reps should become familiar with the firm's operation and employees. Many firms are using mentoring programs to help salespeople feel comfortable in their new jobs.

In order to retain salespeople, companies must integrate them fully into the firm. The desire for social acceptance in the work group is so strong that the recruit who fails to gain it will probably quit. The sales manager can help employees initiate relationships by bringing the new employees together with their co-workers in social situations.

KEY TERMS

Application form
Assessment center
Assimilation
Behavior-based interview
Bona fide occupational qualifications (BFOQs)
Credit report
Employment testing
Experience requirements
Guided interview
Hiring
Job previews
Mentor
Nondirected interview
Performance-based interview
Personal interview
Reference
Resume
Situation-based interview
Socialization
Socioenvironmental qualifications
Stress interview
Validation

1. In the application form that an aptitude testing firm has prepared for sales positions, the following questions are asked. In each case, what do you think is the purpose of the question?
   a. What is the most monotonous task you ever did?
   b. In people you like, what do you like about them?
   c. What has been the outstanding disappointment in your life?
   d. What is your best friend's strongest criticism of you?

2. How may the limitations of the interview be eliminated, reduced, or counterbalanced?

3. Prepare a series of questions an interviewer might ask the applicant so that the company can determine (a) How badly the applicant wants or needs the job (b) Whether or not the job furnishes the applicant with the success he or she wants in order to realize his or her goals in life? (c) Whether or not the applicant will work hard enough to achieve his or her potential.

4. What are the advantages and disadvantages of using videoconferencing (e.g., Skype) to interview sales candidates?

5. If you had to choose between the following two sales recruits, which one would you hire and why?
   a. One has scored very high in terms of the quality of his interview, but not very well on the series of employment tests to predict qualities the firm thinks are necessary for success.
   b. The other person did well on the employment testing, but not very well in the personal interview.

6. Can you eliminate the personal biases and prejudices of interviewers so that they will conduct an interview impartially? Explain your answer.

7. Suppose that halfway through your interview for a job in which you are very interested, the interviewers says, "I don't think you are right for this job." How would you respond?

8. What is the point of asking a recruit during an interview, "How many golf balls would it take to fill the swimming pool at the Summer Olympics?"

9. Give examples of two situation-based interview questions that would be related to a candidate's ability to handle objections.

10. Many sales managers claim that the real factor that determines whether people will be successful in selling is their motivation for hard work. Where is this motivational factor measured in employment testing? How should sales managers determine a person's motivation to do a good job?

11. Some managers believe that the reference is not very helpful as a selection tool. Do you agree with this appraisal? If so, why do you think it continues to be used by virtually every firm that is hiring salespeople or other employees?

12. How could a candidate's ethical standards be evaluated in the interview process?

13. One recruit you want to hire stands out above all the others you interviewed. You make her an offer that is standard throughout your medium-sized company, which has a commissioned sales force of 33 reps. The recruit wants a higher initial salary for the first year before going onto commission. Normally, all trainees are paid $3,000 a month plus expenses for the first year. The recruit demands $3,500. The average commissioned sales rep makes $90,000 a year after four years in the field. What would you do?

14. A sales manager made the following statement: "I don't lose any sleep over it when one of my reps leaves for another position. Generally, it's the people who don't quite fit in who leave." Evaluate this manager's statement.

15. This chapter describes three different types of mentoring programs. Which one do you think is best and why?

EXPERIENTIAL EXERCISES

1. Ask 10 of your peers what are or will be the most important considerations in their job search decisions. Then develop a brief questionnaire that asks respondents to rank the factors you uncovered from your discussion with your peers (e.g., "Rank the criteria below according to their importance to you in accepting a job.").

   a. Administer this questionnaire to 20 of your fellow students, and summarize the results of the report.

   b. Administer the questionnaire to 20 *recruiters* who visit your campus to hire for sales internships and jobs. Note that you may have to change the wording of the questionnaire to something like: "Rank the criteria below according to the importance that you feel students will place on them in their job searches." Summarize the results in a brief report.

   c. Finally, compare the responses of the recruiters to the responses of your peers. Discuss the similarities and differences.

2. Interview three recruiters from three different companies (These should be companies with whom you will *not* have interviews). Ask them to describe the qualities they are looking for in the candidates they interview. Ask them what questions, exercises, and/or other strategies they use to get at this information.

3. Visit three online job sites (e.g., CareerBuilder.com, Monster.com) and report on what services in addition to job listings each one provides. For example, many of them provide advice on how to search for and get a job. Elaborate on what you find.

4. Visit the websites of three Fortune 500 companies and answer the following questions:

   a. What specific information is provided that may be considered part of the pre-employment socialization process?

   b. Which of these companies does the best job of pre-employment socialization through its website? Why do you think this is so?

DELTA PRODUCTS COMPANY
Selection of Sales Representation

"We were formerly employed at TRW—Jim was in microelectronics marketing as a salesperson, and I worked inside to provide technical assistance and service to Jim's accounts. We were a team. Our division was directly hit with the defense and aerospace reductions due to that recession a few years ago. We were terminated. They call us displaced workers." Christina Alvarez and her partner Jim Reynolds were explaining their sales proposition to Tom Shilling, marketing manager for the Delta Products Company.

Alvarez continued, "But we have had enough of working for other companies. We decided to form our own manufacturers' rep company: Pacific Technical Sales. We will do for other companies exactly what we did for TRW. That is, we will sell microelectronic devices, except we will do it as independent agents for a commission instead of a salary and all the benefits. And we'll do it for several noncompeting companies. We will not sell anything for another company that you are prepared to make. No conflicts of interest!"

Jim Reynolds came in on cue. "We propose to represent your firm in California, Arizona and Nevada for a commission base of 5 percent. That rate will be renegotiated for significant contracts in which highly competitive bidding is encountered."

Tom Shilling asked, "And what about business that walks through our door in which you played no role?"

Alvarez replied, "Each week we would furnish you a list of the firms that we have contacted, and we would be protected on those accounts for six months. Everything is spelled out in this portfolio, which explains who we are, what we have done, and what we can do for you."

"I know you need time to consider our proposal, for it is a departure from your previous policy of having your own salesperson in the field. However, since your local sales rep no longer is with you and market conditions have changed considerably, we think you should consider retaining our firm instead of hiring another salesperson," Reynolds declared. "Is it convenient for you to see us next Monday morning at 11 for your answer?"

Tom Shilling studied his *very full* Outlook calendar and replied, "Monday is really bad for me. I'm all jammed up. Besides, I need more time to consult with the boss about it. This would be a pretty big change for us to make. I can hire salespeople without talking it over with anyone, but you are another matter. No, I'll have to do a lot of talking with some people before I can give you an answer. Let's make it next Thursday morning at 11."

Alvarez and Reynolds departed as Shilling rose and cordially walked them to the front door. He said, "I'll take your portfolio home tonight and give it a close look, and tomorrow I'll get with Mr. Gross, our president, about it."

Shilling intended to encourage the two people because he faced a serious problem trying to maintain field sales representation in the declining, highly competitive markets being faced.

Delta Products Company designed and manufactured small electronic devices for other manufacturers that incorporated them into whatever products they made. It did business all over the world; international sales accounted for 35 percent of its business. Sales in California, Arizona, and Nevada had accounted for about 10 percent of the company's sales a decade ago, but had dropped to only 4 percent more recently because of the firm's historical dependence on sales to firms in the defense and aerospace industries. Shilling had already started strong sales programs to solicit business from new accounts outside the defense/aerospace industry.

However, the cost of the field sales force had become a burden. Shilling had terminated the firm's salesperson, Herb Hawkins, for the California/Arizona/Nevada region. Hawkins' selling costs had soared way out of line because of a significant drop in sales in the region. His total selling costs last year had been $192,466, of which $85,000 had been his salary. No bonuses had been paid since his performance had been below expectations. The bulk of his expenses had been for automotive and entertainment costs. Hawkins had been with Delta since its inception twenty years ago. He was its leading producer for years when his territory was the focus of much defense and aerospace activity.

In a rather disturbing meeting with Hawkins, Shilling had reviewed the situation with him and declared that the company could no longer afford $192,000 to cover his territory. He then told Hawkins that the firm could afford to pay only 5 percent of sales for field-selling costs. Based on Hawkins recent sales volume, this meant an annual cost of $116,000. Consequently, Shilling had told Hawkins that his next year's salary would be cut to $50,000 plus some bonuses for meeting quotas, with an expense allowance not to exceed $60,000. No more lavish entertaining and no more paying more than $30,000 for a car. Hawkins had a strong preference for driving vehicles costing well in excess of what could be deducted for income tax purposes.

Herb Hawkins had rejected the offer. He was 63 years old, and since the combination of his company pension plan, his savings, and Social Security would exceed what was being offered him, he decided to take early retirement.

Shilling did not immediately begin a search for Hawkins' replacement. He felt that he could use the savings from not having a salesperson in the area to help meet his budget deficits for the year. He was in no hurry to replace Hawkins since he felt he and the staff could serve the existing accounts from the home office in Redondo Beach, California. However, while attending a trade show, Shilling had occasion to renew acquaintance with Brian Snowcroft, with whom he had worked closely when they both were at Hughes Aircraft several years ago. He thought highly of Snowcroft's talents and knowledge of the industry. He recalled Snowcroft's background: He had graduated from Arizona State with a degree in electrical engineering. After starting to work for Hughes, in Tucson, Arizona, on a classified technical project, he had been thrust into contract relationships because of his excellent customer skills. He enjoyed great success with Hughes but was about to be put adrift due to the cutbacks Hughes was making. He had only three more months before he was going to be on the street looking for work.

Shilling told Snowcroft of his situation with Hawkins and asked him if he would be interested in it. Snowcroft did not say no, and he was not indignant when told of the reduced compensation package. He was told he would not have to move to Redondo Beach but could cover the territory from his home in Tucson. It was left that, if Snowcroft was interested in the job and wanted to talk about it some more, he would call Shilling.

Sunday night Tom Shilling settled down in his lounge chair to study the Alvarez-Reynolds proposal. He was impressed with it. Friday afternoon he had called a friend of his at TRW to ask her to investigate the records of both Alvarez and Reynolds at TRW. She had reported back within the hour that their records were spotless. They were both well thought of and highly recommended. They had been terminated only because of the cutback of all employees.

As Shilling was thinking about the matter, the telephone rang. It was Brian Snowcroft. He had been laid off that afternoon, much sooner than he had anticipated. He was now interested in the job. However, he said that he would have to have a minimum salary of $65,000 to be able to survive financially. He said that he had been making in excess of $85,000 a year for the past five years. With his high fixed costs plus having two kids in college, he needed more than $65,000 a year to stay financially above water.

The two men talked for more than 30 minutes about the job and the situation. Shilling let Snowcroft know that he was also under great financial pressure and was being forced to make some cutbacks that he was reluctant to make, but such were the times. Shilling signed off by saying that he would get back to Snowcroft the following week.

In a way, Shilling was grateful that Snowcroft had called, for it helped him focus his thinking on the problem at hand. The thought crossed his mind that perhaps he should abandon efforts to fill the position with an experienced salesperson and hire a beginner right out of an engineering college, someone he could pay a beginning salary of perhaps 35 or 40 thousand a year, plus bonuses if warranted. However, he wondered if the additional delay of having to start a search for a college graduate might upset his boss, who had indicated some apprehension over the firm's lack of a sales rep in the area. Shilling did not want to look indecisive.

Tom Shilling rose from his chair to go to the window to gaze at the Pacific Ocean below him as he pondered the problem.

Question:

1. What course of action should Tom Shilling follow regarding the vacant position?

2. If Tom Shilling were to decide to hire a college graduate for this position, which of the five categories of selection tools would you recommend to him? Which ones would you not use? Explain your answer.

BAY AUTOMOTIVE PARTS CENTER
Selection of Inside Salesperson

"The job calls for someone with a great telephone voice and an easy way of talking with people. I want someone our customers will really want to talk with," Bill Monk, owner of Bay Automotive Parts Center, declared to Linda Monk, his partner and spouse.

Linda was in charge of office operations, which included handling all incoming sales orders. Bill handled the outside sales operations, and the couple's three children—Ken, Kay, and Kate, ages 25, 27, and 29, respectively—ran the distribution center. Kate was in charge of purchasing and inventory management. Kay managed warehouse operations and order picking. Ken managed the receiving and shipping department. Much to their parents' dismay, none of the Monk offspring had much interest in the sales end of the business.

Each time an opening on the three-person inside sales force came up, Linda had pressured her children to get some experience in sales. She thought that their taking turns on the inside sales desk would be good training. They resisted her overtures. They maintained that it was too important a job for their inexperienced efforts. Moreover, none of the children was blessed with a good speaking voice. Consequently, Bay Automotive was looking for an inside salesperson to fill the vacancy that developed when Sal Nunzio retired.

Bay Automotive Parts Center of Baltimore, Maryland, was a large independent distributor of automotive parts in the Chesapeake Bay area, with sales in excess of $25 million a year. It had an outside sales force of five reps who called on local area garages and parts dealers. Bill Monk handled the significant accounts himself. However, on a day-to-day basis, the bulk of the orders came in by telephone to people who took the orders. The three inside salespeople handled the incoming orders, but usually there were times during the day when Linda and/or Bill would have to handle some overload calls.

Linda, resigned to selecting a new inside salesperson, had considered 11 people for the job, 2 people from within the firm and 9 recruited from other sources. From those people, Linda had narrowed her choices to three people, each of whom represented different prototypes for the job.

First, there was Larry, an older man with considerable experience in the automotive business, both in repair and in parts sales. For the previous two years, he had worked the inside desk for a parts distributor in Detroit. He quit that job to move to Baltimore to be closer to his children and grandchildren. He knew the auto parts business and was considered by his previous employers to be a reliable employee. He could go to work immediately with little training. The firm's compensation package, which was slightly below the market for such jobs, was satisfactory to him. He was ready to go to work.

The second person under consideration was Dorothy, who was working in a telemarketing "boiler room" selling health insurance. She was good at it, but she disliked what she was selling. She voiced serious concerns about the scripts she had to read to the prospects. She had said in her interview, "I want to sell legitimate products to people who really need them."

Dorothy was a local person who had graduated a few years ago from the University of Maryland, majoring in the dramatic arts. Her speaking voice and stage presence were superb. She was quick-witted and able to handle herself quite well with all sorts of people. While she had shown a slight surprise at Bay Automotive's compensation package, she seemed to accept it. Linda wondered how long Dorothy would stay interested in the job. But she thought that whatever that time would be, it would be well worth it for what she and the other people learn from her about telemarketing. Linda secretly hoped some of Dorothy's polish would rub off on Kay and Kate.

The third person being considered was Steve, who had worked for Bay Automotive for more than 10 years in various capacities. He was currently filling orders and reported to Kay Monk. When he learned of the vacancy, Steve came to Linda and said he wanted the job. He was sure he could do it, he wanted the higher earnings, and he wanted to get into sales and develop his skills. He had been a loyal worker with good work habits. The Monks held him in high regard and really wanted to help him but were not certain that this was the best way to do it—for either him or the firm. While Steve had helped out on incoming sales calls when things got too busy for the regular crew to handle, he was not famous for having a melodious voice.

Linda assembled what she had developed on each of the candidates for the job and laid the information before the family after an evening meal. An extensive discussion followed. Each candidate had his or her supporters. Ken really liked Dorothy, but for the wrong reasons. Finally, Bill said, "As I see it, it comes down to a question of (1) Do we hire an old parts pro who knows what to do and can do it now? (2) Do we go for the modern telemarketing professional who might be able to teach us a thing or two? Or (3) Do we reward our loyal employee and friend who wants to improve himself? Is that it?

They all nodded in agreement and then tried to avoid making a decision.

Question:

1. What are the pros and cons of each candidate?

2. Who should be selected for the job? Explain your answer.

UNIVERSAL COMPUTERS
Evaluation of Hiring Procedures

Fran Long, branch sales manager, walked into her office at Universal Computer's southeastern regional headquarters in Atlanta, Georgia. She had spent the previous week in the field working with some of her sales reps who were having trouble with some key accounts. While she had kept in close contact by telephone with her office staff during the week, her paperwork had stacked up. The in-basket was overflowing. She groaned as she surveyed the work ahead of her that morning, but she got to it immediately. She turned the basket upside down and began processing the paper—first in, first dealt with.

After Long had read and processed several intercompany memos, suddenly a letter from Sharon Altman caught her attention. Altman, a marketing major, had graduated from one of the state's universities with an outstanding record while working full time in the school's computer department. After on-campus interviews, Altman was invited for a series of personal interviews at the company's Atlanta offices. She made an excellent impression on everyone in the company who had interviewed her, and everything on her resume checked out satisfactorily. Consequently, she was offered a job as a sales trainee at the market rate for such people. She was given two weeks to accept or decline the offer that had been made in a letter sent to her three days after her interview. She had been informed verbally that she would be receiving the offer. She had requested and been granted the two weeks to answer.

After working through all the nice commentary about how great Universal was and how much she was impressed with Fran Long and all the people she had met, Sharon Altman got to the bottom line—she had accepted a sales job with another firm.

Long was displeased. She had made a great effort to recruit Altman and thought that she had been successful. Altman had given no indication that she was considering another job. Long considered calling her immediately to find out what happened, but she looked at the stack of papers to be processed and decided to postpone taking any action that day. She wanted to think about it for a while.

Fifteen documents later, she was looking at another letter rejecting a job offer she had made to a young man from North Carolina. His story was about the same as Altman's. An outstanding prospective sales reps was made an offer when he indicated that he wanted one. Long was puzzled by this rejection because the young man fit the stereotypical person the company was famous for hiring. He was a Universal man from his haircut down to his shoes. What's going on here, Long wondered.

By noon Long had finished with the in-basket and wished she had stayed home. Three more people to whom job offers had been made unexpectedly rejected them to accept other opportunities. Long knew she had a problem on her hands, because hiring good people was the lifeblood of the business. The firm had been built on its ability to attract, train, and keep a highly effective sales force.

Universal Computers was one of the world's largest computer companies, with offices in every major city around the globe. Its growth and profitability had been the envy of the international business world. Unfortunately, during the previous two years it had encountered financial difficulties as its revenues suffered from competitive intrusions into its markets as well as from a sluggish economy. Management had made massive cutbacks in budgets and personnel. Changes in top management rocked the business world. The price of its stock dropped by more than 50 percent.

The company's sales management program had been copied extensively by its competitors. *Universal* was a household word. Fran Long thought, "You just don't reject an offer from us, particularly in these tough times. And above all, you don't play games with us." She recognized that these recruits had used the Universal offers for bargaining with other firms. She had used the same tactic in reverse when she came to work for Universal 10 years previously.

With five sales trainee positions to fill, Long had interviewed 22 people for the openings. There were eight other recruits who were considered acceptable to hire, but they were not nearly as promising as the recruits who had received the offers. She arranged for a meeting that afternoon with everyone involved in the selection process.

After explaining what had happened to the offers that they had made, Long said, "I want to discuss three things right now: What went wrong? What should we do right now? And how do we keep this same thing from happening in the future?"

The discussion was spirited, with each person having some opinions. The group thought that there was nothing wrong with its selection process. The procedures that had worked so well for years were followed. Those recruits were given the royal treatment. No insincerity had been detected; all of the recruits seemed to be bona fide candidates.

The group wondered if they made a mistake by not putting more pressure on the recruits. Perhaps they should not give them so much time to consider the offer, and maybe they should have gotten a verbal acceptance before making a written offer, and maybe they should have gotten a verbal acceptance before making a written offer.

"Good deeds never go unpunished!" observed Long's operations manager. He continued, "We were nice guys. Maybe we should quit being so nice. Competition is getting rough, as we well know, and that holds true for people as well as markets."

Fran's assistant demurred. "Do we really want to hire anyone who really doesn't want to work for us? I think not. I just can't see pressuring anyone to come to work for us. It hasn't come to that, has it?"

Long nodded and asked, "To what extent have our current competitive and financial problems played a role in this matter? Let's face it; we avoided all discussion of it with these people. We pretend it doesn't exist. But it does. Should we get it out on the table and talk about it with these people, or would that be washing our dirty linen in public?" She did not wait for an answer but instead hurried on to the immediate problem: "How do we go about making the next offers? Should we bring them in to Atlanta again and get their acceptance on the spot? If we don't fill these five slots, will we look bad in New York when this year's sales training program begins?"

After her impassioned speech, Long quietly wondered if Universal should be hiring available bodies to fill slots instead of waiting until the right people could be hired. After all, the world wouldn't end if they weren't able to fill their sales trainee positions with college graduates. She knew that there were a lot of good people on the streets looking for jobs.

Questions:

1. What are your thoughts as to why the applicants rejected Universal's job offer?
2. If Fran Long wants to hire five trainees from those who have already been interviewed, how should she do it?
3. If you were in Fran Long's position, exactly what actions would you take?

PACIFIC PAPER PRODUCTS
Indoctrination of New Salespeople

"I'm getting too old for this job. Everything seems to have changed. I don't seem to be able to manage things the same way I used to," Mo Martin complained to his longtime friend Bernie, who was a bit weary of Mo's never-ending complaints about the ways of the modern world.

Mo Martin, vice president of sales for Pacific Paper Products, had started his career in sales with the paper division of Weyerhaeuser, the huge wood products company, when he graduated from college over thirty years ago. After completing the company training program, he was assigned to the firm's Southern California regional office where he enjoyed a stellar sales career through a combination of hard work and a large fast-growing territory. Weyerhaeuser was known as an excellent company to work for, and Mo was enjoying much success in his sales career. However, he became progressively dissatisfied with his status at Weyerhaeuser, because his peers in his training program were being promoted into various management positions while he was still selling. He kept asking his boss about it, and he was continually told that the company felt that his superior selling skills would best benefit the company if he remained in selling. He was given several large key accounts for which he was solely responsible. One of those accounts was Pacific Paper, a paper wholesaler. Mo eventually became close friends with its owner, who persuaded Mo to work for him as vice president of sales.

Mo started with Pacific Paper after 12 years with Weyerhaeuser. He established himself as an excellent sales manager by most indexes one might want to use: sales increases, profit margins, selling costs, turnover, and modernization of the sales system.

Mo's traditional management style was to develop close personal relationships with his people. There was much socializing among the sales force that was located in the Southern California region. Sales meeting were often held in Palm Springs or San Diego, at which golf tournaments were usually featured. The company sponsored several charity celebrity golf tournaments at which the salespeople played significant roles by inviting various key customers to play.

Mo spent much time in the field working closely with the sales reps. He tried to spend at least one day every three months with each of the firm's 33 sales reps. Every birthday, anniversary, wedding, graduation, or other memorable event in a rep's family was recognized with appropriate gifts or cards.

The sales group was diverse, with 10 reps from minority groups and four women. The first woman was hired about ten years ago. Mo was aware that the women had not assimilated into the sales force very well at all, even though their collective sales performance was good. As he had said when asked why he had hired them, "They were the best of the applicants."

He normally went out of his way to help new sales reps become part of the work group. He kept close daily contact with new reps, helping them with whatever personal problems they were encountering in changing their jobs. He had made personal loans to some new reps who were having financial troubles. Mo said, "They can't sell effectively if they're worried about their family or finances. Anything I can do to help them become effective salespeople and happily accepted in our work group will eventually pay us big dividends."

However, Mo had quickly detected that his management style was not well accepted among the women he had hired. Although they had not come to him as a group, individually they had let him know that they did not play golf and did not like to go to a bar with him to talk over the day's sales calls. Moreover, they were not really interested in socializing that much with the other sales reps, or even having much ado made over their birthdays. Mo had held a surprise birthday party for Ruth Spencer on her 40th birthday. She was not amused, as they say, and she let him know about it.

Since they exchanged confidences almost daily—they were neighbors and socialized extensively—Bernie was well aware of Mo's problems. Bernie kept observing that times had changed and Mo had to change with them. "What worked for you before may not work for you now. Maybe some people only want to work for you; they don't want to be your buddies. They only wanted a job, not a social life," Bernie told him.

"Yeah, I know you're right, but how about me and what I want? I enjoy my job so much because it's so much fun working and playing with my people. If I can't have fun and do it my way, why do it? Maybe I should take early retirement and say to heck with it."

"Hold the phone, Mo. Don't go off the deep end just yet. I know someone who might be able to help you with your problem. I met this woman management consultant who specializes in advising managers on these matters. Talk to her. And talk to some other people, too. I think there are some things you can do to get some perspective on your situation."

Questions:

1. Critique Mo's approach to management given the chapter's discussion on assimilation and socialization. That is, what does he do well? In what ways can he improve?

2. What advice would you give Mo Martin?

ENDNOTES

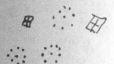

[1] This information was posted on the private news service Reddit on August 1, 2014, and retrieved by the author on May 20, 2016 from the following URL: this https://www.reddit.com/r/jobs/comments/2cbubq/pg_one_million_applicants_for_3000_job_openings/

[2] The discussion on Procter & Gamble's hiring process is based on information retrieved from the company website on May 20, 2016 – from the following URL: http://pgcareers.com/apply/our-hiring-process/

[3] James H. Leigh, Neil C. Herndon, Donna Massey Kantak, "Effects of Customer Gender and Mode of Dress on Service Response Received in Retail Establishments," *Journal of Marketing Channels*, Oct-Dec2013, Vol. 20 Issue 3/4, pp. 239-259.

[4] William Cron, Greg W. Marshall, Jagdip Singh, Rosann L. Spiro, and Harish Sujan, "Salesperson Selection, Training, and Development: Trends, Implications, and Research Opportunities," *Journal of Personal Selling & Sales Management*, Spring 2005, pp. 123-37.

[5] George F. Dreher and Thomas W. Dougherty, *Human Resource Strategy: A Behavioral Perspective for the General Manager* (New York: McGraw-Hill Higher Education, 2001), p. 107.

[6] Dreher and Dougerty (2001) ibid…

[7] Mark McMaster, "Ask SMM," *Sales & Marketing Management*, December 2001, p. 58.

[8] Dan Hanover, "Hiring Gets Cheaper and Faster," *Sales & Marketing Management*, March 2000, p. 87.

[9] Crohn et al, "Salesperson Selection, training, and Development."

[10] Geoffrey Brewer, "Professionally Speaking," *Sales & Marketing Management*, February 1996, p. 27.

[11] Elana Harris, "Reducing the Recruiting Risks," *Sales & Marketing Management*, May 2000, p. 18.

[12] For additional information on evaluating and using psychological tests in the selection process, see "Standards for Educational and Psychological Testing," from the American Psychological Association, Washington, DC; and "Principles for Validation and Use of Personal Selection Procedures," from the Society for Industrial and Organizational Psychology Association Inc., a division of the American Psychological Association in Arlington Heights, IL.

[13] Brian J. Hoffman, Colby L. Kennedy, Alexander C. LoPilato, Elizabeth L. Monahan, Charles E. Lance, "A Review of the Content, Criterion-Related, and Construct-Related Validity of Assessment Center Exercises," *Journal of Applied Psychology*, July 2015, Vol. 100 Issue 4, pp. 1143-68.

[14] Hiram C. Barksdale Jr., Danny N. Bellenger, James S. Boles, and Thomas G. Brashear, "The Impact of Realistic Job Previews and Perceptions of Training on Sales Performance and Continuance Commitment: A Longitudinal Test," *Journal of Personal Selling & Sales Management*, Spring 2003, pp. 125-38.

[15] Ginger Trumifio, "Recruiting Goes High Tech," *Sales & Marketing Management*, April 1995, pp. 42-44.

[16] Karsten Strauss, "The 12 Best Internships for 2016," *Forbes.com*, February 24, 2016, p. 1.

[17] Formal or Informal Mentoring: What Drives Employees to Seek Informal Mentors? Daniel T. Holt, Gergana Markova, Andrew J. Dhaenens, Laura E. Marler, Sharon G. Heilmann, *Journal of Managerial Issues*, Spring/Summer2016, Vol. 28 Issue 1-2, pp. 67-82.

[18] Minna Rollins, Brian Rutherford, and David Nickell, "The Role of Mentoring on Outcome Based Sales Performance: A Qualitative Study from the Insurance Industry," *International Journal of Evidence Based Coaching and Mentoring*, Vol. 12, No. 2, August 2014, pp. 119-33.

[19] Michele Marchetti, "A Helping Hand," *Sales & Marketing Management*, August 2005, p. 45.

7

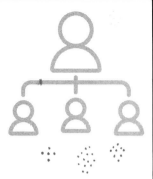

Sales Training

A few weeks after graduating from college, Angela Sebo began her sales position with Liberty Mutual Insurance.[1] Angela spent the entirety of her first four months in training. During this time, she traveled to different centralized training facilities for face-to-face courses that each lasted a week or two. In addition, she took a variety of online courses offered by Liberty Mutual, and studied hard to prepare for a variety of licensing exams that allow her to legally sell insurance in Ohio, her state of residence. At the end of this time period, Angela became officially licensed and began to sell insurance policies.

This initial phase of the Liberty Mutual training program involves significant costs to the company. These costs include a variety of travel/lodging expenses, licensing exam fees, instructional materials, and of course a well-paid training staff. Not only did Liberty Mutual pay for all of this, the company also compensated Angela with an annual straight-salary of $50,000.

When this initial training program phase was over, Angela began to sell Liberty Mutual insurance policies to customers—but the training was not done. At this point, a sales coach was assigned to Angela. The sales coach was an experienced Liberty Mutual salesperson that provided on-the-job guidance through a close, one-on-one relationship that lasted for a few years. The coach received additional compensation for accepting the coaching role. Of course, Angela's direct supervisor (her branch manager) also provided significant guidance and support through this period.

After a few years—if all of these training initiatives go well—Angela will become a high performing salesperson. Her training, however, will continue in a variety of ways. There is a continual new stream of products, regulations and issues that agents must be kept up to date on. Consequently, Liberty Mutual provides ongoing training in all of these areas.

Liberty Mutual Insurance understands that its training program is an important part of its success. Yes, recruiting and selecting the right people is important, but strong new hires will only develop into high performing salespeople through proper training. Further, Liberty Mutual believes that training is also important for its experienced salespeople, too.

THE VALUE OF SALES TRAINING

As product life cycles have become shorter and relationships between companies and their customers have become more complex, training for salespeople has become more important than ever before. Most sales executives agree that training is a critical factor ensuring the salesperson's success. The salesperson's product knowledge, understanding of customer needs, and selling skills are directly related to the amount of training that he or she receives. As shown on Figure 7-1, sales training provides *value* to firms in that it leads to greater selling effectiveness, better customer relations, and improved organizational commitment and retention.[2]

Companies spend a great deal of money on sales training, which they view as an essential means of protecting the investments they have made in their sales forces. In fact, the American Society for Training & Development (ASTD) reports that U.S. companies spend $15 billion per year on sales training, or over $2,000 per salesperson per year.[3]

Training professionals, however, argue that often companies are not spending their training budgets wisely and, as a result, their training is not as effective as it could be. Indeed, many salespeople report that the training they receive is ineffective or less than useful.[4] Customers, too, often feel that the salespeople who serve them are not very effective. Thus, it is apparent that many sales training programs are not imparting the skills salespeople need to achieve success.

Experts believe that the value of sales training programs can be improved if the designers effectively deal with the following four key challenges that are currently facing sales organizations.[5] First, salespeople's roles are becoming increasingly complex as they must effectively collaborate with and offer service to many individuals in the buying organization. Second, the designers of sales training programs need to do a better job of demonstrating the return on investment of what they teach. Third, training programs must do a better job at keeping up with the changes in technology associated with sales force automation/CRM systems. And fourth, salespeople are not adjusting to the increased global emphasis and cultural diversity within and around organizations—and so the programs must do a better job at teaching salespeople to be culturally competent.

It also should be noted that companies frequently try to use training to solve problems it cannot actually solve.[6] For example, reps may be performing

FIGURE 7-1
Sales Training Value

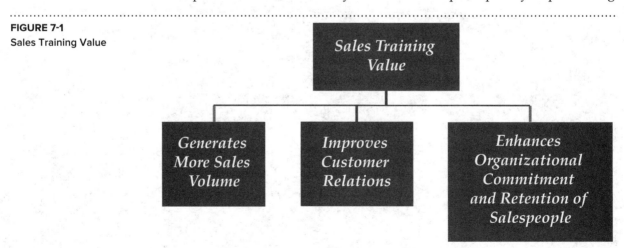

poorly because the company is selecting the wrong *type* of person for the job, not because those reps are poorly trained. If sales are low, it may be due to a poor marketing strategy—a problem beyond the scope of sales training. Training is not a panacea, but it can lead to significant improvements in performance if it is properly designed, implemented, and reinforced. In the remainder of this chapter, we discuss how to design, deliver, and reinforce an effective sales training program.

SALES TRAINING AND STRATEGIC PLANNING

Many aspects of sales training are affected by the company's strategic marketing plan. Conversely, the sales training program—when properly coordinated with the firm's marketing objectives and strategies—can help the company implement that plan.

In today's competitive marketplace, customers are demanding more and more from their suppliers in terms of quality and service. In response to these pressures, firms are placing greater strategic emphasis on developing long-term partnerships with their customers. Rather than just selling products and services, salespeople are expected to build relationships and provide solutions to their customers' problems. As a result, the selling process has become ever more interactive and situation-specific. Salespeople have to know more about the product and more about the customer. Many firms have adopted team-selling strategies in order to respond to customers' expectations. In these strategies, the salesperson works much more closely with people from other areas in the firm, such as manufacturing, engineering, and research. As a result, sales training has become much broader in scope, covering topics such as quality management, teamwork, and other interpersonal skills necessary for building relationships.

The firm's marketing strategies and objectives provide the basis for establishing sales training objectives. For example, a marketing objective of increasing market share by 20 percent calls for one kind of training program, and the objective of maintaining market share by providing better service to existing customers calls for a different kind. Training provides the knowledge and skills needed to achieve business objectives.

If a company makes a major change in its sales organizational structure, an intensive training program for experienced sales reps may be needed. This sort of situation occurred when Pfizer acquired Pharmacia and trained 3,000 sales representatives on 18 products in three U.S. sites in one week.[7]

TRAINING ASSESSMENT

In the **training assessment** phase, sales executives must ask themselves four questions:

- What are the training program objectives?
- Who should be trained?
- What are the training needs of the individual rep?
- How much training is needed?

The following sections look at each question in turn.

What are the training program objectives?

Most companies expect to influence the productivity of their field sales organizations through the design and delivery of their training programs. But training programs may have other objectives as well. They include a lower employee turnover rate, better morale, more effective communication, improved customer relations, and better self-management. These objectives are shown in Figure 7-2 and described below.

- **Increased sales productivity.** Companies try to improve their return on sales investment by improving the productivity of their salespeople. This can be done by increasing sales per salesperson or by lowering costs. Training is frequently used to accomplish greater sales per salesperson and sometimes used to lower costs.

- **Lower turnover.** Good training programs lower employee turnover in part because well-trained people are less likely to fail. A well-thought-out training program prepares trainees for the realities of a life in sales—including the fact that discouragement and disappointment are to be expected early in a sales career. The trainee who can handle the early problems is less likely to become discouraged and quit.

- **Higher morale.** Closely tied to turnover is the matter of morale. People who are thrust into the business world without proper training or preparation are likely to suffer from poor morale. Lack of purpose is another reason for poor morale. Hence, a major objective of a sales training program should be to give trainees some idea of their purpose in the company and in society.

- **Improved communication.** Training is used to ensure that salespeople understand the importance of the information they provide to the company concerning their customers and the marketplace. They need to know how the information will be used and how it affects the performance of the firm.

FIGURE 7-2
Objectives of sales training program

- **Improved customer relations.** A good training program helps trainees become aware of the importance of establishing and maintaining good customer relations. They should learn how to avoid overselling, how to determine which products are needed, and how to adjust complaints.
- **Improved self-management.** Management has become increasingly interested in how employees use their time. The goal is to learn how to produce more output from the relatively few hours available for working. Salespeople must be organized and allocate their time effectively in order to be successful.

Technological advances in recent years have provided sales reps with great opportunities to improve their productivity. Computers, including both laptops and smartphones, are playing an increasingly important role in selling. They allow the rep to access the company's databases and communicate with the operating sales system. Properly used, they can be of immense benefit. However, the reps must learn how to use the new technology.

Who should be trained?

Obviously, newly hired company salespeople require some training. How much they need will be discussed in the next section. In addition, sales organizations should train experienced salespeople, customers and sales managers. The need for training among the existing sales force is not so obvious, but usually at least some salespeople are struggling to achieve their objectives. They need help, and the company can profit by giving it to them.

Of course, things continually change. New products are introduced, markets shift, and buyers come and go. These and other changes require retraining the sales force to handle the new developments. But even without such changes, every salesperson can benefit from appropriate sales training. Even the most experienced or skilled salesperson can benefit from refresher courses. Sales training is most effective with those reps who have a strong desire and commitment to learn coupled with a specific lack of skills or knowledge. Remember that experienced reps need to know how the training will benefit them before they will embrace it.

Generally speaking, a company will achieve its best investment return when it gives priority to training the middle 60 percent of its sales force (see Figure 7-3). However, salespeople who are in the top 20 percent of a field sales force also can benefit from training, and the return on those training dollars may be substantial as these reps often account for a proportionately higher percent of margin dollars.[8] Sales reps who are consistently in the lowest 20 percent of the organization may be in the wrong job; and so, the manager must make the tough decision to terminate the rep.[9]

At times it is also important to train people who are not the company's employees, especially those customers that resell the product, like independent manufacturers' representatives, distributors, and dealers. For example, manufacturers' representatives promote those products that are easiest to sell or that have the highest commissions. Experience shows that the products that are easiest to sell are those that the rep knows best. Usually the rep is most familiar with the products that are best supported by their manufacturers. These resellers want and expect support from the companies they represent. Firms that give it to them send several valuable messages: We want you to make money with

FIGURE 7-3

Best return on investment in
the training of salespeople

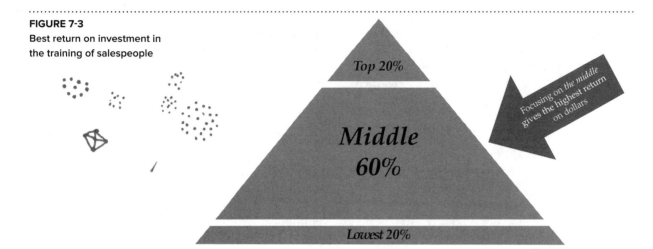

our line; we will support you in the best way we can; and we want you to be part of our organization.

Some customers who are *users* of the product should also be trained, especially when the product is complex. For example, one medical equipment and supply company will not allow any physician to buy or use its products until the physician has gone through the company's training program. This policy is part of the firm's program to lessen medical product liability litigation. It has worked; the company has had not suits to date.

Although the focus of this chapter is on the training that sales managers should provide their salespeople, it seems obvious that sales managers need training as well. In fact, the return on investment is arguably higher when training managers (as opposed to salespeople), because the improved performance of managers can have an impact on their entire *team* of salespeople. Further, the sales management landscape has become increasingly complex in recent years with increased globalization and advances in technology—so it has become even more important for sales organizations to effectively train their sales managers.[10] These programs focus on a variety of supervision and leadership issues, including how to recruit and hire excellent salespeople; how to coach and motivate the team; how to accurately forecast sales; and how constructively evaluate performance.

What are the training needs of the individual rep?

To say that the purpose of a training program is to increase sales productivity is so general that it serves only as a hazy guidepost for making decisions. The manager must break down the broad objectives into *specific goals* for the individual rep, such as improving product knowledge, prospecting methods, probing, or relationship building. Meeting these separate goals should result in achieving the broad objectives.

The assessment of training needs, the most important step in designing a sales training program, provides the starting point for setting training goals and designing the program. The company uses the analysis to identify weaknesses in selling skills and then designs programs to eliminate these weaknesses.

Training for an Experienced Sales Rep

Adam Dark, general sales manager for Shiderlots Elevator, had a problem. One of the company's veteran account managers, Carmen Weekly, had announced her refusal to attend any sales training courses. Shiderlots had seen sales and customer satisfaction slip in some of its key territories over the last two years. This had prompted Adam to hire an outside training specialist to conduct a three-day sales seminar for the account managers in his branch. Adam hoped that through the use of case studies, videos, and role-plays, his reps would improve on their interpersonal and overall selling skills.

Carmen Weekly, however, didn't like the idea. She told Adam Dark, "I've been one of this company's top salespeople for 23 years. The last thing I need is to leave my territory for a week just to get some silly training. Leave the training to the new kids. I lose commissions when I'm not out there selling. Five days out of the territory is money out of my pocket.

In reviewing Carmen Weekly's performance over the last several years, Adam had to admit that Weekly was one of Shiderlots' top sellers. After graduating from a Midwestern community college, Weekly started her sales career in the life insurance industry. In her third year on the job, she sold one of Shiderlots' executives an insurance policy. The executive was so impressed with Weekly that he offered her an account management position at Shiderlots.

Over the course of her tenure with the company, Weekly has won five "Account Manager of the Year" awards. Although many people within Shiderlots feel that Weekly is not much of a team player, Shiderlots' VP of Sales boastfully refers to her as his "Lone Wolf Superstar."

Question: How should Adam Dark handle this situation with Carmen Weekly?

Setting these specific objectives also

- Helps the trainer and trainee focus on the purpose of the training.
- Guides prioritization and sequencing of training.
- Guides the choice of training methods.
- Provides a standard for measuring training effectiveness.

Naturally, the objectives of any segment of a sales training program will vary depending on the nature of the trainee. The program designed to convert an inexperienced recruit into a professional account manager will be more comprehensive than a program intended to refresh the selling skills of an experienced salesperson or update the existing sales force on new products.

Standardization and Customization

Some training programs, such as those for inexperienced reps or those concerning new products or policies, can be provided to all of the salespeople in a *standardized* form. However, a significant portion of the training for experienced reps should be based on identifying the needs of the individual and then *customizing* a curriculum to meet those individual needs. It is also possible to let your sales reps suggest their own ways to improve their skills.

Sources of Information

Companies can and should use many sources to gather the information concerning their training needs. The most frequently used source is managerial judgment. While managers' assessments may be accurate, it is important for a firm to systematically collect information from a number of other sources as well. Performance measures, such as sales volume, number of calls, selling expenses, and customer complaints, can help managers assess training needs.

Interviews with or surveys of salespeople and customers also can provide valuable insights. For example, executives at Factiva, a joint venture between Dow Jones and Reuters that provides competitive information to businesses, first met with managers to define roles and competencies. Then they asked all members of the 300-person sales force to grade themselves on each of the competencies. This enabled Factiva to identify the areas in which the salespeople felt they needed more training.[11]

Some companies use customer questionnaires as the basis for identifying individual training needs. Each salesperson delivers the questionnaires to a selected group of customers, who are asked to assess the importance of a variety of skills to the selling relationship and to rate the salesperson's application of these skills.

Another method of assessing training needs is to conduct a **difficulty analysis** of the sales job. In this analysis, the sales manager attempts to discover what difficulties his or her staff encounters in the field. Then the company can devise proper training to help overcome those problems. The manager conducts the difficulty analysis by going into the field and interviewing sales reps about their problems. Frequently, the manager reviews a series of calls in which the reps failed to get orders and attempts to discover just what caused the failure. If the analysis discloses that reps are picking poor prospects, for example, they would be given additional training on prospecting.

How much training is needed?

The amount of training needed depends on the training objectives. A half-day program might suffice to introduce reps to a new promotional program, whereas two or three days might be needed to teach them the features and benefits of a new product or service. A program with the objective of improving the sales reps' customer orientation may require three or four days, but a program designed to teach basic selling skills to inexperienced recruits may take as long as six months.

Generally, inexperienced recruits need to learn not only about their companies and the products they are selling but also about basic selling techniques. Recruits who have had sales experience may require less basic training but may have inadequate knowledge of specific selling techniques that are most appropriate for their current selling assignment. This situation would call for considerably more training.

Most training programs for new hires last from two to six months, with costs often exceeding $100,000 per rep. As you might expect, the more technical the products are, the longer and more expensive the training for new recruits. Travel and lodging costs can be greater than facilitator fees.[12]

In the case of continual training, there is a trade-off between the gains that should result from training and the lost sales that may result from the rep's absence from the field. Of course, the long-term perspective suggests that the

CONSIDER THIS...

More Training Isn't Always Better: Measuring SFV (Salesperson Future Value)

Because training is expensive and time consuming, there comes a point where *additional training for a given salesperson* does not make sense. The problem is determining exactly when this is.

Recent sales research has demonstrated that training should stop at the point when the *salesperson's future value* (SFV) to the firm is optimized. This can be determined through data analytics.

In other words, sales organizations can measure SFV by analyzing variables such

as each salesperson's performance, age, tenure with the company, and the expected long-term value of the salesperson's customers.

As of now, this approach is largely theoretical; and so is not regularly used by many sales organizations to determine training schedules. However, the sources below suggest that this might become much more common in the near future.

SOURCES: V. Kumar, Sarang Sunder, and Robert P. Leone, "Measuring and Managing a Salesperson's Future Value to the Firm," *Journal of Marketing Research*, 51 (October 2014), pp. 591-608.

benefits from training will eventually outweigh any short-term losses. But there is a limit to how long and how often you can pull a rep out of the field and not affect the level of customer service.

PROGRAM DESIGN

In the **program design** phase, the following questions must be answered:

- Who should do the training?
- When should the training take place?
- Where should the training take place?
- What should the content of the training be?
- What teaching methods should be used?

Who should do the training?

Regular line executives, staff personnel, and outside specialists may all serve as trainers. Another option is to have the training done online through an interactive website. Any one or a combination can be used successfully. It is not uncommon for a firm to use all of these, each for different purposes. For example, Fastenal has a series of programs for its sales personnel through its Fastenal School of Business—including several online courses, face-to-face sessions led by staff trainers at a variety of regional sites, and of course the daily interaction with the supervising managers (i.e., line executives) at the Fastenal stores. This includes Fastenal's phase one sales training for part-time sales personnel, and then a separate, more comprehensive phase two sales training once the employee moves to a full-time sales position.

In the choosing of trainers, it is very important to remember that the quality of the teaching itself will have a greater impact on what is learned than the content of the training.

Line Personnel

Line personnel are those who supervise the salespeople, including direct supervisors and/or any other higher-level executive that has formal line authority. This includes field supervisors, territorial managers, and sales managers who are in direct command of the sales force. Having one of the bosses train the salespeople is quite common. The advantages and disadvantages are discussed below.

Similarly, numerous firms have made effective use of peer training. They set up situations in which rookie salespeople are partially trained by their more experienced peers on the sales force. One survey reports that 75 percent of managers use their top reps to help train other reps.[13] It works well if the sales force is skilled and has a vested interest in developing the new person's selling ability. Even though these peers typically do not have line authority, trainees generally view their more experienced and successful colleagues in a way that is similar to how they view their supervisors. As referenced in the introduction to this chapter, these peer trainers are sometimes called coaches.

One of the key advantages of having line personnel do the training is that they are more likely to have successful sales experience; and so, their words carry much more authority than those of staff people or outside specialists. Having the boss do the training achieves a certain unity of action because afterward there can be no mistaking what the supervisor expects. Furthermore, recruits can be trained to sell the way the manager wants them to sell. Line executives who train their own salespeople can evaluate each person's ability better than administrators who do not participate in the training program can. Also, better rapport can be established between the executive and the sales force, since training affords a wonderful opportunity to become acquainted.

The potential disadvantages of using line personnel are lack of time and lack of teaching ability. The pressures of other activities may force managers to give, at best, only partial attention to the training program. This can be harmful to trainee morale. Also, a line executive may know a great deal about selling but be unable to teach others about it. Neither of these disadvantages is serious, however, since both can be remedied by proper managerial action. Line administrators can be given the necessary time for training. And teachers are not necessarily born; they also can be trained.

Staff Trainers

Staff trainers can be hired specifically to conduct training programs, or staff people who hold other jobs in personnel, production, or office management can take this on. We will focus on the full-time sales trainer, since use of other staff personnel ordinarily is not recommended. Members of the personnel department are seldom qualified to conduct a sales training program. They may be involved in certain phases of the instruction, such as furnishing company information or handling the physical arrangements of the program. However, entrusting them with the technical details of the training program is generally unwise.

A trainer specifically hired to handle the training program can attend to the details, prepare the necessary materials, and give trainees the attention they need. Frequently, it is less expensive to hire a specialized staff-training officer than it is to add the additional line executives needed to allow them more time for training activities.

In theory, the staff trainer lacks control over the trainees and does not speak with the authority of a line executive. However, in practice, this is an academic point, since the trainees know that the trainer has the backing of the boss.

Companies incur additional cost in maintaining a separate training department. The median salary of the trainer alone can be $60,000 per year, depending on his or her qualifications. This limits the number of firms that can hire a sales trainer; smaller companies cannot afford the cost.

Outside Training Specialists

One survey of firms showed that 39 percent of them use outside training specialists to provide at least part of their training.[14] Some small and medium-sized firms often turn the entire training of their sales reps over to outside firms, primarily because they lack the resources to provide the training internally.

Practically every large city has firms that specialize in sales training. Their scope varies widely. Some will establish and administer an entire training program, whereas others specialize in teaching specific sales techniques. Training firms may specialize in a very narrow field. For example, some organizations do nothing but train real estate brokers or pharmaceutical reps or advertising account reps.

The key to successfully using an outside specialist is to select the one that is right for your firm. The following steps can help ensure that you do so:

* Set specific objectives for the training.
* Select a trainer who has sales experience.
* Select a trainer who has expertise in the area of your training need.
* Select only those programs that allow you to customize.
* Get references.
* Preview or audit the program.
* Ask for specifics on what results your company can expect.

Self-development programs are also important in training a sales force. Many firms pay part or all of the cost of approved educational programs or seminars. Sometimes they furnish subscriptions to educational services and newsletters. The basic idea is that the company benefits from having well-educated employees.

When Should The Training Take Place?

There are two basic attitudes toward the timing of training. Some executives believe that everyone placed in the field should be fully trained, not only in product and company knowledge but also in selling techniques. Training programs for new salespeople may last from a few weeks to a year or more before the salespeople are sent into the field. Sales managers may have trainees work for a while in either production or service to acquire product knowledge.

Other managers want recruits to exhibit a desire to sell before investing in training them. Some insurance companies require a new agent to sell a certain amount of life insurance before going to a sales school. The first training program is only a basic course. After that, the agent must again go into the field and sell successfully before attending more advanced schools for underwriters.

This philosophy has considerable educational and managerial merit. From the educational point of view, it is much easier to training people who have had some field experience versus those who have none. People who have experience in facing problems are eager to find solutions to them. If many prospects have said that the price is too high, for example, reps will be eager to find out how to cope with that objection. From a managerial point of view, weak salespeople are usually eliminated if they must sell before being trained. By putting new employees in the field first, the manager can determine how much and what type of training they really need.

The only trouble is that people who might have been successful had they been given proper instruction may be eliminated by the push-them-off the dock method. To avoid this trouble, companies should use delayed training only when product knowledge is easily acquired; the prospect does not require a polished selling approach; and customers are sold only once, with each sale being of little importance to total volume. If a sales rep botches a particular sale, the company is not seriously injured.

The need for training does not end with completion of the initial program. Most sales authorities see training as a continual function. It never ceases; it only changes form. Salespeople periodically need refresher courses. IBM, for example, strongly encourages its salespeople to develop education plans and to take advantage of the training courses that IBM provides as well as courses offered externally. It has a reimbursement plan for those who participate.[15]

Where Should Training Take Place?

The decision on the training program's location involves the extent to which it should be centralized. Unless there is some reason for centralizing training in one location, it should be decentralized. Compared to training in the field, centralized training is usually more expensive and requires more organizational effort.

Decentralized Training

Decentralized training can take several forms: (1) field sales office instruction, (2) use of senior salespeople, (3) on-the-job training, (4) sales seminars or clinics, or (5) self-guided assignments.

The advantages of decentralized sales training are many. First and foremost, it is usually less expensive than centralized training. The trainee remains in the field to work while learning, and the company avoids the substantial expense of supporting both the trainee and a central school staff.

Second, there is definite educational merit to decentralized training. Education requires time. Studies prove that cram courses are inefficient since the students quickly forget much of what they learn. A decentralized program can match instruction to the speed at which the trainee can learn the material. The limit on how much effective training can be accomplished in the shorter time frame of a centralized program has caused Xerox, Motorola, ARCO, and many other companies to decentralize training efforts as much as possible.

Third, decentralized training has considerable managerial benefits because the branch manager or an assistant is usually directly responsible. If the branch managers do a good job, trainees gain confidence in their leadership. At the same time, the managers can evaluate each of the trainees through direct observation.

Many companies are turning to self-guided Web-based instruction. Not only are these programs cost-effective and self-paced, but they also can be customized to address the training needs of the individual rep. This is particularly useful for continual training. This method will be discussed further in a following section of this chapter.

A major disadvantage of decentralized training, and it is a big one, is that the branch or field manager may not be able to perform the training role properly. Time demands, combined with lack of training skills or the desire to train, may make the field manager an inept trainer. Also, if complex or expensive equipment is needed in the training program, it may not be available in the field. For example, an intraocular lens company had to set up an operating room to train its reps about eye surgery.

Centralized Training

Centralized training may take place in organized schools or in periodic sales meetings at a central location, often the home office. Some large companies that hire many sales reps each year maintain permanent centralized sales schools. Technology services company NCR's training camp, called Sugar Camp, is an example of such an installation. Xerox's International Training Center in Leesburg, Virginia, is another. Smaller concerns typically conduct one or two sales schools a year in the home office, each lasting three or four weeks.

In centralized training, highly skilled personnel are usually available to teach. Also, proximity to the plant or the home office allows the trainees to become acquainted with home-office personnel and manufacturing facilities. It is important for them to meet the top executives. Centralized training certainly saves executive time because it eliminates travel. Also, a centralized school normally has more formal facilities for training than are available in the field. The needed equipment and materials are handy for the instructor's use. Another significant advantage is that the trainees can get to know one another. An esprit de corps can develop among the members of the class, and this is conducive to good morale.

From an educational standpoint, housing trainees at a central location, so they are not subject to the distractions of home life, has some merit. They can focus attention on learning how to be better salespeople.

Centralized training has two main weaknesses. First, as noted above, it is expensive to take people out of the field and support them while training. Second, the amount of time a person can be kept at a central training location is limited. Moreover, trainees eventually become bored. When boredom sets in, education stops. Also, some people do not want to be away from their families for extended periods.

Many companies overcome the disadvantages of using either centralized or decentralized training by designing a program that incorporates both. Companies usually provide some centralized indoctrination training first and then supplement this with some field training.

WHAT SHOULD THE CONTENT OF THE TRAINING BE?

A training program for newly hired salespeople should focus on the following **training content** areas, which tend to overlap to some degree:

1. Company orientation—Company technology (e.g., learning the CRM system)
2. Product knowledge
3. Market/customer knowledge
4. Sales process (how to sell)
5. Organizational skills (managing time, workplace stress, conflict, etc.)

Company orientation covers the wide variety of firm-specific topics that newly hired salespeople need to know to effectively function in the job. For this part of training, salespeople learn about the firm's policies and procedures regarding employee pay and benefits, including information on health insurance, retirement plans, hours of work, attendance, vacation, sick leave, dress code, expense reimbursement, sexual harassment, alcohol/drug use, grounds for dismissal, privacy issues associated with internet/telephone use, and other human resources issues. Training on company orientation is greatly facilitated by a well-organized employee handbook (See the box on **Employee Handbook**).

Company orientation should also cover various technology issues associated with a sales job at that firm. For example, new salespeople need to understand how to acquire, use and ultimately return any laptops, cell phones, automobiles, and/or other equipment that is issued to them. And more importantly, salespeople must be trained on how to use the customer relationship management (CRM) system used by their firm. This type of training is important as salespeople are not necessarily savvy technology users—although younger, freshly-out-of-college salespeople are more likely to adapt more quickly to technology. Many firms outsource this training through the CRM provider. For example, Salesforce.com offers a number of courses—both online and face-to-face—that users can take for a fee.[16]

The next training content area is **product knowledge,** which is the understanding and technical expertise that salespeople have about the products they sell. The amount of time spent on this aspect of training depends on both the complexity of the product and experience of the newly hired salesperson. Pharmaceutical products and various medical devices, for example, are quite complex; and thus, take hours and hours of training time. New hires who have just graduated from college require more product knowledge than a new hire who has already acquired years of experience working in the industry (e.g., for a competitive company).

Increasingly, **market/customer knowledge** is an important part of sales training. This is defined as the understanding that salespeople have about the needs of their customers. Like with product knowledge, the amount of time spent on this content area must be increased with more complex industries and less experienced new hires. Recall that in this era of relationship selling, salespeople are expected to be consultants to their customers. In other words, they must *understand* the customer's business, and then demonstrate how the product can help the customer be more efficient. Yes, understanding the product is important, but often most competitive products are very similar to each other; and so, customers buy the product from the salesperson with the highest

CONSIDER THIS...

The Employee Handbook

Most organizations maintain an employee handbook, which is a useful source of information that facilitates the *company orientation* phase of training. In fact, many organizations require their new employees to sign and submit a document indicating that they have read and understand all company policies and procedures found in handbook, and accept the terms.

Laws of both the state and federal government—along with an increased number of lawsuits brought forth by employees against their company—provide a strong rationale for why *all firms* should establish and clearly communicate policies and regulations to their workforce.

The firm's human resources group is responsible for keeping the handbook up-to-date, and generally revises it on an annual basis. Sales managers should have a sound working knowledge of the contents, staying abreast of any revisions.

Following is an example of the Table of Contents of an employee handbook:

1. Welcome
1.1. History, Goals & Culture
1.2. Purpose of Handbook
1.3. At-Will Employment
2. Workplace Commitments
2.1. Equal Opportunity Employ
2.2. Sexual Harassment
2.3. Drug Free/ Alcohol Free
2.4. Open Door Policy
3. Policy and Procedures
3.1. Professional Conduct
3.2. Dress Code
3.3. Payday
3.4. Company Property
3.5. Privacy
3.6. Personnel Files

4. Employment Classification
4.1. Exempt
4.2. Non-Exempt
4.3. Part-Time/Full-Time Status
5. Attendance Policies
5.1. General Attendance
5.2. Tardiness
5.3. Breaks
6. Leave Policies
6.1. Vacation
6.2. Sick Leave
6.3. Family & Medical Leave Act
6.4. Holidays
6.5. Jury Duty/Voting
6.6 Military Leave
6.7. Leave of Absence

7. Work Performance
7.1. Expectations
7.2. Reviews
7.3. Insubordination
8. Discipline Policy
8.1. Disciplinary Action
8.2. Procedures
8.3. Termination
9. Employee Health and Safety
9.1. Workplace Safety
9.2. Workplace Security
9.3. Emergency Procedures

10. Benefits
10.1. Health Insurance
10.2. Retirement Plans
10.3. Worker's Compensation
10.4. Disability
11. Termination Policies
11.1. Voluntary Termination
11.2. Final Paycheck
11.3. COBRA
11.4. Exit Interview
12. Acknowledging Receipt
12.1. Employee Copy
12.2. Employer Copy

SOURCE: National Federation of Independent Business website. Retrieved May 11, 2016 from www.nfib.com.

quality insight. That is, customers want salespeople to help them identify creative new ways to increase revenue, cut costs, enter new markets and alleviate risk in a manner that has never occurred to the customer. This can only be provided by salespeople who are well-trained in market/customer knowledge.

The next content area involves teaching new hires *how to sell*, which relates to the steps of the **sales process** discussed in Chapter 3. Some people believe that this cannot be done because salespeople are born (not made). However,

CONSIDER THIS...

Five Myths about Salespeople

Myth #1	**Salespeople are born—not made.** This simply is not true. The great sales forces of today, such as those of Salesforce.com, IBM, Procter & Gamble, are all based on excellent sales training programs. These firms often hire recent college graduates who are largely without sales experience or skills and teach them how to sell.
Myth #2	**Salespeople must be good talkers.** On the contrary: Good salespeople are good listeners. Salespeople of today must understand the customer's business—and the only way that happens is if they *listen* to customer concerns.
Myth #3	**Selling is a matter of knowing the right techniques or tricks.** There are no tricks or magic selling techniques. Selling is more a matter of providing solutions for customers—and again, that stems from understanding the customer's business; and then conscientiously working hard to provide superior service.
Myth #4	**A good salesperson can sell ice to an Eskimo.** Selling is not about convincing customers that they need something when they don't. Good selling starts by finding someone who needs the product and can afford it. In other words, good salespeople call on good prospects.
Myth #5	**People don't want to buy.** On the contrary, people do want to buy products—but only if those products help them solve problems.

that is a misperception—or a myth (see **Five Myths** box)—that stems from a misunderstanding about what professional selling is. It is true that some people are born "talkers"—but selling is much more complicated than that. There is a best way of doing almost every single aspect of the sales process, and those professional selling behaviors can be *taught* to any hard-working individual willing to take on the responsibility to learn and grow. Certainly, the vast majority of sales trainers believe that this is so.

For the purposes of training on how to sell, the sales process is often broken down into topics that relate to the various steps of the sales process. For example, Dale Carnegie Training, a well-known outside specialist training company, offers multiple course modules on each of the following topics: (1) uncovering selling opportunities through effective prospecting, (2) acquiring customers through pipeline and territory management, (3) building rapport that leads to trust, (4) generating interest by asking insightful questions, (5) presenting solutions to customer problems, (6) understanding and overcoming objections, (7) gaining customer commitment, and (8) following up to develop key accounts.[17] These modules map onto the eight steps of the sales process from chapter 3.

The final content area is **organizational skills**, which relates to a wide variety of coping-with-the-job topics, such as how to manage time and how to deal with workplace stress and conflict. This is especially important for salespeople given that they must facilitate the efficient interaction among so many different people. In other words, salespeople service multiple people from both their own firm and the customer firm. These people include purchasing agents, engineers, supply chain professionals, product designers, accountants, production personnel, and a range of other executives—possibly even the company president. As discussed in the first chapter, salespeople must learn to deal with the stress that is generated from their very large role sets.

WHAT TEACHING METHODS SHOULD BE USED?

Several different teaching methods may be used to present material in a sales training program (see Figure 7-4). Keep in mind that not all methods of presentation are equally effective for all parts of the training. The best format requires blending the topic and the audience. For example, Ecolab, a supplier of commercial cleaning products, blends classroom training, e-learning, videos, and field trips into their training program.[18]

Lectures
The lecture method can allow trainers to present more information in a shorter time to a larger number of students than any of the other techniques. Selling techniques are best taught by participation methods, but a *limited* number of short lectures introducing students to the underlying problems and principles can be extremely helpful in most sales training programs. Similarly, company information and some product knowledge can be presented in published material, but some lecturing is usually necessary as well. Also, a lecture is frequently the best way to present a basic outline of a subject. Merck's pharmaceutical reps spend about 90 percent of their training in the classroom, where they are taught

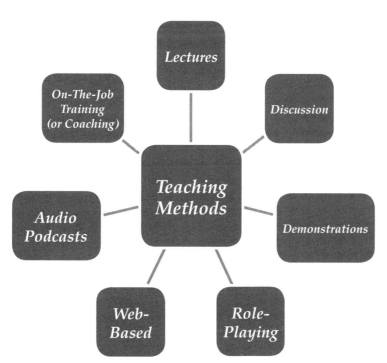

FIGURE 7-4

Teaching Methods used in Sales Training

the scientific principles of medicine. Merck believes that this enables its reps to maintain peer-to-peer discussions with physicians.[19]

Discussion

Discussion should play a large role in any sales training program, since it gives the students an opportunity to work through their own problems. It is also a very good method for encouraging experienced sales reps to share best practices with less-experienced reps.

Discussions can take several forms. Many are simply open talks on various topics between the teacher and the students, with the teacher controlling the discussion and stimulating it. However, cases, roundtables, and panels also can be used to stimulate and facilitate discussions.

The box labeled "Let's Play Zodiak" presents a very creative method of using board games to teach sales concepts. These games have been used by Motorola, Novartis, and other companies to train their sales reps.[20] Aesop.com, a Web marketing consultancy, uses another novel approach—a book club. Each salesperson is required to read a certain book before meeting for an hour of discussion. Aesop reps have read such selections as Jay Conrad Levinson's *Guerrilla Marketing* and the Chinese classic by Sun Tzu, *The Art of War*. These discussions often leap from the literature to day-to-day business strategies and foster camaraderie as well.[21]

Demonstrations

Demonstrations can be used to great advantage in teaching both product knowledge and selling techniques. What better way to teach how a product operates than to actually demonstrate its use? Instead of just telling trainees about the different types of questions that can be used to probe for information, for example, instructors can perform a skit or set up a simulation that demonstrates the questions in a given context. Trainees can be shown how to handle innumerable selling situations that are difficult to describe. Whirlpool Corporation provides its salespeople with a unique type of demonstration. Small groups of newly hired reps live for two months in a house that is equipped with Whirlpool appliances, where they learn by using these

CONSIDER THIS...

Let's Play Zodiak

In order to teach basic financial literacy to salespeople, several sales organizations use a board game simulation called Zodiak. The game is provided by a sales training company (an outside specialist) and is typically played by members of a sales team for one full day.

In playing Zodiak, salespeople analyze customers' financial and strategic information, perform sensitivity analysis for increased prices and value-added services, and deal with shareholder demands and customer complaints.

In other words, Zodiak helps salespeople understand their customers' business strategies, including how they go to market and how they make money. This takes the fear out of finance, and creates a better awareness of the role salespeople play for their customers."

SOURCE: Paradigm Learning, http://www.paradigmlearning.com, Accessed May 13, 2016.

appliances in their daily lives.[22] Sometimes these skills and knowledge are demonstrated with the use of videos.

Role-Playing

Many companies use role-playing to teach selling skills. In role-playing, the trainee attempts to sell a product to a hypothetical prospect. Often these role-plays are video recorded and critiqued by the trainer and/or peers. In handling the role-playing sessions, the trainer must explain the importance of taking criticism the right way. Students must be convinced that the critiques will help them become more effective. They must realize that many problems have no cut-and-dried answers and that the suggestions they receive will give them other options to handle problems. This type of learning-by-doing education can be highly effective in teaching selling techniques, particularly in initial training programs. Some companies such as Du Pont use role-playing on a continual basis to *practice* critical, issue-oriented sales calls just prior to making these calls.[23]

Role-playing and analysis is also an effective technique for teaching growth-related skills such as adaptability, emotional intelligence, creativity, and coping. Peer assessments of fellow salespeople may identify a salesperson's ineffective or even offensive behaviors of which s/he is not aware. Weaknesses in growth skills can be overcome with repeated practice in scenarios that simulate real situations. Companies such as Coca-Cola and Johnson & Johnson are using role-playing and critiques to teach some of the growth-related skills.[24]

Web-based Training

Many companies are turning to Web-based training to save money or to reach employees in far-flung global locations. The biggest advantage to Web-based training is cost—not having to bring people together eliminates not only travel, lodging, and meal costs but also instructor salaries. Studies show that online training takes 50 percent less time and costs 30 to 60 percent less than other forms of training.[25] IBM plans to move 35 percent of its training online and estimates that the company has already saved $100 million in its implementation of e-learning programs.[26] However, the push to online training is not just because of the dollar savings; it also is fueled by rapid spread of information and the need for salespeople to keep pace with constant change. It also keeps reps in the field. When they can go online when it is convenient for them and move at their own pace, they don't lose selling time.

Most companies such as IBM and AT&T are using a blend of online training and face-to-face training.[27] Often the online training focuses on basic skills and knowledge, such as introductory tutorials and new product or customer updates. Face-to-face training can then be reserved for teaching and practicing more advanced skills. In some companies such as Gallo Winery, most of the training is done online.[28]

There are some pitfalls in using online training. It is easy for the reps to either put it off when they are busy or not do it at all if they feel it is not specific to their needs. However, these problems can be offset by making sure that the information is relevant, by setting time limits for completion, by testing results, and by rewarding progress and completion.

Audio Podcasts

Most sales representatives do lots of driving between accounts, and many companies feel that this driving time can be translated into professional development through the use of podcasts or other audio recordings. Companies such as General Motors and IBM provide their sales forces with podcasts that cover a wide range of topics.[29] Selling techniques, time management, and motivational speeches are a few of the topics typically covered. Because these are on-demand audio, sales reps can learn at their own pace.

On-the-Job Training (or Coaching)

On-the-job training is the most popular form of sales training. Generally, the procedure is for the trainee to observe the sales manager (or possibly a senior rep) making several sales calls. The sales trainee, in turn, makes several calls while the supervisor observes. The supervisor and trainee discuss what took place during that call and what the trainee could have done more effectively. This type of one-on-one interaction in the field, which consists of extensive verbal feedback and role modeling, is known as **coaching.** This approach places the student in a more realistic situation than any of the other techniques do. Usually this method is used as the final stage of the trainee's sales education and it is used as a form of continual training. AT&T, GE, and Boise Cascade Office Products all hold their sales managers responsible for the continual coaching of their sales reps.[30]

Mentoring is a more informal type of on-the-job training frequently used by companies. A mentor in a training program is usually an experienced rep who is paired with a new trainee. As in the assimilation phase of the staffing (discussed in Chapter 6), the mentor provides advice and support to the new hire. Both Boeing and IBM say they get some of their best training results when they pair a seasoned veteran with a beginner.[31]

REINFORCEMENT

Most salespeople won't change their behaviors as a result of training unless there is some ongoing **reinforcement.** In fact, as noted earlier in the chapter, Xerox found that most of its salespeople retained only 13 percent of the information learned in training after 30 days unless it was reinforced. Yet in many companies, reinforcement doesn't occur as frequently as it should, largely because managers don't place a priority on this activity. They don't have time, they are uncomfortable, or they don't know how to provide constructive feedback—and rarely are they recognized or rewarded for their efforts in the skill development area.[32]

There are many ways to reinforce training, including all of the original training methods we have discussed. The most frequently used method is for the sales manager to serve as a coach, reinforcing training efforts during actual calls. Some companies use senior salespeople to coach new reps. Some companies follow up the training session with refresher classes. Boston Scientific Corporation provides follow-up sessions for its five-day training seminar in 13 cities around the globe.[33] Other companies use Web-based methods to reinforce formal training sessions. These methods lower the costs of reinforcing training. Whatever the method, it is important to build some type of reinforcement into the overall training program.

TRAINING EVALUATION

Finally, during the **training evaluation** phase, sales executives must assess the effectiveness of their training programs. Evaluation is necessary to determine the value of the training and to improve the design of future programs. In evaluation, executives must decide what outcomes will be evaluated and how these outcomes will be measured. The outcomes must be measured against the objectives for which the training was designed. Outcomes generally fall into one of the following four categories:[34]

- **Reactions.** These outcomes indicate, in a subjective manner, whether those who participated in the training thought it achieved the stated objectives and generally whether it was worthwhile. Reactions may be measured by having participants complete questionnaires or, less formally, by recording verbal comments from the trainees, their supervisors, or the training staff.
- **Learning.** This outcome equates to how much information was absorbed and usually involves giving the trainee some type of test. There may be "before" and "after" tests or just one test taken after the training is completed.
- **Behavior.** This outcome provides an assessment of whether the trainee has changed in substantial ways. The appraisal of behavior is usually conducted by a supervisor who can observe the rep directly. It also may include self-assessment or input from customers.
- **Results.** These are indicators of whether the training is transferring to improved performance results. This is the ultimate test of whether the benefits of training outweigh the costs. Such measures as increased sales and profitability, better customer retention and penetration, and numbers of new accounts can be used to assess bottom-line results.

Although companies are spending billions of dollars on training, many are not taking the time to critically evaluate their training effectiveness, and/or do not know how to measure training effectiveness.[14] Too many companies rely on testing reactions to training or learning. While it is important to measure reactions and factual knowledge as part of a systematic evaluation program, it is just as important to use other types of measures too. Otherwise, the sales manager will not be able to relate training outcomes to performance in the field.

SUMMARY

A successful training program consists of four phases: training assessment, program design, reinforcement, and evaluation. Training is an important factor contributing to the success of salespeople. A good program begins by establishing program objectives and then determining who should be trained. The company must then identify individuals' training needs. This is the key to how much training will be needed.

During the program design phase, the company must decide who will do the training, where and when it will be conducted, what topics will be covered, and what methods will be used. While line personnel have distinctive advantages as sales trainers, they often lack the essential teaching skills. Thus, training is often the responsibility of staff sales trainers. Many companies also use outside training specialists to provide part of their training.

New reps need enough initial training to do a respectable job. However, there are advantages to delaying training until the new person has some experience that can be carried into the classroom. Although initial training is often conducted centrally, continual sales training is often provided in the field.

Among the different methods used to train salespeople are lectures, discussion, demonstrations, role-playing, Web-based training, audio podcasts, and on-the-job training techniques such as coaching and mentoring.

It is very important that companies provide a method for systematically reinforcing their training programs. Otherwise, salespeople are unlikely to change their behavior.

Increasingly, top management is demanding that training programs prove their worth. Training outcomes generally fall into four categories: the reactions of the salespeople, their learning, their behavioral change, and their performance results.

KEY TERMS

Centralized training	Mentoring	Training assessment
Coaching	On-the-job training	Training content
Decentralized training	Program design	Training evaluation
Difficulty analysis	Reinforcement	

QUESTIONS AND PROBLEMS

1. "I don't have any training program. I just hire salespeople who have already proved successful for other companies and turn them loose. I let the big corporations do all my training for me and then just hire away their best people." This was the attitude expressed by the sales manager of one relatively small office-machine firm. Is this a sound policy? What are some of the strengths and weaknesses of this position?

2. "Salespeople are born, not made. It's futile to try to train a person to be a salesperson, so I don't." How would you answer a sales manager who said this to you if you were trying to get him or her to hire you as a sales trainer?

3. "The school of hard knocks is the best training school for salespeople. I just shove them off the dock. Those who have it in them will learn selling on their own, and those who don't have it in them—well, we don't want them around the company anyway." How would you answer a manager who said this?

4. How can the sales manager keep top-notch sales reps interested in continual training programs?

5. You have been made sales trainer for a firm with 125 salespeople. How would you determine their specific training needs?

6. What kind of training is needed for a salesperson who has been promoted to a sales management position?

7. If you were designing a five-week sales training program, how many days would you devote to each of the five content areas of training (Company orientation, Product knowledge, Market/customer knowledge, Sales process, Organizational skills)? Explain and defend your answer.

8. You read an article about an outside training specialist and liked what you read. You feel that hiring this specialist may be beneficial to you in your job as sales trainer to Large, Inc. Unfortunately, you know only what this one article said. You want to know much more. Exactly what you want to learn about this outside specialist?

9. How would you motivate a manager to spend more time reinforcing the skills new reps practiced in the formal training program?

10. How could a manager influence the adaptability of her salespeople?

11. How could you prove the cost-effectiveness of your sales training program?

EXPERIENTIAL EXERCISES

1. Identify a business and a position within it that interacts with the public. For example, you could choose a loan officer or a teller in a bank; a bagger, meat cutter, or checkout clerk at a grocery store; a sales clerk at a Gap store; or a sales rep for a local beer distributor. Talk to people within and outside the company who deal with the person in that position, and talk to some of the people who currently hold that position. Then prepare a written assessment of the typical training needs of a new person for that position.

2. Interview a sales professional about the sales training in her or his company. Describe the program, focusing on the following elements: who and how many participate, what content is covered, who conducts the training, what techniques are used, how long it lasts, where it is conducted, what costs are associated with the training, whether there is any reinforcement after the training, and how the training is evaluated.

3. Assume that you are a sales manager for a medium-sized company that wants to contract with an outside supplier to provide sales training in the area of selling skills for new reps. Using one of the Internet search engines, such as Google, identify suppliers of such sales training. List the Web addresses of these suppliers and describe the programs they provide.

SUNRISE CLEANERS
To Train or Not to Train

Sunrise Cleaner Company's sales have been expanding rapidly in the past several years and are expected to continue increasing throughout the next several years. In order to meet this demand, Mickie Parsons, Sunrise's sales manager, has hired a number of sales representatives and expects to hire about 6 to 10 salespeople per year in the foreseeable future.

In the past, Sunrise hired only experienced reps, but lately the company has been recruiting at universities and hiring recent marketing graduates. While the new grads don't have experience, they often have a high level of motivation and a good understanding of overall marketing planning. However, the less-experienced reps need more training—on both company policies and sales procedures—before they are effective in making sales calls.

Consequently, Parsons is designing an intensive, two-week training program that will provide the necessary training at the lowest possible cost.

Currently, Sunrise does not have a training program. The new hires just spend a week in a territory with an experienced rep, and then they are given their own territory. While this system was satisfactory with experienced people, it is not adequate for the inexperienced people the company is now hiring.

Mickie Parsons has suggested to the president of Sunrise, Keat Markley, that the company institute a one- or two-week training program at company headquarters. Parsons has suggested two options. The first option is to hire a staff recruiter/trainer who would spend half of his or her time on recruiting and the other half on training. The new staff specialist would be paid a salary of about $70,000 a year—so the added cost with respect to the training responsibilities would be $35,000 a year.

The second option is to contract with an outside company that specializes in sales force training. That company would provide a specialist to set up and conduct a training program at a cost of approximately $15,000 per week (or $30,000 for two weeks, which is the expected length of the program).

Parsons was just concluding her presentation to Keat Markley. "I feel that a training program would increase the average annual sales per rep a minimum of 5 percent. So on average, our reps generate one million dollars in sales volume. With this program, we expect that will increase to an average of $1,050,000 per rep."

Markley replied, "I am not convinced that the training would improve performance enough to justify the costs. First, keep in mind our cost of goods sold is about 50%, so only half of that increased sales is profit. And the training costs also include many expenses that you have not yet mentioned. For example, we would have to pay for travel and lodging for all the new hires to be at company headquarters for two weeks, plus I'm sure there will be significant training materials costs. I just want to be sure that the sales increase would more than cover all of the training expenses."

Parsons started calculating these costs in her head. She knew that bringing a rep into headquarters would cost $250 per person for travel and roughly $1,000 for lodging and meals for the two week period. She expected that the training materials would add $100 per rep, and that the audio visual equipment might run $500 per training session. These costs would be relevant to both options.

Markey suddenly had a thought for a third option: "Have you ever thought about developing an online training program? Everything I read says that the top companies are moving toward this—and I heard they save bundles in the process."

Parsons, who had already looked into the online option, replied, "These online programs have significant upfront costs. We'd need to develop a customized program, and that would cost a minimum of $350,000 to develop. Of course, once it's in place, the cost to keep it going would be minimal—I'd guess $2,000 a year to keep it updated. Besides, I think an online program works best for refresher training or for introducing new product information, not for teaching basic selling skills. Face-to-face is much better for that. So in other words, I don't see any way we would get the 5 percent increase in sales with an online program."

"Well, okay," said Markley, "you put together an analysis that considers the profit or loss of all

three of these options; and then make a sound recommendation to me."

Mickie Parsons headed for her office to crunch the numbers. She knew that Mr. Markley would want to make an informed decision, and was relying on her recommendation.

Questions:

1. What is the expected profit/loss of each of the three options for training?
2. Which of the three training options is best for Sunrise Cleaners? What is the reasoning for your recommendation?
3. What characteristics of Sunrise Cleaners make online training (as opposed to face-to-face) more/less attractive? Discuss.

IMAGINATIVE STAFFING, INC. (A)
Training Program for a Selling Team

"I'm not sure what's going on around me right now, but it seems as if somebody is trying to tell me something." Angie Roberts, CEO of Imaginative Staffing, Inc., of New York City, was expressing her thoughts to her assistant, Nicole Gamin. Roberts didn't wait for an answer but continued, "I met some marketing professor at a party the other night, and he seemed to think he was holding a class about what's new in selling. He kept babbling something about team selling. I wasn't sure what he was talking about at first. Maybe he had some professional ball team he wanted to sell to someone with more dollars than sense. But then I caught the drift that he was talking about a way to make sales presentations.

"Then last night, I read an article in one of the trade journals about team selling. To top it off, my daughter informed me that she was forming a team with some of her Girl Scout friends to sell their cookies this year. Is there some kind of message for us in all this?" Roberts asked Gamin.

Gamin smiled and answered innocuously, "Maybe so!" She had a long list of daily agenda items to go over with her boss and really didn't want to get involved with a discussion about the merits of team selling. "Now let's go over what must be done today."

"You're putting me off because you don't like me to mess up your plans for the day. Well, it won't work. I want to know more about team selling, so put it on the agenda somewhere for today," Roberts insisted.

"All right, you're having lunch with your executive committee. Let's put it on the agenda for that meeting." Gamin evidently had said the right thing because her boss immediately got down to the business at hand, planning the day. Mondays were always busy. Not only did all departments start each Monday with a short meeting to plan the week, but the head of each department met with the CEO for lunch, during which company-wide matters were discussed. Roberts felt strongly that these Monday lunches were important. They allowed her not only to learn what was going on in the company but also to foster communications between her and the other managers in the organization.

Imaginative Staffing, Inc., was a temporary-services firm in New York City. Formed in 1990, it had grown to $17 million in revenues. Besides herself and her assistant, Nicole Gamin, the company had a chief financial officer, a sales director, 6 account managers, an operations manager, 8 sales support personnel, 5 administrative assistants, and a receptionist.

One reason Roberts had perceived the team-selling messages was that for some time she had been frustrated by the length of time it took to close a sale with a good prospect. On average, it took about six months of hard work to make a sale to a major customer. One of the sales reps would make the contact and do all of the selling, sometimes with the help of the sales director if the situation seemed to warrant it.

Large and small corporations made extensive use of temporary help for one or more of several reasons: (1) to fill in for workers who, for some reason, were unable to work; (2) to handle overload conditions; or (3) to take care of seasonal peak workloads. In the current legal environment, many organizations were reluctant to hire permanent employees until there was a clear-cut, long-term need for them. Such factors as benefit packages, insurance, unemployment claims, and termination difficulties made management think seriously about hiring people as employees.

The lunch meeting proceeded smoothly as the group ate and disposed of the agenda items in order. When the last item, team selling, came up, members of the group looked at each other with puzzlement. What was it about? Only Susan Borland, the sales director, knew what team selling was. She was not eager to take the lead in the discussion, preferring instead to sit back to find out what was on Roberts' mind. She did not have long to wait.

The CEO began, "You may wonder why I have put this item on the agenda, so I'll not keep you wondering. For some time, I have not been satisfied with our selling effort. It seems to take too much time to gain the confidence of prospective accounts to the extent that they feel comfortable with us. We are relatively new in this market. They don't know us. I've heard and read about team selling as a system that might be of use to us. I want to know exactly what it is and if it is something we should be using."

"It's interesting that you bring this up today because I just had a breakfast meeting with a sales team for Colony Cablevision," Susan Borland said. She continued, "As you know, I'm on the board of directors of my homeowners' association. We have more than 1,000 homes in our planned development, most of whose owners individually subscribe to a cable television system at an average cost of about $45 a month. Now we have been approached by Colony to enter into a bulk billing deal in which all the homeowners will be billed by the association at an attractive price, less than $20 a month for the package. Well, they flew in one of the top managers from their home office to join with the local manager, the local technical engineer, the local marketing manager, and the person who would be our account manager. Each of them made a presentation, and I must say it was effective. I think the board bought it. Anyway, at the time I wondered if this was something we should be doing."

The meeting was interrupted by the receptionist informing several of the managers that their 1:30 appointments were waiting. As they stood up to leave, Roberts asked Borland to prepare a plan for developing and training a sales team for the group to consider at some meeting in the near future.

Susan Borland had been with the company from its beginning. In the early days, she did whatever needed to be done, but as the firm grew and was able to hire people to do specific jobs, she devoted more and more of her time to sales. At first, she was the firm's only salesperson, but as the company grew, she was able to hire more sales reps and she spent increasingly more time in the office, yet she still helped the sales reps whenever they needed it. She was interested in her assignment and intended to get on it that afternoon with the help of her assistant, Judy Morgan.

After briefing Morgan about the team-selling assignment, Borland told her to research the subject. "Find out everything you can about it and who is using it."

That evening, Borland was talking about the day with a friend and the conversation drifted into team selling. The friend, a sales rep for a leading software company, was familiar with the concept since his firm used it to sell to important accounts. He advised, "Don't put too many people on the team, or things can get confusing to the prospect. On one of our first team sales calls, we had seven people in there pitching. It was a disaster. The prospect was overwhelmed with information, much of which was useless. Our people weren't trained. We had some of the programming people in there, and you can imagine their selling skills. They just wouldn't talk about what the prospect wanted to hear; they just talked in their lingo."

Susan Borland listened. She had already decided who should be on the sales team, but now she realized that some of these people would require training.

Questions:

1. Should Imaginative Staffing, Inc., adopt a team-selling system for selling to important accounts?

2. If so, who should be on the team?

3. What training would be needed by the team? To what extent should the team's presentation be planned?

ENDNOTES

[1] The chapter introduction is based on interviews with Liberty Mutual executives. Angela Sebo is a fictional, composite character created to represent a typical new hire.

[2] Vijay Lakshmi Singh, Ajay K. Manrai and Lalita A. Manrai, "Sales Training: A State Of The Art and Contemporary Review," *Journal of Economics, Finance & Administrative Science,* June 2015, Vol. 20 Issue 38, pp. 54-71.

[3] Jennifer J. Salopek, "The Power of the Pyramid," *Training and Development,"* 63 (May 2009), 70–75.

[4] Felicia Lassk, Thomas N. Ingram, Florian Kraus, and Rita Di Mascio, "The Future of Sales Training: Challenges and Related Research Questions," *Journal of Personal Selling & Sales Management,* Winter 2012, Vol. 32 Issue 1, pp. 141-154.

[5] Lassk, et al.

[6] Mark McMaster, "Is Your Training a Waste of Money?" *Sales & Marketing Management,* January 2001, pp. 42-48.

[7] Susan Silbermann, "How Culture And Regulation Demand New Ways To Sell," *Harvard Business Review,* Jul/Aug2012, Vol. 90 Issue 7/8, p104-105.

[8] Julie Barker, "Too Good to Ignore," *Sales & Marketing Management,* March 2005, pp. 38-40.

[9] Lee Salz, "Do You Know the Right Time to Fire a Sales Person?" *Eyes on Sales,* Sep 27, 2011. Retrieved from the sales blog: http://www.eyesonsales.com/content/article/do_you_know_the_right_time_to_fire_a_sales_person

[10] Thomas L. Powers, Thomas E. DeCarlo and Gouri Gupte, "An Update on the Status of Sales Management Training," *Journal of Personal Selling and Sales Management,* 30 (4) Fall 2010, pp. 319-326.

[11] Andy Cohen, "From the Ground Up," *Sales & Marketing Management,* November 2000, p. 23.

[12] Ian Altman, "How Much Does Sales Training Cost?" *Forbes,* December 1, 2014. Retrieved from http://www.forbes.com/sites/ianaltman/2014/12/01/how-much-does-sales-training-cost

[13] Julia Chang, "Making the Grade," *Sales & Marketing Management,* March 2004, pp. 26-28.

[14] "2005 Industry Report," *Training, December 2005, pp. 26-28.*

[15] The HR Chally Group, "The Customer-Selected World Class Sales Excellence Ten-Year Research Report," 2003, p. 59.

[16] Information on training courses offered by Salesforce.com was retrieved on the company website (http://salesforce.com) on May 13, 2016.

[17] Information on training courses offered by Dale Carnegie Training was retrieved from the company website (http://www.dalecarnegie.com/) on May 12, 2016.

[18] Julia Chang, "The Premium Blend," *Sales & Marketing Management,* April 2004, p. 19.

[19] Elana Harris, "Best at Sales Training," *Sales & Marketing Management,* July 2000, p. 68.

[20] Paradigm Learning, http://www.paradigmlearning.com, Accessed May 13, 2016.

[21] Mark McMaster, "Training Places," *Sales & Marketing Management,* October 2001, p. 43.

[22] Betsy Cummings, "Welcome to the Real Whirled," *Sales & Marketing Management, February 2001, pp. 88-89.*

[23] Jay Kennedy, "Practicing Sales Excellence," *Sales & Marketing Management Executive Report,* March 5, 1997, p. 6.

[24] Julia Chang, "Born to Sell?" *Sales & marketing Management,* July 2003, pp. 34-37.

[25] Malcolm Fleschner, "Business Class," *Selling Power,* September 2001, p. 133.

[26] McMaster, "Is Your Training a Waste of Money?" pp. 42-48.

[27] "2005 Industry Report," *Training,* December 2005.

[28] Julia Chang, "Experts in the Field," *Sales & Marketing Management,* October 2005, p. 19.

[29] Lauren Hahn, "Tuning Up Sales Skills," *Sales & Marketing Management,* March 2006, p. 17.

[30] The HR Chally Group, p. 56.

[31] Kevin Dobbs, "Training on the Fly," *Sales & Marketing Management,* November 2000, p. 96.

[32] Rackham and Ruff, *Managing Major Sales,* p. 130.

[33] Slade Sohmer, "Emerging as a Global Success," *Sales & Marketing Management,* May 2000, p. 125.

[34] Donald Kirkpatrick, *Evaluating Training Programs: The Four Levels* (New York: Berrett-Koehler, 1992).

[35] Ashraf Attia, Earl D. Honeycutt Jr., and Mark P. Leach, "A Three-Stage Model for Assessing and Improving Sales Force Training and Development," *Journal of Personal Selling & Sales Management,* Summer 2005, pp. 253-68.

8

Motivating a Sales Force

All motivation is self-motivation. Salespeople cannot be motivated unless they want to be. At the same time, sales managers can create an environment that unleashes salespeople's inner motivation, such that the reps are more likely to work hard toward achieving their sales goals.

Sales contests are often used to create such an environment. However, the typical problem with contests is that the same, top-sellers tend to always win—and so, the majority of the salespeople do not even try because they feel they have very little chance of winning the contest. This is why Dan McGraw, Founder of the gasoline app Fuelzee, prefers sales contests that reward his account managers for their *effort*. In one case, Fuelzee awarded a $100 gift card every week to the team member that received the most "no's," which was tracked by the company's CRM system. McGraw's reasoning is that the more no's you get, the closer you are to getting a yes. The contest practically doubled the number of outbound calls, demonstrated to everyone how effort leads to more reward, and generated more sales volume. Further, it was a fun event that motivated the entire team.

MOTIVATION—WHAT IS IT?

To better understand the behavioral concept of motivation, let's first ask: Why do people act as they do? Or: Why do people act at all? The answer: People seek, consciously or unconsciously, to attain rewards that fulfill or satisfy some physiological or psychological need. All behavior starts with an aroused, or stimulated need, such as hunger. So, if hungry, a person will put forth effort to receive a reward (or food) that satisfied their hunger.

These needs may originate within the person, or they may be stimulated by an external force. You may simply become hungry, for example, or you may see an ad for food that makes you hungry. In either case, once the need is aroused, you will be motivated—you will want to take some action.

Consequently, we define **motivation** as the desire to put forth effort toward a goal in order to receive a reward that fulfills a need. To motivate the sales force, a sales manager must first understand the needs of each sales rep, and then must know what specific rewards satisfy those needs. This is not easy—especially given that each salesperson is different.

Dimensions of Sales Motivation

Motivational effort is generally thought to include three dimensions: intensity, persistence, and choice.[1] *Intensity* refers to the amount of effort the salesperson expends on a given task; *persistence* refers to how long the salesperson will continue to put forth effort; and *choice* refers to the salesperson's choice of specific actions to accomplish job-related tasks. For example, a salesperson may decide to focus on a particular customer (choice). She may increase the number of calls she makes on this customer (intensity) until she gets the first order (persistence). As noted in Figure 8-1, the choice of a specific action may affect the intensity and persistence. Likewise, intensity may affect how long a salesperson persists at a specific task.

The sales job consists of a large variety of complex and diverse tasks. Because of this, it is important that the sales rep's efforts be channeled in a direction consistent with the company's strategic plan. Therefore, the *direction* of the salesperson's effort is as important as the intensity and persistence of that effort.

FIGURE 8-1
Motivational effort

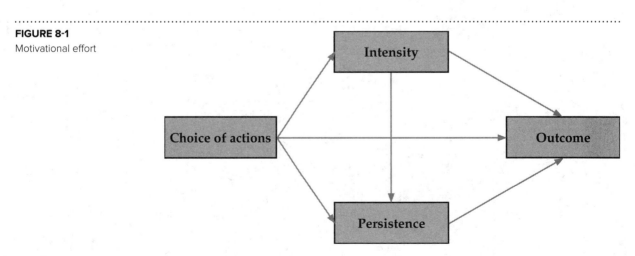

Motivation and Strategic Planning

A sales manager concerned with motivating salespeople finds that the most complex task is getting them to expend effort on activities consistent with the strategic planning of the firm. Many salespeople don't need external stimulation to work hard and long; their internal needs motivate them to do so. However, every sales rep must be externally motivated to perform actions that support the strategic objectives of the firm. For example, if a company's strategic plan calls for changing its customer mix, a sales staff must be motivated to change its allocation of calls in a way that is consistent with the strategic change. The first step in making this happen is for the sales manager to provide each salesperson with a new plan for calling on a different set of customers.

IMPORTANCE AND DIFFICULTY OF MOTIVATION

Motivating salespeople is important for a firm. After all, salespeople generate the revenue that is necessary to stay in business; and this not likely to happen with an unmotivated sales force. In addition, motivating salespeople is difficult. First, salespeople tend to spend most of their time on their own, away from the office (where the sales manager is). Further, each salesperson is a unique individual, and so sales managers have to be especially sharp to understand what makes each one tick. Finally, company goals are always changing and today's marketplace is quite dynamic; so what works today may not work tomorrow!

Unique Nature of the Sales Job

Salespeople experience a wonderful sense of exhilaration when they make a sale. But they also must frequently deal with the frustration and rejection of not making the sale. Even very good reps don't make every sale. Also, while many customers are gracious, courteous, and thoughtful in their dealings with salespeople, some are rude, demanding, and even threatening.

Salespeople spend a large amount of time by themselves calling on customers and traveling between accounts. This means that most of the time they are away from any kind of support from their peers or leaders, and they often feel isolated and detached from their companies. Consequently, they usually require more motivation than other workers do to reach the performance level management desires.

Individuality of Salespeople

Sales reps have their own personal goals, problem, strengths, and weaknesses. Each rep may respond differently to a given motivating force. Ideally, the company should develop a separate motivational package for each sales rep, but a totally tailor-made approach poses major practical problems. In reality, management must develop a motivational mix that appeals to a whole group but also has the flexibility to appeal to the varying individual needs.

A related point is that the sales reps themselves may not know why they react as they do to a given motivator, or they may be unwilling to admit what these reasons are. For example, a salesperson may engage in a certain selling task because it satisfies her ego. Rather than admit this, however, she will say that she is motivated by a desire to serve her customers.

Diversity in Company Goals

A company usually has many diverse sales goals, and these goals may even conflict. One goal may be to correct an imbalanced inventory (by having the reps focus on selling one particular item due to excess capacity); another goal may be to have the sales force do missionary selling to strengthen long-term customer relations. These two goals conflict somewhat and require different motivating forces. With diverse goals, such as these, developing an effective combination of motivators is difficult.

Changes in Market Environment

Changes in the market environment can make it difficult for management to develop the right mix of sales force motivational methods. What motivates reps today may not work next month because of changes in market conditions. Conversely, sales executives can face motivational problems when market conditions remain stable for an extended time. In this situation, the same motivators may lose their effectiveness.

BEHAVIORAL CONCEPTS OF MOTIVATION

Finding an effective combination of motivators may be easier if a sales manager understands some of the behavioral factors that affect sales force motivation.

The motivational process begins with an aroused need, but, as depicted in Figure 8-2, three conditions must exist before an unfulfilled need leads to enhanced sales performance.[2] First, salespeople must feel that the rewards are *desirable*—that is, that they will satisfy some need. Second, they must believe that the rewards are tied to performance, and they must understand exactly what performance is required to get the rewards. Finally, sales reps must believe that the performance goals on which the rewards are based are attainable. In other words, the reps must feel that if they expend effort, they can achieve the goals that have been set for them.

Consequently, managers must understand each of their salespeople before developing motivational programs. Such programs often fail because they appeal to the wrong needs. Several motivational theories offer classification

FIGURE 8-2
Motivational Conditions

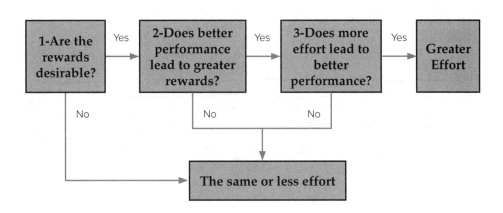

systems that can help managers recognize and understand different kinds of needs. The next section discusses expectancy theory, Maslow's hierarchy of needs theory, Herzberg's dual-factor theory, role theory, and attribution theory.

Expectancy Theory

Expectancy theory builds on the idea that needs provide the starting point for understanding an individual's motivation. However, it goes several steps further by explaining all the conditional links described in Figure 8-2. These links, which are called valence, instrumentality and expectancy, are explained in detail in the following sections.

Is the reward desirable?

The extent to which a salesperson desires a reward is known as **valence.** Valences must be strong for reps to be motivated; which means that the company and/or sales manager should offer rewards that are desirable. This is not easy because each rep is unique and has a different combination of needs. Therefore, company rewards and incentives desired by one rep may not be valued by another. Too often, sales managers do not know the relative value placed on various incentives by their salespeople. Past research has shown that managers believe that compensation is the most important motivator of salespeople; however, salespeople report that what motivates them most is *interesting work*—or at least that is what they say![3]

Assume that a given sales rep, working under a straight salary compensation plan, has reached her sales goal. Suppose the reward is a congratulatory pat on the back from management and a formal recognition award for the best sales performance of the period. This rep may say to herself, "This honor award would be fine if I were bucking for a promotion or if I wanted to boost my status, but what I really want is more money—a nice bonus or a salary increase for my outstanding performance." At the end of this thought process, the rep decides that the reward for reaching her goal is not desirable—so why put forth any effort? Management in this case should consider establishing monetary rewards for those reps on straight salary who meet their sales goals.

When determining the level of valence (or desirability of a reward), salespeople tend to look at what other reps are getting. If they perceive that they are being treated unfairly, then the rewards are not as motivating. If first prize for the sales contest is a trip to Florida, valence will be lower if last year's winner won something much nicer (e.g., a trip to Hawaii).

Does better performance lead to more reward?

In addition to valence, sales reps must also believe that the reward is tied to higher performance. This is called **instrumentality.** If the rewards are pretty much the same regardless of how good or bad a rep's performance is, then these rewards will not be effective motivators (due to low instrumentality). Also, salespeople must understand exactly what they must accomplish in order to get the particular reward.

Sales managers must design a reward structure in which greater rewards are tied to better performance. The evaluation process should be linked to the reward system, and sales managers should make every effort to keep the process as objective as possible. The goals should be clear, concise, and measurable.

Every sales rep should be made aware of the criteria and the process that will be used to evaluate them.

One clear way to tie reward to performance is by using a commission compensation package (as opposed to straight salary). In other words, instrumentality tends to be strong if salespeople make a certain percent of the sales volume they generate. Chapter 9 covers compensation plans in greater detail.

Does more effort lead to better performance?

The third link of expectancy theory is called **expectancy**, which is the perception that greater effort leads to greater performance. It follows that salespeople will only work harder to try to sell more product if they believe that their increased effort will result in more sales. Low expectancy could be the result of a poor training program. That is, salespeople may have inadequate product knowledge, and so they avoid contacting customers because they do not feel qualified to demo the product.

Salespeople are not always accurate in assessing the effort/performance link. Suppose, for example, a salesperson believes that making a greater number of calls will lead to improved performance, when in fact what the rep really needs to do is to improve the quality of the calls or to call on a different mix of customers. This rep may be motivated to make the additional calls, but such effort will not lead to significantly improved performance. Salespeople must have accurate perceptions of which activities will lead to improved performance. Similarly, they must correctly understand the reasons for their successes and failures. The sales manager can directly impact motivation by clarifying exactly what type of effort will lead to greater performance.

So again, expectancy theory holds that salespeople will only be motivated if *all three* elements of the theory are strong: valence, instrumentality and expectancy. That is, salespeople will only generate more effort (1) if the rewards are desirable, (2) if greater performance is linked to the rewards, and (3) if greater effort is linked to performance.

Maslow's Hierarchy of Needs Theory

In his **hierarchy of needs theory**, Abraham H. Maslow proposed five levels of needs that every individual seeks to satisfy.[4] The theory holds that individuals are first concerned with physiological needs, which are at the bottom of the pyramid in Figure 8-3. Once these needs are fulfilled, individuals then start to worry about safety needs, then social needs, and so on. Occasionally, a previously satisfied need (e.g., job security) may become unfulfilled (loss of job); that need will then take precedence again over the higher-level needs.

According to Maslow, the highest-level needs of self-actualization are fulfilled through self-development, challenge, and other intrinsic rewards. The lower-level or more basic needs (esteem, social, safety, and physiological) can be fulfilled through either extrinsic or intrinsic rewards. **Extrinsic rewards** (such as pay and recognition) are provided by others. **Intrinsic rewards** come from performing the task itself. For example, a salesperson's feeling of accomplishment that comes from landing a big account is an intrinsic reward. The bonus the salesperson receives for landing that account is an extrinsic reward. A survey of over 500 salespeople found that those who earn the most are those who least prefer cash as an incentive, and those who earn the least prefer cash over other incentives.[5]

As shown in Figure 8-3, there are a variety of sales management actions or rewards that can help satisfy the various needs. As discussed before, different salespeople have different needs; and so, sales managers are better motivators when they understand the various needs of their sales force. For example, a sales manager might know that threatening to fire a particular account manager will arouse safety needs (which are fulfilled through job and income security); and thus motivate him or her to work harder. Alternatively, this same action might motivate another account manager to find another, safer position with a different company.

Dual-Factor Theory

Another theory of motivation, developed by psychologist Frederick Herzberg, also is based on the idea that people have needs that they will seek to satisfy through their behavior.[6] However, Herzberg's dual-factor theory groups sources of satisfaction and dissatisfaction into only two groups: **hygiene factors** and **motivation factors**. The theory holds that job satisfaction and job dissatisfaction act independently of one another.

Examples of hygiene factors, which correspond to Maslow's lower-order needs, are company policies, supervision, basic compensation and working conditions. They are called hygiene factors because they deal with the condition of the work environment rather than the work itself. An absence of hygiene factors causes dissatisfaction among the workers—and many complaints. However, these factors do not provide the incentive for salespeople to work harder.

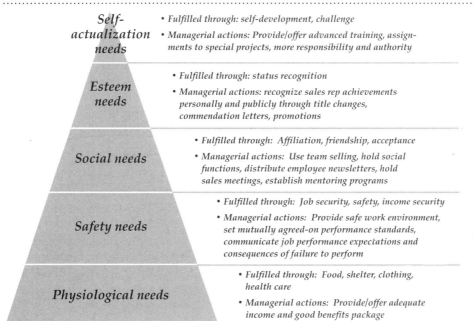

FIGURE 8-3

Maslow's Hierarchy of needs and possible sales management actions

Motivation factors, which correspond to Maslow's higher-order needs, include recognition, pay raises and commission tied to performance, responsibility, challenge, and opportunities for growth. The theory holds that these are the factors that can motivate a salesperson to higher performance.

The dual-factor theory discusses these four possible combinations:

1. High Hygiene, High Motivation—Highly motivated salespeople who are satisfied with their jobs; this is the ideal situation.
2. High Hygiene, Low Motivation—Salespeople are happy with their jobs, but uninspired. The job is viewed merely as a paycheck.
3. Low Hygiene, High Motivation—An exciting, challenging job that motivates salespeople to work hard, but there are many complaints due to low compensation and poor working conditions.
4. Low Hygiene, Low Motivation—Salespeople complain and are not motivated; this is the worst possible scenario.

Sales managers are successful if they can steer their sales force toward the high hygiene and high motivation situation. A number of academic studies provide strong support for the dual-factor theory of motivation.[7]

Role Theory

Role theory concerns the social roles people occupy and the various behaviors that are appropriate to those roles. As noted above, salespeople must understand exactly what they must do in order to improve their performance. However, this is often difficult because much of their job activity involves dealing with people outside the company (namely, customers) and because they usually work with little or no direct supervision. As a result, there can be considerable role ambiguity and role conflict in the salesperson's role. Note that these are the two dimensions of role stress discussed in the first chapter.

Role ambiguity results when sales reps are not sure what is expected of them. For example, reps may be uncertain of whether or not they have the authority to meet price competition or to grant credit. They may be unclear about their organizational relationship with staff executives. A marketing research manager may ask the reps to perform some duties in the field; the reps may not know how much time and energy to devote to such requests.

Role conflict stems from two sources. One source is that a sales rep is trying to serve two masters: the company and the customer. Because these two often have different and conflicting interests, a rep can get caught in the middle. For example, a customer wants lenient credit terms, but the credit manager wants to deal in short-term credit with stringent terms. Or a customer expects gifts and lavish entertainment, but the rep's management, fearful of bribery accusations, wants to cut back on these items.

Another potential source of conflict lies in the varying demands placed on the sales reps by different groups within their own companies. For example, the marketing department may push the reps to follow up on leads generated by visitors leaving their contact information on the company website, but the sales department wants the reps to concentrate on existing customers.

Sales managers must make sure that all salespeople understand what is expected in their respective roles. Writing clear and detailed job descriptions and letting the sales force participate in setting their own goals are ways of decreasing role ambiguity and conflict.

The importance of having the sales force know what is expected of them and how to handle various situations goes beyond improved performance. Research has demonstrated that when salespeople have a clear understanding of their roles, not only is their performance higher; their job satisfaction is also higher and their propensity to leave is lower.[8]

Attribution Theory

According to attribution theory, salespeople usually attribute their successes and failures to one or more of the following reasons: Ability, effort, strategy (or tactics), luck, or difficulty of the task.[9] Sales reps will be motivated to do different things, depending on the **attributions** for success or failure they have made. For example, if a salesperson feels that he did not reach his goals because he did not put forth enough effort, he will be motivated to work harder—to work more hours and/or to call on more accounts. However, if he feels that he lost sales because of the particular presentation he was using, he will change his strategy by adapting his presentation. Changing strategies is sometimes called "working smarter."

If sales reps feel their failures are due to lack of ability, they should be motivated to seek advice or help. But sometimes they will instead increase their effort to compensate for their lack of ability. If they feel that the difficulty of the task contributed to their failure, they may be motivated to work harder and/or smarter. However, if they feel that the task is impossible, or that the goal is unreasonable, they will be frustrated and less motivated. Figure 8-4 summarizes these attributions and their impact on selling behavior.

Through training, counseling, and day-to-day coaching, sales managers can help their people both recognize which activities lead to improved performance and make correct attributions for success and failure. They also can set attainable goals. More important, sales managers themselves must understand that encouraging their salespeople to work harder is not the only path to success, nor necessarily the best one. Motivating sales reps to understand customer

FIGURE 8-4
Salespeople's perceived reasons for failure and their motivational impact

differences, think about alternative sales strategies, and be adaptive when the situation calls for it may lead to better results than will simply telling them to try harder.[10]

SALESPERSON CHARACTERISTICS

Personal characteristics of the salespeople have a big impact on their needs, their evaluation of rewards, and their perceptions of the conditional links described in the various motivational theories discussed. We briefly discuss three categories of these characteristics: demographics, psychological traits, and experience.

Demographics. Age, family size, income, and education all affect the value that salespeople place on various rewards. For example, sales reps relatively satisfied with their current income level may be more interested in such things as status, freedom, and self-development than in pay and benefits. Others, less satisfied, may be very concerned about their income levels. Salespeople with greater education may place a higher value on opportunities for training and advancement than others.

Psychological traits. Some psychological traits are linked to how the sales rep evaluates rewards. For example, a rep with a high need for achievement will be motivated by greater responsibility and challenge. Other traits affect the person's perceptions of the effort/performance link. Salespeople with high levels of self-esteem, for example, will feel confident about their efforts to improve performance.

Experience. Another factor that affects salespeople's perceptions is experience. The more experience they have in sales, the more understanding reps will have about what kind of effort leads to improved performance and about what performance levels are necessary to attain the rewards they desire.

CAREER STAGES AND THE PLATEAUED SALESPERSON

Many managers agree that salespeople's needs change as they progress through their careers, and research supports this.[11] The following four career stages are related to demographics discussed in the previous section:

- In the **exploration stage** of their careers, salespeople are in their early to mid-20s in entry-level positions—and much more likely to switch jobs. They are interested in advancement and growth opportunities, yet are prone to skepticism about their future in sales.
- If they choose to pursue a sales career, salespeople—now in their late 20s or early 30s—move to the **establishment stage**, during which they become more committed to their occupations. Typically this is also the time when family responsibilities become greater; so money and benefits become much more important. Status, recognition, and intrinsic job satisfaction are important as well.
- In the **maintenance stage**, salespeople are valuable to the company as they are generally top performers. Because they have been in the same position for several years, these salespeople sometimes feel frustrated over limited promotion opportunities. Job security, job enrichment, and status enhancement are key motivators.

- In the **disengagement stage**, salespeople are mentally preparing for retirement. This group is typically in their 40s or 50s—but this varies. While they still know how to be successful, they have often lost the desire to sell. They withdraw psychologically; lose interest in their jobs; and so their performance often slips.

Those salespeople in the disengagement stage are often referred to as **plateaued salespeople**. This group is a challenge for sales managers to motivate. Often these people have performed well in the past, but they reach a point where they seem to lose the drive to sell or even the interest in striving for new goals. This is a significant problem for most sales managers.

Plateaued salespeople are not performing to expectations, and it is very difficult to get them to do so. Yet managers are hesitant to terminate them because they are likely to have developed very strong relationships with a few important customers. In fact, they may still generate a large number of sales with these customers without trying very hard.

Causes. The lack of upward mobility is the number one cause of plateauing. Salespeople faced with limited opportunities for promotion see their careers coming to a standstill. Other reasons are boredom, perceptions of unfair treatment, and general burnout. Also, these salespeople are often satisfied with their current compensation, and no longer driven to make more money.

CONSIDER THIS...

Motivating Laggards, Core Performers and Stars

The typical sales force has a handful of low performers that we call Laggards, and a handful of high performers or Stars. Those Core Performers in the middle are by far the largest group, which is why wise sales managers introduce motivational programs that inspire this group. Research shows that these three groups are each motivated by different types of rewards.

Laggards are motivated by more frequent (e.g., quarterly) bonuses, and the social pressure of having a high-quality pipeline of new sales talent

Core Performers are motivated by multi-tier targets, with the low tier relatively easy to attain, the middle tier harder to attain, and the top tier very difficult to attain. The tiers act as stepping stones that are helpful in guiding core performers up the curve.

Stars are motivated by no cap commissions, and sales contests with several prizes (experts say that the number of prizes should equal the number of stars in the sales force).

SOURCE: Thomas Steenburgh, Michael Ahearne, "Motivating Salespeople: What Really Works," Harvard Business Review. Jul/Aug2012, Vol. 90 Issue 7/8, p70-75.

Symptoms. There are early signs of plateauing. Sales reps who have done so in the past may no longer prospect hard enough or follow through. They seem to be sick or absent more than they used to be, and they work fewer hours. They seem to lack energy, time, enthusiasm, creativity, and a sense of humor. Their paperwork may become sloppy, and the sales manager may get more complaints from their customers. Usually these reps are not keeping abreast of new products and technologies. They relish the past and resist changes.

Possible solutions. The first step for a good solution is to recognize the symptoms early. Then it is important for the sales manager to discuss the situation with the rep. The manager must identify the problem and set clear performance expectations. If the rep does not improve his or her performance, then more creative solutions may be necessary. One solution is to give the plateaued salesperson a new assignment, such as coaching new salespeople, gathering competitive intelligence, surveying customers for new product ideas, or developing a new territory. The new responsibilities may relieve the boredom and/or provide a challenge that would excite and motivate the rep. Another alternative is to shift accounts, which forces the sales rep out of a comfortable territory that requires little maintenance into one where he or she must start over. It is the manager's responsibility to take action to get these people out of their ruts. Their experience and skills are too great to waste.

SELECTING EFFECTIVE COMBINATIONS OF MOTIVATIONAL TOOLS

It is difficult to predict exactly what will motivate any given salesperson, but sales managers should begin by getting to know each rep as an individual in order to understand his or her specific needs. Only then will the sales manager design an effective motivational program. Some companies feel that personal goals are such an important motivator that they tie the achievement of bonuses to both sales goals and personal goals.[12] Every motivational program should have some elements within it that can be tailored to the individual's needs. The starting point for a successful motivational program is to establish specific performance objectives that have been agreed on and can be measured by both the manager and the salesperson.

Given a set of performance objectives, managers must determine the most effective combination of motivation methods for their salespeople. Motivational tools may be divided into two categories: **financial rewards** and **nonfinancial rewards.** Each type is outlined in Figure 8-5. Notice that the basic sales management tasks of leadership, training, planning, and evaluating also are considered part of the motivational mix. Because each of these is discussed in separate chapters, the discussion that follows focuses primarily on the financial and nonfinancial rewards.

FINANCIAL REWARDS

While all jobs involve some form of financial reward, usually in the form of a salary, sales jobs differ in that they may provide additional kinds of financial rewards, often aligned with behavior or performance.

Financial Rewards	Other Elements
• Basic compensation plan	• Leadership and supervision
○ Salary	• Sales training programs
○ Commissions	• Sales mentoring
○ Bonus payments	• Sales planning elements
○ Benefits	○ Forecasts
• Sales contests	○ Budgets
Nonfinancial Rewards	○ Quotas
• Recognition awards such as pins, trophies, certificates	○ Territories
	• Evaluation of salesperson's performance
• Praise and encouragement from management	• General management elements
• Job enrichment	○ Organizational structure
• Opportunity for promotion (this also may be a financial reward)	○ Management's leadership style
	○ Channels of communication
• Sales meetings and conventions	○ Corporate culture

FIGURE 8-5
Specific elements in the motivational mix

Compensation

Money is often used as an incentive for salespeople. A survey found that 69 percent of the companies surveyed use cash as an incentive and that salespeople like to receive cash. Surveys show that salespeople *prefer* pay raises and cash incentives over any other type of motivational program. Yet only 15 percent of salespeople surveyed say that they are *motivated* by the expectation of financial reward.[13] Therefore, relying on additional compensation to motivate your salespeople may not always be effective. The design of sales force compensation plans is discussed in the next chapter.

Other Financial Rewards

Many companies offer their salespeople performance incentives that are not in the form of cash but that would cost the reps a significant amount of money if they were to buy these things for themselves. Companies such as Lexmark, Grainger Industrial, and Panasonic use merchandise and travel to encourage their reps to improve their performance. In order to appeal to varying preferences, Lexmark and other companies have individualized their incentives. They use a points-based program in which salespeople earn points toward merchandise they may select from a catalog.[14]

Some companies rely on **experience-based incentives.** Shred-it, a document destruction company headquartered in Toronto, Canada, gave 14 reps a trip to a NASA space camp, where the reps learned to pilot a space ship and experienced weightlessness. Ford Motor Credit sent three salespeople from each of its top 15 dealerships to fly T-6 fighter planes, pairing each rep with an experienced pilot.[15] Many of the incentives described here are used in conjunction with sales contests, described next.

Sales Contests

The financial and nonfinancial rewards are often attached to **sales contests**, which are short-term incentive programs that use prizes and awards to motivate sales reps to achieve specific goals. Contests are a popular motivational device.

CONSIDER THIS...

Creative Sales Contest Ideas

According to some experts, sales contests are only effective if they engage the salespeople through fun and excitement. For example, consider this idea:

Lucky Duck: For this contest, the office has a tub with floating ducks, each of which has a hidden number that corresponds to a prize. Prizes might be small, medium or big. Upon achieving the performance goal, the salesperson pulls a duck and is immediately rewarded with the related prize.

What are the pros and cons of this type of approach to sales contests?

SOURCE: Tomek Jordan, "Sales Contest Ideas to Motivate Your Sales Team," *Repignite Sales Blog*, Retrieved from the following URL on June 22, 2016: https://repignite.com/2014/01/sales-contest-ideas-to-motivate-your-sales-team/

Fastenal Company has a variety of sales contests throughout the year, one of which is the Bounty Hunter Program that recognizes and rewards high performing districts on a weekly basis. The Fastenal sales contests are often co-sponsored by manufacturers, which pay out a **spiff**—or bonus money—to each rep that reaches a specific sales goal. For example, Fastenal sales reps might get a bonus for selling a certain number of DeWalt power tools—and the spiff could come from DeWalt. On occasion, free trips or vacation packages are also offered to the winners.

A contest should have a clear-cut purpose, such as something management wants the sales force to do that it isn't doing. Contests are best used to achieve such specific goals as getting new accounts, selling newly-introduced products, or relieving certain overstocked inventory positions.

In planning and conducting a successful contest, managers must design the contest, select the prizes, and promote the contest.

Contest design

The contest should be designed so that each person has an equal opportunity to win. If the average or poor reps learn that the top producers win all the prizes, they will silently withdraw from the competition. Opportunity to win may be equalized through the use of quotas or by allowing for differences in territories and selling abilities. The rep who makes the greatest improvement relative to others is the winner. In this way, even the poorest salesperson has a chance to win.

A variation of the design described above is an **open-ended contest**, in which there is no limit to the number of people who can win by meeting their preset goals. In this way, people are competing only with themselves. This is in contrast to a **closed-ended contest**, in which there are a limited number of winners. Volvo of Canada has successfully used an open program, whereas Optimus Solutions, an IT services provider, tends to rely on closed programs.[16] Another method of broadening the opportunity to win is to use a **tiered contest.** In this type of program, two or more levels of prizes are awarded. If salespeople perform at or above a certain level, they get a certain prize—say, a trip to the Bahamas. This can be used in conjunction with an open-ended contest in which everyone can win.

The Sales Contest

Desi Carroll, a Shiderlots account manager, was angry. She wanted to know what Adam Dark planned to do about the sales contest. Although the $15,000 award had already been delivered to one of her colleagues, Carroll felt the prize was actually hers.

It had been only a year ago that Adam Dark had dreamed up the idea of a $15,000 contest for his sales force. Having just introduced a new type of service contract designed for shopping malls, the company was interested in seeing sales get off to a quick start. Adam had suggested a sales contest, the company's first, whereby the account manager selling the most contracts to the designated target market would receive a check for $15,000—hand-delivered over a private luncheon with Shiderlots' president, Rosann Speer.

Having developed the guidelines, Adam then informed his team of the contest, which would last for nine months. The reaction from the sales force was quite enthusiastic; in the first month alone, the new line's sales exceeded company projections.

With one month to go in the contest, Desi Carroll appeared to be well on her way to winning the prize. She had worked extremely hard identifying and calling on the shopping malls in her territory, and landed a handful of small- to medium-sized new accounts. Her efforts appeared to be paying off when, out of the blue, her fellow salesperson Johnny Lear, delivered a huge new contract from Polaris Fashion Place, the large shopping complex on the north side of the city. Polaris had long been established with Shiderlots key competitor; so it was quite surprising.

With that order, Lear was able to secure the contest; and so, one month ago he had his lunch with the president, during which he received the $15,000 check. This week, however, came a startling development. It seemed that Polaris Fashion Place had decided to cancel the order—just a few days before it was to start. Of course, Polaris had not yet paid its bill.

When asked by Adam Dark about the cancellations, Johnny Lear expressed shock and disappointment, but still felt the $15,000 prize belong to him. "I sold those orders within the contest time frame, fair and square! It's not my fault that the Polaris people changed their minds at this point—I had nothing to do with it. I followed the contest rules very carefully, and was the legitimate winner."

Desi Carroll, however, disagreed. "Lear played this contest like a fiddle! I'll bet this was a bogus order from the start. Heck, Johnny's brother-in-law works in management over at Polaris. I think it was a setup. I want that $15,000 luncheon with the president," demanded Carroll.

Question: What should Adam Dark do to resolve this dilemma?

RUNNING CASE
Shiderlots
Elevators, Inc.

Contest prizes and promotion

Contest success depends to a great extent on the attractiveness of the prizes (see the chapter's earlier discussion about valence and expectancy theory). Cash prizes, merchandise, and travel are frequently used as incentives. Cash prizes have the advantage of giving the rep the greatest choice in how to use the prize. On the other hand, travel and merchandise are more visible and interesting to promote and publicize. Also, as noted above, several studies have found noncash prizes to be more effective than cash prizes for motivating sales reps.[17] As noted earlier, one way to increase the choice associated with merchandise is to use a point system in which the winners earn points toward merchandise they may select from a catalog. At Sprint, the salespeople can choose from a wide variety of merchandise or travel, but they also can choose to get reimbursed for individualized "lifestyle" items including home renovations or plastic surgery.[18]

The sales contest and the prizes that will be given out should be widely and continually publicized through the duration of the contest. At least 10 percent of the budget for the contest should be spent on promotion. The goal is to keep everyone excited.

Objections to contests

While contests can increase sales and boost morale, they also may have some unintended effects. Frequently, sales contests lead to undesirable selling methods, such as overstocking, overselling, and various pressure tactics. In the short run, such tactics may enable a sales rep to win the contest, but in the long run, they can cause trouble. Many executives object to contests on the grounds that they create morale problems. To some extent, the open-ended and tiered programs can alleviate the possible morale problems.

One of the biggest objections to sales contests is that a decline in sales almost inevitably occurs afterward. The sales force cannot keep up the high level of activity indefinitely. Also, some crafty sales reps "stockpile" orders by getting customers to delay orders in the period just before the contest begins. Many questions have been raised about the long-run benefits of a contest. If a contest has achieved wider distribution and new dealerships, a long-run benefit should occur. But if the contest has focused mainly on sales volume, its long-range value is questionable. Lack of permanent accomplishment is not necessarily bad, however. For instance, many contests are designed for short-run purposes such as selling out an overstocked inventory item.

In summary, then, contests can be effective motivators, but they must be carefully and thoroughly designed to encourage participation by the greatest number of people.

NONFINANCIAL REWARDS

Managers often assume that financial incentives are the best motivators and that developing a good compensation package is the only thing they must do to motivate their sales force. However, evidence suggests that sales reps are motivated by both financial and nonfinancial incentives. A variety of factors—including job enrichment, recognition, promotion, encouragement, and praise—motivate performance. These factors are discussed below.

Job Enrichment and Support

Salespeople thrive on challenge. One way managers can challenge reps is to give them greater responsibility, authority, and control over their jobs. Also, most people like to have variety in their job-related tasks. Doing the same things over and over again quickly becomes boring to someone who is seeking challenge.

Varying some aspects of the sales job can provide a stimulus for increased levels of motivation. Together, increases in responsibility and variety are known as **job enrichment**. Some companies offer sales contest winners the prize of lunch and/or a coaching session with a high level company executive.[19] This is a form of job enrichment, and is motivating for salespeople striving to get ahead.

Additionally, like everyone else, salespeople want to feel that they are performing a meaningful task that will make a significant contribution to their companies and/or to those around them. Managers must make sure that each salesperson understands the importance of his or her contribution to the company's performance. Finally, salespeople also must be given adequate support in the areas of training, technology, and information to be able to compete in today's high-tech market.

Recognition and Honor Awards

A fundamental principle of good human relations is that individuals who deserve commendation must be given full recognition. Most salespeople enjoy public recognition of their accomplishments. Plaques, pins, or certificates can be used to recognize accomplishment levels. Furthermore, most managers report that they are effective in reinforcing desired behaviors and motivating high performance.[20]

Recognition programs are most effective when they include approximately half of the company's salespeople. If too many people receive them, the awards lose their value; if too few receive them, the awards may be viewed as too hard to achieve. The awards should be publicized and presented in a public ceremony or banquet. Involvement by top management adds significance and prestige to the award.

Many company develop clubs for outstanding producers or those who meet certain goals. Membership in such clubs usually bestows on high achievers the right to various recreational diversions in addition to the ego-gratifying recognition connected with just being in the select group. The life insurance industry has long had its Million Dollar Round Table to recognize agents who sell that amount of life insurance each year. Xerox has its President's Club where 18 percent of top performers go away on a five-day trip to the top resorts around the world.[21] Membership in such clubs is valued highly by most reps, who consider it a major career accomplishment. Nominating your top salespeople for awards by industry or trade groups is another excellent way to recognize top performance. As noted aptly by a regional director of marketing and sales executives, "Internal recognition is great, but nothing is better than getting recognized by your peers across several industries."[22] It is really difficult to give too much recognition to anyone.

Promotions

Title changes can be another source of motivation. Changing a rep's title from sales representative to senior sales representative—or VP of sales—can indicate the rep's accomplishment, and be a point of pride for salespeople. Changing a job title costs a company virtually nothing, and so some argue that it is a wise decision with a higher return on investment than any other recruiting and retention tool. At the same time, there has been some backlash against inflated titles, especially for relatively low-level salespeople.[23] Of course, the possibility of legitimately being promoted into a *sales management position* is a motivating factor for many salespeople.

Encouragement and Praise

The easiest and least expensive form of motivation is personal encouragement and praise from the manager. Small things such as a personal note, a pat on the back, or a thank-you for a job well done go a long way. Most reps like to feel that someone knows and cares about how much extra effort went into heading off the competitive threat to the company's largest account or how hard they tried, even though they didn't get that new account. Research suggests that sales managers do not understand how motivating regular encouragement and praise can be.[24]

Customer Feedback

Customer feedback is a very powerful motivator because it lets the salesperson see the direct impact of his/her efforts. To find out what customers think, companies usually survey the customer by phone or e-mail and ask them to rate how satisfied they are with the sales process and the salesperson. Sometimes, customers are asked to provide ratings relative to competitive reps, on various dimensions of performance. These surveys are often part of the company's evaluation process of its reps, which is discussed further in Chapter 16.

Corporate Culture

Some companies have very supportive corporate cultures in which they provide support to their employees that goes beyond the training and technology directly related to their jobs. According to the Society for Human Resource Management's annual benefits survey, 54 percent of companies now offer flextime, and 36 percent allow telecommuting.[25] Medtronic goes above and beyond to provide a healthy work environment—it provides its salespeople with flextime scheduling, on-site fitness centers, free health screenings, adoption assistance, massage therapy rooms, and even meditation rooms. These perks motivate Medtronic account managers to stay loyal to the company.[26]

SALES MEETINGS

Sales Meetings are one of the most commonly used methods of motivating salespeople. Most companies have one or more sales meetings a year, and some have them as frequently as once a week. The most important aspect of the sales meeting is communication. Being able to interact with management and with fellow reps makes reps feel like part of a team. More important, increased communication between salespeople and their managers leads to improved performance.[27] Unfortunately, salespeople often complain that sales meetings are a waste of their time.[28]

Purposes of Sales Meetings

Management can use sales meetings to communicate the company's long term goals and strategic objectives and to explain how important the salesperson's role is in achieving these goals. This instills self-esteem and pride in the reps and helps them identify with the company. This kind of communication is

CONSIDER THIS...

Keys to Successful Sales Meetings

Too often, salespeople think that meetings are a waste of time. Here are ten ways to change that, and make the weekly sales meeting useful and productive:

1. Focus on one or two key issues—don't try to cover every topic.
2. Salespeople love recognition, so be sure to praise top performers.
3. Be well organized, and distribute the agenda ahead of time.
4. Start and end on time, making sure meetings never last more than 75 minutes.
5. Do not focus too much on the issues of just one salesperson during the meeting.
6. Allow for discussion and input—meetings should be never be one-way communication.
7. Limit the amount of time for listing updates, which can get boring.
8. Do not leaving things hanging—reach agreement on the issues discussed.
9. Have at least one "personal growth/training" exercise to improve selling skills.
10. Build morale by establishing team goals.

SOURCE: Mark Hunter, "10 Secrets to a Successful Sales Meeting," *Forbes.com*, September 22, 2014

particularly important for salespeople who are often physically isolated from their companies. In many companies, the reps rarely see each other except at sales meetings. Thus, the meetings enable them to develop friendships and build team spirit and solidarity.

Sales meetings also are used to inform reps about product changes and new products, to explain new advertising and marketing programs, to provide training, and to inspire the sales staff to work harder and smarter. Meetings such as these can help the sales staff understand what is expected, improve their knowledge and skills, and build confidence in their efforts to succeed. Some meetings are held primarily for the purpose of recognizing and rewarding salespeople's performance.

Planning for Sales Meetings

A poorly planned sales meeting is probably worse than no meeting at all. A boring, tedious meeting in which salespeople have no opportunity to interact and participate can be demoralizing. This problem can be avoided by careful planning, by using speakers who are effective communicators, and by asking a variety of communication formats. Videos, small-group discussions, role-playing, demonstrations, and questions-and-answer sessions all can be effective communication methods. Soliciting input from the reps about what they think should be covered in the meeting can help as well. Follow-up to ensure that the key points of the meeting are reinforced is important as well. For other ideas, see the box entitled "Keys to Successful Sales Meetings."

MOTIVATION AND PERFORMANCE

It is important to remember that motivation—the desire to expend effort—is not the only requirement for successful sales performance. Salespeople must have the *ability* to perform as well as the motivation to do so.

The ability to perform sales tasks can be acquired or learned through training and experience. Some companies hire only experienced, proven salespeople who already have the necessary skills. But when companies hire inexperienced people, management must provide the training for them to gain the necessary skills. It is not enough for the reps to be motivated; they also must know how to do what is expected of them.

Recruiting and selection procedures are also important. In hiring *inexperienced* people, companies must be careful to select those with an aptitude for learning sales skills. In hiring *experienced* people, they must be certain that those selected have the desired set of skills. It is also important in both cases to select people whose needs are consistent with the demands or rewards of the particular sales job.

The motivational program must be integrated with the entire sales management program. A good motivational program will not compensate for poor recruiting, selection, and training. Motivational policies must be a part of a well-planned and well-executed sales management program.

SUMMARY

All human behavior starts with motivation. That is, the reason people act in a certain way is that they are motivated to do so. Motivation is the desire to expend effort to fulfill an aroused need. Sales managers are interested in the effort salespeople desire to expend on various activities or tasks associated with the sales job.

Sales executives generally agree that effective motivation of a sales force is essential to the success of any sales organization. The problem lies in finding the right combination of motivators for any given group of salespeople. Motivating a sales force is difficult because of the unique nature of the sales job. Also, each rep is an individual who responds in his or her own way to a given motivator. Another motivational difficulty occurs when there is a conflict in management's sales goals. Finally, changes in the market or selling environment pose motivational problems.

To motivate salespeople, managers must first understand their needs. Expectancy theory, Maslow's hierarchy of needs theory, Herzberg's dual-factor theory, role theory and attribution theory all help managers understand the kinds of needs salespeople have. In addition, these theories explain the conditional links between effort, performance, and rewards.

Managers must make sure that salespeople not only know what is expected but also understand what kinds of activities will lead to better performance. Managers should know how each of their salespeople evaluate rewards, and create an environment where (1) greater effort leads to higher performance, (2) performance is linked to rewards, and (3) the rewards are distributed fairly and desired by the salespeople.

Management's task is to select the right combination of motivators—the right motivational mix for a given sales force. This is difficult because each salesperson is unique due to his or her particular set of demographics, psychological traits, and other personal characteristics. Also, salespeople depending on which of the four career stages they are in: exploration, establishment, maintenance or disengagement. It is especially challenging to motivate plateaued salespeople.

Motivational tools fall into two categories: (1) financial rewards, such as compensation, travel, merchandise, and sales contests; and (2) nonfinancial rewards, which include job enrichment, recognition and honors, promotions, encouragement and praise, and support from the corporate culture. Sales meetings are another method commonly used to motivate salespeople.

It is important to remember that motivation is only one component of successful sales performance. Motivational policies must be incorporated into a well-planned and well-executed sales management program.

KEY TERMS

Attributions	Extrinsic rewards	Nonfinancial rewards
Attribution theory	Financial rewards	Open-ended contest
Closed-ended contest	Hierarchy of needs theory	Plateaued salespeople
Disengagement stage	Hygiene factors	Role ambiguity
Dual-factor theory	Instrumentality	Role conflict
Establishment stage	Intrinsic rewards	Role theory
Expectancy	Job enrichment	Sales contests
Expectancy theory	Maintenance stage	Sales meetings
Experience-based incentives	Motivation	Spiff
Exploration stage	Motivation factors	Tiered contest
		Valence

QUESTIONS AND PROBLEMS

1. Define motivation and explain why it is particularly important for salespeople.
2. Which is more important, the *strength* of a salesperson's beliefs about the effort/performance link or the *accuracy* of those beliefs?
3. What types of role conflicts are salespeople likely to experience?
4. Why do salespeople experience more role ambiguity than other occupations?
5. What can a sales manager do to reduce a salesperson's role ambiguity? How can role conflict be reduced?
6. Explain why persistence is an important dimension of motivation for the sales position.
7. Would providing salespeople with flextime and/or on-site child care by a motivational factor for a rep who has young children or would it just make the rep feel committed to the organization? Explain using Herzberg's dual-factor theory.

8. Explain what kind of behavioral changes can be expected if a salesperson attributes failures to luck, effort, strategy, ability, or task difficulty.

9. Explain how the sales manager should handle a rep who is one of the company's best performers but is constantly driving all of the other reps crazy with her combative, haughty attitude.

10. "If you pay a salesperson enough, you will have a well-motivated salesperson." Do you agree? Explain.

11. Explain how motivation is related to each of the following aspects of managing a sales force:

    a. Supervising the sales force.

    b. Setting sales quotas.

    c. Recruiting and selecting salespeople

    d. Designing the expense-payment plan.

12. If you were a district sales manager, how would you motivate the following sales reps?

    a. An older salesperson who is satisfied with his present earnings level. He plans to remain as a career sales rep and retire in six years.

    b. An excellent salesperson whose morale is shot because he did not receive an expected promotion. He has been with the company for five years.

13. A sales manager once said, "Motivating salespeople is the same as babying them. I am careful to hire only motivated people. This way I don't have to worry about motivating them. Good sales reps don't need any motivation from me—they motivate themselves." What do you think about this philosophy?

1. Interview a sales manager, asking what motivates three or four individual reps under his or her supervision. Then interview these same reps (one at a time) and ask them what motivates them. Compare the reps' responses with those of the manager.

2. Design sales contests for different types of salespeople. That is, design one for those who sell advertising for your local school paper, for a local copying service, for a local beverage supplier, for a telemarketing firm, for your school's telemarketing fund-raising group, and/or for a school organization.

3. Interview 10 of your friends and ask them to describe an experience-based incentive that would motivate them to try to improve half of their next semester's or quarter's grades by one letter, while maintaining their grades in their other courses.

4. Assume that you have just been promoted into a sales management position and (because you sold your sales management text after graduation) need some information on how to motivate the sales reps who are reporting to you. Do an internet search for such information and report on what you find.

5. Assuming you are still in the sales management role described above, search the internet for sales training seminars that address motivational issues. Describe these programs and give your assessment of whether they would help motivate your sales reps.

DIAMOND HOUSEWARES
Problems with a Veteran Account Manager

"It's time to talk about Dan. He's not cutting it, not getting the job done these days. You've been protecting him, but I just called up his numbers on our CRM—he hasn't hit quota for two years. He serves some of our most important accounts. Why haven't you done something about it before this?" Kurt Diamond, CEO of Diamond Housewares, demanded of Dave Mitchell, the company's sales manager.

Diamond Housewares had been formed 40 years ago by Kurt Diamond's father to sell a line of imported products for the home. As the years passed, the company began to develop its own products and have them manufactured by subcontractors. As plastic and rubberized goods increasingly displaced metal products in the housewares industry, the company purchased a financially distressed, local plastic injection molding company in Chicago, Illinois. It began making some of its own products. Kurt Diamond focused on production and product development. Sales were left in the hands of Dave Mitchell.

Diamond housewares was financially sound and highly profitable due to the steady introduction of new products that found ready market acceptance. The company did little advertising, preferring instead to spend its promotional money at the houseware industry's trade shows. It maintained sales office and showrooms in the major trade marts. Dan Ricker was the account manager working from the Dallas Trade Mart, an important market for the company. One of his key accounts was Costco.

Dan Ricker had been hired right out of college. He was a marketing major from the University of Oklahoma. Ricker's father and Diamond's father had been close friends, so Ricker and Diamond had known each other most of their lives, but they were not considered close since they had contrasting personalities. Diamond was an introvert and socialized little, whereas Ricker had an outgoing personality and many friends. Ricker developed a highly profitable business for the company in the southwestern territory by working long and hard developing the department stores and the emerging mass distributing firms as accounts.

Dave Mitchell was more than a little surprised at Kurt Diamond's sudden interest in Dan Ricker. It was the first time Diamond had taken any interest in the sales force for a long time. Usually he had something to say only when sales were down, which fortunately they seldom were, or when one of the company's new products flopped. Of course, any product failure was the fault of the sales force and had nothing to do with the product! Mitchell understood how that game was played, which was one reason he had kept his job for so long. He had joined the company more than two decades ago, and had been sales manager for about 10 years. Actually, Dan Ricker had been offered the sales manager position ahead of Mitchell—but Ricker turned it down because he was afraid it would be a pay cut. Being paid on straight commission, Ricker had earned substantially more than the sales manager did. However, that had changed in recent years as his performance declined.

Mitchell paused after Diamond stopped talking and then said, "Do you want an answer, or was that just some therapy we went through?" He didn't wait for a verbal answer. One was written on Diamond's face. "OK, no need to give you the Dan Ricker history. We both know how much he has done for us. He's been a top producer for years, and he has been loyal to us. Time and again, some competitor has tried to lure him away, but he never bit. So don't you think we should cut him a little slack, give him time to work out his problems?"

Diamond replied, "I recall a punch line that went 'What have you done for me lately?'" Then he asked, "What do you mean problems? What's going on?"

"Evidently, more things than Dan can handle all at once. First, you remember his daughter Kay and that guy she married. We, he lost his job as a pharmaceutical rep, and hasn't been able to find another one. He's been out of work for a year. They had to sell their home and have moved in with Dan, two kids and all. So now Dan is out about $40,000 a year trying to keep Kay's family intact. If that wasn't enough, his son Matt has gotten into some serious legal trouble with substance abuse and that's also costing Dan a lot of money and worry. To top that off, I'm not so sure about his health. He's not that old—in his early fifties—but he's been dragging a bit and doesn't look too good to me."

Mitchell shook his head as he continued, "I've talked with him about his problems, but what can I say? I haven't got any solutions for them, but I am hopeful these problems will work themselves out. Dan's no fool, and he's working on them. Then he'll be back with us full-time."

Diamond responded, "Come on, give me a break. Dan Ricker is a has-been. He's burned out and tired. Tired of working. Tired of hustling." He continued, "If you don't do something, we'll be losing some key customers...I'm worried."

The discussion was suddenly interrupted by a telephone call for Dave Mitchell. It was from the buyer at Costco.

Questions:

1. What should Dave Mitchell do about Dan Ricker?

2. Pretend you're Dan Ricker. What would you do in response to what was recommended in the first question?

BIOLAB PHARMACEUTICAL COMPANY
A Quest for Motivational Skills

"How did your interview go today? Are you going to get that promotion you want?" Hobie Dobbs asked his spouse, Kathryn. Although they had been married less than a year, Hobie had been paying close attention and had learned when silence was a definitive answer to one of his questions. This was clearly one of those times. Nothing was said, but nothing had to be said, for anger and frustration were etched in Kathryn's face. She dropped her briefcase on the floor rather loudly as she headed for the refrigerator in search of some moral support. Hobie followed and ventured a suggestion, "The Ben & Jerry's ice cream is at the bottom of the freezer."

It worked. After the second spoonful, Kathryn said, "I couldn't believe it. There he sat telling me that I'm not properly motivating my reps. That I cannot be promoted until I learn how to motivate people better. Me, Katie O'Brien. My career is being threatened by a bozo who tells me I can't motivate people well enough to suit him."

Kathryn O'Brien, a senior sales rep for Biolab Pharmaceutical Company, supervised five junior sales reps in her St. Louis, Missouri, territory. She had worked for the company for three years and had an excellent record. Each year she was one of the company's top producers. She was well liked by her peers and subordinates. It seemed to everyone that Kathryn was well on her way to a great management career with Biolab.

Biolab Pharmaceutical Company was a huge, international manufacturer of ethical drugs most noted for its biological and blood-related products. Kathryn reported to Ed Simpson, district manager, who also worked out of the St. Louis office. Thus, Simpson had more opportunity to observe Kathryn at work than was the case in the relationships between most district managers and their senior salespeople.

Hobie also worked for the company in customer service; he was a pharmacist who could be called on an inbound 800 number by any physician, druggist, or sales rep for product and application information. He and Kathryn become good telephone buddies in her early days with the firm because she relied on him for information.

"Gee, that's kind of general, isn't it? Exactly what does he mean when he says you can't motivate people? You sure don't have any trouble motivating me." Hobie paused and then continued, "Did you try to pin him down? Ask him what he was talking about? Get some specifics?"

"Yeah, it was like pulling teeth. He squirmed and had trouble looking me in the eye. He really didn't want to get into it with me, but I wouldn't leave until I understood what he was talking about. He kept saying that my five sales reps were not performing well enough to suit him. He thought they should be producing more results and that the reason they weren't was that I was not motivating them to work harder. He said that they just were not making the calls and making the efforts that they should be."

"And that's your fault, is that it?" Hobie asked. "Who hired them, who trained them, who sets all the compensation policies? But since they made you the senior rep over them, everything is your fault, I suppose. Can you get rid of reps who aren't performing up to expectations?"

Kathryn responded, "NO, I can only write them up, give them a bad evaluation."

"Have you done that?" Hobie asked.

Kathryn explained, "NO, and I won't. It's true they aren't setting the world on fire, but they're doing all right, about average for trainees. They are busy learning the business right now at their stage of development and I don't see why I should put more pressure on them than they have right now. First, learn the business, then when they know what they are doing they can start working harder."

"Seems reasonable to me. Did you tell Simpson that?"

"Are you kidding? I was so mad I couldn't think, let alone speak. Besides I don't agree with his ideas of motivation. He keeps giving us those bubba stories about how his old football coach used to motivate him and those other players to go out and die for dear old Mizzou. Then he starts talking about his Marine Corps days and how they motivate people—pride, don't let your buddy down, and all that. He's from another world. Well, we sell drugs to physicians for about 40 hours a week. We're not fighting for our lives and we sure aren't trying to beat the brains out of the competition."

"You seem to know how *not* to motivate your reps. Now, what do you think *will* motivate them?" Hobie asked.

"I don't want to talk about it anymore tonight. I want to think about it. I'll tell you tomorrow morning what I am going to do." And with that, Kathryn declared the meeting over.

The next day began much earlier than usual because Kathryn was eager to get her conflict with Simpson behind her. Confrontation was to be the order of the day. She had decided to attack Simpson's evaluation of her motivational skills directly with him instead of appealing it to his superior, as she had a right to do under company policy. She was not interested in getting embroiled in the company's cumbersome bureaucratic processes. She would attack this threat right at its source—and if her effort failed, she would resign. She had good reason to believe that she could get a similar job with a competitor, so she was not worried about being unemployed.

She laid out her plans to Hobie, who listened carefully, saying nothing until she was through talking. Then he asked, "And what are you going to tell Simpson about your motivational philosophies and skills that will change his evaluation of you? What makes you think he is really interested in what you think about how to motivate your people? He seemed to be focused on your reps' input efforts. Hard facts! From what you tell me about him, what reason do you have for thinking that he can change his mind about anything? And by the way, what are you going to say about your motivational philosophies?"

Kathryn responded, "First, I am going to insist that the sales reps' basic motivational structure is pretty well set when we hire them. If they're lazy, we're not going to be able to change it. Furthermore, all sales management literature indicates that a firm's basic compensation plan provides the bulk of its motivational thrust. Add the training program to the mix, and I maintain that, as a senior salesperson, sort of a bargain-basement supervisor, I have little power to really motivate the reps. Consequently, he is evaluating me on something over which I have little control.

"Next, I know how the game is played. I may win something on appeal, but that will be the real end of my future with the firm. I would have dirtied the nest, made waves, or whatever you call it. I would be tagged a militant, and that would be that. So if my career is not to be with Biolab, so be it. The quicker I get out, the better. It would be foolish to stay around and let this guy do a job on me. I don't need it, and I don't have to take it. So that's the way it's going to be."

Hobie smiled. He knew it was going to be an interesting day.

Questions:

1. Do you approve of Kathryn's plan of action? If so, why? If not, what changes would you suggest she consider making?

2. Do you agree with Kathryn's philosophies of motivation? If so, why? If not, what are your philosophies of motivation?

INTERNATIONAL CHEMICAL INDUSTRIES
Use of Motivational Funds

The following memo from George McCall, vice president of sales operations at International Chemical Industries, was distributed to all regional and district managers:

> Each manager should be prepared to give a short presentation to the group during our national sales meeting next week about how the motivational fund for his or her area was spent last year. Being new to the organization, I want to familiarize myself with what we are doing in this important area. Moreover, it seems to me that many of you may be doing some things that would be of interest to other managers.

Underlying McCall's memo was a hidden agenda: McCall was suspicious that much of the firm's motivational fund was being squandered on ineffectual motivational tactics. He wanted to open up the subject not only to discover what was going on but also perhaps to develop some uniformity to what everyone was doing.

International Chemical Industries produced and distributed basic chemicals, such as nitrates, sulfur, and potassium, around the globe. It was one of the world's largest chemical concerns. Its U.S. operations were directed from offices in Houston, Texas. The U.S. sales operations were divided into five regions, each of which contained five districts. Thus, there were to be five regional managers and 25 district managers at the meeting the following week.

Historically, management budgeted 3 percent of its sales volume of $722 million for the costs of managing sales operations. Of that amount, 83.3 percent was allotted to field-selling costs, which included the salaries and expenses of both the field sales reps and their field managers. The costs of the regional and district sales offices were covered by the remainder of the sales budget. From that amount, area managers were allotted a small fund of approximately 0.02 percent of sales that could be used for motivational purposes in any manner they desired. For example, the district manager for Chicago spent $70,000 last year on a special motivational program for the area's five reps (Chicago accounted for 5 percent of the company's U.S. sales volume, or about $36 million). Each rep who achieved quota for the year received a free trip for two people, all expenses paid, to St. Thomas in the Virgin Islands. All reps won and went together with their spouses for a most successful holiday. The manager planned to institute another such program for the coming year.

The response to McCall's memo was good. The managers seemed to take delight in relating how they spent their motivational fund. It seemed to McCall that they were in competition with each other to see who could come up with the most innovative plan. McCall was pleased to learn that they had been putting their motivational funds to good use. He also was pleased with the attitudes of the managers. Morale seemed to be high. The managers seemed to relate to each other exceptionally well, except for two isolated cases about which McCall had been made aware by his predecessor and for which he was taking steps to remedy.

In summarizing what he learned from the managers' presentations, he categorized the managers' programs into three groups. Twelve of the district managers had developed some sort of program to reward the sales reps' total effort for the year much along the lines of the Chicago district's program. Seven of the managers used the money for shorter special-purpose programs such as contests to encourage certain desired behavior such as pushing certain products or getting new accounts.

One such program stood out in McCall's mind since it particularly impressed him at the time. The manager of the New York office had become concerned with the tendency of the reps to concentrate on the firm's established accounts. He wanted them to make more calls on potentially new accounts. To that end, he designed a contest to reward those reps who not only called on prospective accounts but also managed to make them new customers. Since it usually took many calls on a prospective account before a sale was made, the contest had been conducted over a two-year period.

Six of the managers used the money for doing several smaller, short-run, action-oriented, one-shot deals. For example, the manager of the Charlotte, North Carolina, district walked into the office one midsummer day waving two season tickets for the city's professional basketball team. She announced, "These go to the person who brings in the first new account this month." This resulted in a flurry of new account activity and a dispute between two reps over who brought in the first new account. The manager settled the argument by giving both of them two season tickets. She made two reps happy. McCall was impressed with her savvy in handling what could have been a sticky situation.

On another occasion, she walked in and announced that if the district met its quotas for the quarter, all reps and their families would be treated to a long weekend outing on a chartered boat out of Wilmington. The district sales volume had not been up to plan, but that quickly changed as everyone started working hard for their boat rides.

McCall was not sure which of these models was best for the company, in either the short run or the long run. He had heard some of the managers talking about how much they liked learning about what the other managers were doing with their motivational money. He wondered if such information should be included in the company's monthly newsletter. How would such information be used? Would a rep in Chicago pressure the manager for a contest that provided season tickets to the Bulls or Bears games after learning of the Charlotte program?

After due consideration, McCall felt that the money was being well spent and wondered if it should be increased. He had several questions: What returns were being realized from those expenditures? How could he build a case to his superiors for increasing the motivational funds budget? Should he do it across the board or test it by giving an increased budget to a district manager representative of each of the three types of programs that were evidenced?

Questions:

1. What should George McCall do about the firm's motivational fund?

2. What policies should George McCall establish regarding the motivational fund?

ENDNOTES

[1] Ruth Kanfer, "Motivation theory and industrial and organizational psychology," in *Handbook of Industrial and Organizational Psychology*, ed. M.D. Dunnette and Leaetta M. Hough (Palo Alto CA: Consulting Psychologists Press, 1990), Vol. 1, 2nd edition, pp. 75-170.

[2] These conditions are based on expectancy theory concepts developed by Victor H. Vroom, *Work and Motivation* (New York: John Wiley & Sons, 1964), and others; Edward C. Tolman, *Purposive Behavior in Animals and Men* (New York: Appleton-Century-Crofts, 1932); and Kurt Lewin, *The Conceptual Representation and the Measurement of Psychological Forces* (Durham, NC: Duke University Press, 1938). Expectancy theory as a framework for explaining salesperson motivation was popularized by Orville C. Walker, Gilbert A. Churchill Jr., and Neil M. Ford, "Motivation and Performance in Industrial Selling: Present Knowledge and Needed Research," *Journal of Marketing Research*, May 1977, pp. 156-68.

[3] Kenneth A. Kovack, "Employee Motivation, Addressing a Crucial Factor in Your Organization's Performance," working paper, George Mason University, Fairfax, Virginia, 1997.

[4] Abraham H. Maslow, *Motivation and Personality*, 2nd ed. (New York: Harper & Row, 1970), chapters 307.

[5] Vincent Alonzo, "Money Isn't Everything," *Sales & Marketing Management*, January 1999, p. 28.

[6] Frederick Herzberg, Bernard Mausner, and Barbara B. Snyderman, *Motivation to Work*, 2nd ed. (New York: John Wiley & Sons, 1959).

[7] Marcus Buckingham and Curt Coffman, *First, Break All The Rules* (New York: Simon & Schuster, 1999).

[8] Jagdip Singh, "Striking a Balance in Boundary-Spanning Positions: An Investigation of Some Unconventional Influences of Role Stressors and Job Characteristics on Job Outcomes of Salespeople," *Journal of Marketing*, July 1998, pp. 69-86.

[9] Andrew Dixon, Rosann L. Spiro, and Lukas P. Forbes, "Attributions and Behavioral Intentions of Inexperienced Salespersons to Failure: An Empirical Investigation," *Journal of the Academy of Marketing Science* 31 (Fall 2003), pp. 459-68.

[10] Jeong-Eun Piercy, David W. Cravens, and Nikala Lane, "Adaptive Selling Behavior Revisited: An Empirical Examination of Learning Orientation, Sales Performance, and Job Satisfaction," *Journal of Personal Selling & Sales Management*, Spring 2003, pp. 239-47.

[11] Fred C. Miao, Donald J. Lund, and Kenneth R. Evans, "Reexamining The Influence Of Career Stages On Salesperson Motivation: A Cognitive And Affective Perspective," *Journal of Personal Selling & Sales Management*, Summer2009, Vol. 29(3), pp. 243-255.

[12] Melanie Berger, "Setting Personal Goals for Employees," *Sales & Marketing Management*, February 1997, pp. 35-36.

[13] Libby Estell, "Economic Incentives," *Sales & Marketing Management*, October 2001, p. S4; and Vincent Alonzo, "Motivating Matters," *Sales & Marketing Management*, January 1999, p. 28.

[14] Mark McMaster, "Personalized Motivation," *Sales & Marketing Management*, May 2002, p. 16.

[15] Mark McMaster, "Wowing the Sales Force," *Sales & Marketing Management*, June 2001, p. 67.

[16] Ron Donoho, "It's Up! It's Good!" *Sales & Marketing Management*, October 2004, pp. 24-29.

[17] Julia Chang, "Trophy Value," *Sales & Marketing Management*, October 2004, pp. 24-29.

[18] Libby Estell, "Economic Incentives."

[19] Marci Martin, "3 Proven Ways to Motivate Your Sales Team," *Business News Daily*, April 5, 2016. Retrieved from the following URL on June 21, 2016: http://www.businessnewsdaily.com/7051-how-to-motivate-sales-team.html

[20] Mary Litsikas, "Maximize Incentive ROI," *Sales & Marketing Management*, January/February 2006, p. 16.

[21] Julia Chang, "Happy Sales Force, Happy Returns," *Sales & Marketing Management*, March 2006, pp. 32-33.

[22] Julia Chang, "Best of the Best," *Sales & Marketing Management*, June 2005, p. 18.

[23] John Sullivan, "Exciting Job Titles Can Be Powerful Recruiting and Retention Tools," *ERE Media*, August 13, 2012. Retrieved from the following URL on June 21, 2016: http://www.eremedia.com/ere/exciting-job-titles-can-be-powerful-recruiting-and-retention-tools/

9

Sales Force Compensation

HubSpot is an inbound marketing firm that has had a lot of success since it was founded one decade ago. With almost $200 million in annual sales and a successful IPO, this startup employs several hundred salespeople who provide a variety of online marketing tools to thousands of business customers. Mark Roberge, who is credited with building HubSpot's large sales team, says, "When I look back on the various strategies I used to grow our sales force from zero to several hundred people, I realize that one of the biggest lessons I've learned involves the power of a compensation plan to motivate salespeople—not only to sell more, but to act in ways that support a startup's evolving business model and overall strategy." Specifically, HubSpot revised its compensation plan to fit each of the three stages that the company went through in its early years: customer acquisition, customer retention and success, and sustainable growth.[1] Companies should review their compensation plans once a year to ensure that they are consistent with the organization's direction. In this chapter, we study sales force compensation, suggesting ways in which sales executives can design effective compensation plans.

Sales force compensation should be structured to provide the following two elements:

1. Financial compensation
    a.   Direct payment (money)
    b.   Indirect payment (paid vacations, health insurance, etc.)
2. Nonfinancial compensation
    a.   Opportunity to advance in the job
    b.   Recognition inside and outside the firm
    c.   Enjoyment of the job

Most of our discussion in this chapter will deal with *direct payments of financial compensation.*

The compensation problem is twofold. A company must determine both the level of earnings and the method of paying its sales force. By **level of earnings**, we mean the total dollar income paid to each salesperson for a given period of time. The **method of compensation** is the plan by which the reps earn or reach the intended level, and this includes choices between salary, commission, and/or bonus.

SALES FORCE COMPENSATION AND STRATEGIC PLANNING

A close relationship exists between a company's strategic marketing planning and its sales force compensation plan. The compensation plan has a direct bearing on the successful *implementation* of the marketing plan. For an example of this relationship, assume that a manufacturer of industrial machinery is planning to enter a new geographic market to increase the firm's overall market share. On the one hand, a straight salary compensation plan probably would help to implement this strategy. On the other hand, a stronger incentive—perhaps a large commission—might be necessary when the strategy calls for aggressive selling to liquidate excess inventories. If the company is a high-risk, new venture, then its compensation should reflect that same high risk with large incentives for success. If the company is a mature, well-established firm, then a more stable compensation plan with a lower percentage of at-risk income should be used.

To get salespeople to aid in successfully implementing the company's strategic marketing plan, management needs to coordinate its sales compensation plans with the company's goals. But it is surprising how often a firm has a sales compensation system that is at odds with management's stated goals. Many firms, for example, say they want a sales compensation plan that "emphasizes profitability," yet they maintain a commission component based on sales volume rather than on gross margin or some other measure of profit.[2]

Management also should recognize that companies and their market positions change over time. Consequently, a sales compensation plan also should change to reflect the company's evolution in its business environment. One type of pay plan is needed when a firm is just getting started and it wants to reach and maintain a certain level of sales revenue. Another type of plan will be required later when the company is realigning territories, introducing new products, and adding new channels of distribution or new types of intermediaries. The compensation plan should match the culture of the company.

As we noted in Chapter 2, companies are changing the way they do business. Successful companies today focus on providing problem solutions and developing long-term relationships with their customers. Sales efforts must shift to reflect these changes; and because sales efforts must change, compensation plans must be revised as well. Instead of being rewarded for selling as much as possible and winning market share, salespeople will be rewarded for building relationships with customers, keeping customers longer, and increasing the value of each one.

OBJECTIVES OF A COMPENSATION PLAN

The objectives of a good compensation plan, which are shown in Figure 9-1, may be viewed from the perspective of the company as well as from the perspective of the individual salesperson. These objectives are not mutually exclusive; and in some situations, one goal may conflict with another. All, however, are valuable guidelines for a sales executive to recognize and follow.

The Company's Perspective

The company has a strategy (or multiple strategies), financial objectives, and operational objectives. In the best of circumstances, they all align with the

FIGURE 9-1
What a Good Sales
Compensation Plan Should
Do

company's mission or goal. Similarly, it is important for the sales compensation plan to provide the sales force with incentives to act in ways that align with the company's objectives and strategies.

Motivating Salespeople

Companies want to encourage salespeople to reach and exceed their goals. Thus, compensation plans are designed to motivate salespeople to perform. According to a recent survey of sales and marketing executives, 20 percent of them rated their companies' compensation plans as very successful, but the remaining 80 percent of those surveyed reported their plans as not successful or at best only somewhat successful.[3] Clearly, designing a plan that motivates salespeople to meet or exceed their goals is not an easy task.

Correlating Performance with Rewards

Correlating performance with rewards is an ideal that most companies constantly seek yet seldom achieve. There is often a weak link between pay and performance. In most cases, rewards are given for results, but this can be very problematic. A person can work very hard (expending much effort) but get few results—and therefore little reward. This can happen even when the minimal results are due to factors beyond the control of the salesperson. In reverse, we all know of situations where seemingly little effort has brought big results and consequently big rewards.

Another problem is that many companies do not differentiate the top performers enough from the average performers. Experts recommend that the incentive potential for outstanding performance should be three times the average incentive payout.[4]

Control Salespeople's Activities

A good plan should act as an unseen supervisor of a sales force by enabling management to control and direct the sales reps' activities. Research has demonstrated that the compensation plan should explicitly recognize different dimensions of the position.[5] Today, this usually means motivating the reps to ensure a fully balanced selling effort, that is, a *total* selling job. The compensation plan must offer incentives flexible enough to cover such varied tasks as full-time selling, missionary work (defined in Chapter 1 as involving building goodwill and relationships without soliciting orders), or controlling selling expenses. Compaq Computer's sales managers base 20 to 40 percent of their reps' compensation on individualized sales objectives, such as directing a rep to work with a specific new account, increasing sales of a specific product line, or improving customer satisfaction.[6]

Ensuring Proper Treatment of Customers

Companies will be increasingly competing on the basis of customer service. A seller's ability to maintain strong, long-term relationships with customers depends largely on providing customer service that results in a high level of customer satisfaction. A good compensation plan is one that motivates salespeople to treat customers properly, thus providing customer satisfaction. Enterprise Rent-A-Car is one of many companies that link customer feedback scores to compensation—but to do this, companies must be careful. The measure of customer satisfaction must be stable and reliable. In addition, the sales manager should make sure salespeople are not gaming the system.[7]

Attracting and Keeping Competent Salespeople

A good pay plan helps a company build the quality of its sales force because it assists in attracting high caliber reps. A sound plan also should *help to keep* desirable people. In fact, if the company does not have a cutting-edge compensation plan, it is likely to lose its best salespeople to competition.

Being Economical Yet Competitive

From the management's standpoint, a compensation plan should be economical to administer. A firm whose compensation expenses are disproportional to its revenues will have to increase the price of its product or suffer decreased profit margins. Most firms, however, want to keep their sales force expenses in line with those of competitors. It is not always easy to balance being economical with being competitive.

Staying Flexible Yet Stable

A compensation plan should be sufficiently flexible to meet the needs of individual territories, products, and salespeople. Not all territories present the same opportunity. A representative in a territory where the company is the leader should ordinarily not be compensated by the same method as a rep in a newly entered district. Some companies, such as FleetBoston Financial Corporation, are using individual pay plans, in which each salesperson is allowed to choose what percentage of his or her compensation should be straight salary and what percentage should be incentive based.[8] Flexibility also is needed to adjust for differences in products. Some products are staples and can be sold by taking orders for frequent repeat sales. Others are sold one to a customer and thus require much creative selling.

At the same time, the basic plan should possess stability. The basic pay plan should contain features that enable a company to meet changing conditions without having to change the basic plan. For example, the basic plan may include three categories of commission rates—high, medium, and low percentages—to reflect differences in profitability among products. However, a product category may be changed from time to time as competition and other external factors affect its profitability. These category reassignments can be made without changing the basic pay plan at all.

The Salesperson's Perspective

The salesperson's perspective may differ from the company's perspective, but in some instances it may overlap.

A Secure Income and an Incentive Income

Every plan should provide a regular income, at least a minimum level. The principle behind this point is that sales reps should not have to worry about how to meet living expenses. If they have a bad month, if they are in seasonal doldrums, or if they are sick and cannot work for a period, they should have some income. However, this steady income should not be so high that it lessens the desire for incentive pay.

In addition to a regular income, a good pay plan should furnish an incentive to elicit above-minimum performance. Most people do better when offered a reward for some specific action than when no incentive is involved. It should be noted that it is not possible to design a workable system that offers the greatest degree of both security and incentives. The concepts are mutually incompatible. In practice, the company must develop a compromise structure.

Simplicity

Simplicity is a hallmark of a good compensation plan. Sometimes simplicity and flexibility are conflicting goals—that is, a plan that is simple may not be sufficiently flexible, and a plan with adequate flexibility may achieve that goal at the expense of simplicity. However, the plan should be simple enough for salespeople to understand readily; they should be able to figure out what their incomes will be. In general, there should be no more than three measures combined to calculate the reps' compensation. Sometimes companies need to adjust their compensation plans, especially new plans; but too much tweaking leads to confusion and frustration for the salespeople.

Fairness

A good compensation plan must treat all salespeople fairly. Nothing will destroy salespeople's morale faster than feeling that their pay is inequitable. One way to ensure fairness in a plan is to strive to base it as much as possible on measurable factors that are controllable by the sales force. The next section covers this point further. It is also possible to put online all of the incentive compensation information such as individual progress toward targets and payouts, thus achieving a high level of transparency.

Choice

Salespeople want to have choices in how they are compensated. They want these choices because they are at different stages in their careers or because they have differences in the amount of risk with which they are comfortable. Many firms, such as FleetBoston Financial, mentioned above, are offering salespeople a choice of compensation plans. The most common choice given to salespeople is what percentage of their compensation will be salary based versus commission based.

DESIGNING A SALES COMPENSATION PLAN

The steps in designing a pay plan for sales force are shown in Figure 9-2. However, before designing a new pay plan or revising an existing one, a sales executive should review a few fundamental points. Specifically, we present the following four useful generalizations:

1. **There are inherent conflicts in the objectives of most compensation plans.** Sales executives want a plan that maximizes the sales reps' income and at the same time minimizes the company's outlay. Or they want one plan to give the sales force security and stability of income as well as incentive. In each situation, the desires are diametrically opposite. The best a manager can do is to adjust the pay plan until a reasonably satisfactory balance between objectives can be found.

2. **No single plan fits all situations.** Consequently, a firm should have a plan tailor-made for its own specific objectives. There may be considerable similarity in the general features of plans used by several firms, but the details should reflect the individual objectives of each company. Many companies also need more than one compensation plan because of differences in types of sales jobs, territories, or products.

3. **It is very important to achieve external parity in salespeople's earnings.** Management should pay its sales force at a level competitive with salespeople in other firms. This information is readily available and well-known by the salespeople inside the industry. Or alternatively, doing an internet search for "annual compensation survey for salespeople" returns a number of relevant sources.

4. **Management should solicit suggestions from the sales force regarding the compensation plan.** It is critical to get input from salespeople because they are more likely to accept a plan if they were consulted about it during its design and development.

FIGURE 9-2
Steps in Designing a Sales Compensation Plan

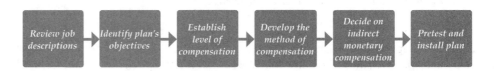

With these fundamental points in mind, the sales executive can begin to design a compensation plan. The first two steps are to review job descriptions and then identify objectives.

Review Job Descriptions

A carefully crafted, detailed job description is an important input to either designing a new compensation plan, or revising an established one. This should disclose the exact nature, scope, and probable difficulty of each job. A separate description should be included for each selling position, such as sales engineer, missionary salesperson, or sales trainee. The job descriptions indicate the services and abilities for which the business is paying.

Identify Specific Objectives

Part of the job of designing a compensation plan is deciding *specifically* what it is intended to accomplish. It is not enough to say that the goal is to get an honest day's work for a day's pay or to attract good people. These are examples of the broad, general type of objective referred to earlier—objectives *every* plan should attempt to accomplish. The following are examples of specific objectives:

- Increase profits by 10 percent.
- Increase sales volume of a certain class of products by 10 percent.
- Increase volume at existing accounts.
- Improve customer satisfaction.
- Stimulate missionary work.
- Develop a new territory.

Compensation should be based primarily on factors that (1) salespeople can *control* and (2) the company can *measure*. However, most factors contributing to sales success are only partially or not at all controllable by the sales force. Salespeople have some control over their sales volume, for instance, but this control is limited by product attributes and company pricing policies. The point is that a firm should try to base most of each salesperson's compensation on factors over which the rep has a maximum of control.

The next step is to give as much consideration as possible to the elements that the company can measure. Sales, selling expenses, calls made, new accounts brought in, displays set up, and gross margin contributed are all easily measured. In contrast, such activities as improving customer satisfaction and training dealer salespeople are not as easily evaluated. Even so, companies should develop some kind of measurement for activities that contribute to long-term relationships with customers.

ESTABLISHING THE LEVEL OF COMPENSATION

One of the two key tasks in designing a pay plan is to determine the **level of compensation** (the other—to develop the *method*—is discussed in the next section of this chapter). The level of compensation means the average earnings of the salespeople over a given period. In many respects, the level is more important than the method. People usually are more interested in *how much* they've earned than in *how* they earned it. To the company, the level of income is the

....

RUNNING CASE

Shiderlots

Elevators, Inc.

Reps Selling Too Many Low-Profit Products

Over the past several days, sales manager Adam Dark had been conducting his annual performance reviews of his account managers. Overall, the sales and profit results were satisfactory, but Dark was concerned about a particular issue with several of his account managers.

Total sales volume for all of these account managers was satisfactory, but Dark was struck that they had not opened up hardly any new accounts for several months. That is, almost all of their sales were being generated from *existing* customers. The good part about this is what it said about retention; and Dark often preached to his sales force how it is much more efficient to retain existing customers than it is to acquire new customers.

At the same time, he felt that his account managers should have a dual-focus on both retention *and* acquisition. Dark called up one of his more experienced account managers, Carrie Duffner, and asked her, "Why aren't you more focused on getting new accounts?"

Duffner responded, "Well, I don't really see why I would do that. It's easier for me to develop my existing accounts. I have great relationships with them; I thoroughly understand their needs. It just doesn't pay for me to spend my time with the unknown prospects. It's more time consuming and high risk."

After the conversation, Dark kept thinking about how Duffner said, "…it just doesn't pay." And he also remembered how company president, Rosann Speer, recently asked Dark whether or not he had any ideas about how to improve the compensation plan for the sales force.

Currently, the account managers' compensation is a combination of salary and incentive—with the incentives simply tied to generic sales and profits. Dark knew that a good compensation plan can control salespeople's activities to achieve the company's strategic goals. He began to get some ideas.

Question: How might the compensation plan be revised to help fix this problem?

direct sales cost. Management is interested in the compensation level because that is what attracts most salespeople. If reps believe that they will not be able to earn enough, they probably won't be attracted to the job regardless of the method used. Conversely, they may take a job that pays well even though the firm does not offer the combination of salary and commission they prefer.

There is no clearly prevailing pay rate for sales jobs, as there is for certain office or factory jobs. According to a recent survey by the U.S. Bureau of Labor Statistics, sales representatives for wholesalers and manufacturers of technical and scientific products make an average annual wage of $89,170, including base salary plus commission.[9] Compensation varies widely by industry. Retail sales workers can make less than $30,000 per year; whereas salespeople in the enterprise-tech industry tend to earn much more than that (see the box entitled "Top Earning Salespeople").

The *method* of compensation has a bearing on the *level* of compensation. Salespeople who work under a straight salary plan typically earn less than reps who are paid a straight commission or some combination of salary and commission.

The level of sales compensation also is closely related to the *experience* of the salesperson. This is understandable because the more experienced representatives have usually developed more skills. As a result, their productivity should be higher.

CONSIDER THIS...

Top Earning Salespeople

According to a popular jobs and recruiting site, salespeople in the enterprise-tech industry can earn big money – with the top performers regularly making over $400,000 per year. The top ten tech companies in terms of what they pay their salespeople are on the table below. As shown, the base salary is typically about $100,000, and the commission can be more than twice that.

Tech Company	Median Total Pay	Median Base Salary
1. SAP	$235,000	$110,000
2. Cisco	$211,000	$ 93,000
3. CA Technologies	$210,000	$110,000
4. EMC	$200,000	$100,000
5. Symantec	$197,000	$118,000
6. Microsoft	$191,000	$118,000
7. Salesforce.com	$173,500	$ 90,000
8. Adobe	$162,500	$ 90,000
9. Avaya	$160,000	$ 95,000
10. IBM	$150,000	$100,000

SOURCE: Julie Bort, "Salespeople at these 10 tech companies get paid tons of money," Business Insider blog, July 23, 2015. Retrieved from the following URL on June 28, 2016: http://www.businessinsider.com/what-salespeople-earn-at-tech-companies-2015-7

DEVELOPING THE METHOD OF COMPENSATION

The other key task in designing a sales compensation plan (besides setting the pay *level*) is to develop the **method of compensation**, which relates to *how* the reps will be paid. The building blocks available to management when constructing a sales compensation plan include the following elements:

- Salaries
- Commissions
- Bonuses
- Indirect monetary benefits (e.g., vacation and insurance)
- Expenses

Some of these components are incentives for the sales force; others offer stability and security in earnings; still others may help the firm control sales costs. The more elements used in building a plan, the more complex it is, as shown in Figure 9-4. (Although there is a box for expenses in the figure, ordinarily reimbursement for travel and other business expenses incurred by salespeople

FIGURE 9-4
Building Blocks for a Sales
Compensation Plan

Security	Incentives	Benefits	Expenses
		Others	
		Profit sharing	Others
		Pension	Entertainment
	Profit sharing	Moving expenses	Company car
	Bonus	Insurance	Lodging
Salary	Commission	Paid vacation	Travel

FIGURE 9-4
Building Blocks for a Sales Compensation Plan

should be kept separate from their compensation.) The two elements usually cause enough problems on their own without combining them. Sales force expenses are covered in Chapter 10.

Basic Types of Compensation Plans

Fundamentally, there are only three widely used methods of compensating a sales force:

1. A *straight salary*—a fixed element related to a unit of time during which the salesperson is working.
2. A *straight commission*—a variable element related to the performance of a specific unit of work.
3. Some *combination* of compensation elements (e.g., salary and commission).

In recent years, there has been significant growth in plans that combine salary with an incentive feature. This trend has been primarily at the expense of straight salary and straight commission plans—but there is a wide variation across industries. For example, primary metals firms tend to prefer straight salary plans for their salespeople—as they sell a commodity product with a price that often fluctuates based on factors beyond the salesperson's control. At the other extreme, companies marketing financial services, especially securities brokers, are heavy users of straight commission plans, which provides the necessary incentive to acquire new customers and actively manage their existing customers' portfolios. Surveys of salespeople indicate that the reps themselves strongly endorse some form of combination plan.

Traditionally, sales compensation plans have been geared to generate sales volume and, more recently, profits. Today, however, there has been a shift away from sales volume and high margins toward developing strong relationships with customers by providing them with comprehensive solutions to their problems. As noted in earlier chapters, the salesperson becomes more of a consultant than a transactional seller. Many companies are setting 10 to 25 percent of incentive pay on developing these long-term customer relationships.[10] These firms realize that sales volume alone is a poor indicator of a salesperson's value to the firm.

Customer satisfaction is another important objective for sales organizations. As mentioned earlier in the chapter, Enterprise Rent-A-Car includes customer satisfaction scores as an input into the compensation of their salespeople. Firms using this measure of performance must be sure that the salesperson—rather than the product, its distribution, or some other dimension—is the primary factor influencing the customer satisfaction ratings.

Straight Salary Plans

A **salary** is a direct monetary reward paid for performing certain duties over a *period of time.* The amount of payment is related to a unit of time rather than to the work accomplished. A salary is a fixed element in a pay plan. That is, in each pay period, the same amount of money is paid to a salesperson, regardless of his or her sales, missionary efforts, or other measures or productivity. Companies that sell commodities, such as the oil/gasoline company Marathon Petroleum, tend to use straight salary for their salespeople. This makes sense because the sales volume of commodities is often dependent much more on supply and demand, than it is on what the sales force is doing.

Strengths of Straight Salary Plans

A regular income gives the salesperson a considerable degree of security. A salary plan also provides stability of earnings, without the wide fluctuations often found in commission plans.

The assurance of a regular, stable income can do much to develop loyal, well-satisfied salespeople. Sales forces on straight salary usually have lower turnover rates than those on commission. Also, management can direct the sales force into various activities more easily under a salary plan than under any other method of compensation.

Because people on salary are less likely to be concerned with immediate sales volume, they can give proper consideration to the customers' interests. Also, customers often react more favorably to a salesperson if they know he or she is on straight salary.

Limitations of Straight Salary

A frequent objection to the straight salary plan is that it provides no direct incentive to the sales force. True, a salary plan does not offer the strong, direct incentive that a commission or bonus plan does. However, salary adjustments can provide incentives. Theoretically, salaries could be revised daily or weekly in relation to the salesperson's performance, but this is not practical. The problem is finding a *frequency* of salary adjustment that is practical and that works as an incentive. Companies sometimes do not make adjustments often enough.

Another reason many salary plans fail to provide adequate incentive is that managers fail to adjust the salaries of (i.e., give raises to) those salespeople who deserve to be rewarded. This is because there is no clear-cut understanding among managers of what constitutes satisfactory performance. Another disadvantage of a straight salary is that it is a fixed cost. There is no direct relationship between salary expense and sales volume. When sales are down, the fixed cost of compensation can be burden on the firm.

When straight salary plan is best

Generally speaking, a salary plan is best used when management (1) wants a well-balanced sales job and (2) can supervise and motivate the reps properly. Specific situations suited to the straight salary include the following:

- Sales recruits are in training or are still so new on the job that they cannot sell enough under a commission to earn a decent income.
- The company wants to enter a new geographical territory or sell a new line of products.
- The job entails only missionary sales activities.

CONSIDER THIS...

Drawing Account

Certain straight commission plans utilize a draw and a drawing account. A draw is defined as a cash-advance for future commissions earned. Here is an example of how a drawing account plan might work for a fictional company called ABC Logistics:

Because ABC Logistics wants to guarantee its salespeople a minimum of $36,000 per year, the company has a $3,000 monthly draw. Further, the drawing account is attached to a straight commission plan that is based on gross margin, and has a rate of 25%. In other words, ABC account managers are paid $0.25 for every dollar of gross margin they generate.

Let's consider the following performance and resulting compensation of one account manager named Pat in the first quarter of the year:

Month	Beginning of month payment	Gross margin generated	Commission earned	End of month payment
January	$3,000	$18,000	$4,500	$1,500
February	$3,000	$ 6,000	$1,500	$0 ("owes" $1,500)
March	$3,000	$20,000	$5,000	$500 (if nonguaranteed) $2,000 (if guaranteed)

As shown, Pat the account manager receives the draw of $3,000 at the beginning of every month, no matter what. At the end of the month, any additional commission earned is added to his account.

However, when falling short of the draw, no money is added to Pat's account. In this case, the money "owed" is subtracted from the next month's end-of-month payment if the drawing account is nonguaranteed. Alternatively, the money is "forgotten about" in a guaranteed drawing account.

A drawing account like this makes sense when monthly performance greatly fluctuates—as the draw provides stable monthly income.

Straight Commission Plans

A **commission** is a regular payment for the performance of a *unit of work*. A commission is related to a unit of accomplishment, in contrast to the salary method, which is a fixed payment for a unit of time. Salespeople usually receive commissions according to the factors that are largely under their control. Commission plans generally consist of these two items:

1. A *base* on which performance is measured and payment is made—for example, sales in dollars or units of the product.
2. A *rate*, which is the amount paid for each unit of accomplishment—for example, if a firm pays a five cents in commission for each dollar of sales the rate is 5 percent.

In addition, the straight commission plan may or may not include a provision for advances against future earnings (a drawing account—see box). Essentially, straight commission plans and straight salary plans are diametrical opposites. That is, the strong points of one generally are the weak points of the other.

Advantages of straight commission plans

Probably the major advantage of the straight commission method of sales compensation is the terrific incentive it gives to the sales force. Many firms have no ceiling on the sales reps' commission earnings, so their income opportunities are unlimited. Commission payments also are a strong motivating factor to get the reps to work hard.

A commission plan probably is the best type of pay plan for weeding out ineffective sales reps. Another big advantage to the company is that a commission is a direct expense—that is, an expense is incurred only when a sale is made or some other activity is performed.

Disadvantages of straight commission
The limitations of the commission method mentioned most often can be summed up under one point: It can be difficult to supervise and direct the activities of salespeople because their overriding concern is to sell more, without regard for the interests of the company or the customer. The reps may concentrate on easy-to-sell items and ignore products that are equally or more important to the company, but harder to sell. Customers may be sold more items, or more expensive items, than necessary. Sales reps on commission often disregard any thought of a fully balanced sales job, and management cannot expect them to do missionary work.

Management is not totally helpless to combat some of these problems. In fact, it can exercise considerable control by judiciously modifying commission rates and bases. For example, to deter a focus on easy-to-sell, low margin items, the company can pay a commission on gross profit, thus lowering rates on such products.

When straight commission plan is best
Conditions under which the straight commission method is the best choice include the following:

- A company is in a weak financial position and therefore selling costs must be related directly to sales.
- Salespeople need great incentive to achieve adequate sales.
- Very little missionary work is needed.
- Developing long-term relationships with customers is not required.
- A firm uses part-time salespeople or independent contractors such as manufacturers' reps.

Commission Bases and Rates
When a firm uses the commission method, it must make decisions about commission bases, commission rates, split commissions, and limits on earnings.

The **commission base** refers to the part of performance that will correspond to payment. In other words, what the commission is based on. The most common commission bases are sales in dollars, sales in units, and gross margin (or profit). In other words, commission tends to be based on the sales price of the product, the number of units sold, or on the difference between the sales price and the cost. Switching from a sales volume base to a gross margin base should incentivize the salespeople to work harder to sell high-margin items.

Once the base is chosen, management must determine the **commission rate**, which is the amount paid for each unit of accomplishment. Rates vary among companies, and even across products and/or territories within a single company. For example, Fastenal offers its outside salespeople one commission rate on existing business, and then a higher commission rate that is applied to both increased sales from existing customers and/or sales from new accounts.

The choice of rates is affected by factors such as (1) the level of income desired for the sales force, (2) the price and/or profitability of given products, (3) difficulty in selling a product, or (4) classes of customers. By establishing different rates for different product lines, a company is effectively stressing the profit feature. That is, higher commission rates are paid on the high-margin products to encourage their sales. Conversely, low rates are paid on sales of low-margin products.

Rates may be constant throughout all stages of sales volume, or they may be on a sliding scale, going up or down as sales volume increases. A **progressive rate** increases as the volume increases. For example, each quarter (three-month period), a business may pay 5 percent on sales up to $20,000; 7 percent on the next $80,000 (sales from $20,000 to $100,000); and 10 percent on everything over $100,000.

A progressive rate is intended to offer reps a great incentive in that the more they sell, the more they make on each sale. The company usually can afford this because the larger the sale, the less the overhead charged to each unit of volume. A progressive rate requires careful administration to prevent reps from taking advantage of the system. Reps may postdate or predate orders so that all fall in one period. Thus, they artfully boost their volume during a given period and consequently qualify for a higher rate on the last orders turned in.

A **regressive rate** works in reverse (see Figure 9-5). A firm may pay 7 percent on the first $20,000 of sales in a given period, 5 percent on the next $20,000, and 3 percent on all sales over $40,000. This type of commission plan has some merit if it is hard to get the first order, but reorders come frequently and automatically. A regressive rate also may be used to even out the earnings of all salespeople or to reduce the effect of a windfall sale (which is a large and unexpected order that is not a direct result of something the salesperson did). Managers using a regressive rate must plan carefully to discourage a salesperson from (1) withholding orders at the end of a commission period when they would command a lower rate and then (2) turning them in at the start of the next period.

FIGURE 9-5
Example of Progressive and Regressive Commission Rates

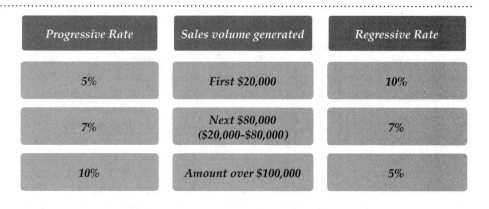

Progressive Rate	Sales volume generated	Regressive Rate
5%	First $20,000	10%
7%	Next $80,000 ($20,000–$80,000)	7%
10%	Amount over $100,000	5%

A **split commission**, dividing the commission between multiple employees, is often used when two or more salespeople work together on a sale. Various situations may call for a decision on the issue. It may take a team of three people to complete a sale of, say, a large technical product. One may be the territorial sales rep, the second a sales engineer or service rep from the home office, and the third the district manager. If a commission or bonus is part of the compensation plan for each of these people, distribution of the credit is a problem. (See the box labeled "Compensating Cross-Functional Selling Teams" for a discussion of other compensation considerations surrounding team selling.)

Geographical location also can complicate the commission division. For example, a salesperson in the Birmingham, Alabama, district may make a sale, but the order is placed through the buyer's home office in Atlanta, Georgia. To further complicate matters, delivery may be made to plants in Nashville and New Orleans, as well as to Birmingham. If each of the four cities is covered by separate sales reps, the sales manager has a real problem in splitting any commission involved.

No simple or generally accepted method exists for handling split commissions. Instead, each firm must feel its own way, using executive judgment to arrive at a policy.

Limits on earnings

Should management place a limit (commonly called a ceiling or a cap) on the earnings of its salespeople? This question will most likely arise when part or all of the compensation plan is based on commission.

Executives who favor caps on salespeople's earnings put forth some compelling arguments. One argument is that no sales rep should earn more than their bosses. Another is that sales reps who earn too much may turn down a promotion into management if it means taking a cut in pay. And yet another is that reps should not benefit from windfall sales—particularly large single orders—especially when they had no influence or control over those sales.

However, the reasons against caps or limitations on sales earnings seem to outweigh the arguments favoring them. The more a salesperson earns, the more the company makes, particularly if the earnings are in the form of a bonus or commission. Recent studies indicate that caps on commissions tend to decrease the motivation and effort of salespeople—especially those who are high-performing reps.[11]

If management does decide to limit the earnings of its salespeople, it can use any of several methods besides establishing a ceiling. One approach is to reduce commissions or bonus payments on all sales. A second is to establish a system of regressive commission rates. Third, windfall accounts may be reclassified as house accounts. These accounts are then turned over to a sales executive who calls on them. Finally, management may even change its basic compensation plan to place less emphasis on the incentive features and more on the fixed element of salary.

Combination Plans

As noted earlier, some form of combination pay plan is used to compensate the majority of all sales forces. Broadly speaking, the purpose of any combination

CONSIDER THIS...

Compensating Cross-Functional Selling Teams

Team selling has gained in both prevalence and importance. It requires the joint selling effort of several people, often from different functional areas within the firm. For example, Hallmark's selling teams include members from marketing, sales, finance, logistics, operations, information systems, and customer service. As a result, designing a compensation plan for a selling team can be a truly challenging assignment.

Several principles should be followed in designing a team-based compensation system:

Shared reward. Some form of shared reward is always necessary. That is, some significant portion of the team members' pay should be variable, based on the team's operating success. But there should be a balance between individually based and team-based compensation.

Role-reward congruence. Each team member contributes in a different way to the team. Therefore, not all of the team members must be measured and paid in the same manner. The specific performance measures used and the percentage that is team based should be chosen in accordance with the tasks performed by the individuals on the team.

Team-member input. For teams to succeed, all of the team members must be committed to the team goals and satisfied with the compensation structure. Therefore, it is important to gather input early in the process from those who will be affected by the pay program.

Peer evaluation. Part of the evaluation of performance should be based on team members' evaluation of their fellow members' contributions to the overall performance of the team. This helps the company recognize individual performance and pinpoint free-loaders.

plan is to overcome the weaknesses of a single method while at the same time keeping its strong points. Most of the combined plans fall within the following three categories:

- Salary plus commission
- Salary plus bonus
- Salary plus commission and bonus

In a combination pay plan, what portion should be incentive and what portion salary? The answer depends on the nature of the selling tasks and the company's marketing goals. The incentive portion should be larger when a company is trying to increase its sales or gross margin, especially in the short run. The salary element should be larger when management wants to emphasize customer servicing, a fully balanced selling effort, or team selling. The incentive portion in combination plans is most often in the 40 percent range.

Combination plans introduce a component that we have not yet discussed—namely, a bonus. The word *bonus* is probably the most loosely used word in the compensation vocabulary. As a result, it is sometimes difficult to accurately assess the extent to which it is used in pay plans. A **bonus** is a lump-sum payment for an above-normal performance. Because of its nature, a bonus cannot be used alone but instead must always be combined with another element such as a salary or commission. Strictly speaking, management need not announce in advance either the amount of the bonus or the basis for distributing it. However, most companies devise sales bonuses to stimulate the sales force to perform specific tasks. Unless they explain the plan in advance, managers will gain nothing by giving a bonus.

The most commonly used basis for paying a bonus is the measure of a salesperson's performance against a quota—a quantitative goal of financial or performance output that will be discussed in the next chapter.

Salary plus commission

The salary-plus-commission plan is used more than any other type of compensation method. Although there is no generally agreed-on percentage split between the fixed and the variable elements, on the average the commission portion accounts for 40 percent of the total compensation (note that in the Top Earning Salespeople box early in the chapter, the average variable portion was 45%). The salary-plus-commission plan provides the advantages of a salary plus the incentive and flexibility features of a commission. KMC Telecom pays its reps a base salary plus commissions that start at 50 percent and run as high as 225 percent depending on the product sold.[12] It should be remembered that the addition of incentive features at the expense of the salary can reduce managerial control over the sales force. In the final analysis, the success of a salary-plus-commission plan—or of any combination plan, for that matter—depends largely on the balance achieved among the elements.

Salary plus bonus

For the company that wants to control its sales force at all times and still offer some incentive, a salary-plus-bonus plan may be the answer. Usually, the salary element constitutes the major part of the total earnings—much more so than in a salary-plus-commission plan. The salary-plus-bonus arrangement is excellent for encouraging some activity for a short time. For example, a company may want to generate new accounts, encourage repeat business, or push missionary work for one product line. Blinds.com initiated a new bonus system that was based on an index of four factors: sales revenue, dollars generated per call, conversion rate and the quantity of calls. Conversion rates jumped from 27 percent to 36 percent, and company revenue increased by $2 million. Further, the new program resulted in an improvement in selling skills and behaviors.[13]

Many companies are using bonuses to reward team performance. If the team achieves its goals, then all of the team members receive a bonus. A few companies even tie bonuses to the accomplishment of personal goals such as losing weight or learning a foreign language.

Salary plus commission and bonus

A number of companies use all three components—salary, commission, and bonus—in their compensation plans. This allows them to have a certain degree of control and to provide an incentive as well as offer a bonus for the accomplishment of a specific goal. For example, a company might pay a base salary, plus a commission based on total gross margin generated, and then a quarterly bonus awarded to salespeople whose customer satisfaction surveys are at a certain level.[14]

Linking the Method to the Objective

As we noted earlier in the chapter, it is very important that the compensation plan be linked to the achievement of specific, *measurable* objectives. The choice of which method to use depends on the specific objectives that have been chosen. To provide examples, we list the specific objectives that were presented earlier and suggest the best methods to achieve them:

- *Increase profits by 10 percent.* Some form of incentive is usually necessary, such as a commission or a bonus.
- *Increase sales volume of a certain class of products by 10 percent.* A higher rate of commission may be paid on sales of the high-margin items or on whichever line of goods the company is pushing.
- *Increase volume at existing accounts.* A bonus may be paid for increasing business at existing accounts by a certain percentage. The bonus could be tied to a quota for repeat business. Alternatively, higher commissions could be paid for repeat business.
- *Improve customer satisfaction.* A bonus is the best way to accomplish this objective, although increases in salary may be used as well.
- *Stimulate missionary work.* Missionary activities may include training dealer salespeople, making demonstrations, or building displays. Some of these efforts can be individually measured, and a bonus can be given for their accomplishment. Efforts that cannot be measured easily may be rewarded by having salary form the bulk of the total compensation.
- *Develop a new territory.* Probably all income should be in the form of salary, at least in the earliest stages of territorial development.

INDIRECT MONETARY COMPENSATION

Today, most salespeople enjoy the same employee benefits as production and office workers in a company. Young people going into selling are more security-conscious than they were years ago, and management is more sensitive to its social responsibility. Sales executives are realizing that rewards are due in two general areas. One is nonfinancial rewards, which include honors, recognition, and opportunities for promotion. These features which were introduced in Chapter 8, help salespeople develop a sense of self-worth and a feeling of belonging to a group.

The other type of reward is an **indirect monetary benefit:** an item that has the same effect as money, though payment is less direct than a salary or commission. Indirect monetary benefits also are referred to as *fringe benefits* or just *benefits.* Almost all companies contribute to or pay all of your medical insurance, life insurance, disability insurance, as well as into a retirement plan. Some companies also provide a profit-sharing and stock purchase plans. Indeed, what were once considered "fringe" benefits are now better considered to be an integral part of the compensation package. These benefits can be equal to 10 to 20 percent of total compensation.

Firms also give their salespeople paid holidays and provide paid vacation time that varies according to the employees' length of service. Paid vacations present a managerial problem in connection with salespeople who work substantially or entirely on commission. These reps usually do not receive vacation pay that equals their commissions. Firms often allow these reps to draw against their future earnings and repay the amount following the vacation. Also, most companies pay a commission to the reps on any sales that come in from their territories while they are on vacation.

Indirect monetary benefits are important in attracting desirable sales applicants. These benefits probably give salespeople a degree of security and make them more loyal and more cooperative than they would be otherwise. Such characteristics undoubtedly have some bearing on a reduction in the turnover rate.

PRETEST AND INSTALL THE PLAN

Once management has tentatively selected the method of compensation, the next step is to pretest the entire compensation plan. This involves determining how the proposed plan would have operated if it had been in effect during the previous few years. Management can estimate what the company's cost would have been and what income would have been earned by the salespeople. Pretesting a compensation plan is a simulation exercise that can easily be done on a computer. No amount of pretesting will answer all questions, however. If the new plan had been in effect, sales might have been quite different.

The commission features of a plan are easier to pretest than the salary elements are. If the base salary is increased 20 percent, it is hard to say how much more effective the missionary work will be or how much harder the sales force will work. However, managers can make several calculations regarding the commission elements. By assuming various levels of sales for each line of product, management can compute what the compensation cost will be.

The following **compensation equation** can be used to calculate the total compensation of a salesperson:

Compensation = base salary + commission + bonus

Where Commission = Amount of Commission Base Generated × Rate of Commission

For example, let's say that an account manager named Sally is in a combination salary plus commission compensation plan with a monthly base salary of $4,000, and a commission rate of 6% of dollar sales. How much should Sally be compensated if she sold $25,000 last month?

Answer: $4,000 + ($25,000) × ($0.06/dollar sales) = $5,500

If the pretest goes well, the firm should install the plan by introducing it to the sales force.

Introducing the Plan to the Sales Force

A change in a compensation plan—especially a major one—can create a real culture shock for the sales force. Often in the wake of such a change, salespeople believe that management is simply trying to reduce selling costs. Thus, they look on any changes in the pay plan as a way to lower the sales reps' earnings.

Consequently, management should develop and introduce any new plan very carefully. Ideally, the salespeople are involved in the design at the very beginning of the process and provided critical feedback throughout the process. However, even though the reasons for changing the previous plan may have been thoroughly and candidly discussed, managers should announce the plan well in advance of when it is to take effect. Sometimes a company will phase in a new plan over a period of time—three or six months or even a year. This phasing-in period gives the salespeople a chance to adjust to the new plan—that is, to buy into the new system.

Because companies have been changing their incentive systems more frequently and because incentive systems have become more complex than ever before, some companies such as Hewlett-Packard, Lexmark, and Johnson & Johnson are outsourcing the administration of their incentive plans. Companies that provide these services include Oracle, Synergy, and Trilogy.

In general, whether it is an existing plan or a new plan, it is important to precisely monitor each salesperson's progress on a continuing basis. This serves to let the manager know whether the salesperson is meeting his or her own financial expectations; it also serves to signal the manager as to whether the salesperson is meeting performance expectations.

The final step is to make certain the entire plan will be evaluated frequently to prevent it from becoming outmoded. A common mistake is to spend so much time and money developing a good compensation system (or selection or training program) and then allowing the system to become outdated. As noted at the beginning of this chapter, companies should audit their compensation plans annually. This is a sound management practice that ensures that a compensation plan aligns with changes in the strategic direction of the firm.

SUMMARY

Compensation is the most widely used method for motivating a sales force. Most of our discussion in this chapter involved direct payments of financial compensation. When building a compensation plan, management must determine both the level of earnings and the method of paying the sales force. The sales force pay plan has a significant influence on the implementation of a company's strategic marketing plan.

From the company's perspective, the general goals of a good compensation plan are to (1) motivate salespeople, (2) correlate a salesperson's efforts and results with rewards, (3) control salespeople's activities, (4) ensure proper treatment of customers, (5) attract and keep competent salespeople, (6) be economical yet competitive, and (7) be flexible yet stable. From the salesperson's perspective, a good compensation plan (1) provides a steady income and an incentive income, (2) is easy for the sales rep to understand and simple for the company to administer, and (3) is fair.

When designing a pay plan, a company should first review its job descriptions to see what the reps are being paid to do. Then management should set specific goals for the pay plan. Compensation ideally should be based on items that (1) the sales force can control and (2) the company can measure objectively.

A major step in building a compensation plan is to establish the *level* of pay for the salespeople. Another major step in designing a compensation plan is to determine the *method* of compensation. Fundamentally, there are only three methods for compensating a sales force: (1) a straight salary, (2) a straight commission, and (3) some combination of compensation elements (salary, commission, and bonus). Some form of a combination plan is used the majority of all sales forces.

A straight salary plan ensures a regular, stable income for the sales force. It enables management to direct the sales force into a variety of activities. The main drawback to a straight salary plan is that it does not provide any direct incentive to the sales force. It is also a fixed cost to the company. Generally speaking, a straight salary plan is best used when management (1) wants a fully balanced sales job and (2) can supervise the salespeople so that they are properly motivated.

The main advantage of a straight commission plan is the tremendous incentive it gives the sales force to do what the commission is based on. To management, a straight commission plan is a variable expense. Under a straight commission plan, it may be difficult to direct the activities of the salespeople. There are several situations in which a straight commission plan is best. With a straight commission pay plan, management must decide on the base and rates for paying the commission. Also, policies are needed regarding split commissions and drawing accounts. Management also must decide whether it will limit its sales reps' earnings.

Combination pay plans typically are a compromise designed to retain as much as possible the strong points and to overcome the weaknesses of straight salary or straight commission. Combination plans include some type of bonus paid for above-normal performance. These bonuses are often tied to quotas, which are performance goals.

Most sales compensation plans also include indirect monetary benefits such as paid vacation time and company insurance plans. The final steps in designing a pay plan involve pretesting the plan, introducing it to the sales force, installing the plan, and evaluating it periodically.

KEY TERMS

Bonus	Drawing account	Progressive rate
Commission	Indirect monetary	Regressive rate
Commission base	benefit	Split commission
Commission rate	Level of earnings	Salary
Compensation equation	Method of	
Draw	compensation	

QUESTIONS AND PROBLEMS

1. Explain three alternative reasons, in addition to not matching the company strategy, that a compensation plan may not be successful.

2. As stated in this chapter, two broad goals of a sound compensation plan are (a) to control and direct sales force activities and (b) to ensure proper treatment of customers. Can these goals be reached by use of any managerial tool or activity other than a good pay plan?

3. Rank the following types of sales jobs by total earnings, showing which type you feel should have the highest level of compensation, which is second, and so on. Justify your rankings.

   a. Missionary sales for a large soap company

   b. Sales for a steel manufacturer

   c. Pharmaceutical sales

   d. Sales by appliance wholesalers to retail stores

   e. Life insurance sales

   f. Sales for a software manufacturer

   g. Sales for a manufacturer of children's clothes, calling on retail department stores and other clothing stores

   h. Sales for a firm selling conveyor systems

4. What might be some of the difficulties of letting salespeople develop their own goals for their sales volume (i.e., their own quotas)?

5. In 2012, a firm hired several college graduates for sales jobs at a yearly salary of $47,000. In 2016, most of these people were making a salary of about $57,000. In 2016, the same company hired more graduates for entry-level sales, and paid them $56,000 a year. Thus, the people with no experience received almost the same pay as those with four years' experience. Discuss the problems involved in this situation and suggest remedies.

6. Assume that salespeople's earnings in a certain firm have no limit and that a good sales rep can earn more than some of the company's sales managers. What incentive do these salespeople have to move into management? Especially consider those for whom a promotion means a decrease in income.

7. Give some specific examples of how each of the following factors can influence a company's choice of a sales force compensation plan:

   a. Caliber of the salespeople

   b. Nature of the job

   c. Financial condition of the company

8. Suggest a specific type of compensation plan that may be used to solve each of the following three problems often faced by sales managers:

   a. Salespeople tend to overemphasize the easy-to-sell parts of multiple product lines in an effort to build sales volume; other, more profitable lines are forced into the background.

b. Salespeople are not taking time to develop new accounts.

c. To improve a company's long-term position, salespeople should be doing more missionary work and developing long-term customers to meet expected competition.

9. What is the economic justification underlying the progressive commission rate? Is there any economic justification for a regressive rate? Which of the two rates is better for stimulating a sales force?

10. What plan would you recommend for each of the following companies in handling split commissions?

a. A manufacturer of sheets, pillowcases, towels, and related items sells to a department store chain. The order is placed through the chain's buying offices in New York. Delivery is made to stores throughout the country on an order from the department manager in each store. The manufacturer's salespeople call on the units of the chain located in their territories.

b. A manufacturer of oil-well-drilling equipment sells to main offices and drilling locations. Salespeople in the area where the product is delivered must service the item.

11. What do you think would be some potential problems in having team members rate each other as part of their performance evaluation?

12. In what respects would a compensation plan differ among salespeople for the following firms?

a. A manufacturer of small airplanes used by executives

b. A wholesaler of office equipment and supplies

c. An automobile dealer

EXPERIENTIAL EXERCISES

1. Call 10 different firms and ask them to identify the methods they use to compensation their salespeople. Discuss whether or not the differences across firms make sense.

2. Ask 20 of your friends what portion of their compensation they would like to be salary (a fixed component) and what portion they would like to be some type of incentive (commission or bonus). Try to determine why different people have different preferences in this regard.

3. Visit career websites and other internet sources to compile data on current salary levels for salespeople in different industries and different parts of the country.

4. Assume your current salary is $50,000 in your hometown; then calculate the equivalent salary in three different parts of the country using the following CNN Money website: http://money.cnn.com/calculator/pf/cost-of-living/

FALCON ENTERPRISES, INC.
Revising a Sales Force Compensation Plan

Over the past few months, Scott Paluch, vice president of sales and marketing at Falcon Enterprises, Inc., and Ron Fogarty, the sales manager reporting to Paluch, had periodically been discussing the compensation plan currently used for their company's sales force. Both men agreed they had been talking long enough, and it was time to take some action.

Falcon Enterprises was a relatively small West Coast firm with sales last year of $20 million. Falcon manufactured and marketed two types of carpet cleaning machines for industrial users: a basic commercial vacuum cleaner and the more powerful extractor. Using the extractor to clean carpet was a relatively slow but efficient process. It was equipped with a very powerful motor, a water tank, and a bucket that held the debris. The commercial vacuum cleaner was the usual type of vacuum with a bag. Its advanced features included a protected belt that prevented it from breaking if the brushes got stuck on some object. Both products were high quality and relatively expensive. Falcon sold these products to industrial distributors for the following prices: $8,000 for the extractor and $3,000 for the vacuum cleaner. Falcon's manufacturing costs for these products were $5,200 for the extractor and $2,400 for the vacuum cleaner.

The industrial distributors, which were typically janitorial supply houses, marked up the price 15 percent and resold the units to industrial users. Most of the industrial users were janitorial maintenance firms that cleaned carpets in office buildings, schools, hospitals, and hotels/motels. The distributors also sold to building contractors and to companies (other than supermarkets) that rented carpet-cleaning equipment.

The Falcon sales force consisted of 10 people who worked out of their homes throughout the West Coast. Their direct supervisor was Ron Fogarty, the sales manager. These salespeople were paid on a straight commission basis, which was 6 percent of dollar sales. Further, they paid all of their own expenses. Fogarty said that the company used this compensation and expense plan because Falcon was a small firm and was trying to keep its operating costs as low as possible. By paying a straight commission, the company made its sales compensation expense a variable cost. Also, Fogarty believed that by being paid a straight commission, the people tended to work harder. They had no big salary to fall back on.

The Falcon sales rep's job consists of two sets of activities. The first involved finding distributors (janitorial supply houses) and selling the Falcon cleaners to them. These were the wholesalers that sold to the janitorial maintenance firms that cleaned offices and other buildings. The second set of job duties involved activities to make the distributor's selling effort more effective.

To get a distributor to carry the Falcon line, a sales rep would first go to a janitorial service that cleaned several office buildings. The rep would give a sales presentation that included a demonstration of the product and then secure an order. The rep took this order to the distributor. With orders from the final user already secured, it would be easier to get the distributor to carry the Falcon products.

Once the distributor agreed to handle Falcon products, it was the sales rep's job to keep that distributor actively and effectively selling those products. Because most of these distributors also carried other brands of carpet cleaners along with the Falcon products, the reps were constantly trying to persuade the distributors to promote the Falcon line over competing brands. This meant that the Falcon reps had to make frequent calls on their distributors.

To effectively sell the extractors, the reps usually had to conduct sales demonstrations at night. Carpet cleaning was a wet process and therefore took time to dry. If the demonstration was done in the evening, the carpet could dry overnight and not interfere with the business working day. Also, janitorial cleaning crews did most of their work at night. Since they were the final buyers of the Falcon extractors, demonstrations had to be directed toward them. Most of the time, the distributors were not willing to put in this extra effort. As a result, the Falcon salespeople had to convince the distributors of the need for these night demonstrations in order to maintain sales of Falcon products.

Three factors had triggered Paluch's and Fogarty's discussions of their sales compensation plan. First, Fogarty noticed that some of the sales reps were showing signs of dissatisfaction with their jobs. He was concerned because he knew that any decline in the sales reps' morale would adversely affect their working relationships with their distributors.

Second, Fogarty was increasingly concerned that the existing compensation plan failed to motivate the salespeople to do a complete sales job. The straight commission on net sales, he believed, did little to get the sales reps to make night demonstrations or to spend time with the industrial users—the janitorial maintenance firms. Fogarty said that the plan did not stimulate long-range planning by the reps nor did it build lasting relationships with the distributors.

The third factor leading to the compensation discussions was a concern that the current plan did not provide the sales reps with enough of an incentive to sell the extractors ahead of the vacuum cleaners. The extractors generated significantly more profit for the firm than did the vacuum cleaners. However, the extractors required significantly more time and effort to sell, so the reps tended to focus more on selling the vacuum cleaners. In fact, about 80 percent of sales stemmed from vacuum cleaners and only 20 percent from extractors. Both Paluch and Fogarty felt like the percent should be closer to 50-50.

Paluch felt that the current plan was generally working well. He believed that morale problems should be approached through changes in the sales training program. Paluch talked to Denise Cole, the manager of sales training, about morale problems. Cole had done some research in attitude measurement and change. She conducted sales training seminars for Falcon's distributors as well as for the sales force. Fogarty felt that these seminars were beneficial. He said, however, that they were not enough to handle the problems related to the declining morale and lack of a complete selling job.

Cole believed that any problem in this situation was not the fault of the compensation plan. She noted that the 6 percent straight commission on sales volume was standard in the industry and that the Falcon reps were making good money. Paluch, in looking for a compromise, suggested increasing the commission rate another 1 or 2 percent—to a total of 7 or 8 percent. He believed that this added incentive might offset the growing problems.

Fogarty felt uneasy with both Cole's and Paluch's proposals. He wondered about introducing a salary element into the plan, and/or perhaps switching the base of commission from sales volume to something else. Paluch was open to different suggestions, but he was anxious to settle the compensation questions. He felt that Falcon had a good sales force. Many of the reps had been with the company for several years and Paluch did not want to lose them now. Consequently, he asked Ron Fogarty to come up with a solid proposal regarding the sales force compensation plan.

Questions:

1. Given the data provided in the case, what is the compensation of the average Falcon salesperson?

2. Make a specific recommendation for a new, better compensation plan for the Falcon Enterprise sales force.

3. What will the average Falcon salesperson make under your new plan?

ID SYSTEMS, INC.
Directing Salespeople Efforts through a Compensation System

"Today, world crime escalates daily, with terrorism and hijackings almost commonplace. Bombing, kidnapping, and electronic fraud dominate both national and international news. Add to that the less dramatic, but damaging, cost of white-collar crime, and the conclusion is clear: Never before has absolute identification been so important."

That is the theme of ID Systems, Inc., manufacturer of personal identification systems. The three main product areas are cardkey systems, proximity reader systems, and retina-scanning devices. The cardkey security systems control who is permitted to enter a defined area and during what time of day they may enter. Each card is coded by means of a microchip within the card. The cards cannot be duplicated, as some with magnetic strips can. The proximity reader systems are based on a concept similar to the cardkey systems. However, instead of carrying a card that must be inserted into a system, the user simply carries a plastic plate, about one inch by two inches, that activates the lock at a certain distance from the door. The retina-scanning device is based on the fact that every pair of eyes has a unique pattern of blood vessels. The identification system compares the retinal scan with a template of characteristics stored in a memory bank. When the template is matched with an acceptable degree of accuracy, access is granted.

The average cardkey or proximity system sells for about $3,000 per door, and the retina scan is around $25,000. The average sales for the company is $60,000 to $75,000. Last year, ID Systems, with sales of $72 million, controlled 30 percent of the U.S. security market. Its two closest competitors are Schlage (with 20 percent of the market) and Boye (with 15 percent). Seventy-five additional companies each has 3 to 4 percent; and another 200 companies, which are not Underwriter's Laboratory (UL) approved, have approximately 5 percent of the market. The demand for security identification systems is exploding, and the market is expected to have sales of $4.4 billion in three years. ID Systems, whose products are becoming more and more high tech with each new design or improvement, is in an excellent position to compete in the changing marketplace. Its product line is the trend of the future, and its potential for sales is enormous.

ID Systems' sales force consists of 24 salespeople divided into six districts across the United States. Each district has a sales manager, an electrical engineer, and a sales support engineer. There is also an international sales zones. International sales, all through an independent distributor network, comprise 73 percent of ID's sales.

Each sales rep is expected to make 16 calls and to quote four jobs in a week. The sales rep makes the initial call and determines what the customer needs and what will satisfy those needs. Then the sales engineer does a "walk-through" with the rep to make sure the design is technically feasible.

The territories are designed to equalize potential, and each rep has a quota of $1.5 million per year. The compensation is a base salary of $34,000 plus progressive-rate commission based on sales. Reps receive 5 percent of sales for sales of $800,000 and under; 8 percent for $800,000 to $1.5 million; and 10 percent for sales over $1.5 million.

Cheryl Sites is the vice president of sales for ID Systems. She began her career with the company as a sales rep, progressing through the positions of district manager and regional manager. She has been the vice president for several years and is well respected for her market knowledge and sense of fairness in dealing with employees.

Recently, Sites has been struggling with a serious problem of how to implement a new marketing and sales strategy. ID Systems has been growing at a healthy rate for the past 10 years. This growth has come primarily from skimming the more profitable and larger accounts on the market. Management realized that there is a tremendous amount of untapped business and that much of it is located in areas of relatively low population that the sales force does not heavily penetrate. On the one hand, realistically, it would be difficult for the existing salespeople to cover the more densely populated parts of their territories as well as the outlying areas. On the other hand, these areas by themselves do not have enough volume to support a full-time rep. Therefore, the company decided to establish a distributor network to supplement the direct sales by the reps.

The salespeople have been given the task of identifying and supporting the distributors for their own territories. The reps are each supposed to have sales of $300,000 each year through their distributor networks. They must locate the distributors, get them set up, support them with their service, and maintain a working relationship with them. They also are expected to help train the distributors' employees.

Cheryl Sites agreed with the new strategy. She felt that it made sense from an overall strategic perspective. She also felt that, in the long run, ID's salespeople would benefit from the opportunity to develop a greater sales base through the distributor network. However, her salespeople seem to view the new strategy from a short-term commission perspective. While the sales reps received the same commissions from sales through their distributors, the prices to the distributors are generally discounted by 40 percent off the normal selling prices. As the reps see it, they are getting significantly less for selling the same amount of product. Furthermore, they know that it takes a lot of additional effort initially to get the distributor set up and that the ongoing support requirements are going to be greater. They do not want to spend time with distributors when they feel they can continue to do well without them.

The reps also do not want the distributors stealing sales from them. Even though the distributors would be selling in areas that the ID reps have not had time to cover, the reps would technically be giving up some of the potential in their territories. If these concerns were not enough, one of the reps said to Sites yesterday, "Why should I help find my own replacement?" Apparently, many of the reps are threatened by the establishment of a dealer network. They envision ID eventually selling exclusively through distributors and having reps who merely service these distributors. Sites also is concerned that if she pushes the reps into setting up some distributors, they may set them up, but they won't support them very well. This could give ID a bad name, making it difficult to establish additional distributors.

Sites is considering her options. Her preference is to find some way of motivating the current reps to support the establishment of the distributor network. One way is to change their compensation to provide some short-term incentive to establish and support the distributors. She is not certain what that incentive should be, and she is not certain, given the reps' attitude, whether it would work. Another alternative is to hire several new reps whose only responsibility would be to set up and sell through the distributors. Of course, the current reps wouldn't like this idea either. Finally, she could recommend to management that ID change its strategy of establishing a distributor network at this time.

Question:

1. Should Cheryl Sites recommend a change in strategy? If not, what steps should she take to implement the new strategy?

IMAGINATIVE STAFFING, INC. (B)
Compensating a Sales Team

Susan Borland, sales director, and her assistant, Judy Morgan, had been assigned the task of developing a program for team-selling the company's services to prospective accounts. As they dug into their task, they encountered particular difficulty with the matter of how to pay the team.

Imaginative Staffing, Inc., is a temporary-services firm in New York City that supplies temporary workers to firms located in the five boroughs. Formed in 1998, it had grown to $17 million in revenues. Besides Angie Roberts, the president, and her assistant, Nicole Gamin, the company had a chief financial officer, a sales director, four sales reps, an operations manager, 10 account managers, five administrative assistants, and receptionist.

One reason Roberts had become aware of the team-selling concept was that, for some time, she had been frustrated by how long it took to close a sale with a good prospect. On average, it took about six months of hard work to make a sales to a major customer. One of the sales reps would make the contact and do all of the selling, sometimes with the help of the sales director if the situation seemed to warrant it.

Large and small corporations made extensive use of temporary help for any of several reasons: (1) to fill in for workers who, for some reason, were unable to work; (2) to handle overload conditions; or (3) to take care of seasonal peak workloads. In the current legal environment, many organizations were reluctant to hire permanent employees until there was a clear-cut, long-run need for them. Such factors as benefit packages, insurance, unemployment claims, and termination difficulties made management think seriously about hiring people as permanent employees.

Susan Borland and Judy Morgan had decided that a selling team should usually consist of at least three people: a sales rep, the person who would be the account's manger, and one person from top management. There was considerable debate on two issues: Should someone from the sales director's office be on the team (Borland or Morgan)? And who in top management should be involved? In particular, much consideration was given to Angie Roberts's role. Should the president be part of a sales team on an important sale, or would that undermine the development of the company's salespeople?

In any event, the matter of paying the people became an issue. Borland thought that there should be no special compensation plan for the selling team. "After all," she said, "they are paid a salary for their work and they all get substantial bonuses at the end of the year depending on how much profit we have made. If they sell more, they'll get paid in their year-end bonus."

Morgan demurred. "Two problems here: Delayed payment provides little immediate incentive, and the impact on a person's bonus by any one sales would be slight. I think we need to build some push into this team-selling concept by giving the victors some of the spoils."

Under the existing system, a sales rep who brought in a new account was paid a commission of 10 percent of that account's billings for the first year. The commission was paid at the end of the month in which the money was received from the account. Thereafter, the sales rep received 1 percent of the account's billings. The account manager who took over the managing of the new account was paid a salary plus 1 percent of her account's billings. The company would not accept any account with billings less than $10,000 a year. It had slightly more than 500 active accounts, of which about 100 had billings totaling approximately $11 million. The typical new account started out with billings of about $12,000 for the first year, and it grew as it gained experience with the company.

It was part of the account manager's job to develop each account's use of the firm's services. This usually involved getting to know the account's special needs and problems, and then developing programs for using temporary employees to solve them. It often involved recruiting people with special skills who could work as needed for different accounts. For example, one client required people with the ability to read music. Another required people fluent in Russian.

The reps and the account managers had been receiving earnings based on customer billings. Consequently, both Susan Borland and Judy Morgan anticipated problems with them if those earnings were threatened by the team-selling concept. Why would they want to adopt a new selling system that would threaten their earnings? Clearly, they would have to see the system as a way to increase their earnings. Another problem automatically arose. If the reps and the account managers received incentive compensation based on account billings, how would that affect the attitudes of the other team members? Wouldn't they also want some pay based on the productivity of their work? If that was to be, then how much?

Questions:

1. Should the president be part of the selling team when appropriate?

2. Should the team receive compensation for its productivity, or should the teamwork be considered part of the job?

3. If you feel that a productivity compensation plan for the sales team is called for, design one.

ENDNOTES

[1] Mark Roberge "The Right Way to Use Compensation," *Harvard Business Review*, April 2015. Retrieved from the following URL on June 30, 2016: https://hbr.org/2015/04/the-right-way-to-use-compensation-2

[2] Paul R. Dorff, "Designing Compensation Plans to Boost Sales Performance," *National Productivity Review*, Summer 2000, pp. 73-77.

[3] "2006 Compensation Study," *Sales & Marketing Management*, 2006, p. 25.

[4] David Cichelli, *Compensating the Sales Force,* McGraw-Hill Education; 2 edition (July 8, 2010).

[5] Sunil Erevelle, Indranil Dutta, and Carolyn Galantine, "Sales Force Compensation Plans Incorporating Multidimensional Sales Effort and Salesperson Efficiency," *Journal of Personal Selling & Sales Management*, Spring 2004, pp. 101.12.

[6] Michelle Marchetti, "Pay Changes Are on the Way," *Sales & Marketing Management*, August 2000, p. 101.

[7] Rob Markey, "The Dangers of Linking Pay to Customer Feedback," *Harvard Business Review*, September 8, 2011. Retrieved from the following URL on June 28, 2016: https://hbr.org/2011/09/the-dangers-of-linking-pay-to

[8] Andy Cohen, "What Keeps You Up at Night?" *Sales & Marketing Management*, February 2000, pp. 26-27.

[9] Bureau of Labor Statistics, Occupational Employment and Wages for Sales Representatives, Wholesales and Manufacturing, Technical and Scientific Products. May 2015. Retrieved from the following URL on June 28, 2016: http://www.bls.gov/oes/current/oes414011.htm

[10] Julia Chang, "Passing the Buck," *Sales & Marketing Management*, November 2004, p. 18.

[11] Thomas Steenburgh and Michael Ahearne, "Motivating Salespeople: What Really Works," *Harvard Business Review*, July-August 2012.

[12] Betsy Cummings, "The Perfect Plan," *Sales & Marketing Management*, February 2002, p. 53.

[13] Emma Johnson, "How To: Motivate Your Sales Staff," *Success.com*, July 4, 2011. Retrieved from the following URL on June 28, 2016: http://www.success.com/article/how-to-motivate-your-sales-staff

[14] Eilene Zimmerman, "Quota Busters," *Sales & Marketing Management*, January 2001, p. 59.

chapter

10

Sales Force Quotas and Expenses

"Setting quotas is a challenge because you can never really win. If the goal is too easy, you pay more than you should. On the other side, if you set it too high, your sales reps don't make any money, and they'll leave."[1] This quote, by the president of the payroll services company SurePayroll, demonstrates how the opening topic of this chapter completes our previous discussion of motivation and compensation. Quotas are very powerful motivators, and can be a significant part of a salesperson's compensation.

After quotas, this chapter covers the topic of how firms and salespeople deal with travel and entertainment expenses. This, too, relates to our ongoing discussion of motivation and compensation. While expenses are not directly tied to compensation, they may be thought of us an indirect benefit. Certainly, a good expense plan can help salespeople be successful as it provides the means for them to get to know and better understand their customers by interacting with them in social situations (e.g., at a business meal, a ballgame, the golf course, etc.).

SALES QUOTAS

A **sales quota** is a performance goal assigned to a marketing unit for a specific period of time. The marketing unit may be a salesperson, a branch office, a district or region, or a dealer or distributor. For example, each sales rep might be assigned a specific sales goal for the coming three-month period. This quota goal may be stated in dollars, product units, or selling activities. The specified time period usually is a month, a quarter, six months, or a year; but it may be for as short a period as a week. A marketing unit's quotas also may be established for individual products and/or types of customers. When salespeople achieve their quotas, they often receive some sort of reward for their performance.

Most companies are satisfied with the overall effectiveness of their quota programs, yet see room for improvement. The most commonly stated goal by sales executives is to have 60 to 70 percent of their salespeople meet or exceed quota. But this is not quite achieved; on average only 49 percent of salespeople make quota.[2]

Relation to Sales Potential

A quota is often tied to the *sales potential* associated with the marketing unit. However, a quota is *not* the same as sales potential. Often marketing plans and/ or the characteristics of the sales rep—skills, experience—are such that a particular territory cannot reach its full sales potential. In those cases, the only way a salesperson would ever "make quota" is if the quota was set to be significantly *less* than the sales potential of that territory. Sales potential is covered in more detail later in the chapter.

Management usually sets volume sales quotas so that their total equals the sales budget or forecast. Thus, if all the reps reached their quotas, the sales budget would be met. This is *management by the numbers;* if everyone reaches "their number," the company fulfills its operational plan.

Sales Quotas and Strategic Management

Sales quotas help in planning and evaluating sales force activities. When setting sales quotas, the sales managers should consider the goals and strategies developed in the marketing planning. If the marketing goal is to increase market share, then the quota should be based on total sales of one or more products. However, if the goal is to increase a company's return on investment or net profit as a percentage of sales, then the quota should be based on gross margin (or profit)—not total sales. Thus, good sales quotas can help effectively implement the strategic plans.

Additionally, sales quotas also can help guide the sales reps' activities, sometimes with unintended consequences. For example, quotas that are too high can cause sales reps to pressure and overload the customers. Quotas that are too low will not serve to motivate the reps.

Finally, sales quotas are a widely used basis for evaluating sales force performance. Salespeople who meet their quotas are judged to be performing adequately in the activity the quota is based on. Thus, quotas can have a big impact on a salesperson's morale. Because of these strategic and behavioral considerations, it is important that management do the best job possible when setting quotas.

PURPOSES OF SALES QUOTAS

Sales quotas serve several useful purposes, as shown in Figure 10-1 and discussed below.

Indicate Strong or Weak Spots in the Selling Structure

When accurate quotas are established for each territory, management can determine the extent of territorial development by whether or not the quota is being reached. If the sales total significantly exceeds the predetermined standards, management should analyze the reasons for this variance. If the sales in a district fail to meet the quota, this failure tells management that something has gone wrong. Of course, it does not tell *why* the failure occurred. It may be that competition is stronger than expected, the salespeople have not done a good selling job, or the potential was overestimated.

Furnish Goals and Incentives for the Sales Force

In business, as in any other walk of life, individuals usually perform better if their activities are guided by standards and goals. It is not enough to say to a salesperson: "We expect you to do a good selling job." It is much more meaningful to express this expectation in a quota that is very specific (perhaps in a given dollar sales volume of a particular product, or in the number of new accounts to be acquired during the next month). This goal is generally set at a performance level that is perceived to be satisfactory—so a salesperson who consistently achieves his or her quota is doing well. The vast majority of companies use quotas as a measure by which salespeople are judged.

Control Salespeople's Activities

A corollary to the preceding point is that quotas enable management to direct the activities of the sales force more effectively than would otherwise be possible. Through the use of the appropriate type of quota, executives can encourage a given activity such as selling high-margin items or getting orders from new customers. The salespeople are not likely to know which area of activity should be stressed unless management tells them. For example, a small business might set an activity quota of 15 calls to potential clients per day, plus to meet in person with at least six prospects per week.

Evaluate Productivity of Salespeople

Quotas provide a yardstick for measuring the general effectiveness of salespeople. By comparing a rep's actual results with his or her quota, management can evaluate that person's performance. Quota performance also provides guidance for field supervisors by indicating areas of activity where the sales force needs help. Decisions on whether to give salespeople promotions or raises are often based largely on their performance in relation to their quotas.

Improve Effectiveness of Compensation Plans

A quota structure can play a significant role in a sales compensation system. Quotas can furnish incentives to salespeople who are paid straight salary. A sales rep knows, too, that a creditable performance in meeting assigned quotas reflects favorably on him or her when it is time for a salary review.

In some cases, salespeople receive a bonus if they achieve a certain quota or they may receive a commission on all sales above some preset level (or quota) of sales. At Disney, for example, the salespeople earn commissions if they exceed ambitious quotas set by the company for the number of hotel rooms booked.[3]

Inequities in territorial potential may cause inequities in compensation unless a firm establishes a quota system. In one territory, a person may get a $1,500 monthly salary plus a 5 percent commission on sales over a quota of $10,000. In a district that presents low potential and a more difficult selling job, the salesperson may have the same arrangement, except that the commission starts when the rep reaches a quota of only $7,000 each month.

Control Selling Expenses

Management can often encourage expense control by the use of expense quotas alone, without tying them to the compensation plan. Some companies gear payments for the salespeople's expenses to a quota. For instance, a business may pay all the expenses of an account manager up it 8 percent of sales. Other companies may set an expense quota and let the salespeople know their effectiveness is being judged in part by how well they meet it.

Evaluate Sales Contest Results

Sales quotas are used frequently in conjunction with sales contests. Salespeople rarely have equal opportunities in a contest unless management makes some adjustment to compensate for variation in territorial potentials and workloads. Using the common denominator of a quota, management can ensure each participant a reasonably equal chance of winning, provided the quota has been set accurately.

TYPES OF QUOTAS

The most frequently used types of sales quotas, as outlined in Figure 10-2, are those based on

- Sales volume
- Activities
- Gross margin (profit)
- Expenses
- Some combination of the above

The type of quota that management selects depends on several factors, including the nature of the product and the market. Let's assume a company has too much of one product in its inventory—and wants to correct that. This company might introduce a sales volume quota to incentivize the salespeople to sell that item, and thus reduce the surplus stock. Alternatively, if management wants

FIGURE 10-1
Purposes of sales quotas

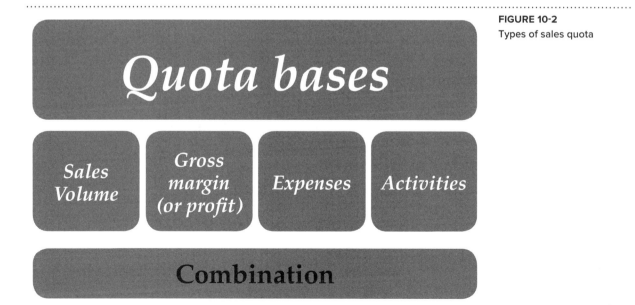

FIGURE 10-2
Types of sales quota

to develop a new territory, it should probably set an activity quota focused on calling on new accounts. These specific types of quotas are defined in detail in the following sections.

Sales Volume Quotas

Undoubtedly, the most widely used type of sales quota is one based on sales volume. A **sales volume quota** may be established for a geographical area, a product line, a customer, a time period, or any combination of these bases. Ordinarily, it is more effective to set a monthly or quarterly quota than an annual one. Some high-performance sales organizations even set daily sales quotas.

Even when a company sells a large number of products, it may be feasible to group them into a few broad lines and then set unit quotas for each line. For example, an appliance wholesaler may set unit goals for small appliances in one group, white goods (refrigerators, stoves, washers) as a second group, and electronics (televisions, computers) as a third line.

Management uses volume goals because they are simple to understand and easy to calculate. Many sales managers still regard sales volume as the only real measure of an account manager's worth to the company. However, sales volume alone does not tell the full story of a salesperson's productivity and effectiveness. It does not indicate the profit generated by the person's efforts. Nor does it measure the extent to which the salesperson has done a fully balanced sales job. In fact, volume quotas discourage balanced activities by the sales force because they stress volume to the detriment of nonselling activities.

Gross Margin (or Profit) Quotas

Many companies set quotas based on gross margin or net profit (we use these two terms synonymously). These goals may be established on many of the same bases as a volume quota. For instance, a gross margin quota may be set for a salesperson, a branch, or a group of products. The preference some companies show for **profit quotas** instead of volume quotas reflects management's recognition of the importance of profit as compared with volume.

High-volume performers are not necessarily the best sales reps for company interests. Easy-to-sell items may be low-margin items. Unless the firm controls these reps, they may decrease company profits every time they increase their volume. They may be emphasizing the sales of unprofitable items or sales to unprofitable customers.

One significant drawback to gross margin or profit quotas is the possibility that friction may arise between management and the salespeople. The salespeople may not understand how their quotas were calculated, and may not be able to measure their progress during the quota period. Another limitation is that the rep has no control over some of the factors on which the quota is based. For example, unexpectedly high production costs may leave the company with little or no profit on a certain item.

Generally, a compromise approach is to base the quota on a rep's contribution to profit. Contribution to profit is commonly called **contribution margin**, which is the amount left after deducting a salesperson's direct (or controllable) expenses from gross margin. Cost and profitability are covered in more detail in Chapter 14.

Expense Quotas

Some companies attempt to encourage a profit consciousness by establishing a quota based on the rep's travel and other expenses. Sometimes, the expense quota is related to sales volume or to the compensation plan. A sales rep may be given an expense quota equal to 4 percent of sales. That is, direct expenses, such as travel, entertainment, food, and lodging, must not exceed 4 percent of net sales volume.

Expense quotas probably encourage a salesperson to be more aware of costs and profits than volume goals. Nevertheless, it seems that an expense quota is a negative approach to the problem. A rep's attention may be devoted more to cutting expenses than to boosting the sales of profitable products.

Activity Quotas and Customer Satisfaction

One way to decrease the overemphasis on sales volume is to establish a quota based on activities or behaviors. Management may select from such tasks as (1) daily calls, (2) new customers called on, (3) orders from new accounts, and (4) product demonstrations made, and (5) displays built. An **activity quota** sets quantifiable expectations for specific activities. When properly established and controlled can do much to stimulate a fully balanced sales job. This type of quota is particularly valuable for use with missionary salespeople. Probably the principal difficulties in administering an activity quota are, first, to determine whether the activity actually was performed and, second, to find out how effectively it was done. The logic is sound. Sales result from doing a lot of things right—making many calls on the right people, giving demonstrations, opening new accounts, suggesting new or additional products. Thus, if the manager wants to build the sales volume, a way must be found to encourage salespeople to do the basic things that result in sales.

Customer satisfaction is a nontraditional type of performance goal that has become very popular among many companies. Nortel, AT&T, and Siebel Systems survey their customers about their sales reps' performance on such dimensions as responsiveness, product knowledge, ability to integrate customer requirements with product solutions, repeat purchases, and overall satisfaction.[4] The resultant customer service satisfaction score is benchmarked against a target score and used to determine a portion of the rep's performance reward. Siebel earmarks 40 percent of each salesperson's incentive compensation for achieving target scores on customer-reported satisfaction. At JD Edwards, a global e-business solutions provider, 20 percent of each rep's target earnings is based on twice-yearly customer satisfaction surveys. The rep's score, between one and ten, determines the percentage of bonus he or she receives, from 75 to 125 percent.[5]

Combination Quotas

Companies that are not satisfied with any single type of quota may combine two or more types. Traditional quotas may be combined with nontraditional ones. As an example, a firm may want to establish a quota based on one activity, a customer satisfaction score, plus gross margin on the products sold. See an example in Figure 10-3.

A combination quota seeks to use the strong points of several types of quotas, but frequently such a plan is limited by its complexity. Also, a salesperson may overemphasize one element in the quota plan. In this illustration, for example, the rep could achieve quota by reaching 100 percent of the gross margin quota, 200 percent of the quota for product demonstrations, and do *virtually nothing* to secure orders from new accounts. Sales managers should be aware that this type of gaming of the system might occur, and consider whether or not that is detrimental to the company.

CALCULATING QUOTA ATTAINMENT

As shown in Figure 10-3, the calculation of whether or not an account manager has achieved quota is straight-forward. If the ratio of [actual performance / quota] is less than 1 or (100 percent), then the individual has not achieved quota. If the ratio—or percent of quota attained—is 100 percent or greater, then quota has been achieved. For combination plans, the percentages of quota attained for all the elements are simply averaged. The example in Figure 10-3 is one in which the individual has fallen short of quota (because the average of 97 percent is below 100 percent).

Note that calculating an expense quota is different because the goal is to be below the quota. For example, if the expense quota is $1,000, and the salesperson has spent $900—then that salesperson is 10 percent below the quota; but that is good as it is exceeding quota, so the percent of quota attained is 110 percent. The equation for this is:

$$2 - [\text{ actual performance} / \text{quota}] = 2 - [900/1{,}000] = 1.1 \text{ or } 110 \text{ percent}$$

FIGURE 10-3
Combination Quota

	Quota	Actual	Percent of Quota Attained
Gross margin, all products	$30,000	$25,000	83%
Product demonstrations made	120	135	117%
Customer satisfaction score	10	9	90%
Average			97%

BASIS FOR SETTING A SALES VOLUME QUOTA

The sales volume quota illustrates quota-setting procedures well because it is the most commonly used type. However, the same procedure can be used for the other types. Fundamentally, two general approaches may be used to set volume quotas:

- Quotas are set in conjunction with territorial sales potentials.
- Quotas are set on the basis of considerations other than sales potentials, such as past sales, executive judgment, salesperson determination, or compensation design.

Quotas Based on Sales Potential

One common practice in quota setting is to relate quotas directly to the territorial sales potentials or forecasts. The sales potential is the estimated total industry sales that the company would ideally realize in a given territory. The sales forecast is what the company realistically expects to get given the current circumstances. Consequently, the forecast is typically a bit lower than the potential. Both the potential and the forecast for total company sales are often built by piecing together the estimates calculated for each territory.

Thus, if the territorial sales potential or forecasts have already been determined and the quotas are to be related to these measures, the job of quota setting is largely completed. For instance, let's assume that the sales potential in territory A is $300,000, or 4 percent of the total company potential (and let's say that the potential and forecast are equal in this situation). Then management may assign this amount as a quota for the salesperson who covers that territory. The total of all territorial quotas then would equal the company sales potential.

Adjustments to Potential-Based Quotas

In some cases, management chooses to use the estimate of potential as the starting point in determining the quota. These potentials are then adjusted for one or more of the factors discussed below.

Human factors

A quota may have to be adjusted downward because an older salesperson is covering the district. The rep may have done a fine job for the company for years but is now approaching retirement age and slowing down because of physical limitations. It would not be good human relations—or ethical—to discharge or force the person into early retirement. Nor would it help the rep's morale to be assigned an unreachable quota. Sometimes such reps are given smaller territories with correspondingly lower quotas. Likewise, sometimes new reps are given lower quotas for the first few years until they reach a greater level of competence. Giving younger reps more attainable quotas will help build their confidence and keep their morale high.

Psychological factors

Management understands that it is human nature to relax after a goal has been reached. Therefore, some sales executives set their quotas a little higher than the expected potential, just in case some reps can do better than expected. On the other hand, management must not set the goal unrealistically high. A quota that is too far above potential can discourage the sales force. The ideal psychological quota is one that is a bit above the potential but can still be met and even exceeded by working effectively.

Compensation

Some companies relate their quotas basically to the sales potential but adjust them to allow for the compensation plan. In such a case, the company is really using both the quota and the compensation systems to stimulate the sales force. As an example, one organization may set its quotas at 90 percent of potential. It pays one bonus if the quota is met and an additional bonus if the sales reach 100 percent of the potential.

Quotas Based on Factors other than Potential

A company that does not wish to set its sales quotas in relation to territorial potentials has these alternatives:

- Quotas may be set strictly on the basis of past sales.
- Quotas may be determined by executive judgment alone.
- Quotas may be related to the compensation plan.
- The salespeople may set their own quotas.

Past sales

In some organizations, the motto is "Beat last year's figures." As a result, sales volume quotas are based strictly on the preceding year's sales or on an average of sales over a period of several years. Management sets each salesperson's quota at an arbitrary percentage increase over sales in some past period. About the only merits in this method of quota setting are computational simplicity and low-cost administration.

However, a quota-setting method based on past performance *alone* is subject to severe limitations. This method ignores possible changes in a territory's sales potential. General business conditions this year may be depressed in a district. Thus cutting the sales potential. Or promising new customers may have moved into the district, thus boosting the potential volume.

Basing quotas on previous years' sales may not uncover poor performance in a given territory. A person may have had sales of $100,000 last year, and the quota is increased 5 percent for this year. The salesperson may even reach the goal of $105,000. However, the potential in the district may be $200,000. This salesperson may perform poorly for years without management's recognizing that a problem exists. Quotas set on past sales also ignore the percentage of sales potential already achieved. Assume the sales potential in each of two territories is $200,000 and rep A's volume was $150,000 last year while rep B's was $210,000. It may not be realistic to expect each to increase sales the same percentage over last year's figures.

Moreover, "chase your tail" quotas—in which the more the reps sell, the more they are supposed to sell—destroy morale and ultimately cause top producers to leave the company.

Executive judgment

In setting quotas for sales reps, some companies rely entirely on what they refer to as executive judgment, which is more precisely called *guesswork*. Executive judgment is usually an indispensable ingredient in a sound procedure for setting quotas, but to use it *alone* is certainly not recommended. Even though the administrator may be very experienced, too many risks are involved in relying solely on this type of opinion-based approach that does not refer to quantitative market measures.

Compensation design

Earlier in this chapter, we discussed the idea of relating compensation to volume quotas based on potential. Quotas also may be used in compensation plans without any relation to potential. As a case in point, a company may prefer to pay its sales representatives by straight commission. However, management realizes that the reps prefer a salary-plus-commission plan. Therefore, the company adopts a combination plan, with a salary of $1,200 per month and a commission of 6 percent on all sales over $20,000 a month. By using the quota, management in effect achieves its preference for a straight commission because no commission is paid until the salary is recouped (6 percent of $20,000 equals $1,200).

Salespeople setting their own quota

Some companies place the quota problem in the laps of the sales representatives by letting them set their own performance goals. The rationale for this move is that the salespeople are closer to their territories than management and thus can do a better job. Also, setting their own quotas allows the reps to reflect their individual abilities. Finally, if sales reps make the decisions about their own goals, they will have higher morale and strive more to attain the quota.

From a practical standpoint, however, this method can be problematic. Sometimes salespeople do not have access to the necessary information. Also, some salespeople—especially *inexperienced* salespeople—tend to be optimistic about their capabilities and the opportunities in their districts. Therefore, they may set unrealistically high quotas. Then, as the period goes on and it becomes evident that they cannot reach the goal, a serious morale problem may develop. Alternatively, they may "sandbag," suggesting a lower quota, knowing that they are likely to beat it.

ADMINISTRATION OF SALES QUOTAS

Usually the sales department is responsible for establishing the sales quota, and no approval of a higher executive is needed. Within the sales organization, the task may rest with any of several executives. The chief sales executive may be responsible for setting the total company quota. But the individual breakdown may be delegated down through the regional and district managers. Or territorial sales potentials may be given to the district managers, and they set the salespeople's quotas. Many attributes found in good compensation plans, territorial designs, and other aspects of sales management also are found in good quota plans, as seen in Figure 10-4.

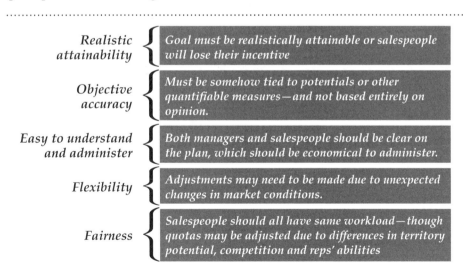

Realistic attainability	*Goal must be realistically attainable or salespeople will lose their incentive*
Objective accuracy	*Must be somehow tied to potentials or other quantifiable measures—and not based entirely on opinion.*
Easy to understand and administer	*Both managers and salespeople should be clear on the plan, which should be economical to administer.*
Flexibility	*Adjustments may need to be made due to unexpected changes in market conditions.*
Fairness	*Salespeople should all have same workload—though quotas may be adjusted due to differences in territory potential, competition and reps' abilities*

FIGURE 10-4
Characteristics of a good quota plan

Typical administrative weaknesses

Companies that do not use sales quotas may justify their position by citing various limitations in a sales quota system. Generally speaking, however, these limitations are not *inherent* in the system. Instead they are *administrative* weaknesses that reflect management's failure to utilize the characteristics of a good quota plan.

Probably the major criticism of quotas is that it is difficult or even impossible to set them accurately. This point may be justified in some cases. Perhaps a company sells a new product for which very little marketing information is available, or a firm sells a product that requires several quota periods to elapse before the sales is consummated. In order to achieve greater accuracy, companies frequently adjust quotas during the year. This can be very discouraging to the sales reps and should be avoided unless it is a planned part of the compensation program. However, just because a company cannot set a goal that is 100 percent statistically correct is no reason for management to abandon the entire project. The solution for improving accuracy is to set quotas for shorter periods so that you can make periodic adjustments.

In other instances, quotas are not used because management claims they lead to high-pressure selling and generally emphasize some activities at the expense of others. These criticisms may well be justified if a sales volume quota is used alone. A quota also may overstress a given selling or nonselling activity. However, these are indications of planning or operating weaknesses. They are not inherent disadvantages of quotas.

Gaining Sales Force Acceptance of a Quota Plan

A final essential ingredient in a well-planned and well-operated quota system is its wholehearted acceptance by the sales force. Salespeople often are suspicious of quotas, either because the purposes are not apparent or because there are questions about the factors underlying the plan. The purposes of the quota, the bases on which the quota is set, and the method used in the process should be explained to the reps. When the quota is ready for formal installation, the sales force will probably be more inclined to accept it if they have had a hand in its development. Management also stands to gain by soliciting ideas from salespeople, who may introduce considerations that escaped management's notice.

Salespeople should be kept informed about their progress toward meeting the performance goal. Conferences and correspondence with the reps often are necessary. The sales force also needs some incentive to reach the goal. This may come from a bonus for achieving the quota or from some other direct link with the compensation plan. Management should make it clear that quota performance is reflected in periodic merit ratings, salary review, or considerations for promotion.

SALES FORCE EXPENSES

One sales manager observed that, even when properly managed, sales force expense accounts are a nuisance and, when improperly managed, they can amount to grand larceny. This may be an unusually sour view of the situation. However, it points up the problem of establishing and administering a plan for controlling travel and other business expenses incurred by the sales force.

Salespeople are among the few company employees who are allowed to spend the company's money—and the amount they spend can be quite substantial. As of June 2016, the cost per salesperson for *meals and lodging alone* averaged about $207 per day in a typical metropolitan area such as Atlanta.

SALES FORCE EXPENSES AND STRATEGIC PLANNING

Expense account policy is one element in a firm's strategic marketing plan. New enterprises are often financially unable to bear the fixed costs of their reps' selling expenses. Entrepreneurs want all costs to be variable—that is, related to sales volume. Thus, as a matter of strategy, start-up companies will likely offer reps a deal in which the reps pay all their own selling costs in exchange for a higher rate of commission. Reps who accept this deal hope it will allow them to make more money than they could make if the company paid selling expenses. One fact is certain: If the reps pay their own expenses, there will be little waste.

In contrast, some firms hope to woo customers by treating them lavishly. The adroit use of entertainment can lure a customer into the company's fold to stay. Other firms want to develop an image of prosperity. They require their salespeople to go first class in their travel and in relationships with accounts.

Often firms use expense account policy as a strategic tool for recruiting many financially strapped college graduates. One of the most recent strategic trends is the willingness of companies to pay for items that can lead to increases in salesperson productivity. For example, many firms are willing to pay 100 percent of the cost for such things as laptops, smart phones, and various other hardware and software. This trend is expected to continue as more and more firms adopt sales automation.

INTERNAL REVENUE SERVICE REGULATIONS

Income tax laws significantly affect how much salespeople spend on travel, entertainment, and gifts to customers. Congress and the Internal Revenue Service (IRS) have progressively tightened the regulations on the deductibility of such expenses on income tax returns. Although most travel and lodging expenses are wholly deductible, the government has strictly limited the deductibility of business *entertainment* expenses associated with "wining and dining" the customers. Specifically, only 50 percent of legitimate business entertainment expenses and only 50 percent of business meal expenses can be deducted when computing a firm's income tax. Furthermore, the tax deductibility of business gifts is limited to $25 per year for each recipient. Moreover, tax auditors often scrutinize travel and entertainment (T&E) expenses closely because experience has shown that there is a high probability of error in T&E expenses. Thus, it is important to keep careful records of all expenses.

LEGITIMATE TRAVEL AND BUSINESS EXPENSES

Management should specify in writing the expenses for which the company will pay—not only the broad expense categories, such as transportation or lodging, but also the details within each category. For example, management may reimburse sales reps only for coach fare in the case of air travel or for only the cheapest lease on a rental car. *All* items relating to travel should be clarified beforehand.

There is no unanimous agreement on what constitutes a legitimate expense for reimbursement, but we can generalize about major categories of expenses. With regard to allowable items, a good general policy is that the salesperson should be reimbursed for (1) *business expenses* incurred in connection with work and (2) *personal expenditures* that would not have been necessary otherwise. Telephone, Wi-Fi fees, and other *communication* costs are considered legitimate business expenses, as are *office supplies* and *stenographic services*. *Transportation* costs incurred on the job also are considered business expenses and are usually covered in full. Personal expenses include all *lodging* costs incurred while the salesperson is away from home overnight on business. Companies also usually cover the cost of out-of-town *meals*, but they frequently limit the amount per meal. The specific allowance or payment for each day is called a **per diem**. For example, the average per diem cost in Atlanta is $207 (or $138 for lodging and $69 for meals).[6] Figure 10-5 shows the percentage breakdown of U.S. per diem costs associated with lodging, meals and automobile expenses.

Undoubtedly, the most controversial of all expense categories are *entertainment* and *gifts.* The prevailing practice seems to be to allow all necessary and reasonable entertainment expenses. There may be limits in the form of per person maximums on allowable items, such as meals and theater tickets. Or the entertainment may be restricted to taking a client out to a meal, which is the most popular method of entertainment.

The advent of the 50 percent IRS limit on the deductibility of entertainment expenses has dampened management's enthusiasm for entertaining. Additionally, the soaring costs of entertainment have made most companies reappraise their entertainment policies. Giving business gifts is a long-standing practice, but limits on the tax deductibility of business gifts have altered the gift-giving practices of many companies. Surveys show opinions divided on gift giving. Some firms do it because they like to. Other organizations would like to end the practice but feel they would suffer competitively. Many firms limit their gifts to the holiday season. Also, some organizations do not allow their buyers to accept any gifts—even small ones. For examples, Wal-Mart strictly forbids its buyers to accept a gift—even a can of Coke—from any salesperson.[7]

FIGURE 10-5
U.S. Salesperson per diem costs
SOURCE: *Sales & Marketing Management,* April 2001, p. 11

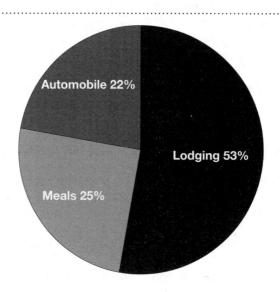

Reduction in Travel Expense

Adam Dark had just finished reading a memo from the president's office, instructing all branch managers to reduce their travel and entertainment (T&E) expenses. No percentage reductions were specified, nor were the sales managers given any details as to how reductions were to be achieved. Adam realized that his sales force actually had above average T&E expenses in the past few years, and so he felt that he was being called out to some extent. His biggest worry was how he might cut these costs without unduly hurting the morale of his account managers.

Dark knew that many other companies were struggling with this same cost-reduction problem. In fact, he was just talking to one of his customers about this. The customer firm formerly provided first-class air transportation for their employees who traveled, but a new policy required everyone (executives included) to fly economy class. However, this tactic would not help the Shiderlots situation as Dark's account managers did not have to fly to visit their Columbus-area clients—they drove.

Dark looked over the most recent month's list of expenses. The number one expense was related to automobiles. There were also significant expenses associated with (1) taking clients out to restaurants—and these were *very nice* restaurants, and (2) taking clients to various Columbus-area sporting events, including several Columbus Bluejackets hockey games. Although there were no golf outings on the list, he knew that the greens fees would start to show up as soon as springtime arrived.

Dark knew that he did not have a choice in the matter. He would be in big trouble with the home office if he did nothing about this. He just did not know what to do.

Questions: What are three specific actions that Dark could take to reduce T&E expenses with his account managers? How might he introduce these ideas in a way that doesn't damage his account managers' morale?

RUNNING CASE
Shidcrlots
Elevators, Inc.

CHARACTERISTICS OF A SOUND EXPENSE PLAN

A well-conceived and well-executed expense plan has certain general characteristics. Naturally, no perfect plan exists. Every plan has inherent limitations.

No Net Gain or Loss for the Reps

The expense plan should be designed so that employees neither profit nor lose. A sales rep should net the same income working on the road as at home—an ideal difficult to achieve in practice.

Some firms give sales reps expense allowances in lieu of compensation. Employees often prefer an increase in a nontaxable expense account to a raise in taxable salary or commissions. However, this practice is unwise for at least two reasons. First, it tends to nullify the control feature of a good compensation plan. Second, it encourages people to violate tax laws. An expense account is nontaxable only to the extent that it reimburses the employee for legitimate business expenses. If a salesperson receives reimbursement for bogus expenses, that reimbursement should be treated as income and taxed.

Equitable Treatment of the Reps

Sales reps should be able to maintain approximately the same standard of living on the road as at home. They should not have to sacrifice comfort to stay within expense limits. To ensure equitable treatment, sales managers should recognize differences in travel expenses among the different territories. Costs may be higher in an Atlantic Seaboard territory than in the Great Plains, for example.

No Curtailment of Beneficial Activities

A good expense plan should not hamper the performance of selling duties, nor should it curtail activities beneficial to the company. A plan that attempts to set selling expenses as a percentage of sales may discourage a rep from developing a new territory. If all expenses are limited to 1 percent of sales, for instance, no one would be eager to go into new territories, where expenses often are abnormally high in relation to early volume.

Minimal Detail and Administrative Expense

A sound expense control plan should be simple and economical to administer. Clerical and administrative expenses should be minimized. Often, expense reports either require too much unnecessary detail or duplicate information requested elsewhere.

Clarity

A good expense plan should be clear enough to prevent misunderstandings between management and the sales force. One way for managers to reach this goal is to consult the sales force when establishing or revising an expense-control plan. Management should explain the plan to the sales force in detail and in writing before putting it into effect. The plan should be especially clear about the timing of reimbursement. The company should pay promptly or, better yet, make an advance payment available to those who need it.

Company Control of Expenses and Elimination of Padding

A good plan controls expenses and curtails padding. However, *control* is not synonymous with *stinginess.* A sales manager should be able to get all the benefits of control without damaging sales force morale by adopting a Scrooge-like approach.

Expense account padding is a prevalent problem most sales managers face at one time or another. In fact, experts say that the typical company loses 5 percent of its annual revenue due to fraud and abuse by employees, and that 15 percent of this loss is due to expense account padding.[8] This adds up to millions of dollars in annual losses for the typical Fortune 500 company.

Padding is often a *symptom* of a problem in another area. Managers' good judgment in other areas will prevent salespeople from abusing their expense accounts. Recognition of achievement, a good training program, and an adequate compensation plan are practices that help eliminate expense account padding.

METHODS OF CONTROLLING EXPENSES

First, management must decide whether the company will pay for sales reps' field-selling costs or have the reps pay their own expenses out of their earnings. Almost all firms pay for travel and business expenses if salary is an element in the compensation plan. If the salespeople pay all their own expenses, chances are that they are compensated by the straight commission method.

Salespeople Pay Own Expenses

Salespeople who are compensated by straight commission often pay their own selling expenses. Management usually figures into the commission a certain percentage of sales for the field sales expense. It offers the total commission amount to the sales rep and says, in effect, "What's left over after you pay your costs is yours." The main reason for this is that some people paid a straight commission might be tempted to cheat on an expense account during periods of lean sales. Also, from management's standpoint, the plan is simple and costs nothing to operate.

There are also at least two reasons that a salesperson might prefer to pay his or her own expenses. First, such a plan offers freedom of operation—they don't have to explain their expenses to management. Second, many reps gain income tax advantages when paying their own expenses. They can deduct more expenses than if their earnings and expenses are separated by the company.

When salespeople pay their own expenses, however, the results may not be what management wants. A company loses considerable control over the activities of the sales force. For example, salespeople are not likely to travel long distances to call on and entertain prospective new accounts who do not offer immediate sales potential.

Unlimited-Payment Plans

The most widely used method of expense control is the **unlimited-payment plan**, in which the company reimburses salespeople for all legitimate business and travel costs they incur while on company business. There is no limit on total expenses or individual items, but salespeople are required to submit itemized accounts of their expenditures.

The main advantage of the unlimited-payment method of expense control is its flexibility. Cost differentials between territories, jobs, or products present few problems under this plan. Flexibility also makes the plan fair for both salespeople and management, assuming that reps report their expenditures honestly and accurately. Furthermore, this plan gives management considerable control over the salespeople's activities. If sales executives want a new territory developed or new accounts called on in out-of-the-way places, the expense plan is no deterrent.

However, an unlimited-payment plan may not allow management to accurately forecast its direct selling costs. The unlimited feature is an open invitation for some people to be extravagant or to pad their expense account with unjustifiable items. The plan offers no incentive for a salesperson to economize.

It is debatable whether the unlimited-payment method leads to more or fewer disputes between management and the sales force other than expense-control systems. The unlimited feature should reduce the number of disagreements, but friction may arise if management questions items on the expense reports. Probably a manager's greatest need in an unlimited-payment plan is to establish a successful method of controlling the expenses. Certainly a sales manager should analyze the expense reports to determine what is reasonable and practicable.

Limited-Payment Plans

A **limited-payment plan** may take either of two forms. In one form, the plan places a limit on the amount to be reimbursed *for each expense item.* For example, a company may pay a maximum of $140 per day for lodging and $51 for meals and incidental expenses (M&IE), the latter of which is broken down into $11 for breakfast, $12 for lunch, $23 for dinner, and $5 for incidental expenses (incidental expenses include fees and tips given to porters, baggage carriers, and hotel staff). In the other form, the plan provides a *flat sum for a period of time,* such as a day or week. One company may allow $180 a day; another firm may set its flat sum at $900 a week. Management typically—though not always—sets different limits for each salesperson to account for territorial cost differentials. After all, it is much more expensive to travel in New York City than in Fort Wayne, Indiana.

Setting limits on expense payments has some advantages. Limited-payment plans are especially suitable when salespeople's activities are routine and travel routes are repetitive. Then the expenses can be more accurately forecast. These maximum expense forecasts then aid in budget planning. Also, knowing in advance what the limits are should reduce expense-account disputes between management and the sales force, particularly if both sides perceive the limits to be fair.

The sales manager's major problem in administering a limited-payment plan probably is establishing the limits for each item or time period. Management may study past reports to determine the mileage salespeople typically cover each day. It may examine hotel directories to establish limits on lodging. A separate study should be conducted for each territory to ensure that the plan reflects regional cost differentials. Also, management should monitor the program to ensure that the limits reflect a territory's current structure. Salespeople should be included in these various deliberations, because limited-pay plans are good only if the sales force believes the limits are equitable.

Companies typically encounter several other problems in limited payment plans. High-caliber salespeople may object to limits on expenses because they feel that the company does not trust them. Also, the system can be inflexible. A salesperson may have some unusual expense, such as an entertainment item he or she could not escape without losing the account. If entertainment is not an allowable expense, the salesperson may not be reimbursed. Some companies avoid such inflexibility by allowing these unusual expenses if they are reported separately with an explanatory note.

When management sets limits for each item, the plan may be hard to control. Reps may switch expenditures among expense items—that is, they may attempt to recoup money spent in excess of the limit for one item by padding the claim for some other item. Also, the plan cannot prevent a cheater from economizing on some expenses and then padding the account up to allowable limits.

Combination Plans

The advantages of both the limited and unlimited plans can sometimes be realized by developing a control method that combines the two. Management may set limits on items such as food and lodging, for example, but place no ceiling on transportation. Another combination method is an **expense-quota plan.** Under this system, management sets a limit on the total allowable expense, but the ceiling is related to some other item on the operating statement, such as net sales. For example, a quota of $2,000 may be set for a month because monthly sales are expected to be $40,000. Expenses can be tied to sales even more directly by allowing salespeople a monthly expense account not to exceed 5 percent of their net sales. The compensation plan can play some part in this expense-control system by paying a bonus if the rep keeps expenses at an amount under quota.

Expense-quota plans do have the advantage of enabling management to relate sales force expenses to net sales. In this method, management has some control over this direct selling cost. Furthermore, the reps have some operating flexibility within the total expense budget. Reps who have been made expense-conscious are not likely to be wasteful.

CONTROL OF SALES FORCE TRANSPORTATION

One significant selling expense with little room for discretion is the cost of transportation. Transportation expense decisions are usually clear-cut because they are based on the costs and the nature of the selling environment. The salesperson who covers Manhattan might prefer to use taxis or the subway over an automobile. However, in Los Angeles, an automobile is a must. The situation

CONSIDER THIS...

Expense Report Abuse— What to Watch For

Sales managers are often responsible for analyzing the expense receipts submitted by their salespeople. This is an important responsibility. Not only can it save the company significant amounts of money on travel and entertainment expenses, it sets the tone for ethical behavior for the employees of the company.

There are many ways that salespeople can cheat on their expense plans. Here are four common schemes that managers should look out for:

1. Double billing (e.g., submitting a duplicate receipt one month after ini-

tial reimbursement)

2. Mischaracterizing an expense item that is not allowed under company rules (e.g., hiding alcohol on a receipt when the company has a no alcohol for lunch policy)

3. When exceeding the limit on a single item, salespeople sometimes split the item up into two parts (so that the smaller items fall under the allowable limit).

4. Inflating a bona fide expense (e.g., adding tips that were never paid)

SOURCE: Tracy Coenen, "Expense Report Abuse: Much Ado about Nothing?" *Fraud Files Forensic Accounting Blog*, April 17, 2015. Retrieved from the following URL on June 29, 2016: http://www.sequenceinc.com/fraudfiles/2015/04/expense-report-abuse-much-ado-about-nothing/

largely dictates the transportation required. Some aspects of this are open to managerial control.

Every year, the Internal Revenue Service issues the standard mileage rates. This is the rate that can be used to calculate the deductible costs of operating a vehicle, but also is typically the amount that salespeople who own their own car are reimbursed. The most recent standard mileage rate is 54 cents per mile.[9] As shown in the graphic entitled "IRS Standard Mileage Rates," this rate has fluctuated a fair amount over the past ten years due to varying fuel costs and other factors.

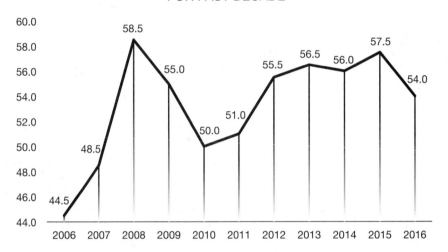

IRS STANDARD MILEAGE RATES
FOR PAST DECADE

Ownership or Leasing of Automobiles

Since most sales travel is done by automobile, a car has become almost standard equipment. Management may provide company-owned cars or leased vehicles, or salespeople may use their own cars. No one policy for car ownership is best under all conditions. The final decision rests on a consideration of the following factors:

- Size of the sales force. With a small sales force, a company achieves simplicity and economy either by having salespeople use their own cars or by leasing cars for them. Only when its sales force is large does a company generally find it advantageous to own the cars.
- Availability of centralized maintenance and storage facilities. If a company maintains centralized vehicle storage and repair facilities, it is in a good position to furnish the sales force with cars.
- Unusual design required. Some companies require that the cars used by their salespeople be a special color, have a specially constructed body, or carry some form of company advertising. Sometimes the vehicle must double as a sales car and a delivery truck. In these situations, the company should furnish the cars.
- Control of car's operating condition. If the company furnishes the car, management is in a better position to demand that it be kept presentable.

The company probably can provide cars that are newer than the average salesperson's own car. However, salespeople may take better care of their own cars than they do of company-owned or leased vehicles.

- Personal preferences. Some people are financially able and willing to furnish their own cars for work. When salespeople *must* provide the cars, however, management runs the risk of losing good applicants. Some reps may not want to drive their own cars for company business, or they may not have suitable cars.

- Annual mileage. A salesperson's average annual mileage influences the automobile ownership decision. The more miles driven, the more advantageous it becomes for the company to own the cars. The point of indifference varies depending on the cars used and the company's auto-expense allowances. Suppose the company pays a flat 50 cents per mile auto allowance and that management has calculated the cost of owning the preferred model to be $6,000 a year, plus 20 cents a mile. Under these circumstances, the point of indifference would be 20,000 miles. If salespeople covered less than this mileage, management would probably encourage them to own the cars.

- Operating cost. It is hard to say definitely which of the three alternatives—employee-owned, company-owned, or company-leased—offers the lowest operating cost. It depends to a great extent on rental costs, number of miles driven, and method of reimbursing the sales force. It also is difficult to measure some indirect costs of company ownership, such as the administrative expense of operating the system.

- Investments. If the company is not in a strong financial position or does not want to make the investment, it can lease cars or have the salespeople provide their own.

- Administrative problems. One major administrative question that comes up when the company furnishes cars is whether they should be available for the salesperson's personal use and, if so, to what extent. Most companies allow salespeople to use company cars for personal transportation. Management may or may not suggest some limits. If a company adopts a no-limit policy, reps may choose not to buy their own cars, or they may use the company car as a second family car.

   Use of a company car for private purposes is another indirect monetary payment, the same as group insurance or a paid vacation. Some businesses ask the rep to pay for the gas when driving the car for personal use. Others pay all expenses for both business and private use. Some ask that operating expenses be paid only on long personal trips such as vacations.

Leasing—as opposed to owning or buying—is the easiest way for a company to put its sales force on wheels, and has become increasingly popular in recent years. The sales executive does not have to be a transportation expert, and the firm avoids the problems of buying the car, maintaining it, and later reselling it. Leasing especially makes financial sense when the company wants to turn over the cars frequently (i.e., every year or two). [10]

Reimbursement Plans for Employee-Owned Cars

Salespeople who use their own cars on company business are often reimbursed for the cost. Three separate types of expenditures are involved in owning and operating a car. One type is *variable costs*, which are generally related directly to the number of miles driven. Examples of variable-cost items are gasoline, oil changes, tires, and normal service maintenance. A second class of expenditures is *fixed costs*, which tend to be related to time rather than miles driven. Fixed costs include depreciation, license fees, and insurance. The third group, *miscellaneous expenses*, is difficult to standardize. Typical items are tolls, parking, and major repairs. Usually miscellaneous costs are not incorporated into one of the ordinary automobile expense-control plans. These items are listed separately on the expense account.

Salespeople may be reimbursed for using their cars on company business by some kind of a fixed-allowance plan or by a flexible-payment method.

Fixed-Allowance Plans

The **fixed-allowance plan** may be based on either mileage or time. Under mileage, the employee is paid the same amount for each mile driven on company business. The flat rate per mile is used by more companies than any other major plan, although there is a trend toward more flexible methods. Under the other type of fixed-allowance plan, a flat sum is paid for each period of time, such as a week or a month, regardless of the number of miles driven. The reimbursements cover both fixed and variable automobile costs.

Fixed-allowance plans have several advantages. They are generally simple and economical to administer. Salespeople know in advance what they will be paid. Also, if payment is based on a flat allowance for a given period of time, the company can budget this expense in advance. People who drive few miles (5,000-10,000 per year) prefer it because they can generally make money under such a plan.

The criticisms of fixed-allowance plans are so severe, however, that we wonder why they remain popular. Generally speaking, the plans are inflexible and may be unfair—some salespeople may benefit, while others lose. The fixed sum for a given time period can be reasonably good only if everyone travels in a routine fashion and costs are the same in each territory. Similarly, the flat-mileage allowance is equitable only if all reps travel about the same number of miles in the same type of cars under the same operating conditions. These conditions are highly unlikely and unrealistic.

Consider the inequities introduced, for example, by variations in the number of miles driven. In the operation of a car, some costs are fixed regardless of the number of miles driven. Therefore, the greater amount of driving, the more miles over which to amortize the fixed costs. In other words, the fixed costs per mile decrease as the total mileage increases. Under a fixed allowance per mile, every additional mile works to the financial benefit of the salespeople. An example is outlined in Figure 10-6. Assuming annual fixed costs of $8,000, variable costs of 25 cents per mile, and a mileage allowance of 50 cents, the results are shown for various annual mileages. A salesperson who drives 10,000 miles per year receives $5,000, when the total costs are $10,500. Thus, the rep's earnings are reduced by $5,500 in this scenario. At the other extreme, a salesperson who drives 50,000 miles gets $25,000, which is a gain of $4,500 over his or her actual costs. If the salesperson were paid a fixed sum per month, similar inequities would result but in reverse. That is, a payment of $600 per month would benefit the low-mileage traveler at the expense of the person who drove many miles in a year.

Annual Mileage	Fixed Cost	Variable Costs at 25 Cents/Mile	Total Costs	Per-Mile Costs	Payment to Salesperson at 50 Cents/Mile	Gain or Loss to Salesperson
10,000	$8,000	$2,500	$10,500	$1.05	$5,000	-$5,500
20,000	$8,000	$5,000	$13,000	$0.65	$10,000	-$3,000
30,000	$8,000	$7,500	$15,500	$0.52	$15,000	-$500
40,000	$8,000	$10,000	$18,000	$0.45	$20,000	$2,000
50,000	$8,000	$12,500	$20,500	$0.41	$25,000	$4,500

FIGURE 10-6

Example of Results of Flat-Rate-Per Mile Plan under Varying Mileages

Flexible-Allowance Plans

To avoid the inherent weaknesses in a fixed-allowance system, companies have developed several **flexible-allowance plans.**

A *graduated-mileage* rate plan pays a different allowance per mile depending on the total miles driven in a time period. For example, one firm might pay 50 cents a mile for the first 15,000 miles driven in a year and 30 cents for every mile over 15,000. Mileage allowances are graduated downward to reflect the fact that total costs per mile decrease as mileage goes up. Although a graduated plan corrects some of the faults of a flat-rate method, it usually does not consider differences in territorial costs and types of cars.

Under a plan that *combines an allowance per time period with a mileage rate,* management figures automobile allowances in two parts. Thus, the differences between fixed and variable costs of owning and operating a car are reflected in the payment. To cover fixed costs, the company makes a flat payment for each given time period, such as a week or a month. In addition, variable costs are reimbursed by mileage allowances, which usually are flat rates although they could be graduated. For example, one company pays $600 a month plus 30 cents a mile; another pays $450 a month plus 30 cents a mile over 750 miles a month.

A widely recognized and respected plan was developed by the founder of Runzheimer International, which is a company that can be hired to manage a company's automobile reimbursement program. In one of its programs, Runzheimer divides the United States into several geographic regions and then computes the total annual costs, which include ownership and operating expenses for cars in each of these regions. As an example, Figure 10-7 shows the cost allowances for a midsized car in St. Louis, Missouri.

In some respects, the **Runzheimer plan** gives the same results as the graduated mileage system in that the more miles driven, the smaller the per-mile allowance. However, this plan is much more accurate because payments reflect variations in types of cars, miles driven, and territorial operating costs. In an analysis of a midsized car, for instance, the annual fixed costs were estimated to be $11,114 in Detroit, but only $7,131 in Sioux Falls, South Dakota. Note that Runzheimer has utilized mobile technology and created an app that makes it easy for salespeople to keep track of their automobile mileage. Overall, this plan seems to be the most equitable and accurate method available for paying salespeople for the use of their cars.

Annual Fixed Costs		
1.	Annual vehicle costs	$8,600
2.	Insurance	1,800
3.	License and registration	150
4.	Personal and property tax	398
5.	Total fixed costs	10,948
6.	71.4% of fixed costs	7,816
Operating Costs per Mile		
7.	Miles per gallon	23
8.	Fuel price per gallon	$2.118
9.	Fuel and oil per mile	$0.102
10.	Maintenance per mile	$0.062
11.	Tires per mile	$0.020
Standard Cost Reimbursement		
A.	Fixed cost per month	$651.33
B.	Operating cost per mile	$0.184

SOURCE: Runzheimer International website: www.runzheimer.com

OTHER METHODS OF EXPENSE CONTROL

Selling costs loom large in the expenses of most firms. Of course, salespeople's compensation is the largest selling cost, but the cost of travel and entertainment can also be very significant. Following are a few ways of controlling these travel and entertainment expenses.

Training and Enforcement

Right from the start, management should teach salespeople how the company expects them to spend its money. Any violators of company expense policy should be subject to immediate reprimand or something stronger. Otherwise, the sales force will assume that management will overlook expense account abuse.

Some firms make it quite clear from the beginning that expense account fraud will be a basis for dismissal. Moreover, these firms include a section in their job performance evaluations appraising how wisely a salesperson spends company money. A salesperson who wants a position in management should develop a reputation as an honest person who is careful with company money. Management may tolerate some character flaws in its people, but dishonesty is not one of them.

Credit Cards

Many firms use credit cards to control various expense items. For example, Fastenal provides its salespeople with a company fuel card for gasoline. By accepting credit card charges only from a designated list of hotels and restaurants, for example, a company can control where its salespeople sleep and eat. Also, salespeople who use company credit cards need to carry less money when they travel, thus reducing the risk of loss or theft.

The Expense Bank Account

In some instances, companies place an undue burden on representatives who have to pay their expenses and then wait for reimbursement. Salespeople may have to finance three or four weeks of expenses—that is, $2,000 to $4,000. To avoid this, some firms place a certain sum, say $2,000, in a checking account for each member of the sales force. Expenses of each salesperson are then drawn from that accounts. When the account needs replenishment, or at regular intervals, the salesperson files an expense report. Upon approval of the report, the company deposits enough in the checking account to bring it back up to the initial sum.

Change in Nature of Entertainment

The costs of entertaining customers have skyrocketed to ridiculous levels in many areas. It is easy to spend over $1,000 entertaining a client for one evening in New York or Los Angeles.

Consequently, home entertainment, quiet dinners, or small parties offer attractive alternatives to the manager or salesperson seeking lower entertainment costs. The salesperson will include out-of-pocket costs directly associated with the party in the normal expense account. Some firms have simply stopped taking clients to Broadway shows or treating them to an expensive night on the town.

Related to this, the insurance industry has become especially competitive as new online companies, such as Progressive and Geico, have been successful with a model that involves no face-to-face interaction with customers. Consequently, traditional companies, like State Farm and Liberty Mutual, have been forced to cut back on travel and entertainment expenses for its salespeople.[11]

Telemarketing/Email

High travel and entertainment costs have led many firms to move more toward interacting with their customers by phone and/or email. Of course, this type of communication is not as personal, but it is much, much less expensive.

Along the same lines, salespeople are increasingly pushing their smaller customers to make purchases through the company's website because the transaction costs are lower. Both buyer and seller can benefit because many buyers would much rather spend a few minutes placing an order on the internet or over the phone than waiting to meet with their sales rep or listening to a sales pitch by an account manager. Both parties seek transactional efficiency.

Careful Travel Planning

Many large companies have a travel manager whose job it is to minimize travel expenses by careful advanced planning. With the help of a travel manager, salespeople and their managers can coordinate their routes to accomplish as much business as possible on each trip, and to reduce travel costs.

Some firms whose people must travel extensively by air have developed in-hour travel agencies to help lower travel costs. These firms also carefully study the costs of flying from different airports under different conditions. Prices vary greatly, even from day to day, depending on when one travels, how far in advance reservations are made, how long the traveler stays, which airline and route are selected, and what the competitive situation is at the time.

Some firms also have established the position of *fleet manager*, whose responsibility it is to purchase cars, fuel, and maintenance services. Other companies outsource their fleet management. Runzheimer International (discussed previously in this chapter) and Element Financial are examples of companies that provide this service.

SUMMARY

A sales quota is a sales performance goal. It serves such purposes as (1) indicating strong and weak spots in a company's selling structure; (2) furnishing a goal and an incentive for the sales force; (3) improving the effectiveness of compensation plans; (4) controlling selling expenses; and (5) evaluating sales contest results.

Sales volume (in dollars and in product units) is the most frequently used basis for setting quotas. Other commonly used bases are gross margin, net profit, contribution to profit, selling expenses, selling activities, customer satisfaction, or some combination of these.

There are several common ways of setting quotas. One is to base them on territory potential; another is to base them on past sales. Sometimes they are set without any direct relationship to potential or past sales, such as using executive judgment or compensation design considerations, or even by letting the salespeople set their own.

The handling and control of expense accounts is one of the most sensitive areas in sales management. Expense accounts are strictly regulated by the Internal Revenue Service, which stipulates in some detail what is and is not tax deductible. Management should identify in writing, and in detail, what expenses it will cover for salespeople. Normally, salespeople are reimbursed for their business expenses plus some personal costs that would not have been necessary if they were at home. A sound expense plan should be simple to administer, neither enrich nor impoverish the salespeople, and control the level of selling expenses.

Management must decide if the company will pay for the sales force's field-selling costs or if the salespeople should pay their own expenses. Salespeople working on straight commission often pay their own expenses. Under any other compensation plan, however, the company should pay the salespeople's expenses as an item separate from the compensation plan.

In the most widely used expense-control plan—the unlimited-payment plan—salespeople are reimbursed for all legitimate expenses, but they must itemize expenses and document certain large expenditures. Under a limited-payment plan, management either sets limits for certain items (such as food, lodging, and entertainment) or else provides a fixed total allowance for some time period.

A company should develop a plan for controlling the sales force's transportation costs. When salespeople travel by car, management must decide whether to own or lease the cars, or to have the salespeople use their own cars. If the salespeople use their own cars, the company should formulate a program to reimburse them. Often some form of fixed allowance per mile or per time period is used. However, the preferred method is to develop some system of flexible allowances that considers the variation in the miles each salesperson drives and the costs of driving a car in the particular location.

The greatly increased costs of travel and entertainment have encouraged most companies to attack such expenses aggressively by several means. In many cases, entertainment has been curtailed, and sales managers have found less expensive ways for their salespeople to interact with customers. Travel plans are now more carefully monitored to limit costs than was previously the case.

Finally, given that travel and entertainment expenses are such large expenses, sales executives have recommended changes in the nature of entertainment and used the following to better control these costs: training and enforcement, credit cards, expense bank accounts, telemarketing, and careful travel planning.

KEY TERMS

Activity quota
Contribution margin
Expense-quota plan
Fixed-allowance plan
Flexible-allowance plans
Limited-payment plan
Per diem cost
Profit quota
Runzheimer plan
Sales quota
Unlimited-payment plan
Volume quota

QUESTIONS AND PROBLEMS

1. Should quotas be used in each of the following cases? If so, what type of quota do you recommend and what should be the length of the quota period?
   a. Missionary salesperson for a candy bar manufacturer
   b. Salesperson for manufacturer of industrial central heating and air-conditioning units.
   c. Salesperson for manufacturer of room air conditioners for home
2. A luggage manufacturer uses volume quotas for its sales force.
   a. What effective measures may this firm use to encourage its salespeople to do non-selling tasks such as setting up dealing displays or prospecting for new accounts?
   b. How can the customers be protected against overstocking, high-pressure selling, and other similar activities by this manufacturer's sales force?
3. One apparel manufacturer established volume quotas for its salespeople. Last year's quota was 20 percent higher than it was ten years ago. The

sales force seemed perfectly happy with the new quota. Salespeople were paid a straight commission of 5 percent on net sales. Under what circumstances would this type of quota work?

4. "The expense-control plan should enable our representative to maintain (at no extra cost to them) the same standard of living while on the road that they enjoy at home," said the sales manager of a metals products manufacturer. Discuss the implications of this statement.

5. What factors should management consider when deciding what method to use for controlling and reimbursing salespeople's expenses? Give some examples of how each factor might influence the decision.

6. A company's dire need of a replacement part had shut down its production line. A salesperson in the supplier's office was told to deliver the part as quickly as possible. She did so in record time, but in the process she received a ticket for speeding. On her expense account, the rep applied for reimbursement of the $150 fine. As her sales manager (who approves her expenses), what would you do?

7. A petroleum firm with a sales force of 300 people planned to sell its fleet of company-owned cars and have the salespeople furnish their own cars instead. What problems are involved in this change?

8. The petroleum firm noted in Question 7 was trying to decide which method to use to reimburse the salespeople for the use of their cars on business. Each rep traveled about 15,000 miles a year. The company was computing the costs on the assumption that they all drive midsized cars. The following payment methods were under consideration. What would be the total annual cost to the firm under each of the three proposals?

    a. A straight 50 cents a mile

    b. $300 a month plus 18 cents a mile

    c. The Runzheimer plan (see Figure 10-7). Assume that the 300 salespeople were evenly divided among territories based around Detroit and St. Louis.

9. In lieu of a salary increase last year, a television manufacturer granted its sales force the privilege of using company cars for any personal purposes, and the company paid all expenses. Previously, the firm had strictly prohibited any personal use of these cars. Discuss all aspects of this policy decision.

10. A publishing company was considering leasing small Chevrolet or Dodge cars instead of paying its present 50 cents per mile to salespeople for using their personal cars. Several of the salespeople were driving economy cars and were willing to take less than 50 cents per mile in order to keep from changing cars. What should the company do?

11. The major U.S. airlines have frequent-flyer plans, which offer awards (free flights or upgraded seat) after a person has accumulated a certain number of miles flying on a given airline. In the case of salespeople who accumulate miles on business travel, who should get these awards—the salespeople who did the traveling or their companies who paid for the trips? If you give the awards to the salespeople, should the awards be considered taxable income to them?

EXPERIENTIAL EXERCISES

1. Contact a local car dealer to compare the costs of leasing or buying a fleet of 10 cars. Assume that the cars will be midsize American cars and that the salespeople will average 30,000 miles per year.

2. Contact sales managers from five different companies. Ask them to explain how they establish sales quotas; and discuss what they like and do not like about their quota system.

3. Contact sales managers from five different companies. Ask them to explain the expense reimbursement plan for their salespeople. Discuss what they like and do not like about this plan

ANGELINA FASHIONS
Proposed Change in Expense Plan

Ms. Hartman, sales manager of Angelina Fashions, had been requested by Mr. Marshall, president, to review the firm's method of handling salespeople's expense accounts. Mr. Marshall had voiced the opinion that the company was being overly generous to its sales force without any valid reason.

Angelina Fashions was founded in 1992 by Mr. Marshall for the purpose of manufacturing and distributing a relatively small line of high-styled, expensive, women's coats, jackets, and suits. By virtue of having some rather talented designers, the company had grown rapidly to become a $20 million (in annual sales) company. The product was sold directly to exclusive women's clothing boutiques by 10 highly experienced salespeople. Since it was necessary in the initial stages of the business to keep selling expenses in line with sales volume, the firm had adopted the policy of paying a flat 6 percent commission on all sales, with the salespeople paying all of their own expenses. So, on average, the annual compensation was $120,000 per salesperson.

This combination compensation-expense plan had proved to be highly satisfactory to both the company and the salespeople in the past. For instance, Matt Walker, sales representative in the southeastern states, was an enthusiastic support of the plan. He said, "It's the only way to sell. I really watch my expenses this way and what I don't spend is mine."

In recent years, however, Mr. Marshall had become increasingly bothered by the dollar amount of selling expenses. Because there were ten salespeople, total dollar selling costs last year were about $1,200,000 (or 6 percent of company sales revenue). From his knowledge of what the salespeople actually spent for expenses in the field, Mr. Marshall knew that their take-home pay was substantial. He knew that Matt Walker's

actual expenses would run approximately $32,000 a year $11,200 for transportation and $20,800 for field living costs. This meant that Mr. Walker was easily taking home a minimum of $88,000. He wondered if the company would be better off if it lowered the commission rate paid to the salespeople and assumed responsibility for all expenses. He asked Ms. Hartman to study the situation and prepare recommendations on it.

Ms. Hartman had sounded out the sales force regarding the idea of the company's assuming responsibility for expenses and had found that the entire sales force was strongly opposed to the idea. Ms. Hartman liked the present system since it was easy to administer; she was not bothered by having to audit or handle expense accounts. In addition, Ms. Hartman enjoyed managing a sales force with high morale. She did not want to do anything that would possibly disturb the rather easy position she now had. She fully realized that at present her sales force required practically no management at all. About the only contact she had with them was the two conventions each year at which the new season's lines were introduced. Other than that, the salespeople completely managed themselves and were all performing excellently. Turnover had been nonexistent; the company had not lost a single salesperson since it started. On the other hand, Ms. Hartman realized that Mr. Marshall was an extremely dominant and aggressive individual whose ideas and opinions were not to be put aside lightly.

Hence, Ms. Hartman had formulated three alternative plans for handling compensation and expenses:

1. Plan number one consisted of reducing the commission rate to 4 percent on sales volume with the company paying all expenses.

2. Plan number two consisted of reducing the commission rate to 3 percent plus a bonus

of 1 percent of all sales upon attainment of a sales volume quota set at $2,000,000 for the year. The firm would pay all expenses.

3. Plan number three provided for a $40,000 annual salary for each salesperson, plus a 5 percent commission on all sales over $1,200,000. Again, the firm would pay all expenses.

When Mr. Marshall saw these plans, he objected strongly, because he felt that some form of limited expense accounts would be necessary; otherwise the salespeople would merely pad their expenses to make up for the reduced compensation.

Mr. Marshall suggested that plan 3 could be adopted with the following changes: a 4 percent commission rate on sales over $1,200,000; plus, a flat-sum expense account of $20,000 per year per person.

Ms. Hartman knew that the sales force would not be happy with any of the proposals, but they would be particularly incensed by the fixed-expense plan. Further, she knew that the salespeople gained some tax advantages from the present system and that they would not look kindly upon having those advantages discontinued.

Questions:

1. What would the typical salesperson earn in total compensation under the four plans being proposed?

2. Which of these four plans makes the most sense for Angelina Fashions? Explain your answer.

3. Create your own compensation plan that you think would be best. Be sure to include a recommendation for how to handle expenses.

4. How would you approach Mr. Marshall to convince him to go with your own (the best) plan?

PAN PACIFIC TRADING COMPANY
Expense Account Auditing Policy

Kate Cook, sales manager for Pan Pacific Trading Company, wondered what was bothering Larry Cheng, the company's controller. He had asked for a meeting with her concerning sales department expense accounts.

The Pan Pacific Trading Company of San Francisco imported a wide range of consumer products, gift items, apparel, and jewelry from the Pacific Rim nations. Its customers were department stores, gift shops, chain specialty stores, and any other merchant who found the goods attractive. The company's product policies had been most aggressive. It would import anything that management felt would make a good profit. Some of the items defied classification. One profitable item for the Christmas season was a novelty from Taiwan—a plastic flower that danced to music.

Since the markets for the firm's imports were so diverse, the company had to encourage buyers for smaller operations to come to Pan Pacific's sales offices. Consequently, the company maintained sales offices at the home office in San Francisco and at the major marts in such cities as New York, Chicago, Dallas, Los Angeles, and Atlanta. Each office was under the direction of a regional sales manager who had the major responsibility of developing that regions' markets. The regional managers were paid a modest salary supplemented with a strong incentive system of bonuses that resulted in average earnings in excess of $150,000 a year. Each sales office also had an in-house salesperson who kept the office open each day. There were usually two or three other salespeople who worked large accounts in addition to the regional manager.

Everyone was in the office on "market days." While the apparel trades held a few market weeks during the year, usually six, the gift trades were different. For example, in Dallas, every Friday was market day for gift buyers. In addition, several well-attended gift market weeks were held each year. Moreover, the daily traffic that stopped by the sales offices was surprisingly large. Many different merchants who sold the kind of things imported by the company visited the sales offices.

Larry Cheng had requested a two o'clock meeting, and Kate Cook noted that he was prompt as usual. He marched into her office with his large brown attaché case firmly in hand. After the perfunctory greetings, he asked, "Can I spread my papers on your table?" Cook nodded while wondering what this was all about. She resented Cheng's failure to tell her the subject of the meeting. Cook had nearly said so when Cheng made the appointment, but she had decided she would be better off not knowing what was to be discussed. That way, she could always stall and divert Cheng by saying, "Hey, you just sprung this on me. I'll need some time to study it." Cook took pride in her tactical skills, which had served her well as she rose in the company.

Cheng began, "I don't know where to start. Your sales department expense accounts are not only way out of line, but they're illegal. If the IRS audits us, they'll disallow a lot of your expenses. And I mean yours and your department's."

Cook interrupted, "Does Mr. Tsai know of this meeting and your concern with our expense accounts?" Tsai was the founder and president of the company. Cook wanted to discover Cheng's power base and find out how much cloud he was carrying in his crusade for lower and cleaner expense accounts. This was not a new issue with him. Cook and Cheng had this same conversation every year near tax time.

Cheng answered, "No, this is my area of responsibility. I don't run to the boss every time there's a problem. You know he doesn't want to hear about our problems. He only wants to hear about our solutions to them."

Cook knew that Tsai was not too sympathetic to Chang's close adherence to IRS code. When Cook had brought the expense account issues to Tsai before, he had told her, "In some ways, it is an advantage to have Cheng the way he is; it keeps us on our toes. He will make certain we know what we are doing. On the other hand, he may be of less use than he could be, because he does not believe in our cause. We'll wait and see if he becomes a problem." Cook then understood that Tsai would not appreciate any expense account problems being dumped into his lap. Thereafter she handled issues as they arose.

"Come on, Larry, you're talking generalities. Get down to specifics. I can't make decisions on such generalities."

"There are so many specifics."

"I don't care how many there are. If you want me to do something about each one of them, you'll have to list them. Get me a document that itemizes each of your concerns so I can start to deal with them." Cook smiled to herself. She had just bought some time to think about the problems that would be on that list. She knew exactly the things that were bothering Cheng. She knew the law and IRS policy. She had even gone out of her way to take a seminar on handling expense account deductions for income tax purposes. She knew it was an important part of her job and she was not about to let any accountant push her anywhere she did not absolutely have to go.

Cook also understood the company's tax compliance philosophies. While Tsai insisted on absolute compliance with all laws of the lands in which the company did business, he also recognized that there were many gray areas in which the laws were subject to great differences of interpretation and administration. He saw no reason to penalize his company by attempting to interpret any law in favor of whatever government was involved. He pushed the law to the limit when necessary and then backed off or compromised if the government forced him to do so. Neither he nor Pan Pacific Trading had ever been charged with any misdeeds. He had told Cook, "Tax audits are inevitable. Count on them! Play the game as tough as you can, but keep good documentation. If a dispute arises, our professional people will settle it as best as they can depending on the documentation we provide them.

Cheng persisted, "Fine. You'll have your itemized list tomorrow. But now I want to tell you the areas that are going to cause us some real problems down the line. First, there's the matter of the cars that everyone drives and deducts. It is quite clear in the law that the government does not want to subsidize the driving of luxury cars. The IRS doesn't feel you need to be driving a Cadillac to do business. Now, you and all of the regional managers and sales reps are driving luxury cars, and the end result is that the company is paying for them. Get our automotive expense account policy within the law!"

Cook did not like Cheng's tone or attitude. She coolly replied, "What we do is not illegal. As I recall, when we began our present policy, no one questioned its legality." She wondered what was bothering Cheng so much about the cars they were driving. She really liked her BMW. Then she recalled that Cheng drove a Ford. She also realized that perhaps the biggest danger to the company in the matter was Cheng's attitude toward the company's policy. Just after Congress altered the tax code to limit the deductions for the depreciation of automobiles, the company changed its method for handling auto expenses. It started giving each sales manager and salesperson a flat expense allowance per year generous enough to allow them to drive luxury cars. She knew that several salespeople rented their cars. She did not know how they handled their tax treatment since such matters were the private, personal concern of each person. The allowance varied depending on the person and the territory. The New York allowance was much lower than the allowance for Los Angeles because the New York salesperson did not own a car. She either used public transportation or rented a car when needed. Cook was given a $15,000 annual allowance. It was treated as income and reported to the IRS on her W-2 form. She then had to take the deductions for its business use. She preferred this system, as did all the other managers and reps. Some members of top management had similar car allowances. Larry Cheng did not.

Cheng continued, "And then there is the matter of your entertainment costs. They are excessive. Any auditor will scream at some of your claims. The New York rep's last expense account claimed that she spent $950 entertaining one customer one evening in New York City. That's nonsense! And,

Kate, I didn't intend to say anything, but those expense reports of yours on that trip you and Ms. Tsai took to Japan . . . well."

Cook knew he was referring to that $4,500 meal they reported when they entertained several of their Japanese suppliers one evening at a fancy Tokyo restaurant on the Ginza. She said nothing about it to Cheng, however, because she knew she could beat him on that one if he even so much as mentioned it in the itemized list of grievances. Then Cheng launched into the subject of the limitations for entertainment in the tax code.

"We need to reexamine our attitudes toward entertainment now that we can only deduct 50 percent of its costs. We are now having to absorb half of our already outrageous entertainment expenses as nondeductible expenses."

Cook dismissed Cheng by saying, "I've got to run to a meeting now. I'm eager to see your list."

Questions:

1. How should Kate Cook handle this problem with Larry Cheng?

2. Is the company's auto expense policy in violation of the IRS code?

3. Evaluate Larry Cheng's concern with the seemingly high costs for entertainment. What would you do to avoid such high entertainment costs?

ENDNOTES

[1] Susan Greco, "What's a fair sales quota in 2010?" *Inc.com*, January 4, 2010. Retrieved from the following URL on June 30, 2016: http://www.inc.com/articles/2010/01/surepayroll-michael-alter-setting-fair-sales-quotas.html

[2] The Alexander Group, "2015 Sales Quotas Practices Survey," 2015, p. 4.

[3] John F. Yarbrough, "Walt Disney Company," in Geoffrey Brewer and Christine Galea, "The Top 25," *Sales & Marketing Management*, November 1996, p. 48.

[4] Eilene Simmerman, "Quota Busters," *Sales & Marketing Management*, January 2001, pp. 58-63.

[5] Ibid.

[6] Per diem rates obtained from the travel website of the United States General Services Administration (GSA): http://www.gsa.gov/portal/content/104877

[7] Walmart's statement of ethics found retrieved from the following URL on June 29, 2016: https://www.walmartethics.com/

[8] Liz Galst, "A Little Extra on the Road," *The New York Times*, November 16, 2010, p. B4.

[9] 2016 Standard Mileage Rates for Business, Medical and Moving Announced. This article is dated December 17, 2015, and was found on the IRS website at the following URL: https://www.irs.gov/uac/newsroom/2016-standard-mileage-rates-for-business-medical-and-moving-announced

[10] Jean Murray, "Leasing a Company Car for Business Use," *About.com blog*, February 29, 2016. Retrieved from the following URL on June 30, 2016: http://biztaxlaw.about.com/od/carleaseexpense/fl/Leasing-a-Company-Car-for-Business-Use.htm

[11] Beth Healy, "Amid high profits, Liberty Mutual cuts benefits," *Boston Globe*, August 27, 2013. Retrieved from the following URL on June 30, 2016: https://www.bostonglobe.com/business/2013/08/26/liberty-mutual-cuts-retiree-benefits-retirement-contributions-for-rank-and-file/XMSd5ORv6WFVaH2ZrTzJ8I/story.html

11

Leadership of a Sales Force

"Managers do things right, but leaders do the right thing," is a famous quote about leadership.[1] The job of sales managers is especially difficult because they must do both! That is, they must go back and forth between the little details of management and the big picture of leadership.[2]

This starts with having **vision**—in other words, a clear idea of where the sales force is going, and the ability to describe that idea in exciting terms so salespeople buy into it. In addition, good sales managers have high performance expectations for their salespeople, yet they also must inspire them to work together as a team to reach—and often surpass—those expectations. These sales managers are generally excellent role models, who lead by example. They are hard-working, honest individuals who genuinely care about the welfare of their subordinates. This creates an environment of mutual trust and respect between the salespeople and manager.

Contrary to what some might believe, research indicates that leadership ability can be learned.[3] But first, sales managers must understand what leadership is. In sales, **leadership** is defined as those activities performed by sales managers to influence salespeople to achieve goals that contribute to the success of the entire organization.[4] As suggested above, these activities include a variety of "big picture" behaviors such as articulating a vision, leading by example, and inspiring teamwork. It also involves taking care of the details through more mundane, supervisory tasks such as making sure everybody understands his or her job responsibilities.

There is not one, definitive profile of a sales manager who is a successful leader. At the same time, these leaders tend to share certain characteristics and skills, and to exhibit a certain leadership style (or combination of leader behaviors). Gaining insight into leadership is key to the ultimate success of a sales manager.

LEADERSHIP CHARACTERISTICS AND SKILLS

Identifying potential leaders is not easy. An individual's leadership qualities aren't always indicated by the performance of his or her administrative unit. As depicted in Figure 11-1, leadership effectiveness is based on a combination of personal characteristics, managerial skills and behaviors, and the situation. Personal characteristics and managerial skills that affect leadership potential are discussed below, and situational factors are discussed in the next main section of the chapter.

Personal Characteristics

Self-Confidence.   Leaders must believe in themselves. To inspire confidence in others, they must set an example. In a sales organization, they must have confidence in their abilities and beliefs in order to face the challenges and problems inherent in the sales manager's position.

Initiative.   Leaders are independent self-starters who take initiative. They take charge. Leaders welcome change and create change. They are willing and eager to take the risks associated with change.

Energy.   Leaders usually have high energy levels. They are industrious, stepping forward when something needs to be done. Leaders must manage a wide variety of activities and relationships among people—such management takes a lot of energy. Also, a very energetic person is perceived by others as highly motivated and enthusiastic. This behavior is contagious and spreads to those surrounding the leader.

Creativity.   Leaders need creativity and imagination. The organization looks to its leaders for solutions to problems—a challenge that often entails creativity and new approaches.

Maturity.   Effective leaders must be more interested in the well-being of their organization and the development of their people than in their own self-importance or domination of others. Such an interest is a sign of maturity.

Managerial Skills

Problem-Solving Skills.   Most managers spend a significant amount of time resolving problems. Effective leaders identify specific problems and their causes; they formulate and implement solutions. Such leaders must anticipate, analyze, and make decisions.

Interpersonal Skills.   Interpersonal skills bear heavily on leadership capabilities. Leaders must discover what best motivates each salesperson. To do this, leaders establish good working relationships with their people. They know and treat each salesperson as an individual. This does not mean that leaders necessarily become good friends with every salesperson—often they cannot and should not. Instead, leaders develop good business relationships. Leaders also must establish good working relationships with superiors.

Communication Skills. Communication skills are a critical component of effective leadership. Setting goals, organizing, forecasting, staffing, training, motivating, supervising, evaluating, and controlling the sales force all involve communication. The sales manager continuously transmits information from upper management to the sales force and from the sales force to upper management. This information must be accurate, clear, concise, and timely. An effective leader must have good oral and written communication skills.

Persuasive Skills. Good leaders rely more on persuasion than on power. They persuade people to do what they want instead of threatening or coercing them. Their ability to persuade is based on the fact that their subordinates admire and respect them.

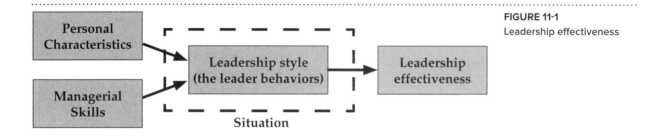

FIGURE 11-1
Leadership effectiveness

LEADERSHIP STYLE[5]

Possessing certain characteristics and skills gives the manager the potential to be an effective leader, but more is needed for that potential to become a reality. Ultimately, the measure of good leadership is how the manager behaves. In other words, what the leader does is more important than who she or he is. Good leaders use a wide variety of managerial or leadership behaviors. The combination of behaviors that a manager typically uses is known as that manager's **leadership style.** Most behaviors tend to be consistent with one of two distinct styles of leadership: transactional leadership and transformational leadership.

Transactional Leadership

In a sales context, **transactional leadership** generally refers to those supervisory activities regarding the day-to-day operation and control of the sales force. In other words, transactional leadership equates to supervision. It is a reactive style of leadership that centers on the exchange—or the give-and-take—between the sales manager and salesperson. Sales managers who are effective transactional leaders appropriately provide **verbal feedback** in the form of rewards and punishments to their salespeople. For example, when a salesperson makes a big sale, the sales manager praises her (gives her a verbal reward). When a salesperson shows up late for a meeting, the sales manager points out his mistake (gives him a verbal punishment).

Transactional leaders exhibit **task orientation**—a short-term focus on getting the job done. This orientation generally involves one-way communication; the leader tells salespeople what to do and how, when, and where to do it. That is, transactional sales managers know the right way to do things and are excellent supervisors. They inform, monitor, and clarify company rules, policies, and procedures to their sales force.

The transactional leadership style relates to the working relationship between the sales manager and salesperson. The sales manager who checks with his or her salespeople each morning to see what their plans are for the day is *directly* supervising their activities. Many other managerial actions constitute *indirect* supervision, such as auditing expense accounts or appraising sales performance.

Management versus Leadership

Sales managers must be more than *managers*; they also must be *leaders* of their sales force. The following table outlines the key differences in terms of the behaviors associated with the two roles—both of which are important.

Managers...	Leaders...
1. Use transactional leadership style	1. Use transformational leadership style
2. React to what has just happened	2. Take proactive steps to avoid future problems
3. Focus on short-term issues, putting out fires one at a time	3. Build a team that works together toward a long-term vision
4. Provide reps with feedback, such as praise for a job well done	4. Are role models who lead by example—they don't just bark orders
5. Use one-way communication to explain policies	5. Listen/respond to the concerns of everyone via two-way communication
6. Do things right	6. Do the right thing

Transformational Leadership

Transformational leadership transforms the basic values, beliefs, and attitudes of followers such that they are willing to perform at levels above and beyond your expectations. Individuals exhibiting this style are usually referred to as **charismatic leaders.**[6] These are exceptional leaders who make a meaningful difference in the performance levels of their followers. Whereas transactional leaders focus primarily on short-term problems, transformational leaders take proactive steps in anticipation of the future. In other words, they don't just know the right way to do things; they also know the right things to do. Furthermore, they genuinely care about those they lead. They use two-way communication, and they are always open to listening to the concerns of each follower.

Described below are four transformational leader behaviors that are especially relevant for sales managers.

Articulate a vision

Transformational leaders create a common, compelling vision for guiding the future of their companies. They articulate a vision that describes an exciting, challenging future for their salespeople and the company. They get people to work toward a common end, even sometimes at the expense of their personal goals.

Of course, the vision for the sales organization typically stems from the company's overall mission as described by the president or chief executive officer. This does not mean, however, that articulating a vision is not the sales manager's responsibility. The sales manager breaks down the overall mission statement into usable sales tools and objectives for the salespeople. In other words, the sales manager should communicate the big picture to salespeople in ways that make sense for them. This is not easy to do. One estimate is that only about 20 percent of companies have a clearly identifiable mission statement that sales managers understand and effectively articulate to their sales teams.[7]

Fostering group goals

Fostering group goals means promoting cooperation—encouraging followers to work together toward a common goal. An organization greatly benefits when leaders successfully persuade followers to sacrifice their own personal goals for the sake of the team.

In this era of team selling, it is especially critical for sales managers to build teamwork through identifying the goal of the group. Transformational leaders must convince each salesperson that she or he cannot operate as a lone wolf. Salespeople must help each other. The strong performers, for example, should be asked to help the inexperienced, low-performing salespeople. In addition, sales managers must encourage their salespeople to recognize the importance of nonsales personnel. Customers have come to expect salespeople to provide solutions to their business problems, but this can only be done when salespeople work closely with engineers, manufacturing specialists, and other co-workers.

Provide a Role Model

Transformational leaders do not merely bark orders—they exhibit **role modeling,** or leading by example. They behave in a manner that is consistent with the values they espouse and with the goals of the organization. Leaders who demonstrate high levels of honesty can expect their salespeople to be honest, too. Similarly, those who exhibit a strong work ethic inspire their subordinates also to work hard.

There are many specific ways in which sales managers can be effective role models for their salespeople. Because they want their salespeople to listen to customers, sales managers themselves listen to the thoughts and concerns of their salespeople. For similar reasons, sales managers present a professional image through appropriate dress and grooming and prompt arrival to meetings and appointments. Perhaps the most important way in which managers can serve as role models is to personally demonstrate proper selling techniques so that salespeople see how sales calls should be handled.

Provide Individualized Support

Finally, transformational leaders genuinely care about and respect their subordinates. They oversee their individual development and are concerned about their personal feelings and needs. As we noted in Chapter 8, on motivation, each person tends to have a unique set of needs and capabilities. Thus, providing **individualized support** is a difficult, time-consuming task for any leader. At the same time, it is an important task—especially in a sales context. Sales managers should take the time to learn about each salesperson's background, family, hobbies, and so on. This information may help the manager know how to address specific problems that arise. Because salespeople are under heavy emotional demands due to the inevitable ups and downs associated with selling, most of them greatly appreciate and respond to a sales manager who shows true concern for their individual needs.

SITUATIONAL LEADERSHIP

Obviously, a sales manager cannot use all behaviors all the time with all salespeople. What makes a sales manager an excellent leader is **situational leadership**—that is, the ability to tailor leadership style—transformational or transactional—to the needs of the current situation and the individual salesperson.

Figure 11-2 lists four different situations and indicates appropriate leader behaviors for each. For a newly hired, inexperienced salesperson, the sales manager must first engage in a heavy dose of transactional leadership. New salespeople need to learn a great deal about the rules and procedures associated with the job; thus, the sales manager must engage in extensive one-way communication focused on informing and clarifying. Verbal feedback in the form of both praise and constructive criticism is also essential in this situation. At the same time, elements of transformational leadership are critical for these new salespeople. In particular, the sales manager should be a role model by accompanying the salesperson on sales calls and demonstrating proper selling technique; and the manager should provide individualized support to show genuine care and concern for these individuals, who might be overwhelmed by the many challenges of a brand new job.

A burned-out veteran salesperson whose performance has plateaued or dropped also responds to the subtle encouragement associated with individualized support. In addition, this individual should be made to feel like part of a team striving to achieve a specific goal or vision. Ideally, the sales manager describes the process in a way that makes the veteran salesperson excited again about working toward a common goal with fellow salespeople. The manager should make a point to offer specific praise for what he or she does well, but too much verbal feedback can sound condescending. After all, this is an experienced salesperson who already knows the basics of the selling process and the rules of the company, so this situation requires only minimal amounts of transactional leadership.

Figure 11-2 also refers to an unstable, crisis environment, which is the norm for certain industries such as computer software. In this situation, it is critical for the sales manager to communicate the seemingly ever-changing vision to the salespeople in a way that makes sense for them. Further, the manager should serve as a calm, hard-working role model who readily accepts and adapts to the inevitable changes.

Finally, in some situations, the absence of leadership might be most appropriate. Many individuals seek sales jobs because they like the autonomy. That is, they like being their own boss. When these salespeople perform at high levels, smart leadership may involve only an occasional update of the vision or overall goals of the organization. Of course, this hands-off approach would not be effective for team-selling situations, in which salespeople must be encouraged to work together (i.e., through fostering group goals).

LEADERSHIP AND STRATEGIC PLANNING

We believe that the leadership ability of sales managers is critical to the success of sales organizations, but not everybody shares this view. Many firms, particularly smaller ones with limited resources, provide little guidance and

FIGURE 11-2
Critical Leader
Behaviors for
Different Situations

Situation	Transactional Leader Behaviors		Transformational Leader Behaviors			
	Informing basic rules	Verbal feedback	Articulating a vision	Fostering group goals	Providing a role model	Individualized support
Newly hired, inexperienced	√	√			√	√
Plateaued veteran; low performance due to burnout		√	√	√		√
Unstable situation, crisis environment			√		√	
High-performing, likes autonomy			√			

supervision for their sales force. The strategic marketing plan for these firms calls for the recruitment of experienced, proven performers who are essentially left alone to do their jobs.

An important factor in this strategic planning with regard to leadership is the importance of any one sale to the firm's welfare. If each sale is vitally important to the firm (as it is for Boeing Aircraft given that what they sell is priced at millions of dollars), leadership is critical and thus each salesperson will be closely supervised. If a single sale or even a single territory is not so important to total corporate well-being, then top management is not likely to spend much money hiring and developing accomplished leaders as sales managers. The leadership decision is a portion of the overall strategic decision as to how important the sales force is in accomplishing the firm's goals.

TOOLS AND TECHNIQUES OF LEADERSHIP

Compared to other business executives, sales managers face unique challenges in providing leadership to their subordinates. Perhaps the best method of leading a sales force is through one-on-one personal contact, but this is not always feasible. An account manager might work out of his or her home in a territory that is hundreds of miles away from the closest co-worker. To be an effective leader, a sales manager must therefore use a combination of tools and techniques to interact with salespeople. These include personal contact, sales reports, telecommunications, printed aids, sales meetings, and other indirect supervisory aids.

Personal Contact

Typically, the sales manager visits salespeople on the job and tries to help them with whatever problems are evident. This is sometimes called **coaching**, which is covered in more detail in Chapter 7. The manager's objectives and activities when traveling with a salesperson vary, but generally they include assisting in selling difficult customers or settling grievances, training, and evaluating. It is

CONSIDER THIS...

Ethics and Leadership

In recent years, a number of business scandals were caused by leaders that engaged in immoral, self-serving actions. This generated interest in the concept of ethical leadership.

Ethical leaders are defined as those perceived to be "...fair and principled individuals who care about people and society at large, are honest and trustworthy, and thus demonstrate ethical behavior both personally and professionally. The ethical leader exhibits moral management by actively attempting to influence followers' ethical behavior. This is accomplished by communicating an ethics and values message, role modeling acceptable behavior, and using rewards and punishment to hold individuals accountable for ethical behavior." (Schwepker, p. 294).

This style of leadership, which in many ways overlaps with transformational leadership, has been found to have a number of positive benefits for sales organizations, including greater job satisfaction and organizational commitment, which leads to salespeople who are more likely to stay with the organization and be productive.

SOURCES: Charles H. Schwepker, "Influencing the salesforce through perceived ethical leadership: the role of salesforce socialization and person–organization fit on salesperson ethics and performance," *Journal of Personal Selling & Sales Management,* December 2015, Vol. 35 (4), pp. 292-313; and James B. DeConinck, "Outcomes of ethical leadership among salespeople," *Journal of Business Research,* May2015, Vol. 68 (5), pp. 1086-1093.

important to remember that when the sales manager or supervisor accompanies the salesperson on a sales call, that salesperson should still take the lead in directing the conversation and moving from one agenda item to another.

When riding with their salespeople in order to train and evaluate them, managers should take care to observe a variety of things. The following questions should be kept in mind:

- Is the salesperson prepared for the call?
- Does the salesperson understand the customer's business and specific needs?
- Does the salesperson treat customers respectfully and honestly?
- Does the salesperson know the competition?
- Is the salesperson skillful at gaining commitment?

Spending time in the field observing, asking thoughtful questions, and discussing strengths and weaknesses are all important coaching behaviors. This type of personal contact is arguably the primary role of a sales manager.[8]

Sales Reports

Sales Reports provide records for monitoring and evaluating salespeople's activity. These reports usually include the number of calls made, number of orders taken, miles traveled, days worked, new prospects called on, and new accounts sold. As a supervisory tool, the sales report is a silent enforcer of company policy. Salespeople who know they must account for all their activities will feel more secure and comfortable if they stay within company policy.

Frequently, salespeople are required to submit a **call plan,** which includes both their travel itinerary and their strategies for calling on each customer for the upcoming period. The call plan forces salespeople to organize their activities. These plans show, for example, whether the salespeople are routing themselves properly, calling on the various classes of customer in the right ratio, and/or developing appropriate objectives for their calls.

Advancements in technology have had a great impact on how salespeople submit call plans and receive sales reports. For many sales organizations, the process is automated through customer relationship management (CRM) systems, which were discussed in Chapter 2. The programs typically provide access to in-depth information on a variety of salesperson performance indicators, and also on customer problems and needs as well as on competitive activity. Monitoring this information makes the sales manager a more effective leader. Further, CRM systems help salespeople be more productive. For example, the technology gives salespeople the means to easily and quickly quote prices, write contracts, track orders, and provide product and marketing information.

CRM programs significantly improve both the quality and accuracy of sales report information. Companies that have implemented CRM systems generally report significant improvements in sales force productivity and management effectiveness. The challenge for sales managers is to motivate their salespeople to use the CRM program to its fullest potential. Managers should encourage salespeople to enter relevant data into the program on a regular basis (typically every day). This reporting activity should be evaluated and rewarded as one of the salesperson's primary responsibilities.

Information Communication

Communicating information is a challenge for sales managers given that their salespeople might live and work hundreds of miles away from them. Advances in technology have had a great impact in this area. Thanks to CRM systems, the internet, smart phones, tablets, and other related technology, there are a wide variety of ways to send and receive voice messages, data, text, images, and even video. That is, it is much easier today to send information over long distances.

Because this information communication is so important in the sales context, companies equip their salespeople with the latest smart phone, tablets, and laptops loaded with sophisticated software. This is done by almost all sales organizations today for the following reasons:

- **Better customer and industry information.** The technology allows salespeople and their managers to access complete customer histories and industry information anywhere, at any time.
- **Selling assistance.** The technology provides electronic libraries of product information and enhanced capabilities for analyzing customer problems. Price quotes, bids, proposals for service, and installation agreements can be generated automatically.
- **Sales support.** The technology allows salespeople to enter and track orders very accurately. It also allows salespeople to handle correspondence with customers efficiently.
- **Reporting responsibilities.** Salespeople can submit their call plans and reports, expense reports, and other market intelligence much more easily.
- **Communication.** As suggested above, technology enables sales managers to be in constant communication with their salespeople regardless of

where they are. This includes both real-time communication through conversation, text-messaging, and screen-sharing, and asynchronous communication through e-mail and voice messages.

In summary, advances in technology have helped sales organizations in many ways. Not only does technology improve salesperson performance, it also makes it easier for sales executives to provide leadership from afar.

Published Materials

Sales manuals, bulletins, company newsletters, and other regularly published materials can also be effective tools in leadership. These can be either printed or digitally produced. A good sales manual tells salespeople what to do in various circumstances. Some questions can be answered just as effectively in a publication as they can through personal contact.

Meetings

Sales meetings, which were discussed in Chapter 8, are another means used to provide leadership. During sales meetings, managers often explain new procedures, policies, and programs to the sales force. Increasingly, companies hold annual sales meetings that are built around a unique but relevant theme. This makes the topics more compelling and memorable to the sales team. For example, Continental Tire North America surprised its reps with a military "boot camp" theme for a recent meeting. Sales executives were dressed in army fatigues and portrayed drill sergeants as they talked about military strategy in the war against competitors. The goal of these thematic gatherings is to get the salespeople motivated and energized.[9]

Indirect Supervisory Aids

Several other leadership tools can be called **indirect supervisory techniques.** They have inherent supervisory powers and work automatically toward company goals—and they can be exceptionally effective. Unlike the other supervisory methods, these indirect techniques travel everywhere with the sales force. They include:

- **Compensation plans.** By far the most important automatic leadership tool, the compensation plan encourages salespeople to do those things that will maximize earnings.
- **Territories.** Establishment of specific sales territories tells salespeople what areas they are responsible for.
- **Quotas.** By setting quotas for various product lines or for certain classes of customers, the sales manager can guide sales force activities into desired channels.
- **Expense accounts.** Policies on expenses automatically guide sales force behavior by limiting the amount salespeople can spend on certain activities.
- **Sales analysis procedures.** Using sales analysis procedures (discussed in the later chapters), management can evaluate the performance of each salesperson and then guide or assist the salespeople who need help on certain points.

The specifics of these indirect supervisory aids are generally guided by the sales organization's **control system**, which refers to the firm's general approach to monitoring, directing, evaluating, and rewarding salespeople. The control system for a given sales organization falls on a continuum ranging from outcome- to behavior-based control. Firms with **outcome-based control** involve very little monitoring, directing, and evaluating, and reward their salespeople through mostly incentive-based (i.e., commission) compensation plans. Quotas based on sales volume are used extensively, and travel and entertainment expenses are often paid by the salesperson. In a sense, this approach replaces leadership with indirect supervisory aids.

On the other end of the continuum, sales managers in a **behavior-based control** system are expected to actively engage in both transactional and transformational leadership (or, in other words, situational leadership). These sales managers extensively monitor, direct, and evaluate their salespeople, who are paid a relatively high portion of salary (i.e., less commission). These salespeople also receive more nonfinancial rewards such as praise and recognition. According to a number of research studies, behavior-based control is superior to outcome-based control.[10] Of course, this points to the importance of a sales manager's leadership skills. The specific, positive outcomes of effective leadership are described in the next section.

CONSIDER THIS...

Leading the Working-from-home Salespeople

Increasingly, salespeople work from their home, and this presents leadership challenges for sales managers. Following are some tips on how sales managers can provide effective leadership to their telecommuters:

- **Share tribal knowledge.** Working from home means that the salespeople are not included in the casual, day-to-day interpersonal communication that occurs with colleagues at the home office; and this can create a feeling of not knowing what is happening. Sales managers can improve this situation by regularly and deliberately sharing information through webinars, Skype interactions, virtual small group meetings, etc.
- **Schedule regular meetings.** Some salespeople almost never visit the rest of their team, and this leads to a feeling of isolation. The sales manager should schedule real, face-to-face visits where the salespeople can get to know the other salespeople as well as the home office staff.
- **Virtual Ride-a-longs.** When working together from a branch office, sales managers often accompany their salespeople on sales calls—but this does not happen very often when salespeople work from home. Technology can allow the sales manager to participate in virtual presentations and phone conversations with clients. This participation can lead to the manager providing a great deal of useful information and feedback to the salespeople.

SOURCE: Anthony Iannarino, "How to help remote salespeople sell better," *The Sales Blog*. Retrieved from the following URL on July 1, 2016:
HTTP://THESALESBLOG.COM/2012/10/21/HOW-TO-HELP-REMOTE-SALESPEOPLE-SELL-BETTER/

CONSIDER THIS...

Mentoring the Sales Force

Many sales organizations provide additional leadership to their salespeople through a mentoring program. Typically, mentors are assigned to newly hired salespeople for the purposes of career training and sales skill development, and also as a means for socialization and acclimation.

Mentors can come from three distinct sources: (1) manager mentors from within the organization, (2) peer mentors from within the organization, and (3) mentors from outside the firm. Research has examined the effect of different mentoring strategies on two important outcome variables: sales performance and intention to leave. The results demonstrate that mentoring can be a powerful leadership tool.

The best strategy is using manager mentors from within the organization, as it led to higher performance and lower intention to leave among the salespeople. Using outside mentors also led to higher performance, yet these salespeople were much more likely to quite the organization. Using peer mentors from inside the organization made the salespeople less likely to leave but did not improve their performance. Finally, salespeople with no mentors at all were low on performance and more likely to quit their job.

Questions: Do these results make sense to you? Are there any circumstances under which you would support peer mentors? How about outside mentors? Discuss.

SOURCE: Anthony Iannarino, "How to help remote salespeople sell better," *The Sales Blog*. Retrieved from the following URL on July 1, 2016:
HTTP://THESALESBLOG.COM/2012/10/21/HOW-TO-HELP-REMOTE-SALESPEOPLE-SELL-BETTER/

OUTCOMES OF EFFECTIVE LEADERSHIP

The right combination and amount of leadership can result in a number of positive leadership outcomes for the sales organization: well-trained salespeople, trust among salespeople, citizenship behaviors, better performance, and sales force morale.

Well-trained salespeople

As an effective leader, the sales manager provides a vision that should clarify what the salespeople are expected to do. Further, verbal feedback and role modeling by the sales manager show salespeople *how* to do it. In other words, the right combination of leader behaviors can do much to develop an inexperienced recruit into a productive salesperson. As we noted in Chapter 7, the most helpful sales training takes place over a period of time and is best done in the field while salespeople are actually facing day-to-day problems. Thus, great leaders are great trainers, and the first important outcome of effective leadership is a highly trained sales force.

Trust among Salespeople

Excellent leaders genuinely care about their subordinates and effectively persuade them to work together as a team. This leads to an environment of **trust**, which is when salespeople have faith in the reliability, truth, ability, or strength of their sales managers—*and vice-versa*. Such an environment is critical for the success of any organization. Only when salespeople trust and respect each other can they successfully work together toward a common goal. Further, salespeople who trust their supervisor have significantly higher job satisfaction, and are less likely to quit.[11] A renowned leadership expert has written "Trust is the lubrication that makes it possible for organizations to work."[12]

Citizenship Behaviors

Salespeople managed by great leaders are likely to engage in **citizenship behaviors,** which are voluntary behaviors that are not part of a formal job description yet are important to the success of the firm. The following are examples of key citizenship behaviors that salespeople might exhibit:

- Offering tips and encouragement to a struggling new salesperson.
- Showing up to work on time and never missing a meeting.
- Tolerating problems without complaining.
- Volunteering to serve on a community service committee.
- Being courteous and respectful of the rights of others.

These are activities that salespeople are generally not trained—or even asked—to do. Further, the sales manager would not punish salespeople for failing to do these activities. At the same time, citizenship behaviors have been shown to be related to overall sales force productivity.

Better Performance

Some sales managers believe that direct supervision stimulates salespeople to do better work. However, there is a limit to how much an employee can be prodded without becoming resentful. For some salespeople, just knowing that management is aware of their efforts can be beneficial. Conversely, performance seems to suffer when salespeople know that management has no means of knowing what they are really doing.

It is important to most salespeople to know that someone in the organization cares about and recognized the work they do. If the supervisor is adept, just the fact that he or she is in personal contact should have a good effect on performance.

Sales Force Morale

Effective leadership results in a well-trained, higher-performing sales group whose members trust and help each other as they work together toward a common goal. This combination of positive outcomes equates to higher **group morale** throughout the sales force. Group morale involves a sense of common purpose and a belief among members that group goals can be attained.

Group attitudes toward work are important for both economic and social reasons. From the economic standpoint, productivity is likely to be higher in groups whose members have relatively good morale. It does not always follow that high morale results in high productivity, however. A group may have a good attitude but poor results. Nevertheless, productivity is usually higher for employees who have good mental attitudes toward their jobs. From a social point of view, people who develop negative attitudes toward work can make life miserable not only for themselves but also for those around them. Life is too short to be spent working in an unpleasant environment. The proposition that leaders should promote good morale for its own sake certainly has merit.

In order for group morale to be high, each individual in the group must first be satisfied with his or her job. **Job satisfaction**—sometimes called *individual morale*—is the individual salesperson's emotional and evaluative feelings toward various dimensions of the job. These dimensions include pay, promotions, security, benefits, and co-workers. In other words, a salesperson will not be generally satisfied with his job if he is unhappy with one or more of these dimensions. At the same time, individual job satisfaction is hardly sufficient for group morale. In a situation where salespeople hate each other but get paid a high salary for doing very little work, job satisfaction could be quite high throughout the sales force. This group, however, could not be said to have high group morale.

Some job satisfaction dimensions might be outside the sales manager's control. For example, in many firms, a mid-level sales manager has very limited input into the overall compensation levels of salespeople. Nevertheless, effective leadership by the manager can go a long way toward increasing individual job satisfaction and, ultimately, group morale.

PROBLEMS ENCOUNTERED IN LEADERSHIP

Certain leadership and supervisory problems are commonly encountered when managing salespeople. They include poor performance, substance abuse, expense account abuse, other unethical behavior, and sexual harassment.

Poor Performance

When salespeople are not performing up to standards, the best solution is not to fire them but rather to help them become productive employees Often these salespeople have received extensive training, so correcting the problem is less expensive than replacing them. Also, because of possible discrimination suits, prudent managers will make sure that they have done everything within reason to help failing employees—firing them should be a last resort.

Although many managers find it difficult to criticize their subordinates, it is often possible to correct a problem just by giving immediate feedback about the problem behavior. This constructive feedback should take place as soon as the manager notices the problem. Managers should be very specific about what the problem is and what the salesperson must do to correct it. The following steps should be followed in providing effective feedback.[13]

1. State the problem.
2. Get the salesperson's agreement on the problem.
3. Listen to the salesperson's assessment of the problem.
4. Consider extenuating circumstances.
5. Design an action plan for improvement
6. Get the salesperson's agreement on the action plan.

If the salesperson's performance does not improve as a result of immediate feedback, the manager should review the problem in a formal performance appraisal;

then the manager and salesperson should agree on a plan for improvement. The manager must make it very clear that poor performance is not acceptable. Each step should be documented with written memos detailing what took place. If the problem continues, the manager should set up a counseling session to review all the previous attempts to encourage improvement. The salesperson should be given a specified time period to show improvement. If the salesperson has not improved by the specified time, then the manager, with all of the appropriate documentation, must demote or terminate the salesperson.

A Sales Rep Objects to Harassment

RUNNING CASE
Shiderlots
Elevators, Inc.

Lisa Unser, Shiderlots Account Manager, called her sales manager Adam Dark and requested an urgent meeting. Unser was having problems with one of her largest customers, Jeff Vasel from Easton Hospital. Although she was one of Adam's top account managers, Unser's current troubles did not come as a total surprise to Dark. As he prepared for the meeting, Dark reviewed the history with this account.

Easton Hospital was a large and important client of Shiderlots for at least 10 years, but Mr. Vasel became the key contact there just four years ago. At that time, Shiderlots account manager Diane Buschman serviced the account. Just a few months later, however, Buschman suddenly quit her job Shiderlots. Dark did not fully understand why, and never got around to getting the full story.

A bright young account manager named Neal Darling was hired to replace Buschman. Darling has gone on to become a solid performer, but his approach did not work with Jeff Vasel. Just a couple months later, Vasel was threatening to move the business of Easton Hospital to Shiderlots' main competitor. Darling worked hard to make him happy, but nothing was working.

Adam Dark approached an acquaintance of his who was one of Vasel's coworkers. "Jeff Vasel likes lady reps. I guess he feels more comfortable buying from a woman," said the friend to Dark.

It was then that Adam Dark, under pressure from top management to save the account, decided to have Lisa Unser switch a couple accounts with Neal Darling. For a time, the plan seemed to work very well as all sides seemed happy. But this recent phone call from Lisa was concerning.

At the meeting, Dark could immediately see that Lisa Unser was very upset. "The problem is that Vasel keeps making passes at me, and yesterday asked me to join him for the weekend at his lake house. He's a 48-year-old rich and powerful bachelor who expects all the women he meets to fall madly in love with him. I've been totally professional with him since the day I joined the account, but I can't take any more of his antics. I'm done with that account—I can't take it anymore," Unser said.

Questions: How well has Adam Dark dealt with this situation up to this point? What should Dark do now?

Substance Abuse

One of the most difficult personnel issues that sales managers encounter is when a salesperson has a problem with **substance abuse**, which is the overindulgence in or dependence on alcohol, drugs or some other addictive element. Unfortunately, some sales jobs lead to excessive drinking because they constantly put the salespeople in social situations where drinking is expected. Such jobs are terrible risks for people who cannot handle the temptations of alcohol.

Surveys indicate that the problems of drug and alcohol abuse among workers are pervasive and costly. A U.S. government study found illicit drug use among 7.7 percent of the nation's workforce, and among 9.1 percent of salespeople. The same study reported heavy alcohol use among 7.5 percent of the nation's workforce—but just 4.1 percent of salespeople.[14] The fact that heavy alcohol use among salespeople is significantly below the national average is surprising as it contradictions longtime convention wisdom. Nevertheless, even if it affects only a few salespeople, substance abuse can still represent a big problem for sales managers. The performance of salespeople who are alcoholics or drug abusers almost always suffers. Their work habits are usually poor, and the quality of their work is often unacceptable.

Detection

The signs of alcohol abuse (the odor, for example) can be more obvious than drug abuse, but both may be difficult to detect. If managers do not have day-to-day contact with their salespeople, the problem may go undetected for some time. Still, there are warning signs: alcohol on the breath, slurred speech, missed appointments, missed work, and declining performance. Excessive use of alcohol or drugs also may exhibit itself in certain behaviors at company functions and conventions.[15]

Many firms make job offers to applicants contingent on their passing a drug test. Regardless of whether or not the firm uses substance abuse testing, sales supervisors should become familiar with the signs and symptoms of abuse so they can detect any problems as early as possible.[16]

Dealing with abuse

The use of illegal drugs on the job is, of course, never allowed; the consumption of alcohol, which is a legal substance, may be allowed in certain situations, such as entertaining customers. However, the abusive use of either alcohol or drugs almost invariably leads to performance deficiencies. It is the performance deficiency, not the abuse itself, that the supervisor should address first.

The salesperson should be told that he or she must rectify the performance deficiency or be subject to termination. Then the manager can explore the reasons for the deficiency with the salesperson. When it is possible to get an admission of an abuse problem, the sales manager can recommend that the salesperson seek assistance from a professional substance abuse program. Sales managers should not attempt to provide counseling—they are rarely trained to deal with these problems. If salespeople refuse treatment or do not make satisfactory progress in the treatment, and if their performance does not improve, termination may be appropriate.

Some companies have formal policies for dealing with alcohol and drug abuse, but many do not. If there is no company policy, sales managers should develop their own formal, written policies. These policies should be clearly communicated to the sales force.

Expense Accounts

As noted in Chapter 10, expense accounts can lead to costly problems for management. The folklore of selling is full of fictional sales expense accounts. Expense account policies should be clearly set forth when salespeople are hired. Companies that expect the sales force to be honest should make it clear that cheating on an expense account is grounds for dismissal. Then they consistently back up that policy with action.

A sales manager who discovers discrepancies in a salesperson's expense account should review the situation with the salesperson to be certain there is not simply an error or a misunderstanding of allowable expenses. Some managers simply disallow expenses they feel are not in order. Others go over the expense report with the salesperson, putting the salesperson on notice that the expense reports are being watched. But such matters are sensitive, and the sales manager must deal with each case as the situation warrants.

Unethical Behavior

Padding expense accounts is one type of unethical behavior. But there are others—for example, recommending unnecessarily high product quality levels or inventory levels, selling out-of-production items without informing the customer, or providing misleading information on competitors. Sales managers who overlook such unethical practices are asking for trouble. While the immediate consequences of allowing such behavior may not seem too great, this practice will likely result in more serious long-term consequences such as lawsuits and negativity publicity.

Managers must take immediate action to put an end to unethical behavior. The same steps suggested earlier for problematic performance should be followed in correcting unethical behavior.

Sexual Harassment[17]

In 1980, the Equal Employment Opportunity Commission (EEOC) issued guidelines that interpret **sexual harassment** as a form of discrimination. Since that time, the number of sexual harassment cases filed has steadily increased. A typical Fortune 500 company spends millions of dollars a year dealing with sexual harassment. The costs stem from a variety of factors, including the investigation of sexual harassment claim; reduced productivity; increased turnover and absenteeism; and, of course, payments of monetary compensation to victims. It is important that sales managers take proactive steps not only to recognize and put a stop to harassment that does occur but also, and perhaps more important, to prevent it from occurring in the first place.

The EEOC defines sexual harassment as follows.

Unwelcome sexual advances, request for sexual favors, and other verbal or physical conduct of a sexual nature constitute sexual harassment when any of the following criteria are met:

1. Submission to such conduct is made either explicitly or implicitly a term or condition of an individual's employment;

CONSIDER THIS...

Workplace Romance

"The best advice I have for people to stay out of trouble is to not start an office romance, but that seems to be increasingly difficult as we spend more time at work than anywhere else," says a renowned labor and employment lawyer.

Indeed, nearly 2 out of 5 U.S. workers admit to being romantically involved with a coworker, and more than half of salespeople say they have known of a romantic relationship between their *sales manager* and a fellow salesperson on their team. Relationships between managers and subordinates have the greatest potential to cause significant problems.

First, such relationships can hurt the morale of the sales team—particularly if the manager shows favoritism to the salesperson he or she is dating. Worse, if the relationship ends bitterly, the company may be open to sexual harassment charges. Such lawsuits can not only cost millions in legal and settlement fees, but also result in negative publicity that tarnishes the company's reputation.

Despite the many problems, only 15 percent of companies have any written policy regarding workplace relationships. Legal experts recommend for companies to require employees to disclose such relationships—especially supervisor-subordinate relationships. This can protect the company from sexual harassment lawsuits.

SOURCES: Kathryn Buschman Vasel, "Here's Your Guide to Dating in the Workplace," *FOX Business*, February 13, 2014; Betsy Cummings, "An Affair to Remember," *Sales & Marketing Management*, August 2001, pp. 50-57.

2. Submission to or rejection of such conduct by an individual is used as a basis for employment decisions affecting that individual;

3. Such conduct has the purpose or effect of unreasonably interfering with an individual's work performance or creating an intimidating, hostile, or offensive working environment.

Typically, sexual harassment involves two people who work for the same firm—for example, a sales manager harassing a subordinate salesperson. In addition, if a sales manager is romantically involved with a subordinate salesperson and grants favors to (e.g., promotes) that person, then colleagues of that salesperson might have grounds for sexual harassment lawsuit. This is especially true if the girlfriend or boyfriend who was promoted is less qualified than others (see the box "Workplace Romance").

A form of sexual harassment relatively unique to sales organizations is **third-party harassment,** which means that the harassment is done by someone *outside the firm.* That "someone" is most often a customer. In these cases, sales managers have a responsibility for taking immediate corrective actions in response to all such incidents. These actions may include reassigning the salesperson to a new customer or territory; requesting that the customer stop the inappropriate behaviors; and, if the customer will not commit to refraining from such behaviors, closing the account.

One sales executive reported to the author that third-party sexual harassment does happen from time to time, and that this is always difficult to deal with. In a recent incident, the executive learned of inappropriate behavior exhibited toward his salesperson by a customer at a manufacturing facility. The sales executive contacted the plant manager, explained what happened, and allowed the customer firm to deal with it internally. The salesperson was given the option to continue calling on the account or not. The salesperson chose to continue calling on the account, and the inappropriate behavior stopped.

Sales managers must be proactive in creating an environment that does not tolerate harassment. In fact, the selling firm may still be liable even if the sales manager did not know about the sexual harassment—but *should have known about it.*

Fastenal distributes its sexual harassment policy to all new employees, and the policy is covered in the first phase of training. This is the norm. A firm's sexual harassment policy should be comprehensive, and include statements about the behaviors that are prohibited; the penalties for misconduct; the procedures for making, investigating, and resolving complaints; and procedures for education and training. Sales managers should understand these policies and ensure that they are followed.

SUMMARY

Leadership—a process in which one person influences other people's behavior toward the accomplishment of specific goals—is essential for a sales manager to be effective. Effective leaders tend to possess similar personal characteristics, such as high levels of self-confidence, initiative, energy, creativity, and maturity. In addition, effective leaders possess advanced managerial skills, including the ability to solve problems, communicate, persuade, and understand what motivates each salesperson.

Leadership style refers to the specific set of leader behaviors that sales managers put forth in a given situation. There are two distinct styles: transactional leadership and transformational leadership. Transactional leadership involves those supervisory activities regarding the day-to-day operation and control of the sales force. It presents a short-term, task-oriented focus on getting the job done. Transactional leaders provide one-way communication to salespeople in the form of verbal feedback, letting them know what they are doing right and wrong.

Transformational leadership changes (transforms) the basic values, beliefs, and attitudes of followers such that they are willing to perform at levels above and beyond expectations. Those who use this style are outstanding leaders—usually referred to as charismatic. The primary transformational leader behaviors are articulating a vision of the future, fostering group goals, being a role model, and providing individualized support.

Both transactional and transformational leadership can be an effective way to lead salespeople. The situation determines the appropriate style or combination of styles. The best sales managers instinctively know the right mix of leader behaviors to use for any given situation.

The best way to lead a sales force is through face-to-face, personal contact. Due to distance or lack of time, however, sales managers must supplement personal contact with other tools and techniques of leadership. These include sales reports, information communication, sales meetings, published materials, and indirect supervisory aids.

A number of positive outcomes result from the right combination and amount of leadership. First, the salespeople are generally better trained and the work environment is characterized by mutual respect and trust among all employees. This in turn leads to higher-performing salespeople who are more likely to engage in citizenship behaviors. Finally, the right leadership leads to a sales force with high group morale.

Some frequent problems encountered by leaders include poor performance, substance abuse, expenses misappropriation, other unethical behavior, and sexual harassment. Each problem needs to be dealt with proactively to avoid potentially serious consequences.

KEY TERMS

Behavior-based control	Individualized support	Task orientation
Call plan	Job satisfaction	Third-party harassment
Charismatic leaders	Leadership	Transactional leadership
Citizenship behaviors	Leadership style	Transformational
Coaching	Outcome-based control	leadership
Control system	Role modeling	Trust
Fostering group goals	Sales reports	Verbal feedback
Group morale	Sexual harassment	Vision
Indirect supervisory	Situational leadership	
techniques	Substance abuse	

QUESTIONS AND PROBLEMS

1. What are the personal characteristics necessary for an effective leader? Will possessing these characteristics alone ensure success as a manager? If not, what other elements need to be considered?

2. What specific leader behaviors (from the two leadership styles) would you use in the following situations? Why?

   a. Terry is one of your best sales representatives. She has eight years of experience and has proved her abilities many times.

   b. Diane graduated with a marketing degree within the past year, but she has limited sales experience.

   c. John is a veteran employee. In recent months, however, you notice his performance stagnating.

3. How has the revolution in technology (high-speed computers, e-mail, the Internet, etc.) affected the way sales managers lead their salespeople?

4. Bill Jolton, an account manager for a large national soap company, informs his immediate supervisor that he is quitting at the end of the month. The supervisor is surprised to learn this, since she thought that Jolton was doing a good job and was happy with his work. The supervisor would like to keep Jolton with the firm, for she thinks he shows exceptional promise. How should the supervisor handle the situation?

5. As manager for ABC Company, Rocky Farlow oversees 15 sales reps. Farlow is an outstanding transactional leader, but he is hopelessly ineffective as a transformational leader. Is this a problem? Why or why not?

6. A sales manager of a large metropolitan automobile dealership required his sales force of eight people to meet each morning at 9:00am for about 30 minutes to plan their activities for the day. During this meeting, he asked each salesperson to tell what he or she intended to accomplish that day. Were these meetings sound? What was the manager's goal in setting up such meetings?

7. What are some specific ways in which sales managers can be role models to their salespeople? List several distinct ways.

8. What is the difference between job satisfaction and morale? Is it possible to have high job satisfaction but low morale?

9. You notice that Mike, one of your account managers, has been consistently unproductive for the past two months. You have heard rumors indicating that Mike may be abusing alcohol or drugs; however, no proof is available. What actions should you take? Why?

10. One of your account managers, Nancy, claims that one of her colleagues has been sexually harassing her and she has asked you to do something about it. You have talked to Bill, but he denies it. What should you do now?

EXPERIENTIAL EXERCISES

1. Pick a classmate and describe what personal characteristics, skills, and/ or behaviors this person exhibits that would make him or her an effective leader. Also describe any characteristics and/or behaviors that would make this classmate less effective.

2. Interview two business managers whom you know to determine whether each is more of a transactional leader or a transformational leader (Hint: it might be useful to ask them how frequently they use certain behaviors to direct the efforts of their salespeople). Describe the differences and similarities between the two managers.

3. Can a sales manager learn how to be a leader? A variety of consulting/ training companies say, "Yes, and we can teach them!" Use search terms such as "leadership training," "sales coaching," and/or "sales management," and do an online search to find websites of a few companies that have programs to teach leadership skills. Describe the program and comment on whether or not you think it would be effective.

4. Visit the websites of the National Institute on Drug Abuse (www. drugabuse.gov) and the National Institute on Alcohol Abuse and Alcoholism (www.niaaa.nih.gov). What are the signs that a person has a substance abuse problem? What do these sites tell you about how a sales manager can detect and deal with drug and alcohol abuse?

SPECTRUM HEALTI I, INC.
Leadership in a Crisis Situation

"Okay, we are now officially in a crisis," Cara Bakelin said out loud to herself. She knew she was about to face the toughest leadership challenge of her career—but she was not sure how she would handle it.

After a successful seven-year career in the field, Cara now has been district manager for Spectrum Health for just over two years. She supervises 10 territory medical device sales reps across her district, the state of Maine. But this is new, because just last week she was the supervisor of 12 reps. Two were laid off by Spectrum as part of its initiative of reducing its U.S. sales force by 24 percent. According to Jack Lord, Spectrum's new CEO, the layoffs were necessary to stay competitive. "This will make us a leaner, more efficient organization," Jack wrote in a memo. Cara knew that other factors contributed to the decision to eliminate salespeople. These included a downturn in the economy, specific government cutbacks of health care funding for most of Spectrum's customers, and the emergence of a tough foreign competitor.

Spectrum Health, Inc., is a $3.2 billion medical equipment manufacturer. The company produces a wide range of medical supplies and devices for health care providers such as physicians, hospitals, and health maintenance organizations. Products range from expensive heart-lung machines to inexpensive stethoscopes, thermometers, and wound closure products.

Cara Bakelin felt that the morale of her sales force was never especially high. The reps were unique individuals who did not seem to interact much with each other. They were each motivated by different goals. She never sensed any animosity among them and had been hopeful that somehow she could make them more of a team. But in her first two years on the job, she has focused primarily on learning her administrative duties, such as quantitative analysis, forecasting, and budgeting.

In fact, the sales executive who performed her recent evaluation told Cara that she needed to do a better job communicating with her salespeople—especially through coaching and individual contact. She told the executive, "I've never been good with that touchy-feely stuff, but I'll try to do better!"

Cara also had been told that her unit's overall sales levels were disappointing. Market research indicated that Spectrum held a 5.2 percent share of the market in Maine. This was well below the company's current national average of 8.5 percent market share.

What stood out more than anything else was Cara's unit's lack of success in selling the more expensive health care products, such as the heart-lung machine. To effectively sell such complex devices, team selling is required. That is, Spectrum reps must coordinate the efforts of engineers, cardiopulmonary experts, and other high-tech colleagues.

Cara knows she is in a very difficult situation. She needs to try to improve the morale of an underachieving group of people who have a long history of not being committed to anything other than their own individual goals. Further she has to do this in a tough business climate in which the company is laying off her salespeople. Commitment to the organization is clearly at an all-time low among reps. How can she get these reps excited about working toward a common goal when they do not trust the company?

Even before the announced layoffs, Cara had taken the advice of superiors and booked more of her work time for individual contact with her reps. In fact, she has devoted next week exclusively to this. She will address all 10 reps first thing Monday morning in a one-hour sales meeting. She then plans to spend the rest of the week, through Friday, coaching them individually. She plans on accompanying at least some of them on sales calls.

Her first challenge is to decide what kind of leadership to provide to—and how much time to spend with—each of her 10 reps. After reviewing her reps' unique needs and talents, Cara feels that they can be categorized into five distinct groups:

1. Two reps, Kristi and Kraig, are high performing and experienced. They sell all Spectrum products the way they should be sold. In fact, they are the only two reps who consistently sell the big items such as the heart-lung machine. This success stems in part from the close bonds that the two have formed with some of the nonsales (technical) people at Spectrum.

2. Four reps, Allen, Ashley, Andrew and Art, are solid performers but lone wolves. The performance is average to above average across these four reps. Cara appreciates much of what they do, but she is disappointed in their sales of big-ticket items such as the heart-lunch machine. These reps love their jobs, especially the autonomy. They generally have little interaction with others at Spectrum, including both sales and nonsales personnel.

3. Two reps, Daniel and Debra, are low performing rookies. Actually, these two reps have been with Spectrum for almost one year now. They are the only two reps left that Cara personally hired (two other reps she hired were laid off). They are bright and energetic, but they still lack experience. Cara feels they could be much better performers if they improve their selling technique.

4. One rep, Erin, is a mediocre-performing misfit. To Cara, Erin stands out as being a loner among the loners. The reps are generally not very close to each other, but Erin seems to be the least interactive. Her sales levels are a bit higher than those of the rookies, but they should be since she has been with Spectrum for almost five years. Erin never seems happy. Cara suspects this stems from the fact that she was born and raised on the West Coast, over 3,000 miles away.

5. Finally, the one remaining rep, Robert, is a low-performing, burned out veteran. Now approaching 60 years old, Robert was a solid performer in years past. Since Cara became sales manager, however, Robert's performance has dropped significantly. Cara gets the sense that Robert is looking forward to his retirement; and, in fact, she is, too.

Cara wants to develop a strategy for effective leadership of her sales force. She understands that there are different styles of leadership, and that most leader behaviors are either transactional or transformational. She also understands that her leadership style should be appropriate for the current crisis situation. Cara wants to develop a specific plan of action for each of the five groups of salespeople, but she needs your help.

Questions:

1. What is the general message that Cara Bakelin should give all the reps in the Monday morning meeting?

2. What are the specific leader behaviors that Cara Bakelin should exhibit toward each of the five groups of reps? Be specific, and defend your answer.

KAPFER EQUIPMENT COMPANY
Declining Performance of a Good Account Manager

"Johnny's been one of our outstanding salespeople for the past 10 years. I can't believe what I've just learned," Tom Grant, sales manager, said to Jackie Kapfer, partner and co-manager of the Kapfer Equipment Company of Lincoln, Nebraska.

"And what is that?" Jackie asked.

"He's been moonlighting on us for the past six months. He's a partner in an apartment construction project over in Sioux City with an old buddy of his. That's why his sales have been so bad these past few months. He's not working full-time for us anymore."

Kapfer Equipment distributed a wide line of heavy-duty equipment, machines, and tools to the construction trades, governments, mining companies, and the oil industry in a five-state area around Nebraska. Its customers were anyone who had a large-scale construction project to build. The company had long and good relationship with the 15 manufacturers it represented. Its lines included such items as crawler tractors, excavator-shovels, motor graders, cranes, backhoes, off-highway trucks, loaders, rollers, compactors, conveyors, pavers, and asphalt equipment.

The company had been founded by Otto Kapfer in 1940 and passed to his son, Max, in 1965. Max's two children, Dirk and Jacklyn, had taken over the enterprise 20 years ago upon Max's retirement. Dirk worked with the suppliers and the service side of the business while Jacklyn, who was called Jackie by everyone but her mother, ran daily operations.

Each person on the 22-member sales force sold the entire line of products and services to every type of customer in his or her assigned territory. It was a difficult job because it included many different types of products and customers.

John Knight had joined the company 15 years ago, after five years as a salesperson for Caterpillar. Prior to that he had worked as an engineer in heavy construction, mostly building the interstate highway system. He had graduated from Iowa State University in with a degree in civil engineering.

Since John had developed many valuable contacts in the Omaha area from his work for one of the area's largest construction companies, he was assigned that territory. He met his quotas the first year and exceeded them by 23 percent the second. He became the company's second most productive account manager, consistently exceeding his sales quotas. Tom Grant had considered him managerial timber. It was thought that he might become sales manager if Tom ever left the company or was promoted to a higher position in the company.

Jacklyn asked, "How did you find out about John's apartment project?"

"Well, six months ago his sales fell 30 percent below quota. He blamed the economy but said that things would pick up soon, that I shouldn't worry. Well, when somebody tells me not to worry, that's when I really start worrying. I pulled out his activity reports. He wasn't making the calls as he used to make them. Something was wrong. And you know we require a report on every situation in which we don't get the order but some other company does. I knew of some business that John Deere had sold that we bid on, so I looked for the report on it. No reports! So I go see him."

Jackie asked, "Why didn't you call him in? Why waste your time going over to Omaha?"

"Because all the evidence would be in Omaha. It's easy for a guy to lie to you in the office. In the field where the bodies are buried it's easier to get to the truth. I went to his house unannounced. No one was there, but a neighbor told me that John was probably at his apartment project. She gave me the address. I went over and caught him red-handed, working on the roof with his partner. Did he ever look sheepish?"

Tom paused for effect and then continued, "He came down and we had a long, very frank talk. I was so mad I wanted to fire him on the spot. If he wasn't so big, I might have decked him. I kept my cool, but he knew I was mad.

"His story was that he got caught in the apartment project by the real estate recession. Initially, he was only an investor in the deal his friend had put together, but they ran into trouble. Their permanent financing collapsed when the bank got into some trouble with the Feds. Also, the insurance company that was furnishing the construction money was about to pull the plug on them, so they had to get the project finished fast for what little money they had. So John and his partner had been working to complete the project to save themselves. He insisted that it would be done in a month and that he would then be back at work at full speed. He pleaded for his job. He said he really liked to work for us. He also said he

would continue to do an outstanding job for us if we would just give him a little room right now to get out of the mess he was in."

"What did you say to that?" Jackie asked.

"I told him how I felt about how he had treated us and how he had used very bad judgment. However, I said that I would think about it and let him know my decision tonight."

"And what have you decided?"

"I decided to talk it over with you and Dirk first. After all, he has been one of the company's valuable earning assets. You wouldn't like it if I sold the warehouse out from under you without you knowing it, would you?"

Jackie replied, "Look, I know you have made up your mind what you want to do. So tell me and I'll put in my two cents' worth if I feel like it."

Questions:

1. Should John Knight be fired?
2. Discuss/explain how you would handle the situation if you were Tom Grant.

[1] This quote is often attributed to leadership author Warren Bennis, who wrote, *On Becoming A Leader*, Addison-Wesley Publishing Company, 1989. Chapter 2 in this book discusses the differences between managers and leaders.

[2] Robert I. Sutton, "True Leaders Are Also Managers," *Harvard Business Review*, August 11, 2010.

[3] Paul Hunting, "Developing Natural Leadership," *British Journal of Administrative Management*, May/June 2001, pp. 28–29; Susan Johnstal, "Successful Strategies for Transfer of Learned Leadership," *Performance Improvement*, August 2013, Vol. 52 (7), pp. 5–12; Duff McDonald, "Can you learn to lead?" *New York Times,* April 12, 2015, p. ED17.

[4] Thomas N. Ingram, Raymond W. LaForge, William B. Locander, Scott B. MacKenzie, and Philip M. Podsakoff, "New Directions in Sales Leadership Research, *Journal of Personal Selling & Sales Management*, Spring 2005, pp. 137–54.

[5] The leadership style section is based to a large extent on Scott B. MacKenzie, Philip M. Podsakoff, and Gregory A. Rich, "Transformational and Transactional Leadership and Salesperson Performance," *Journal of the Academy of Marketing Science,* Spring 2001, pp. 115–34.

[6] Channoch Jacobsen and Robert J. House, "Dynamics of Charismatic Leadership: A Process Theory, Simulation Model, and Tests," *Leadership Quarterly,* Spring 2001, pp. 75–112.

[7] Betsy Cummings, "Getting Reps to Live Your Mission," *Sales & Marketing Management,* October 2001, p. 15.

[8] Steven Rosen, "Are Your Sales Managers Effective Sales Coaches?" *Sales & Service Excellence Essentials*, June 2016, Vol. 15 (6), pp. 24–24.

[9] Betsy Cummings and Amy Moerke, "Meeting Masters," *Sales & Marketing Management*, March 2004, pp. 36–38.

[10] Nikolaos Panagopoulos and Sergios Dimitriadis, "Transformational leadership as a mediator of the relationship between behavior-based control and salespeople's key outcomes: An initial investigation," *European Journal of Marketing,* 2009, Vol. 43 (7/8), pp. 1008–1031; and Luiza Rodrigues, Cristina Alencar; Filipe Coelho, and Carlos M.P. Sousa, "Control mechanisms and goal orientations: evidence from frontline service employees," *European Journal of Marketing,* 2015, Vol. 49 (3/4), p350–371.

[11] Jay Prakash Mulki, Fernando Jaramillo, and William B Locander, "Effects of Ethical Climate and Supervisory Trust on Salesperson's Job Attitudes and Intentions to Quit," *Journal of Personal Selling and Sales Management,* Winter 2006, pp. 19–26.

[12] Warren G. Bennis, *Managing the Dream: Reflections on Leadership and Change* (Cambridge, MA: Perseus, 2000).

[13] Tom Quick, *Making Your Sales Team No. 1* (New York: AMACOM, 1992).

[14] U.S. Department of Health and Human Services Substance Abuse and Mental Health Services Administration, *Worker Drug Use and Workplace Policies and Programs: Results from 1994 and 1997 NHSDA* (Rockville, MD: U.S. Department of Health and Human Services, 1999).

[15] Wayne Friedman, "That Demon Alcohol," *Sales & Marketing Management*, December 1996, pp. 42–47.

[16] A number of nonprofit and/or government sponsored organizations provide extensive information on issues surrounding substance abuse problems. For example, visit the websites of the National Institute on Drug Abuse (www.drugabuse.gov) and the National Institute on Alcohol Abuse and Alcoholism (www.niaaa.nih.gov).

[17] This discussion is based to a large extent on the following articles: Cathy Owens Swift and Russell L. Kent, "Sexual Harassment: Ramifications for Sales Managers," *Journal of Personal Selling & Sales Management,* Winter 1994, pp. 77–88; and Leslie M. Fine, C. David Shepherd, and Susan L. Josephs, "Insights into Sexual Harassment of Salespeople by Customers: The Role of Gender and Customer Power," *Journal of Personal Selling & Sales Management*, Spring 1999, pp. 19–34.

12

Forecasting and Budgets

The foundation of the planning efforts of most companies is a sales forecast. The importance of sales forecasting is clearly shown at Otis Elevator Company, a world leader in the development and marketing of elevators and moving stairway systems. According to Heinz Dickens, Sales Manager of International Operations at Otis, sales forecasting for him begins with estimates of sales for the coming year. These are provided by salespeople and sales managers in the company's territories. Many of the sales territories include whole foreign countries.

Otis, like many large companies, uses its sales forecasts to allocate resources across different functional areas. Production uses sales forecasts to develop production schedules and quantity requirements and to regulate inventories; finance uses them to set operating budgets and to project cash flows; human resources uses them to establish hiring levels; and marketing uses them to allocate resources across different marketing activities.

Sales forecasting at Otis is not an exact science, says Dickens. The international division often makes adjustments to the forecast for elevators and moving stairways as unforeseen events surface, such as wars and changes in governments. These events can dampen or stimulate sales of the company's products. Otis tries to improve forecasting accuracy by including many different types of information in the sales forecasts. For example, the company compiles monthly reports on the progress of negotiations with its potential customers. "Though we may be off-target sometimes," says Dickens, "our manufacturing operation would come to a standstill if we did not produce a reasonably good sales forecast."

The problem confronting Otis Elevator year after year is how to develop an accurate sales forecast that helps managers make sound business decisions. In this chapter, we will help you understand the importance of forecasting, illustrate types of forecasting methods firms use, and discuss several guidelines on the selection of a sales forecasting method.

SALES FORECASTING AND STRATEGIC AND OPERATIONAL PLANNING

A company must establish its marketing goals and strategies—the core of a marketing plan—before it makes a sales forecast. The sales forecasts will differ according to whether the marketing goal is to liquidate inventory or to expand the firm's market share by aggressive advertising or some other goal.

Once the sales forecast is prepared, it becomes the key factor in all *operational* planning throughout the company. Forecasting is the basis of sound budgeting. Financial planning for working capital requirements, plant utilization, and other needs is based on anticipated sales. The scheduling of all production resources and facilities, such as setting labor needs and purchasing raw materials, depends on the sales forecast. The sales forecast also plays a critical role in sales force planning. The sales forecast helps sales executives determine the budget for the department; it also influences sales quotas and compensation of salespeople.

If the forecast is wrong, the plans based on it also will be wrong. For example, if it is overly optimistic, the organization can suffer great losses because of over-expenditures in anticipation of revenues that are not forthcoming. If the sales forecast is too low, the firm may not be prepared to provide what the market demands. This means that the company will be forgoing profits and giving its competitors a bigger market share. Clearly, valid sales forecasts can play a major role in the success of the company.

FIGURE 12-1
Market Potential vs. Sales Potential

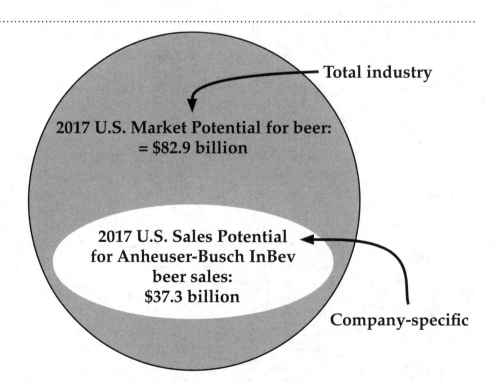

Total industry

2017 U.S. Market Potential for beer:
= $82.9 billion

2017 U.S. Sales Potential for Anheuser-Busch InBev beer sales:
$37.3 billion

Company-specific

THE BASIC IDEAS USED IN FORECASTING

Before we discuss the methods used in forecasting, we need to define and explain some of the basic terms used in forecasting sales. Because the terms are closely related and used loosely in business, they frequently cause misunderstandings among managers.

Market Potential and Sales Potential

What do we mean when we speak of a potential market for a product? **Market potential** is the total expected sales of a given good or service for the *entire industry* in a specific market over a stated period of time. To be complete and meaningful, the definition of market potential (and sales potential and the sales forecast, which we will discuss next) must include four elements:

1. The item being marketing (the good, service, idea, person or location).
2. Sales for the entire industry in dollars or product units.
3. A specific time period.
4. A specific market delineated either geographically, by type of customer, or both

For example, a reasonable estimate of the market potential for beer in the United States in the year 2017 is $82,895 million—or 24,016.5 million liters in terms of volume.[1] Note that this statement about the market potential of beer includes information on each of the four points discussed above. The market potential for beer also could be stated for markets more specific than the United States, such as U.S. blue-collar men, Ohio white-collar women, men and women ages 21-25 in Florida, and so on.

Sales potential refers to the maximum share (or percentage) of market potential that an individual firm can reasonably expect to achieve. For example, Anheuser-Busch InBev with its portfolio of brands that include Budweiser, Corona and Stella Artois, has about a 45 percent market share in the United States.[2] It is therefore reasonable to estimate AB InBev's 2017 sales potential in the U.S. for all of its beer brands to be $37,303 million (or 45% of the market potential). When we speak of a company's sales potential, we must again specify the product, market, and time period.

As shown in Figure 12-1, market potential is a total-industry concept, whereas sales potential refers to products of an individual firm. Thus, we may speak of the "market potential" for light beer and the "sales potential" (or market share) for AB InBev's Bud Light. Market potential and sales potential are equal in the case of a monopoly. In most industries, however, market potential and sales potential are different, since there are many firms competing in the market. As discussed in Chapter 13, it is sales potential that is a key input into the process of designing territories.

Sales Forecast

A **sales forecast** is an estimate of sales (in dollars or units) that an individual firm expects to achieve during a specified forthcoming time period, in a stated market, and under a proposed marketing plan. A company may make a forecast for an entire product line or for individual items within the line.

Sales may be forecast for a company's total market or for individual market segments.

At first glance, the company's sales potential and sales forecast may appear to be the same, but usually that is not the case. The sales potential is what would be achieved under ideal conditions. The sales forecast typically is less than the sales potential for many different reasons. The company's production facilities may be too limited to allow the firm to reach its full sales potential. Also, the firm's financial resources may not be adequate enough to allow it to realize the full sales potential in the current period.

ESTIMATING THE POTENTIAL FOR A MARKET AND SALES

Under conditions of great uncertainty, such as those that exist when a firm is trying to market an innovation, it is very difficult to develop accurate forecasts. Estimates are often inaccurate. If the innovation hits a market favorably, the projections will probably prove to be too low; if it misses the market, the sales projections will prove to be insufficiently conservative.

The three fundamental techniques for estimating market and sales potentials for a product are market-factor derivation, surveys of buyer intentions, and test markets. Each of these methods is based on an analysis of the customer. Therefore, we will first describe the customer analysis and then discuss each method.

Customer Analysis

A **customer analysis** identifies and clearly defines the target market, determines customer needs, and then explains how the product satisfies those needs. The starting point in this process is to determine who will use the product and to identify all possible characteristics of those users. A distinction must be made between the person who *buys* the product and the individual who actually *uses* it. The market potential is based on the individual or firm for which the product is intended. Although many women buy shirts for men, the market potential for men's shirts is determined by the number of men users, not by the number of women buyers.

Are the users household consumers, industrial users, or both? If they are household consumers, the seller may want to classify them further by demographics such as age, sex, marital status, area of residence, income, occupation, religion, and education. Lifestyle information also may be used, such as the types of exercise and recreation in which the user is interested. In the case of businesses selling to businesses, the seller must collect information on the types and quantities of products potential buyers manufacturer and sell to their end users. Managers must gather the names and positions of the persons influencing the purchase decision, as well as information about the company's competitors. Most companies have compiled such information through periodic contact with their customers or through the use of marketing research.

Performing a customer analysis also requires a determination of why customers are buying the product and what their buying habits are. Most products purchased to fulfill some need. Understanding these needs can improve the accuracy of a company's market potential estimate and sales forecasts. For example, consumer sensitivity to the prices of grocery products has resulted in greater sales of private-label (i.e., store-brand) products and, in response to consumers' concerns about price, consumer product giants such as Procter & Gamble and Unilever routinely chop prices of their products to stay competitive. Price also plays a major role in forecasting demand in areas outside of grocery products. For example, fluctuating prices in the oil industry can have a major impact on the forecasted dollar sales volume on gasoline. In all these cases, the understanding that price plays an important role in purchase decision will help the companies produce accurate forecasts.

Market-Factor Derivation

The **market-factor derivation** method for determining the size of a potential market begins with a market factor. A **market factor** is an item or element in a market that (1) causes the demand for a good or service or (2) is otherwise related to that demand. To illustrate, the annual birthrate is a market factor underlying the demand for playpens. That is, this element is related to the number of playpens that a manufacturer can sell. Using the birthrate as a market factor, a manufacturer of playpens would estimate the sales potential for playpens as follows:

Estimated number of births per year	4,000,000
Times: Percent who buy playpens	X 0.33
Market potential	1,320,000
Times: Potential market share	X 0.30
Sales potential	396,000

An independent supermarket operator in Denver, Colorado, computed the store's sales potential by using an estimate of food and beverage sales in the Denver metropolitan area (about $4.897 billion) as the market factor.[3] The store did not sell to the entire area but rather appealed only to a region in which about 15 percent of the population resided. So the operator estimated the market potential to be about $734.7 million. Since three other large supermarkets plus some smaller stores competed in that same area, the operator set 20 percent as the store's probably share of the market. Therefore, the sales potential was $146.9 million for the year.

Denver food sales	$4,897,791,000
Times: Percent of market covered	X 0.15
Market potential	$ 734,668,650
Times: Potential market share	X 0.20
Sales potential	$ 146,933,730

This market-factor derivation technique for determining market and sales potentials has several advantages. First, the validity of the method is high. The method is usually founded on some valid statistics that have relatively little error. Other favorable aspects of this technique are that it is fairly simple, requires little statistical analysis, and is relatively inexpensive to use.

It should be noted that the market-factor method, like the other methods of estimating potentials, can be used as the basis of the sales forecast. In order to forecast sales, the company must estimate what portion of its sales potential it can reasonably expect to achieve in a given period.

Surveys of Buyer Intentions

The **survey of buyer intentions** technique for determining potentials consists of contacting potential customers and questioning them about whether or not they would purchase the product or service at the price asked.

One manufacturer contemplating the production of an aluminum playpen for babies used this technique. The playpen was to be made exactly like the ordinary wooden playpens on the market, except that aluminum tubing would be used instead of the wooden bars. The manufacturer established that it would be satisfied if it sold 5,000 aluminum playpen units per year. Since the cost of the unit would be higher than that of the wooden units, the manufacturer wanted to know two things. First, how many people would buy such a product if it were placed on the market at the retail price of $59.95? Second, what did customers think the price of such a product should be?

The manufacturer conducted a survey through personal interviews with 240 parents of infants. The results showed that 170 of the 240 (approximately 71 percent) were interested in such a product. However, they also indicated that the price would have to be $39.95 to capture that size of market. The average (mean) price quoted ($45) would eliminate half of the respondents who showed interest in the product. Still, 10 people (4 percent of the market) said they would be interested in purchasing the product at the retail price of $59.95.

The survey indicated that only about one-third of all families with infants purchase playpens. Thus, the total market potential for the $59.95 aluminum playpens would be approximately 52,800 units. This figure was derived by multiplying the total number of births per year (4 million) by one third- (0.33) and taking 4 percent of the result. This simple calculation showed the manufacturer that market interest in the playpen well exceeded the goal of selling 5,000 units and was therefore sufficient to warrant further investigation.

The primary advantage of surveys of buyer intentions is that the method is based on information obtained directly from the people who will ultimately purchase or not purchase the product. Major disadvantages of this method are its cost and its time-consuming execution. For the sales manager who needs a quick idea of the market potential of a product, the survey method is not suitable. If a manufacturer intends to distribute nationally, consumer surveys can easily run into thousands of dollars and take three to six months to complete. Furthermore, surveys of buying intentions are hazardous undertakings. It is easy for the respondents to say that they would buy a certain product, but the acid test is whether or not they actually do.

Test Markets

Test marketing involves introducing and marketing a new product in a market that is similar to the company's other markets. For example, Indianapolis, Indiana, and Columbus, Ohio, are often used as test markets by companies because their socioeconomic and demographic profiles are similar to the profiles of many other cities in the United States. The demand for the product in the test market will then be used to forecast sales of the product in other markets.

Although the test marketing takes considerable time and money, it is probably the most accurate method of estimating the sales potential for certain products. The reason is that a test market actually requires the buyers to spend their money. The other methods discussed require an estimate of what share of the market the product will achieve. Frequently, these estimates are merely guesses. The test market eliminates the guessing.

In the world of new ventures, venture capitalists view the first stage of development in which the product is initially offered for sales as a test market. Jerry Zimmer started ZDC, a computerized system for managing and measuring the energy used in master-metered apartment houses, in Boulder, Colorado, with just a $60,000 initial investment. He sold about $1 million worth of his systems in the Denver market area during ZDC's first year of operation. On the basis of that test, the company was able to raise an additional $500,000 to expand market coverage. The first several years of the life of many new products is essentially a test market that proves that people will buy the product and that it is profitable.

The one obvious advantage of the test-marketing technique is that it results directly in a sales potential for products under consideration. However, test marketing requires a considerable amount of effort and time before results are known. Products that require extensive investment in fixed assets before they are introduced to the market cannot be evaluated by this method. Similarly, test markets provide poor evaluations of products that require time to gain acceptance or have a low rate of consumption. Test marketing is used mainly when a relatively small number of units can be produced at a minimum cost.

TERRITORY POTENTIALS

Once the company has determined total sales potential, the sales manager usually wants to divide that potential among the various territorial divisions. This allows the manager to allocate selling efforts properly and to evaluate the relative performance of each district. The usual method for this is to use some pertinent market factor of index broken down by small areas.

A **market index** is a market factor expressed as a percentage, or in some other quantitative form, relative to some base figure. A market index may be based on two or more market factors. For example, one **buying power index** is based on three factors—population, effective buying income, and retail sales.[4] This index, like many other published indexes, provides information broken down in many ways: regions of the country, states, cities, counties, and metropolitan areas. This index is primarily designed to aid the executive in allocating activities among areas.

Figure 12-2 provides an example of how the buying power index is used to allocate total sales potential among territories. A manufacturer of men's suits determined that national sales potential for its suits was $25 million for the next year. Management then determined the percentage of national retail

FIGURE 12-2
Division of Sales Potential among Territories Using Retail Sales as a Market Index

Territory	Percentage of Total Retail Sales*	Territorial Sales Potential $25M x Col 1 x 100
New England	5.6	$1,400,000
Middle Atlantic	13.1	$3,275,000
East North Central	15.3	$3,825,000
West North Central	7.2	$1,800,000
South Atlantic	18.5	$4,625,000
East South Central	5.4	$1,350,000
West South Central	11.6	$2,900,000
Mountain	6.9	$1,725,000
Pacific	16.5	$4,125,000
TOTAL	100.0%	$25,000,000

* From "Survey of Buying Power Index," *Sales & Marketing Management,* September 2005, p. 62.

sales that occur in each of the manufacturer's nine sales territories and multiplied the percentage by $25 million to yield sales potential on a territory-by-territory basis.

In forecasting sales for industrial products or business-to-business goods or services, companies often use the **North American Industry Classification System (NAICS)** developed jointly by the United States, Canada, and Mexico to replace the former U.S. Standard Industrial Classification (SIC) system. Under NAICS, businesses are divided into numerically ordered categories. Each firm is assigned a four-digit number on the basis of its main line of business. Then data collected by most government agencies are classified and published by those numbers. For example, as shown in Figure 12-3, NAICS 325 contains all firms in the chemical manufacturing industry. The pharmaceutical and medicine segment of that industry carries the four-digit number 3254. The pharmaceutical preparations companies are numbered 325411. By referring to 3254 in NAICS, companies selling products to pharmaceutical firms can discover how many firms (potential customers) are included in that

FIGURE 12-3
North American Industry Classification System (NAICS)

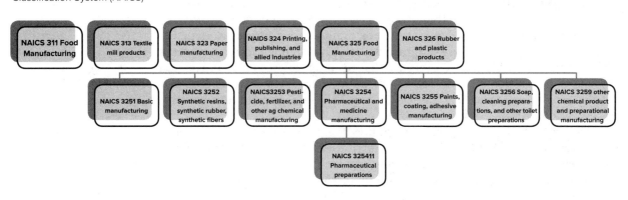

category, where they are located, what their sales volumes are, how many employees they have, and much more. Much of the information can be used to help estimate potentials. Anyone doing research in industrial marketing should become familiar with NAICS data.

Firms also can use experts to meet their data needs. A large number of commercial data supply and marketing research companies provide businesses with information that can help them with their forecasting needs. Scanning technology has enabled retail firms to provide their vendors with data to help them forecast sales. Walmart provides weekly forecasting data to well over half of its approximately 5,000 vendors through its electronic data interchange system.[5]

SALES FORECASTING

After determining the market or sales potential for a product or service, management can make a sales forecast. This is an essential step in sales planning, and the sales executives are highly involved. At Liberty Mutual, area managers are responsible for forecasting sales across their region, which typically spans an entire state or two. A Liberty Mutual area manager is an executive that supervises several branches, each of which is headed by a branch manager that oversees about 10 salespeople. In other words, the forecasting is responsibility is given to a high-level individual—which points to its importance to the firm. Forecasting is also a difficult, time-consuming activity.

Difficulty of Sales Forecasting

The difficulty of developing an accurate sales forecast varies from situation to situation. When sales of a product are very stable from one period to the next, a sales forecast for an upcoming period is not difficult to perform. When sales of a product fluctuate dramatically from period to period, accurate sales forecasts are difficult to develop. Accurate sales forecasts are also difficult to attain for new products, since a historical sales record is lacking. Developing a sales forecast for an existing product is less difficult, since managers have some historical data to guide them.

Sales Forecasting Periods

Although it varies widely from company to company, sales forecasts are commonly made for periods of three months (quarterly), six months, or one year. Usually the sales forecasting period coincides with the firm's fiscal year since the fiscal year is used as a basis for planning expenditures. However, some firms find that their operations cycle is considerably shorter than a year and prefer to forecast for that cycle. At Fastenal, the district manager looks at market trends and makes a series of forecasts for each store in the district. This includes a projection of sales for each of the next four quarters—but these forecasts are adjusted up or down each month. Not surprisingly, the forecasts for the impending quarter are more accurate than the forecasts for the later quarters.

Firms usually undertake long-run sales estimates to plan capital expenditures. Top management often seeks knowledge about the long-term sales outlook before undertaking any plant expansion. When the forecasting horizon is short (one year or less), forecasting accuracy is likely to be greater than when the forecasting period is long.

Factors Influencing the Sales Forecast

The sales forecast must take into consideration changes that have occurred or are anticipated that may affect sales. These changes can be placed in four general categories:

- Marketing plans
- Conditions within the industry
- Market conditions
- General business conditions

Marketing plans

Any changes in the price structure, channels of distribution, promotional plans, products, or other internal marketing policies may influence future sales. The forecaster must estimate the quantitative extent of these influences. He or she may know, for example, that the firm will soon have to raise prices. Although this action will reduce unit volume, total dollar volume might go up or down, depending on the product's price elasticity. Thus, formulating a realistic sales forecast is impossible without taking price changes into consideration. If the firm planned to alter its channels of distribution or its advertising expenditures, these actions also would influence future sales.

Conditions within the industry

A firm obtains its sales volume from total industry sales. Therefore, any change within the industry has an impact on the firm. Whatever volume new producers in an industry gain must come from existing companies. Thus, the sales forecast for those companies may have to be revised downward. If a competitor is planning to redesign its line of products, the firm must consider the possibility that the competitor may obtain a larger share of the market during the coming period.

Market conditions

If basic demand factors are in a slump, the future sales of the firm will be affected. The firm's manager must be aware of any basic changes in the primary demand for the industry's output. An analysis of future market conditions is particularly important if the concern sells to relatively few industries.

Mor-Flo, a manufacturer of solar water heaters, saw its sales potential suddenly multiply several times during a natural gas shortage. And, when the price of gasoline increases, the sales potentials for the makers of compact cars can expand significantly—as the sales of large cars, SUVs, and other gas guzzlers go down.

General Business Conditions

A major influencing factor in future sales development is the general state of the economy. Basically, many of the methods of sales forecasting are simply reflections of overall opinion of what the general economy will be like during the coming period.

SALES FORECASTING METHODS

The following methods may be used to forecast the sales of a product or service. The methods can be placed in three general categories. Survey methods rely on the opinions and judgments of experts, such as salespeople, sales executives, and the customers who will be making purchase decisions. Twelve percent of all industries use survey methods. Mathematical methods apply mathematical and statistical techniques to historical data to forecast sales. These methods, used by 68 percent of industries, are the most popular. Operational methods take information about the marketing plans, financial requirements, and/or the company's capacity to derive a sales forecast. These methods are used by 20 percent of industries.

- Survey methods:
  - Executive opinion
  - Sales force composite
  - Buyers' intentions

- Mathematical methods:
  - Moving average models
  - Exponential smoothing models
  - Regression models

- Operational methods
  - Test markets
  - "Must-do" calculations
  - Capacity-based calculations

Figure 12-4 shows the sources of the data for the various methods. Surveys of buyer intentions and test markets were discussed earlier in the chapter, as they are methods that are used both for estimating potentials and for forecasting sales. They will not be discussed again, but each of the other methods is explained below.

METHOD	SOURCE OF DATA
Executive opinion	Executives and managers
Sales force composite	Salespeople
Survey of buyer intentions	Customers
Moving average models	Historical sales data
Exponential smoothing	Historical sales data
Regression analysis	Historical sales and other data
"Must-do" calculations	Company operations
Capacity-based approach	Company operations
Test markets	Company operations

FIGURE 12-4
Sources of data for sales forecasting methods

Executive Opinion

The **executive opinion** method of forecasting is the oldest and simplest technique known. It consists of obtaining the views of top executives regarding future sales—views that may or may not be supported by facts. Some executives may have used forecasting methods, such as those we will discuss soon, to arrive at their opinions. Others may have formed their estimates largely by observation, experience, and intuition.

The forecasts made by the executives are averaged to yield one forecast for all executives, or the differences are reconciled through discussions among executives. For example, executives at Wyeth, a large pharmaceutical firm, use this approach in geographical areas and for products where forecasting software does not exist. Executives review monthly shipments and orders to arrive at sales forecasts for the geographic areas and products. The final forecast is then used to develop a financial plan for the coming year.[6]

The major advantage cited for this technique is that it is quick and easy to do. Perhaps because it is easy to use, the executive opinion method is especially popular among small- and medium-sized companies.

Despite its popularity, the executive opinion approach has several disadvantages. Many managers consider this method to be highly unscientific, little more than educated guesses. Many managers also argue that the executive opinion method requires too much management time since differing forecasts must be reconciled before a final forecast is made. Finally, the opinions of highly placed executives (and/or executives with strong feelings) may influence the final forecast more than executives who are more knowledgeable about the company's products.

The Delphi technique

A highly publicized technique developed by the Rand Corporation for predicting the future and for forecasting sales is the **Delphi technique,** which a variation of executive opinion. In administering a Delphi forecast, a company selects a panel of experts, who are typically managers from various functional areas inside the firm (although key customers, supplier and other outside industry experts may also be on the panel). Each expert is asked to make a prediction on what company sales will be in the forthcoming time period. The resulting set of forecasts is fed back to the whole panel. The experts are then asked to make another prediction on the same matter, with the knowledge of the forecasts of the others on the panel. This process is repeated until the experts arrive at some consensus. The Delphi method is used by 15 percent of those who use executive opinion to formulate their forecast.[7]

Sales Force Composite

The **sales force composite** method is based on collecting an estimate from each salesperson of the level of products they expect to sell in the forecast period. The estimate may be made in consultation with sales executives and customers and/or based on the salesperson's intuition and experience. The individual forecasts are then aggregated to yield an overall forecast for the firm. This method places the responsibility for making the forecast in the hands of those who have to make it happen and who are closest to the market. Sales quotas and compensation that are based on sales force composite forecasts are likely to be regarded as fair by the salespeople.

However, salespeople are often poor forecasters. Depending on the circumstances, they tend to be either optimistic or pessimistic. Rookie salespeople tend to be overly optimistic—perhaps in an attempt to impress the executives. On the other hand, when quotas or other types of goals are based on the forecast, salespeople may purposely underestimate future sales. This way, the goal is easier to attain, and so they are more likely to look good and perhaps receive their bonus compensation. In addition, although salespeople may understand their particular customers and territory better than anybody, they are often not as knowledgeable as executives—especially in terms of the broader economic and company forces at work. Finally, sales force composite is a time consuming activity for both management and the salespeople involved. Management must be on the lookout for both the high and low estimates that tend to come in—and correct for those.

Moving Average Technique

The simplest way to forecast sales is to predict that sales in the coming period will be equal to sales in the past period. Such a forecast assumes that the conditions in the last period will be the same as the conditions in the coming period. It is likely, however, that the factors affecting sales change from period to period. Hence, it makes sense to take an average of sales from several periods to construct the sales forecast for the coming period. This approach is called the **moving average technique.** The moving average technique takes the following form, where t is the current time period and n is equal to the number of past periods being averaged:

$$\text{Sales}_{t+1} = 1/n \; (\text{sales}_t + \text{sales}_{t-1} + \dots + \text{sales}_{t-n})$$

In other words, sales_{t+1} is forecasted sales in the coming time period, sales_t is sales in the present time period, sales_{t-1} is sales in the period immediately past, and so on. The sales of the designated periods are summed and then divided by the number of periods to yield the average. When a forecast is developed for the next period, the sales total in the oldest period is dropped from the average and is replaced by actual sales in the newest period, hence the name *moving average.* The forecaster determines how many periods will be included in the average.

An example of the moving average technique is shown in Figure 12-5 for a toy manufacturer. Historical/actual sales from the past four periods are shown. Assume that we are at the end of November 2016, and so we need to develop a forecast for December 2016. The two-period moving average of $81,000 was determined by averaging sales in the present period and the previous period. Note that the two-period moving average forecast for November 2016 would be

	8/2016	9/2016	10/2016	11/2016	12/2016*
Actual $ sales →	$80,000	$84,000	$83,000	$79,000	
		Two-period moving average ($79,000 + $83,000)/2 =			$81,000
	Three-period moving average ($79,000 + $83,000 + $84,000)/3 =				$82,000

FIGURE 12-5
Forecasting December Sales Using Moving Average Method

* December 2016 represents *the next* time period (so current time is the end of November).

$83,500, yet actual sales turned out to be $79,000. The three-period moving average for December 2016 is $82,000 as it was the average of sales in September, October and November. Note the slight difference in forecasted sales between the two averages, which is to be expected given that an additional period was used to calculate the three-period model.

The most significant advantage of the moving average approach is that it is easy to compute. Moving average models provide accurate forecasts for products with stable sales histories; but the forecasts are less accurate for products that experience dramatic changes in sales, since the sales forecast is based on an average of sales from several different periods. Moving average models are also unable to reflect the impact of factors that arise in the forecasted period that were not present in previous periods. For example, the moving average model could not predict a significant decrease in sales for the toy manufacturer due to the unexpected entry of a strong competitor into the market.

Exponential Smoothing Models

The **exponential smoothing model** is closely related to the moving average technique for sales forecasting. In moving average models, the sales total in each of the past periods has the same impact on the sales forecast. Using an exponential smoothing model, the forecast can allow sales in certain periods to influence the forecast more than sales in other periods.

The general form of the exponential smoothing model is:

$$\text{Sales}_{t+1} = L * (\text{Actual sales}_t) + (1-L) * (\text{Forecasted sales}_t)$$

The exponential smoothing model argues that forecasted sales in the coming time period (i.e., Sales_{t+1}) is equal to actual sales in the present period times a smoothing constant (L) plus (1—L) times what had been the sales forecast in the present period. The key difference between the exponential smoothing model and the moving average technique lies in the application of the smoothing constant (L), which translates into a weighted average of the most recent actual sales with the most recent forecast. A smoothing constant with a high value (such as, L=0.8) allows for the most recent actual sales to influence the sales forecast more than sales in earlier periods, whereas a constant with a low value (such as, L=0.2) allows earlier periods to influence forecasted sales more. The forecaster determines the value of the constant based on a review of the data and on his or her intuition and knowledge about the similarity between conditions in the forecasted period and conditions in previous periods.

Returning to the toy manufacturer example, Figure 12-6 shows exponential smoothing forecasts for December 2016 under two different smoothing constants. Note that the sales forecast for November has been added—so, actual sales in November of $79,000 were one thousand dollars less than what had been forecast. We then calculate two separate exponential smoothing forecasts for December 2016—one with L=0.3 and one with L=0.7. As discussed above, the higher smoothing constant results in a forecast that is closer to the most recent actual sales (and the lower smoothing constant leads weights the earlier periods).

One significant advantage associated with the exponential smoothing model over the moving average technique is that the forecaster can determine the degree to which a particular period can affect forecasted sales. A significant disadvantage associated with the exponential smoothing model is that the selection of

FIGURE 12-6
Forecasting December
Sales Using Exponential
Smoothing

	8/2016	9/2016	10/2016	11/2016	12/2016*
Actual $ sales →	$80,000	$84,000	$83,000	$79,000	
Forecasted $ sales for November 2016 →				$80,000	
Exponential smoothing forecast with L=0.3 = 0.3x79,000 + 0.7x80,000					$79,700
Exponential smoothing forecast with L=0.7 = 0.7x79,000 + 0.3x80,000					$79,300

* December 2016 represents *the next* time period (so current time is the end of November).

the smoothing constant is somewhat arbitrary. Despite this limitation, exponential smoothing models are used by a large number of companies to forecast sales

Regression Analysis

The final mathematical forecasting technique that we will discuss is called **regression analysis**. This technique is often used to project sales trends into the future. Unlike moving average and exponential smoothing, regression can result in a forecast that extends an upward (or downward) trend, and so it can result in a sales forecast that is higher (or lower) than actual sales ever have been. Regression analysis analyzes the historical relationship between some predictor variable and sales; and gives us an equation to forecast sales. In a simple linear regression, the relationship between sales (Y), and predictor variable (X) is shown through the following equation that represents a straight line:

$$\text{Sales } (Y) = a + bX,$$

Where a is the constant and b equals the slope. If one were to graph the relationship between sales and the predictor variable (with sales on the vertical axis), then the constant is the point on the vertical axis where the regression line starts. The slope is the amount that sales changes for every unit increase in the predictor variable. The resulting line will fit the actual data as well as possible—that is, the regression line cuts through the actual sales data points better than any other line that could be drawn.

To better understand this, let's consider a regression analysis to forecast year 7 sales for ABC Company. The following table shows actual sales and the number of salespeople that ABC Company has had in each of the six years it has been in business:

Year	# of reps	Sales
1	2	300,000
2	4	400,000
3	4	500,000
4	10	1,000,000
5	12	1,100,000
6	13	1,200,000
7	??	??

Using year as the predictor variable, the regression analysis generates a constant a=40,000, and a slope b=202,857.[8] The slope suggests that sales increases $202,857 every year. The year 7 sales forecast is $1,460,000, which can be calculated by plugging 7 into the regression equation (40,000 + 202,857x7). See Figure 12-7 for a graphical representation of this forecast.

Alternatively, one could use number of reps as the predictor variable. When doing this, the regression analysis generates a constant a=127,803, and a slope b=82,960. The slope suggests that sales increases $82,960 for every rep that works at the company in a given year. In order to calculate the year 7 forecast with this regression analysis, one must first determine how many reps will be working for ABC Company in coming year. This can be estimated through consulting the firm's marketing plan. Let's say that ABC Company's marketing plan involves opening up one new territory, and so will have 14 reps in the coming year. Consequently, the year 7 forecast is $1,289,238 or 127,803 + 82,960x14. See Figure 12-8 for a graphical representation of this forecast.

A key advantage of regression is that it allows forecasters to experiment with "what-if scenarios." Like with the example above, one could ask: What will sales be if we hire 15 reps? What if we hire 17 reps? And so on. To make these what-if scenarios especially helpful toward strategic planning, multiple predictor variables are used and typically based on elements of the marketing mix (e.g., advertising expenditures, number of retail outlets, etc.). Note that when more than one predictor variable is used within the same regression analysis—this is called **multiple regression.**

"Must-Do" Forecasts

Often management forecasts what volume of sales it needs to accomplish certain goals. For example, sales forecasts for new products are difficult to develop because historical sales data do not exist. Hence, firms often decide that

FIGURE 12-7

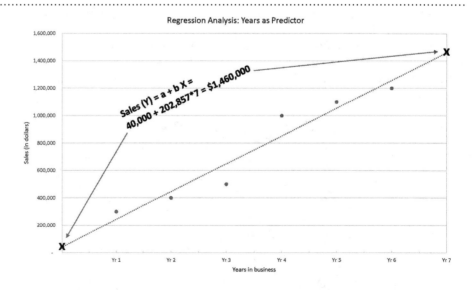

Regression Analysis: Years as Predictor

Sales (Y) = a + b X = 40,000 + 202,857*7 = $1,460,000

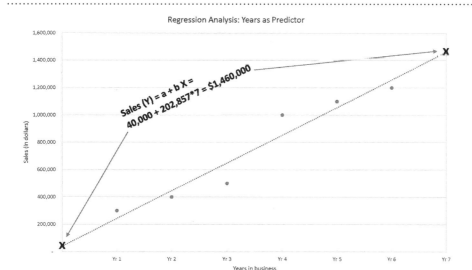

FIGURE 12-8

a reasonable forecast is the sales that must be achieved for a firm to reach its break-even point. In other words, a **must-do forecast** is based on the sales volume needed to generate sufficient cash to cover fixed and variable costs. At other times, management may forecast a level of sales volume that will allow it to achieve some profit goal.

For example, one new consulting service enterprise budgeted its total overhead costs at $165,000 for the first year. The entrepreneur desired a profit of $60,000, which would represent her salary. Given that the product was a service, there were no costs of goods sold. Thus, she projected sales at $225,000 for the year and proceeded to plan on that basis.

Capacity-Based Forecasts

Sometimes a firm's market is such that it can sell everything it can make or buy. Thus, its capacity becomes its sales forecast. For example, the owner of a highly acclaimed restaurant developed a **capacity-based forecast** of sales according to how many seats the restaurant had: 120 seats at 30 tables. The restaurant had a dinner-only format in which only two seatings per evening were planned. Thus, a total of 240 people could be served in each of the 300 nights a year the restaurant was open. There was a waiting list to eat at the restaurant during each night, so empty seats would not be encountered. The average ticket with drinks was forecast at $30. Hence, sales for the year were projected at $2,160,000 ($30 times 240 people times 300 nights).

SOME GUIDING PRINCPLES FOR FORECASTING

Sales forecasting is a very difficult task. There are some guidelines available to managers that can enhance the accuracy of the sales forecast. They are summarized in Figure 12-9.

Fit the Method to the Product/Market

Some forecasting techniques work better than others for some products and in some markets. To develop accurate forecasts, it is important to use the most appropriate method. Ocean Spray Cranberries provides a good example of this. The company serves consumers using supermarket chains in the United States and Canada. All of Ocean Spray's product sales are captured in retailer scanning data, so the company has ample historical data from which to build a sales forecast. Forecasters at Ocean Spray employ quantitative techniques, like moving average models, to achieve forecasts for more than 300 different products. The company knows demand for cranberries can be seasonal, so it takes steps to account for seasonality. The forecast is used for procurement purposes and for supply, replenishment, and revenue planning.[9]

Use More than One Method

One way to improve the accuracy of a sales forecast is to use multiple forecasting techniques. For example, the Lockheed Martin Aircraft and Logistics Center (LM) uses times series techniques (like exponential smoothing models) and regression analysis to forecast sales. The regression analysis is used because of the need to predict demand more accurately. For example, LM employs environmental, industry, and economic factors into its forecasts to enhance accuracy.[10] Similarly, executive opinion could be combined with a mathematical method, such as exponential smoothing, to develop a forecast.

Minimize the Number of Market Factors

In market analysis, simplicity has great virtue. The more factors on which an analysis is based, the more difficult it is to determine exactly what affects the demand for a product. Often the inclusion of many factors in a market index results only in the duplication of a few basic forces. One drug manufacturer computed a market index from the following factors: (1) number of drugstores, (2) population, (3) number of physicians, (4) income, (5) number of hospital beds, and (6) number of people older than 65. Actually, this market index essentially was based on two elements—population and income. Several of the supposed market factors were merely surface indicators of these two basic forces. The number of physicians in an area is a reflection of the population and income of that area. Similarly, the number of drugstores and the number of hospital beds usually depend on population.

Additionally, a large regression analysis model presents the forecaster with many statistical problems and, because of its size, actually can inhibit an understanding of the factors that build sales of the product. A good approach is for the forecaster to discuss the factors that affect sales of the company's products with salespeople, executives, and customers and then to develop a model consisting of a relatively small set of factors believed to affect sales.

Recognize the Limitations of Forecasting

Managers must be comfortable with the limitations of forecasting. As noted earlier, forecasts will be more accurate for some products than for others, and in some situations than in others. For example, forecasts are very difficult when the product is innovative and few similar products exist in the market or when the demand for the product is highly variable from period to period. Furthermore, a company can develop a good forecast for the period but fall short of forecasted sales because the company did not implement the marketing plan very well.

Use the Minimum/Maximum Technique

Sound research strategy dictates the use of both minimum and maximum estimates in all computations in order to obtain a range of variations. Analysts should work up one set of estimates that assumes the worst possible developments in each of the calculations. In doing this, they compute the lowest probably potential market for the product. At the same time, they should estimate what the market potential would be should all things be favorable. They also may prepare other estimates, each based on varying assumptions between the two extremes.

Understand Math and Statistics

The development of a sales forecast typically involves the use of statistics and mathematics. A sales manager should be sufficiently acquainted with statistical techniques to recognize any serious errors in the material presented.

REVIEW THE FORECASTING PROCESS

The company should review the forecasting process periodically. The first step in the review is to determine the accuracy of past forecasts to learn if changes are needed in the way forecasts are made. If the company finds that sales forecasts are significantly different from actual sales in the period, it should undertake a review of the sales forecasting process before making any more forecasts.

The evaluation process then should review the data used in sales forecasting. Poor data collection methods can decrease the quality of the data used for forecasting, or the data may be inappropriate for forecasting sales of the product. For example, a large farm-implements company forecast sales according to data provided by sales executives; over the years, it found the forecasts to be very inaccurate. After a review of the situation, the company decided to collect data from customers instead of its executives and found that the accuracy of its sales forecasts improved significantly.

It should be noted that the determination of the sales forecasts and sales budgets should be an iterative process. As mentioned at the beginning of this chapter, the sales forecast provides the basis for preparing detailed sales budgets. However, the amount that the company plans to spend on marketing has a significant impact on the amount of sales the company will be able to achieve. Therefore, changes in marketing expenditures must be incorporated into the preparation of the sales forecasts. In the remainder of this chapter, we discuss the procedures for estimating potential and forecasting sales.

RUNNING CASE
Shiderlots
Elevators, Inc.

Account Managers Underestimate Sales Forecasts

On November 15 each year, Adam Dark was required to submit to top management a forecast of sales for the coming year. To that end, on September 30, the account managers received kits and detailed instructions about how to use the enclosed forms to generate sales forecasts for each of their territories. The company's overall sales forecast was then a composite of the account managers' forecasts. Since the company sold to a relatively small number of large customers that were well known to the account managers, Dark thought the system worked quite well. Actual sales each year were within plus or minus 10 percent of the sales forecast.

All of the company planning, including setting sales quotas, was then based on those sales forecasts. These sales quotas became important because sales force bonuses were awarded according to how well the account managers performed in relationship to their quotas. Thus, each salesperson's forecast was carefully appraised by management. If it appeared to be off-base, Dark would go over it with the account manager, and the two would come to some agreement about what sales from her or his territory would be.

As the two top salespeople stepped up to receive their awards at the company holiday party, where year-end bonuses were distributed, an account manager named Scott Stevens yelled from the back of the room, "Sandbaggers!" There was some laughter and some embarrassment.

Adam Dark said nothing at the time, but a couple days later he found himself alone with Stevens. "What was that sandbagging business all about?" Dark asked him.

"Come on, Adam," Stevens replied. "Don't play innocent with me. Everyone knows the game and how to play it. Those two award winners are just better than others at selling you their forecasts."

Dark let the matter drop without comment, but he was deeply bothered by the implication that he was being conned by these two account managers.

Question: What should Adam Dark do about this matter?

DEVELOPING BUDGETS

The budgetary process and its offspring, the budget, are the very core of the planning-control structure of most large companies. At the end of each year at most firms, top management requires the organization to prepare a plan for operations during the coming year. Each operating unit (marketing, sales productions, finance, research, etc.) develops its operational plans according to the basic sales and profit targets for the year provided by top management. Each department head then develops a detailed plan of what the unit must do to achieve these goals. The plan also includes a detailed itemization of the costs of doing those things—the projected costs. The projected costs ultimately are the basis for the unit's budget. The budgetary process is a complex, time-consuming managerial task. It is not much fun. But it must be done!

The sales forecast provides the basis for developing company operating plans. Everything is keyed to the level of expected sales activity. The budgets are essentially based on the sales forecast. If the forecast is wrong, the resulting budgets will have to be revised often to reflect actual sales results.

A budget is simply a tool, a financial plan that an administrator uses to plan for profits by anticipating revenues and expenditures. By using various planning procedures, management hopes to guide operations to a given level of profit on a certain volume of operations.

PURPOSES OF BUDGETING

The budget is very important for the successful operation of the sales force. It serves several purposes, including planning, coordination, and evaluation— each of which is discussed in this section.

Planning

Companies formulate marketing and sales objectives. The budget determines how these objectives will be met. The budget is both a plan of action and a standard of performance for the various departments. Once the budget is established, the department can begin organizing to realize that plan. This is especially important for salespeople. It is through a detailed breakdown of the sales budget among products, territories, and customers that salespeople learn what management expects of them.

Coordination

Maintaining the desired relationship between expenditures and revenues is important in operating a business. We might say that the objective of a business is to "buy revenues" at a reasonable cost, and a budget establishes what this cost should be. If sales of $5 million are forecast, management can establish how much it can afford to pay for that revenue. If the company wants a profit of 10 percent on sales, then $4.5 million can be paid to buy the $5 million in revenue. Part of the $4.5 million would go to the production and administrative departments and another portion would be available to operate the sales department. Thus, the budget enables sales executives to coordinate expenses with sales and with the budgets of the other departments. The budget also restricts the sales executives from spending more than their share of the funds available for the purchase of revenues. In sum, the budget helps to prevent expenses from getting out of control.

Evaluation

Any goal, once established, becomes a tool for evaluation of performance. If the organization meets its goals, management can consider the performance successful. Hence, the sales department budgets become tools to evaluate the department's performance. By meeting the sales and cost goals set forth in the budget, a sales manager is presenting strong evidence of his or her success as an executive. The manager who is unable to meet budgetary requirements is usually less well regarded.

DETERMINING THE SALES BUDGET

Determining expenditure levels for each category of selling expense is very difficult. Two methods for determining budget levels are discussed below: the percentage-of-sales method and the objective-and-task method.

Percentage-Of-Sales Method

Many managers plan and control their enterprises by percentages. Using this method, the manager multiplies the sales forecast by various percentages for each category of expense. The products of these calculations then become the dollar amounts budgeted for the respective categories. The manager might derive the percentages used for each category from his or her experience and/or feelings about what portion of the sales dollar can or must be spent on each business function to achieve the desired profit. The percentages also might be based on published industry averages for expense categories. Sales managers should use these published averages only as guidelines that must be adjusted to reflect the unique aspects of the particular organization. However they are derived, the percentages are then used in controlling sales and their costs.

Of course, there are not guarantees that the percentage-of-sales method will lead to optimal performance. In fact, the expense allocations determined by this method will follow the direction of change in sales. If sales are forecasted to decline, for example, then the budget allocations for all expense categories will decrease as well—yet this may or may not be the optimal allocation to counter the sales decline. Additionally, the effectiveness of this method is dependent on the firm's having accurate sales forecasts. Despite the limitations of the method, the manager knows that if expenses are kept within their percentage budgets, final operations will come out as planned.

Objective-and-Task Method

In the objective-and-task method of budgeting, the manager starts with the sales objectives, which are specified in the sales forecast. Then the manager determines the task that must be accomplished in order to achieve the objectives, and estimates the costs of performing those tasks. These costs will be reviewed in light of the company's overall profit objective. If the costs are too high, the manager may be asked either to find a different way of achieving the objective or to adjust the original objective. This iterative process continues until management is satisfied with both the objectives and the means of achieving them. Many firms use some variation of the objective-and-task method.

The American Marketing Association, a nonprofit association of marketing professionals and academics, uses an objective-and-task method to develop its budget. Its budgeting process starts with forecasts of membership revenue and publication sales. Then the senior managers estimate the costs of the programs designed to achieve the forecasted revenues. If the projected expenses exceed revenues, the managers make adjustments in costs, programs, and revenues until the budget is balanced.

BUDGETS FOR SALES DEPARTMENT ACTIVITIES

Sales executives are responsible for formulating three basic budgets: the sales budget, the selling-expense budget, and the sales department administrative budget.

The Sales Budget

The **sales budget** is the revenue or unit volume anticipated from sales of the firm's products. This is the key budget. It is the basis of all operating activities in the sales department and in the production and finance areas. The validity of the entire budgetary process depends on the accuracy of this one sales budget. If it is in error, all others also will be in error.

The sales budget is based on the sales forecast but calls for extreme detail. It must account for every single product sold by the firm. Little good comes from telling production planners that $100,000 worth of small parts will be needed. The planners must be told specifically what small parts will be needed, in what quantities, and when.

Managers estimate the sales of each product and often make separate forecasts for each class of customer and each territorial division. Budgets for territories and classes of customers usually are of interest only to sales executives. Other departments normally need only the sales budget for product divisions.

To some extent, a sales budget can become a self-fulfilling prophecy. You predict that 100 units of Model 101 will be sold in January, so 100 units are produced to be sold in January. Sales of that item may then fall short of the goal, but they cannot exceed it, for that's all there is to sell. Moreover, there is considerable pressure to make the planned sales figure a reality. Thus, once the sales budget is set, management digs in to make it become a fact.

The Selling-Expense Budget

The **selling-expense budget** anticipates the various expenditures for personal-selling activities. These are the salaries, commissions, and expenses for the sales force. This is not a difficult budget to develop. If the salespeople are on a straight commission, the amount of the revenue allotted for compensation expenses will be determined by the commission rate. Experience usually indicates how much money must be set aside for expenses. If salespeople are paid a salary, the process merely requires compiling the amounts, taking into consideration any raises or promotions to be made during the coming period. Any plans for sales force expansion also should be anticipated in this budget.

The selling-expense budget must be closely coordinated with the sales budget. Suppose the sales budget calls for the introduction of a new product line that requires considerable retraining of the sales force and the addition of a new service department. The expense budgets must reflect those needs. What will it cost to accomplish each line in the sales budget? That is essentially the question the sales manager must answer in preparing the selling-expense budgets that will accompany the sales budget.

The Administrative Budget

In addition to having direct control over management of the sales force, the typical sales executive is also an office manager. Ordinarily, the staff includes sales department secretaries and office workers; the total staff can be large. There may be several assistant sales managers, sales supervisors, and sales trainers under the sales manager. Managers must make budgetary provisions for their salaries and their staff. They also must budget for such operating expenses as supplies, rent, heat, power and light, office equipment, and general overhead. These costs constitute the **administrative budget**.

THE BUDGET PROCESS FOR THE FIRM

The first step in the budgetary process is to translate the sales forecasts into the work that must be done to achieve the forecasts. This is no easy task. The firm may want to introduce a new line of whoozits, since widgets are now obsolete. What does that mean in terms of the people needed (staff requirements)? What will it do to office expenses, field-selling costs, trade show commitments, and so on?

Each administrative unit must determine how much money it will need to meet the performance goals set for it. This is usually done by (1) surveying each of the activities the unit must perform, (2) determining how many people will be required to accomplish the job, and (3) figuring what materials and supplies will be needed for those people to do the job properly.

Many sales managers use the previous year's budget as a starting point. Then they take into account any changes in sales strategies and what those will cost to implement. They also get as much information as possible from their salespeople about changes in their territories that may necessitate changes in the budget. The various sales department budgets are compiled into one major budget that is forwarded to the financial executive, who disseminates the information to the other departments.

As described earlier, everything starts with the sales budget. From it, data flow in five directions. Figure 12-10 shows the flow of information from one budget to another. In addition to providing the basis for the various sales department budgets—such as advertising, selling expenses, and sales office expenses—sales budget figures also flow directly to the production department. Here the total production budget is established, and from that the various

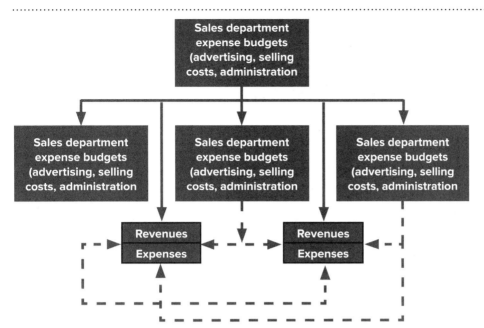

FIGURE 12-10
Flow of information from
sales budget to other
budgets

materials and labor budgets are determined. The financial officer also uses anticipated sales figures from the sales budget to prepare the cash and the profit-and-loss budgets. The cash budget is a tool used to determine how many dollars will flow into and out of the firm each month. This budget is necessary because of the time lag between expenditure and receipt of funds. It is necessary to lay out money for materials, labor, advertising, and selling expenses many months prior to selling the merchandise. Then, after sales of the goods, it may be several months before the firm receives cash. The financial officer must ensure that the firm has sufficient cash to enable it to finance the lag between the expenditure and receipt of funds.

The financial officer also uses the anticipated net sales figure as the beginning of the profit-and-loss budget. The budgets for sales department expenses, production, and general administrative expenses all flow into the profit-and-loss and cash budgets to determine the expected costs of operation. Thus, all budgets are summarized in the profit-and-loss and cash budgets. Errors in the sales department budgets have twofold effect on the financial plan. First, revenues will not be correct. Second, expenses will be out of line because the sales budget determines the production and administrative expenses.

The due dates on various budgets must be staggered if the budgeting program is to be a success. The sales department budget must be in the hands of the financial officer before final preparation of the production budget, since the production budget is completely dependent on the sales budget. Compiling all the budgets into the overall cash and profit-and-loss budgets can be done only after all other work on the plans of the organization has been completed.

Meetings, compromises, and much hand-wringing are all part of the budgeting process. It is a give-and-take process among the managers of various functional units. That is, managers fight for what they believe is necessary to meet departmental goals, and generally start out by asking for more than they believe they will get. Few managers relish working on tight budgets, yet in well-managed organizations all budgets are right. This is because having a limited budget can motivate managers into paying closer attention to what funds are available, and avoiding unnecessary expenses.

Every aspect of this process has become more efficient with the use of CRM programs. This technology, for example, allows managers to make changes in one part of the budget and see the impact of those changes on all other parts of the budget immediately.

Finally, sound planning procedures dictate that all administrative heads sign off on all plans and budgets. That is, they must all agree that they will make it happen.

BUDGET PERIODS

Budgets are commonly created for yearly, semiannual, and quarterly periods. Some firms prepare budgets for all three periods; others prefer to operate on an annual basis, thereby reducing the amount of paperwork.

The quarterly budget forces a reappraisal of the firm's position four times a year, thereby decreasing the likelihood that operations will get out of control. Many companies find a quarterly system advisable because it coordinates roughly with their operations conversion cycle. Garment makers usually have four conversion cycles per year. That is, they put out four different lines of goods, one for each season, and find it convenient to budget for each selling season. The main advantage of a short planning period is that it is more likely to be accurate than a long one. The shorter the forecasting period, the less likelihood there is that the estimate will be disturbed by unforeseen developments. In deciding which period to use, a firm must balance the degree of control with costs of compiling the budgets.

MANAGING WITH BUDGETS

Once prepared and in operation, the budget becomes one of the manager's regularly used tools. The previous month's actual sales and expenses come back from the accounting department by the middle of the present month. All figures that are over budget are marked for attention. Some of the accounts may be over budget for understandable reasons; the manager knows those reasons and either accepts them or expects them to be corrected in the near future. If the manager does not know why an account is significantly over budget, he or she will investigate the overage and take corrective action if necessary.

SUMMARY

The sales forecast is the basis of most corporate planning. From the forecast, the company plans activities and determines production levels. Should the forecast be in error, management may face serious consequences.

The company sales forecast is often based on market potential and the sales potential of the products it sells. Thus, the forecasting process begins with the market potential, which can be determined using (1) market-factor estimations, (2) surveys of buyer intentions, and/or (3) test markets. Once the market potential is calculated, a firm can then calculate its sales potential. Finally, territory potentials can be determined by using a market index to breakdown the firm's sales potential among the territories.

Good forecasting rests on a careful analysis of the factors that affect sales of the product. A perceptive analysis of buyers or end users and their reasons for purchase or use should play a significant role in the sales forecasting process. The impact of changes in the firm's marketing plans must also be incorporated into the forecast.

Many different sales forecasting methods are available to managers. One group is more subjective as the methods rely on surveys of executives, customers, and the sales force to derive the forecast. A second group applies mathematical methods to company records or historical data to yield a sales forecast. A third group employs methods linked to the operation of the company to forecast sales. Each of the forecasting methods possesses both advantages and disadvantages that are important for forecasters to understand.

The budget is a financial plan that the manager uses to plan for profits by anticipating revenues and expenditures. Budgeting serves several purposes: planning, coordination and control, and evaluation. There are primarily two methods of budgeting. First is the percentage-of-sales method, whereby expenses are estimated as a percentage of sales. Second is the objective-and-task method, where the manager determines the tasks necessary to achieve the objectives and then estimates the costs of performing these tasks. Both methods rely on developing an accurate sales forecast.

There are three basic budgets for the sales department. These are the sales budget, the selling-expense budget, and the administrative budget.

The budgetary process begins in the sales department with the formulation of a sales forecast. From that figure, a detailed sales budget is developed that contains the expected sales of each item in the product line. The production budgets and the selling-expense budgets are developed from the sales budget.

Once the sales forecast and budgets are developed, they become the standard by which the manager judges performance.

KEY TERMS

Administrative budget
Buying power index
Capacity-based forecast
Customer analysis
Delphi technique
Executive opinion
Exponential smoothing model
Market factor

Market-factor derivation
Market index
Market potential
Moving average technique
Multiple regression
North American Industry Classification System (NAICS)

Regression analysis
Sales budget
Sales force composite
Sales forecast
Sales potential
Selling-expense budget
Survey of buyer intentions
Test marketing

QUESTIONS AND PROBLEMS

1. Indicate what market factor or factors you would use to estimate the market potentials for each of the following products: Tiger Shark golf clubs, Scott's fertilizer, Chrysler automatic swimming-pool cleaner, Mohawk carpeting, Smith's ski goggles, and McGraw-Hill economics textbooks.

2. After one year of market testing, the manufacturer of a new food product had sold 4,800 packages in the test city of Louisville, Kentucky. Assuming that the test market is representative of the whole nation, determine national sales of the product.

3. In general, how do sales forecasts based on surveys differ from forecasts based on mathematical methods?

4. Use exponential smoothing with a smoothing constant of 0.8 to predict period 7 sales based on the data below. Then forecast sales with a smoothing constant of 0.2. (Note: the sales forecast for period 6 was 40).

Period					
1	2	3	4	5	6
24	32	44	24	30	42

5. In exponential smoothing, when should the smoothing constant be large? When should it be small?

6. What are some of the pitfalls in conducting test markets?

7. The following regression model was developed by a professor to help the owner of a restaurant predict sales:

Sales = 70.0 + 46.5X_1 + 208.5X_2

Where Sales = $ sales per month, X_1 = Advertising expenditure per month, and X_2 = $ value of coupon.

   a. Forecast sales if the owner decides to spend $500 on advertising and offers a coupon for $5 off one meal for parties of two or more in a month.

   b. Forecast sales if the owner decide to spend $400 on advertising and offers a coupon for $10 off one meal for parties of two or more in a month.

8. A university professor developed a model for predicting the sales of windmills to supply power for businesses and homes. Describe at least five factors that could be in the model.

9. A company's best-selling product line possesses a highly variable sales pattern according to company records. Which sales forecasting technique should be used to provide an accurate sales forecast for the product in the coming period?

10. Sales volume was forecasted at 16,000,000 monthly units, but ultimately sales was one percent more than that. If the average unit costs is $0.92, what does the 1 percent overforecast cost the company on a yearly basis?

11. If total expenses must be reduced by 10 percent, should an across-the-board cut or selective reduction be used? If selective, how should the selection be made?

12. You feel your salespeople are underpaid. You requested a large increase in the budget for them, but it was denied in conference with the other vice presidents, who all wanted pay increases for their people. You still feel strongly that more money is needed if the sales force is to be kept effective. What would you do about the situation?

13. Your CEO demands that you sign off on an operational plan and budget that you feel is totally unrealistic. What would you do?

EXPERIENTIAL EXERCISES

1. Develop an estimate of the market potential for a business in your community using one of the methods described in the chapter.

2. Develop an idea for a new consumer product. Develop an estimate of the market potential for this using census data.

3. Assume that you are the national sales manager for a company that sells heavy-duty mining equipment to the mining industry in Minnesota, Wisconsin, and North and South Dakota. This company wishes to expand its operations into other parts of the country, and the CEO has asked you to develop potential estimates for the remaining states. Assume that typically a firm would spend $100,000 per $1 million in sales on the type of equipment you sell. Visit the U.S. Census Bureau website (www.census.gov) to develop these estimates. Look for the most recent economic census.

ANDROS INTERCOM
Revision a Sales Forecasting Approach

"I am very concerned about the accuracy of our sales forecasts in recent years. Last year, for example, we underestimated sales by 16 percent. Based on the faulty sales forecast, we ordered less material from our suppliers and scheduled less production early in the year, causing us to miss many sales opportunities. I wouldn't be so concerned, but the year before we underestimated sales by 21 percent! I realize sales forecasting is a complex exercise and events can pop up that can dramatically affect a company's sales during the year, but we should be doing a better job in this area. Fay, I want to see some improvement in the coming year." Dinos Andros, founder and president of Andros Intercom, was speaking to Fay Philmus, vice president of sales for Andros. Fay had been in her position only three months, but Dinos was the second person at Andros Intercom to complain to her about the poor forecasts. The first person, John Richman, vice president of finance, was equally blunt in his desire to see the company's sales forecasts improve. He had said, "A new salesperson, a new forecaster: good."

Dinos now continued, "Let's meet in two weeks, say, on Tuesday the 25th, at 10, to discuss how you plan to forecast sales for the coming year. I'll have John Richman and Ray Forge from production attend as well, to hear what you have to say." Andros Intercom has been in existence for 20 years, manufacturing and marketing internal wall-based communications systems for new homes throughout the states of Maine and New Hampshire. The communications systems are designed so that people in one room can easily talk to people in other rooms or talk to people outside the home. Andros offers its customers a variety of systems, depending on the type of home and the needs of the homeowner. The company, headquartered in Bangor, Maine, prides itself on making the highest quality internal communications systems while offering customers competitive prices. Through clever marketing of its top-quality but affordable systems, Andros has become the market leader in the Northeast and has enjoyed record profits in each of the last three years.

In response to the president's request, Fay spent a good part of the next week working with her assistant, David Moss, on examining the old forecasting techniques used by the company to forecast company sales over the past 14 years or so. The two managers then worked on developing a new forecasting system for Andros in the week before the meeting. To make a convincing argument on how Andros should forecast in the future, Fay and David assembled a PowerPoint presentation for the meeting.

The 25th finally arrived. Fay and David walked into a crowded conference room for the 10:00 a.m. presentation. "Good morning, Fay," Dinos said. A few other people in the room mumbled their hellos.

"Good morning. I brought my assistant, David Moss, with me for today's meeting. David helped develop forecasts for Spancom and AT&T before joining us about six months ago, and he has helped develop today's presentation." After several people greeted David, Fay started the presentation.

"I would like to begin by reviewing how we have performed our sales forecasts in the past few years. Three methods were employed to develop the final forecast. One involved obtaining information from top executives in the company, based on their intuition, experience, and observations of the business environment. I believe this method was a favorite of my predecessor, who sought to have top management partially responsible for the sales forecast." Several people in the crowd snorted with amusement. "Another method involved obtaining information from each of the company's sales representatives. The salespeople's forecasts were then aggregated to yield an overall forecast for the company. Finally, we had our salespeople survey our customers to determine their purchase intentions for the coming year. The three independent forecasts were combined to yield an overall sales forecast for the year.

"In light of our poor forecasting performance at Andros in recent years, we would like to propose another approach, called regression analysis. Regression analysis is a mathematical technique in which sales, the variable we are trying to forecast, is related to one or more predictors of sales, say, price and advertising. Applying regression analysis to a database will produce a regression line, captured by an equation, that represents all of the data points. The equation is as follows:

$$y = a + b_1x_1 + b_2x_2 + b_3x_3$$

where y is unit sales; x_1, x_2, and x_3 are the values of the three predictor variables (i.e., the amount of money spent on advertising, the price of the intercom, and the number of housing starts), b_1, b_2, and b_3 are the slopes or coefficients that reflect the change in unit sales for every unit increase in the particular predictor variable; and finally, a is called the constant or y-intercept. To forecast, you just plug in the values for x_1, x_2, and x_3 and multiply them by their respective coefficients, sum them, and then add the constant (or subtract it if it is negative).

"For example, let's consider a multiple regression model with just two predictor variables that looks like: $y = 10 + 2x_1 + 3x_2$—to calculate a forecast with this model requires the forecaster to plug in values for the two relevant values for x_1 and x_2. Let's say these values are 40 and 50. In this case, sales would equal 240 (or 10 + 80 + 150). Get it?"

Fay paused for a moment and then continued. "Please note that this approach recommends dropping sales forecasts developed by the individual salesperson and company executives and eliminating purchase intention data from our customers in the forecasting process. After speaking with a variety of people on this issue, it seems the salespeople were being less than candid about their sales forecasts and those of their customer by underestimating demand for our products to help them meet their quotas."

"Wait!" cried one manager. "You are recommending that we move away from using the input of our customers, our sales force, and our executives? These are people who know our business from top to bottom. I'm sorry, but I don't trust a mathematical approach that is untested and hard for most of us to understand."

Another manager said, "I understand it. By using regression analysis, you're just saying that the future is going to be like the past. But I question that! My salespeople may be overly pessimistic about sales prospects sometimes, but they do provide us with some valuable information on future sales."

Fay replied patiently, "We are not recommending this approach. We are offering it as an alternative to existing sales forecasting approaches. We feel using regression analysis is a much simpler sales forecasting approach and one that will produce an accurate forecast. Hear me out on this for a minute." Fay then posted a PowerPoint slide containing the data shown in Table 12-1A. "The regression model we developed using data from company records and the U.S. government argues that sales are affected by the dollar amount spent on advertising by Andros, the average prices for our products after discounts have been taken by our customers, and the number of housing starts in Maine and New Hampshire. Advertising and price are variables that we manipulate to build sales, while housing starts is a good variable to use because our systems are placed almost exclusively in new homes. To develop a forecast, we ran the multiple regression model using the *linest* function in Microsoft Excel. It's easy to figure out how to do it—for example, there are websites and YouTube videos that show you."

"This approach can forecast better than we have been forecasting in the past?" asked one manager.

"If the regression analysis is well conceived, we believe error can be cut significantly," Fay stated. "Here is the database we are using to develop the regression model. After entering the data in the format shown above, the model produced a sales forecast that is very close to our actual sales levels in past years."

Fay stopped a minute to let the audience absorb her presentation. "So there it is. My team and I have given you one approach for forecasting sales. Please let us know which approach you think Andros should take. We can either try the old approach again this year or go with something different, like the approach we have presented to you today. We will support your decision either way," Fay concluded.

"Wait a second," John Richman exclaimed. "You and your team are supposed to be the experts, yet you are telling us, the nonforecasting crowd, that we are the decision makers? I think you should make the forecasting decision and we'll live with it, at least until we can determine the accuracy of the forecast."

"I agree," said Dinos Andros. "Why don't you prepare a document for us by this time next week, showing which forecasting approach you recommend and why you selected the approach? We must put this baby to bed in a hurry, given that our planning period is coming up soon. Sound OK, Fay?"

"Our recommendation will be on your desk in one week," Fay said.

After she returned to her office, Fay thought about the meeting and wondered which forecasting approach she would recommend. Many of the managers in the meeting seemed leery of a mathematical approach to sales forecasting. "Should I just plow ahead with regression analysis, which I think will work, even though it includes a technique that seems to scare people, or should I use an approach that is familiar and understandable to management?" she thought.

Questions:

1. Assume that in 2017, Andros will spend $1.1 million on advertising, sell its products for an average of $3,300, and that there will be 36.0 thousand housing starts. Run a multiple regression analysis [you'll have to do some internet research to learn how to conduct a multiple regression (e.g., using Excel's linest function), and then calculate the constant and coefficients (or slopes) for the three predictor variables]. What is the 2017 sales forecast using this approach? Show the regression equation.

2. Describe the advantages and disadvantages associated with both the old (subjective) approach and the new (mathematical) approach to sales forecasting. Discuss the accuracy of both approaches.

3. Based on your analysis, which approach do you recommend? Explain.

TABLE 12-1A: Andros Intercom: Forecasted Sales

Year	Unit Sales y	Advertising ($ millions) x1	Price x2	NH & ME Housing Starts x3
2002	559	.20	3,005	11.0
2003	648	.30	2,985	11.0
2004	661	.32	2,878	11.1
2005	682	.33	3,013	12.5
2006	870	.40	2,799	13.0
2007	885	.41	3,100	13.0
2008	849	.51	2,913	14.2
2009	1,045	.50	2,888	16.4
2010	1,115	.51	2,999	19.5
2011	1,251	.57	2,794	20.7
2012	1,302	.59	2,819	22.2
2013	1,444	.60	2,883	22.1
2014	1,542	.60	2,851	23.0
2015	1,443	.59	3,082	32.4
2016	1,990	.80	3,003	32.3

Revision of Sales Forecasting Model

"It seems to me that our forecasting system, which we have been so proud of for so many years, has sprung a leak. Our forecasts used to be on the money. Now suddenly we missed by 18 percent two years ago and 22 percent last year. Business was better than we thought it would be, so we missed a lot of sales by underplanning production. Something seems to be wrong and it's causing us to lose market share because we don't have enough inventory to supply the demand. What are we doing about it, Pat?" David Haeppner, president of Precision Tools, Inc., of Salt Lake City, Utah, was talking to Pat Michaels, the company's vice president of sales operations.

Precision Tools, Inc. designed, made, and distributed a wide line of specialized machine tools used in light manufacturing operations. Most of the firm's products were computer driven; thus, the firm also was involved in developing the software needed for operating the machines.

Ten years ago, the firm's market analyst had developed a relatively simple model for forecasting the demand for the firm's products based on the payroll and employment statistics of the firms included in the SIC categories of the company's target markets. Management became increasingly comfortable with its forecasting model, which provided excellent forecasts for a while. However, the model underestimated sales by 22 percent last year. It was not known how much more the company could have sold had it been prepared for the unexpected demand.

One sales rep was heard to say, "If this is a recession, let's have more of it." While the firm's customers had reduced their payrolls and employment, their manufacturing activities were increasing. Their increased profits were encouraging their purchase of machine tools. Thus, business was good for Precision Tools, contrary to what its forecasting model had predicted.

In response to the president's question, Pat Michaels replied, "I have asked Cori Newman to develop a new forecasting system for us since it has become obvious that the previous relationship between employment and our sales has changed."

"Call her in! I want to know where we now are and where she is in her thinking." David Haeppner handed the phone to Pat Michaels as he dialed the extension.

Cori Newman had joined the company as market analyst after working for Microsoft, a software developer in Orem, Utah, for four years in its marketing research group. She was a graduate from Brigham Young University's MBA program. She quickly responded to the request for her presence in the executive conference room and took with her the portfolio of work she had already done on the forecasting problem.

After observing the usual courtesies, Newman began. "As we have suspected, the relationship between employment and machine tool demand has changed. This is a common problem encountered in all forecasting models based on an analysis of historical relationships. Relationships change! We can easily reformulate our existing forecasting equation to determine whatever new relationship evolves between employment and machine tool demand, but probably that new equation would have to be repeatedly revised.

"I also would like to point out that sales forecasts tend to become self-fulfilling prophecies. If the forecast is low, that is what the company will likely sell. A high forecast likely increases sales through the combined forces of more inventory and more marketing pressure." Newman noted that her audience was receptive so far to her thoughts. She continued, "We have some alternatives. We could ask our customers about their plans for buying our tools the coming year. Academics call it surveying buyers' intentions. We could do it since our total number of customers is not large. The salespeople would contact all of their accounts to find out what they plan to buy for the next budget. Then the salespeople summarize what they discovered and make a forecast of their sales. We then summarize all of the salespeople's forecasts to come up with our own. One advantage of this procedure is that we can develop forecasts in more detail, by product lines."

"Then you're recommending that we abandon our mathematical approach to forecasting and go to a survey method. Is that right?" the president asked.

"Not necessarily. I am trying to give you an idea of the different approaches we can use and let you make the decision," Newman replied.

"Whoa! I have trouble with that. You're supposed to be the expert in market analysis, not us. We hired you to tell us what you think we should do. I want a recommendation from you without any equivocation." Pat Michaels firmly told Cori Newman what was expected of her. Newman was inwardly shaken by Michaels' aggressive position but tried to maintain her composure. She replied,

"Very well, you'll have my recommendation in writing Monday morning." After exchanging the usual parting words, she returned to her office to begin what would be a hectic weekend.

She mulled over the other forecasting alternative that she had not been allowed to present at the meeting. She had been about to tell her bosses that she could develop another mathematical model based on data other than employment. She would have to do a lot of statistical work to locate and validate such a series of information, but, after all, that was her job.

Cori Newman wondered if she should recommend continued use of a forecasting method with which management was familiar or if she should recommend switching to the survey of customers' buying intentions system.

Question:

1. What forecasting method should Cori Newman recommend that Precision Tools adopt?

[1] Beer Industry Profile: United States. *MarketLine Industry Profile, Beer in the United States.* 4/1/2015, pp. 1–38.

[2] Jason Notte, "These 11 brewers make over 90% of all U.S. beer". *MarketWatch.com.* Jul 28, 2015. Retrieved from the following URL on July 2, 2016: http://www.marketwatch.com/story/these-11-brewers-make-over-90-of-all-us-beer-2015-07-27

[3] "2005 Survey of Buying Power," *Sales & Marketing Management*, 2005, p. 73.

[4] "Survey of Buying Power," *Sales & Marketing Management*, September 2005, p. 62.

[5] Chaman L. Jain, "Business Forecasting in the 21st Century," *Journal of Business Forecasting,* Winter 2005–2006, p. 9.

[6] Daniel Kiely, "Forecasting Process at Wyeth-Ayerst Global Pharmaceuticals," *Journal of Business Forecasting, Winter* 2001, pp. 7–9.

[7] Jain, "Benchmarking Forecasting Models," p. 10.

[8] The constant and slope were calculated using the =LINEST function in Microsoft Excel, but understanding how to calculate these numbers is beyond the scope of this textbook.

[9] Sean Reece, "Forecasting at Ocean Spray Cranberries," *Journal of Business Forecasting*, Summer 2001, pp. 6–8.

[10] Dan Carter, "Forecasting at Lockheed Martin Aircraft and Logistics Center," *Journal of Business Forecasting, Fall* 2001, pp. 9–10.

13

Sales Territories

Brett is an account manager who has a longtime, successful relationship selling to Holly. When Holly leaves her company, she joins another firm and wants to continue to buy from Brett. The problem, however, is that Holly's new company is no longer in Brett's sales territory. Rather, the new company is located in the sales territory that belongs to Brett's fellow salesperson, Susan. Brett and Susan argue over who should service this account, and thus earn the commissions. If you were their sales manager, how would you settle this dispute?

When this scenario was presented on an online sales blog[1], sales professionals fiercely debated the issue, with about an equal number of arguments on both sides. Although this was a fictional case, this type of conflict about sales territories happens frequently in sales organizations. Territories create other problems, too. It's not uncommon for salespeople to complain that their territory is too small, too spread out, or unfair in some other way.

If sales territories cause so many problems for sales managers, then why have them? That is the question that this chapter attempts to answer.

NATURE OF TERRITORIES

A **sales territory** comprises a number of present and potential customers, located within a given geographical area and assigned to a salesperson, branch, or intermediary (retailer or wholesaling intermediary).

In this definition, the keyword is *customers* rather than *geographical.* To understand the concept of a sales territory, we must recognize that a market is made up of people, not places—people with money to spend and the willingness to spend it. A market is measured by people times their purchasing power rather than in square miles.

Benefits of Territories

A company, especially a medium- or large-sized one, can derive several benefits from a carefully designed territorial structure. An overview of six key benefits[2] is provided in this section, and shown in Figure 13-1.

Enhanced customer coverage

When a sales territory is too large, potential important customers are overlooked. The salesperson simply does not have enough time to call on all customers. Creating territories is a way for management to *control* salespeople's activities such that all customers are served in a more efficient manner.

Reduced travel time and selling costs

With no geographic territories, salespeople inevitably crisscross each other as they travel to and from their accounts. The result? Salespeople spend more time traveling and less time selling; and the firm spends too much money in automobile/fuel expenses.

Opportunity for more equitable rewards

Imagine two salespeople who are equal in both ability and motivation. Yet one salesperson would earn much more commission than the other if assigned to a territory with significantly higher potential. This is hardly fair! Sales organizations should reward the salesperson and not just the territory.

Aids evaluation of sales force

With well-designed territories that are equal with respect to both sales potential and workload, sales managers can more easily and fairly evaluate their salespeople's performance. Each person's actual performance is typically compared to a territorial potential or quota.

Increased sales for the sales organization

Many firms have some territories that are too big and others that are too small. These firms should redesign their territories to be equal. Sales will go down for salespeople with previously big territories. These lost sales, however, will be more than offset by the sales increases of the other salespeople (this is discussed later in the chapter—see Figure 13-6).

Increased morale

In general, good territory design results in productive salespeople who efficiently serve satisfied customers and who are being evaluated and rewarded in

FIGURE 13-1
Benefits of Good Territory
Design

a fair manner. This in turn leads to increased morale, which benefits the sales organization in many ways—not the least of which is through reduced turnover.

Potential Problems with Territories

A common problem with territorial structure of a sales organization is that the territories are poorly designed—and in need of revision because some territories are much better than others. Often, the territories are well-designed *at the start*, but then sales executives fail to monitor and react to changes in the market. Over time, some territories gain potential customers at a faster rate than other territories. Some territories might even lose customers. Eventually, territories that once were fair and equal become unbalanced in terms of their sales potential. And so, instead of generating the six benefits described in the previous section, the territory design is the cause of *problems* in these areas (i.e., it results in low morale, etc.). This is why sales executives must consider revising the territorial structure on a regular basis. More detail on revising territories is provided later in this chapter.

When Territories Are Unnecessary

In select circumstances that typically involve small-sized companies, sales territories are not necessary. For example, formal territories may not be needed for a small company with a few people selling only in a local market. In this case management can plan and control sales operations without the aid of territories and still enjoy many benefits of a formal structure. Automobile dealerships and commodity and security brokers usually do not assign their salespeople to territories.

In addition, lack of territories may be justified when personal relationships (including friendships or family connections) play a large part in the market transaction. This plays a part in explaining why there are no territories for the approximately 20 salespeople selling Liberty Mutual Insurance products in Columbus, Ohio. In fact, these salespeople—who are divided between two branches, one on the east side and one on the west side of the city—are actually licensed to sell throughout the entire state. At the same time, the branch managers encourage their salespeople to focus on clients on their side of the city.

Geographic territories are also not needed when the salespeople primarily make contact with customers over the telephone, as would be the case for Total Quality Logistics. In TQL's Cincinnati headquarters, there are hundreds of salespeople who service customers from all over the country. The company's CRM system efficiently keeps track of which customer belongs to whom.

DESIGNING TERRITORIES

Many sales professionals argue that the ideal goal in territorial design is to make all territories equal with respect to both sales potential and workload. **Sales potential** relates to the expected level of sales in the territory for a given period of time; and so corresponds to the size and number of customers in the territory. **Workload** relates to the number of calls and the amount of traveling necessary to effectively cover the territory, and so corresponds to the number of customers as well as the total number of square miles. To achieve equality with both sales potential and workload is very difficult given the differences in density of population across the country. However, many sales executives typically strive to be as close as possible to this goal when designing territories.

This ideal goal makes sense for the sake of being fair to all the salespeople. Also, it is easier for sales managers to evaluate and compare their subordinates' performance when all territories are the same. Equal opportunities also reduce disputes between management and the sales force and generally tend to improve workers' morale. However, it may not be a good strategy when there are large individual differences among the salespeople. In fact, some companies purposefully design smaller territories for their inexperienced, rookie salespeople, and then gradually increase the potential and workload as their skills improve.

Changing market conditions put continuing pressure on companies to revise and adjust their territories. Different procedures may be used to design the territories. However, a company's territorial structure is influenced by the potential business in the firm's market and by the workload required or sales expected of its sales force. One plan for establishing or redesigning territories includes the six steps in Figure 13-2.

Determine Basic Control Unit for Territorial Boundaries

When designing territories, the first step is to select a geographical **control unit** as a territorial base. Commonly used units are states, counties, cities, zip code

FIGURE 13-2
Procedure for designing
sales territories

areas, and metropolitan areas (see Figure 13-3). A typical territory may comprise several individual control units. One person's territory may consist of four metropolitan areas; another's may be three states. The unit should be small for at least two reasons. First, a small control unit helps management realize one of the basic values of territory design—the geographic pinpointing of potential. Second, the use of small control units makes it easier for management to adjust the territories. If an organization wants to add to one person's territory and reduce another's, a county unit facilitates the adjustment better than a state unit.

States

Territorial systems built around states are simple, inexpensive, and convenient. Territories may be built around states if a firm has a small sales force covering a national market and uses a selective distribution policy. A luggage manufacturer on the West Coast that sells directly to a limited number of selected retail accounts, for example, uses the state unit with success.

However, for most companies, states do not serve well as control units for territories because customers often ignore state lines. An Oregon-Washington boundary ignores the fact that many consumers and retailers in southern Washington buy in Portland, Oregon. Trade from Alton and East St. Louis, Illinois, gravitates to St. Louis, Missouri, rather than to any Illinois city.

Counties

For companies that prefer to use a political subdivision as a territorial base, the *county* may be the answer. In the United States, there are almost 3,100 counties but only 50 states. Smaller control units help management to design territories that are equal in potential and to pinpoint problem areas. Many kinds of statistical market data (population, retail and wholesale sales, income, employment, and manufacturing information) are available on a county basis.

FIGURE 13-3
Territorial control units

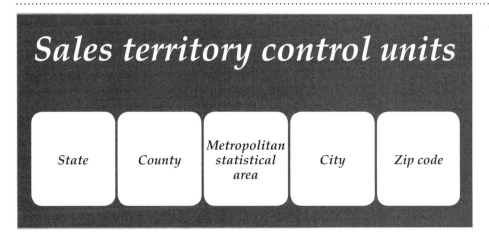

Sales territory control units

| State | County | Metropolitan statistical area | City | Zip code |

The only serious drawback to the county unit is that it is still too large for some companies. A manufacturer or a wholesaler may want to assign several salespeople to cover one county because the potential is far too much for one person to handle. This situation may prevail in such counties as Los Angeles, Cook (Chicago), Wayne (Detroit), or Cuyahoga (Cleveland). It then becomes necessary to divide the county into a series of territories, and some smaller control unit is needed.

Cities and zip codes

In the past, such firms as wholesalers of food, drugs, and tobacco often used a *city* as a control unit, because most of the market lay within urban limits. In fact, in many instances, even the city was too large, and firms used several salespeople within a single city. Then some sub-city unit was needed, and precincts, wards, or census tracts were used.

Postal zip code areas are one particular sub-city unit widely used when an entire city is too large to use as a basic control unit. By using zip code areas, a company works with geographical areas that ordinarily have a high degree of economic, social, and cultural homogeneity. However, it is difficult to get much statistical market data for geographical units smaller than a county or city.

Metropolitan statistical areas

Many companies have found that a significant share of their market has shifted to suburban and satellite cities outside the major central city. These firms have been aided tremendously by the delineation of *metropolitan statistical areas (MSAs)*. The federal government has identified and established the boundaries for about 380 of these areas.[3] An MSA is an economically and socially integrated unit with an urbanized area of at least 50,000 people. The MSA boundary lines are defined by one or more counties. For example, the MSA containing Santa Rosa, California, which is in Sonoma County, is defined by the area of that one county. Alternatively, the MSA containing Cincinnati, Ohio, includes the area of 15 surrounding counties, including counties in nearby Kentucky and Indiana. So, an MSA may cross state lines.

Because an MSA is defined in terms of counties, a vast amount of market data is available. MSAs are small in land area—about two-thirds of U.S. counties are not in any MSA. However, over 80 percent of the nation's population live within one of the 380 MSAs. Consequently, MSAs constitute lush, concentrated markets for many consumer and industrial products. Because of this market potential, some firms assign territories that consist of a number of metropolitan areas. They encourage their salespeople to work only in the defined MSAs, and to skip the areas outside and between them.

Determine Location and Potential of Customers

Management should determine the location and potential of both present and prospective customers within each selected control unit. Sales records should indicate the location of *present* customers in each control unit. *Prospective* customers can be identified with the aid of company salespeople plus outside sources, such as online directories (e.g., thomasnet.com), subscription lists from trade journals, trade associations, and credit rating firms (e.g., Dun & Bradstreet, Inc.).

Once the customers are identified, management should assess the potential business it expects from each account. Management then can classify these accounts into several categories based on their potential profitability to the seller. This step furnishes some of the necessary background for determining the basic territories.

Determine Basic Territories

The third general step in designing sales territories is to establish a fundamental territory based on statistical measures. This can be accomplished by using either the buildup method or the breakdown method. Under the **buildup method**, territories are formed by combining small geographical areas based on the number of calls a salesperson is expected to make. This method is driven by the goal to *equalize the workload* of salespeople. The **breakdown method** involves division of the whole market into approximately equal segments based on sales potential. Thus, this method focuses on *equalizing sales potential.*

The steps of the buildup method and the breakdown method are presented in some detail in the following section; and are shown in Figure 13-4—side by side for comparison purposes.

Buildup method

Several variations are possible in establishing territories by building up from the basic control unit. Usually, however, these variations depend on some type

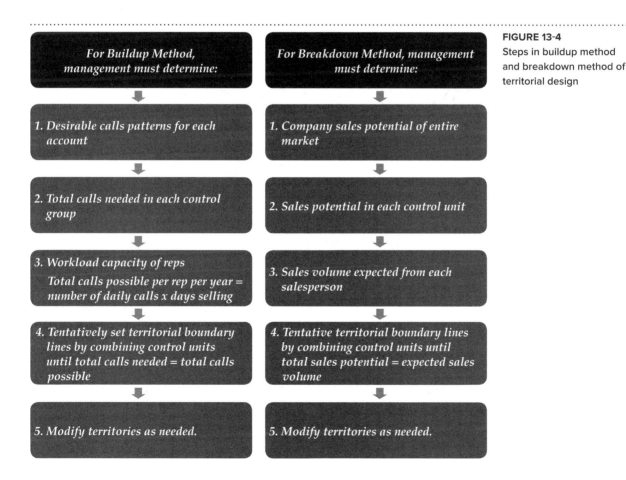

FIGURE 13-4
Steps in buildup method and breakdown method of territorial design

For Buildup Method, management must determine:

1. *Desirable calls patterns for each account*

2. *Total calls needed in each control group*

3. *Workload capacity of reps*
   Total calls possible per rep per year = number of daily calls x days selling

4. *Tentatively set territorial boundary lines by combining control units until total calls needed = total calls possible*

5. *Modify territories as needed.*

For Breakdown Method, management must determine:

1. *Company sales potential of entire market*

2. *Sales potential in each control unit*

3. *Sales volume expected from each salesperson*

4. *Tentative territorial boundary lines by combining control units until total sales potential = expected sales volume*

5. *Modify territories as needed.*

of customer analysis and study of the salespeople's workload capacity. A suggested procedure is outlined in the following paragraphs:

1. **Determine optimal call frequencies.** Management should establish optimal **call frequencies** for each account. In other words, management must determine how many times per year an account should be visited. The call frequency is affected by the sales potential, the nature of the product, customer buying habits, the nature of competition, and the cost of calling on a customer. Thus, the call frequency is primarily determined by the profitability of the account. The optimal call frequencies can be determined using several different computer models or estimated using managerial judgment. Figure 13-5 is an example of how management might divide its customers into three classes based on profitability. Class A accounts are the most profitable and are called on twice a month. Class B accounts are visited monthly, and Class C accounts bimonthly.

2. **Determine the total number of calls needed in each control unit.** By multiplying the number of each type of account in the control unit by the number of calls that type of account requires, we can determine the total number of calls needed in each control unit. Assuming that metropolitan areas are the control unit, and using the call frequencies shown in Figure 13-5, it can be seen that metropolitan area X requires 630 calls per year and area Y requires 660.

FIGURE 13-5

Example of call frequency for different customer classes

Customer class	Call frequency	Metropolitan Area X		Metropolitan Area Y	
		No. of accounts	No. of calls per year	No. of accounts	No. of calls per year
A	2 per month	10	240	5	120
B	1 per month	25	300	15	180
C	1 every 2 months	15	90	60	360
		50	630	80	660

3. **Determine workload capacity.** A salesperson's **workload capacity** is the average number of calls a salesperson can make in a day times the number of days in a year that the salesperson will make calls. The number of calls a salesperson can effectively make in one day depends on several factors. One is the average length of time required for a call. This is influenced by the number of people to be seen on each call and the amount of missionary work to be done. Another factor is the amount of travel time between customers. For example, for salespeople that work eight hours per day where the average length of call is an hour, and the average travel time is 15 minutes, six calls per day is possible. If that salesperson works 250 days per year, then the annual total number of calls would be 1,500.

Continuing with the example in Figure 13-5, a salesperson who can make 1,500 calls per year could call on both area X and area Y and still have time for accounts that require a total of about 210 calls a year [1,500—(630 + 660) = 210]. A salesperson could cover any number of customers who, in total, required 1,500 calls a year.

The box labeled "Factors Influencing Workloads and Territory Size" presents a number of factors that influence either the number of calls a salesperson can make or the optimal call frequency.

4. **Draw tentative territorial boundary lines.** The final step is to accumulate enough contiguous territorial control units until the yearly number of calls needed in those control units equals the total number of calls a salesperson can make (the workload for one salesperson). A company has a choice of places from which to start this grouping. On a national scale, a firm that groups contiguous metropolitan areas into territories may start in Maine and work south to Florida, then go back to Ohio and again work south to the Gulf of Mexico. Another firm, using county control units, may start each territory with a county that includes a major city and then complete a given territory by fanning out in all directions until the necessary number of contiguous counties are included. Other organizations group counties or metropolitan areas around a branch office or plant.

   Often, unless it splits a control unit, a company is unable to group contiguous control units so that the number of calls needed equals the number that one salesperson can make. In our earlier example, metropolitan areas X and Y together required 1,290 calls. However, no metropolitan area may be contiguous to X or Y that can be covered with approximately 210 calls, the number needed to create a normal load of 1,500 visits per year.

   In most cases like this, it is best not to split the control unit. Rather, the territory can be made a little smaller or bigger than the rest. However, sometimes this may cause significant sales potential inequities among territories. If this is the case, splitting the control unit may be the best option. This is a matter of managerial judgment.

5. **Modify the tentative territories as needed.** The tentatively drawn boundary lines of a given territory may need to be adjusted due to special considerations. For example, the competition may be particularly strong in one control unit and require more intense effort from the salesperson than in other control units. The salesperson in this area may need to have a smaller territory so that he or she can make more calls on fewer customers.

Breakdown method

The breakdown method breaks down the sales potential of the entire market to design territories. The steps for this procedure are shown in Figure 13-4, and described below.

1. **Determine sales potential.** The first step is to determine what sales volume the company can expect in its entire market. This is done using one of the forecasting procedures described in Chapter 12.

2. **Determine sales potential in each control unit.** To obtain the sales potential in each control unit, a market index (as described in Chapter 12) can be multiplied by total sales potential to allocate it among the various control units.

3. **Determine the sales volume expected from each salesperson.** In this step, management must estimate how much each salesperson

must sell to have a profitable business. A study of past sales experience and a cost analysis are often used to determine this information. For example, assume that the cost of goods sold and distribution costs are estimated to equal 70 percent of sales; direct selling costs are $30,000; and management wants to earn a profit of 10 percent of sales. Then it can be shown that each salesperson must sell a minimum of $150,000.[4] Of course, on the basis of experience, management may feel that each salesperson can and should sell twice as much. Therefore, expected sales volume is set at $300,000.

4. **Draw tentative territorial boundaries.** The final stage in the statistical phase of the breakdown method is to divide the entire market so that each salesperson has about the same potential. The potential has already been established for each of the basic territorial control units. Therefore, management needs to assign enough contiguous units to each salesperson so that he or she has at least $300,000 of sales potential. In other words, the sales potential of the territory should be equal to or greater than the sales volume expected from each salesperson. The boundaries of each territory should coincide with the borders of the control units.

5. **Modify tentative territories as needed.** As in the buildup method, the tentatively drawn boundary lines may need to be adjusted due to special considerations with regard to that geographic area.

USING TECHNOLOGY IN TERRITORY DESIGN[5]

Sales managers are increasingly using mapping software to design and realign their sales territories. This is much faster and more comprehensive than cranking out the breakdown or buildup method by hand. The technology is known as a **geographic information system (GIS).** GIS provides an in-depth understanding of a sales territory by combining multiple layers of information about that territory and then presenting it in an easy-to-comprehend graphic or map. A complete GIS consists of the following four elements:

1. **Software.** GIS requires software that can store, analyze, and graphically display information about the sales territory. Features and prices vary greatly. Low-end business mapping programs are practically free, while high-end software capable of running simulations and optimizing territories can cost thousands of dollars.

2. **Hardware.** A standard desktop computer, running on a Windows operating system, is typically sufficient. A quality color printer is also necessary.

3. **Data.** Generally speaking, the GIS output will be more valuable as the amount of inputted data about the territory (i.e., the layers of information) increases. The data include image data such as aerial photographs or satellite images as well as data about customer locations, call frequencies, sales, potentials, and so on.

4. **Trained people.** Finally, an individual with training—or at least practical experience—with GIS must operate the system. Training ranges from

CONSIDER THIS...

Factors Influencing Workloads and Territory Size

Territorial design depends basically on the company's sales potential and the workload of its sales force. Consequently, management should identify and measure the factors influencing these workloads. Two companies, each selling in markets of comparable potential and geographical size, may have quite different territorial structures simply because of a difference in the salespeople's workloads.

- **Nature of the job.** A salesperson's call patterns are influenced by the nature of the job. A salesperson who only sells can make more calls per day than one who must do considerable amount of missionary work along with the selling.
- **Nature of the product.** The nature of the product also can affect a salesperson's call pattern. A staple convenience good (canned foods with a rapid turnover rate may require more frequent calls than would an industrial product (conveyor belts) with very limited repeat-sale business. Similarly, a complex technical product may require long calls and numerous presale and post-sale calls.
- **Stage of market development.** When a company enters a new market, its territories typically are larger than those in markets where the firm is well entrenched—even though the market potential is comparable in the old and new regions. A large geographical area is needed initially to yield an adequate volume of business.

- **Intensity of market coverage.** If a firm wants mass distribution, it will need smaller territories than if it follows a selective or exclusive distribution policy.
- **Competition.** No general statement can be made about the net effect competition has on territory size. If management decides to make an all-out effort to meet competition, then territorial borders will probably be contracted. Salespeople will be instructed to intensify their efforts by increasing the frequency of calls and the length of time spent with each account. However, competition may be so fierce, or the territorial markets so overdeveloped, that the company is not going to make much profit in the territory. It therefore may decide to expand the geographical area, and have the salesperson call only on selected accounts.
- **Ethnic factors.** A company may adjust its territorial boundaries in large cities because of the market concentration of certain cultural groups that tend to speak their native language more so than English. For example, a company might call on retailers operated by those of Cuban heritage clustered in specific Miami zip codes. And so, it makes sense to design territories around those neighborhoods so that a salesperson that speaks the Cuban dialect of Spanish can be hired to call on them.

CONSIDER THIS...

Sales Territories For Pharmaceutical Sales Reps

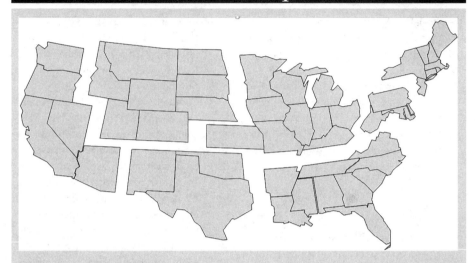

In the United States, sales territories for the pharmaceutical industry are typically organized using the following terminology and structure:

- The 48 contiguous states are divided into 5 to 10 geographic *regions,* similar to those shown on the map. Each region is supervised by a regional manager.
- Every region is then divided into several *districts,* each supervised by a district manager. Less populated states, such as Maine, many represent one entire district. More populated states, such as Massachusetts, are likely to be split into several districts. (Boston alone might consist of two or three districts.)
- The districts are then divided into 8 to 12 *territories,* each typically covered by a single pharmaceutical sales representative. Larger pharmaceutical companies might assign two or more reps to a territory with each one specializing in a specific product or customer group. For example, one rep might call on doctor's offices in the territory, while the other calls on hospitals.

SOURCE: David Currier and Jay Frost, "On the Right Path: Sales Careers in Pharma," *Pharmaceutical Executive,* July 2001, pp. 16-19.

formal university GIS programs to self-paced learning via a workbook, CD-ROM, or website. GIS has become such a critical part of strategic planning that some companies have created a new position: geographic information officer.

Companies have increasingly relied on GIS business mapping software to create, analyze and realign sales territories. Budget Rent-A-Car Corporation, for example, used this technology to examine the several territories in its western U.S. region, which consist of a 75-person sales force covering 10 states. Information about the locations and sales revenues of current and potential customers was inputted from various internal and external databases. The computer analysis of the data resulted in territories defined with pinpoint accuracy. The end result was that Budget's salespeople are now more efficient as prospective new accounts are easier to find. Further, the whole process is done in considerably fewer worker-hours compared to the previous method. Budget has no plans to go back to plotting and analyzing territories manually.

ASSIGNING SALESPEOPLE TO TERRITORIES

Once the sales territories have been established, management can assign individual salespeople to each one. Up to this point, we have implicitly assumed that the salespeople have equal selling abilities, and that each person would perform equally well in any territory. Obviously, this is not a realistic assumption.

In any given sales force, the salespeople may differ in selling effectiveness. They also vary in experience, age, physical condition, initiative, and creativity, as well as in selling skills. A salesperson may succeed in one territory and fail in another, even though the sales potential and workload are the same in both. For example, in a territory where a large number of the customers are engineers, a salesperson with a technical background may be highly effective. Sales performance also may be influenced by differences in local customers, religion, and ethnic background.

As referenced earlier, some companies intentionally design some sales territories so that they are *unequal* in size, as measured by the salesperson's workload or the territorial sales potential. Note that this contradicts the often-stated "ideal goal" of designing territories that are equal with respect to workload and potential. However, these unequally sized territories accomplish two purposes. One is to accommodate some of the above-noted differences among salespeople. The other is to give executives some flexibility in managing their sales forces. For example, many firms intentionally design a small territory for beginners or sales trainees. Then, as the rookies progress in skill and performance, they are moved (or promoted) to progressively larger and more lucrative territories. Similarly, some companies may initially assign salespeople to territories that are in remote, undesirable locations. Later, these salespeople can be promoted to better territories closer to their homes or offices.

REVISING SALES TERRITORIES

As companies and markets change, territorial structures may become outdated and need revision. In fact, studies indicate that over half of all sales territories need to be realigned because they are either too large or too small; and that optimizing territory design can increase sales from 2 to 7 percent—without any other change in sales strategy.[6] Sales executives should review their territories at least once a year to see if they need to be realigned. Some sales organizations review territories more often than that.[7] However, before making any boundary adjustments, management should be certain that the danger signals noted below are the result of poor territorial design, and not of poor administration in other areas. The problem may lie in the compensation plan, in adequate supervision, or a poor quota system.

CONSIDER THIS...

Tracking salespeople with GPS technology on their smartphones

Some of the same advances in technology that make it easier for sales organizations to create well-designed sales territories can be used to electronically monitor the sales force. Consider the case of an account executive from a company called Intermex Wire Transfer:

Intermex required all of its salespeople to download an app called Xora onto their smartphones, and insisted that they keep their phones turned-on and with them 24/7—so customers could contact them. This app allows the company to track its salespeople's locations, determine whether they are covering their territories efficiently—and even monitors how fast they are driving. One salesperson felt that being monitored this way was unnecessary and excessive—*especially during nonwork hours*. This salesperson de-installed the app, and soon was fired!

This salesperson has filed a lawsuit against her former employer, claiming invasion of privacy and wrongful termination.

Increasingly, employees are mixing business and personal hours—given that they are expected to be on call 24/7. Given this, which side are you on?

SOURCE: Greenfield R. Testing Workers' Digital Privacy Protections. Bloomberg BusinessWeek [serial online]. May 25, 2015; (4428):33-34. Available from: Business Source Complete, Ipswich, MA. Accessed July 9, 2016.

Indications of Need for Adjustment

Frequently, sales potential outgrows a territory, and as a result the salesperson skims the territory rather than covering it intensively. When out-of-date measures of potential are used, the performance results can be quite misleading. In a fast-growing territory, for instance, one salesperson's volume may have increased 100 percent over a four-year period, the largest increase of any salesperson in the firm. Management praises that person highly as the model of a good performance. Actually, that salesperson may have been doing a very poor job because the territorial potential increased 200 or 300 percent during that time. The company really was losing its former share of market because the territories were not small enough to encourage thorough coverage.

Sometimes the selling task changes. Anheuser-Busch found that its customers were demanding more and more value-added services, leaving the company's salespeople with less time to sell. So the company made the territories smaller and hired new salespeople, giving each one more time to sell.[8] At the same time, sales organizations are under constant pressure to increase productivity. This has forced some firms—especially those in volatile industries such as telecommunications and automotive—to downsize their sales force.[9] The sales professionals left behind must service more customers in larger territories. They are overworked and stressed because they cannot adequately cover their territory. In these cases, the need for adjustment is clear, but the executives believe they lack the resources to fix the situation. This is often short-sighted.

At the other end of the scale, territories may need revising because they are too *small*. They may have been set up that way, or changing market conditions may have caused the situation. The territories should be realigned, which might involve moving control units away from a territory that is too large and into

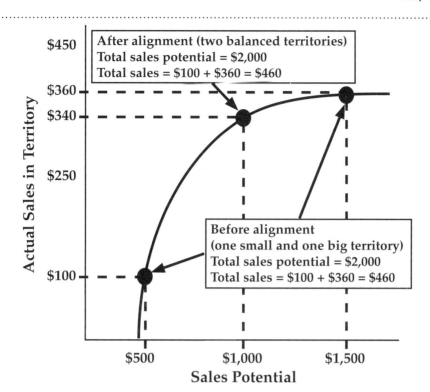

FIGURE 13-6
The relationship between sales potential and actual sales is positive, but with diminishing returns
SOURCE: Adapted from PK Sinha and Andris Z. Zoltners, "Sales-Force Decision Models: Insights from 25 Years of Implementation," Part 1, *Interfaces* 31, no. 3 (May-June 2001), pp. S8-S44.

the small territory. This makes sense because in an excessively large territory, the workload is too much for one salesperson to handle and so certain accounts are not adequately covered. Of course, the realignment will result in less sales for the salesperson in the larger territory. However, the lost sales will be more than offset by the sales gains of the other salesperson. This is demonstrated in Figure 13-6. As this graph shows, actual sales in a given territory increase as the sales potential of that territory increases, but there are diminishing returns. So, balancing two territories can result in a significant increase in sales—even when total sales potential is unchanged.

Another indication of the need for adjustment is overlapping territories, which is a problem found in many sales organizations. This generally has evolved informally from previous boundary revisions. To illustrate, salesperson Carter originally had as a territory the three West Coast states California, Oregon, and Washington. As its sales potential grew, this territory was divided in two. Carter kept California and a new rep, McNeil, was assigned Washington and Oregon. However, Carter also was allowed to keep certain preferred accounts in what is now McNeil's territory. The reason for this decision was that Carter had spent much time developing the accounts. The customers like Carter, and they might switch to a competitor if Carter does not call on them. Management therefore allowed the overlap to develop in the territories. However, the company planted the seeds for future morale problems because, eventually, McNeil is likely to chafe under the arrangement. Overlapping territories generally result in higher costs and selling inefficiencies, and thus should be corrected as soon as possible.

Similarly, sales managers should not allow one salesperson to call on customers in a territory that is assigned to another one. This is known as **claim**

jumping, which is a term that became common during the California Gold Rush over 150 years ago (i.e., when someone illegally took over a miner's plot of land to which a gold claim had been staked). When practiced by salespeople, claim jumping—especially when it is excessive—*may be* another indication for territorial adjustments. This is especially true when a salesperson has done a thorough job in his or her territory and still has the time to go into another one. This is a sign that the territory is too small. The increasing costs, inefficiencies, and friction among the salespeople that can develop when one cuts into another's territory should be obvious.

RUNNING CASE
Shiderlots
Elevators, Inc.

Claim jumping by account manager formerly in a territory

Adam Dark, sales manager for Shiderlots Columbus, Ohio, area, had just finish a call from Ann Moser, one of his account managers. This was the third call in six months that that Dark had received from Moser concerning the same problem. She was upset because of what she called claim jumping by Kyle Velasco, the Shiderlots account manager in an adjoining territory. That is, Velasco was selling to some Shiderlots customers in Moser's territory. Moser's territory covered several counties on the south side of the city. Velasco's territory was to the north of Moser's (just south of downtown Columbus).

Prior to two year ago, both of these territories constituted one large unit that was covered by Velasco. But the territory had grown too large in potential for one account manager to cover. Velasco was skimming the market, relying on establish accounts, rather than intensively developing the growing potential. The territory was split. Velasco chose to keep the northern section, and Moser was hired to take over the southern counties.

Velasco had been with the company for 12 years and did well—consistently ranking as one of highest performers in Columbus. His accounts generally spoke well of him, and Dark rarely received any customer complaints about Velasco. Moser also had done well since she had joined Shiderlots. She had a good record in opening new accounts and retaining the existing accounts that once were Velasco's. Customer feedback reported that she was very service-oriented.

Over the past couple years, however, Velasco continued to sell to a couple of his old accounts in what is now Moser's territory. Initially, the plan was to transfer these accounts over to Moser *eventually*, but this has not yet happened. Velasco is now claiming that Shiderlots would probably lose these accounts if he did not service them. He was close friends with the key contacts in these accounts, and in fact golfed with them regularly.

This situation was infuriated Ann Moser. She felt that Velasco was undermining her in the eyes of these customers. She told Dark that Velasco was simply a claim jumper and that he was using his good-old-boy network to take business away from her. She reminded Dark that these accounts generated a lot of commission, and so Velasco's activities were taking money out of her pocket. She was particularly upset that Dark apparently had done nothing in response to her previous two phone calls about the same issue.

Question: How should Adam Dark respond to Ann's Moser's charges?

Why Are So Many Sales Territories Unbalanced?[10]

As explained above, the problem of unbalanced territories is prevalent among sales organizations. Experts have estimated that over half (55 percent) of sales territories are either too big or too small, and that the typical sales organization could significantly improve its sales by optimizing territory alignment. There are several reasons why so many sales organizations are in this predicament.

First, organizations too often give the responsibility of designing and revising territories to the local sales manager. This manager is typically too busy with other responsibilities to do an adequate job of aligning territories within his or her district. Further, many times the boundaries are not designed optimally, and the manager has no control over this.

A second reason is that organizations often fail to have good definitions of what constitutes a good alignment. The goal should be equalizing potential and workload across all territories, but many sales executives fail to understand this. Further, many sales executives fail to understand how much the overall sales performance can increase by bringing the territories into balance. Experts demonstrate that properly aligned sales territories can increase an organization's sales by 2 to 7 percent.

Finally, sales executives have a tendency to put the individual desires of salespeople ahead of what is best for the organization. That is, salespeople often resist change and are more comfortable calling on their existing accounts than they are trying to establish new accounts. Sales managers acquiesce because they are afraid that good salespeople will be offended and leave the organization. Managers are especially reluctant to offend the veteran salespeople with whom they have had a long relationship. Of course, taking away accounts from salespeople becomes much more offensive to them when they are being paid on a commission basis.

Ironically, high morale was identified as a key benefit of good territory design toward the beginning of this chapter. However, sales executives often hesitate to make needed adjustments in territorial boundaries for fear of hurting sales force morale. In fact, many of the problems—overlapping territories, for instance—are a result of management's trying to avoid friction. It is important for firms to continue to realign territories for the sake of what's best for the sales force as a whole. The motivation levels of individual reps can be better maintained by demonstrating that the process is fair. Specifically, the sales manager should ask salespeople for input in the realignment process, assure salespeople that they are being treated the same as everyone else, and provide salespeople with transitional funding so that their total compensation does not significantly drop.[11]

TERRITORIAL COVERAGE—MANAGING A SALESPERSON'S TIME

After designing territories and assigning salespeople to each one, management then should plan how the salespeople will cover their territories. In effect, managing territorial coverage is an exercise in managing the time of each salesperson. Time management is becoming increasingly important as companies continue looking for ways to control their field-selling costs.

In addition to scheduling their time, sales managers are often involved in routing the salespeople. Computer technology is often used for this. In fact, when sophisticated computer modeling is used to design territories, the average travel time for the sales force is typically reduced by 10 to 15 percent.[12] Of course, this leads to a more productive, higher-performing sales force.

Routing the Sales Force

Routing is the managerial activity that establishes a formal pattern for salespeople to follow as they go through their territories. This pattern is usually indicated on a map or list that shows the order in which each segment of the territory is to be covered. Although routing is referred to as a managerial activity, it is not done only at some executive level. Often a firm asks its salespeople to prepare their own route schedule as part of their job.

Reasons for routing by management

Managerial routing of the sales force should reduce travel expenses by ensuring an orderly, thorough coverage of the market. Studies indicate that it is not at all unusual for salespeople to spend one-third of their daily working hours traveling. At that rate, a salesperson is not even inside a customer's office for four months out of a year.

Proponents of management's handling of routing believe the typical salesperson is unable to do the job satisfactorily. They feel that salespeople will look for the easiest, most pleasant way to do their jobs, although this may not be the most effective way. Left to their own routing devices, they will backtrack and crisscross their territory in order to be home several nights a week.

The map of Texas in Figure 13-7 illustrates a problem that often occurs when management allows salespeople to route themselves. Let's assume a salesperson

FIGURE 13-7

Problems when salespeople route themselves: Area B is neglected
Source: The HR Chally Group, Ten Year Research Report, *2002.*

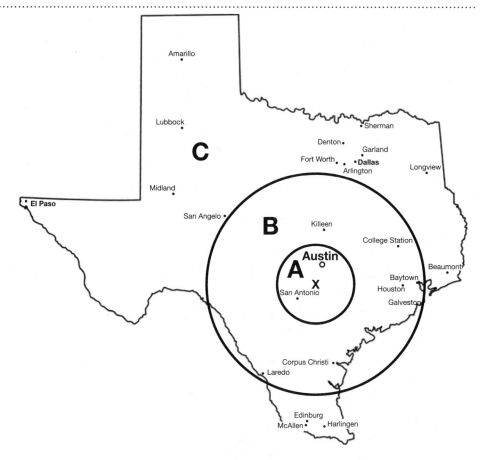

named Townes lives between Austin and San Antonio (at the X), and his territory is all of Texas. In Area A, which includes San Antonio and Austin, Townes can do a full selling job and still easily get home at night. Actual sales in A approximate the area's potential. Sales to accounts in area C, which includes El Paso, Amarillo and Dallas, also approximate the potential. This is because when Townes covers area C, he is resigned to being away overnight; so, he gets a hotel room and concentrates on doing a creditable selling job. Area B, which includes Houston, is the problem area—it's close enough that Townes chooses to come home at night, but it's far enough away that he tends to work less than a full day (so he can get home at a reasonable hour). Sales in area B are well below potential.

Objections to routing

Many sales executives feel that routing reduces people's initiative and restricts them in an inflexible plan of territorial coverage. They believe that a salesperson in the field is in the best position to decide the order in which accounts should be visited. Market conditions often are very fluid. Therefore, it would be a mistake to set up a route plan and prevent a salesperson from making expedient changes to meet some situation. High-caliber salespeople usually do not need to be routed, and they may resent it if a plan is forced on them.

Factors conducive to routing

Before deciding to route its sales force, management should consider the nature of the product and the job. If the call frequencies are regular and if the job activities are reasonably routine, planning a person's route is easier than if visits are irregular. Salespeople for drug, grocery, tobacco, or hardware wholesalers can be routed without serious difficulty. In fact, to attempt an irregular call pattern with a given customer can result in loss of the account. A grocery or hardware retailer, for instance, plans his buying on the basis of a salesperson's call, say, every Tuesday morning. If this retailer cannot depend on the salesperson's regular call, the buyer may seek another supplier.

Procedure for establishing a routing plan

In order to establish a routing plan, the present and prospective accounts should be spotted on a map of the territory. Then the daily call rates and the desired call frequency must be determined for each account. This information may have already been determined during the territory design process. With all this information available, the actual establishment of routes is reasonably mechanical. For example, Figure 13-8 shows examples of two common patterns of routing: hopscotch and cloverleaf. In both of these examples, the salesperson starts covering the territory from the center, moves out toward the boundary, and then returns to the center (the territories are split up into four areas—but in reality, it could be more or less than that depending on the size and shape of the territory).

When call frequencies differ among accounts, management may employ a skip-stop routing pattern. That is, on one trip, a salesperson may visit every account, but on the next trip this salesperson may call on only a third of the accounts—the most profitable third.

Routing salespeople effectively is another sales operational area that is ideal for computer application. A number of computer models have been designed to help management determine the one route through a territory that will minimize either total travel time or travel cost. Portatour, Badger Maps, and Sales

FIGURE 13-8
Examples of two routing
patterns
*Source: The HR Chally
Group*, Ten Year Research
Report, *2002.*

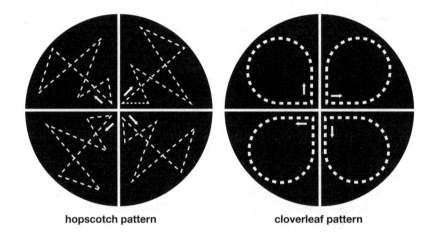

hopscotch pattern   cloverleaf pattern

Navigator are three examples of smartphone apps that are used for this.[13] The sales organization's CRM and/or SFA software programs are also applied to optimize this function.

SUMMARY

A sales territory is comprised of a number of present and potential customers located within a geographical area. This area is assigned to a salesperson or to an intermediary. There are several benefits to be derived from establishing sales territories. However, formal territories may not be needed in a small company with a few salespeople selling in a local market.

Different procedures are available for designing sales territories, and some of these approaches involve sophisticated mathematical models. Basically, however, a company's territorial structure depends on (1) the potential business in the company's market and (2) the workload required from the sales force. The plan we propose includes three broad steps: The first step is to select a geographical control unit to serve as a territorial base. Commonly used control units are states, counties, cities, zip code areas, and metropolitan statistical areas (MSAs). The second step is to determine the location and potential of each customer. The third step is to determine the basic territories, which can be accomplished manually by either the buildup or breakdown method.

Using the buildup method, management determines the desirable call frequencies for each customer and the daily call rate for the salesperson. Contiguous control units are then combined until the total annual calls needed in the territory equal the total number of calls the salesperson can make in a year.

Under the breakdown method, we start with sales forecasted for the total market and allocate it to the control units based on some type of market index. Then the sales volume expected from each salesperson is determined. With this input, management can set its basic territories by combining control units until the total potential in those units at least equals the expected sales from each salesperson.

Alternatively, the basic territories can be determined by a computerized process based on a geographical information system (GIS). A complete GIS system requires software, hardware, territory data, and trained personnel.

After the territories have been established, management must assign individual salespeople to each one. As companies and markets change over time, the territorial structures may become outdated and need revision. Revising boundaries is usually a very difficult job. A key principle that management should follow is to avoid overlapping territories.

Once sales territories are designed and salespeople are assigned to them, management should turn its attention to planning how the salespeople will cover their territories. This often involves routing, which is the managerial activity that establishes a formal pattern for salespeople to follow as they go through their territories. This can save salespeople time and greatly increase their efficiency. However, high-caliber salespeople usually do not need to be routed, and they may resent it if a plan is forced on them.

KEY TERMS

Breakdown method	Control unit	Sales potential
Buildup method	Geographic information	Sales Territory
Call frequencies	system (GIS)	Workload
Claim jumping	Routing	Workload capacity

QUESTIONS AND PROBLEMS

1. What control unit would you recommend in establishing sales territories for the following companies? Support your recommendation.
   a. Manufacturer of laptops
   b. Food broker
   c. Appliance wholesaler
   d. Manufacturer of textile machinery
   e. Manufacturer of outboard motors
   f. Lumber wholesaler

2. The text discussed several qualitative factors that may affect a territory's sales potential and thus necessitate a change in the statistically determined boundaries. How can variations in competition or ability of the sales force be reflected in square miles, trading areas, or other geographical measurements of territories?

3. Is it discriminatory to consider ethnic factors when assigning salespeople to territories?

4. Since it is impossible to equate territories perfectly, should the manager use them to provide promotions for good people? For example, should the best salespeople be given the choice areas?

5. What are some of the signals indicating that a company's territorial structure may need revising?

6. Assume that a territory's potential has increased to the point where the area should be realigned to form two territories. Properly developed, each of the two new units should bring an income equal to what was previously earned in the one large territory. Should management assign the same salesperson, who formerly had the combined territory, to one of the new ones? Or should the salesperson be transferred to an entirely different area before the division is attempted?

7. Salespeople normally are prohibited from going outside their territorial boundaries in search of business. Sometimes, however, a customer located in one territory will voluntarily seek out a salesperson or branch office located in another one. Perhaps this customer can realize a price advantage by buying outside his or her home area. What should be the position of the seller in these situations? Should it reject such business? Should it insist the order be placed in the territory where the customer is located? If the order is placed in the foreign territory, should the salesperson in the customer's home territory be given any commission or other credit?

8. If a company has several branches and insists that each of its suppliers send the same salesperson to all branches, what problems are involved? What course of action do you recommend for firms that sell to the company in question?

9. Territories A and B are right next to each other. Aaron Andrews is assigned to sales territory A, which is so large that Andrews cannot call on all the customers on a regular basis. Bob Burton is assigned to sales territory B, which is so small that Burton can adequately cover it by working only four days a week. Discuss the pros and cons of moving part of territory A into territory B in order to make them equal with respect to workload and potential.

10. In the process of revising territories, many firms do not allow a salesperson to keep any former accounts if they are outside his or her new territory. One hardware wholesaler realigned its territories. Then the company found that it faced the loss of some good customers because they said they would do business only with the wholesaler's sales rep who had been calling on them for years. Should the wholesaler make an exception and allow this rep to keep these accounts outside the new territory? Is the loss of these good accounts the only other alternative?

11. "Routing is a managerial device for planning and controlling the activities of the sales force." Explain the function of routing in relation to each of the concepts in this statement.

12. Under what conditions is a firm most likely to establish route plans for its sales force?

13. Under what circumstance should a customer be allowed to access the supplier's internal database?

EXPERIENTIAL EXERCISES

1. Assuming that Hallmark has 150 U.S. account managers, provide your recommendations for the allocation of these salespeople across sales territories. Be sure to base your recommendation on a relevant market factor or factors.

2. Call 10 companies and ask the sales manager (1) when the company last revised its sales territories and (2) what the catalyst or reasons were for the action.

3. Assume you are the national sales manager for a brand-new pharmaceutical company that specializes in the manufacturing and marketing of arthritis drugs. Your first job is to create 25 sales territories across the United States (you are in the process of hiring 25 salespeople). The sales potential of a given market closely parallels the number of senior citizens in that market. Go to the website for the U.S. Census Bureau (www.census.gov) to find the relevant information—using the 48 contiguous U.S. states as the control units. In other words, create 25 sales territories in the U.S. that have an approximately equal amount of potential based on the number of people who are 65 years old and above living in the states. Explain which territories are the best and the worst.

4. Google the search term: *GIS sales territories* to learn more about how a geographic information system can help a sales organization create, realign, and manage its sales territories. Identify a few GIS companies that you could hire to help you do this. Which company do you recommend? Explain your answer.

VILLAGE BEDS
Realigning Sales Territories

Lee Flicker was the newly hired national sales manager for Village Beds. It was his first day on the job and he was a bit overwhelmed by all he had to do. One significant problem, however, jumped out at him as a high priority: His new company's sales territories were seriously out of balance and realignment was long overdue.

A relatively small company in the health care equipment industry, Village Beds, manufactured a line of beds especially designed for nursing homes. Village Beds was started just 20 years ago in Toledo, Ohio, by its current president, Steve Moser. Before founding the company, Moser had been a nursing home administrator for more than 20 years. This gave him insight into the many problems that both patients and staff had with standard nursing home beds. He developed his new line of beds with these problems in mind. Although expensive, Village Beds have an excellent reputation in the industry for durability, quality, and value.

Moser, however, was not an expert at designing a sales and marketing team. The initial sales territories were developed arbitrarily and were changed only by necessity as Village Beds grew and hired more salespeople. Currently, the company has a sales force of just seven salespeople, who call directly on nursing home companies across the United States. Compensation, which is a combination salary plus commission, varies greatly across the seven salespeople.

Table 13-1A outlines the current situation, including key statistics for the seven sales territories and reps. The sales territories were clearly out of balance. Not only could Lee Flicker quickly discern this from looking at the statistics, but he had already heard complaints. During his first phone call to her, Mary Jones, sales rep in the central district, had told him that the inequity of the sales territories was causing morale problems for her and others. Flicker already had a lead on three experienced salespeople he could hire. He decided that moving from 7 to 10 territories was a logical,

manageable first step. The problem was how to draw the boundary lines. Village Beds had always used states as control units, and he saw no reason not to continue doing that.

Flicker was concerned about his salespeople's reaction to any realignment plan. Many of the salespeople had close ties to certain customers whom they would hate to leave behind. Also, it was inevitable that he would reduce the territory size for some. He was especially worried about the reaction from Max Harris, who had sold Village Beds in the Midwest territory for over 15 years. The Midwest not only had potential that far exceeded any other territory, it was also the territory in which Village Beds was best known given its Ohio headquarters. Harris also happened to be a close personal friend of Steve Moser, the company president.

Flicker had a spreadsheet file containing the various statistics for each state or control unit (see Table 13-1B). He sat down at his computer and began the task of realigning territories. He wanted to do it right. His goal was to create 10 territories that were as equal as possible with regard to sales potential and workload. In addition, he wanted to minimize the changes to the existing territories in order to keep the current seven salespeople happy.

QUESTIONS:

1. What is the best way to realign the existing seven territories into 10 new territories? (Use of a spreadsheet is strongly advised)

2. Should the current seven salespeople be consulted for the realignment plan? Or should the new territories be created without their input?

3. To which of the new territories should Max Harris and the other current salespeople be assigned? To which of the new territories should the three new reps be assigned? Explain your reasoning.

TABLE 13-1A Selected Statistics for Current Sales Territories

Territory	Total population	Population 65 years & older	No. of nursing homes	Last year's sales	Square miles
T1: New England (NY, NJ, MA, CT, ME, RI, NH, VT)	41,313,324	5,446,964	2,142	$11,928,455	123,409
T2: Mid-Atlantic (PA, MD, WV, DE)	20,169,484	2,892,892	1,205	$4,507,086	82,022
T3: Midwest (OH, IL, MI, MO, IN, WI, MN, KY, IA, KS)	65,326,238	8,341,166	5,396	$41,204,566	581,589
T4: Southeast (FL, NC, VA, GA, TN, AL, LA, SC, AK, MS)	63,432,088	8,363,438	3,332	$6,256,858	483,920
T5: Southwest (TX, OK, NM)	26,121,520	2,732,645	1,643	$3,227,755	458,376
T6: Central (CO, NE, UT, ID, MT, SD, ND, WY)	12,332,667	1,367,003	972	$4,660,451	742,629
T7: West (CA, AR, WA, OR, NV)	50,316,057	5,575,266	1,942	$7,390,888	548,400
SUM TOTAL	279,011,378	34,719,373	16,632	$79,176,059	3,020,345

TABLE 13-1B Selected Statistics for the States

Territory	Total population	Population 65 years & older	No. of nursing homes	Last year's sales	Square miles
New York	18,976,457	2,447,963	669	$3,663,807	49,112
New Jersey	8,414,350	1,110,694	364	$2,021,557	7,790
Massachusetts	6,349,097	857,128	505	$2,756,465	8,262
Connecticut	3,405,565	469,968	254	$1,443,459	5,006
Maine	1,274,923	183,589	126	$752,734	33,128
Rhode Island	1,048,319	152,006	97	$577,578	1,213
New Hampshire	1,235,786	148,294	83	$449,781	9,283
Vermont	608,827	77,321	44	$263,074	9,615
Pennsylvania	12,281,054	1,915,844	771	$2,812,552	45,310
Maryland	5,296,486	598,503	251	$998,299	10,455
West Virginia	1,808,344	276,677	141	$537,602	24,231
Delaware	783,600	101,868	42	$158,633	2,026
Ohio	11,353,140	1,509,968	999	$7,631,590	41,328
Illinois	12,419,293	1,502,734	858	$6,379,888	56,343
Michigan	9,938,444	1,222,429	436	$3,164,047	58,513
Missouri	5,595,211	755,353	545	$4,172,142	69,709
Indiana	6,080,485	753,980	561	$4,286,717	36,185
Wisconsin	5,363,675	702,641	420	$3,247,697	56,145
Minnesota	4,919,479	595,257	427	$3,348,955	84,397

continued

Territory	Total population	Population 65 years & older	No. of nursing homes	Last year's sales	Square miles
Kentucky	4,041,769	505,221	304	$2,422,933	40,411
Iowa	2,926,324	436,022	466	$3,603,715	56,276
Kansas	2,688,418	357,560	380	$2,946,882	82,282
Florida	15,982,378	2,812,899	728	$1,319,299	58,681
North Carolina	8,049,313	965,918	413	$783,635	52,672
Virginia	7,078,515	792,794	289	$527,526	40,598
Georgia	8,186,453	785,899	364	$724,878	58,390
Tennessee	5,689,283	705,471	349	$631,836	42,146
Alabama	4,447,100	578,123	228	$449,421	51,718
Louisiana	4,468,976	518,401	332	$618,187	47,720
South Carolina	4,012,012	485,453	179	$327,695	31,117
Arkansas	2,673,400	374,276	250	$489,341	53,183
Mississippi	2,844,658	344,204	200	$385,039	47,695
Texas	20,851,820	2,064,330	1,179	$2,313,575	266,874
Oklahoma	3,450,654	455,486	383	$759,958	69,903
New Mexico	1,819,046	212,828	81	$154,222	121,599
Colorado	4,301,261	417,222	223	$1,107,862	104,100
Nebraska	1,711,263	232,732	232	$1,100,870	77,359
Utah	2,233,169	189,819	92	$416,221	84,905
Idaho	1,293,953	146,217	84	$394,800	83,574
Montana	902,195	120,894	103	$500,924	147,047
South Dakota	754,844	107,943	112	$559,037	77,122
North Dakota	642,200	94,403	87	$405,000	70,704
Wyoming	493,782	57,772	39	$175,737	97,818
California	33,871,648	3,590,395	1,344	$5,131,090	158,648
Arizona	5,130,632	666,982	139	$507,877	114,007
Washington	5,894,121	660,142	268	$1,060,689	68,126
Oregon	3,421,399	437,939	145	$522,767	97,052
Nevada	1,998,257	219,808	46	$168,464	110,567
SUM TOTAL	279,011,378	34,719,373	16,632	$79,176,059	3,020,345

Sources: 2000 U.S. Census (www.censu.gov); Centers for Medicare and Medicaid Services (www.medicare.gov)

ATHENIAN PRESS, INC.
Redesigning Sales Territories

Steve Womble, the sales manager for the Athenian Press, was reviewing the quarterly summary for advertising sales and was concerned by the results, which showed a slight decrease from the previous quarter. More important, ad revenues for the past two years were showing a disturbing trend. Not only had the company not made its targeted growth of 2 percent, but sales were down over the past two years by 7 percent. While Womble felt that a small part of this trend might be attributed to more intense competition in recent years, he felt that most of the decrease in sales was due to the need for change in the sales organization. The market had been changing in terms of both rapid growth and increased customer expectations. Womble, who had recently been promoted to his current position, felt that Athenian Press had not responded to these changes.

Athenian Press, Inc., founded in 1945, publishes a daily newspaper and a Sunday paper that serve the community of Athens, Tennessee, home of the company's main office. The target market contains the central Tennessee counties of McMinn and Meigs plus major portions of Monroe and Hamilton counties. These counties comprise a market of more than 300,000 people.

The *Athenian Daily* has a circulation of 49,582 subscribers. In an average day, more than 60 percent of the adults in the area read this paper. The *Athenian Sunday Journal* has a circulation of 83,621 and is read by approximately 89 percent of the market adults at least once per month.

As with most newspaper publishers, a major source of Athenian's revenue is the amount of advertising sold. Generally, advertisements comprise more than 60 percent of any newspaper, and the size of the paper is determined by the number of advertisements it includes. Most of these advertisements are purchased by retail store merchants to increase customer awareness and to advertise special promotions. The Athenian Press has 800 active accounts and employs eight retail salespeople to call on these merchants. The salespeople report directly to the sales manager. Each salesperson is assigned to a specific territory. Within their territories, salespeople are given a great deal of independence and freedom. Athenian also employs three inside salespeople who are responsible for serving those who place ads in the classified section. These salespeople also report to the sales manager.

Competition for retail advertisements is strong in this area. The Athenian papers compete with several other papers for the advertisements. The *Knoxville Journal* currently holds about 8 percent of the market, while the *Chattanooga Free Press* has 4 percent and the *Tennessean*, published in Nashville, has 2 percent. The paper also competes against local radio and television stations for the ads of the retail stores. However, its greatest competitor is ADCO Mailing. ADCO is a company that produces advertising fliers distributed by mail. To compete with these fliers, the *Athenian Daily* prints a weekly newspaper insert that contains coupons from the local merchants.

A salesperson for the Athenian Press has three main responsibilities. The first and most important is to meet with the customers on a regular basis to solicit their advertising. Each salesperson is expected to make 10 to 15 calls a day and to spend 30 to 60 minutes per call. For the very active accounts (approximately 50 percent of the accounts), the salespeople are supposed to schedule regular weekly meeting times to discuss the weekly order. For the less active accounts, the salespeople are expected to stay in regular contact by making appointments once or twice per month. Each salesperson is responsible for approximately 100 of these active accounts. For accounts that advertise only infrequently, salespeople are directed to make unscheduled calls when they have time available. The salespeople's second responsibility is to make all of their customers aware of upcoming promotions. If the newspaper is running a special section on dining out, the sales force is responsible for contacting all local restaurant owners to suggest that they may want to be included. The third responsibility is to look for new accounts in their territories. The salespeople must meet with the owners and/or managers of any new stores as soon as they are under construction to inform them of Athenian's services and encourage them to advertise.

Once an order has been taken by a salesperson, the salesperson is in charge of making preliminary sketches of the ad according to the specifications of the customer. These sketches are then sent to the art department, which develops the final copy. The business department is responsible for all billing and accounting; but if a problem arises with bill collection, the salesperson contacts the customer to try to resolve the issue.

The compensation for the salespeople consist of salary and commission plus a yearly bonus based on performance. Salary makes up 60 percent of their total income, and commissions account for the remaining 40 percent; the bonuses are added to this base. The average compensation of $32,000 is considered competitive for this size newspaper, and the salespeople are relatively satisfied with their compensation levels. Sales trainees are paid a straight salary. New reps are given a brief indoctrination to the company before being assigned to "shadow" an experienced salesperson for two weeks. After this period of observing an experienced rep, they are assigned to a territory.

Steve Womble establishes yearly quotas for the salespeople and conducts their annual evaluations. On a continuing basis, he monitors their call reports and meets with each salesperson at least once a month to discuss his or her progress. Each week, the entire sales force has a breakfast at which they share problems and ideas.

Recently Womble had completed a careful analysis of the salespeople's current activities. He concluded that the sales force was not spending enough time with its customers. First of all, each salesperson can spend only about 60 percent of his or her time in the field because of the reps' responsibility of creating the preliminary sketches of the ads. Second, because of the number of accounts

salespeople must service, they are not spending as much time as they should with each customer. Additionally, the 15 or 20 minutes it takes to travel between each account also limits the amount of time they can spend with each customer. As a result, most customer calls are brief and less frequent than they should be, and very little time is devoted to calling on new accounts.

Convinced of the need for change, Womble came up with several options that he discussed with his boss, Linda Gruhn, and with his salespeople. One alternative was to assign the task of creating preliminary sketches to someone other than the salesperson, thus freeing up a significant amount of the salesperson's time. Specifically, art department personnel could perform this task. However, the salespeople felt strongly that the sketches were often needed to close the sale, and they wanted to keep that part of the sale under their control. They also worried about the necessity for increased coordination between themselves and the artists. Finally, as one salesperson said to Womble, "I really enjoy that part of my job because it requires creativity and imagination. Take that away and it won't be as much fun."

Another possibility was to hire additional salespeople and realign the territories so that each salesperson would be responsible for fewer accounts. The salespeople's reaction to this option was not surprising: They all felt that this was a threat to their sales volumes and thus to their commissions as well. Additionally, Linda Gruhn told Womble that he must be able to justify hiring any additional salespeople before she would approve it.

A final possibility was for Womble to take over selling to several of the largest accounts, thus giving the salespeople more time with the remaining accounts. This would decrease the time Womble could spend on his managerial duties, but he felt he could handle 8 to 10 of these accounts and still provide the salespeople with an adequate amount of supervision. Needless to say, the salespeople were not in favor of this option, which they saw as a threat to their commissions.

Question:

1. What action should Steve Womble take? Be sure to support the decision you recommend with the appropriate analysis.

[1] Lee B. Salz, "The Sales Management Challenge," *Sales Architects* sales blog, on the following URL retrieved on July 10, 2016: https://www.salesarchitects.com/smc/who-owns-a-referral-when-it-is-outside-an-assigned-sales-territory/

[2] The six benefits of good territory design are based primarily on Andris Z. Zoltners and Sally E. Lorimer, "Sales Territory Alignment: An Overlooked Productivity Tool," *Journal of Personal Selling & Sales Management,* Summer 2000, pp. 139–50.

[3] Wikipedia contributors. "List of Metropolitan Statistical Areas." Wikipedia, The Free Encyclopedia. Wikipedia, The Free Encyclopedia, 3 Jul. 2016. Web. 9 Jul. 2016.

[4] The equation is as follows: Sales = cost of goods sold + direct costs = profit. Algebraically, it is $(1x - 0.7x) = \$30,000 = 0.1x$, which is solved as \$150,000.

[5] This section was largely based on information from *GIS Lounge,* which is an information portal focused on the field of geographic information systems. This organization's website is www.gislounge.com, the purpose of which is to provide introductory text for issues relating to GIS as well as interesting news items, tips, and resources for the geospatial field. This site is run by Caitlin Dempsey Morais, and was accessed by the author on July 1, 2016.

[6] Andris A. Zoltners, PK Sinha, and Sally Lorimer, "Why Sales Teams Should Reexamine Territory Design," *Harvard Business Review,* August 7, 2015. Accessed July 9, 2016, from: https://hbr.org/2015/08/why-sales-teams-should-reexamine-territory-design

[7] Tim Donnelly, "How to Set UP Sales Territories," *Inc.com,* September 2, 2011. Accessed on July 9, 2016 from: http://www.inc.com/guides/201109/how-to-set-up-sales-territories.html

[8] Sarah Lorge, "Marking Their Time," *Sales & Marketing Management,* September 1997, p. 105.

[9] Tammy Joyner, "The Collateral Damage of Cutbacks," *Atlanta Journal-Constitution,* October 20, 2002, p. 1F.

[10] This section is based on PK Sinha and Andris A. Zoltners, "Sales-Force Decision Models: Insights from 25 Years of Implementation," Part 2 *Interfaces* 31, no. 3 (May/June 2001), pp. S8–S44.

[11] Kirk Smith, Eli Jones, and Edward Blair, "Managing Salesperson Motivation in a Territory Realignment," *Journal of Personal Selling & Sales Management,* Fall 200, pp. 215–26.

[12] Sinha and Zoltners, "Sales Force Decision Models…"

[13] Sarah Leung, "The Right Route Planning App: Our Top 3 Picks," *Handshake sales blog,* March 17, 2015. Retrieved from the following URL on July 10, 2016: https://www.handshake.com/blog/route-planning-apps-for-sales-reps/

14

Sales Volume Analysis

Perry Marshall is a Google AdWords expert who runs a successful marketing consulting firm. He says that a key to his success is turning away customers! In fact, this is something that he not only does himself, he also encourages his clients to do the same. "We're all tempted to waste our time trying to please all of our customers instead of the most lucrative ones," says Marshall, who categorizes customers into the three groups. First, there is the top 20 percent of customers who generate 80 percent of the profits. Second, there is the middle group that generates the rest of the profits. The third group is the bottom 10 to 20 percent of customers that actually cost money to service. His advice is to "...paddle away from the 20 percent of your customers who cause problems, and focus on the 20 percent who buy the most from you."[1]

Marshall's advice is a consequence of the 80/20 principle, which this chapter covers in detail. To identify the top customers that this principle refers to, sales managers must conduct an analysis of sales volume. This analysis is part of a three-step process that involves planning, implementation and evaluation of performance. Plans are made; they are put into operation; and the results are evaluated. The new plans for the next cycle are prepared, based in part on what was discovered in the preceding evaluation.

STRATEGIC RELATIONSHIP BETWEEN PLANNING AND EVALUATION

As shown in Figure 14-1, planning, implementation, and performance evaluation are particularly interdependent activities in the sales force management process. Planning comes first, and sets forth what *should be* done. After the plan is implemented, evaluation shows what *really was* done. These activities are tightly connected, and represent an endless cycle. To Illustrate, let's assume that an organization has done a good job of strategic sales force planning. But without an effective evaluation, management cannot tell (1) whether its plan was effectively implemented, (2) to what degree it has been successful, or (3) what the reasons are for the plan's success or failure. In effect, the lack of adequate evaluation can virtually cancel out the value of strategic planning. It's like deciding to go someplace but never knowing when, or if, you arrived there.

A performance evaluation without prior strategic planning is equally useless—and may even be dangerously misleading. Without planning guidelines, a salesperson may think that she or he is doing well by stressing the sale of high-margin products. However, management may prefer that this rep concentrate on opening new accounts or performing more missionary selling activities. If management does not set goals for its salespeople (planning), then what bases can it use for evaluating the salesperson's performance? Without a par for the course (i.e., a standard of performance), how can management know whether a salesperson is doing a satisfactory job?

Truly, planning and performance evaluation are strategically interrelated and interdependent. Evaluation both follows and precedes planning. Evaluation follows the planning and operations of the current period of company activity. Actual performance is measured against predetermined standards. Then evaluation precedes and influences the planning for the next period's operations. To illustrate, let's say that evaluations show the company's gross margin declined because of a heavy sales volume in low-margin products, or there was a decline in the share of total sales coming from new accounts. These evaluation results can influence management when it prepares the next period's plans for sales force training, supervision, and compensation.

Relation of Performance Evaluation to Sales Control

Many writers and business executives refer to the subject of this chapter as *sales control* or *control of sales operations.* We do not use such a label because we believe it is a misleading and unrealistic use of the term *control.* Control is not an isolated managerial function. It permeates virtually all other managerial activities. For example, management controls its sales force by means of the compensation plan, quota system, territorial structure, and expense-payment plan. Control also is exercised through the training program, sales contests, supervision, and other devices.

INTRODUCTION TO SALES FORCE PERFORMANCE EVALUATION

Evaluation of sales force performance is a broad term that covers (1) the analysis of sales volume—the topic of this chapter, (2) marketing cost analysis and profitability analysis—the topics of Chapter 15, and (3) various analytical

measures used to evaluate an individual salesperson's performance—the topic of Chapter 16.

As established in earlier chapters, a trend toward relationship selling exists in today's sales organizations. In other words, sales organizations work toward developing long-term relationships with existing customers and growing those relationships into major accounts. The end-result is that, relative to 30 years ago, a given firm's customers tend to be fewer in number but larger in sales volume. In fact, firms are sometimes better off eliminating direct business contact with small, low-volume customers.[2] Performance evaluations help sales organizations identify (and then focus on) those customers with the greatest potential. Clearly, companies must have the ability to effectively evaluate performance if they are to remain competitive in today's business environment.

A Marketing Audit: A Total Evaluation Program

An audit is a review and evaluation of some activity. Therefore, a **marketing audit** is a comprehensive, periodic review and evaluation of the marketing function in an organization—its marketing goals, strategies, and performance. A fragmented evaluation of some marketing activities may be useful, but it is not a marketing audit. It is only part of such an audit.

A complete marketing audit is an extensive project that provides an ideal for management to work toward. It is expensive, time-consuming, and difficult. But the rewards can be great. Management can identify its problem areas in marketing. By reviewing its strategies and tactics, the firm can keep abreast of its changing marketing environment. Any marketing successes also should be analyzed so that the company can capitalize on its strong points.

A traditional audit in accounting is an after-the-fact review. However, a marketing audit is also used to evaluate the effects of alternatives *before* a decision is reached. Thus, the audit becomes an aid in decision making. Further, a marketing audit done correctly should anticipate future situations as well as review past one.

A Sales Management Audit

A marketing audit covers an organization's entire marketing system. A company also can apply the audit concept to major divisions *within* the marketing system. Thus, for example, a company might conduct a physical distribution audit or an advertising audit. Or, as is pertinent to this book, management can audit the personal selling and sales management activities in a company's marketing system. Thus, like a marketing audit, a **sales management audit** evaluates a firm's *sales* objectives, strategies, and tactics. The *sales* organization and its policies, personnel, and performance are appraised.[3]

The Evaluation Process

The evaluation process—whether it is a complete marketing audit or only an appraisal of individual components of the marketing program—is essentially a three-stage task, as seen in Figure 14-2. Management's job is to:

1. Find out *what* happened—get the facts by comparing actual results with budgeted goals to determine the variations.
2. Find out *why* it happened—determine what specific factors in the marketing program accounted for the variations.
3. Decide *what to do* about it—plan the next period's activities to improve on unsatisfactory conditions and capitalize on favorable ones.

Much of our discussion in Chapters 14 and 15 is devoted to the first step—that is, explaining the techniques for determining *what* happened. Yet the task in the second step—finding out *why* variances occurred between plans and actual results—is much more difficult and time-consuming. It is relatively easy to discover that sales of *product A* declined 10 percent last year in the western region when management had forecast a 5 percent increase. The real problem is to identify *why* this variation between actual and forecasted sales occurred. Was the forecast in error? Or does the reason lie in the countless possibilities among the elements of the marketing mix or the myriad aspects of sales planning and operations?

Our reason for devoting significant space to the first step is that you cannot decide *why* something occurred if you first don't know *what* occurred. Many companies don't know *what* happened. That is, they have not analyzed their sales and cost performance results in any significant detail. This is surprising because the first step in the evaluation process is actually the easiest, especially with the ready-availability of information through CRM technology.

FIGURE 14-2
The Evaluation Process

Components of Performance Evaluation

Because of the time, cost, and difficulty involved in a full marketing audit, sometimes it is more reasonable to evaluate the separate components of the marketing mix. An evaluation of field-selling efforts involves an appraisal of sales volume results, related marketing expenses, and the performance of individual salespeople. These components are sufficiently independent so that management can conduct one or two evaluations without the need to do all of them. One company may decide to analyze its sales volume but not its marketing costs. Another firm may study various ratios involving sales force activities without making any detailed sales or cost analyses.

A **sales volume analysis** is a careful study of a company's records as summarized in the net sales section of its profit-and-loss statement. It is a detailed study of the dollar or the unit sales volume by product lines, territories, key accounts, and general classes of customers. A sales volume analysis may be expanded to include a corresponding study of cost of goods sold. The result is an analysis of its gross margin, also broken down into such segments as products or territories. A **marketing cost analysis** continues from the analysis of sales volume. It is a study of the marketing expenses to determine the profitability of various marketing segments in the organization.

In a general sense, the two types of analyses are component parts of a detailed study of a company's operating statement. In effect, a sales volume analysis (SVA) and a marketing cost analysis (MCA) together constitute a marketing profitability analysis (MPA). Or look at it this way:

$$\text{SVA} + \text{MCA} = \text{MPA}$$

PERFORMANCE EVALUATION AND MISDIRECTED MARKETING EFFORT

A marketing profitability analysis is one step that may be taken to correct the misdirected marketing effort found in many companies today.

The Nature of Misdirected Marketing Effort: The 80/20 Principle

A company does not enjoy the same rate of net profit on every sales. In most firms, a large proportion of the customers (or orders, or territories, or products) accounts for a small share of the profits. This relationship between selling units and profits has been characterized as the 80/20 principle. That is, 80 percent of the orders, customers, territories, or products contributes only 20 percent of the sales volume or profit. Conversely, the other 20 percent of these marketing units accounts for 80 percent of the volume or profit. In actuality, it seldom is exactly 80/20—but it almost always is *approximately* true.

The 80/20 principle leads to a discussion of how marketing efforts are misdirected. That is, too often firms spend so much time with a certain number of small customers that they lose money on them! Alternatively, firms sometimes do not realize who their most important customers are…and ignore them at their peril. Fastenal, on the other hand, understands the 80/20 principle, which is why the company identifies the top 20 accounts in every district so that high level executives at Fastenal can call on and get to know these key customers.

LivHome is another example of a company that understands the 80/20 principle. This Los Angeles-based home health care provider regularly calculates the lifetime value of each customer by collecting and evaluating information about recency, frequency, and monetary value of purchasing patterns. This information is used to create distinct segments of various customer profiles. LivHome then directs its salespeople to call on those segments most representative of loyal, deep-pocketed customers likely to generate the significant sales volume over the long haul.[4] The 80/20 situation stems from the fact that marketing efforts and costs are to some extent related to the *number* of marketing units (territories, products, customers) rather than their *actual* or *potential sales volume and profit.* A firm may have one salesperson and one branch office in each territory, with all the attendant expense, regardless of the volume obtained from these districts. For every order received, the seller must process a purchase order, invoice, and a payment check—whether the order is for $10 or $1,000.

Reasons for Misdirected Effort

Because they lack sufficiently detailed information, many executives are unaware of the misdirected marketing effort in their firms. They do not know what percentage of total sales and profits comes from a given product line or customer group.

Total sales or costs on an operating statement are often inconclusive and misleading (see Figure 14-3). More than one company has shown satisfactory overall sales and profit figures, but when these totals were subdivided by territory or products, serious weaknesses were discovered. A manufacturer of plastic products showed an overall annual increase of 12 percent in sales and 9 percent in net profit on one of its product lines one year. But when management analyzed these figures, the sales change within each territory ranged from an increase of 19 percent to a decrease of 3 percent. In some territories, profit increased as much as 14 percent; in others, it was down 20 percent.

FIGURE 14-3
Total sales figures may hide
significant problems

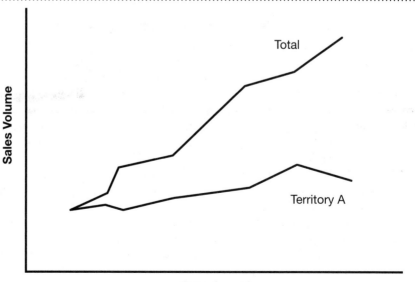

There is a more fundamental reason for misplaced marketing effort. Sales executives must make decisions even though their knowledge of the exact nature of marketing costs is inadequate. In other words, management lacks:

1. Knowledge of the disproportionate spread of marketing effort.
2. Standards for determining
   a. What should have been spent on marketing.
   b. What results should have been obtained from these expenditures.

As an example, a sales executive really does not know exactly how much to spend on sales training, marketing research, or sales supervision. Even more troublesome is that management has no yardstick to determine whether the results of these expenditures are satisfactory. If a firm adds 10 missionary salespeople or employs field supervisors where none existed before, the executives ordinarily cannot say how much the volume or profit should increase. Nor can they compare the value of two expenditures. Assume that a company spends $200,000 on a contest for the sales force. No one can say how much additional volume this expenditure will bring, as compared with spending the same amount on advertising or on sales training, for example.

The Need for Detailed Data

Sales administrators who want to analyze sales volume may find they lack detailed data. The sales department works largely with figures supplied by the accounting department. But these records are rarely itemized sufficiently for the sales managers. Before managers can make a worthwhile analysis, they must establish a system to supply the sales department with the necessary facts.

The possible classifications of sales data and the combinations of these breakdowns have almost no limit. The following are some widely used subdivisions for reporting and analyzing sales:

- **Sale territories.**
- **Salespeople.** If each salesperson has a district, an analysis of sales volume by territory also serves for individual salespeople.
- **Products.** Reports may be in dollars and/or physical units for individual products or lines of products.
- **Customers.** Management may classify the volume by the individual customers, key accounts, industrial groups of customers, or channels of distribution.
- **Size of order.**

BASIS FOR ANALYZING SALES VOLUME

The sales volume of a firm should be analyzed in a variety of ways. First, a firm's total sales volume should be examined with respect to previous points in time. In addition, the sales volume should be broken down by territory, by product, and by customer class. The following sections provide more details on how to approach these analyses.

Total Sales Volume

A reasonable place to begin a sales analysis is with the *total sales volume*—the combined sales of all products in all territories for all customers. This readily available figure gives an overall picture of how the company is faring. However, the *trend* in sales is usually far more important to administrators than the volume for any given year. Two trends—the trend of the company's sales over a period of years and the trend of the company's share of the total industry market—are especially important.

A study of total sales volume is probably the easiest of all types of analyses. The only data needed are (1) the annual sales figures for the company over the past several years and (2) the annual industry sales in the geographic market covered by the firm. From these figures analysts can determine the company's share of the market.

Figure 14-4 shows the sort of information developed in a total sales volume analysis for the Colorado Ski Company. This concern carries two basic product lines: ski equipment (skis and accessories) and a limited line of ski clothes (ski pants and parkas). The company manufactures some of these items and purchases others from outside sources to sell under Colorado Ski's brand. The firm sells to two classes of customers—sporting goods stores and specialty ski shops—in some of the major ski markets in the nation. Annual sales in 2016 were $27 million.

An analysis of the company's volume shows that sales have generally increased each year since 2007, with the exceptions of 2011 and 2013. So far, the picture looks encouraging. However, industry figures shed a different light on the situation. The industry's sales also have increased since 2007, but at a more rapid rate than Colorado's volume. As a result, the company's share of the market has steadily declined. Looking at the 10-year picture, management finds that its sales have increased 80 percent but its share of the market has declined 25 percent.

After management has uncovered the facts as shown in Figure 14-4, the next step is to determine the reasons for the decline in the company's market position. The possible weaknesses in Colorado Ski's operation are almost limitless. On the one hand, something may be wrong with the product line itself, such as styling, construction, or color. Some aspects of the pricing structure

FIGURE 14-4
Information Used in Analysis of Total Sales Volume, Colorado Ski Company

Year	Company volume (in millions)	Industry Volume (in millions)	Company's Share of Market
2016	$27.0	$360	7.5%
2015	25.2	390	6.4
2014	23.4	360	6.5
2013	20.4	312	4.0
2012	21.0	300	8.2
2011	19.2	234	8.3
2010	19.8	240	8.9
2009	19.2	216	8.9
2008	18.0	180	10.0
2007	15.0	150	10.0

may be the problem. The weakness may lie in some phase of advertising, such as the choice of media or the ads themselves. Then the entire area of sales force management can be examined. On the other hand, it may be that all of Colorado Ski's operations are as good as ever but that the competitors have made improvements. Possibly there are more competitors. Or some of these firms may have significantly improved their product, distribution, or promotional effectiveness.

Sales by Territories

Companies usually can do an analysis of *total* sales volume easily and inexpensively. However, its value to management is limited because it tells so little about the details of a firm's marketing progress. Only the aggregate picture emerges and the separate parts remain submerged. One step toward uncovering these parts is the common practice of analyzing sales by territories. Management wants to identify which territories are strong and which are weak in relation to potential. A company must find out *which* territories are weak before it can determine *why* they are weak.

One reasonably simple, inexpensive procedure for analyzing sales volume by territories involves the following four steps:

1. Select a market index that indicates with reasonable accuracy what percentage of total sales should be obtained from each sales territory. For example, one firm may use retail sales as an index. If 10 percent of the total national retail sales were in the Midwestern district, then 10 percent of the company's sales also should come from that district. Or, if the firm sells in only eight southeastern states, then the total retail sales in the eight-state area would be equated to 100 percent. If 22 percent of retail sales in the eight states were tallied in Alabama, then 22 percent of the sales in the company also should come from Alabama.

2. Determine the company's actual total sales in dollars or units during the period being studied.

3. Multiply the territorial index by the total sales figure to determine the goal in each district.

4. Compare actual regional sales with the regional goals to see how much variation has occurred.

An example of this procedure is developed in Figure 14-5. The five territories in the western division of the Colorado Ski Company are being analyzed. Colorado Ski's total sales in the western division were $13.5 million distributed

Territory	Market Index (percent)	Sales Goals ($000)	Actual Sales ($000)	Performance Percentage	Dollar Variation ($000)
A	27%	$ 3,645	$ 2,700	74	$-945
B	22	2,970	3,690	124	+720
C	15	2,025	2,484	123	+459
D	20	2,700	2,556	95	-144
E	16	2,160	2,070	96	-90
Total	100%	$13,500	$13,500		

FIGURE 14-5
Analysis of territorial sales volume in five-territory western division, Colorado Ski Company, 2016

among five territories, as shown in the column headed Actual sales. Sales were $2,700,000 in territory A. The goal in territory B was 22 percent, or $2,970,000, and so on.

A performance percentage is computed by dividing actual sales by the territorial goal. A rating of 100 percent in the district means that the area turned in its predetermined share of the company's business. Figure 14-5 shows that territories B and C did much better than expected. Territories E and D were a shade below par, and A fell considerably short of expectations.

It is not enough to study the *percentage* by which an area's sales are over or under the goals. The more important measure is usually the *dollar volume*. It is possible that the district may be only a few percentage points under par. However, because the territorial potential is very large, these few percentage points may represent a significant sum of money.

A market segment that is below par—its actual performance does not reach its goal—may be called a *soft spot*. In sales management, the **soft-spot principle** states that an administrator reaps the largest possible gain by working with the weakest segments of the organization. Thus, a sales manager in the Colorado Ski Company should devote the most attention to territory A because it has the greatest need for improvement. By the same token, it is doubtful that even considerable attention could improve B and C very much. Already they are far above their goals. Probably the main benefits from a study of B and C would be to determine (1) why they apparently are so successful and (2) whether this information can be used to improve A.

Once management has identified the strong and weak territories, the next task is to determine the *reasons* for the relative performances. Territory A may be doing poorly because competition is particularly effective or because some aspects of Colorado Ski's operation are especially weak. Although the soft-spot principle says to focus on improving the weakest territory, it is always possible that a territory is beyond repair (although this is a rare occurrence). That is, a sales manager sometimes has to make the tough choice to withdraw from a particular market—and focus energy on territories with better potential for growth.

Sales by Products

The 80/20 principle applies to products as well as to territories in many companies. Very often, most of the products in a company's line account for a small percentage of total volume or profit. Conversely, a few products may bring most of the volume. There is not necessarily a relation between volume and profit. Products that account for a large proportion of the volume may or may not contribute a corresponding percentage of the net profits.

Several types of volume analyses by product lines may be helpful to management. The first is simply a summary of present and past total sales divided into individual products or groups of products. An appliance manufacturer may want to study the sales trend for each individual product. A hardware wholesaler, however, would be content to group thousands of products into divisions such as housewares, plumbing goods, and electrical equipment.

If industry figures are available for each product line, they may provide a yardstick for a company to measure its own sales performance by products. For example, assume that the sales of *product A* are decreasing in one firm. Its management need not be too concerned if, over the same period, the industry's sales have decreased at about the same rate.

A further refinement is to study the sales of each product line in each territory. In this way, management can determine the geographical market in which each product is strong or weak. *Product A's total* sales may be up 10 percent over last year, but in the southwestern region, A's volume is down 14 percent. Once these facts are known, an administrator can try to determine the reasons for the variations and then make the necessary corrections.

An analysis of sales by product lines also can be used to refine the territorial analysis discussed in the preceding section. Figure 14-5 showed that territory A was 26 percent under par. Territories B and C were 24 percent and 23 percent above par, respectively. By investigating the product sales in these districts, management can better isolate the reasons for these variations.

In Figure 14-6, market indexes were applied to Colorado Ski's actual volume of $13.5 million to establish targets for products in the five western territories. Note that the total sales goal for territory A is $3,645,000 (which corresponds to the goal from Figure 14-5). This analysis breaks that goal down by product with skis contributing $1,629,000; ski accessories accounting for $270,000; and so on.

In Figure 14-5, we found that the company was short of its sales goal in territory A by $945,000, or 26 percent. However, this shortage was not distributed equally among all four products. Further analysis by product lines showed that the sales of ski pants and parkas were the primary sources of the shortages. The company failed to reach its target by $540,000 and $450,000, respectively, for those two products. Sales of skis actually were $81,000 over the performance standard.

Territory B as a whole was $720,000 over its goal figure. However, sales of parkas fell $90,000 (about 12 percent) short of the goal. Volume in skis, accessories, and ski pants was above the target figure in each of these product categories.

As part of its sales volume analysis by products, management must decide what to do about low-volume products and products that did not meet their sales goals. Figure 14-6 suggests that ski pants and parkas in territory A and parkas in territory B seem to be soft spots in terms of sales goals. Thus, these products seem to provide the best opportunity for improvement.

Management's initial thought may be to drop low-volume products. But before taking such a drastic step, the company should consider other factors. A cost analysis will aid in these decisions. If the product is a losing proposition for the company, this would be a strong point in favor of dropping the item. In some cases, however, a low-volume product must be kept whether or not it is profitable. It may be needed to round out a line, and customers may expect the company to carry the item.

Sales by Customer Classifications

A company is even more likely to find the 80/20 principle in operation when sales are analyzed by customer groups. It is not unusual to find that a small percentage of customers accounts for a major share of total volume. Typically, a firm sells to many accounts on a marginal or even unprofitable basis.

A firm can analyze its volume by customer groups in several ways. It may classify accounts on an industry basis. An oil company may group its customers into *industry divisions,* such as service stations or marine, farm, transportation,

FIGURE 14-6
Analysis of Product Sales
Performance in Two
Territories, Colorado Ski
Company, 2016

Product	Territory A ($000)			Territory B ($000)		
	Goal	**Actual**	**Variation**	**Goal**	**Actual**	**Variation**
Skis	$1,629	$1,710	+$ 81	$1,263	$1,620	+$357
Accessories	270	234	−36	222	360	+138
Pants	900	360	−540	765	1,080	+315
Parkas	846	396	−450	720	630	−90
Total	$3,645	$2,700	−$945	$2,970	$3,690	+$720

industrial, and governmental agencies. Another basis of classification is by *channels of distribution.* A sporting goods manufacturer may group its accounts by sporting goods wholesalers, department stores, and discount houses. A third classification is on the basis of *accounts,* or just the key accounts. Any of these three groups may be cross-classified. An oil company may want to analyze its sales to key accounts in the service-station industry group, for example.

Customer classifications usually should be analyzed for each territory and for each line of products. In one company, it may be that sales to wholesalers are satisfactory on an overall basis, although sales to wholesalers may be particularly poor in one territory. An oil company may assume that a given industry market that accounts for 10 percent of total sales also contributes about 10 percent of the volume of each product line. However, an analysis may disclose that this industry accounts for 18 percent of the volume in *product A,* but only 5 percent in *product B.*

Combining the previously listed types of analyses provides even more in-depth information to guide sales organizations. For example, Figure 14-7 shows a **customer probability cube** for a given territory for a firm with four products and *n* number of customers.[5] This analysis helps predict what customers will buy and when. The cube indicates that customer C1 has a 90 percent change of buying product P1 in the first quarter of the year (Q1). Equipped with this information, salespeople can call on the appropriate customer and can emphasize the right product, at the right time. Of course, this helps firms to properly allocate marketing effort. This type of analysis is much more readily available with the help of advanced sales force automation software discussed in the next section.

The Insufficiency of Sales Volume Analysis

A sales volume analysis alone usually does not furnish enough information to the sales department. Furthermore, the data produced may be misleading. A study may show, for example, that the dollar *volume* of *product A* is 20 percent greater than the sales of *product B.* Yet, if the company were to determine the gross margin or net profit of the two products, management would find that B's dollar *profit* is 10 percent higher than A's. A full-scale sales and cost study—a marketing profitability analysis—is ideal, but it is also likely to be difficult and costly. Further, while an analysis of volume alone has its limitations, it is better than no analysis at all. In spite of the acknowledged value of a marketing cost and profitability analysis, the most widely used measure of sales performance continues to be sales volume.

A compromise between a volume analysis and a full-scale marketing cost study is to expand the volume analysis to include the cost of the merchandise

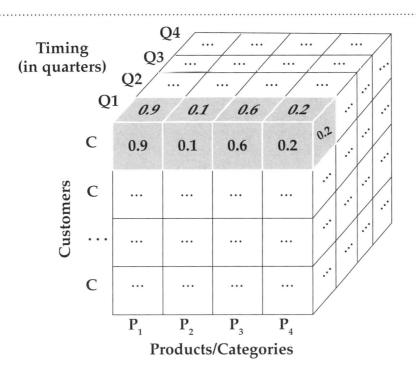

FIGURE 14-7

Customer probability cube shows salespeople what to sell, when, and to whom... SOURCE: V. Kumar, Rajkumar Venkatesan, and Werner Reinartz, "Knowing what to sell, when, and to whom," *Harvard Business Review*, March 2006, pp. 131-37. Reprinted with permission of *Harvard Business Review*. Copyright ©2006 by the Harvard Business School Publishing Corporation; all rights reserved.

sold. Thus, management ends up with a gross margin analysis by territories, products, or customer groups with relatively little additional expense. The next chapter provides much more details on marketing cost analysis.

SALES FORCE AUTOMATION AND PERFORMANCE EVALUATION

In recent years, sales organizations increasingly have relied on **sales force automation (SFA)** software to manage information. This makes performance evaluation much easier and faster. SFA is typically a single part of an overall customer relationship management (CRM) system, and thus analyzes information from a variety of the firm's different business functions (e.g., sales, marketing, accounting, purchasing, manufacturing).

Research shows that company executives are generally satisfied with recent implementations of SFA—although the amount of training required for salespeople to learn the system has tended to be underestimated.[6] Salespeople that use this type of technology are shown to perform at higher levels than those who do not.[7] The technology gives salespeople access to information that enables them to better understand customers and then to make specific recommendations to solve customer problems. This leads to closer relationships between the salesperson and his or her customers.

Salespeople, however, are sometimes resistant to SFA initiatives. To gain their salespeople's acceptance, sales managers must first explain and demonstrate how SFA will help improve sales productivity. In addition, management should exhibit a definite commitment to the technology and should be sure to involve the sales force in designing a program for implementation. These are important managerial actions, because sales force acceptance is necessary for the success of any SFA initiative. The value of the SFA analysis to the sales organization absolutely depends on the reps' ability and willingness to regularly enter data about customers, orders, and expenses; and salespeople will only do this if management offers the right support.[8]

One of many SFA success stories is Boehringer Ingelheim, which is one of the largest pharmaceutical companies in the world. To be successful, this company must develop close, collaborative relationships with its wide range of customers, which include general practitioners, a variety of physician specialists, and influential hospital professionals. Before implementation, customer information was kept in a confusing, decentralized set of databases that made it hard for salespeople to access relevant information. The SFA system, which in this case is an Oracle product, gave all sales and marketing personnel quick and ready access to critical customer information. The end result was a measurable increase in both customer satisfaction and retention. In the words of one Boehringer Ingelheim executive, the system "…makes certain we are seeing the right customers, at the right time, using the most productive methodology. That scheduling information can also be seamlessly shared with others throughout the organization. Furthermore, just prior to each visit, the sales professional can quickly view a real-time summary of the customer's situation from their laptop."[9]

SUMMARY

The sales force management process involves an endless cycle of planning, implementation and performance evaluation. A marketing audit, which is key to performance evaluation, is a comprehensive periodic review and evaluation of the marketing system in an organization. A sales management audit evaluates sales objectives, strategies, and tactics.

The evaluation process is essentially a three-stage task. First, find out *what* happened—actual results are compared with budgeted goals. Second, find out *why* it happened—what factors accounted for the variation between goals and results. Third, decide *what to do* about the situation—that is, plan next period's activities.

Because of the time and cost needed for a full-scale marketing audit, many companies evaluate only the major components of their marketing programs. One such performance evaluation includes an analysis of (1) sales volume, (2) marketing costs, and (3) salespeople's performance. A sales volume analysis combined with a marketing cost analysis constitutes a marketing profitability analysis.

Performance evaluation is a key tool in reducing the misdirected marketing effort in an organization. Misdirected marketing effort means that a company is expending much effort but getting relatively few results. The 80/20 principle illustrates misdirected marketing effort. That is, marketing efforts (costs) are related to the *number* of marketing units (territories, products, customers), rather than the *sales volume* or *profit* derived from these marketing units.

The basic reasons for misdirected marketing efforts are that management lacks (1) knowledge of the disproportionate spread of marketing effort and (2) reliable standards for determining (a) what should be spent on marketing and (b) what results should be derived from these expenditures.

A sales volume analysis is a study of a company's actual sales volume compared with the budgeted sales goals. This volume analysis should be done in great detail. That is, the company's sales should be analyzed in total and also by territory, products, customer groups, salespeople, and order size. In each of these subdivisions, the company's performance should be compared with industry figures. In this way, management can measure its performance against the competition.

Detailed sales performance analysis has been improved immeasurably by advances in computer and Internet-related technology. Sales force automation (SFA) software, for example, helps sales organizations manage information efficiently. SFA, which is typically a part of a firm's CRM program, makes performance evaluation much easier and faster than ever before.

KEY TERMS

Customer probability cube	Marketing cost analysis	Sales management audit
Marketing audit	Sales force automation (SFA)	Sales volume analysis
		Soft-spot principle

QUESTIONS AND PROBLEMS

1. Explain the relationship between planning and evaluation in the management process.

2. Explain the concept of a marketing profitability analysis.

3. What is the 80/20 principle, and how does it apply to sales performance evaluation?

4. If a firm's volume is increasing each year by a satisfactory percentage, is there any reason for a firm to go to the expense of a volume analysis?

5. As a result of sales volume analysis, many firms have eliminated some of their products or customers. Yet in several of these cases, the sales volume has *increased* after the market cutback. How do you account for this result?

6. A territorial volume analysis indicated that a firm's sales had increased at about a 10 percent rate for the past three years in a given district. Is this conclusive evidence that the company's performance is satisfactory as far as sales volume is concerned in the given territory?

7. A company with 15 territories found that *product A* accounted for 40 to 50 percent of the sales in 13 of the districts. But this product brought in only

about 20 percent of the volume in the remaining two territories. What factors might account for the relatively low standing of *product A* in the two territories?

8. Is it possible for a product, territory, or class of customer to be far below par but still not deserve much executive attention? Give examples.

9. Should salespeople be furnished with complete statistics, not only on their own performances but on the performance of other salespeople as well?

10. If a company made a *territorial* volume analysis and found some subpar territories, how might these facts affect the following activities relating to salespeople?

    a. Supervision

    b. Compensation

    c. Training

11. If a firm analyzed its sales volume by *customer classes*, how might the results affect the supervision, compensation, and training of the sales force?

12. What can sales managers do to ensure that their salespeople readily accept and properly use sales force automation (SFA) software?

EXPERIENTIAL EXERCISES

1. Ask a local store manager to discuss with you (and possibly show you) the reports that he or she uses to track the store's performance as well as the performance of various product categories and salespeople.

2. Contact a salesperson and discuss the product and customer data reports that he or she uses to plan selling strategies and evaluate performance effectiveness.

3. Explore Salesforce.com, which is a sales force automation (SFA) website. How do sales managers benefit from using it? How do salespeople benefit? Using sales force automation as a search phrase, find other, similar SFA websites/products. Discuss the pros and cons of Salesforce.com compared to some of these competitive products you found.

SEAL RITE ENVELOPE COMPANY (A)
Analysis of Sales Volume

"You're drowning in data. Haven't you anything better to do around here than reading those reports? You're wasting so much paper, the next thing I know the environmentalists will be picketing the place," exclaimed Max Chernak, Seal Rite Envelope Company's new president. He had stopped by the office of Rose Douglas, the firm's sales manager for the past seven years, to visit with her. His opening remarks were a reaction to the two-foot-high stack of SFA reports spread out in front of Douglas on her desk. She stopped scanning them and looked up as Chernak walked in.

Chernak was smiling as he commented on the pile of paper before her, but Douglas had been warned previously by an acquaintance who had worked for Chernak in another company that he was not a big believer in paperwork. She recalled the words, "He likes to keep things simple. He doesn't spend much time in his office. He always seems to be around. Delegation is not one of his favorite concepts."

The Seal Rite Envelope Company of St. Louis, Missouri, manufactured and distributed a wide line of paper envelopes of all weights, sizes, and paper stock. Its sales force sold to printers, paper wholesalers, and large organizations with their own operations throughout the Midwestern states.

Douglas was rather proud of her sales analysis system, which she had developed using data from the company's sales force automation (SFA) program. All sales orders were classified by the stock numbers of the products bought, who bought them, who sold them, when they were bought, and how much gross margin was realized from the order. The data were for the previous week and previous month, all compared with sales for the same periods the previous year. Any significant changes in performance were automatically highlighted for her attention by the program. A report of each week's sales orders and shipments

was delivered to her email account each Sunday morning so she could study it in preparation for the Monday morning sales meeting. The reports were automatically generated every week by the SFA program. Douglas typically spent one to two hours carefully going through the report every Sunday afternoon.

Douglas felt obliged to defend her system for analyzing sales. "I find it helpful to have the facts about what has happened before I go into my weekly sales meeting every Monday morning. I know who is selling and who isn't. I know what is selling and what isn't. And I know how much we're making on everything we sell and on every order."

"I see. Knowledge is power. Is that it?" Chernak asked.

Douglas nodded slightly; she understood she was under attack. Had she been too aggressive in defending her system, considering that she hardly knew Chernak? She wondered.

The new president was not a person who avoided confrontation. He rose to the challenge. "OK! I see that something is highlighted on that page you're looking at. What is it?"

"Well, it seems that the sales of item number 2510 are down significantly for the month compared to last year. We sold hardly any of it last week. Let's see, 2510 is our heavy-duty, brown, 12-inch by 18-inch mailing envelope," Douglas said as she read from the reports.

"So what?"

"What do you mean, so what?"

Chernak said, "I mean, so what? So what is the significance of that information? So what are you going to do about it?"

Douglas knew she was in a bit of trouble, but she could not back down. "I'll make inquiries of the sales force to see if any of them has an explanation. Is something wrong with our product or its pricing? Is it just a random event? Does it reflect a change in market requirements? I'll keep my eye on it to see if anything develops that warrants taking some action."

Chernak replied, "That's what I call micromanagement. How many of such items are there in that report that will require you to do something? Don't answer that! I'm afraid of the answer. We seem to be on different wavelengths. I only want to know a few things, such as our gross margins by broad product lines and by salesperson. And, of course, I want to know total dollar sales, gross margins, and expenses. But I would lose all perspective if I had to deal with that volume of information you are processing each week. And what about the costs? Are they worth it? Well, as long as the profit performance of your operation keeps doing as well as it has, you can stare at that paper as long as you like if that's the way you get your kicks."

As Chernak left her office, Douglas was a bit upset by the president's attitude toward her sales analysis system. She had been taught that if she took care of the details, the totals would take care of themselves. She had found that by having good, recent information about all aspects of sales, she gained power in the organization. Her people had learned not to challenge her since she could always pull out data to support her position. She wanted people to know that she was on top of her job.

Douglas decided to think about the matter for a while and ask some other people about her system before doing anything about it. As she looked at the stack of paper in front of her, a troubling thought crossed her mind. Was she spending too much time analyzing these SFA reports? Was it all worth it?

Questions:

1. How should Rose Douglas evaluate the effectiveness of her sales analysis system?

2. What would you recommend she do in response to the situation in which her boss obviously disagrees with her attitudes toward analyzing SFA reports?

ENDNOTES

[1] Perry Marshall, "The 80/20 Rule of Sales: How to Find Your Best Customers," *Entrepreneur com,* October 9, 2013. Retrieved from the following URL on July 4, 2016: https://www.entrepreneur.com/article/229294

[2] Paul Smith, "Only Some Customers Are King," *New Zealand Management,* April 2000, pp. 24-26.

[3] For an excellent explanation of a sales management audit, including a detailed outline of its elements, see Alan J. Dubinsky and Richard W. Hansen, "The Sales Force Management Audit," *California Management Review,* Winter 1981, pp. 86-95.

[4] Mark McMaster, "A Lifetime of Sales," *Sales & Marketing Management,* September 2001, p. 55.

[5] V. Kumar, Rajkumar Venkatesan, and Werner Reinartz, "Knowing what to sell, when, and to whom," *Harvard Business Review,* March 2006, pp. 131-37.

[6] Houda Khlif and Rim Jallouli, "The Success Factors of CRM Systems: An Explanatory Analysis," *Journal of Global Business & Technology,* Fall 2014, Vol. 10(2), pp. 25-42.

[7] See both Gary K. Hunter and Williams D. Perreault Jr., "Sales Technology Orientation, Information Effectiveness, and Sales Performance," *Journal of Personal Selling & Sales Management,* Spring 2006, pp. 95-113; and Dong-Gil Ko and Alan R. Dennis, "Sales Force Automation and Sales Performance: Do Experience and Expertise Matter?" *Journal of Personal Selling & Sales Management,* Fall 2004, pp. 311-22.

[8] Ronald Jelinek, "All pain, no gain? Why adopting sales force automation tools is insufficient for performance improvement," *Business Horizons,* September 2013, Vol. 56(5), pp. 635-642.

[9] "Boehringer Ingelheim Holland Experiences Significant Increase in Customer Satisfaction in 12 Months Using Siebel Pharma," *BusinessWire.com,* March 15, 2004. Accessed from the following URL on July 5, 2016: http://www.businesswire.com/news/home/20040315005046/en/Boehringer-Ingelheim-Holland-Experiences-Significant-Increase-Customer

15

Cost And Profitability Analysis

Jim Sobeck is president of New South Construction, which is a construction supply house in South Carolina.[1] Sobeck understands that not every sale is a good sale. In fact, he calculated that his cost to process an order is roughly $100. So, let's say a customer calls his store and buys just one item: a Makita cordless drill for $150. Further, let's assume that the cost of that drill to New South was $90, which means that the store made $60 in gross profit in the short-run—but in the end actually *loses* $40 due to the invoice processing cost. This might sound high for a processing cost, but consider that *several* activities are required to get that drill to the customer, including taking the order, retrieving the item from inventory, billing the customer, delivering the product, etc.

This is why Sobeck encourages his salespeople to do what he calls "related item selling," *especially* to customers that place small orders. Some salespeople resist this because they do not want to come across as being "too pushy." However, Sobeck believes that this is actually helpful to customers

when done correctly. "A good salesperson can ask the right questions about the purchase in such a way that the customer isn't offended and the size of the sale grows," he says. Ultimately, those customers are happy because they need those additional items.

And for those customers who insist on a small order? New South Construction charges them an "expedited order charge," which varies depending on how small the order is and when and where it must be delivered.

The last chapter discussed sales volume analyses, which are useful to a point—but they do not tell the whole story. For example, two territories might generate the same sales volume, yet one might be much less *profitable* than the other due to a problem with too many small orders. Consequently, sales managers must also conduct marketing cost analyses in order to determine the relative profitability of the various marketing units, such as products, territories, and salespeople. This is the focus of this chapter.

NATURE AND SCOPE OF MARKETING COST ANALYSIS

A marketing cost analysis, as noted in Chapter 14, is a detailed study of a firm's marketing costs. It is used to discover unprofitable segments and inefficiently performed functions of the company's marketing program. It goes beyond a sales volume analysis to determine the profitability of various aspects of the marketing operation. Thus, it becomes an important part of an overall sales performance analysis.

Various sales department budgets are frequently an integral part of cost analyses. Management often wants to establish a standard of performance (a budget) for some selling expense and then to determine the causes of variation between the actual and budgeted expense.

Marketing Cost Analysis and the Accounting System

Marketing cost analysis differs somewhat in purpose and scope from the usual accounting system in a firm. Accounting seeks to maintain a complete *historical record of company events that in any way have a financial flavor*. Thus, the system provides management with the story of merchandise sales, materials purchased, equipment depreciation, salaries paid, and all other activities relating to finances. Marketing cost analysis is a managerial tool designed more for us in the planning and control of a firm's *future* operations. Of course, an analysis of past financial events often serves as a guide for future operations.

Marketing cost study is *not* usually a part of a company's regular accounting system. It takes up where the accounting system stops. A study of costs is largely analytical and statistical. It is not concerned with the routine accounting practices. The regular accounting system, however, provides virtually all the data necessary to conduct a marketing cost analysis. Therefore, to do an effective cost analysis, the company must maintain a detailed system of account classification. For instance, one account for sales commissions is not at all sufficient to analyze the commissions paid (1) on sales of a given product (2) to selected customers and (3) in a certain territory.

Marketing Cost Analysis Compared with Production Cost Accounting

Marketing cost analysis and production cost accounting help to control costs in their respective areas. Beyond this general similarity, however, the two concepts are markedly different, as the comparison in Figure 15-1 shows.

To summarize this comparison, sales executives want to know the marketing costs by product in addition to the costs for other marketing units. Moreover, these costs are incurred by salespeople who are not under direct supervision and whose job is not totally routine, in contrast to production workers and their machines. Finally, production managers usually know the exact cost-volume relationship between an increase in output and a decrease in cost. A sales manager, on the other hand, wants to know what the effect on volume will be if a given cost is changed. For example, what change in volume would occur if two salespeople were added to the eight now operating in the Dallas district? Sales executives typically cannot determine answers to these questions with nearly the degree of accuracy that production managers can.

FIGURE 15-1

Top Five Customer Complaints about Salespeople

Comparison Factors	Marketing Cost Analysis		Production Cost Accounting
Bases for computing costs	Various marketing units (territory, customer, order size, and product) *More complex*	←→	Unit of product *Relatively simple*
Source of cost incurred	Salespeople in the field *Less exact*	←→	Machines and closely supervised workers *More precise*
Cost-volume relationship	Volume is a function of cost V = f(C) *Difficult to measure*	←→	Cost is a function of volume C = f(V) *Relatively easy to measure*

Source: *The HR Chally Group,* Ten Year Research Report, *2002.*

TYPES OF MAREKTING COST ANALYSIS

A company's marketing costs may be analyzed in three ways:

1. As they appear in the ledger accounts and on the income statement.
2. After they are grouped into functional (also called activity) categories.
3. After they have been allocated to territories, products, or other marketing units.

Analysis of Ledger Expenses

The simplest and least expensive marketing cost analysis is based on studying object-of-expenditure costs as they are recorded in the company's accounting ledgers. The procedure is simply to take the totals for each cost item (sales force salaries, branch office rent, office supplies, etc.) from the ledger accounts and then analyze these figures in some detail. Totals for this period can be compared with similar figures for past periods to determine trends. Management can compare actual expenses with budgeted expense goals. When trade associations disseminate cost information, a company can compare its figures with the industry's averages.

An analysis of ledger-cost items is of limited value because it provides only general information. A study may show, for instance, that sales compensation costs are 4.7 percent of sales, whereas the industry's average for firms of similar size is 6.1 percent. Findings of this nature are of some help in guiding management and controlling the sales force. However, a more detailed analysis is needed to pinpoint the reasons for the trends observed in the company's costs and the variations from industry norms.

In Chapter 14, we introduced the Colorado Ski Company as part of our discussion of sales volume analysis. At this point, in Figure 15-2, we show that firm's 2016 income statement, sometimes called an *operating statement* or a *profit-and-loss statement*.

Analysis of Activity Expenses

In typical accounting records, expenses are classified according to the immediate object of the expenditure. Thus, ledger accounts may be found for such marketing expenses as sales salaries, branch office rent, and advertising costs. However, for a more effective marketing cost analysis, sales executives usually regroup these ledger expenses into various activity classifications. All the

CONSIDER THIS...

Making Customers More Profitable

In all of the following examples, a marketing cost analysis uncovered a hidden cost. Once these costs were discovered, the company reacted with policy changes that made the customer more profitable.

- A chemical supplier gave customers free, last-minute deliveries if the salespeople classified it as an "emergency delivery." On closer examination, the firm discovered that over half the orders were being categorized as "emergencies." Consequently, the supplier instituted a minimal charge for emergency orders, which resulted in an 80 percent reduction in the number of emergencies—saving the firm $4 million a year.
- A building products company discovered that under its free returns policy, the number of returns had increased from 10 percent to 35 percent. The

company changed its policy—still allowing returns, but now charging the customer for return delivery. Customers responded by getting more precise in ordering exactly what they needed, and returns dropped by 50 percent. Company net income increased by one-half percent.

- A magazine publisher discovered that it lost money on small advertisers—as these customers were not paying bills, using a lot of creative resources, and running ads for very short durations. The publisher changed its policy to require prepayment and to restrict its creative services to advertisers that agreed to run the same ad at least six times. This resulted in more profitable transactions, plus happier customers due to the longer ad runs generating more impact.

SOURCE: Paul Hunt, "Use the Pricing Waterfall to Drive Profits," *Pricing Solutions Blog,* February 29, 2016. Retrieved from the following on July 1, 2016: http://www.pricingsolutions.com/use-the-pricing-waterfall-to-drive-profits/

expenses related to a given marketing function, such as warehousing or advertising, are grouped together.[2]

An activity-related expense analysis is a two-step procedure. The first step involves selecting the appropriate activity categories. Each firm should list the major activities that are relevant to its own marketing program. A retail chain, for instance, ordinarily performs activities different from those of a manufacturer of electric generators. A typical list, however, usually includes many of the following expense categories:

- Personal selling expenses: sales force compensation and travel expenses as well as all costs connected with branch sales offices.
- Advertising and sales promotion expenses.
- Warehousing and shipping expenses.
- Order processing expenses: costs of processing sales and purchase orders, billing, and receiving payments.
- Administration expenses: all costs of sales offices, including executives' salaries and travel expenses; marketing's share of company's general administration expenses.

In the second step of an activity-expense analysis, we take each ledger expense and allocate it among the various activity categories. Many of the ledger expenses listed in accounting records cut across several activity groups. Consequently, management must *allocate* a given ledger expense among the appropriate activities. For instance, the ledger account for office supplies must be allocated to each activity group (such as personal selling, advertising, and warehousing) that incurs this expense. A useful tool here is an expense distribution sheet such as the one pictured in Figure 15-3. All the ledger costs are listed vertically in the left-hand column. (Note that these ledger expenses are the same ones shown in the income statement in Figure 15-2.). The activity categories are listed at the top of the columns across the sheet.

Some ledger expenses are easy to apportion because they are direct expenses. That is, the entire amount can be allocated to one activity. In Figure 15-3, advertising salaries of $218,000 were apportioned entirely to the advertising activity. Sales force travel expenses of $372,000 were apportioned entirely to the personal-selling category.

Other expenses are indirect. Thus, they must be apportioned among several activity groups. The main problem in dealing with each indirect expense is to select a basis for its allocation. For example, property taxes may be distributed on the basis of square feet used for each activity. In the Colorado Ski Company example, about 55 percent of the total floor space was in the warehousing and shipping department. Consequently, $66,000 of the property tax expense (55 percent of $120,000) was allocated to this physical distribution activity.

After all individual ledger expenses are allocated, the columns are totaled, and the resultant figures are the activity expenses. In Figure 15-3, the expenses totaled $6.3 million. The total for personal selling alone was $3,847,000. From this type of analysis, the total cost of each activity can be determined accurately. Moreover, a study of an expense distribution sheet each year shows not only which *ledger* costs have increased or decreased, but also the *activities* responsible for these changes. An analysis of activity expenses also provides an excellent starting point for analyzing marketing costs by territories, products, or other marketing units.

Net sales		$27,000
Less cost of goods sold		18,900
Gross margin		8,100
Less operating expenses:		
Sales salaries and commissions	$3,240	
Sales force travel	372	
Supplies and telephone	178	
Media space	870	
Advertising salaries	218	
Property taxes	120	
Heat and light	168	
Insurance	84	
Administrative salaries	930	
Other expenses	120	
Total operating expenses		6,300
Net profit		$ 1,800

FIGURE 15-2
Income Statement, 2016, Colorado Ski Company

FIGURE 15-3

Expense distribution sheet, Colorado Ski Company, 2016 (showing allocation of ledger expense items to activity categories)

Ledger Expenses	Totals	Activity Cost Categories				
		Personal Selling	Advertising	Warehousing and Shipping	Order Processing	Administrative
Sales salaries and commissions	$3,240,000	$3,240,000	—	—	—	—
Sales force travel	372,000	372,000	—	—	—	—
Supplies and telephone	178,000	43,200	22,200	40,900	43,500	28,200
Media space	870,000	—	870,000	—	—	—
Advertising salaries	218,000	—	218,000	—	—	—
Property taxes	120,000	10,000	14,500	66,000	14,000	15,500
Heat and light	168,000	15,300	17,400	100,500	16,200	18,600
Insurance	84,000	12,000	4,200	46,300	14,000	7,500
Administrative salaries	930,000	144,000	62,000	168,000	126,000	430,000
Other expenses	120,000	10,500	11,700	58,300	26,300	13,200
Totals	$6,300,000	3,847,000	1,220,000	480,000	240,000	513,000

Analysis of Activity Costs by Market Segments

The third and most beneficial type of marketing cost analysis is a study of the costs and profitability of each segment of the market. The most common practice in this type of analysis is to divide the market by territories, products, customer groups, or order sizes. A cost analysis by market segment enables management to pinpoint trouble spots or areas of satisfactory performance much more effectively than with an analysis of either ledger expenses or total activity costs.

By combining a sales volume analysis with a marketing cost analysis, a profit-and-loss statement may be prepared for each of the products or market segments. These individual income and expense statements then can be analyzed to determine the effectiveness of the marketing program in each of those segments.

A complete marketing cost analysis by sales territories or some other marketing unit involves the same three-step evaluation procedure outlined in Chapter 14. That is, we determine what happened, why it happened, and what we are going to do about the situation.

To determine *what happened*, the procedure in a cost analysis by market segments is quite similar to the method used to analyze activity expenses. The total of each activity cost (the bottom line in Figure 15-3) is prorated on some basis among each product or market segment being studied. Let's walk through an example of a marketing cost analysis in the three geographic sales regions of the Colorado Ski Company, as shown in Figures 15-4 and 15-5. First, for each of the five Colorado Ski activities, we select an allocation basis for distributing the cost of that activity among the three regions. These bases are shown in the top part of Figure 15-4. Then we determine the number of allocation "units" that make up each activity cost and we find the cost per unit. This completes the allocation scheme, which tells us how to allocate costs to the three regions. To illustrate further:

FIGURE 15-4
Allocation of Activity costs
to sales regions, Colorado
Ski Company, 2016

Activity	Personal Selling	Advertising	Warehousing and Shipping	Order Processing	Administration
Allocation Scheme					
Allocation basis	Direct expense to each region	No. of pages of advertising	Number of orders shipped	Number of invoice lines	Equally among regions
Total activity cost	$3,847,000	$1,220,000	$480,000	$240,000	$513,000
Number of allocation units	-	61 pages	9,600 orders	120,000 lines	3 regions
Cost per allocation unit	-	$20,000 per page	$50 per order	$2 per line	$171,000 per region

Region			**Allocation of Costs**			
Eastern	Units	—	21 pages	3,800 orders	39,500 lines	1
	Cost	$1,070,000	$420,000	$190,000	$79,000	$171,000
Midwestern	Units	—	11 pages	2,500 orders	28,000 lines	1
	Cost	$747,000	$220,000	$125,000	$56,000	$171,000
Western	Units	—	29 pages	3,300 orders	52,500 lines	1
	Cost	$2,030,000	$580,000	$165,000	$105,000	$171,000

- Personal-selling activity expenses are straight forward to allocate because they are direct expenses, chargeable entirely to the region in which they were incurred.
- Advertising expenses are allocated on the basis of the number of pages of advertising run in each region. The ski company purchased the equivalent of 61 pages of advertising during the year at an average cost of $20,000 per page ($1,220,000/61).
- Warehousing and shipping expenses are allocated on the basis of the number of orders shipped. Since 9,600 orders were shipped during the year at a total activity cost of $480,000, the cost per order was $50. Order-processing expenses are allocated according to the number of invoice lines typed during the year. Since there were 120,000 invoice lines processed on the computer, the cost per line was $2 (120,000 x $2 = $240,000 total cost).
- The administration expense of $513,000—a totally indirect cost—is arbitrarily divided equally among the three regions, at a cost of $171,000 per region.

The final step is to calculate the amount of each activity expense that is to be allocated to each region. The results appear in the bottom part of Figure 15-4. We see that $1,070,000 of *personal selling* expenses were incurred in the eastern region, $747,000 was charged to the Midwestern Region, and $2,030,000 to the Western Region. In the case of *advertising*, 21 pages of advertising were run in the eastern region, so that region was charged with $420,000 (21 pages at $20,000 per page). In similar calculations, the Midwestern Region was charged $220,000 for advertising, and the charge to the western region was $580,000. Regarding *warehousing and shipping* expenses, 3,800 orders were shipped to customers in the Eastern region. At a unit allocation cost of $50, eastern's total allocated cost was $190,000. Midwestern's allocated shipping cost was $125,000, and the western region was charged $165,000. For *order-processing* expenses, management found that 39,500 invoice lines went to customers in the eastern region. At $2 a line, this expense came to $79,000. In the case of the *administration* expenses of $513,000, each region was charged $171,000. After the five activity expenses have been allocated among the three sales regions, we can prepare a profit-and-loss statement for each region, as shown in Figure 15-5. The sales volume for each region was determined in our volume analysis in Chapter 14. The cost of goods sold and the gross margin for each region were determined by assuming that the company wide gross margin of 30 percent ($8,100,000/$27,000,000) was maintained in each region.

In summary, Figure 15-5 shows the operating results for each region in the same way that Figure 15-2 reported the income and expense picture for the company as a whole. For example, we see that the eastern region's net profit was 8.6 percent of sales ($770,000/$9,000,000). In sharp contrast, the Midwestern region did rather poorly, actually losing $24,000, or 0.53 percent of sales ($24,000/$4,500,000 = 0.53%).

At this point in our performance evaluation, we have completed the *what happened* stage. The next step is to determine *why* the results are as shown in Figure 15-5. As mentioned earlier, it is extremely difficult to answer this question. In the Midwestern Region, for example, the sales force obtained only about two-thirds as many orders as in the Eastern Region (2,500 versus 3,800). Was this because Colorado did about half as much advertising in the Midwest as in the East? Or does the reason lie in poor selling ability or poor sales training in the Midwest? Or is competition simply much stronger in the Midwest?

After a profitability analysis has determined *why* the regional results came out as they did, management can move to the third stage in its performance evaluation process. That final stage is to determine *what management should do* about the situation. We shall discuss this third stage briefly after we have reviewed some major problem areas in marketing cost analysis.

FIGURE 15-5

Income and Expense Statement, by Sales Region, Colorado Ski Company, 2016

	Total	Eastern	Midwest	Western
Net sales	$27,000	$9,000	$4,500	$13,500
Less cost of goods sold	18,900	6,300	3,150	9,450
Gross margin	8,100	2,700	1,350	4,050
Less operating expenses:				
Personal selling	3,847	1,070	802	1,975
Advertising	1,220	420	220	580
Warehousing/shipping	480	190	125	165
Order processing	240	79	56	105
Administration	513	171	171	171
Total operating expenses	6,300	1,930	1,374	2,996
Net profit (loss)	$ 1,800	$ 770	$ (24)	$ 1,054
Net profit (loss) as percentage of sales	6.7%	8.6%	(0.53%)	7.8%

PROBLEMS IN MARKETING COST ANALYSIS

Marketing cost analyses can be expensive in time, money, and personnel. Today, however, the use of computerized information systems enables management to generate data that are more current, more detailed, and lower in cost than was true in the past. But even the computers so far have not overcome the problems related to cost allocation and the contribution-margin versus full-cost controversy

Allocating Costs

As a foundation for our discussion of cost allocation, let's first distinguish between direct and indirect expenses (note that we use the terms cost and expenses interchangeably).

Direct versus Indirect Expenses.

Direct costs are incurred in connection with a single unit of sales operations. Therefore, they can readily be allocated in total to a specific marketing unit, whether it is a territory, product, or customer group. If the company dropped a given territory or product, all direct expenses tied to that marketing unit would be eliminated. These are expenses that can be separated from other costs. **Indirect costs** are those shared by more than one market segment. In general, most marketing costs are totally or partially indirect.

Whether a given cost is classed as direct or indirect depends on the market segment being analyzed. The cost never remains permanently in one or the other category. Assume that each salesperson in a company has a separate territory, is paid a straight salary, and sells the entire line of products. Sales force salaries would be a *direct* expense if the cost analysis were being made by territories. But the salary expense would be an *indirect* cost if the cost were being studied for each product—because these salaries cannot be separated by product. Similarly, sales force travel expenses would be a *direct* territorial cost but an *indirect* product cost. However, if the advertising was aired on national media and each advertising element (i.e., each television commercial) focused on exactly one product, then advertising expenditures would be an *indirect* territorial cost but a *direct* product cost.

The term **overhead costs** is frequently used to describe a body of expenses that cannot be identified solely with individual product lines, territories, or other market segments. Sometimes, overhead costs are referred to as *fixed costs.* However, it is preferable to think of these items as *indirect costs* as they are not *directly* allocable among territories, product lines, or some other group of market segments.

Difficulty of allocating costs.

A major problem in a marketing cost analysis is that of allocating marketing costs (especially indirect costs) to individual territories, products, or whatever segment of the market is being studied. Actually, the problem of prorating arises at two levels: (1) when accounting ledger expenses are being allocated to activity groups and (2) when the resultant activity costs are apportioned to the separate territories, product, or markets.

A *direct* cost can be allocated in its entirety to the market segment being analyzed. This phase of allocation is reasonably simple. For example, assume that a territorial cost analysis is being made and each salesperson has a territory. Then all of a given salesperson's expenses—salary, commission, travel, supplies, and so on—can be prorated directly to his or her territory. Some of the advertising expense, such as the cost of ads in local newspaper and the expense of point-of-purchase advertising materials, also can be charged directly to a given territory.

However, the majority of costs are common or *indirect* rather than separable, and real allocation problems occur with these expenses. For some costs, the basis of allocation may be the same regardless of the type of analysis made. Billing expenses are often allocated on the basis of number of "invoice lines," whether the cost analysis is by territory, product, or customer group. An invoice line is one item (six dozen widgets, model 1412, for example) listed on the bill (invoice) sent to a customer. Assume that 22 percent of all invoice lines last year related to orders billed to customers in territory A. Then 22 percent of total billing costs would be allocated to that territory. A cost analysis by product line or customer group would use this same allocation basis—number of invoice lines—when apportioning billing costs.

For other costs, however, the basis of allocation would vary according to whether a firm analyzes its costs by territory, product, or customer group. Consider sales force salaries as an example. In a territorial cost study, these salaries may be allocated directly to the district where the people work. In a product cost analysis, the expense probably is prorated on the proportionate amount of working hours a salesperson spends with each product. In a cost analysis by customer classes, the salaries may be apportioned in relation to the number of sales calls on each customer group.

Allocating totally indirect costs.

The last big allocation problem discussed here concerns costs that are *totally* indirect. Within the broad category of indirect expenses, some costs are *partially* indirect and some are *totally* indirect. Many expenses do carry some degree of direct relationship to the territory or other marketing unit being analyzed. Order-filling and shipping expenses, for example, are partially indirect costs. They would *decrease* to some extent if a territory or product were eliminated. They would *increase* if new products or territories were added.

However, other cost items, such as sales administrative or general administrative expenses, are *totally* indirect costs. The cost of maintaining the chief sales executive (salary, staff, and office) remains about the same, whether or not the number of territories or products changes.

Many administrators question whether it is reasonably possible to allocate totally indirect costs. Consider, for example, the problem of allocating general sales manager Cruz's expense to territories. Part of the year, Cruz travels in these districts. The costs of transportation, food, and lodging on the road probably can be allocated directly to the territory involved. However, how should Cruz's salary and office expenses by apportioned among sales districts? If Cruz spends a month in territory A and two months in B, then presumably one-twelfth of these expenses may be allocated to A and one-sixth to B. At the same time, this method may be unfair to territory A. During the month's stay in A, Cruz spent much time on the telephone discussing unforeseen difficulties in territory F. Moreover, how would the company apportion the expenses incurred while Cruz is in the home office and not dealing with the affairs of any one particular territory.

Three methods frequently used to allocate indirect costs are shown in Figure 15-6. Each method reflects a different philosophy and each has obvious drawbacks.

Method	Pros/Cons
1. Divide cost equally among territories or whatever market segments are being analyzed.	Easy to do, but inaccurate and usually unfair to some market segments.
2. Allocate costs in proportion to sales volume obtained from each territory (or product or customer group).	Underlying philosophy is to apply cost burden where it can best be borne. That is, charge a high-volume market segment with a large share of the indirect cost. This method is simple and easy to do but may be very inaccurate. Tells very little about a segment's profitability and may even be misleading
3. Allocate indirect costs in same proportion as the total direct costs. Thus if product A accounted for 25 percent of the total direct costs, then A also would be charged with 25 percent of the indirect expenses.	Again, easy to do but can be inaccurate and misleading. Falsely assumes a close relationship between direct and indirect expenses.

FIGURE 15-6
Methods used to allocate indirect costs

The Contribution-Margin versus Full-Cost Controversy

In a marketing cost analysis, two ways of handling the allocation of indirect expenses are the contribution-margin method (also called contribution-to-overhead method) and the full-cost method. A real controversy exists regarding which of these two approaches is better for managerial control purposes.

In the **contribution-margin method**, only the direct expenses are allocated to each marketing unit (territory, product) being analyzed. These are the costs that presumably would be eliminated if the corresponding marketing unit were eliminated. After deducting these direct costs from the gross margin, the remainder is the amount that unit is contributing to cover total overhead (indirect expense).

In the **full-cost method**, all expenses—direct and indirect—are allocated among the marketing units under study. By allocating all costs, management is trying to determine the net profit of each territory, product, or other marketing unit.

For any given marketing unit, these two methods may be summarized as follows:

Contribution-Margin Method		Full-Cost Method	
	$ sales		$ sales
less	Cost of Goods sold	less	Cost of Goods sold
equals	Gross margin	equals	Gross margin
less	Direct expenses	less	Direct expenses
equals	Contribution margin	less	Indirect expenses
		equals	Net profit

An example of the contribution-margin method is shown in Figure 15-7. The net sales, cost of goods sold, and gross margin are shown for each of the three geographic regions in the Colorado Ski Company. The direct operating costs of the company are allocated among the three regions. These expenses are then deducted from the region's gross margin. The result is each region's contribution to the remaining $2,196,000 of indirect (overhead) costs. The Midwestern Region, for instance, incurred $794,000 in direct costs and contributed $556,000 to the overhead expenses and net profit. If the company eliminated the Midwestern Region, presumably management would save $794,000 in

FIGURE 15-7
Income Statement by
Sales Region, Colorado Ski
Company, 2016, in $000,
Using Contribution Margin
Approach

	Total	Eastern	Midwest	Western
Net sales	$27,000	$9,000	$4,500	$13,500
Less cost of good sold	18,900	6,300	3,150	9,450
Gross margin	8,100	2,700	1,350	4,050
Less direct operating expenses:				
Personal selling	3,082	845	595	1,642
Advertising	732	254	127	351
Warehousing/shipping	160	64	42	54
Order processing	130	43	30	57
Total direct expenses	4,104	1,206	794	2,104
Contribution margin	$ 3,996	$1,494	$556	$ 1,946
Less indirect operating expenses				
Personal selling	765			
Advertising	488			
Warehousing/shipping	320			
Order processing	110			
Administration	513			
Total indirect expenses	$ 2,196			
Net profit	$ 1,800			

direct expenses. However, the region's $556,000 contribution to overhead would then have to be absorbed by the remaining two regions, assuming the indirect costs still totaled $2,196,000.

The full-cost method could be done by taking one more step. The key question will be how to allocate the indirect costs of $2,196,000 across the three territories. Let's use the second method from Figure 15-6, which is to allocate costs in proportion to sales volume. The Eastern Region generated 33.3% of sales (9,000/27,000); the Midwestern Region generated 16.7% of sales (4,500/27,000); and the Western Region generated 50.0% of sales (13,500/27,000). Using this allocation, the full-cost method generates a net profit for each region as follows:

	Total	Eastern	Midwest	Western
Net sales	$27,000	$9,000	$4,500	$13,500
Less cost of goods sold	−18,900	−6,300	−3,150	−9,450
Gross margin	8,100	2,700	1,350	4,050
Less direct operating expense	−4,104	−1,206	−794	−2,104
Less indirect operating expense	−2,196	−732	−366	−1,098
Net profit	$ 1,800	$ 762	$ 190	$ 848

Note that Figure 15-5 also illustrated a full-cost method, but a different allocation of indirect costs resulted in slight variation of net profits across the three regions. For example, the Midwest showed a loss of $24,000 in Figure 15-5, yet it shows a gain of $190,000 net profit above. So which is the right approach? That is up for debate; in fact, this issue raises controversy.

In particular, there is considerable argument over the relative merits of the contribution-margin and full-cost methods. Proponents of the full-cost method contend that the purpose of a marketing cost study is to determine the net profitability of the units being studied. They feel that the contribution-margin approach does not fulfill this purpose. Furthermore, full-cost advocates believe that a contribution-margin analysis may be misleading. A given territory or product may show a contribution to overhead; yet, after the indirect costs are allocated, this product or territory may actually have a net loss (as seen in the Midwestern Region of the Colorado Ski Company).

Contribution-margin supporters contend that it is not possible to accurately apportion the indirect costs among market segments. Furthermore, items such as administrative costs are not related at all to any single territory or product. Therefore, the unit should not bear any of these costs. These advocates also point out that a full-cost analysis may show that a product or territory has a net loss, whereas this unit may be contributing something to overhead (again, the situation in the Midwestern Region). Some executives might recommend that the losing region be eliminated. But they overlook the fact that the unit's contribution to overhead would then have to be borne by other units. Under the contribution-margin approach, the company would keep this unit, at least until a better alternative could be found.

Actually, both approaches have a place in marketing cost analysis. The full-cost method is especially suited for the systematic reporting of historical costs as a basis for future marketing planning. A full-cost analysis is useful when making *long-range* studies of the profitability of various market segments. This type of analysis also can be helpful when establishing long-range policies on product lines, distribution channels, pricing structures, or promotional programs.

The contribution-margin approach is especially useful as an aid to decision making in *short-run* marketing situations. Also, when cost responsibility is directly assignable to particular market segments, management has an effective tool for controlling and evaluating the sales force.

USE OF FINDINGS FROM PROFITABILITY ANALYSIS

So far in our discussion of marketing cost analysis, we have dealt generally with the first stage in the evaluation process. That is, we have been finding out *what happened.* Now let's look at some examples of how management might use the combined findings from both sales volume and marketing cost analyses—the profitability analysis.

Territorial Decisions

Once management has completed its volume and cost analyses, it may decide to adjust territorial boundaries to match their current potential. Possibly the district is too small. That is, the potential volume is not adequate to support the expense of covering the territory. Or it may be too large, forcing the salesperson to spend too much time and expense in traveling.

Management also may consider a change in selling methods or channels in an unprofitable area. Possibly email or telephone selling should be used instead of incurring the expense of in-person selling visits. A company that sells directly to retailers or industrial users may consider using wholesaling intermediaries instead.

A weak territory sometimes can be made profitable by an increase in advertising and sales promotion. Possibly, the salespeople are not getting adequate support. Or competition may have grown so strong that management must be resigned to a smaller market share than formerly.

The problems in poor territories may lie with the activities of the salespeople. They may need closer supervision, or perhaps too large a percentage of their sales comes from low-margin items. They also may simply be poor salespeople.

As a last resort, it may be necessary to abandon a territory entirely, not even using the facilities provided by mail, telephone, or middlemen. Possibly the potential that was once present no longer exists. However, before dropping a territory from its market, a company should consider the cost repercussions. The territory presumably has carried some share of indirect, inescapable expenses, such as marketing and general administrative costs. If the district is abandoned, these expenses must be absorbed by the remaining areas.

Products

When a cost analysis by products shows significant differences in the profitability of the product line, the executives should determine the reasons for the differences. It may be that these profit variations stem from factors (typical order size or packaging requirements, for example) that are firmly set. That is, management has very little opportunity for profit improvement. On the other hand, many low-profit items often do present opportunities for administrative action. A firm may simplify its line by eliminating some models or colors for which there is little demand. Also, simplification allows the sales force to concentrate on fewer items and probably increases the sales of the remaining products.

Sometimes a product's profitability can be increased by redesigning or repackaging the item. Packaging the product in multiple rather than single units may increase the average order size. This will cut the unit costs of order filling, shipping, and packaging. Another possibility is to alter (increase or decrease) the amount of advertising and other promotional help appropriated for the product. Possibly, a change in sales force compensation is needed to (1) increase the sales of profitable items or (2) discourage the sales of low-margin goods.

A low-volume item cannot always be dropped from the line. Nor can a company always drop an item even though it shows an irreducible net loss. The product may be necessary because customers *expect* the seller to carry it. Thus, eliminating the products might damage the firm's relationships with important clients.[3]

Customer/Size of Order

As suggested in Chapter 14 by the 80/20 principle, some customers are much more important to the firm than other customers. In fact, a **profitability analysis** can reveal that selling to and servicing certain customers actually loses money for the sales organization. In such an analysis, Georgia-Pacific's (GP) supply chain team found that it was losing money providing expedited transportation and distribution services to a major customer. After seeing this information, the customer was willing to work more collaboratively with GP in order to lower costs and raise profits. Surprisingly, many companies never bother to do such an analysis and thus have no clue about the relative profitability of their customers.[4]

A key step in this regard is to calculate how much money is spent to get the orders of each customer. A common situation plaguing many companies is the **small-order problem.** That is, often orders are so small that they result in a loss to the company. Many costs such as direct selling or billing are often the same for each order, whether it is for $10 or $10,000. A cost analysis by customer groups is closely related to an analysis by order size. Frequently, a customer class that generates a below-average profit also presents a small-order problem. Sometimes large volume purchasers build up their volume by giving the seller many small individual orders. Management should review both their customer and order-size analyses before making policy decisions in these areas.

Some firms find that certain customers are costing them too much, and thus they end the business relationship.[5] Firing unprofitable customers, however, is not always the right choice. Management first should determine *why* the accounts are unprofitable and *why* the average orders are small, and then consider ways to improve these situations. Several reasons may account for a customer's small orders or unprofitableness. For instance:

- An account buys a large amount in total over a period of a year, but the customer buys in small amounts from several suppliers.
- A company buys a large amount in total and all from one supplier. But this customer purchases frequently, so the average order is small. The increasingly popular just-in-time (JIT) inventory control systems typically involve the frequent delivery of small orders. However, a JIT delivery system is usually a part of a profitable, long-term purchasing commitment. Consequently, both the buyer and seller can benefit from a JIT inventory control strategy.
- An account is small but growing, and a seller caters to it in hope of future benefits.
- A customer is small and, as far as can be projected into the future, will remain small.

There are many practical suggestions for increasing the average size of an order or for reducing the marketing costs of small orders. See Figure 15-8 for examples.

FIGURE 15-8
Ways to increase order size and reduce small-order marketing costs

- Educate customers who buy from several different suppliers. Stress the advantages of purchasing from one supplier.

- For customers who purchase large total quantities in frequent small orders, stress the advantages of ordering once a month instead of once a week. Point out that the buyer eliminates all handling, billing, and accounting expenses connected with three of the four orders. Note further that the buyer writes only one check and one purchase order. In addition, stress that there will be only one bill to process and one shipment to put into inventory instead of three or four.

- Educate the sales force as well as customers. In fact, it may be necessary to change the compensation plan to discourage acceptance of smaller orders.

- Substitute website, direct mail or telephone selling for sales calls on unprofitable or small-order accounts. Or continue to call on these accounts, but less frequently.

- Shift an account to a wholesaler or some other type of intermediary rather than dealing directly.

- Drop a mass-distribution policy and adopt a selective one. This new policy may actually increase sales because salespeople can spend more time with profitable accounts.

- Establish a minimum order size.

- Establish a minimum charge or service charge to combat small orders.

RETURN ON INVESTMENT: AN EVALUATION TOOL

The concept of **return on investment (ROI)** is another useful managerial aid in evaluating sales performance and in making marketing decisions. The following formula can be used to calculate return on investment:

$$\text{ROI} = \frac{\text{Net Profit}}{\text{Sales}} \times \frac{\text{Sales}}{\text{Investment}}$$

The first fraction expresses the rate of profit on sales. The second fraction indicates the number of times the total investment (assets employed) was turned over. By multiplying the investment turnover by the rate of profit on sales, the ROI is determined.

Two questions may quickly come to mind. First, what do we mean by *investment?* Second, why do we need two fractions? It would seem that the sales component in each fraction would cancel out, leaving net profit divided by investment as the meaningful ratio.

To answer the first query, consider a firm whose operating statement shows annual sales of $1 million and a net profit of $50,000. At the end of the year, the balance sheet reports

Assets	$600,000	Liabilities		$200,000
		Capital stock	$300,000	
		Retained earnings	100,000	400,000
			$400,000	$600,000

Now, is the investment $400,000 or $600,000? Certain the ROI will depend on which figure we use. The answer depends on whether we are talking to the stockholders or to the company executives. The stockholders are more interested in the return on what they have invested—in this case, $400,000. The ROI calculation then is

$$\text{ROI} = \frac{\text{Net Profit } \$50,000}{\text{Sales } \$1,000,000} \times \frac{\text{Sales } \$1,000,000}{\text{Investment } \$400,000}$$

Management, on the other hand, is more concerned with the total investment, as represented by the total assets ($600,000). This is the amount that the executives must manage, regardless of whether the assets were acquired by stockholders' investment, retained earnings, or loads from outside sources. Within this context, the ROI computation becomes:

$$\text{ROI} = \frac{\text{Net Profit } \$50,000}{\text{Sales } \$1,000,000} \times \frac{\text{Sales } \$1,000,000}{\text{Investment } \$600,000} = 8.33\%$$

$$5\% \quad \times \quad 1.67 \quad = 8.33\%$$

Regarding the second question, we use two fractions because we are dealing with two separate elements: the rate of profit on sales and the rate of capital turnover. Management really should determine each rate separately and then multiply the two. The rate of profit on sales is influenced by marketing considerations—sales volume, price, product mix, advertising effort. The capital turnover is a financial consideration not directly involved with costs or profit—only with sales volume and assets managed.

To illustrate, assume that our company's profit doubled with the same sales volume and investment because management operated an excellent marketing program this year. In effect, we doubled our profit rate with the same capital turnover:

$$\text{ROI} = \frac{\text{Net Profit } \$100,000}{\text{Sales } \$1,000,000} \times \frac{\text{Sales } \$1,000,000}{\text{Investment } \$600,000} = 16.67\%$$

$$10\% \qquad \times \qquad 1.67 \qquad = 16.67\%$$

As expected, this 16.67 percent is twice the ROI calculated earlier.

Now assume that we earned our original profit of $50,000 but that we did it with an investment reduced to $500,000. We cut the size of our average inventory and closed some branch offices. By increasing our capital turnover from 1.67 to 2, we raise the ROI from 8.33 percent to 10 percent, even though sales volume and profits remain unchanged:

$$\text{ROI} = \frac{\text{Net Profit } \$50,000}{\text{Sales } \$2,000,000} \times \frac{\text{Sales } \$2,000,000}{\text{Investment } \$500,000} = 10.0\%$$

$$2.5\% \qquad \times \qquad 3.3 \qquad = 10.0\%$$

Assume now that we increase our sales volume—let us say we double it—but do not increase our profit or investment. That is, the cost-profit squeeze is bringing us profitless prosperity. The following interesting results occur:

$$\text{ROI} = \frac{\text{Net Profit } \$50,000}{\text{Sales } \$2,000,000} \times \frac{\text{Sales } \$2,000,000}{\text{Investment } \$600,000} = 8.33\%$$

$$2.5\% \qquad \times \qquad 3.3 \qquad = 8.33\%$$

The profit rate was cut in half, but this was offset by a doubling of the capital-turnover rate, leaving the ROI unchanged.

USE OF RETURN ON ASSETS MANAGED TO EVALUATE FIELD SALES MANAGERS

A variation of the ROI concept is the concept of **return on assets managed (ROAM).** The ROAM concept is particularly useful for evaluating the performance of district sales managers, branch managers, or other managerial segments of a field sales organization. ROAM modifies the factors in the traditional ROI equation to make them appropriate for the organizational segment being analyzed. If management is evaluating sales district performance, for instance

CONSIDER THIS...

Measuring Is the Easy Part

Sales force automation and customer relationship management systems allow marketing and sales executives to measure profitability more frequently and more comprehensively than ever before. This presents the problem, however, of figuring out what to do when a marketing program or unit is found to be unprofitable. That is, measuring ROI of a given territory is only the first step. Profits will not improve until something is done about those territories that are performing poorly. Sales organizations must go beyond the measurements and take a hard look at why numbers are bad. Thanks to technology, finding what is not working is now easy to do. Fixing the broken strategy is the hard—but necessary—part!

SOURCE: Kevin J. Claney and Randy L Stone, "Don't Blame the Metrics," *Harvard Business Review*, 83, no. 6 (June 2005), pp. 26-28.

presumably the sales volume in each district is readily available. For the profit figure in the equation, management can determine the contribution margin in each district. That is, from a given district's sales, we deduct the cost of goods sold and all operating expenses directly chargeable to a district. In the "investment" section of the ROI equation, we substitute the assets employed—that is, the "assets managed"—hence the acronym ROAM instead of ROI. In a sales district, the assets managed consist of the average accounts receivable and the inventory carried to serve that district. The net result of these changes is the following equation:

$$\text{ROAM} = \frac{\text{Contribution margin}}{\text{District sales volume}} \times \frac{\text{District sales volume}}{\text{Average accounts receivable} + \text{Inventory}}$$

The usefulness of the ROAM concept as an executive evaluation tool depends on whether the assets in the equation are controllable by the executive being evaluated. If a district sales manager has little or no control over the assets employed in a district, it is not valid to hold the executive accountable for the return earned on those assets. The lack of asset control by individual salespeople is a reason that ROAM should *not* be used to measure the performance of individual salespeople.

With asset control, however, district sales executives and other field sales managers can improve their ROAM percentage by influencing sales volume, contribution margin, or district asset investment. Thus, field sales managers can use the ROAM concept when considering the addition of new customers or products in their districts. In effect, return on assets managed is an analytical tool that facilitates the delegation of profit responsibility to territorial sales managers.[6]

SUMMARY

A marketing cost analysis is a detailed study of a company's distribution costs. It is undertaken to discover which segments (territories, products, customers) of the company's marketing program are profitable and which are not. A marketing cost analysis is a part of a company's evaluation of its marketing performance.

In marketing cost analysis, we need to understand the differences between accounting-ledger costs and activity-category costs. Another useful distinction is the one between direct and indirect expenses. In a marketing cost analysis, one of the major problems is the difficulty of allocating costs. Management must allocate ledger accounts into activity categories. Then each total activity cost must be allocated to the marketing segment (territory, product, customer group) being analyzed. Cost allocation is especially difficult in the case of indirect expenses.

The difficulty of allocating indirect costs leads to the contribution-margin versus full-cost controversy. In the contribution-margin approach to marketing cost analysis, only the direct costs incurred by the marketing unit (territory or product, for example) are allocated to that unit. The unit's gross margin minus its direct costs equals the amount the unit contributes to pay the company's overhead (indirect expense). In the full-cost approach, all costs (direct and indirect) are allocated to the various marketing units being studied. In this way, management tries to determine the unit's net profit.

The company's marketing costs can be analyzed in three ways. One way is to analyze the costs as they appear in the accounting ledgers and on the company's income statement (or profit-and-loss statement). A second approach is to analyze the marketing costs after they have been allocated to activity categories. The third type occurs after each activity cost has been allocated to the sales territories, products, or other marketing units being studied.

The types of analyses we have summarized tell management *what happened*. Then the executives must try to determine *why* these results occurred. Finally, management must decide *what changes* are needed in the marketing program to correct the misdirected effort.

A marketing cost analysis can be especially useful in identifying and remedying the small-order problem that occurs in so many firms.

Return on investment (ROI) is another tool that management can use in evaluating sales performance and in making marketing decisions. A variation of the ROI concept is ROAM, return on assets managed. The ROAM concept is especially useful for evaluating the performance of field sales managers.

KEY TERMS

Contribution-margin method

Direct costs

Full-cost method

Indirect costs

Overhead costs

Profitability analysis

Return on assets managed (ROAM)

Return on investment (ROI)

Small-order problem

QUESTIONS AND PROBLEMS

1. Explain the similarities and differences between marketing cost analysis and production cost accounting.

2. Is an analysis of expenses as recorded in a company's accounting ledgers better than no cost analysis at all? What specific policies or operating plans may stem from an analysis of ledger expenses alone?

3. A national manufacturer of roofing and siding materials has 40 salespeople. Each has his or her own territory and sells all three of the firm's product lines. They sell primarily to wholesalers and large retailers in the lumber and building materials field. The company wants to make a *territorial analysis* of marketing costs. When allocating the following costs across the territories, what bases do you recommend? (i.e., explain the allocation basis of each as was done in Figure 15-4)

   a. Sales force salaries

   b. Sales force travel expenses

   c. Sales force commissions paid on gross margin

   d. Salaries and expenses of three regional managers, each of whom oversees 10 to 15 of the salespeople

   e. Sales training expenses

   f. National television advertising

   g. Local newspaper advertising

   h. Billboard advertising

   i. Billing

   j. Shipping from three regional factories

   k. Marketing research

   l. Chief sales executive's salary and office expenses

4. The company in the preceding problem wants to analyze its marketing cost by *product lines.* Suggest appropriate bases for allocating the above-listed cost items to the three product groups.

5. What supporting points could be brought out by the proponents of each side in the full-cost versus contribution-margin controversy over allocation of indirect marketing costs? Which of the two concepts do you advocate? Why?

6. In an analysis of expenses grouped by activities, a manufacturer noted that last year the firm's direct selling expenses (sales force compensation, travel expenses, branch office expenses, etc.) increased significantly over the preceding year. Is this trend necessarily an indication of weaknesses in the management of the sales force?

7. Each of the following firms made a territorial cost analysis and discovered it had some districts that were showing a net loss. What actions involving the sales force do you recommend each company take to improve its situation?

   a. Hardware wholesaler, covering six southeastern states

   b. Paint and varnish manufacturer

   c. National business machines manufacturer

8. What actions involving its sales force can each of the following firms take if they discover unprofitable products in their lines?

a. Distributor of electrical goods

b. Flower seed producer

c. Manufacturer of small power tools

9. "Large-annual-volume customers never present a small-order problem while low-annual-volume customers always create small-order problems." Do you agree?

10. To determine return on investment, we multiply two fractions: net profit/sales and sales/investment. Why two fractions? That is, why can't we cancel out the sales factor in each fraction and simply divide net profit by investment?

11. Explain how the ROAM concept may be used to evaluate the profit performance of a territorial sales manager.

EXPERIENTIAL EXERCISES

1. Call sales managers from 10 different companies. Ask them how the performance of their sales districts are evaluated; that is, ask what measures—such as total sales, gross profit margin, ROI, or ROAM—are used.

2. Call sales managers from three companies to determine the process by which they develop their sales budget (sales and selling expenses). Ask them about the difference between the sales forecast process and the sales budget process.

3. A company's website can be used as a strategic tool to increase order size and, thus, reduce small-order problems. For example, the PremierConnect program of Dell Computer (dell.com) is one such example. Search the internet and find other examples of company that are doing this.

SEAL RITE ENVELOPE COMPANY (B)
Profitability Analysis

As Rose Douglas, Seal Rite Envelope Company's sales manager, scanned a printout of a profitability analysis of the company's customers, she had in mind that a previous CRM analysis had indicated that the firm's direct selling costs per call were $110 for the company's $22 million sales volume last year. Since the firm's average gross margin was about 25 percent, the salespeople had to get an average order of $440 for each sales call they made. Even then, a $440 average order just covered the direct selling expenses. That still left the overhead expenses uncovered. She could quickly see from the data in front of her that she had some problems.

Wanting more data on the profitability of customers by their size, she again turned to her CRM and extracted the information shown in Table 15-1A. She did not like what she saw. She recalled a lecture in college given by an old marketing professor who loved to talk about misdirected marketing efforts. At the time, she thought that he was hopelessly out of date. No firm in modern times could possibly allow such situations to develop. Now she wished she had paid more attention to the lecture, for she suspected that she had a problem with just such misdirected marketing efforts.

Questions:

1. What problems are indicated from the data in Table 15-1A?

2. What should Rose Douglas do about those problems?

TABLE 15-1A

Seal Rite Envelope Company, 2016

Annual Customer Volume ($000)	Number of Accounts	Number of Calls	Sales (% of total)	Gross profit (% of sales)	Selling Expense (% of sales)	Operating Profit (% of sales)
Over $200	4	256	10.9	15.9	4.0	11.9
$100-200	4	274	2.9	23.6	9.5	14.1
$50-99.9	32	1,344	11.7	19.8	10.2	9.6
$40-49.9	24	1,011	5.4	18.4	10.2	8.2
$30-39.9	25	1,158	4.0	21.8	9.6	12.2
$20-29.9	63	3,114	8.5	22.8	10.9	11.9
$10-19.9	157	4,725	13.2	23.9	13.4	10.5
$5-9.9	349	7,021	15.7	25.9	16.8	9.1
$4-4.9	235	2,639	5.0	29.0	19.3	10.3
$3-3.9	309	3,233	5.2	31.6	21.9	9.7
$2-2.9	569	4,212	7.1	31.2	25.3	5.9
$1-1.9	842	6,360	6.9	30.4	34.3	23.6
Under $1	871	6,345	3.5	30.9	75.3	244.4
No sales	688	2,001	0.0	0.0	0.0	0.0
Total or average	4,172	43,693	100	25.0	20.1	5.0

ENDNOTES

[1] The opening scenario is based on: Jim Sobeck, "How to Prevent Small Orders from Eating Away at Profits," *ProSales Magazine*, March 14, 2011. Retrieved from the following URL on July 4, 2016: http://www.prosalesmagazine.com/business/sales/how-to-prevent-small-orders-from-eating-away-at-profits_o

[2] For an excellent report on the usefulness and effectiveness of analyzing expenses by activity groupings, see Thomas H. Stevenson, Frank C. Barnes, and Sharon A. Stevenson, "Activity-Based Costing: An Emerging Tool for Industrial Marketing Decision Makers," *Journal of Business & Industrial Marketing*, 1993, Vol. 8 (2), pp. 40-52.

[3] Remko Van Hoek and Kevin Pegals, "Growing by Cutting SKUs at Clorox," *Harvard Business Review*, April 2006, p. 22.

[4] Remko Van Hoek and David Evans, "When Good Customers are Bad," *Harvard Business Review*, September 2005, p. 19.

[5] Paul Smith, "Only Some Customers Are King," *New Zealand Management*, April 2000, pp. 24-26.

[6] For a discussion of the limitations of the ROAM concept that may influence its applicability and a proposal for an alternative evaluation tool, see William L. Cron and Michael Levy, "Sales Management Performance Evaluation: A Residual Income Perspective," *Journal of Personal Selling & Selling Management*, August 1987, pp. 57-66.

chapter

16

Evaluating a Salesperson's Performance

At Liberty Mutual, branch managers conduct two formal evaluations of each of their salespeople every year. Increasingly, Liberty Mutual has moved away from focusing the review on how much these salespeople *sell*. Instead, the managers discuss *the inputs* that should lead to successful selling, such as time management skills, product knowledge, how many customers they talk to every day, and how they go about talking to these customers. By introducing this behavioral component into its evaluation process, Liberty Mutual is better able to identify their agents' weaknesses, and address them in a way that improves their future performance.

This is why regular performance evaluation is one of the most critical responsibilities of sales managers. It is not, however, easy. Performance evaluation is a time-consuming and sometimes unpleasant activity. Especially difficult is dealing with low-performing salespeople who must be told how and why their performance is unacceptable. To do this well, the manager must put into practice many of the processes that we have discussed in various chapters of this book—including training, motivation, and leadership.

This chapter presents the methods and measures that sales managers should use to systematically and objectively assess the performance of their individual salespeople. After examining the nature and purposes of this managerial activity, we outline a program for evaluating sales performance. The last section of the chapter is a case example of how one sales manager interpreted the performance data of three salespeople.

NATURE AND IMPORTANCE OF PERFORMANCE EVALUATION

Appraising a salesperson's performance is a part of the managerial function of evaluation. It is part of a marketing audit. Management compares the results of a person's efforts with the goals set for that person. The purpose is to determine what happened in the past and to use this information to improve performance in the future either by taking corrective actions or by rewarding good performance. The evaluation system also is one of the means by which managers *direct* the activities of their salespeople.

Concept of Evaluation and Development

Evaluation has an added dimension when viewed from the perspective of evaluation and development of individual salespeople. Within this wider context, management engages in a counseling activity rather than in a cold statistical analysis. Certainly management wants to measure past performance against standards to identify strengths and weaknesses in the firm's marketing system, particularly as a basis for planning. But this activity is optimized only if it also is brought to the personal level of the salesperson. It should serve as a basis for the person's self-development and as a basis for a sound company program to guide and develop the personnel.

Concept of Evaluation and Direction

If salespeople are aware of the criteria by which they will be evaluated, they will try to do things to improve their performance on these criteria. For example, if one of the goals of the company's strategy is to improve customer satisfaction, then this goal should be included in the evaluation process. This will serve to *direct* the efforts of the salespeople toward this goal. If the salespeople are aware that customer satisfaction will be an important dimension of their evaluation, then they will try to improve their customers' satisfaction.

Importance of Performance Evaluation

A good performance review can be a major aid in other sales force management tasks. Promotions and pay increases can be based on objective performance data rather than on favoritism, subjective observations, or opinions. Weaknesses in field-selling efforts, once identified, may be forestalled by incorporating corrective measures in training programs. On the other hand, management can identify the sales techniques of the outstanding performers with an eye toward having other salespeople adopt them. Performance evaluations also may uncover the need for improvements in the compensation plan. For instance, the existing plan may focus too much effort on low-margin items or too little attention on nonselling (missionary) activities.

Performance analysis especially helps in sales supervision. It is difficult to effectively supervise someone without knowing what the person is doing correctly or incorrectly, and why. If a salesperson's sales volume is unsatisfactory, for instance, a performance review will show it. Moreover, the evaluation may help identify the cause—whether the salesperson has a low daily call rate, does not work enough days per month, calls on the wrong prospects, has trouble with the sales presentation, and so on.

An effective procedure for appraising the work of an individual also can help morale. Any person who knows what he or she is expected to do and has some benchmarks for measuring accomplishments feels more secure. A performance evaluation should ensure that salespeople who deserve favorable recognition receive it, and those who deserve criticism are handled appropriately. The salesperson with the highest sales volume is not necessarily the best one and may not even be doing a good all-around job. To reward this person on the basis of sales volume alone can hurt the morale of others in the sales force. Similarly, morale suffers if management criticizes a salesperson for low volume when the contributing factor was low territorial potential or unusually stiff competition. A performance-appraisal system should forestall and help correct such situations.

By evaluating the salespeople's achievements, management helps them discover their own strengths and weaknesses. This should motivate them to raise their levels of performance. Like most people, salespeople seldom can make an effective self-evaluation. In fact, when asked to rate themselves, low-performing salespeople tend to overestimate their performance, while high performing salespeople tend to underestimate their performance.[1] Further, even when salespeople do understand their performance is unacceptable, they often are not able to determine the reasons for this poor productivity.

Difficulties Involved in Evaluating Performance

Many duties assigned to salespeople cannot be measured objectively, and some tasks are difficult to evaluate even on a subjective basis. A manufacturer's representative is supposed to service the firm's accounts; a wholesaler's sales rep is told to avoid high-pressure selling; all salespeople are supposed to build goodwill with customers. Even with close field supervision of the sales force, these tasks can be evaluated only subjectively. And, if management does not closely supervise the salespeople in the field, it may be virtually impossible to measure results from some of these duties.

By the same token, however, many tasks of a seemingly subjective nature can actually be quantified. A salesperson's tendency to pressure or oversell customers, for instance, might be measured by tallying canceled orders, lost accounts, and reorders.

The wide variety of conditions salespeople work under makes it difficult for management to compare their productivity. There is no satisfactory method for equating territorial differences in potential, competition, or working conditions. It is difficult to compare the performance of city salespeople with rural salespeople, for example. Even if the districts are equal in potential, they are not comparable in other ways.

Sometimes performance evaluation is difficult because the results of a salesperson's efforts may not be evident for some time. A district's improved position may show up only after a salesperson has been working there for a year or more. Furthermore, when two or more people are involved in making a sale or in servicing a customer, it usually is difficult to give individual credit for results.

Importance of a Good Job Description

In the task of sales force evaluation, as we have seen for so many other sales force management activities, a good job description is critical. Evaluators must

CONSIDER THIS...

An International Perspective

Sales executives that work from the headquarters of an international company should be culture-sensitive when evaluating salespeople in other parts of the world. For example, a performance appraisal approach that works well in the United States might not be effective in India or Germany. This is why it is critical for U.S. executives to take the time to learn and understand the particular marketing and selling styles that work best in other countries.

Most American sales managers promote a "can-do" spirit among their salespeople, encouraging them to be enthusiastic and optimistic. In Japan, however, a salesperson with this selling style is in danger of coming across as a noisy braggart.

Another accepted evaluation approach in the United States is for sales managers to be less authoritative—acting more like coaches than bosses. In fact, 360-degree feedback assessments involve subordinates giving constructive criticism to their superiors. In many Latin American countries, however, employees are not at all comfortable with this approach, and react much better to a boss who is a strong authority figure.

SOURCE: "Pop Quiz," *Sales & Marketing Management* January 2004, p. 20.

work from the reference point of a statement about *what* a salesperson is supposed to do. Otherwise, they are not in a good position to determine *whether* or *how effectively* the job was done.

PROGRAM FOR EVALUATING PERFORMANCE

This section suggests a five-step procedural system for evaluating sales force performance (see Figure 16-1). The program is complete, but it is also expensive and time-consuming.

Step 1. Establish Some Basic Policies

Preliminary to the actual evaluation, management should set some ground rules. One question that calls for a decision is: Who will participate in the evaluation? Several executives normally are involved. One of the most likely is the salesperson's immediate superior—perhaps a field supervisor, a district manager, or a branch manager. The boss of the immediate supervisor also is likely to be involved. Many companies today find benefits in using an employee assessment known as 360-degree feedback, which is especially effective in team environments.[2] This technique involves getting evaluative feedback from an employee's peers, subordinates, and clients, as well as superiors.

Certainly, the salesperson being evaluated should participate actively, usually with some form of self-evaluation. Involving salespeople in the development

FIGURE 16-1
Procedure for evaluating salespeople

1. Establish basic policies → 2. Select evaluation basis → 3. Set performance standards → 4. Compare performances to standards → 5. Discuss results with salespeople

of their objectives creates a greater sense of responsibility and commitment on the part of the salespeople. In some firms, the manager and salesperson identify and negotiate specific goals for the upcoming period. Then the salesperson and manager sign a performance agreement that specifies these goals as the performance standards. This ensures that there will be no misunderstandings about what is expected. This process is often called **management by objectives.**

Another policy decision concerns the frequency of evaluation. Figure 16-2 presents results of a survey of a wide cross-section of sales organizations. As shown on the chart, 19 percent of firms do not even conduct a formal performance evaluation with their salespeople. Of those sales organizations that do evaluate their salespeople, most do it at least on a quarterly basis, and some do it even more frequently than that.[3] Fastenal salespeople undergo an evaluation on a monthly basis. The evaluation scorecard is generated automatically by the Fastenal CRM program. Synygy Inc., a software company, makes a point to have dozens of performance reviews with its salespeople every year. According to Synygy's vice president of sales, "If you don't communicate frequently, they don't know where they stand, or how well they're doing on performance improvement."[4] Although the time and costs required to conduct more frequent evaluations must be balanced against the benefits, the improvements in performance generally outweigh the costs.

Step 2. Select Bases for Evaluation

One key to a successful evaluation program is to appraise a salesperson's performance on as many different bases as possible. To do otherwise is to run the risk of being misled. Let's assume that we are rating a salesperson, Ryan, on the basis of the ratio of selling expenses to sales volume. If this percentage is very low compared to the average for the entire sales force, Ryan probably will be commended. Yet Ryan actually may have achieved that low ratio by failing to prospect for new accounts or by otherwise covering the territory inadequately. Knowing the average number of daily calls Ryan made, even in relation to the average call rate for the entire sales force, does not help us very much. By measuring Ryan's ratio of orders per call (batting average), we learn a little more, but we still can be misled. Each additional piece of information—sales volume,

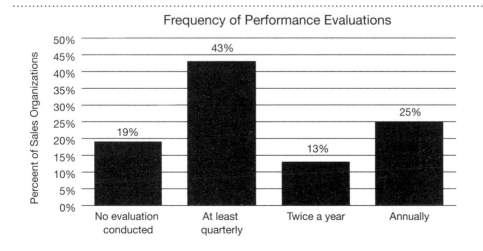

Frequency of Performance Evaluations

FIGURE 16-2
Frequency of Performance Evaluations
SOURCE: Based on a survey of over 200 salespeople in Linda S. Pettijohn, R. Stephen Parker, Charles E. Pettijohn, and John L. Kent, "Performance Appraisals: Usage, Criteria and Observations," *Journal of Management Development* 20, no. 9 (2001), pp. 754-71.

plus average order size, plus presentation quality, and so on—helps give a clearer picture of Ryan's performance.

When selecting the bases on which to evaluate salespeople, it is important to remember that the evaluation serves two purposes. One is to recognize and reward people for a job well done; the other is to develop a clear understanding of the salesperson's performance in order to help him or her improve. Salespeople are more likely to respond to and learn from the evaluation when they perceive it to be fair. Consequently, it is important for sales managers to clearly communicate the bases on which salespeople will be evaluated. Some even feel that salespeople should be involved in selecting the bases. Studies show that when salespeople buy into the evaluation process, their satisfaction toward all aspects of the job tends to be higher.[5]

Bases of evaluation fall into two general categories: output measures and input measures. Both types of measures should be used to get a complete picture of the salesperson's performance.

Output measures

Output measures relate to the salesperson's results—sales volume, gross margin, number of orders, and so on. A list of some output factors ordinarily used as evaluation bases is shown in Figure 16-3. These measures are often used to make some meaningful comparisons. One salesperson may be compared to another, performance this year may be compared to performance for last year, performance may be compared to a goal or target, the salesperson's share of the market may be compared to that of competitors, and so on.

Each of these measures can be further broken down by type of product, customer type, or channel of distribution, and similar comparisons can be made. Breaking the information down by various subcategories may provide

FIGURE 16-3
Output Factors Used as
Evaluation Bases

- Sales volume
  - In dollars and in units
  - By products and customers
  - By email, telephone, and personal sales calls
- Sales volume as a percentage of
  - Quota
  - Market potential (i.e., market share)
- Gross margin by
  - Product line, customer group, order size
- Orders
  - Number of orders
  - Average order size
  - Batting average (orders/calls)
  - Number of canceled orders
- Accounts
  - Percentage of accounts sold
  - Number of new accounts
  - Number of accounts with overdue payment

some insights into the salesperson's performance that otherwise would be overlooked. If the salesperson's performance is below average, it may be that the problem can be isolated to one type of selling situation or to one category of product. If a manager can pinpoint the cause of a performance problem, it becomes much easier to find a solution to alleviate that problem.

All of the output bases are *quantitative* measures. To a large extent, the use of these quantitative measures minimizes the subjectivity and biases of the evaluator. Quantitative properties are also relatively easy to measure. However, since they consider results *only*, these measures may not provide an equitable base on which to compare the performance of one salesperson to another.

Problem of data comparability

Ideally, a salesperson should be judged only on factors he or she can control. Management should identify the uncontrollable factors and take them into consideration when appraising an individual's performance. The sales potential in a territory, especially in relation to size and number of customers, is a good example of an uncontrollable factor. The greater sales potential in one territory versus another may make it easier for the salesperson in the first territory to reach his or her goals while the salesperson in the second territory struggles to meet the same goals. Differences in competitive activity or physical conditions among territories also must be considered when comparing performances. Usually, there are territorial variations in the amount of advertising, sales promotional support, or home-office technical service available to customers. These and several other factors make it difficult to compare performance data. This is one of the reasons for considering information on inputs or efforts as well as results.

Input measures

Two types of **input measures** are used in the evaluation process. The *quantitative* measures focus on the salesperson's measurable behaviors or activities. The number of calls a salesperson makes in a day and the number of e-mails sent to prospects are examples of quantitative input measures. Figure 16-4 lists the more commonly used factors. Tracking these factors is considered so important by Bell South Cellular that 25 percent of its sales managers' quarterly bonus is based on how closely they monitor their salespeople's activities.[6]

The second group of input measures is the *qualitative* factors. These factors measure such things as the quality of the salesperson's presentation, product knowledge, customer relations, and the salesperson's attitude. Figure 16-5 lists other qualitative factors that are often used in the evaluation process.

Both the quantitative and the qualitative input factors are based on behaviors that are usually under the salesperson's control. Therefore, they are less subject to criticisms concerning inequities among the salespeople. But the most important value in using these measures is that they are usually critical in locating trouble spots. Assume that a salesperson's output performance (average order size, gross margin, and so on) is unsatisfactory. Very often the cause lies in the certain behaviors over which the salesperson has control

Research has demonstrated that an evaluation system that emphasizes behaviors more than outcomes has a number of positive effects on the salesperson's overall performance.[7] For example, the more behavior-based the evaluation system, the more the salesperson is willing to cooperate as part of the sales team and the more the salesperson is committed to the organization. With such a system, the salesperson places greater emphasis on implementing adaptive strategies. Of course, outputs cannot be ignored. In fact, it has been shown that evaluation systems that measure *both* inputs and outputs lead to higher sales and profits.[8]

Ratio measures

Most of the quantitative measures discussed above can be combined to create **ratio measures** that can be used for evaluative and comparative purposes. Orders/calls, expenses/sales, and sales/orders are some of the more common ratios managers use to evaluate and compare the performance of salespeople.

A quantitative evaluation of a salesperson's performance often involves the various elements of the following equation:

$$\text{Sales} = \text{Days worked} \times \frac{\text{Calls}}{\text{Days worked}} \times \frac{\text{Orders}}{\text{Calls}} \times \frac{\text{Sales}}{\text{Orders}}$$

$$\text{Sales} = \text{Days worked} \times \frac{\text{Call}}{\text{rate}} \times \frac{\text{Batting}}{\text{average}} \times \frac{\text{Average}}{\text{order}}$$

If the sales volume for a salesperson is unsatisfactory, the basic cause must rest in one or more of these four factors. An analysis such as that done in Figure 16-7 can help focus the manager's attention on the trouble spot so that additional detailed investigation can pinpoint the salesperson's exact difficulties.

Sources of information

When choosing factors to use as bases for a performance evaluation, management should select only those for which data are available at a reasonable cost. The four main sources of information are company records, the salespeople themselves, field sales managers, and customers.

FIGURE 16-4
Quantitative Input Factors Used as Evaluation Bases

- Calls per day (call rate)
- Days worked
- Selling time versus nonselling time
- Direct selling expense
  - In total
  - As percentage of sales volume
  - As percentage of quota
- Nonselling activities
  - Advertising displays set up
  - E-mails/letters written to prospects
  - Telephone calls made to prospects
  - Number of meetings held with dealers and/or distributors
  - Number of service calls made
  - Collections made
  - Number of customer complaints received

- Personal efforts of the salespeople
  - ○ Management of their time
  - ○ Planning and preparation for calls
  - ○ Quality of sales presentations
  - ○ Ability to handle objections and to close sales
  - ○ Inputting information into SFA/CRM system
- Knowledge
  - ○ Product
  - ○ Company and company policies
  - ○ Competitor's products and strategies
  - ○ Customers
- Customer Relations
- Personal appearance and health
- Personality and attitudinal factors
  - ○ Cooperativeness
  - ○ Resourcefulness
  - ○ Acceptance of responsibility
  - ○ Ability to analyze logically and make decisions

FIGURE 16-5
Qualitative Input Factors Used as Evaluation Bases

Company records are the main source for data on most of the quantitative *output* factors. By studying sales invoices, customers' orders, and accounting records, management can discover much about a salesperson's volume, gross margin, average order size, and so on. Most firms fail to make optimum use of their records for evaluation purposes. In the past, the information often was not recorded in usable form for a performance evaluation. Firms found it was too expensive and time-consuming to tabulate and present the data in usable form. However, most companies today use the CRM or SFA system to collect, analyze, and report data in a form useful for evaluation—and so the information is much more readily available.

Reports submitted by the sales force are an important source of information, particularly for performance *input* factors. The regular use of call reports, activity reports, and expense reports can provide the necessary data on the salespeople's work. The Achilles' heel in using salespeople reports for evaluation is that the information is only as good as the accuracy, completeness, and punctuality of their reporting efforts. This is often a serious problem.

As a rule, sales supervisor and other sales executives regularly travel with the salespeople in the field. The managers observe the salespeople during sales calls on customers. This allows the administrators to make a firsthand appraisal of their subordinates' performance with customers.

Customers can be used as a source of evaluation information in one of two ways. The more common method is to gather information submitted by customers on a voluntary, informal basis. Unfortunately, this usually takes the form of complaints, because customers rarely report commendatory performance by salespeople. Increasingly companies are actively soliciting opinions from customers on a regular basis. Some companies ask their customers such questions as *How well does the salesperson analyze your needs?* And *How well does the salesperson build trust?* The customer is certainly in the best position to answer these kinds of questions.[9] However, some firms don't use customers as a source of data. They feel that customers often give excessively good reviews to protect the salespeople they like.[10]

Step 3. Set Performance Standards

Setting standards is one of the most difficult phases of performance evaluation. The standards serve as a benchmark, or a par for the course, against which a salesperson's performance can be measured. Also, standards let a salesperson know what is expected and serve as a guide in planning work. Standards must be equitable and reasonable; otherwise, salespeople may lose interest in their work and confidence in management, and morale may decline. If the standards are too high or too low, using them to evaluate performance will be worthless or even harmful.

Standards for many of the output (results) factors can be tied to company goals for territories, product lines, or customer groups. Such performance measures as sales volume, gross margin, or market share probably already have been set.

It is more difficult to set performance standards for the effort (input) factors. A careful time-and-duty analysis of sales jobs should give management some basis for determining satisfactory performance for daily call rates, displays arranged, and other factors. Another approach is to use executive judgment based on the personal observations of those who work with the salespeople in the field.

To measure the efficiency of a company's selling effort, management must balance the output against the input. Consequently, a firm should develop standards for such output/input ratios as sales volume/calls, orders/calls, gross margin/order, and sales volume/expenses.

Once the standards have been set, it is critical that these standards be communicated to the salespeople. Even if the salespeople were involved in establishing the standards, they should be formally communicated to the salesperson. This ensures that there are no misunderstandings about the benchmarks against which the performance will be judged.

Step 4. Compare Performance with Standards

The accumulated information must be interpreted. This step involves comparing an individual's performance—both efforts and results—with the predetermined standards.

Interpreting quantitative data

Some quantitative factors ordinarily used as bases for performance appraisal were shown in Figures 16-3 and 16-4. The following discussion shows how these factors can be used with the performance standards in step 3 to evaluate the salesperson's performance.

Sales volume and market share

The first criterion most sales managers use to judge the relative performance of salespeople is the dollar sales volume that they generate. Some executives believe that the salesperson who sells the most merchandise is the best salesperson, regardless of other considerations. Unfortunately, sales volume alone may be a poor indicator of a salesperson's worth because it may not correspond to contribution to profit—let alone customer relations.

Sales volume can be a useful indicator of performance, however, if it is analyzed in sufficient detail and with discretion. For evaluation purposes, a salesperson's total volume may be studied by product line, by some form of customer grouping, or by order size. Even then, the volume figures are not very meaningful unless they can be related to some predetermined standard of acceptable performance, volume quota for each product line or customer group, for example.

Another important evaluation factor is the salesperson's **market share**, which relates to how dominant the salesperson is in his or her territory compared to competitors. Specifically, market share can be computed by dividing the salesperson's sales volume by the territorial market potential. Here again, the data are more useful if share of market can be determined for each product line or customer group.

Management must be cautious when comparing market share performance of one person with another. Salesperson A may get 20 percent of the market in his district, while person B captures only 10 percent of her market. Yet B may be doing a better job. Competition may be far more severe in B's district. Or the company may be giving A considerably more advertising support.

Gross margin

The definition of **gross margin** is the difference between sales and cost of goods sold. Consequently, a sales manager generally should be more concerned with the amount of gross margin the salespeople generate than with their dollar sales volume. This is because gross margin is a much better measure of a salesperson's effectiveness because it gives some indication of the salesperson's ability to sell high-margin items. Since the prime objective of most businesses is to earn a targeted return on investment, a person's direct contribution to profit is a logical yardstick for evaluating performance.

Management can reflect its gross margin goals by setting volume quotas for each product line. In this way, the company can motivate the sales force to achieve a desirable balance of sales among the various lines. Then, even though the salespeople are later evaluated on the basis of sales volume, this evaluation will automatically include gross margin considerations.

As an evaluative yardstick, gross margin has some limitations, however. When management ignores selling expenses, there is no way of knowing how much it costs to generate gross margin. Thus, salesperson A may have a higher dollar gross margin than person B. But A's selling expenses may be proportionately so much higher than B's that A actually shows a lower contribution margin. Furthermore, a salesperson does not fully control the product mix represented in his or her total sales volume. Territorial market potential and intensity of competition vary from one district to another, and these factors can influence the sales of the various product lines.

Number and size of orders

Another performance measure combines the number of orders and the size of orders obtained by each salesperson. The average sale is computed by dividing a salesperson's total number of orders into his or her total sales volume. This calculation may be made for each class of customer to determine how the salesperson's average order varies among them. This analysis discloses which salespeople are getting too many small, unprofitable orders, even though their total volume appears satisfactory because of a few large orders. The analysis also may show that some salespeople find it difficult to obtain orders from certain classes of customers but make up for this deficiency by superior performance with their other accounts.

Call rate

A key factor in sales performance is the **call rate**—the number of calls made per day. A salesperson ordinarily cannot sell merchandise without calling on customers; generally, the more calls the more sales. Salesperson A makes three calls a day, but the company average is four for salespeople who work under reasonably comparable conditions. If management can raise A's call rate up to the company average of four, his sales should increase by 33 percent.

For evaluation purposes, a salesperson's call rate can be measured against some other predetermined standard. Customer wants and needs are an important input to this, as research shows that there are significant benefits when the salesperson's call frequency matches what the buyer perceives as ideal.[11] Discretion must be exercised in interpreting a salesperson's call rate, however. Call rates are influenced by the number of miles traveled by the salesperson and by the number of customers per square mile in the territory.

Usually, in a given business, a certain desired call rate yields the best results. At Fastenal, the goal for outside salespeople is to call on 15 customers per day. If the salesperson falls below this rate, sales decline because the salesperson is not seeing enough prospects. If the salesperson calls on too many prospects, sales also may decline since he or she probably does not spend sufficient time with each one to get the job done.

Batting average

A salesperson's **batting average** is calculated by dividing the number of orders received by the number of calls made. The number of calls made is equivalent to times at bat in baseball; the number of orders written is equivalent to the hits made. As a performance index, the batting average discloses ability to locate and call on good prospects and ability to close a sale. A salesperson's batting average should be computed for each class of customers called on. Often, a salesperson varies in ability to close a sale with different types of customers.

Analysis of the call rate in relation to the batting average can be quite meaningful. If the call rate is above average, but the number of orders is below normal, perhaps the salesperson is not spending enough time with each customer. Or suppose the call rate and batting average are both above standard, but the average order is small. Then the sales manager may work with the salesperson—showing him or her how to make fewer but more productive calls. The idea here is to raise the size of the average order by spending more time and talking about more products with each account.

Direct-selling expenses

The sum of compensation (salary, commission and bonus), benefits and travel and entertainment expenses for each salesperson make up the bulk of **direct-selling expense**. These total expenses are often expressed as a percentage of sales. Also, the expense-to-sales ratios for the various salespeople can be compared. Or management can compute the cost per call for each salesperson by dividing total expenses by the number of calls made.

In a performance evaluation, these various cost indexes may indicate the relative efficiency of the salespeople in the field. However, management must interpret these ratios carefully and in detail. An expense-to-sales ratio, for instance, may be above average because the salesperson is (1) doing a poor job, (2) working in a marginal territory, (3) working in a new territory doing a lot of prospecting and building a solid base for the future, or (4) working a territory that covers far more square miles than the average district. A salesperson with a low batting average usually has a high cost per order. Similarly, the one who makes few calls per day has a high ratio of costs per call.

Routing efficiency
Dividing the miles traveled by the number of calls made gives the average miles per call. This figure either indicates the density of the salesperson's territory or measures **routing efficiency**. If a group of salespeople all have approximately the same size and density of territories, then miles per call is a significant figure for indicating each one's routing efficiency. Suppose five salespeople selling for an office machines firm in a metropolitan area vary considerably in the number of miles traveled per call. Then the sales manager may have reason to control the routing of those who are out of line.

Evaluating qualitative factors
When the evaluation is based on qualitative factors, the personal, subjective element comes into full play. This can be good or bad. With qualitative measures, sales managers can give considerable weight to factors not easy to capture quantitatively. These factors include, for example, civic virtue, sportsmanship, and other citizenship behaviors that are not part of the formal evaluation process.[12] Because these are important behaviors for the sales force, the sales manager is not wrong to take them into account. So in certain cases, some might argue that qualitative measures of performance are better at capturing all aspects of a salesperson's performance.

In other situations, subjective evaluations are less accurate than quantitative assessments. Problems can stem from either the manager's personal bias or the type of evaluation form used. There is an almost limitless variety of evaluation forms. Often each manager develops whatever form seems appropriate for the situation. Evaluation forms often have one or more of the following problems:

1. First is **halo effect**. Evaluators may be biased by a generalized overall impression or image of the person they are evaluating. If the manager does not like the way a salesperson dresses, for instance, that attitude may bias all aspects of the manager's evaluation. Similarly, the manager who is impressed with a person's sales ability also is likely to rate other aspects of the person's performance highly. Halo effect can happen with both good and bad evaluation forms—however, it is more likely to occur with evaluation forms involving vague, poorly defined dimensions of performance.

2. Second, some rating forms generally overvalue inconsequential factors and undervalue truly important ones. The sales manager should be

FIGURE 16-6
A behaviorally anchored
rating scale for evaluating
team participation

Evaluate the salesperson's performance on TEAM PARTICIPATION (check one):				
___Unwilling to participate. At times may work against team goals	___Can be expected to participate in team efforts only to the extent required.	___Usually willing to cooperate and participate in team efforts	___Can be expected always to cooperate and contribute to the team objectives. Tries hard to help make the team successful.	___Can be expected to go beyond what is normally expected to help the team achieve its goals.

interested in the salesperson's ability to make money for the firm, not whether the individual is socially adept or impressively dressed. In evaluations, it is essential for the manager to keep in mind what is important and what is not. Often, when a former employee files a legal case involving discrimination in hiring, firing, and promotion, the key point is that the manager based evaluations on unimportant factors.

3. Third, most subjective evaluation forms force the evaluator to make judgments on some factors without a valid basis for doing so. Lacking valid information, the evaluator tends to allow halo effect to take over.

In addition, firms face two even more serious problems. First, many raters refuse to give poor ratings to salespeople who deserve them because of fear of reprisal. As one executive put it, "Who knows what the future holds? The person I downgrade today may be my boss tomorrow." Such managers fail to see any personal advantage in giving accurate ratings. Yet, in any good management evaluation program, a manager's ability and willingness to accurately appraise people is a key factor in that executive's rise in management. A second serious problem is that some people just don't get along. In these cases, evaluators have difficulty being fair.

Most performance evaluation forms use **behaviorally anchored rating scales (BARS)** as a way to subjectively evaluate each salesperson's performance on a variety of dimensions. A BARS instrument contains detailed descriptions of the subject's behavior to guide the evaluator's numerical rating of that person. A sample of a BARS question assessing team participation with a five-point response scale is shown in Figure 16-6. It is important to remember, however, that no amount of instrument sophistication can overcome the basic weaknesses inherent in subjective rating systems.

Step 5. Discuss the Evaluation with the Salesperson

Once the salesperson's performance has been evaluated, the result should be reviewed in a conference with the sales manager. This discussion should be viewed as a counseling interview, in which the manager explains the person's achievements on each evaluation factor and points out how the results compared with the standards. Then the manager and the salesperson together may try to determine the reasons for the performance variations above or below the standards. It is essential to discuss the manager's ratings on the qualitative factors and to compare them with the salesperson's self evaluation on these points. On the basis of their review of all evaluation factors, the manager and the salesperson can then establish goals and an operating plan for the coming period.

An Account Manager Objects to His Evaluation

In December each year, Shiderlots' sales manager Adam Dark accesses the CRM system and prints out a comprehensive performance report on each account manager. The report includes both qualitative and quantitative assessments on a wide variety of outputs and inputs to performance. From this information, Dark writes a letter to each account manager summarizing how well he or she had done during the year, and suggesting ways that future performance might be improved.

It was not one of Dark's favorite jobs, but Shiderlots top management was committed to formal evaluation programs. He knew there would be repercussions from his letter to Greg Zimmer. Neither Zimmer's numbers nor Dark's observation of his performance could prompt much praise. In fact, Dark wanted to replace this account manager, but was being constrained because of company policies.

About 32 seconds after opening Dark's evaluation letter, Greg Zimmer phoned him angrily.

"This is a bunch of garbage you cooked up to justify getting rid of me. If you want to fire me, then do it, but don't insult my intelligence by expecting me to buy this rubbish!" Zimmer challenged.

"I rather expected that you would be coming in to see me. Let's sit down and go over the items you disagree with one by one. We do have excellent records and statistics on what you have done and sold in comparison with the other account managers," Dark said calmly.

"I'm not talking numbers. I know the numbers stink and I'm not happy about them either. I am talking about comparing noncomparables. It is patently unfair to compare me with the other account managers. Being the new kid on the block, I was handed a bad territory. Why was it open? The guy in it before me told me why he quit, and I am fighting the same lack of potential and competitive conditions," Zimmer said.

Dark was well aware that one particular competitor was extremely strong in that area as they were located there. Stalling for time, he asked, "What do you want me to do?"

"I want some understanding of my situation and consideration in my treatment. This evaluation in my file is the kiss of death for any future here. It says I stink. It says I can't plan my work or penetrate the market. It says I can't sell. And that isn't so!" Zimmer fumed.

Questions: What should Adam Dark say and/or do in response to Greg Zimmer's request? What changes in the evaluation procedure might help?

RUNNING CASE
Shiderlots
Elevators, Inc.

The performance-evaluation interview can be a very sensitive occasion. It is not easy to point out a person's shortcomings face to face. People dislike being criticized and may become quite defensive in this situation. Some sales executives resist evaluation interviews because they feel these discussions can only injure morale. The concern is real and valid. They reason, "Why stir up trouble when you are basically happy with the person's performance?" On the other extreme, some sales managers make a point to rank all salespeople from best to worst (see the box titled "Pros and Cons of Ranking Salespeople").

CONSIDER THIS...

Pros and Cons of Ranking Salespeople

Although controversial, many sales organizations regularly display forced sales rankings of all their salespeople—from first to last. Is this a good idea? Here are some pros and cons...

Pros—People who like the rankings say:

- "Salespeople are competitive. Just like in sports, everyone wants to know where each team or individual stands."
- "Forced ranking makes it clear to everyone what is considered excellent, average, and poor performance."
- "Salespeople will work harder to move up in the rankings. We had one salesperson move from #73 to #56 to #23 to #3 in just three years."
- "We don't have to deliver the bad news. People at the bottom know where they stand on the 'wall of shame.' They get embarrassed and many leave of their own accord.

Cons—Those who don't like rankings say:

- "It creates internally focused rivalries—and salespeople soon forget that the competition is out in the marketplace, not within the company among peers."
- "An 'every man for himself' attitude develops, hindering the teamwork needed to serve customers effectively and beat competition."
- "Rankings make a large fraction of salespeople feel like failures in a visible, public way."
- "Delivers bad news in an impersonal way, and allows weak managers to avoid confronting poor performers and having frank discussions with them on how to improve their performance."

SOURCE: Andris A. Zoltners, PK Sinha, and Sally E. Lorimer, "How to Manage Forced Sales Rankings, *"Harvard Business Review* July 27, 2011. Retrieved from the following URL on July 7, 2016: https://hbr.org/2011/07/forced-rankings-salespeople

Unperceptive managers often lose sight of subordinates' virtues and strengths and criticize unimportant factors. One key factor in management is learning to use people's virtues to the best advantage while not allowing their weaknesses to hurt the firm.

USING EVALUATION DATA: AN EXAMPLE

The case example in this section illustrates the computations, interpretation, and use of several quantitative evaluation factors, both input (efforts) and output (results).

The Colorado Ski Company distributes four lines of products nationally: skis, ski accessories, ski pants, and ski parkas (the latter two lines are limited). The firm sells to two basic classes of customers: sporting goods stores and specialty ski shops. The company uses its own sales force to reach these customers directly. The three account managers are paid travel expenses plus a straight commission of 5 percent on sales volume.

For purposes of a performance evaluation, the sales manager of the Colorado Ski Company has divided the products into two basic lines: skis and ski accessories (equipment) and ski pants and parks (clothing). The retailers' usual initial markup on these product is 50 percent of the retail selling price. There are no significant variations among products in the gross margin percentages realized by the Colorado Ski Company.

The sales manager is especially interested in the performance of three account managers: Joe, who sells in the Rocky Mountain region (a huge territory); Gus, selling in the Pacific Northwest; and Paula, who covers the New England market. Much of the quantitative performance data for Joe, Gus and Paula is summarized in Figure 16-7. On the basis of an analysis of these data, the sales manager is trying to decide (1) which of the three did the best job and (2) which particular points should be discussed with each person to improve performance.

If the sales manager of the Colorado Ski Company looked just at the sales production of these three people, he would have to conclude that Joe was best by far. He might even consider replacing Paula, since her volume looks very weak in comparison. However, after comparing each account manager's volume against the market potential, it is evident that Paula sold a larger share of her market than did either Joe or Gus.

Joe's Sales Performance

The sales manager could see that Joe had worked the fewest number of days (220), made the fewest calls (700), and took the fewest orders (500). He also spent more money than the others ($48,000) and traveled far more miles (60,000). The sales manager can make some allowance for this because Joe's territory, the Rocky Mountain region, is more spread out and sparsely populated than either Gus's or Paula's territory.

Joe's batting average (0.714) is certainly adequate, and his average order ($2,400) is more than satisfactory. In fact, it is astonishingly high in comparison with the others ($1,133 and $612). The sales manager can justify this. The tremendous market potential ($6 million) in Joe's territory, in comparison with the number of customers evidently located there, would naturally result in a high average sale. Joe evidently has done a satisfactory job of covering potential prospects. It appears that the market potential per dealer in the Rocky Mountain region is far higher than in the other areas in the country. This would explain why he could take such large orders. Joe makes a little over three calls per day, which is relatively low in comparison to the others (3.75 and 4.80). However, it is not sufficiently out of line to cause any action to be taken, in light of his territory. The large number of miles per call is again indicative of the territory.

Considering expense per sales dollar, it *appears* that Joe is the most efficient account manager, since he spends only 4 percent of sales for expenses. The account managers are paid a straight commission of 5 percent of sales, which brings Joe's total cost of selling to 9 percent. However, the sales manager can see that this low expense ratio is simply a function of his abnormally high sales, which, in turn, are a result of his large market potential.

Joe's cost per call ($68.57) and cost per order ($96) seemed exceedingly high in comparison with those for the other two. He worked 20 fewer days than Gus and 10 fewer than Paula. Granted that he traveled 15,000 miles more than Gus, the cost of those miles at 26 cents a mile would be about $3,900, which leaves something to be explained. The sales manager probably should investigate Joe's expense accounts. Expenses are usually related to the number of days worked

FIGURE 16-7

Evaluation of Performance

	Joe Jackson			Gus Dean			Paula Burns			Total		
	Equipment	Clothing	Total	Equipment	Clothing	Total	Equipment	Clothing	Total	Equipment	Clothing	Total
Total sales (000)	$480	$720	$1,200	$220	$460	$680	$240	$280	$520	$940	$1,460	$2,400
Sporting goods stores	320	440	760	160	320	480	100	160	260	580	920	1,500
Ski shops	160	280	440	60	140	200	140	120	260	360	540	900
Total calls made			700			900			1,100			2,700
Sporting goods stores			300			500			500			1,300
Ski shops			400			400			600			1,400
Total orders taken			500			600			850			1,950
Sporting goods stores			150			450			400			1,000
Ski shops			350			150			450			950
Days worked			220			240			230			690
Expenses			$48,000			$40,000			$36,000			$124,000
Miles traveled			60,000			45,000			35,000			140,000
Total market potential (millions)	$2.00	$4.00	$6.00	$1.20	$2.40	$3.60	$1.20	$1.20	$2.40	$4.40	$7.60	12.00
Sporting goods stores	1.60	2.40	4.00	0.80	1.60	2.40	0.72	0.64	1.36	3.12	4.64	7.76
Ski shops	0.40	1.60	2.00	0.40	0.80	1.20	0.48	0.56	1.04	1.28	2.96	4.24

	Joe Jackson			Gus Dean			Paula Burns			Total		
	Sporting Goods Stores	Ski Shops	Total	Sporting Goods Stores	Ski Shops	Total	Sporting Goods Stores	Ski Shops	Total	Sporting Goods Stores	Ski Shops	Total
Average order	$5,087	$1,257	$2,400	$1,067	$1,333	$1133	$650	$578	$612	$1,500	$947	$1,231
Batting average	0.500	0.875	0.714	0.900	0.375	0.666	0.800	0.750	0.773	0.679	0.769	0.722
Calls per day			3.18			3.75			4.80			3.90
Miles per call			86			50			32			52.00
Expense per sales dollar			4.0%			5.9%			6.9%			5.2%
Cost per call, excluding commission			$68.57			$44.44			$32.72			$45.92
Cost per order, excluding commission			$96.00			$66.67			$42.23			$63.59

	Joe Jackson			Gus Dean			Paula Burns			Total		
	Equipment	Clothing	Total	Equipment	Clothing	Total	Equipment	Clothing	Total	Equipment	Clothing	Total
Total percent of market	24.0%	18.0%	20.0%	18.3%	19.0%	19.0%	20.0%	23.3%	21.7%	21.4%	19.2%	20.0%
Sporting goods stores	20.0%	18.0%	19.0%	20.0%	20.0%	20.0%	13.9%	25.0%	19.1%	18.6%	19.8%	19.3%
Ski shops	40.0%	17.5%	22.0%	15.0%	17.5%	16.7%	21.4%	25.0%	25.0%	28.1%	18.2%	21.2%

and miles traveled. They are not related directly to sales volume; it costs as much to take an order for $100 as one for $600. A large market potential that results in large sales can cause the expense-to-sales ratio to be misleading. Thus, Joe's high sales volume caused his expense ratio to appear low, when in reality he was spending too much money making calls.

Let's analyze Joe's selling effort with regard to products and customers. He has a more difficult time getting orders from a sporting good store (0.500) than from a ski shop (0.875) even though his average sales to sporting goods stores ($5,087) is fantastically high. The sales manager may wonder if this is part of Joe's batting average problem. Possibly in attempting to sell sporting goods stores so much merchandise, he simply scares some of them away. However, the sales manager should be cautious here. In total, it is better that Joe continue to sell a high average order to sporting goods stores and settle for fewer orders than to bring both figures to average.

The sales manager may want to investigate Joe's high average order to sporting goods stores. It may be that a few large discount sporting goods stores in the territory are placing huge orders with Joe. This may be no reflection at all on his ability to build up an order. Therefore, if his batting average could be raised in the sporting goods field, possibly no loss would occur at all to the average order. Then the result would be a higher sales volume. It is something to investigate.

Another thing the sales manager may notice: Joe seems able to sell equipment (24 percent of the potential) better than he sells clothing (18 percent of potential). He is well above average in his ability to sell skis, particularly to ski specialty shops (40 percent of potential), but he is below average in attention to clothing (17.5). This may be just a reflection of his basic interest. He may prefer to talk about skis, bindings, and poles rather than about pants and parkas. The sales manager should mention to Joe that he should be doing a bit better in his sales of clothing. However, Joe is not sufficiently below par in any category for the sales manager to be unduly concerned.

Gus's Sales Performance

Probably the first thing the sales manager would note about Gus's sales performance is his apparent inability to sell to ski shops. He is closing only 37.5 percent of these calls, whereas the company average is 76.9 percent. On the other hand, he has an extremely high batting average in getting orders from sporting goods stores (90 percent). The sales manager may conclude that Gus speak the language of the nonskiing owner of a sporting goods store but does not communicate well with a ski expert. The sales manager may consider a conference with Gus to talk over the needs or problems of the ski shop owner and how they differ from those of the sports shop. Gus may not be sufficiently trained in the technical aspect of skiing to answer the questions and gain the confidence of the ski professional. Gus's expenses seem to be in line with the company average, and his calls per day are satisfactory. While Gus is not achieving par with regard to market share, the deviation is not significant enough to warrant any conference on the matter.

Paula's Sales Performance

Paula seems to do fairly well in getting orders from both sporting goods stores and ski shops. But her average order ($612) is significantly below the company average ($1,231). This indicates a problem area. The sales manager probably wants to determine first if these low average orders are a function of the size of Paula's customers or whether this truly reflects her inability to sell merchandise. The fact that Paula made 1,100 calls with the smallest market potential indicates that her average customer is considerably smaller than those of the other account managers. The sales manager may become alarmed at Paula's relatively high expense of sales. However, he should realize that this is caused by the limited sales potential. Paula's cost per call and cost per order are the lowest of the three, indicating that her expense accounts are not out of line with her efforts.

It should be obvious to the sales manager that Paula works hard; she makes almost five calls per day. This factor helps to explain several of the others. Her high call rate probably explain her low cost per call and the relatively large number of calls she makes. It also may explain why she does not sell much per order. Perhaps she does not spend sufficient time with each customer. On the other hand, the number of miles per call (32) indicates that her territory is relatively dense, and this alone may be the reason she can make almost five calls per day. She spends less time traveling between calls than the other two salespeople.

While a sales manager might at first consider discharging Paula, a detailed analysis shows that she is doing as well as, if not better than the other two account managers. Her costs for efforts undertaken are lower. Also, she achieves a larger percentage of the business available to her. Her key problem, which is that her territory has limited market potential, is beyond her control.

The Sales Manager's Decisions

In conclusion, the sales manager probably will undertake several different projects. First, he may try to get Joe to work a few more days in the year. It is understandable that this account manager is tempted to do a little loafing. He has a comfortable annual income, and leads the sales force in sales. However, Joe's territory has a tremendous sales potential. If he does not want to service it properly, the company can cut it in half, giving each salesperson a $3 million potential to work with. This would still result in two territories of larger potential than that worked by Paula. Also, the sales manager may investigate why Joe does not sell to more sporting goods stores.

With Gus, the sales manager probably will focus his entire attention on why ski shops are such an obstacle. He probably needs additional instruction on the technical aspects of skiing. The sales manager may want to ask Paula why she does not sell more skis to sporting goods stores. That is about her only real weakness, outside of her low average order. Certainly, the sales manager should investigate the reasons for Paula's low average order. However, as previously noted, this may not be the result of poor selling ability.

SUMMARY

A fair and accurate evaluation of the company's sales force is a critical and difficult task. The manager's appraisal of the salespeople is important not only because pay and promotions should be based on such rating, but also because good supervision and training should be based on an objective evaluation of the salesperson's performance. However, the task is difficult. Subjective methods leave much to be desired, as managerial biases may distort the ratings.

The factors affecting a person's performance are many and varied. Moreover, many of those factors are beyond the person's control. It is critical that a person be evaluated only on factors over which he or she has control.

First, management should set some basic policies on the evaluation of the sales personnel. It should establish who will do the rating, when and how often it will be done, how the results will be used, and on what bases people will be rated. Both output and input factors should be measured in the process. Output factors include measures such as sales, orders taken, gross margins realized, new accounts, and lost accounts. They are all quantitative. The input factors are both quantitative and qualitative. Calls per day and days worked are examples of quantitative measures. Sales presentation quality, product knowledge, and customer relations are examples of qualitative factors.

By comparing the quantitative input and output measures, various efficiency ratings can be developed. The basic performance equation is:

Sales = Days worked x Call rate x Batting average x Average order

By factoring each element in the equation, the sales manager can obtain a good picture of what each salesperson is doing and why he or she is successful or unsuccessful. Company records are the basic source of information needed for such evaluations.

The qualitative factors are more difficult to measure. The evaluator's subjective biases may influence his or her ratings of these factors. The use of a well-designed merit rating form can help in the measurement of these factors.

Next, some standards must be developed. Relative standards such as what other groups are doing are widely used. However, there is a place for some absolute standards such as total selling costs and days worked.

Finally, performance must be compared with the standards and the evaluation must be discussed with the salesperson.

KEY TERMS

Batting average
Behaviorally anchored rating scales (BARS)
Call rate
Direct-selling expense

Gross margin
Halo effect
Input measures
Management by objectives

Market share
Output measures
Ratio measures
Routing efficiency
Sales volume

QUESTIONS AND PROBLEMS

1. How can a sales manager determine the accuracy of salespeople's reports?
2. How can a sales manager determine the differences the salespeople encounter in the severity of competition in each territory?

3. How should a manager decide what weights to place on the quantitative versus the qualitative factors in an evaluation?

4. What are some of the indexes a sales manager can use to evaluate the degree to which each salesperson is covering the assigned territory.

5. As sales manager for a baby food concern, you want to evaluate the ability of your salespeople to attain good shelf space in grocery stores. How would you do this?

6. How can a sales executive determine the ability of each salesperson to regain lost customers?

7. An owner-manager of a medium-sized apparel manufacturing company proclaimed, "Don't bother me with all that evaluation hogwash. Just give me sales volume and a good bottom line and I'm as happy as a horse in clover. I am making so much money now that I can't spend it all. So why should I waste my time and effort massaging such numbers?" How would you reply to this owner?

8. How can an evaluation system be used to direct the efforts of salespeople?

9. "The importance of sales force evaluation increases with the size of the sales force and management's distance from it." Comment.

10. Should citizenship behaviors play a role in the evaluation of salespeople? If so, how much?

EXPERIENTIAL EXERCISES

1. Ask the sales managers from three different companies how they evaluate the performance of their salespeople. Copy any forms they use. Compare the procedures and provide your evaluation of which firm is doing the best job of evaluation.

2. Contact salespeople from three different companies. Ask them to explain how their performance is evaluated and whether these evaluations are tied to their compensation. Also ask them whether they think their evaluations help them improve their performance and whether or not they think the evaluations are fair.

3. Search the Internet until you find an evaluation for designed to assess the performance of an outside salesperson. What are the strengths and weaknesses of the form?

4. Go to https://www.surveymonkey.com/mp/survey-templates/ -- and evaluate the survey template for Employee Performance Review. Revise this online survey to make it appropriate to evaluate the account managers of Colorado Ski Company (Paula, Gus and Joe). Is this online service useful for sales organizations? Discuss.

LORRIE FOODS, INC.
Designing an Evaluation System

Lorrie Foods, Inc., is a privately owned wholesales food distributor that has served the Gainesville, Florida, market for several decades. It commands a 60 percent share of the Gainesville market, with annual sales of $6 million and profits of approximately $1 million. It is a small, loosely structured firm that employs 20 people. Top management consists of the general manager, Tom Adair; a marketing manager, Jennifer Walters; and a sales manager, Warren Gottlieb. Recently, the company changed ownership. Both Adair and Walters are new to the firm. Gottlieb has been with the firm for 17 years and remains under the new management as the top-ranking sales executive.

Lorrie Foods has three main product lines: food, paper, and chemicals. Food products include packaged goods, canned foods, and drinks. They represent 70 percent of Lorrie's business. Paper products, which include disposable items such as paper plates, cups, and napkins, account for 25 percent of sales. The remaining 5 percent comes from sales of chemicals such as floor cleaning solutions and kitchen and bathroom supplies.

At the current time, Lorrie has approximately 800 active, major accounts. This customer base, which is very stable, consists of institutions such as hospitals and educational facilities, restaurants, churches, fraternities, sororities, and other organizational groups such as the Scouts. These accounts are served by six outside salespeople. There are another 200 to 300 accounts that are not considered major accounts. Many of these accounts are offices that purchase only paper products and chemicals. Their business is solicited by six telephone salespeople, known as the inside sales group.

Although Lorrie has significant market share, there is strong competition in the Gainesville market. Most of the competition is based in Jacksonville, but there are several national competitors as well, such as Continental Food Services and Kraft. Lorrie is currently the only wholesaler in the immediate area. However, Lorrie soon will not be the only local service supplier. The third-largest independent food distributor in the nation, Bower Foods, headquartered in Georgia, is planning to enter the market as a full-service warehouse wholesaler. Bower's anticipated entry is the primary driving force behind the reorganization at Lorrie.

Tom Adair, Jennifer Walters, and Warren Gottlieb have worked together to establish a set of strategic objectives for the marketing and sales operations. In order of importance, they are (1) greater profitability through deeper penetration of the existing market and new product introductions; (2) greater cooperation between the field salespeople and inside sales; (3) increased market feedback from the salespeople; and (4) greater non-price competition. Walters and Gottlieb have both been charged with the responsibility of improving the efficiency and effectiveness of the sales force in achieving these goals. At the current time, Gottlieb is working to establish an evaluation program for his salespeople.

The field salespeople are responsible for calling on their largest accounts two to five times per week. They are expected to make contact with the remainder of their accounts less frequently; but for those accounts that are seen less, the salesperson is expected to stay in touch through frequent phone contacts. In addition to managing their established accounts, the salespeople also must solicit the business of new accounts. They are also encouraged to bring customer and competitive information back to the sales manager. The phone salespeople have responsibility for servicing the smaller accounts as well as handling all customer-order data entry (their own and that of the outside salespeople) and processing all customer complaints.

The field and phone salespeople are compensated differently. The field reps are given a salary (which is the same for all) plus a commission, which can amount to as much as 60 percent of their pay. They also can earn additional incentives in the form of dollars or prizes from Lorrie's suppliers. For example, a supplier may offer $4 for every carton of its product sold. Lorrie would receive $2 and the individual rep would receive the remaining $2. Other suppliers give points for products sold, which then can be turned into vacations or other merchandise by the rep. Phone sales reps are paid a flat salary with no incentives based on sales.

Currently, the evaluation of salespeople is done by Warren Gottlieb on a rather informal basis. Each salesperson has monthly activity reports indicating the level of sales and profits for his or her territory. In addition, Gottlieb has recently instituted a month chart of personal goals for each rep that can be compared to actual performance. Gottlieb believes in management by objectives. He counsels his people to set realistic goals and then helps each rep attain those goals.

Gottlieb and Walters both realized that the current evaluation policies were inadequate. They agreed there was a need to establish specific time periods for the evaluations and that these should be tied to an annual review of performance as well as salary. However, the two managers were at odds with each other when it came to deciding what criteria should be used in evaluating the outside salespeople.

As Gottlieb told Walters, "The primary goal should be to tie our reporting of sales and profits into a formal evaluation of the rep. This would become the primary input for considering raises." Gottlieb believed that the salespeople should be evaluated primarily on the basis of sales and profit contribution because that is what drives the company's bottom line. "We just need to formalize what I've been doing all along."

Walters felt that Gottlieb was wrong. In fact, she felt that the salespeople's sales and profit should play a minor role in their evaluations and reward. Rather, she felt that greater weight should be placed on their behaviors. For example, she wanted to include criteria such as the degree to which the rep provides frequent, high-quality customer feedback; cooperates with the inside sales phone rep; performs the administrative aspects of the job in a timely fashion; and is customer oriented. She argued, "The large percentage of commission pay encourages and rewards them for sales. They don't need any more incentive to sell, but they do need to be motivated to do the more complete selling job. It is these nonselling activities that will help us maintain our position in the marketplace.

Gottlieb didn't buy it. He felt, first, that these criteria were not necessarily related to good sales performance, and, second that the evaluation of these "behaviors" would be too subjective. More important, he also knew that the administration of such a program would be very costly in terms of both time and money.

Questions:

1. Who is right, Warren Gottlieb or Jennifer Walters? Defend your answer.

2. If you were designing the new evaluation program for Lorrie's sales force, what specific criteria would you use to evaluate the performance of the salespeople?

SEAL RITE ENVELOPE (C)
Evaluation of Inside Sales Telemarketing Reps

After several weeks of considerable discussion with top management about the company's misdirected marketing efforts, Rose Douglas, the company's sales manager, had been given permission to begin an inside sales telemarketing program to lower the costs of covering smaller customers. It had been disclosed by an analysis of customer sales volume in relationship to the company's costs of selling to them that the company was spending too much money covering a large number of small accounts while not giving enough attention to the highly profitable large customers.

Seal Rite Envelope Company made and marketed a wide line of envelopes. It sold directly to printers, wholesalers, and corporations with printing facilities. The availability of relatively low-cost printing equipment combined with computer-generated copy had resulted in many companies maintaining in-house printing operations that often were quite large.

Douglas classified the firm's customers into four categories: (1) printers, (2) paper wholesalers, (3) companies buying envelopes for routine mailing purposes, and (4) companies buying envelopes for sales promotional purposes. Companies in the last category required considerable attention, for their needs were diverse and continually changing. A decision had been made to increase the coverage of the larger customers in the last category and make fewer calls on smaller firms in other categories. However, to replace the direct field calls that were being redirected and to give better support to the entire sales effort, Douglas had been given permission to develop a telemarketing group to handle both outbound and inbound sales programs.

To that end, she had hired six people who were being trained by a telemarketing consultant experienced in such programs. Initially, three of the telephone salespeople would be assigned to handle inbound calls from customers on the company's 800 number line. Such calls would vary from requests to have a sales rep call immediately to deal with some pressing need of the customer to a reorder of some envelope the firm was using. The outbound sales calls would be to customers with frequent needs for envelopes and to smaller customers with infrequent needs.

A callback dating system had been developed. Each customer's usage rate was studied by the sales rep covering that account so that the customer could be contacted a short time before it needed to reorder envelopes.

Douglas was trying to figure out how she was going to evaluate these new telephone sales reps. Could all the reps be evaluated as a group with no distinction between the inbound and outbound telemarketers? Or would she have to evaluate the three inbound people against each other and do the same with the outbound sales reps? She wondered in what way these new telemarketers could be evaluated against the outside sales reps. Would it be a case of trying to compare oranges and apples?

Her box, Max Chernak, the president, had asked for a complete report on the telemarketing program when Douglas finalized her plans for it. He had specifically mentioned that he was eager to learn how she intended to evaluate the program.

At the company's Christmas party, Rose Douglas had an opportunity to talk with Steve Hunter, the firm's top sales rep, about the telemarketing program that was soon to be online. She chose to sound him out on some of the questions she was pondering. She asked him, "How often do you think inside sales should be evaluated?"

Hunter smiled and answered, "How about hourly?"

She retorted, "Serious, I've got to make some decisions."

"I was serious. It seems to me that one of the real advantages of an inside telephone selling program is that you can continually monitor and evaluate how each person is doing. You can look at each day's efforts and production," Hunter observed.

"I could do that on you guys, too. But when you get too close, random events distort the evaluation. One tough problem during the day could totally ruin a rep's evaluation data. I've got to look over a large enough span of time that I can get a valid reading of the person's performance. I was thinking about monthly evaluations. What do you think?"

"I told you what I think. I'd be evaluating each day's work. A lot of bad things can happen in a month," Hunter said as he left to say hello to Max Chernak.

Rose Douglas wandered over to the corner where the company's controller was trying to look inconspicuous. Somehow the ensuing conversation turned to evaluation programs. They spent some time talking about the different bases on which the new people could be evaluated, such as time on the telephone, calls attempted, calls completed, orders taken, size of orders, total volume, and errors made. Douglas was somewhat bothered by the controller's emphasis on making many short calls. She was more concerned with what she called meaningful calls, that is, that the person talk long enough to the customer to get the job done. It had been her experience as a salesperson that if she kept the customer talking long enough, she received additional orders as the customer thought of other things that were needed. Her experience was that some customers just liked to talk with her. She was reminded of a lecture she once heard about the social aspects of the sales call. The professor had maintained that a sales call was partly a social event at which social amenities should be observed. He had maintained that the sales rep should leave neither too soon nor too late. Douglas wondered if all of this would be changed in telephone selling: Would

the customers want to talk, or would efficiency be the order of the day? Should she acquire some mechanical means of measuring the number and length of the telephone calls?

Howie Masters, a foreman in the cutting room, strolled up to Rose Douglas to make idle conversation, but Douglas had other ideas. She knew that Masters was a nut about computer and electronics. She told him about the telemarketing program being developed and asked "Would it be difficult to record each telephone call so we can tell how the salespeople are doing and help them improve?"

Masters quickly responded, "no problem at all. All sorts of equipment are available to do the job. You want me to set it up for you?"

"Let me think about it and get back to you. Thanks for offering," Douglas responded. She wondered if any problems would arise if the phone calls were recorded. She knew that there were some laws governing such things, but she speculated that there had to be some way around any legal or ethical problems involved with recording the calls. She had read that other firms did it.

Suddenly, Douglas became somewhat angry with herself, thinking that she was spending too much time contemplating relatively minor matters when she was not certain what she wanted to measure. She admonished herself to focus more on the content of the evaluation program and less on its format.

As Douglas drove home from the party, she put together in her mind everything she wanted to put in her report to Max Chernak. She would writ it the next day.

Questions:

1. How often should the inside sales telemarketers be evaluated?
2. Should the calls be recorded?
3. On what bases should the telemarketers be evaluated?
4. Should inside sales be evaluated against the field sales reps? Against each other?

ENDNOTES

[1] Fernando Jaramillo, Francois A. Carrillat, and William B. Locander, "A Meta-Analytic Comparison of Managerial Ratings and Self-Evaluations," *Journal of Personal Selling & Sales Management,* Fall 2005, pp. 315-28.

[2] Silva Karkoulian, Guy Assaker, and Rob Hallak, "An empirical study of 360-degree feedback, organizational justice, and firm sustainability," *Journal of Business Research,* Vol. 69 (5), May 2016, pp. 1862-67.

[3] Brent Green, "Listening to Leaders: Feedback on 360-Degree Feedback One Year Later," *Organization Development Journal,* Spring 2002, pp. 8-16.

[4] Linda S. Pettijohn, R. Stephen Parker, Charles E. Pettijohn, and John L. Kent, "Performance Appraisals: Usage, Criteria and Observations," *Journal of Management Development* 20, no. 9 (2001), pp. 754-71.

[5] Betsy Cummings, "Tell It Like It Is," *Sales & Marketing Management,* August 2001, pp. 59-60.

[6] Charles E. Pettijohn, Linda S. Pettijohn, and Michael d'Amico, "Characteristics of Performance Appraisals and Their Impact on Sales Force Satisfaction," *Human Resource Development Quarterly,* Summer 2001, pp. 127-46.

[7] Michele Marchetti, "Board Games," *Sales & Marketing Management,* January 1996, pp. 43-46.

[8] Richard L. Oliver and Erin Anderson, "Behavior- and Outcome-Based Sales Control Systems: Evidence and Consequences of Pure-Form and Hybrid Governance," *Journal of Personal Selling & Sales Management,* Fall 1995, pp. 1-16.

[9] Ibid.

[10] "What the Number May Not Tell You," *Nation's Business,* January 1996, p. 21.

[11] "Work Week: Customers Rating," *The Wall Street Journal,* May 6, 1997, p. A1.

[12] G. Alexander Hamwi, Brian N Rutherford, Hiram C. Barksdale, and Julie T. Johnson, "Ideal versus actual number of sales calls: An application of disconfirmation Theory," *Journal of Personal Selling & Sales Management,* Summer 2013, Vol. 33 (3), pp. 307-318.

[13] Gregory A. Rich, William H. Bommer, Scott B. MacKenzie, Philip M. Podsakoff, and Jonathan L. Johnson, "Methods in Sales Research: Apples and Apples or Apples and Oranges? A Meta-Analysis of Objective and Subjective Measures of Salesperson Performance," *Journal of Personal Selling & Sales Management,* Fall 1999, pp. 41-52.

Ethics and Laws

Ten years ago, China was an important and fast-growing market for the pharmaceutical industry, and so a number of companies were in fierce competition. A high-level executive for one of those companies, GlaxoSmithKline (GSK), devised a "creative strategy" to gain a competitive edge: offering lavish gifts, such as Rolex watches and exorbitant speaking fees for fictional conferences, to important Chinese healthcare administrators and doctors if they would prescribe GSK drugs. The sales team were actively recruited and trained on how to engage in this questionable activity, which involved laundering money through bogus travel agencies. Of course, this strategy was highly unethical and illegal, and GSK got in big trouble for it. The drug maker was fined hundreds of millions of dollars, several of its executives received suspended prison sentences, and a barrage of negative publicity ensued.[1]

Bribery is one of several unethical, illegal acts that unfortunately have become associated with the sales profession. This textbook has covered many others, including padding expense accounts, lying about competitors, misrepresenting the product to get the sale, overstating profits, etc. Salespeople and sales managers have been known to do all of these things, but this is ironic and unwise. At best, these tactics might work in the short-run, but we argue that they never work in the long-run. And recall from Chapter 2, we are in the relationship era, in which nothing is more important than legitimately earning the customer's trust—and this can only be done through the kind of ethical and legal behavior outlined in this chapter.

BUSINESS ETHICS AND SALES MANAGEMENT

Webster's New Collegiate Dictionary defines **ethics** as "the science of moral duty" or "the science of ideal human character." Ethics are moral principles or practices. They are also professional standards of conduct. Thus, to act in an ethical fashion is to conform to some standard of moral behavior.

Sales managers have important ethical responsibilities with regard to their own actions, as well as the actions of their salespeople. That is, sales managers are often faced with ethical dilemmas in hiring, setting quotas, evaluating, and carrying out many other aspects of their management tasks; and, in addition, they set the tone for the ethical work climate among their salespeople by establishing, communicating, and enforcing the ethical standards they expect their salespeople to follow. Research demonstrates that sales managers have a significant, positive impact on the extent to which their subordinates behave in an ethical manner.[2]

Salespeople are exposed to greater ethical pressures than are individuals in many other jobs. They work in relatively unsupervised settings; they are primarily responsible for generating the firm's revenues, which at times can be very stressful; they are continually faced with problems that require unique solutions, which is also stressful; and they are often evaluated on the basis of short-term objectives. The latter, especially, can cause salespeople to promote short-term solutions to customers' problems that may not be in the customers' best interests. A recent survey of sales managers revealed that nearly half of the managers said their salespeople have lied on a sales call and 75 percent believe the drive to achieve sales goals encourages salespeople to lose focus of customer needs.[3] In another survey, 58 percent of the managers surveyed said that they have caught salespeople cheating on an expense report.[4]

THE LEGAL-ETHICAL CONFUSION

One often reads in the trade press or hears of such matters as price discrimination, bribes, kickbacks, insider trading, or conflicts of interest. These practices are considered evidence of management's deficient ethical code.

These practices may be unethical, but—more important—they are illegal! It is illegal to take or give bribes. It is illegal to participate in insider trading on the securities exchanges. It is even illegal to pad an expense account—this is called *embezzlement*. Indeed, a large portion of the so-called ethical issues raised by critics of business are not really ethical problems at all. They are law enforcement problems.

In the United States, Americans have standardized a partial common code of ethics based on our complex federal, state, and city statutes—the law. Indeed, there are people for whom the law is their code of ethics: If it is legal, it is ethical. To others, just because something is illegal does not make it unethical. Most speeders, for example, see nothing unethical about their driving habits.

However, most people understand that the law cannot possibly cover and regulate all aspects of life—nor should it attempt to do so. They understand the need for a personal code of ethics beyond that covered by the law.

In this chapter, we focus first on ethical questions and then on legal issues. Nevertheless, understand clearly that the line between ethics and law is murky. Our discussion will continually cross over it, back and forth. For example, many laws governing business practices are seldom enforced. One can violate them rather safely to great personal advantage. One business practice that is unfair—and illegal—is to knowingly lie to a customer about a competitor's situation. Another is to discriminate in price in violation of the Robinson-Patman Act. Yet these practices are widespread. Now one's ethical code comes into play. Will you do something that is illegal but to your advantage if you think it is safe to do so? Bear in mind, for example, that insider trading has been widespread for decades, but the law was not enforced until recently. Many practices that at one time were legal are now illegal. The trend is clearly toward higher and more ethical business standards.

An example of a dilemma faced by businesspeople is the case of an outstanding securities sales manager who was hired as president of a highly publicized small investment company. This firm specialized in over-the-counter and penny stocks. The new president came home at noon of his first day at work and told his family, "I quit! It's a scam. These people are crooks." He bailed out. The hundreds of others in the firm were not so foresighted, nor were they fortunate when the Securities and Exchange Commission and the Federal Bureau of Investigation closed in. As one vice president of sales told a class, "It's not a whole lot of fun to be hauled off to jail in the middle of the night in front of your family." The one sales manager's future was saved by a personal code of ethics that would not allow him to become involved with a firm that was doing what he knew was wrong.

THE PRESSURE TO COMPROMISE PERSONAL ETHICS

Most of us have our own personal codes of ethics—what we will and will not do. Often we would prefer not to do certain things; but if we are pressed sufficiently hard, our ethical codes may bend. A person's true ethical code surfaces when he or she is tested under difficult conditions. It is easy to be ethical when no hardship is involved—when one is winning and life is going well. The test comes when things are not going so well—when the competitive pressures build up. The pressure brought on by quotas, pay plans, and a fierce competitive environment breeds unethical behavior.

Some business executives believe that in order to advance in an organization, a person must occasionally do something that he or she would prefer not to do. In a recent survey of sales managers, 89 percent of them acknowledge that they or their salespeople have given gifts in excess of $100 in order to gain favor with potential clients.[5] In a survey of salespeople, nearly half of the respondents admitted to taking part in some illegal or unethical activity, such as deceiving customers, as a result of pressure. The largest number of offenders were from computer and software companies—high-growth, highly competitive industries.[6] This is not to say that individuals involved in such deceptive practices get away with them. Prudential Insurance Company paid $425 million to settle a class action suit for using selling practices that deceived customers. Archer Daniels Midland, the United States' largest miller of corn, soybeans, and wheat, paid a $100 million fine for price fixing. One of its executives pleaded guilty to theft, money laundering, conspiracy, and tax evasion.[7]

For executives who ignore the unethical activities of their salespeople, the consequences are serious—lawsuits, fines, ruined careers, and imprisonment.

The damage to their companies is also great in terms of lost customers and potential customers. So, regardless of the pressure to compromise personal standards, all of the recent evidence suggests that it is not in the best interests of salespeople and sales managers to do so.

THE PROBLEM OF DETERMINING ETHICAL STANDARDS

As individuals, sales managers usually have their own standards of ethical conduct. And they usually abide by these standards in managing their sales forces. Most of us believe we act ethically by our own standards. However, ethical standards are set by a group—by society—and not by the individual. Thus, the group evaluates what you as an individual think is ethical.

The problem is that the group (society) lacks commonly accepted standards of behavior. What is considered ethical conduct varies from one country to another (see the International Perspective box), from one industry to another, and from one situation to another. Looking to the law or corporate policy for guidance often leads only to more gray areas rather than to clearly defined, specific guidelines.

The moral-ethical-legal framework presents special problems for sales executives, more than for most other managers. Entertaining customers in a

CONSIDER THIS...

An International Perspective

Bribery is found in many (perhaps all) cultures and political systems. In fact, in many foreign countries, there is no way a company can hope to make sales without paying fees or "commissions" (translate that as *bribes*) to agents in those countries. Bribery is so implanted in many cultures that various languages have slang words to designate it. In Latin America, it is called the *mordida* (small bite). It is *dash* in West Africa and *baksheesh* in the Middle East. The French call it *pot de vin* (jug of wine). In Italy there is *la bustarella* (the little envelope) left on a bureaucrat's desk to cut the red tape.

However, under the Foreign Corrupt Practices Act of 1977, it is illegal for U.S. companies to offer bribes to foreign officials or candidates. There is a narrow exception for **facilitation payments**, which are relatively small sums of money paid to low-ranking officials to facilitate or expedite the normal, lawful performance of duty. In other words, these are payments that are legal in the host country, and that are *for the purpose of facilitating routine government action* (as opposed to the purpose of directly acquiring the business contract). But again, this is a narrow exception.

It is important to remember that all employees of every U.S. company are subject to the laws of the United States regardless of the country in which they are conducting business. Furthermore, sales managers are held responsible not only for their own actions but also for the actions of their internationally based employees. So any subordination payments made by U.S. companies doing business in any foreign country would be considered illegal and punishable under U.S. law.

SOURCE: Kevin J. Claney and Randy L Stone, "Don't Blame the Metrics," *Harvard Business Review,* 83, no. 6 (June 2005), pp. 26-28.

gambling house, for example, may be either moral or immoral from an individual's point of view. This entertainment may be considered acceptable (ethical) or not depending on the industry's practice. And it may be legal or illegal, depending on whether it happened in Nevada or California.

In some of the situations discussed in the following sections, it is apparent that it will be difficult at times for the manager to decide whether or not a particular action is ethical.

ETHICAL SITUATIONS FACING SALESPEOPLE AND SALES EXECUTIVES

Ethical questions are involved in many of the relationships that sales managers have with their salespeople, their companies, and their customers. A few of these situations are discussed here.

Relations with the sales force

A substantial portion of sales managers' ethical problems relates to their dealing with the sales force. Assume, for instance, that a salesperson has built a territory into a highly profitable district. The salesperson may have even worked under a straight commission compensation plan and paid his or her own expenses. An executive who sees this salesperson's relatively high earnings may decide the territory is too large and therefore must be split. Is this ethical? Yet is it sound management not to split the district if the sales executive believes there is inadequate coverage of an overly large district?

In some companies, management takes over the very large, profitable accounts as *house accounts.* (These customers are sold directly by some executive, and the salesperson in that district usually receives no commission on the account.) The ethics here may be questionable, particularly if the salesperson spent much time and effort in developing the account to a profitable level. Yet management may feel that the account is now so important that an executive should handle it.

Ethical questions often arise in connection with promotions, termination, and references. If there is no likelihood that a sales representative will be promoted to a managerial position, should the salesperson be told? If the sales manager knows that the salesperson is working in expectation of such a promotion, to tell him means to lose him. In another instance, when a managerial position opens up in another region, a sales manager may keep a star salesperson in the present territory despite his or her qualifications and desire for promotion. And what is management's responsibility in giving references for a former salesperson? To what extent is a manager ethically bound to tell the truth or give details about former employees?

Relations with the company

Changing jobs and handling expense accounts illustrate the ethical problems involved in sales executives' relations with companies. When changing positions, a manager may want to take key customers to the new employer. Ethical and legal questions may arise if this executive tries to move these customers to the new firm.

Many times, a sales manager possesses information that could be highly useful to a competitor. Naturally, it is difficult to control the information a manager gives to a new employer. But beyond certain limits, such behavior is clearly unethical.

Ethical questions may arise in the interpretation of expense account policies. Suppose that top management states it will pay only 30 cents a mile to salespeople or sales managers who use their personal cars for company business. Yet a sales manager knows that that actual expenses are much higher than that, may be tempted to pad mileage and then encourage the salespeople to do so, too, to make up the difference. The manager may justify this action by rationalizing that the money is really being spent for business purposes and thus the spirit of the expense account is not being violated. Ethical questions include the following: should sales personnel manipulate expense accounts to protect themselves from the stingy policies of top management? In so doing, they are only recovering money honestly spent in the solicitation of business for the firm. Or should they attempt to get policies changed? Or, failing that, should they change employers rather than commit what they believe are unethical acts?

Relations with customers

Perhaps the most critical set of ethical questions facing sales managers is associated with customer relations. The major problem areas involve are in these three areas: (1) information, (2) gifts, and (3) entertainment.

Information

It is important that salespeople provide their customers with *all* of the information that enables them to make informed decisions. Sometimes salespeople make recommendations that are not in the best interests of their customers. For example, they may neglect to give the customers complete information. To cite one example, several insurance agents were trying to sell new policies to their current policyholders. In doing so, the agents failed to tell their customers that the new policies seemed less expensive than they really were because they were paid for in part by using up the cash value of the older policies.[8]

Sometimes salespeople knowingly sell a higher-priced product when a lower-priced product would have fulfilled the customer's need just as well. *The Journal of the American Medical Association* once showed that pharmaceutical sales reps pushed higher-priced calcium channel blockers for high blood pressure when cheaper diuretics and beta blockers were just as effective.[9]

Gifts

The practice of giving gifts to customers, especially at the holiday season, is a time-honored practice. But today, perhaps more than ever before, the moral and ethical climate of giving gifts to customers is under careful scrutiny. The practice is being reviewed by both the givers and the receivers of gifts. Some firms put dollar limits on the business gifts they allow their employees to give or receive. Other companies are even more strict—Fastenal, for example, has a policy that their salespeople never take a new account or prospect out for dinner. "We want to earn your business, we don't want to buy your business," says a Fastenal sales manager.

The Internal Revenue Service places a limit of $25 a year on the amount that may be deducted for business gifts to any one person. Other firms have stopped the practice of giving holiday gifts to customers. Instead, some of these firms offer to contribute (in amounts equal to their usual gifts) to their customers' favorite charities.

It is unfortunate that gift giving to customers has become so complicated and so suspect. A reasonably priced, tastefully selected gift can express appreciation for a customer's business. Today the problem lies largely in deciding what constitutes "reasonably priced" and "tastefully selected." The following examples illustrate this problem:

- A box of golf balls may be a reasonable holiday gift to give a $5,000-a-year customer. But is a $3,000 premium set of golf clubs a gift or a bribe when giving to a million-dollar customer?
- It is customary for appliance manufacturers to reward their distributor-customers with an all-expense-paid incentive trip to the Bahamas. But is it acceptable for a pharmaceutical company to invite its doctor-customers to Jamaica for an all-expense-paid seminar?
- It is a legal and acceptable practice for a manufacturer to give a department store's sales clerks "push money" to promote the manufacturer's brand. But can this manufacturer rightfully give the head buyer a little something extra for first getting the product into the store?

Fortunately, sales executives have some time-tested guidelines to help them avoid gift giving that is unethical or in bad taste:

- Never give a gift before a customer does business with the firm.
- Do not give gifts to customers' spouses.
- Keep the value of gifts low to avoid the appearance of undue influence on future purchase decisions.
- Follow your company's policy on gift giving.
- Walk away from the business if the customer pushes for something that exceeds these guidelines.[10]

Entertainment

Business entertainment is definitely a part of sales work, and a large portion of the expense money is often devoted to it. Salespeople who spend this money unwisely on accounts with little potential waste time, and their selling costs will be out of line. Indeed, a contributing factor in salespeople's success may be their ability to know the right person to entertain and the nature of the entertainment called for.

Over the years, some useful generalizations have been developed for customer entertainment:

- Entertain to develop long-term business relationships, not one order.
- Keep the entertainment appropriate to the customer and the size of the account.
- Be sensitive to customer attitudes toward types of entertainment.
- Do not rely on entertainment as one of the foundations of the selling strategy—use it only to complement the strategy.

ESTABLISHING AN ETHICAL CLIMATE

It is not realistic for a sales manager to construct a two-column list of practices, one headed "ethical" and the other "unethical." A better approach is to establish a climate within the organization in which every person always consciously tries to make ethical decisions. An **ethical climate** is one in which the employees of the organization believe that typical organizational practices and procedures are ethical. It is important to establish an ethical climate. This is done by enacting policies that specify, discourage, monitor, and correct unethical behavior. Below are some guidelines to help establish an ethical climate.

Take a long-run point of view

Sales executives should understand that ethical behavior is not only morally right but also, over the long run, realistically sound. Too many sales administrators are shortsighted. They do not see the possible repercussions from their activities and attitudes. Whether or not the buyer was deceived or pressured may seem unimportant so long as the sale is consummated—that brush mark of one immediate sale seems unimportant when the entire canvas is examined. Management often does not recognize that such practices can lose customers or invite public regulation. Figure 17-1 provides some questions that may help a sales executive evaluate the ethical status of proposed actions. Furthermore, a recent survey suggests that most customers consider a company's ethical reputation when selecting vendors. In response to this, many companies are encouraging their salespeople to sell their companies' integrity and ethical behavior.[11]

Put guidelines in writing

In recent years, U.S. companies have developed a code of ethics in response to a number of revelations of bribery at home and in foreign business dealings. The **code of ethics** are guidelines for all employees to follow. Liberty Mutual salespeople are required to sign the company's ethical conduct policy *every year*. In general, these guidelines are similar to the standards of conduct adopted by the National Association of Sales Professionals—and shown in Figure 17-2.

Writing a code of ethical conduct is no easy task. Critics claim that such a statement usually is public relations window dressing that covers up a bad situation and corrects nothing. Nevertheless, higher levels of ethical behavior have been found in firms where codes of ethics are in place and enforced.[12] An ethical code that is part of the culture of an organization is likely to affect the decision making of that organization's employees. Such codes lessen the chance that executives will knowingly or unknowingly get into trouble, and they strengthen the company's hand in dealing with customers and government officials who invite bribes and other unethical actions. They also strengthen the position of

FIGURE 17-1
Evaluating the ethical status
of a business decision

1.	Is this sound from a long-run point of view?
2.	Would I do this to a friend?
3.	Would I be willing to have this done to me? (The Golden Rule)
4.	Would I want this action publicized in national media?
5.	Would I tell others about it?
6.	Who is damaged by the action?

ETHICS AND PROFESSIONALISM
I will act with the highest degree of professionalism, ethics and integrity.

REPRESENTATION OF FACTS
I will fairly represent the benefits of my products and services.

CONFIDENTIALITY AGREEMENT
I will keep information about my customers confidential.

CONTINUING EDUCATION
I will maintain an on-going program of professional development.

RESPONSIBILITY TO CLIENTS
I will act in the best interest of my clients, striving to present products and services that satisfy my customers' needs.

RESPONSIBILITY TO NASP
I will share my lessons of experience with fellow NASP members and promote the interests of NASP.

RESPONSIBILITY TO EMPLOYER
I will represent my employer in a professional manner and respect my employers' proprietary information.

RESPONSIBILITY TO COMMUNITY
I will serve as a model of good citizenship and be vigilant to the effects of my products and services on my community.

CONFLICTS OF INTEREST
I will disclose potential conflicts of interest to all relevant parties and whenever possible, resolve conflicts before they become a problem.

LAWS
I will observe and obey all laws that affect my products, services and profession.

SOURCE: National Association for Sales Professionals website: http://www.nasp.com/pr/aboutUs/standardsOfConduct.asp

FIGURE 17-2

Standards of Conduct of the National Association of Sales Professionals

lower-level executives in resisting pressures to compromise their personal ethics in order to get along in the firm.

In addition to providing guidelines for ethical decision making, a code of ethics can contribute to the general ethical climate of an organization if it is endorsed and enforced by top management. Having a code of ethics is a concrete sign that the organization cares about whether or not its employees behave in an ethical manner.

Reinforce the ethical climate

A code of conduct must not only be written; it must be enforced. Salespeople who violate the code should be reprimanded; if they don't cease their unethical behavior, they should be fired. In other words, a code of ethics becomes an effective means of guiding behavior only if it is enforced; otherwise, it is meaningless.

Top managers must serve as ethical role models for employees. They must not only verbally endorse ethical behavior but also practice it. Clearly, salespeople are not going to take any code of ethics seriously if they see their immediate managers and other executives behaving unethically. Unfortunately, many managers do not serve as role models. A national survey of 4,000 business employees found that 25 percent of those responding felt their companies ignored ethical conduct in order to meet business objectives and that 17 percent believed their companies *encouraged* unethical practices.[13]

Provide ethical training

Another means of reducing the occurrence of unethical behavior is for the company to provide ethical training to its employees. Often, sales situations are complex, particularly in international situations. Sales managers or salespeople may want to behave in an ethical manner but may not be aware of the ethical implications of some of their decisions; or even if they are aware, they may not know what is the most ethical action to take in a particular situation. Training—through the use of cases, role plays, and games—can simulate ethical dilemmas. This can increase ethical sensitivity and skills.

PUBLIC REGULATION AND SALES MANAGERS

Public regulation at any level of government—federal, state, or local—touches a company's marketing department more than any other phase of the company's operations. This does not imply that regulation of nonselling activities is unimportant. The Securities and Exchange Commission affects corporate financing, minimum-wage legislation influences several aspects of personnel and labor relations, various measures establish safety regulations for offices and factories, local zoning laws affect plant location, and so on. However, the various regulatory measures that affect areas of marketing—such as pricing, advertising, and personal selling—are the ones that will have the greatest impact on the behavior of salespeople and their managers.

As established by the Federal Sentencing Commission for Organizations in 1991, both the employee and the employee's company are responsible for compliance with federal regulations. That is, the government holds the company responsible for preventing misconduct on the part of its employees. It must establish and communicate standards of behavior to employees, monitor employee conduct, allow employees to report criminal activity, punish those who violate the standards, and take steps to prevent further criminal conduct.[14] Sales managers must ensure that their salespeople are aware of their legal responsibilities. To do this, they must provide training with regard to their legal responsibilities and routinely provide updates concerning the most recent legislation and court decisions.

If a manager believes that the behavior of a particular salesperson may lead to legal problems, the sales manager should take action immediately to make the salesperson cease the questionable behavior.

There are four areas in which sales executives are affected by government regulation of business: price discrimination, unfair competition, the Green River type of municipal ordinance, and cooling-off laws.

Price Discrimination

The Clayton Antitrust Act (1914) and its Robinson-Patman Amendment (1936) are federal laws that generally restrict **price discrimination**, which is when the same product is sold at different prices to different buyers. This means that sales managers cannot allow members of their sales force to indiscriminately grant price concessions. Some customers may demand larger discounts than are normally allowed and threaten to take their business elsewhere if their demands are not met. A seller who grants the unusual discount, assuming no corresponding cost differential to justify the transaction, may (along with the buyer) be violating the Robinson-Patman Act.

In another situation, in order to make a sale, it may be necessary for a seller to absorb some or all of the freight ordinarily paid by the buyer. Care must be taken to ensure that the move is made in good faith to meet an equally low price of a competitor. Firms normally cannot make price guarantees to some customers without making the same guarantees to other competing customers. Let's assume that a firm wants to grant allowances to customers for such things as cooperative advertising or demonstrators. These attractions also must be offered to all competing customers on a proportionately equal basis.

Unfair Competition

Unfair trade practices that may injure a competitor or the consumer are generally illegal under the Federal Trade Commission Act and its Wheeler-Lea Amendment. No specific examples of **unfair competition** are spelled out in these laws. However, a large body of illustrations has built up through the years as the Federal Trade Commission has administered these legislative acts. Offering bribes and providing misleading information to customers have been the focus of many FTC legal actions against firms and their employees.

Bribes

Using **bribes**—the payment of money or gifts to gain or retain a customer—is illegal. Using bribes to gain information about competitors is also illegal. Bribery in selling is an unpleasant fact of life that apparently has existed, in varying degrees, since time immemorial. Blatant bribes, payoffs, or kickbacks may be easy to spot—and they are patently wrong. Unfortunately, today much bribery is done in a sophisticated manner that is not easy to identify. Sometimes the lines are blurred between a bribe, a gift to show appreciation, and a reasonable commission for services rendered.

In sales, the bribe offer may be initiated by the salesperson, or the request may come from the buyer. Usually, the buyer's request is stated in a veiled fashion, and it takes a perceptive salesperson to understand what is going on.

Undoubtedly, bribery will continue to put sales managers and salespeople to the ethical test. If nothing else, sales executives should realize that "everyone else is doing it" is not a valid excuse. The penalties can be stiff for those found guilty of taking or giving bribes.

Misleading information

It is illegal to make false, deceptive, or misleading claims about a product or about the services that accompany that product. If a salesperson makes exaggerated claims about a product and those claims lead to misuse of the product, the seller also may be sued for any property damages or personal injuries arising out of a customer's misuse of the product. Merck & Company has been accused of training its sales representatives to avoid questions about whether one of its drugs (Vioxx) had the potential to increase blood pressure. This led to litigation concerning the drug's role in causing heart attacks, and Merck eventually settled the case for several billion dollars.[15]

Making false, deceptive, or disparaging statements about a competitor or its products is also illegal. Yet such practices are prevalent. The lies may run from fibs about the competitor's financial stability to personal attacks on its salespeople. Regardless of their nature, these actions all have the same purpose of discrediting the competitor. This is illegal and can lead to prosecution, fines, and imprisonment.

The following guidelines help sales managers and salespeople minimize the probability of legal proceedings and increase their chances of defending themselves if a legal complaint is brought against them:[16]

- Always make accurate, understandable, and verifiable statements about the product and its use.
- Avoid making exaggerated claims.
- Ensure that customers have the necessary knowledge and skills needed to use the product in the proper manner.
- Caution (in writing) customers against using the product in an improper manner.
- Review sales literature, warnings, and labels to be sure they are accurate and complete.
- Remind customers to read warning labels.
- Be able to verify any statements made about competitors.

Green River Ordinances

Many cities have enacted **Green River Ordinances**, which restrict the activities of salespeople who represent firms located outside the city. These salespeople may sell door-to-door (in-home), or they may call on retailers or other business establishments. Ostensibly, most of these laws were passed to protect local consumers and businesses from the fraudulent, high-pressure, and otherwise unethical selling practices of outlanders. Such measures not only serve this purpose but also tend to insulate local firms from external competition. Generally, these ordinances require salespeople to have a local license to do business in the town. But it often is difficult for salespeople from some types of outside firms to get the necessary license. While the constitutionality of these laws is highly questionable, they do serve as a deterrent to unethical sales activity.

Cooling-Off Laws

Legislation at the federal, state, and local levels protects consumers against the sometimes unethical sales activities of door-to-door salespeople. Much of the state legislation and Federal Trade Commission (FTC) administrative rulings are of the "cooling-off" type. That is, the regulations provide for a cooling-off period (usually three days) during which the buyer in a door-to-door (in-home) sales may cancel the contract, return any merchandise, and obtain a full refund.

The 1972 FTC rulings apply to all sales of $25 or more. They require the salesperson to inform the customer orally and in writing about the opportunity to "say no to the company even after you have said yes to the salesperson." By 1973, nearly 40 states, as well as several cities, had passed some type of **cooling-off law**. This poses real problems of compliance for national direct-selling companies, which must deal with many different laws and sales contracts.

Account Manager Accused of Passing Confidential Information

RUNNING CASE
Shiderlots
Elevators, Inc.

In their visits to customers, Shiderlots account managers are sometimes given confidential information by the customers' personnel about new products, advertising plans, and other impending new business plans. They also had opportunities to overhear private conversations or to read interoffice correspondence left exposed.

In March, Adam Dark received a call from Brittany Bailey, marketing director of Weston Town Center, a large shopping complex on the west side of Columbus. She was angry. "It *has* to be your account manager who did it! My operations' person, Carl Reston, assures me that there was no one else in his office but your guy, Kevin Kardas, on the day that we discussed the photo contest promotion that we were planning on having in August. In fact, we even remember how Kardas walked off with the draft of our flyer for the event—and then brought it back an hour later with the lame excuse that it had gotten caught under a paper clip behind some of *his* papers. Now, before we even announce it, we see that Polaris Mall is going to have a photo contest in July! We checked, and now know that Kardas has a longtime relationship with Polaris. There's no doubt he revealed that he helped them steal our idea to get on their good side."

Dark wasn't sure how to respond. He managed to get out, "Well, I can't imagine Kevin would do such a thing. He understands that you two are big competitors."

Bailey shot back, "You can't imagine? Why should you be surprised that a person with Kardas' background would do that? You know he has a criminal record, don't you?!"

Adam did know that his account manager Kevin Kardas was an ex-convict. Dark had hired Kardas on the recommendation of Ohio penal officials as a rehabilitation measure. Kardas had been grateful for the chance and had worked hard. And up to now, it had seemed like a great idea as his sales record was well above average.

Dark promised Bailey that he would make a thorough investigation. After getting off the phone with her, Dark immediately contacted Kardas and told him about his angry client. Kardas readily admitted knowledge of the photo contest promotion. He said that Carl Reston had told him all about it. However, Kardas absolutely denied that he passed on any of this information to Polaris Mall. He told Dark that there was no way he "was that stupid…"

Both Weston Town Center and Polaris Mall were important, longtime customers. Dark was not sure what action to take.

Question: What further action should Adam Dark take in this situation?

Current Problems

The advent and rapid growth of direct-response marketing, telemarketing, and Internet marketing have given rise to some new problems that many people feel have certain ethical overtones. Or is it right to send unsolicited promotional material to prospects via email? Is it ethical to bother people at home over the telephone, particularly at night? In reaction to these concerns, the National Do Not Call Registry was created in the United States. This has led to lawsuits being filed against sales organizations that solicit business by calling phone numbers in this registry.[17]

The securities industry is plagued with so-called boiler room operations that use telemarketing techniques to sell financial schemes to people the seller will never know or see. The Securities and Exchange Commission is doing its best to regulate such operations, but it is not an easy task.

SUMMARY

Ethics may be defined as moral standards of behavior. Sales managers and salespeople face many different ethical dilemmas. In the United States, many ethical decisions are actually legal questions. Our system of laws standardizes our interpretation of many ethical situations by making them illegal. However, there are still many situations, not covered by the law, in which ethics becomes an important factor.

It is easy to be ethical when it does not cost you anything—when you are winning. The test comes when things are *not* going well. Then there may be real pressure to compromise your personal ethics. There is an increasing awareness and concern over ethics in selling. Adherence to ethical standards is becoming increasingly important.

The problem is to determine what the ethical standards are. Society lacks commonly accepted standards of behavior. Ethical considerations are involved in many of the relationships sales executives have with their sales forces, their companies, and their customers. Customer relations, especially involving information, gifts, and entertainment, can have serious ethical overtones.

A company may help establish an ethical climate by taking a long-run perspective on business decisions, by developing a written code of ethics that managers are expected to enforce, by providing ethical role models through management's words and action, and by providing ethical training.

Public regulation touches a company's marketing department more than any other phase of the company's operations. Both the employee and the company are responsible for compliance with federal regulations. Government regulation has occurred in several areas that affect sales: price discrimination, Green River Ordinances, and cooling-off laws.

KEY TERMS

Bribes	Ethical climate	Green River Ordinances
Code of ethics	Ethics	Price discrimination
Cooling-off law	Facilitation payment	Unfair competition

1. "We always use a manufacturer's rep to open up a new territory; but once that territory is generating enough revenue to support our own company salesperson, we take it away from the manufacturer's rep—and put our own person in there." Is this an ethical policy?

2. "Let's face it. Our product is no different from that of 20 other competitors. It sells for the same price and for the same terms. We all give the same service. It really doesn't matter to the buyer which of us gets the order. So the only way we can get an edge is through our aggressive entertainment and gift program. We work hard at making our buyers happy with us. They enjoy doing business with us." Do you see any ethical problems involved here?

3. You have managed to hire a particularly qualified person to be your assistant sales manager in Los Angeles. The young man moves there with his wife, who yearns for a singing career. The new assistant sales manager is paid a salary that seemed attractive in his former Kansas City area. Economic and culture shock quickly take their toll as the couple learns the economic facts of life in LA. They find that the equivalent of their $200,000 Kansas City home sells for $900,000 in West Los Angeles. Moreover, the new assistant's job performance is most unsatisfactory. You are thinking of firing him. What are the ethical considerations involved in this situation?

4. What actions must a company take to ensure its compliance with federal regulation?

5. "Sure we promote our windshield replacement service to former customers by emailing them flyers and having our telemarketer call them. Why not? We sell and replace windshields at great values. Our customers are satisfied. We're doing great with the program. So a few people complain. So what? Some people will complain if the sun shines while others complain if it doesn't. We're not in the business to make everybody happy. Besides, it's working well." Evaluate the sales manager's statement and philosophy.

6. As a sales manager, you have been asked to recommend someone for a sales management job with another, noncompetitive firm. You have several salespeople who would be excellent for the position, but you don't want to lose them. The other position would be a definite improvement for them; they will never be able to do so well within your own firm. Would you tell them about the opening? Would you recommend them to the other firm?

7. You are one of the newer salespeople with your company. One of the older salespeople happens to see your expense report and he says to you, "Don't you think these numbers are low?" When you tell him that this is what you spent, he says, "That may be, but you are so far below the average that you are going to call the rest of us into question." How do you respond?

8. As an American citizen managing a large corporation owned by a large foreign trading company, you have been ordered to do some things that you feel are clearly detrimental to the welfare of the U.S. economy. What concerns, if any, would you have in following those orders?

9. You are a salesperson and you happen to over see your manager's expense report for a time period during which he was making calls with you. Clearly he has reported some expenses that are fictitious. He has been with the company for a long time and is a respected manager. What should you do about this?

10. Loyalty is a trait highly valued by most executives. They expect their subordinates to be loyal to them and to the company. When might those loyalties conflict? How much loyalty does an employee owe to a superior? To the company?

EXPERIENTIAL EXERCISES

1. You are a sales manager of a firm that makes electronic circuits. You have been requested to write down your policies on entertaining customers, giving gifts, and handling bribery. State your policies in clear, specific terms so that all people concerned know exactly how you will handle each situation.

2. Speak with a salesperson about an ethical issue that he or she faced as part of the job and ask how she or he deal with the problem. Would you have handled the situation any differently?

3. Visit the website of the national association of sales professionals (www.nasp.com) and evaluate this organization's standards of conduct in terms of whether or not it is an adequate guide for salesperson's behavior, given the situations that they might face in their jobs.

CONCORD OIL COMPANY
Policy on Gift Giving

In October, Mr. A.J. Moye was hired by the Concord Oil Company to fill the position of sales manager. This was his first job in the oil industry; his preceding position had been as sales manager for a small tools manufacturer. Three months after joining Concord, Mr. Moye received the following letter from Mr. Richard McMillan, the Vice President of Materials Management for a large cable manufacturing company, which was an old and highly valued customer of the Concord Oil Company:

> Dear Mr. Moye:
>
> I thank you and your company for the greeting you sent us for Christmas. We also wish you a prosperous new business year. We take the gifts you sent to our purchasing agents as a token of your esteem. However, I must ask you to discontinue this practice in the future. Our company recently decided on new purchasing policies. These policies do not allow our purchasing agents to accept gifts from suppliers. I am sure you will understand our policy.
>
> I am looking forward to a continuation of the good business relations that traditionally exist between our companies.
>
> Yours sincerely,
> RICHARD McMillan
> *Vice President of Materials Management*

Mr. Moye had no idea of Concord's policies and practices concerning gift giving. He therefore showed the letter to his assistant, Mr. Spriggs. Mr. Spriggs told him that Ms. Walters, the former sales manager, had instituted the practice of sending wine as Christmas gifts to purchasing agents of customers, and in some instances also to members of the customers' engineering departments. The size of the gifts varied from 3 to 12 bottles according to the sales volume of the account, the continuity of business relations, and many other factors. In practice, the number of recipients and the size of the gift were determined intuitively in agreement with the salesperson who serviced the particular customer.

In today's business environment, Mr. Moye felt that the practice of giving gifts to customers at Christmas or any other time was potentially an explosive issue, or at least potentially a troublesome matter. Some businesspeople considered gift giving as a form of bribery. They believed that a salesperson should sell a product on its merits—on its ability to satisfy a buyer's needs better than any competitive product could do the job. Other executives feel that gift-giving is a time-honored, and respectable, business practice that can become significant in a buyer-seller relationship, especially when many competitive products are essentially the same.

In any event, Mr. Moye realized that he needed to have a clear-cut policy on gift giving. With that goal in mind, his first step was to understand the existing policy in his company and in the oil industry.

Concord was a medium-sized company located in New Jersey. The company sold a wide variety of oil products for the industrial and institutional markets. Its customer list included both large and small firms in a variety of industries located mainly in the eastern part of the United States. Concord, for example, sold cutting oil to small metal-working firms, asphalt to local paving companies, quenching oil to steel parts manufacturers, and gasoline to local city governments.

Concord's major competitors were three of the largest oil firms in the country, plus seven small- to medium-sized firms that marketed in the same general geographic area as did Concord. The intensity of competition varied among the different products. Concord's policy was to cultivate market niches that were not worthwhile for the big three competitors to bother with. But in the case of some products, such as insulating oil, Concord competed directly with the large firms.

To distribute the products that were in competition with those made by Concord, several of the competitive firms relied heavily on manufacturers' agents. A few of the competitors used their own sales forces for these products.

Concord sold to about 900 accounts through a direct sales force of 11 people who were specialized by customer groups. They were compensated by a small salary plus a commission on net sales. They each had a limited expense account, under which limits were set for each major expense category. Entertainment, for example, was limited to $100 per customer per six-month period; exception could be made, however, to most of the limits.

Mr. Moye learned that Concord's gift-giving practices at Christmastime had changed over the years, largely because there was no definite company policy covering this activity. For the past several years during Ms. Walters's tenure as sales manager, the company had given good imported French or German wines. Ms. Walters always had claimed that wine was the perfect solution to the gift-giving problem. She had told her assistant that "most people enjoy drinking wine, and those who are not wine drinkers like having it around for visitors or for other occasions. The wine we send is of first quality. By ordering it in large quantities, we can get a good discount. And the salespeople don't have to worry about what to give their customers for Christmas. The salespeople can spend their time more usefully in selling, rather than in Christmas shopping for presents for their customers."

The wine was ordered from a nearby wholesale importer who was a distant relative of Mrs. Walters. Mr. Moye found that the wine gifts had cost his company about $25,000, including packaging and mailing, for 9,000 bottles last year.

Because Mr. Moye was new in the oil industry, he decided to get his salespeople's opinion on gift giving, and also to learn from them something about the gift-giving practices in the industry. He found that it was customary for firms to send Christmas gifts to their accounts. The gifts ranged from clocks, watches, gourmet food packages,

liquor, and cigarettes to token gifts like calendars and pocket notebooks. In dollar value, they ranged from under $1 to about $200.

When Mr. Moye suggested the possibility of discontinuing the gift giving, most of the salespeople opposed that idea quite strongly. They expressed their fear of losing business. They claimed that the manufacturers' agents who represented Concord's competitors loomed as a special threat in this matter, because they (the agents) typically gave very expensive gifts.

One salesperson said he would like the opportunity to select the gifts that are given to his customers. Mr. Moye did consider the idea of leaving it up to each individual salesperson to buy and send gifts to his or her customers as the salesperson wishes, but to provide no company reimbursement for these expenditures.

After his investigation was completed, Mr. Moye believed that the gift-giving issue boiled down to one question: do gifts influence the buying decision of Concord's customers? And Mr. Moye was not sure of the answer to that question. He also realized that if he did endorse gift giving, then this move would raise some additional problems. For instance, what dollar value should be set for a gift? If it is too expensive, the gift might smack of bribery or of being ostentatious. Low-cost items like a calendar might be ineffective or even create the negative impression that Concord does not think highly of the customer. Another issue was whether the gift selection should be centralized, which may make it inflexible and impersonal, or should each salesperson pick his/her own gifts—which would personalize the activity but would also take valuable selling time from the salesperson. Finally, Mr. Moye wondered whether the salespeople should pay for the gifts themselves or the company should reimburse them. Since the emphasis in the compensation plan was on commission, one might argue that the salespeople should pay for the gifts, because the gifts will bring more business to the salespeople and thus increase their commissions.

Questions:

1. What policy should Mr. Moye adopt with respect to gift giving?

AMERICAN STEEL CORPORATION
Sexual Harassment

Walter Hester, a sales manager for American Steel Corporation, was distraught by what he had just heard from one of his reps. She had told him that one of her buyers, Mr. Thorne, who was the principal buyer for one of American Steel's most important customers, Commonwealth Industries, had asked her to go with him on a "fishing weekend" to a cabin on a lake in Wisconsin. She told him that she did not feel it was appropriate for him to ask her and that she would not accept his invitation. But he acted offended and pushed the issue, saying that reps from other companies had gone fishing with him and he felt that she should too. He further suggested that she would lose his business if she didn't accept his invitation. She told him that if that was what it took to get his business, she was no longer interested in being one of his company's suppliers.

The rep was Barb Schecter. She had recently graduated from the Kelley School of Business with a degree in marketing. She subsequently accepted a position with American Steel Corporation as a salesperson. After a six-month period in training, she was assigned a territory in the west side of Chicago. She sold many different types of fabricated steel to many different small and large manufacturers. She had received good performance evaluations in her first six months and seemed to enjoy the position. She had told Mr. Hester during her last performance review that she particularly liked the variety of the businesses on which she called and the many different people with varying backgrounds.

Walt Hester was well aware of the federal and state regulations with regard to sexual harassment. He assured Barb that she had handled the situation as well as possible and that her safety and comfort were more important than the business from this account. He also asked her if she felt that she could still call on the account or if she would prefer to be relieved of that particular account or be transferred to another territory. Barb told him that she definitely did not want to be transferred to another territory. She also indicated that it would not bother her to continue calling on Commonwealth even if it meant that she would continue to deal with Thorne, but she would leave the decision with regard to who should handle the account going forward up to him. Hester assured her again that she had done the right thing and that he would consider whether or not she should continue to call on Commonwealth.

Walter Hester was angry with Thorne. He had met him on several occasions and, although he was a little rough around the edges, he seemed to be a reasonable guy. This action was clearly harassment and he really wanted to report it to Thorne's supervisors, but he wasn't sure if this was his best action for several reasons. First of all, Thorne's supervisor might only give Thorne a verbal reprimand or, worse, no reprimand at all. In either case, American Steel might lose the business or, even if Thorne was severely reprimanded, they might still lose the business, which would be a significant loss for American.

Of course, the second issue was whether or not to assign this account to a new rep. Again this wasn't an easy issue. First of all, there is the issue of travel and call time. Asking someone from a contiguous territory to handle this account would be inconvenient and burdensome for another rep. Most of the reps in the Chicago territories were spread about as thin as they could be and still effectively cover their territories. No one would willingly take on an account in the middle of another territory. However, if he let Barb continue to call on this account, Thorne would probably make good on his threat to give the business to a competitor and, worse, Barb may be subject to further harassment. If he reported Thorne to his supervisor, then, depending on what the supervisor's response was, the situation could become even worse.

Question:

1. What actions should Walt Hester take?

ENDNOTES

[1] Hester Plumridge and Laurie Burkitt, "GlaxoSmithKline Found Guilty Of Bribery In China," *The Wall Street Journal,* September 19, 2014. Retrieved from the following URL on July 7, 2016: http://www.wsj.com/articles/glaxosmithkline-found-guilty-of-bribery-in-china-1411114817

[2] Fernando Jaramillo, Belén Bande and Jose Varela, "Servant leadership and ethics: a dyadic examination of supervisor behaviors and salesperson perceptions," *Journal of Personal Selling & Sales Management,* Vol. 35 (2), pp. 108–24.

[3] Erin Strout, "To Tell the Truth," *Sales & Marketing Management,* July 2002, p. 44.

[4] Erin Strout, "Are Your Salespeople Ripping You Off?" *Sales & Marketing Management,* February 2001, p. 59.

[5] Melinda Jensen Ligos, "Gimme! Gimme!" *Sales & Marketing Management,* March 2002, p. 34.

[6] Michelle Marchetti, "Whatever It Takes," *Sales & Marketing Management,* December 1997, pp. 29–38.

[7] Michelle Marchetti, Ibid.

[8] Michelle Marchetti, Ibid.

[9] Catherine Arnst, "Is Good Marketing Bad Medicine?" *BusinessWeek* , April 13, 1998.

[10] Ligos, "Gimme! Gimme!" pp. 36–38.

[11] Jennifer Gilbert, "A Matter of Trust," *Sales & Marketing Management,* March 2003, p. 32.

[12] Charles H. Schwepker Jr., "Ethical Climate's Relationship to Job Satisfaction, Organizational Commitment, and Turnover Intention in the Sales Force," *Journal of Business Research,* October 2001, p. 40.

[13] Charles H. Schwepker Jr., Ibid.

[14] United States Sentencing Commission, *Federal Sentencing Guidelines for Organizations,* 1991.

[15] Alex Berenson, "Merck Agrees to Settle Vioxx Suits for $4.85 Billion," *New York Times,* November 9, 2007, p. A1

[16] Karl A. Boedecker, Fred W. Morgan, and Jeffrey J. Stoltman, "Legal Dimensions of Salesperson's Statements: A Review and Managerial Suggestions," *Journal of Marketing,* January 1991, pp. 70–80.

[17] Les Bowen, "State sues auto glass business for violating Do Not Call Registry," *The Daily Courier,* June 16, 2016. Accessed via http://www.dcourier.com/news/2016/jun/16/state-sues-pv-auto-glass-business-violating-do-not/

COMPANY INDEX

3M Corporation 5, 91, 98, 100

A

A-dec, Inc. 40-41
Accenture 130
Airborne Express 7
Alcoa 7
Anheuser-Busch 336-337, 384
Apple Inc. 4, 34, 41, 46, 66, 71, 120
Archer Daniels Midland 475
ARCO 194
AT&T 89, 97, 139, 164, 201-202, 277
Automatic Data Processing (ADP) 16, 105
Avon Products 5, 18

B

Badger Maps 389
Bell South Cellular 451
Best Buy 18
Blackberry 4
BMW 108
Boehringer Ingelheim 414
Boeing Aircraft 202, 313
Bose Corporation 73
Boston Scientific Corporation 108, 202

C

Careerbuilder.com 133, 135, 172
Cessna Aircraft Company 5
Circuit City 18
Coca-Cola 18, 201
Colgate-Palmolive 18
Compaq Computer Corporation 100, 244
Consolidated Freightways 105
Contempo Design 62
Continental Tire North America 316

D

Dell Computer Company 105, 113
Deloitte 167

DeWalt 224
Dialog 62
Dick's Sporting Goods 2
Disney 274
Dow Jones News/Retrieval 62, 190
Dr Pepper/Seven Up Inc. 133
Du Pont 7, 89, 201
Dun & Bradstreet, Inc. 376

E

Eastman Chemical 105
Ecolab Inc. 40, 199
Element Financial 296
Eli Lilly 3, 6, 169
Enron 18
Enterprise Rent-A-Car 244, 250
Equifax 163

F

Facebook 46, 167
Fastenal Company 17, 31, 58, 93, 119, 150, 191, 224, 254, 325, 343, 405, 449, 456, 478
Fidelifacts/Metropolitan New York 163
Firestone 2
FleetBoston Financial Corporation 245-246
Ford Motor Company 2-3, 6, 33
Ford Motor Credit 223
Fuelzee 211

G

Gallo Winery 201
General Electric 89, 93, 100, 105
General Foods 93
General Motors 134, 202
Georgia-Pacific 7, 434
GlaxoSmithKline 473
Google 120, 167
Grainger Industrial 223

H

Harvard University 2
Heublein, Inc. 41
Hewlett-Packard 93, 98, 105, 260
Home Depot 5, 13, 83
Hostess 6
HubSpot 241

I

IBM 5, 7, 41,46, 93-94, 97, 100, 105, 128, 167, 194, 198, 201-202, 249
IBT Media 38
Indeed.com 135
Inland Steel 7

J

JD Edwards 277
Johnson & Johnson 201, 260

K

Kimberly-Clark 93
Kinko's 16
KMC Telecom 257
Kraft Corporation 18, 89
Kroger 13

L

Levi Strauss & Co. 139
LexisNexis 62
Lexmark 223, 260
Liberty Mutual Insurance 59, 183, 295, 343, 374, 445, 480
LinkedIn 29, 46, 59-60, 120, 136
LivHome 406
Lockheed Martin 352
Lucent Technologies 9, 97, 102

M

Marathon Petroleum 251
Martin Miller's Gin 138

Mary Kay Inc. 7, 46
Medtronic 9, 228
Merck & Company 7, 199-200, 483
Microchip Technology 1
Microsoft 47, 66, 84, 120, 133, 137
Monsanto 100
Monster.com 119, 133, 135, 137
Motorola 4, 89, 194, 200

N

NCR 93, 195
NetSuite 16
New South Construction 421
Nortel 277
Northwestern Mutual Life 167

O

Ocean Spray 352
Optimus Solutions 224
Oracle 260, 414
Otis Elevator Company 335
Owens Corning 5, 83, 105

P

Panasonic 53, 223
Pepsi-Cola 5
Pfizer 185
Pharmacia 185
Portatour 389
PricewaterhouseCoopers 18

Procter & Gamble 92, 150, 198, 339
Prudential Insurance Company 475

Q

Quaker Oats 6, 92
Ralph's 47
Rand Corporation 346
Rubbermaid 156
Runzheimer International 293, 296

S

Salesforce.com 16, 46, 61, 146, 196, 198, 249
Salesgenie 59
Samsung 4
SAP 29, 46, 249
Shred-it 223
Siebel Systems 277
Sony Electronics 18
South-Western Educational Publishing 7
Southern California Edison 100
Sprint 226
State Farm 2-3, 295
SurePayroll 271
Synygy Inc. 449

T

Textron 7, 342
The Office Place 157

The Vollrath Company 66
Thomasnet.com 376
Total Quality Logistics 152, 374
Trilogy 260
Twitter 46, 167

U

UltraPawn 73
Unilever 339

V

Volvo 224

W

Walmart/Wal-Mart Stores 3, 13, 18, 54, 284, 343
Williams Scotsman, Inc. 57

X

Xerox 3, 7, 16, 93, 98, 100, 108, 194-195, 202, 227

Y

YouTube 46, 365

Z

ZDC 341

SUBJECT INDEX

A

Activity quota 273, 276-277
Adaptive selling 63
Administrative budget 357-358, 361
Affirmative action 121-123, 151
Assessment center 150, 163
Assimilation 125, 166-167, 169
Attribution theory 219

B

Background checks 163
Batting average 449, 456
Behavior-based control 317
Behavior-based interview 155
Behaviorally anchored rating scales (BARS) 458
Bona fide occupational qualifications (BFOQs) 129, 151
Book agents 36
Breakdown method 377
Bribes 483
Buildup method 377
Buying center 39, 99
Buying power index 341

C

Call frequencies 378, 389, 456
Call plan 314-315
Call rate 456
Canvassers 36
Capacity-based forecast 351
Central American Free Trade Agreement (CAFTA) 107
Centralized training 195
Charismatic leaders 310
Citizenship behaviors 87, 319
Claim jumping 96, 385-386
Closed-ended contest 224
Coaching 202, 313
Code of ethics 480
Cold calling 58, 60
Combination quota 277-278
Commission 252

Commission base 253
Commission rate 253-254
Communications mix 3, 32
Company orientation 196-197
Company website 137
Compensation equation 259
Complex distribution channels 18
Consultative seller 5, 8
Consultative selling 47
Contribution margin 276
Contribution-margin method 431
Control system 317
Control unit 374-376
Cooling-off law 484
Credit report 163
Customer analysis 338
Customer probability cube 412-413
Customer relationship management (CRM) 16, 315
Customer research 62

D

Decentralized training 194-195
Delivery seller 6
Delphi technique 346
Demographics 30-31, 220
Demography 30-31
Difficulty analysis 190
Direct costs 429
Direct-selling expense 456-457
Disengagement stage 221
Diversity 17, 107, 138-139
Draw 252
Drawing account 252
Drug tests 160
Drummers 36
Dual-factor theory 217

E

E-commerce 3
Economic conditions 31
Educational institutions 137
Employee empowerment 38

Employee handbook 197
Employment agencies 138
Employment testing 158-162
Employment websites 135-136
Equal Employment Opportunity Commission (EEOC) 123, 151
Establishment stage 220
Ethical behavior 18, 480
Ethical climate 480
Ethics 474
Executive opinion 346
Expectancy theory 215
Expense-quota plan 289
Experience-based incentives 223
Exploration stage 220
Exponential smoothing model 348
External environment 30
Extrinsic rewards 216

F

Face-to-face interview 158
Facilitation payment 476
Features 65-66
Financial rewards 222-223
Fixed-allowance plan 292
Flexible-allowance plan 293
Foreign-country intermediaries 107-108
Full-cost method 431
Functional organization 88

G

Gaining commitment 71
General Sales Aptitude Test 159
Geographic information system (GIS) 380
Geographic organization 90
Geographic specialization 90
Global account management (GAM) 97, 108
Globalization 18
Green River Ordinances 484
Gross margin quota 276
Group morale 319

Guided interview 155

H

Halo effect 457
Hidden Objections 70-71
Hierarchy of needs theory 216-217
Hiring and assimilation phases 125
Home-country intermediaries 107
Horizontal organization 88-89
Hybrid sales channels 46
Hygiene factors 217

I

Identifying leads 59
Implication questions 64-65
Independent agents 101-102
Independent sales organizations 101
Indirect costs 429
Indirect monetary benefit 258
Indirect supervisory techniques 316
Individualized support 311
Informal organization 86-87
Input measures 451
Inside sales 3
Instrumentality 215-216
Interest tests 159
Interview focus 155-156
Interview structure 154-155
Intrinsic rewards 216-217

J

Job advertisements 135
Job analysis 126-127
Job description 126-128
Job enrichment 226-227
Job previews 166
Job profile 130
Job qualifications 127, 130
Job satisfaction 320

K

Key account management (KAM) 97
Key account seller 5
Kuder Occupational Interest Survey 159

L

Leadership style 309
Legal aspects of testing 161
Level of compensation 247-249
Limited-payment plan 288
Line organization 57
Line personnel 192
Line-and-staff organization 87

M

Maintenance stage 220
Management by objectives 449
Management by the numbers 272
Manufacturer's agent 102
Manufacturer's representative 102
Market factor 339
Market index 341
Market potential 337
Market specialization 92-93
Market-factor derivation 339
Marketing audit 403
Marketing concept 32
Marketing cost analysis 405
Marketing management 33
Marketing mix 3
Marketing profitability analysis 405
Marketing system 30
Marketing-Orientation Stage 34
Mental intelligence tests 159
Mentor 168
Method of compensation 241, 249
Minority groups 139
Mission 43
Missionary salespeople 6
Motivation 212
Motivation factors 217
Moving average technique 347
Multiple regression 350
Multiple relationship strategies 46-47
Must-do forecast 351

N

National Black MBA Association 139
National Society of Hispanic MBAs 139
Need assessment 63-64
Need-payoff questions 65
New business seller 5
Newspapers 136
Nondirected interview 155
Nondiscrimination 122
Nonfinancial rewards 222-223
North American Free Trade Agreement (NAFTA) 107
North American Industry Classification System (NAICS) 342

O

Objective-and-task method 356-357
Office of Federal Contract Compliance (OFCC) 123, 151
On-the-job training 202
Open communication 38
Open-ended contest 224

Operating statement 423
Organizational skills 198-199
Otis Self-Administering Test of Mental Ability 159
Outcome-based control 317
Output measures 450
Outside sales force 2
Outside training specialists 193
Overhead costs 429

P

Part-time workers 138
Peddlers 35
Per diem / per diem cost 284
Percentage-of-sales method 356
Performance-based interview 157
Personal interview 152-153
Personality tests 160
Physical environment 30
Planning phase 124
Plateaued salespeople 221
Political-legal factors
Pre-Approach 31
Presentation 65
Price discrimination 482-483
Price or Value Objections 69
Problem questions 64
Problems in testing 161-162
Procrastinating objections 70
Product demonstrations 66
Product knowledge 196
Product managers 92
Product specialization 90-91
Product specialization organization 91
Product staff specialization 92
Product/Service Objections 69
Production-Orientation Stage 33
Profit quota 276
Profit-and-loss statement 426, 439
Profitability analysis 405, 412
Program design 191
Progressive rate 254
Promotional mix 3, 32
Prospecting 58
Psychological traits of salespeople 220

Q

Qualifying leads 59-61

R

Ratio measures 452
Recruiting 131
Recruiting evaluation 140
Recruiting phase 124

Recruiting sources 132-133
Referral 133
Regression analysis 349
Regressive rate 254
Reinforcement 202
Relationship marketing 4, 37
Relationship-Orientation Stage 35
Resumes/application forms 152
Return on assets managed (ROAM) 437-438
Return on investment (ROI) 436-437
Role ambiguity 8, 218
Role conflict 8, 218
Role modeling 202, 318
Role stress 8, 218
Role theory 218
Routing 388
Routing efficiency 457
Runzheimer plan 293

S

Sales Aptitude Checklist 159
Sales aptitude tests 159
Sales budget 272, 356-357
Sales contests 223-224
Sales cycle 70
Sales engineers 6
Sales force automation (SFA) 16, 413
Sales force composite 346-347
Sales force diversity 17
Sales forecast 279, 337-338
Sales management 2
Sales management audit 404
Sales meetings 228
Sales pipeline 61
Sales process 57-58
Sales quota 272
Sales reports 314-315

Sales support 5-6, 315
Sales territory 372
Sales volume analysis 405
Sales-Orientation Stage 33-34
Selection phase 125
Selection tools 150
Selling by executives 16
Selling center 100
Selling team 99
Selling-expense budget 357-358
Sexual harassment 323
Situation questions 64
Situational leadership 312
Small-order problem 434
Social responsibility 18. 47
Social selling 45
Socialization 166
Sociocultural factors 31
Soft-spot principle 410
Span of control 86
Spiff 224
SPIN Selling 63
Split commission 255
Staff trainers 192
Straight commission 250, 252
Straight salary 250-251
Strategic account management (SAM) 97
Strategic planning 41
Stress interview 157
Strong-Campbell Interest Inventory 159
Substance abuse 321-322
Survey of buyer intentions 340

T

Task orientation 309
Teaching methods 199

Telemarketing 3
Territorial profit managers 9
Test marketing 340-341
Third-party harassment 324
Tiered contest 224
Total quality management (TQM) 39
Total sales volume 408
Trade journals 136
Training assessment 185
Training content 196
Training evaluation 203
Transaction selling 4
Transactional leadership 309
Transformational leadership 310
Trial close 65

U

Unfair competition 483
Unlimited-payment plan 287

V

Valence 215
Validation 151
Value-added components 4
Verbal feedback 309
Videoconferencing 158
Volume quota 276

W

Wholesale distributors 102
Wonderlic Personnel Test 159
Workload 374
Workload capacity 378
World Trade Organization (WTO) 106